1933

THE COLLEGE BOOK OF PROSE

THE COLLEGE
BOOK OF PROSE

1400 – 1929

COMPILED BY

ROBERT M. GAY
Professor of English, Simmons College, Boston

TOVT
BIEN OV
RIEN

HOUGHTON MIFFLIN COMPANY

BOSTON · NEW YORK · CHICAGO · DALLAS

SAN FRANCISCO

The Riverside Press Cambridge

The Riverside Press
CAMBRIDGE · MASSACHUSETTS
PRINTED IN THE U.S.A.

PREFACE

THE welcome accorded the *College Book of Verse* suggested the preparation of a companion-volume of prose, following the same general design.

I have never looked upon the former volume as precisely an anthology, but rather as a selection of poems illustrating the progress and variety of poetic expression; and, similarly, I have in the present book tried to illustrate the progress and variety of prose, rather than to assemble an anthology of the best prose passages.

By following a chronological arrangement, from the fourteenth century to the present, I have undertaken to suggest each period in its essential character — the ingenuousness of the mediæval, the brave rhetoric of the Elizabethan, the august Latinity of the seventeenth century; but at the same time have attempted to include in each period examples of all the chief styles then cultivated, setting alongside the courtly ornateness of *Menaphon*, for example, the somewhat clumsy straightforwardness of Raleigh's story of the last fight of the Revenge and the manly homespun of Deloney's account of the rise of Simon Eyre.

I have, in fact, thought much more of the book as a whole than of great names and purple patches (though these are represented), and I have included both numerous examples of sustained writing (ten to thirty pages) and examples of as many kinds of writing as possible. I have in general avoided what a friend calls "museum pieces," aiming at freshness as well as quality and interest. The consequence is that there are only four or five specimens in the book that are

10430

usually found in the volumes of readings compiled for survey courses or in the collections of prose selections used in college freshman classes or in the high schools.

In the earlier periods the spelling presented a difficult problem. To have adopted the original spelling throughout would have made the text forbidding to the reader, and yet to ignore the old spelling altogether, as is commonly done, would give him a false notion of the progress of the language. I compromised by printing some pieces, especially when these were short, in the old spelling and, in long selections, printing an unimportant part as it was originally printed, and indicating the fact in a footnote. (See, for example, the final section of the *Book of Balin* and the Epilogue to *Reynard the Fox*.) In modernizing I have as a rule altered nothing but the spelling and punctuation. By reproducing some examples *verbatim et literatim*, it was possible to furnish a survey of the *look* of the language throughout its course, as well as of its vocabulary.

Footnotes have been used more freely than in the *College Book of Verse*. I have attempted especially to identify quotations and allusions, partly because looking up such matters in reference books seems a poor expenditure of time for student or teacher, but principally because the books and authors that a writer refers to are symptomatic of his qualities. The twenty-odd quotations in Hazlitt's *On Going a Journey*, for instance, give a very interesting indication of his favorite reading. And the incessant references to the Bible throughout our literature could best be pointed out by identifying them in footnotes.

It will be seen that progressively more space has been devoted to the successive periods, so that about half of the book is drawn from the nineteenth and twentieth centuries. Narrative and exposition have been included in roughly equal proportions, and, in the later pages, examples of complete tales and stories have been given, together with two complete one-act plays and one or two long passages of sustained narrative from novels. These latter passages are complete units. The limits of space precluded the inclusion of many examples of any one sort, whether of narrative or exposition; but a student can catch the spirit of a type of essay or story as well from one example as from twenty.

The Analytical Index of the *College Book of Verse* has proved so welcome that an index of the same sort has been attempted here. It consists of a catalogue of literary types, forms, technical devices, and rhetorical methods, as well as of subjects, which, it is hoped, will be found a convenience in both composition and literature courses. In the Notes, at the back of the book, I have given such information about the respective selections as might help the reader to adopt a sympathetic attitude towards them. Especially in reading our earlier literature it is important that the student be what a recent writer has called "*then*-minded;" and the notes are designed to help him to become so. Also with this end in view a brief introduction to each section of the book has been included among the notes. In the desire to make the notes readable, I have given very little biographical material, preferring in the small space at my command to refer mostly to the artistic qualities of the selections. By indulging freely in cross-reference and in allusions to other books, I hope to encourage other reading and to suggest subjects for study and for composition. Dates of birth and death are given in the general index.

ACKNOWLEDGMENTS

ACKNOWLEDGMENT must be made to the various publishers who have generously permitted the reprinting of their copyright material. The editor wishes to express his indebtedness to the following publishers:

D. Appleton and Company for the selection from *Prefaces*, by Don Marquis.

Boni and Liveright for the selection from *The Great God Brown*, by Eugene O'Neill, published by Horace Liveright.

Dodd, Mead and Company, Inc., for selections from *Tremendous Trifles*, by G. K. Chesterton, and *Zuleika Dobson*, by Max Beerbohm. Copyright by Dodd, Mead and Company, Inc.

Doubleday, Doran and Company, Inc., for the selection from *Of Human Bondage*, by W. Somerset Maugham, copyright, 1917, by George H. Doran Company, and reprinted by special permission of Doubleday, Doran and Company, Inc., publishers.

Houghton Mifflin Company for selections from the works of Emerson, Lowell, and Thoreau, *Fame's Little Day*, by Sarah Orne Jewett, *Points of Friction*, by Agnes Repplier, *The Dance of Life*, by Havelock Ellis, and *Literature and the American College*, by Irving Babbitt.

Little, Brown and Company for the selection from *Five Plays*, by Lord Dunsany.

Longmans, Green and Company for the selection from *Mysticism and Logic*, by Bertrand Russell.

The Macmillan Company for the selection from *The Crock of Gold*, by James Stephens.

Modern Library, Inc., for the selection from *Tales of Mean Streets*, by Arthur Morrison.

Charles Scribner's Sons for the selection from *Virginibus Puerisque and Other Papers*, by Robert Louis Stevenson.

The Viking Press, Inc., for selections from *Dubliners*, by James Joyce, and *Triumph of an Egg*, by Sherwood Anderson.

CONTENTS

CONTENTS

THE
COLLEGE BOOK OF PROSE

.·.

MIDDLE AGES

TAKE HEDE OF MAYDENS

1398

Men byhove to take hede of maydens: for they ben hote & tendre of complexion; smale, pliaunt and fayre of disposicion of body; shamfaste, ferdefull and mery touchynge the affeccion of the mynde. Touchynge outwarde disposicion they be well nurtured, demure and softe of speche and well ware what they say: and delycate in theyr apparell . . . Their hondes and the uttermeste party of their membres ben full subtyll and plyaunt, theyr voyce small, theyr speche easy and shorte, lyght in goynge & shorte steppes, and lyght wit and heed; they ben sone angry, and they ben mercyable and envyous, bytter, gylefull, able to lerne . . . And for a woman is more meker than a man, she wepeth soner, and is more envyousse, and more laughinge, & lovinge, and the malice of the soule is more in a woman than in a man. And she is of feble kinde, and she makith more lesynges and is more shamefaste, & more slowe in werkynge and in mervynge than is a man, as sayth *Aristotle*.

John Trevisa, translation of Bartholomew de Glanville's *De Proprietatibus Rerum* (1360), printed by Wynkyn de Worde, 1495.

---

hote, hot, fresh.   *ferdefull*, fearful, timid.   *heed*, head.
for, because.   *lesynges*, lies.   *mervynge*, moving.

A PRAYER

O stelliferi conditor orbis.

1377–81

O thou maker of the whele that bereth the sterres, which that art y-fastned to thy perdurable chayer, and tornest the hevene with a ravisshing sweigh, and constreinest the sterres to suffren thy lawe; so that the mone somtyme shyning with hir ful hornes, meting with alle the bemes of the sonne hir brother, hydeth the sterres that ben lesse; and somtyme, whan the mone, pale with hir derke hornes, approcheth the sonne, leseth hir lightes; and that the eve-sterre Hesperus, whiche that in the first tyme of the night bringeth forth hir colde arysinges, cometh eft ayein hir used cours, and is pale by the morwe at the rysing of the sonne, and is thanne cleped Lucifer. Thou re-streinest the day by shorter dwelling, in the tyme of colde winter that maketh the leves to falle. Thou dividest the swifte tydes of the night, whan the hote somer is comen. Thy might atempreth the variaunts sesons of the yere; so that Zephirus the deboneir wind bringeth ayein, in the first somer sesoun, the leves that the wind that highte Boreas hath reft awey in autumpne, that is to seyn, in the laste ende of somer; and the sedes that the sterre that highte Arcturus saw, ben waxen heye cornes whan the sterre Sirius eschaufeth hem. Ther nis no-thing unbounde from his olde lawe, ne forleteth the werke of his propre estat. O thou governour, governinge alle thinges by certein ende, why refusestow only to governe the werkes of

perdurable chayer, eternal throne.   hevene, celestial sphere (heaven).
sweigh, sway, motion.   hir, her, *or* their.   eft ayein, back again.
cleped, called.
tydes, hours (swift because the summer nights are short).
highte, is named.
ben waxen heye cornes, are grown to tall grain.
eschaufeth, warmeth.   hem, them.   his, its.   forleteth, leaves.

men by dewe manere? Why suffrest thou that
slydinge fortune torneth so grete entrechaunginges of
thinges, so that anoyous peyne, that sholde dewely
punisshe felouns, punissheth innocents? And folk of
wikkede maneres sitten in heye chayres, and anoyinge
folk treden, and that unrightfully, on the nekkes of
holy men? And vertu, cler-shyninge naturelly, is hid
in derke derkenesses, and the rightful man bereth the
blame of the feloun. Ne forsweringe ne the fraude,
covered and kembd with a fals colour, ne anoyeth nat
to shrewes; the whiche shrewes, whan hem list to usen
hir strengthe, they rejoysen hem to putten under hem
the sovereyne kinges, whiche that poeple with-outen
noumbre dreden. O thou, what so ever thou be that
knittest alle bondes of thinges, loke on thise wrecchede
erthes; we men that ben nat a foule party, but a fayr
party of so grete a werk, we ben tormented in this
see of fortune. Thou governour, withdraw and re-
streyne the ravisshinge flodes, and fastne and ferme
thise erthes stable with thilke bonde, with whiche thou
governest the hevene that is so large.

Geoffrey Chaucer, translation of Boethius' *De Consolatione
Philosophiae,* Book I, Met. 5. (Written about A.D. 524;
printed by William Caxton, 1480.)

THE LADY OF THE LAND

In English 1410–20

And somme men seyn that in the Ile of Lango is
yit the doughter of *Ypocras* in forme and lykness of
a gret dragoun, that is an hundred fadme of lengthe
as men seyn, for I have not seen hire. And thei

---

entrechaunginges, mutations.
ne ... ne ... ne ... nat, neither ... nor *(the last two negatives increase the
force of the first two).*
shrewes, scoundrels.   *kembd,* combed, trimmed.
whan hem list to, when they choose to.   *erthes,* lands, countries.
party, part.   *thilke,* that same.   *fadme,* fathom.

of the Iles callen hire lady of the lond. And sche
lyeth in an olde castell in a cave, and scheweth
twyes or thryes in the yeer, and sche doth non harm
to no man but yif men don hire harm. And sche was
thus chaunged and transformed from a fair damysele
into lykness of a dragoun be a Goddess that was
clept Deane. And men seyn that sche schal so endure
in that forme of a dragoun unto tyme that a knyght
come that is so hardy that dar come and kisse hire on
the mouth, and than schall sche turne agen to hire
owne kynde and ben a womman agen, but after that
sche schall not lyven longe ... And it is not longe
sithen that a yonge man, that wiste not of the dragoun,
wente out of a schipp, and wente thorgh the Ile til
that he come to the castell, and cam in to the cave and
wente so longe til that he found a chambre, and there
he saugh a damysele that kembed hire hede and
lokede in a myrour. And sche hadde meche tresoure
abouten hire and he trowede that sche hadde ben a
comoun womman that dwelled there to resceyve men
to folye. And he abode till the damysele saugh the
schadewe of him in the myrour. And sche turned
hire toward him and asked hym what he wolde. And
he seyde he wolde be hire lemman or paramour, and
sche asked him yif that he were a knyght, and he
seyde nay. And than sche seyde that he myghte not
ben hire lemman. But sche bad him gon agen unto
his felowes and let make him knyght, and come agen
upon the morwe, and sche scholde come out of the
cave before him, and thanne come and kysse hire on
the mowth. "And have no drede, for I schall do the
no maner harm, all be it that thou se me in lykeness of
a dragoun. For though thou se me hidouse and hor-

Deane, Diana.   _meche_, much.
trowede, thought.   _morwe_, morrow.

rible to loken onne, I do the to wytene that it is made be enchauntement. For withouten doute I am non other than thou seest now, a womman, and therfore drede the nought. And yif thou kisse me thou schalt have all this tresoure, and be my lord and lord also of all that Ile." And he departed fro hire, and wente to his felowes to schippe, and leet make him knyght, and cam agen upon the morwe for to kisse the damysele. And whan he saugh hire comen out of the cave in forme of a dragoun so hidouse and horrible, he hadde so gret drede that he fleygh agen to the schipp, and sche folewed him. And whan sche saw that he turned not agen, sche began to crye as a thing that hadde meche sorwe. And thanne sche turned agen into hire cave. And anon the knight dyede, and sithen hider-wardes myghte no knyght se hire but that he dyede anon. But whan a knyght cometh that is hardy to kisse hire, he schall not dye, but he schall turne the damysele into hire ryght forme and kyndely schapp, and he schal be lord of all the countreyes and Iles above seyd.

The Voyage and Travaile of Sir John Maundeville, from the French (1357–71), in part by Jean de Bourgogne, called Jean de la Barbe.

THE BOOK OF SIR BALIN LE SAVAGE

Before 1470

Of a damoysel whyche came gyrde wyth a swerde, for to   nde a man of suche vertue to drawe it oute of the scabard. Capitulo primo.

After the death of King Uther Pendragon reigneth King Arthur his son, which had great wars in his days,

do the to wytene, make known to thee.   *saugh*, saw.
sithen hiderwardes, from that time till now.
kyndely schapp, natural shape.

for to get all England into his hands; for there were many kings at that time within the realm of England, in Wales, in Scotland, and in Cornwall. So it befel upon a time, when King Arthur was at London, there came a knight and brought the king tidings how that Rience, of North Wales,[1] had reared a great number of people, and were entered into the land, and burnt and slew the king's true liege people. "If this be true," said King Arthur, "it were great shame unto mine estate, but that he were mightily withstanden." "It is truth," said the knight, "for I saw the host myself." Then King Arthur let make a cry, that all the lords, knights, and gentlemen of arms, should draw unto a castle, that was called in those days Camelot, and there the king would let make a council general, and a great joust.

So when the king was come thither, with all his baronage, and lodged as them seemed best, there was come a damsel, which was sent on message from the great lady Lily of Avelion; and, when she came before King Arthur, she told from whom she came, and how she was sent on message unto him for these causes. Then she let her mantle fall, that was richly furred, and then she was girded with a noble sword, whereof the king had great marvel, and said, "Damsel, for what cause are ye gird with that sword, it beseemeth you not?" "Now shall I tell you," said the damsel. "This sword, that I am gird withal, doth me great sorrow and cumbrance; for I may not be delivered of this sword but by a knight; and he must be a passing good man of his hands, and his deeds, and without villainy or treachery, and without treason. If I may find such a knight that hath all these virtues, he may

---

[1] In the *Book of Merlin* (Book I), which precedes this, Rience sends a messenger to Arthur to demand his beard and, upon Arthur's refusal, boasts that he is coming to get it.

draw out this sword of the sheath. For I have been at King Rience. It was told me there were passing good knights, and he and all his knights have assayed it, and none can speed."

"This is a great marvel," said Arthur; "if this be sooth, I will myself assay to draw out the sword; not presuming upon myself that I am the best knight, but that I will begin to draw at your sword, in giving example to all the barons, that they shall assay every one after other, when I have assayed." Then Arthur took the sword by the sheath and by the girdle, and pulled at it eagerly, but the sword would not out. "Sire," said the damsel, "ye need not pull half so hard; for he that shall pull it out shall do it with little might." "Ye say well," said Arthur: "now assay ye, all my barons; but beware ye be not defiled with shame, treachery, nor guile." "Then it will not avail," said the damsel; "for he must be a clean knight, without villainy, and of gentle strain of father's and mother's side." Most of all the barons of the Round Table, that were there at that time, assayed all by row, but there might none speed. Wherefore the damsel made great sorrow out of measure, and said, "Alas! I weened in this court had been the best knights, without treachery or treason." "By my faith," said King Arthur, "here are as good knights as I deem as any be in the world; but their grace is not to help you, wherefore I am displeased."

How Balen, arayed lyke a poure knyght, pulled out the swerde, whyche afterward was cause of his deth.

Capitulo ij.

Then fell it so that time, that there was a poor knight with King Arthur, that had been a prisoner with him half a year and more, for slaying of a knight, which was cousin to King Arthur. The name of this knight was called Balin; and by good means of the barons, he was delivered out of prison; for he was a good man named of his body, and he was born in Northumberland. And so he went privily into the court and saw this adventure, whereof it raised his heart, and would assay it as other knights did; but for he was poor, and poorly arrayed, he put him not far in press. But in his heart he was fully assured to do as well (if his grace happened him) as any knight that there was. And, as that damsel took her leave of King Arthur and of all the barons, so departing, this knight, Balin, called unto her, and said, "Damsel, I pray you of your courtesy, suffer me as well to assay as these lords; though I be poorly clothed, in mine heart meseemeth I am fully assured as some of these other, and meseemeth in my heart to speed right well." The damsel beheld the poor knight, and saw he was a likely man; but, for his poor arrayment, she thought he should be of no worship, without villainy or treachery. And then she said unto the knight, "Sir, it needeth not to put me to any more pain or labour, for it seemeth not you to speed there, as others have failed." "Ah! fair damsel," said Balin, "worthiness and good tatches and good deeds are not all only in arrayment, but manhood and worship is hid within man's person; and many a worshipful knight is not known unto all people; and therefore worship and hardiness is not in arrayment." "By God!" said the damsel, "ye say sooth; therefore ye shall assay to do what ye may."

Then Balin took the sword by the girdle and sheath, and drew it out easily; and when he looked upon the sword, it pleased him much. Then had the king and

tatches, marks, qualities.

all the barons great marvel, that Balin had done that
adventure; and many knights had great despite of
Balin. "Certes," said the damsel, "this is a passing
good knight and the best that ever I found, and most
of worship, without treason, treachery, or villainy,
and many marvels shall he do. Now gentle and
courteous knight, give me the sword again." "Nay,"
said Balin, "for this sword will I keep, but it be taken
from me with force." "Well," said the damsel, "ye
are not wise to keep the sword from me; for ye shall
slay with the sword the best friend that ye have, and
the man that ye most love in this world; and the
sword shall be your destruction." "I shall take the
adventure," said Balin, "that God will ordain me: but
the sword ye shall not have at this time, by the faith
of my body." "Ye shall repent it within a short
time," said the damsel, "for I would have the sword
more for your avail than for mine, for I am passing
heavy for your sake; for ye will not believe that the
sword shall be your destruction, and that is great
pity." With that the damsel departed, making great
sorrow.

Anon after Balin sent for his horse and armour, and
so would depart from the court, and took his leave of
King Arthur. "Nay," said the king, "I suppose ye
will not depart so lightly from this fellowship. I
suppose ye are displeased, that I have showed you
unkindness; blame me the less, for I was misinformed
against you. But I weened you had not been such a
knight as ye are of worship and prowess; and if ye will
abide in this court among my fellowship, I shall so
advance you, as ye shall be pleased." "God thank
your highness," said Balin, "for your bounty and
highness may no man praise half to the value; but now
at this time I must needs depart, beseeching you

always of your good grace." "Truly," said the king, "I am right wroth for your departing; I beseech you, fair knight, that ye tarry not long and ye shall be right welcome to me and to all my barons, and I shall amend all amiss, that I have done against you." "God thank your great lordship," said Balin, and therewith made him ready to depart. Then the most part of the knights of the Round Table said that Balin did not this adventure all only by might, but by witchcraft.

How the Lady of the Lake demaunded the knyghtes heed that had won the swerde, or the maydens hede.   iij.

The meanwhile that this knight was making him ready to depart, there came into the court a lady, that hight the Lady of the Lake, and she came on horseback richly beseen, and saluted King Arthur, and there asked him a gift that he promised her when she gave him the sword. "That is sooth," said Arthur, "a gift I promised you; but I have forgotten the name of my sword that ye gave me." [1] "The name of it," said the lady, "is Excalibur, that is as much as to say Cut-steel." "Ye say well," said the king; "ask what ye will and ye shall have it, if it lie in my power to give it." "Well," said the lady, "I ask the head of the knight that hath won the sword, or else the damsel's head that brought it; and I take no force though I have both their heads, for he slew my brother, a full good knight and true, and that gentlewoman was the causer of my father's death." "Truly," said King Arthur, "I may not grant neither of their heads with my worship; therefore ask what ye will else, and I shall fulfil your desire." "I will ask none other thing," said the lady. When Balin was

---

[1] See the *Book of Merlin,* chap. xxii.   *take no force,* care not.

ready to depart, he saw the Lady of the Lake, that by her means had slain Balin's mother, and he had sought her three years. And when it was told him that she asked his head of King Arthur, he went to her straight and said, "Evil be ye found, ye would have my head, and therefore ye shall lose yours:" and with his sword lightly he smote off her head before King Arthur. "Alas! for shame," said Arthur; "why have you done so? you have shamed me and all my court, for this was a lady that I was beholden to, and hither she came under my safe conduct. I shall never forgive you that trespass." "Sir," said Balin, "me forthinketh much of your displeasure, for this same lady was the untruest lady living; and by her enchantment and sorcery she hath been the destroyer of many good knights, and she was the causer that my mother was burnt through her falsehood and treachery." "What cause soever ye had," said King Arthur, "ye should have forborne her in my presence; therefore think not the contrary, ye shall repent it, for such another despite had I never in my court; therefore withdraw you out of my court in all the haste ye may."

Then Balin took up the head of the lady, and bare it with him to his hostel, and there he met with his squire, that was sorry he had displeased King Arthur; and so they rode forth out of the town. "Now," said Balin, "we must depart; take thou this head and bear it to my friends, and tell them how I have sped, and tell my friends in Northumberland that my most foe is dead; also tell them how I am out of prison, and what adventure befell me at the getting of the sword." "Alas," said the squire, "ye are greatly to blame for to displease King Arthur." "As for that," said Balin, "I will hie me in all haste that I may to meet

me forthinketh, I regret.

with King Rience, and destroy him, either else or die therefore; and if it may hap me to win him, then will King Arthur be my good and gracious lord." "Where shall I meet with you?" said the squire. "In King Arthur's court," said Balin. So his squire and he departed at that time. Then King Arthur and all his court made great dole, and had great shame of the death of the Lady of the Lake. Then the king richly buried her.

How Merlyn tolde thadventure of this damoysel.

Capitulo iiij.

At that time there was a knight the which was the king's son of Ireland, and his name was Launceor; the which was an orgulous knight, and counted himself one of the best of the court, and he had great despite at Balin for the achieving of the sword, that any should be accounted more hardy or more of prowess; and he asked King Arthur, if he would give him leave to ride after Balin, and to revenge the despite that he hath done. "Do your best," said King Arthur, "for I am right wroth with Balin; I would he were quit of the despite that he hath done to me and to my court." Then this Launceor went to his hostel, to make him ready.

In the meanwhile came Merlin to King Arthur's court, and there was told him the adventure of the sword, and the death of the Lady of the Lake. "Now shall I say you," said Merlin, "this same damsel that here standeth, that brought the sword unto your court, I shall tell you the cause of her coming, she was the falsest damsel that liveth." "Say not so," said they. "She hath a brother," [said Merlin,] "a passing good knight of prowess, and a full true man; and

orgulous, proud.

this damsel loved another knight that held her to paramour, and this good knight, her brother, met with that knight that held her to paramour, and slew him by force of his hands. When this false damsel understood this, she went to the lady Lily of Avelion, and besought her of help to be avenged on her brother.

How Balyn was pursyewed by Syr Launceor, knyght of Irelonde, and how he justed and slewe hym. v.

"And so this lady Lily of Avelion, took her this sword, which she brought with her, and told there should be no man pull it out of the sheath, but if he be one of the best knights of this realm, and he should be hard and full of prowess, and with that sword he should slay his brother. This was the cause that the damsel came into this court. I know it as well as ye do. Would God she had not come into this court; but she came never in fellowship of worship to do good, but always great harm, and that knight which hath achieved the sword shall be destroyed by that sword; for the which will be great damage; for there liveth not a knight of more prowess than he is, and he shall do unto you, my lord Arthur, great honour and kindness; and it is great pity he shall not endure but a while, for of his strength and hardiness I know not his match living." So the knight of Ireland armed him at all points, and dressed his shield on his shoulder, and mounted upon horseback, and took his spear in his hand, and rode after a great pace as much as his horse might go: and within a little space on a mountain he had a sight of Balin, and with a loud voice he cried, "Abide, knight, for ye shall abide, whether ye will or nill: and the shield that is tofore you, shall not help." When Balin heard that noise, he turned his horse fiercely, and said, "Fair knight, what will you with me; will ye joust with me?" "Yea," said the Irish knight, "therefore come I after you." "Per-adventure," said Balin, "it had been better to have holden you at home: for many a man weeneth to put his enemy to a rebuke, and often it falleth to himself. Of what court be ye sent from?" said Balin. "I am come from the court of King Arthur," said the knight of Ireland, "that come hither for to revenge the despite that ye did this day to King Arthur and to his court."

"Well," said Balin, "I see well I must have ado with you, which me forthinketh for to grieve King Arthur or any of his court; and your quarrel is full simple," said Balin, "unto me, for the lady that is dead did me great damage, or else would I have been loth as any knight that liveth for to slay a lady." "Make you ready," said the knight Launceor, "and dress you to me; for one of us shall abide in the field." Then they took their spears, and came together as much as their horses might drive, and the Irish knight smote Balin on the shield, that all went shivers of his spear. And Balin hit him through his shield and the hawberk perished, and so pierced through his body and the horse croup; and anon turned his horse fiercely, and drew out his sword, and wist not that he had slain him, and then he saw him lie as a dead corpse.

How a damoysel, whiche was love to Launceor, slewe hyr self for love, and how Balyn mette wyth his brother Balan. *vj.*

Then he looked by him, and was ware of a damsel that came riding full fast as the horse might ride on a fair palfrey. And when she espied that Sir Launceor was slain, she made sorrow out of measure, and said, "O Balin! two bodies thou hast slain and one heart,

and two hearts in one body, and two souls thou hast
lost." And therewith she took the sword from her
love that lay dead, and fell to the ground in a swoon;
and when she arose, she made great dole out of measure, the which sorrow grieved Balin passingly sore,
and he went unto her for to have taken the sword out
of her hand, but she held it so fast, that he might not
take it out of her hand; unless he should have hurt
her; and suddenly she set the pommel of the sword
to the ground, and rove herself thorough the body.
When Balin espied her dead, he was passing heavy in
his heart, and ashamed that so fair a damsel had
destroyed herself for the love of his death. "Alas!"
said Balin, "me repenteth sore the death of this
knight, for the love of this damsel; for there was much
true love betwixt them both," and for sorrow might
no longer behold them, but turned his horse and
looked toward a great forest, and there he was ware by
the arms of his brother Balan; and when they were
met, they put off their helms and kissed together,
and wept for joy and pity. "Then," Balan said, "I
little weened to have met with you at this sudden
adventure; I am right glad of your deliverance out of
your dolorous prisonment, for a man told me in the
Castle of Fourstones that ye were delivered, and that
man had seen you in the court of King Arthur; and
therefore I came hither into this country, for here I
supposed to find you." Anon the knight Balin told
his brother of his adventure of the sword, and of the
death of the Lady of the Lake, and how King Arthur
was displeased with him; "wherefore he sent this
knight after me that lieth here dead, and the death of
this damsel grieveth me full sore." "So doth it me,"
said Balan; "but ye must take the adventure that
God will ordain you." "Truly," said Balin, "I am

right heavy of mind that my lord, Arthur, is displeased with me, for he is the most worshipful knight
that reigneth now on earth; and his love I will get, or
else I will put my life in adventure; for the King
Rience lieth at a siege at the castle Terabil, and
thither will we draw in all haste, to prove our worship
and prowess upon him." "I will well," said Balan,
"that we do so, and we will help each other as brethren ought to do."

*How a dwarfe repreyved Balyn for the deth of Launceor,
and how kyng Marke of Cornewayl founde them, and
maad a tombe over them.*   *Capitulo vij.*

"Now we go hence," said Balin, "and well be we
met." The meanwhile as they talked there came a
dwarf from the city of Camelot on horseback, as much
as he might, and found the dead bodies; wherefore he
made great dole, and pulled out his hair for sorrow, and
said, "Which of you knights have done this deed?"
"Whereby asketh thou it?" said Balin. "For I would
wit it," said the dwarf. "It was I," said Balin, "that
slew this knight in my defence; for hither came he to
chase me, and either I must slay him or he me; and
this damsel slew herself for his love, which repenteth
me, and for her sake I shall owe all women the better
love." "Alas!" said the dwarf, "thou hast done great
damage unto thyself; for this knight, that is here dead,
was one of the most valiantest men that lived, and
trust well, Balin, that the kin of this knight will chase
you through the world till they have slain you." "As
for that," said Balin, "I fear not greatly; but I am
right heavy, that I have displeased my lord, King
Arthur, for the death of this knight."

So, as they talked together, there came a king of
Cornwall riding, which was hight King Mark; and

when he saw these two bodies dead, and understood how they were dead by one of the ij knights above-said, then made the king great sorrow for the true love that was betwixt them, and said, "I will not depart till I have on this earth made a tomb." And there he pitched his pavilions, and sought through all the country to find a tomb. And in a church they found one was fair and rich, and then the king let them put them both in the earth, and put the tomb upon them, and wrote the names of them both on the tomb, how: — "Here lieth Launceor the king's son, of Ireland; that at his own request was slain by the hands of Balin, and how his lady Colombe and paramour slew herself with her love's sword, for dole and sorrow."

How Merlyn prophecyed that two the best knyghtes of the world shold fyght there, whiche were Syr Launcelot and Syr Trystram. *Capitulo viij.*

[*In the forepart of this chapter Merlin prophesies to King Mark concerning the great battle between Launcelot and Tristram, which is related in the* Book of Marvellous Adventures.]

. . . Then said Merlin to Balin, "Thou hast done thyself great hurt, because thou savest not this lady that slew herself, that might have saved her an thou wouldest." "By the faith of my body," said Balin, "I might not save her, for she slew herself suddenly." "Me repenteth," said Merlin; "because of the death of that lady, thou shalt strike a stroke most dolorous that ever man stroke, except the stroke of our Lord; for thou shalt hurt the truest knight, and the man of most worship that now liveth, and through that stroke three kingdoms shall be in great poverty, misery, and wretchedness xij years, and the knight shall not be whole of that wound [in] many years."

Then Merlin took his leave of Balin; and Balin said,
"If I wist it were sooth that ye say, I should do such
perilous deed as that, I would slay myself to make
thee a liar." Therewith Merlin vanished away suddenly: and then Balin and his brother took their leave
of King Marke. "First," said the king, "tell me your
name." "Sir," said Balan, "ye may see he beareth
two swords, thereby ye may call him the knight with
the two swords." And so departed King Marke, to
Camelot to King Arthur; and Balin [and his brother]
took the way toward King Rience, and as they rode
together they met with Merlin disguised, but they
knew him not. "Whither ride ye?" said Merlin.
"We have little to do," said the ij knights, "for to
tell thee." "But what is thy name?" said Balin.
"As at this time," said Merlin, "I will not tell thee."
"It is evil seen," said the knights, "that thou art a
true man, that thou wilt not tell thy name." "As
for that," said Merlin, "be it as it may; I can tell you
wherefore you ride this way, for to meet King Rience:
but it will not avail you, without you have my counsel." "Ah!" said Balin, "ye are Merlin: we will be
ruled by your counsel." "Come on," said Merlin;
"ye shall have great worship, and look that ye do
knightly; for ye shall have great need." "As for
that," said Balin, "dread ye not: we will do what we
may."

How Balyn and his broder, by the counceyl of Merlyn,
toke kyng Ryons and brought hym to kyng Arthur. ix.

Then Merlin lodged them in a wood amongst leaves,
beside the highway, and took off the bridles of their
horses, and put them to grass, and laid them down to
rest them till it was nigh midnight. Then Merlin bade
them rise and make them ready; for the king was nigh

them that was stolen away from his host, with iij score of his best knights: and xx of them rode tofore, to warn the Lady de Vance that the king was coming; for that night King Rience should have lain with her. "Which is the king?" said Balin. "Abide," said Merlin; "here in a straight way ye shall meet with him." And therewith he showed Balin and his brother where he rode. Anon Balin and his brother met with the king, and smote him down, and wounded him fiercely, and laid him to the ground; and there they slew on the right hand and on the left hand, and slew more than xl of his men, and the remnant fled. Then went they again to King Rience, and would have slain him, had he not yielded him unto their grace. Then said he thus: "Knights, full of prowess, slay me not; for by my life ye may win, and by my death shall ye win nothing." Then said these two knights, "Ye say sooth and truth;" and so laid him on a horse-litter. With that Merlin was vanished, and came to King Arthur aforehand, and told him how his most enemy was taken and discomforted. "By whom?" said King Arthur. "By two knights," said Merlin, "that would please your lordship, and to-morrow ye shall know what knights they be." Anon after came the knight with the two swords, and Balan, his brother, and brought with them King Rience of North Wales, and there delivered him to the porters, and charged them with him; and so they two returned again in the dawning of the day.

King Arthur came then to King Rience and said, "Sir king, ye are welcome; by what adventure came ye hither?" "Sir," said King Rience, "I came hither by an hard adventure." "Who won you?" said King Arthur. "Sir," said the king, "the knight with the two swords and his brother, which are two marvellous

knights of prowess." "I know them not," said
Arthur; "but much I am beholden to them." "Ah!"
said Merlin, "I shall tell you, it is Balin that achieved
the sword, and his brother Balan, a good knight;
there liveth not a better of prowess and worthiness,
and it shall be the greatest dole of him that ever
I knew of knight, for he shall not long endure."
"Alas!" said King Arthur, "that is great pity; for I
am much beholding unto him, and I have full ill
deserved it unto him for his kindness." "Nay," said
Merlin, "he shall do much more for you, and that ye
shall know in haste. But, sir, are ye purveyed?"
said Merlin; "for to-morrow the host of Nero, King
Rience's brother, will set upon you or noon with a
great host: and therefore make you ready, for I will
depart from you."

*How kyng Arthur had a bataylle ayenst Nero and kyng
Loth of Orkeney, and how kyng Loth was deceyved by
Merlin, and how xij kynges were slayne.   Capitulo x.*

[*In this chapter, King Nero fights one great battle with
King Arthur and King Lot another.   Both are defeated.
Balin and Balan perform great feats of valor.*]

*Of the entyerement of xij kynges, and of the prophecye of
Merlyn how Balyn shold gyve the dolorous stroke.   xj.*

[*In this chapter, Balin is merely mentioned.   King
Arthur gives the scabbard of Excalibur to Morgan le Fay
for safe-keeping, and Merlin foretells the downfall of
the Order of the Round Table, through the treachery of
Mordred; and also the quest of the Sancgreal.*]

*How a sorouful knyght cam tofore Arthur, and how
Balyn fet hym, and how that knyght was slayn by a
knyght invisible.   xij.*

entyerement, interment, burial.   fet, fetched.

Within a day or two King Arthur was somewhat sick, and he let pitch his pavilion in a meadow, and there he laid him down on a pallet to sleep, but he might have no rest. Right so he heard a great noise of an horse; and therewith the king looked out at the porch of the pavilion, and saw a knight coming even by him making great dole. "Abide, fair sir," said King Arthur, "and tell me wherefore thou makest this sorrow." "Ye may little amend me," said the knight, and so passed forth unto the castle of Meliot. Anon after there came Balin; and, when he saw King Arthur, he alighted off his horse, and came to the king on foot, and saluted him. "By my head," said King Arthur, "ye be welcome. Sir, right now came riding this way a knight making great mourn, for what cause I cannot tell; wherefore, I would desire of you, of your courtesy and of your gentleness, to fetch again that knight, either by force or else by his good will." "I will do more for your lordship than that," said Balin; and so he rode more than a pace, and found the knight with a damsel in a forest, and said, "Sir knight, ye must come with me unto King Arthur, for to tell him of your sorrow." "That will I not," said the knight; "for it will scath me greatly, and now do you none avail." "Sir," said Balin, "I pray you make you ready; for ye must go with me, or else I will fight with you, and bring you by force, and that were me loth to do." "Will ye be my warrant," said the knight, "and I go with you?" "Yea," said Balin, "or else I will die therefore." And so he made him ready to go with Balin, and left the damsel still; and, as they were even afore King Arthur's pavilion, there came one invisible, and smote this knight that went with Balin throughout the body with a spear.

"Alas!" said the knight, "I am slain under your

conduct, with a knight called Garlon; therefore, take my horse, that is better than yours, and ride to the damsel, and follow the quest that I was in, as she will lead you, and revenge my death when ye may." "That shall I do," said Balin, "and that I make vow unto knighthood." And so he departed from this knight with great sorrow. So King Arthur let bury this knight richly, and made a mention upon his tomb how there was slain Herleus le Berbeus, and by whom the treachery was done, the knight Garlon. But ever the damsel bore the truncheon of the spear with her that Sir Herleus was slain withal.

How Balyn and the damoysel mette wyth a knyght whych was in lyke wyse slayn, and how the damoysel bledde for the custom of a castel.   *Capitulo xiij.*

[*In this chapter, Balin is befriended by Sir Perin de Montbelyard, but the latter is soon after slain by Garlon, the invisible knight. Balin is captured in a castle, but is released when the damsel gives a drink of her blood to the lady of the castle, who is sick and can be cured only by the blood of a king's daughter.*]

How Balyn mette wyth that knyght named Garlon at a feest, and there he slewe hym to have his blood to hele therewith the sone of his hoost.   *Capitulo xiiij.*

They rode three or four days, and never met with adventure; and by hap they were lodged with a gentleman that was a rich man and well at ease, and, as they sat at their supper, Balin heard one complain grievously by him in a chair. "What is this noise?" said Balin. "Forsooth," said his host, "I will tell you: I was but late at a jousting, and there I jousted with a knight, that is brother unto King Pellam, and twice

truncheon, butt of a broken spear.

I smote him down; and then he promised to quit me on my best friend, and so he wounded my son, that cannot be whole till I have of that knight's blood: and he rideth always invisible, but I know not his name." "Ah!" said Balin, "I know that knight, his name is Garlon; he hath slain two knights of mine in the same manner, therefore I had rather meet with that knight than all the gold in this realm, for the despite he hath done me." "Well," said his host, "I shall tell you: King Pellam, of Listenise, hath made do cry, in all this country, a great feast that shall be within these xx days, and no knight may come there but if he bring his wife with him, or his paramour; and that knight, your enemy and mine, ye shall see that day." "Then I behote you," said Balin, "part of his blood to heal your son withal." "We will forward to-morrow," said the host.

So, on the morrow, they rode all three towards Pellam, and had xv days' journey or they came thither: and that same day began the great feast, and so they alighted and stabled their horses, and went into the castle: but Balin's host might not be let in, because he had no lady. Then was Balin well received, and brought unto a chamber, and unarmed him; and there were brought him robes to his pleasure, and would have had Balin leave his sword behind him. "Nay," said Balin, "that do I not; for it is the custom of my country for a knight always to keep his weapon with him, and that custom will I keep, or else I will depart as I came." Then they gave him leave to wear his sword. And so he went to the castle, and was set among knights of worship, and his lady afore him. Soon Balin asked a knight, "Is there not a knight in this court whose name is Garlon?" "Yonder he go-

behote, promise.

eth," said the knight, "he with the black face: he is the marvellest knight that is now living, for he destroyeth many good knights, for he goeth invisible." "Ah, well," said Balin, "is that he?" Then Balin advised him long: — "If I slay him here I shall not escape, and if I leave him now, peradventure I shall never meet with him again at such a steven, and much harm will he do, an he live." Therewith this Garlon espied that this Balin beheld him, and then he came and smote Balin on the face with the back of his hand, and said, "Knight, why beholdest thou me so? for shame: eat thy meat, and do that thou came for." "Thou sayest sooth," said Balin; "this is not the first despite that thou hast done me; and, therefore, I will do that I came for." And rose up fiercely, and cleaved his head to his shoulders. "Give me the truncheon," said Balin to his lady, "wherewith he slew your knight." Anon she gave it him, for always she bear the truncheon with her. And therewith Balin smote him through the body, and said openly, "With that truncheon thou hast slain a good knight, and now it sticketh in thy body." And then Balin called to him his host, saying, "Now may ye fetch blood enough for to heal your son withal."

How Balyn fought wyth kyng Pelham, and how his swerde brake, and how he gate a spere wherewyth he smote the dolorous stroke.   *Capitulo xv.*

Anon all the knights arose from the table for to set on Balin; and King Pellam himself rose up fiercely, and said, "Knight, hast thou slain my brother? Thou shalt die therefor, or thou depart." "Well," said Balin, "do it yourself." "Yes," said King Pellam, "there shall no man have to do with thee but myself,

steven, favorable time.

for the love of my brother." Then King Pellam caught in his hand a grim weapon, and smote eagerly at Balin; but Balin put his sword between his head and the stroke, and therewith his sword burst in sunder. And when Balin was weaponless, he came into a chamber for to seek some weapon, and so from chamber to chamber, and no weapon he could find; and always King Pellam followed after him, and at the last he entered into a chamber that was marvellously well dight and richly, and a bed arrayed with cloth of gold, the richest that might be thought, and one lying therein: and thereby stood a table of clean gold, with four pillars of silver that bear up the table, and upon the table stood a marvellous spear, strangely wrought. And when Balin saw that spear, he gat it in his hand, and turned him to King Pellam, and smote him passingly sore with that spear, that King Pellam fell down in a swoon; and wherewith the castle roof and walls brake, and fell to earth, and Balin fell down, so that he might not stir foot nor hand: and so the most part of the castle that was fallen down, through that dolorous stroke, lay upon Pellam and Balin three days.

How Balyn was delyverd by Merlyn, and savyd a knyght that wold have slayn hym self for love.   Capitulo xvj.

Then Merlin came thither and took up Balin, and gat him a good horse, for his horse was dead, and bade him ride out of that country. "I would have my damsel," said Balin. "Lo," said Merlin, "where she lieth dead." And King Pellam lay so many years sore wounded, and might never be whole till Galahad, the haughty prince, healed him in the quest of the Sancgreal; for in that place was part of the blood of our Lord Jesus Christ, that Joseph of Arimathea brought into this land, and there himself lay in that rich bed.

And that was the same spear that Longius smote our Lord to the heart; and King Pellam was nigh of Joseph's kin,[1] and that was the most worshipful man that lived in those days: and great pity it was of his hurt, for thorough that stroke turned to great dole, tray, and teen. Then departed Balin from Merlin, and said, "In this world we meet never no more."

So he rode forth through the fair countries and cities, and found the people dead slain on every side. And all that were alive cried, "O Balin! thou hast caused great damage in these countries, for the dolorous stroke that thou gavest unto King Pellam; three countries are destroyed; and doubt not but the vengeance will fall on thee at last."

[*Balin meets a knight, Sir Garnish of the Mount, dolorously weeping, because his lady has proved false to him. Balin offers to go seek her.*]

". . . I will into the castle," said Balin, "and will look if she be there." So he went in, and searched from chamber to chamber, and found her bed, but she was not there; then Balin looked into a fair little garden, and, under a laurel-tree, he saw her lie upon a quilt of green samite, and a knight in her arms, fast halsing either other, and under their heads grass and herbs. When Balin saw her lie so with the foulest knight that ever he saw, and she a fair lady, then Balin went through all the chambers again, and told the knight how he found her as she had slept fast; and so brought him to the place where she lay fast sleeping.

How that knyght slewe his love and a knyght lyeng by hyr, and after how he slewe hym self wyth his owne swerde, and how Balyn rode toward a castel where he lost his lyf.

Capitulo xvij.

---

[1] *King Pellam*, cf. *Morte Darthur*, Book XVII, ch. 21.
tray and teen, vexation and grief.   samite, rich silk.   halsing, embracing.

And when Garnish beheld her so lying, for pure sorrow his mouth and nose brast out on bleeding, and with his sword he smote off both their heads; and then he made sorrow out of measure, and said, "Oh! Balin, much sorrow hast thou brought to me; for hadst thou not showed me that sight, I should have passed my sorrow." "Forsooth," said Balin, "I did it to this intent, that it should better thy courage, and that ye might see and know her falsehood, and to cause you to leave that love of such a lady. God knoweth I did none other but as I would you did to me." "Alas!" said Garnish, "now is my sorrow double that I may not endure, now have I slain that I most loved in all my life." And therewith suddenly he rove himself on his own sword unto the hilt. When Balin saw that, he dressed him from thence, lest folks should say that he had slain them; and so he rode forth, and within three days he came by a cross, and thereon was letters of gold written, that said, "It is not for no knight alone to ride toward this castle." Then he saw an old hoary gentleman coming toward him, that said, "Balin le Savage, thou passeth thy bounds to come this way; therefore turn again, and it will avail thee." And he vanished away anon, and so he heard an horn blow, as it had been the death of a beast. "That blast," said Balin, "is blown for me; for I am the prize, and yet I am not dead." Anon withal he saw an hundred ladies and many knights that welcomed him with a fair semblance, and made him passing good cheer unto his sight, and led him into the castle, and there was dancing and minstrelsy, and all manner of joy. Then the chief lady of the castle said, "Knight with the two swords, ye must have a do and joust with a knight hereby that keepeth an island; for there may no man pass this way, but he may joust, or he pass." "That is an unhappy custom," said Balin, "that a knight may not pass this way, but if he joust." "Ye shall not have a do but with one knight," said the lady. "Well," said Balin, "since I shall, thereto I am ready; but travelling men are oft weary, and their horses too: but though my horse be weary, my heart is not weary; I would be fain there my death should be." "Sir," said a knight to Balin, "methinketh your shield is not good, I will lend you a bigger; thereof I pray you." And so he took the shield that was unknown, and left his own, and so rode unto the island, and put him and his horse in a great boat. And when he came on the other side he met with a damsel, and she said, "O knight Balin, why have you left your own shield? alas! ye have put yourself in great danger: for by your shield you should have been known. It is great pity of you as ever was of knight, for of thy prowess and hardiness thou hast no fellow living." "Me repenteth," said Balin, "that ever I came within this country: but I may not turn now again for shame, and what adventure shall fall to me, be it life or death, I will take the adventure that shall come to me." And then he looked on his armour, and understood he was well armed, and therewith blessed him, and mounted upon his horse.

How Balyn mette wyth his brother Balen, and how eche of theym slewe other unknowen, tyl they were wounded to death. xviij.

Then afore him he saw one riding out of a castle, a knight, and his horse trapped all in red, and himself of the same colour. And when this knight in red beheld Balin, him thought it should be his brother Balin, because of his two swords; but because he knew not his shield, he deemed that it was not he. And so they

aventred their spears, and came marvellously fast together, and smote other in the shields; but their spears
and their course were so big that it bare down horse
and man, so that they lay both in a swoon; but Balin
was sore bruised with the fall of his horse, for he was
weary of travel. And Balan was the first that rose on
foot, and drew his sword, and went toward Balin, and
he arose and went against him, but Balan smote Balin
first, and he put up his shield, and smote him through
the shield, and tamed his helm; then Balin smote him
again with that unhappy sword, and well nigh had
felled his brother Balan: and so they fought there together till their breaths failed. Then Balin looked up
to the castle, and saw the towers stand full of ladies.
So they went unto battle again, and wounded every
other dolefully; and then they breathed ofttimes, and
so went unto battle: that all the place there as they
fought was blood red. And at that time there was none
of them both but they had smitten either other seven
great wounds; so that the least of them might have
been the death of the mightiest giant in the world.
Then they went to battle again so marvellously, that
doubt it was to hear of that battle; for the great blood-
shedding. And their hawberks unnailed, that naked
they were on every side. At the last Balan, the
younger brother, withdrew him a little, and laid him
down. Then said Balin le Savage, "What knight art
thou? for or now I found never no knight that matched
me." "My name is," said he, "Balan, brother unto
the good knight Balin." "Alas!" said Balin, "that
ever I should see this day." And therewith he fell
backward in a swoon. Then Balan yede on all four,
feet and hands, and put off the helm of his brother,

---

aventred, lowered, couched.   *tamed*, crushed.
unnailed, possibly *unmailed*, i.e., the rings separated or broken.

and might not know him by the visage, it was so full
hewn and bled; but when he awoke, he said, "O Balan, my brother, thou hast slain me, and I thee, wherefore all the wide world shall speak of us both."
"Alas!" said Balan, "that ever I saw this day, that
through mishap I might not know you; for I espied
well both your swords, but because ye had another
shield, I deemed you had been another knight."
"Alas!" said Balin, "all that made an unhappy knight
in the castle, for he caused me to leave mine own
shield to our both's destruction; and if I might live I
would destroy that castle for ill customs." "That
were well done," said Balan, "for I had never grace to
depart from them, since that I came hither; for here
it happed me to slay a knight that kept this island,
and since might I never depart, and no more should ye,
brother, and ye might have slain me, as ye have, and
escaped yourself with your life." Right so came the
lady of the tower with iiij knights and vj ladies, and
vj yeomen unto them, and there she heard how they
made their mourn either to other, and said, "We came
both out of one tomb, that is to say, one mother's
belly, and so shall we lie both in one pit." So Balan
prayed the lady of her gentleness, for his true service,
that she would bury them both in that same place
there the battle was done. And she granted them,
with weeping, it should be done richly, in the best
manner. "Now will ye send for a priest, that we may
receive our sacrament and receive the blessed body of
our Lord Jesus Christ?" "Yea," said the lady, "it
shall be done." And so she sent for a priest, and gave
them their rites. "Now," said Balin, "when we are
buried in one tomb, and the mention made over us how
ij brothers slew each other, there will never good
knight, nor good man, see our tomb, but they will pray

for our 'souls." And so all the ladies and gentlemen wept for pity. And anon Balan died, but Balin died not till the midnight after, and so were they buried both; and the lady let make a mention of Balan, how he was slain by the hands of his own brother: but she knew not Balin's name.

How Merlyn buryed them bothe in one tombe, and of Balyns swerd.   *Capitulo xix.*[1]

In the morne cam Merlyn and lete wryte Balyns name on the tombe with letters of gold that, "Here lyeth Balyn le Saveage, that was the knyght with the two swerdes, and he that smote the dolorous stroke." Also Merlyn lete make there a bedde, that ther sholde never man lye therin but he wente oute of his wytte, yet Launcelot de Lake fordyd that bed thorow his noblesse. And anone after Balyn was dede, Merlyn toke his swerde and toke of the pomel, and set on an other pomel. So Merlyn bad a knyght that stode afore hym handel that swerde, and he assayed, and he myght not handle hit. Thenne Merlyn lough. "Why laugh ye?" said the knyghte. "This is the cause," said Merlyn, "ther shalle never man handle this suerd but the best knyght of the world, and that shalle be Syr Launcelot or els Galahad his sone; and Launcelot with this suerd shalle slee the man that in the world he loved best, that shalle be Syr Gawayne." Alle this he lete wryte in the pomel of the swerd.

Thenne Merlyn lete make a brydge of yron and of stele in to that iland, and it was but half a foote brode, and there shalle never man passe that brydge nor have hardynes to goo over but yf he were a passyng

noblesse, rather, through the power of an amulet given him by the Lady of the Lake.
pomel, pommel, knob at the end of the hilt.
Gawayne, see *Morte Darthur*, Book XX, 21, 22; XXI, 2.
[1] This chapter is given in the old spelling.

good man and a good knyght, withoute techery or vylonye. Also the scaubard of Balyns swerd, Merlyn lefte it on this syde of the iland that Galahad shold fynde it. Also Merlyn lete make by his subtylyte that Balyns swerd was put in a marbel stone standyng up ryght as grete as a mylle stone, and the stone hoved al weyes above the water, and dyd many yeres, and so by adventure it swam doun the streme to the cyte of Camelot, that is in Englysshe Wynchestre, and that same day Galahad broughte wyth hym the scaubard, and encheved the swerde that was there in the marbel stone, hovynge upon the water. And on Whytsonday he encheved the swerde, as it is reherced in the book of Sancgrayll. Soone after this was done Merlyn came to kyng Arthur and told hym of the dolorous stroke that Balyn gaf to kyng Pellam, and how Balyn and Balan foughte to gyders the merveillous batail that ever was herd of, and how they were buryed bothe in one tombe. "Allas!" said kyng Arthur, "this is the grettest pyte that ever I herd telle of two knyghtes, for in the world I knowe not suche two knyghtes." Thus endeth the tale of Balyn and of Balan, two bretheren born in Northumberland, good knightes.

> *Sir Thomas Malory, knight, The Noble and Joyous Book entitled Le Morte Darthur.* Printed by William Caxton, 1485.

AN INTIMATE LETTER

June 1476

To his Kinswoman, Katherine Ryche

Jesus. An°. xvj°.

My nowne hartely belovid Cossen Kateryn, I recomande me unto you withe all the inwardnesse of myn

Sancgraylle, see Morte Darthur, Book XIII, 2.

hart. And now lately ye shall understond that I resseyvid a token from you, the which was and is to me
right hartely welcom, and with glad will I resseyvid it;
and over that I had a letter from Holake, youre gentyll Sqwyer, by the which I understond right well that
ye be in good helth of body, and mery at hart. And
I pray God hartely to his plesour to contenew the
same: for it is to me veray grete comforth that ye so be,
so helpe me Jesu. And yf ye wold be a good etter of
your mete allwaye, that ye myght waxe and grow fast
to be a woman, ye shuld make me the gladdest man
of the world, be my trouth: for whanne I remembre
your favour and your sadde lofynge delynge to me-
wardes, for south ye make me evene veray gladde and
joyus in my hart: and on the tother syde agayn
whanne I remembre your yonge youthe, and seeth
well that ye be none etter of youre mete, the which
shuld helpe you greatly in waxynge, for south than ye
make me veray hevy agayn. And therfore I praye
you, myn nown swete Cossen, evene as you lofe me to
be mery and to eate your mete lyke a woman. And yf
ye so will do for my love, looke what ye will desyre of
me, whatsomever it be, and be my trouth I promesse
you by the helpe of our Lord to performe it to my
power. I can [no] more say now, but at my comyng
home, I will tell you mych more betwene you and me
and God before. And where as ye, full womanly and
lyke a lofer, remembre me with manyfolde recom-
endacion in dyversse maners, remyttynge the same to
my discresscion to depart them ther as I love best, for
south, myn nown swete Cossen, ye shall understand
that with good hart and good will I resseyve and take to
my self the one half of them, and them will I kepe by
me; and the tother half with hartely love and favour

sadde lofynge delynge, serious loving dealing.

I send hem to you, myn nown swete Cossen, agayn, for to kepe by you: and over that I send you the blis- synge that our Lady gave hir dere sonne, and ever well to fare. I pray you grete well my horsse, and praye hym to gyfe you iij of his yeres to help you with all: and I will at my comynge home gyf hym iiij of my yeres and iiij horses lofes till amendes. Tell hym that I prayed hym so. And Cossen Kateryn I thannke you for hym, and my wif shall thanke you for hym here- after; for ye do grete cost apon hym as it is told me. Myn nown swete Cossen, it was told me but late that ye were at Cales to seeke me, but ye cowde not se me nor fynde me: for south ye myght have comen to my counter, and ther ye shuld bothe fynde me and see me, and not have fawtid off me: but ye sought me in a wronge Cales and that ye shuld well know yf ye were here and saw this Cales, as wold God ye were and som of them with you that were with you at your gentill Cales. I praye you, gentill Cossen, comaunde me to the Cloke, and pray hym to amend his unthryfte maners: for he strykes ever in undew tyme, and he will be ever afore, and that is a shrewde condiscion. Tell hym with owte he amend his condiscion that he will cause strangers to advoide and come no more there. I trust to you that he shall amend agaynst myn commynge, the which shalbe shortely with all hanndes and all feete with Godes grace. My veray feithefull Cossen, I trust to you that thowe all I have not re- membred my right worshipful maystres your modyr afore in this letter that ye will of your gentilnesse rec- omaunde me to her maystresshipe as many tymes as

---

horses lofes, horseshoes.   *till amendes,* as payment.
do grete cost apon, spend much money upon.
Cales, a city in Italy. Kathryn has evidently mistaken for it a town of the same name farther north.
counter, office.   *fawtid off,* missed.   *Cloke,* clock.
thowe all, although.

it shall ples you: and ye may say, yf it plese you, that in Wytson Weke next I intend to the marte-ward. And I trust you will praye for me: for I shall praye for you, and, so it may be, none so well. And Almyghty Jesu make you a good woman, and send you many good yeres and longe to lyve in helth and vertu to his plesour. At greate Cales on this syde on the see, the fyrst day of June, whanne every man was gone to his Dener, and the Cloke smote noynne, and all oure howsold cryed after me and badde me come down; come down to dener at ones! and what answer I gave hem ye know of old.

> Be your feithefull Cossen and lofer
>   Thomas Betson.

I sent you this rynge for a token.

To my feithefull and hartely belovid Cossen Kateryn Ryche at Stonor this letter be delyvered in hast.

Stonor Letters and Papers

SCENES FROM REYNARD THE FOX

In Dutch 1479
In English 1481

Here beginneth the History of Reynard the Fox.

In this history ben written the parables, good lerynge, and diverse points to be marked, by which points men may learn to come to the subtle knowledge of such things as daily ben used and had in the counsels of lords and prelates, ghostly and worldly, and also among merchants and other common people. And this book is made for need and profit of all good folk, as far as they in reading or hearing it shall mowe understand and feel the foresaid subtle deceits that daily ben used in the world; not to the intent that men

intend to the marte-ward, intend to go to market.   *lerynge*, doctrine.
mowe, be able to.

should use them, but that every man should eschew and keep him from the subtle false shews, that they be not deceived. Then who that will have the very understanding of this matter, he must oft and many times read in this book, and earnestly and diligently mark well that he readeth; for it is set subtlely, like as ye shall see in reading of it; and not once to read it, for a man shall not with once over reading find the right understanding ne comprise it well; but ofttimes to read it shall cause it well to be understood. And for them that understandeth it, it shall be right joyous, pleasant, and profitable.

How the Lion, King of all Beasts, sent out his mandment that all Beasts should come to his Feast and Court.
Capitulo Primo.

It was about the time of Pentacost or Whitsuntide, that the woods commonly be lusty and gladsome, and the trees clad with leaves and blossoms, and the ground with herbs and flowers sweet smelling, and also the fowls and birds singing melodiously in their harmony, that the Lion, the noble King of all Beasts, would in the holy days of this feast hold an open Court at state; which he did to know over all his land, and commanded by straight commissions and commandments that every Beast should come thither, in such wise that all the Beasts great and small came to the Court save Reynart the Fox: for he knew himself faulty and guilty in many things against many Beasts that thither should comen, that he durst not adventure to go thither. When the King of all Beasts had assembled all his Court, there was none of them all but that he complained sore on Reynart the Fox.

[In Chapters II and III, Isegrim the Wolf and Courtoys the Hound complain of Reynart; in Chapter IV,

Tybert the Cat and the Panther speak for and against him; and in Chapter IV, Grymbart the Dasse (Badger), defends him. While he is speaking, a funeral procession approaches.]

How the Cock complained on Reynart. Capitulo v.

Chanticleer came forth and smote piteously his hands and his feathers; and on each side of the bier wenten tweyne sorrowful hens, that one was called Cantart and that other good hen Crayant, they were two the fairest hens that were between Holland and Arderne. These hens bare each of them a burning taper which was long and straight. These two hens were Coppen's sisters, and they cried so piteously "Alas and weleaway" for the death of their dear sister Coppen. Two young hens bare the bier, which cackled so heavily and wept so loud for the death of Coppen their mother, that it was very hard. Thus came they together tofore the King.

And Chanticleer tho said, "Merciful lord, my lord the King, please it you to hear our complaint and abhor the great scathe that Reynart hath done to me and my children that here stand. It was so that in the beginning of April, when the weather is fair, as that I, as hardy and proud because of the great lineage that I am come of and also had, for I had eight fair sons and seven fair daughters which my wife had hatched, and they were all strong and fat, and went in a yard which was walled round about, in which was a shed wherein six great dogs which had tofore and plucked many a beast's skin in such wise as my children were not afraid. On whom Reynart the thief had great envy because they were so sure that he could none get of them; how well ofttimes hath this fell thief gone round about this wall and hath laid for us in such wise that the dogs have be set on him and have hunted him away; and once they leapt on him upon the bank, and that cost him somewhat for his theft. I saw that his skin smoked. Nevertheless he went his way. God amend it!

"Thus were we quit of Reynart a long while. At last came he in likeness of an hermit, and brought to me a letter for to read, sealed with the King's seal, in which stood written that the King had made peace over all in his realm, and that all manner beasts and fowls should do none harm nor scathe to any other. Yet said he to me more that he was a cloisterer or a closed recluse becomen, and that he would receive great penance for his sins. He showed me his slavyne and pylche and an hairen shirt thereunder, and then said he, 'Sir Chanticleer after this time be no more afraid of me, ne take no heed, for I will eat no more flesh. I am forthon so old that I would fain remember my soul. I will go forth, for I have yet to say my sexte, none, and mine evensong. To God I betake you.' Tho went Reynart thence, saying his Credo, and laid him under an hawthorn. Then was I glad and merry, and also took none heed, and went without the wall for to walk; whereof is much harm comen us, for Reynart lay under a bush and came creeping between us and the gate, so that he caught one of my children and laid him in his male. Whereof we have great harm, for sith he hath tasted of him there might never hunter ne hound save ne keep him from us. He hath waited by night and day in such wise that he hath stolen so many of my children that of fifteen I have but four, in such wise hath this thief forslongen

---

slavyne and pilche, old shoes and skincoat.
sexte, none, prayers and exercises of the sixth and ninth hours (after sunrise).
betake, commend.
male, bag, wallet.   *forslongen,* swallowed.

them.   And yet yesterday was Coppen my daughter,
that here lieth upon the bier, with the hounds rescued.
This complain I to you, gracious King, have pity on
mine great and unreasonable damage and loss of my
fair children!"

How the King spake touching this complaint.

Capitulo vi.

Then spake the King:

"Sir Dasse, hear ye this well of the recluse of your
Eme? He hath fasted and prayed, that if I live a
year he shall abye it. Now hark, Chanticleer, your
plaint is enough. Your daughter that lieth here dead,
we will give to her the death's rite. We may keep
her no longer, we will betake her to God. We will
sing her vigil and bring her worshipfully on earth, and
then we will speak with these lords and take counsel
how we may do right and justice of this great murder,
and bring this false thief to the law."

Tho began they *Placebo domino*, with the verses that
to longen, which if I should say were me too long.
When this vigil was done and the commendation, she
was laid in the pit, and there upon her was laid a mar-
ble stone polished as clear as any glass, and thereon
hewen in great letters in this wise: COPPE CHAN-
TEKLERS DOUGHTER, WHOM REYNART THE
FOX HATH BYTEN, LYETH HIER UNDER
BURYED, COMPLEYNE YE HER FFOR, SHE IS
SHAMEFULLY COMEN TO HER DETH.

After this, the King sent for his lords and the wisest
of his council for to take advice how this great murder and trespass should be punished on Reynart the

Eme, uncle.   *abye*, pay for.
Placebo domino, opening words of the antiphon of the vespers for the dead
    (*Psalm* 116, verse 9).
to longen, belong to.

Fox. There was concluded and appointed for the best that Reynart should be sent for, and that he left not for any cause, but he came into the King's court for to hear what should be said to him; and that Bruin the Bear should do the message.

The King thought that all this was good and said to Bruin the Bear, "Sir Bruin, I will that ye do this message; but see well for yourself, for Reynard is a shrew, and fell, and knoweth so many wiles that he shall lie and flatter, and shall think how he may beguile, deceive, and bring you to some mockery."

Then said Bruin, "What, good lord, let it alone! Deceiveth me the Fox, so have I ill learned my *casus*. I trow he shall come too late to mock me." Thus departed Bruin merrily from thence, but it is to dread that he came not so merrily again.

[*In Chapters VII–X, Bruin the Bear and Tybert the Cat are both tricked by Reynard, who plays upon their greed, the one of honey, the other of mice. They are trapped through his wiles and are sorely beaten by men. The King, enraged, then sends Grimbart the Dasse, who is related to Reynard and for whom Reynard has some affection. In Chapter XI, Reynard comes to court and on the way confesses to Grimbart his sins and promises to be virtuous henceforth. He still, nevertheless, casts longing eyes at the poultry. (Chapter XII.)*]

How the Fox came to the Court and how he excused him tofore the King.   Capitulo xiii.

At the first when it was known in the Court that Reynart the Fox and Grymbart his cousin were comen to the Court, there was none so poor nor so feeble of

---

shrew, malicious deceiver.   *fell,* cruel.
casus, case. Bruin considers himself a keen casuist.

kin and friends but that he made him ready for to complain on Reynart the Fox.

Reynart looked as he had not been afraid, and held him better than he was, for he went forth proudly with his nephew through the highest street of the Court, right as he had been the King's son, and as he had not trespassed to any man the value of an hair: and went in the middle of the place standing tofore Noble the King and said —

"God give you great honour and worship. There was never King that ever had a truer servant than I have been to your good grace, and yet am. Nevertheless, dear lord, I know well that there ben many in this Court that would destroy me if ye would believe these false deceivers and liars lightly. To God mote it be complained how that these false liars and flatterers nowadays in the lord's Courts ben most heard and believed, the shrews and false deceivers ben borne up for to do good men all the harm and scathe they may. Our Lord God shall once reward them their hire."

The King said, "Peace, Reynart, false thief and traitor! How well can ye bring forth fair tales! And all shall not help you a straw. Ween ye with such flattering words to be my friend, ye have so oft served me so as ye now shall well know. The peace that I have commanded and sworn, that have ye well holden, have ye?"

Chanticleer could no longer be still, but cried, "Alas, what have I by this peace lost!"

"Be still, Chanticleer, hold your mouth. Let me answer this foul thief. Thou shrewd fell thief," said the King, "thou sayest that thou lovest me well: that hast thou showed well on my messengers, these poor fellows, Tibert the Cat and Bruin the Bear, which yet ben all bloody; which chide not ne say not much, but that shall this day cost thee thy life. *In nomine Patris et Christi filii.*"

Said the Fox, "Dear lord and mighty King, if Bruin's crown be bloody what is that to me? When he ate honey at Lanfert's house in the village and did him hurt and scathe, there was he beaten therfor; if he had willed, he is so strong of limbs, he might well have be avenged ere he sprang into the water. Tho came Tybert the Cat, whom I received friendly. If he went out without my counsel for to steal mice to a priest's house, and the priest did him harm, should I abye that, then might I say I were not happy. Not so, my liege lord. Ye may do what ye will, though my matter be clear and good; ye may siede me, or roast, hang, or make me blind. I may not escape you. We stand all under your correction. Ye be mighty and strong. I am feeble, and my help is but small. If ye put me to the death it were a small vengeance."

Whiles they thus spake, up sprang Bellyn the Ram and his ewe Dame Olewey, and said, "My lord the King, hear our complaint." Bruin the Bear stood up with all his lineage and his fellows. Tybert the Cat, Isegrim the Wolf, Cuwart the Hare, and Panther; the Boar, the Camel, and Brunel the Goose; the Kid and Goat; Boudewyn the Ass, Borre the Bull, Hamel the Ox, and the Weasel; Chanticleer the Cock, Pertelot with all their children, all these made great rumour and noise, and came forth openly tofore their lord the King, and made that the Fox was taken and arrested.

How the Fox was arrested and judged to death.

Capitulo xiv.

Hereupon was a Parliament; and they desired that

abye, undergo, suffer.　　　*siede*, seethe, boil.

Reynart should ben dead. And whatsomever they said against the Fox he answered to each of them. Never heard man of such beasts such plaints of wise counsel and subtle inventions. And on that other side, the Fox made his excuse so well and formably thereon, that they that heard it wondered thereof. They that heard and saw it may tell it.

How the Fox was led to the gallows.   *Capitulo xv.*

[*Chapter XV tells how the Fox is taken to a tree to be hanged. He is sore afraid, and yet keeps a good countenance and taunts his enemies. But his quick wits are busy with a plan of escape.*]

The Fox said, "Now may my heart be well heavy for great dread; for I see death tofore mine eyen, and I may not escape. My lord the King, and dear Queen, and forth all ye that here stand, ere I depart from this world I pray you of a boone: that I may tofore you all make my confession openly, and tell my defaults all so clearly that my soul may not be acumbred, and also that no man here after bear no blame for my theft ne for my treason. My death shall be to me the easier, and pray ye all to God that he may have mercy on my soul."

How the Fox made openly his confession tofore the King and tofore all them that would hear it.   *Capitulo xvi.*

All they that stood there had pity when Reynart said tho words, and said it was but little request if the King would grant it him, and they prayed the King to grant it him.

The King gave him leave.

Reynart was well glad, and hoped that it might fall better, and said thus:

"Now help, *Spiritus Domini*, for I see here no man but I have trespassed unto. Nevertheless yet was I, unto the time that I was weaned from the teat, one of the best children that could anywhere be found. I went tho and played with the lambs, because I heard them gladly bleat. I was so long with them that at the last I bit one; there learned I first to lappen of the blood. It savoured well; me thought it right good. And after I began to taste of the flesh thereof, I was licorous; so that after that I went to the gate into the wood, there heard I the kids bleat and I slew of them twain. I began to wax hardy after. I slew hens, polaylle and geese wherever I found them. Thus worden my teeth all bloody. After this, I wex so fell and so wroth that whatsomever I found that I might over, I slew all. Thereafter I came by Isegrim, now in the winter, where he hid him under a tree, and reckoned to me that he was mine eme. When I heard him then reckon alliance, we became fellows, which I may well repent. We promised each to other to be true, and to use good fellowship, and began to wander together. He stole the great things and I the small, and all was common between us. Yet he made it so that he had the best deal; I got not my half. When that Isegrim gat a calf a ram or a wether, then grimmed he, and was angry on me, and drove me from him, and held my part and his too, so good is he. Yet this was of the least. But when it so lucked that we took an ox or a cow, then came thereto his wife with seven children; so that unto me might unnethe come one of the smallest ribs, and yet, had they eaten all the flesh thereof, therewithall must I be content; not for that I had so great need, for I have so great scatte

---

licorous, fond of dainty fare.   *polaylle,* poultry.   *worden,* became.
unnethe, scarcely.   *scatte,* treasure.

and good of silver and of gold, that seven wains should not can to carry it away."

When the King heard him speak of this great good and riches, he burned in the desire and covetyse thereof, and said, "Reynart, where is the riches becomen? tell me that."

The Fox said, "My lord, I shall tell you. The riches was stolen. And had it not be stolen, it should have cost you your life and you should have been murdered — which God forbid! — and should have been the greatest hurt in the world."

When the Queen heard that, she was sore afraid and cried loud, "Alas, and weleaway! Reynart, what say ye? I conjure you by the long way that your soul shall go, that ye tell us openly the truth hereof, as much as ye know of this great murder that should have be done on my lord, that we may all hear it!" —

Now hearken how the Fox shall flatter the King and Queen, and shall win both their good will and loves, and shall hinder them that labour for his death. He shall unbind his pack and lie, and by flattery and fair words shall bring forth so his matters that it shall be supposed for truth.

In a sorrowful countenance spake the Fox to the Queen, "I am in such case now that I must needs die, and had ye me not so sore conjured I will not jeopardize my soul, and if I so died I should go therefor in to the pain of hell. I will say nothing but that I will make it good, for piteously he should have been murdered of his own folk. Nevertheless they that were most principal in this feat were of my next kin, whom gladly I would not betray, if the sorrow were not of the hell."

The King was heavy of heart, and said, "Reynart, sayest thou to me the truth?"

"Yes," said the Fox. "See ye not how it standeth with me? Ween ye that I shall damn my soul? What should it avail me if I now said otherwise than truth? My death is so nigh. There may neither prayer ne good help me." Tho trembled the Fox, by dissembling, as he had ben afeared.

The Queen had pity on him, and prayed the King to have mercy on him, in eschewing of more harm, and that he should doo the people hold their peace, and give the Fox audience, and hear what he should say.

Tho commanded the King openly that each of them should be still, and suffer the Fox to say unberisped what that he should.

Then said the Fox, "Be ye now all still, sith it is the King's will, and I shall tell you openly this treason. And therein will I spare no man that I know guilty."

How the Fox brought them in danger that would have brought him to death, and how he got the grace of the King.
Capitulo xvii.

Now hearken how the Fox began. In the beginning he appealed Grymbart his dear Cousin, which ever had helped him in his need. He did so because his words should be the better believed; and that he forthon might the better lie on his enemies. Thus began he first and said:

"My lord, my father had found King Ermeryk's treasure dolven in a pit; and when he had this great good, he was so proud and orguillous that he had all other beasts in despite which tofore had been his fellows. He made Tybert the Cat go into that wild land of Ardenne to Bruin the Bear for to do him homage, and bad him say, if he would be King that he should

---

unberisped, untroubled, unexcited.
Ermeryk or Ermetick, an imaginary king.   *dolven*, dug, buried,

come in to Flanders. Bruin the Bear was glad hereof, for he had long desired it, and went forth in to Flanders; where my father received him right friendly. Anon he sent for the wise Grymbart, mine nephew, and for Isegrim the Wolf and for Tybert the Cat. Tho these five came between Gaunt and the thorp called Yfte, there they held their council an whole dark night long. What with the devil's help and craft, and for my father's riches, they concluded and swore there the King's death. Now hearken, and hear this wonder. The four swore upon Isegrim's crown that they should make Bruin a king and a lord, and bring him in the stool at Akon, and set the crown on his head; and if there were any of the King's friends or lineage that would be contrary or against this, him should my father with his good and treasure fordrive, and take from him his might and power.

"It happed so that on a morrowtide early when Grymbart, my nephew, was of wine almost drunk, that he told it to Dame Sloepcade, his wife, in counsel, and bade her keep it secret. But she anon forgat it, and said it forth in confession to my wife upon an heath where they both wenten a pilgrimage, but she must first swear, by her truth and by the holy Three Kings of Cologne, that for love ne for hate she should never tell it forth, but keep it secret. But she held it not, and kept it no longer secret but till she came to me; and she then told to me all that she heard, but I must keep it secret. And she told me so many tokens that I felt well it was truth; and for dread and fear mine hair stood right up, and my heart became as heavy as lead and as cold as ice. I thought by this a likeness which here aforetime befell to the frosshis

---

Akon, Aachen, Aix-la-Chapelle.   *fordrive*, drive away.
frosshis, frogs.

which were free and complained that they had none lord ne were not bydwongen, for a comynte without a governour was not good, and they cried to God with a loud voice that he would ordain one that might rule them, this was all they desired. God heard their request, for it was reasonable, and sent to them a Stork which ate and swallowed them in, as many as he could find; he was alway to them unmerciful. Tho complained they their hurt, but it was too late; they that were tofore free and were afraid of nobody ben now bound and must obey to strength their king: herefor, ye rich and poor, I sorrowed, that it might happen us in likewise.

"Thus, my lord the King, I have had sorrow for you whereof ye can but little thank. I know Bruin the Bear for such a shrew and ravener, wherefore I thought if he were king we should be all destroyed and lost. I know our sovereign lord the King of so high birth, so mighty, so benign and merciful, that I thought truly it had been an evil change for to have a foul stinking thief and to refuse a noble mighty stately Lion; for the Bear hath more mad folly in his unthrifty head, and all his ancestors, than any other hath. Thus had I in mine heart many a sorrow, and thought alway how I might break and foredo my father's false counsel, which of a churl and a traitor and worse than a thief would make a lord and a king. Alway I prayed God that he would keep our King in worship and good health, and grant him long life, but I thought well if my father held his treasure he should with his false fellows well find the way that the King should be deposed and set aside. I was sore bethought how I might best wit where my father's good lay. I awaited at all times as nigh as I could, in woods, in bushes, in

bydwongen, restrained.   _comynte_, community.

fields; where my father laid his eyen; were it by night or by day, cold or wet, I was alway by him to espy and know where his treasure was laid.

"On a time I lay down all plat on the ground and saw my father come running out of an hole. Now hark what I saw him do. When he came out of the hole, he looked fast about if anybody had seen him. And when he could nowhere none see, he stopped the hole with sand and made it even and plain like to the other ground by. He knew not that I saw it. And where his footspore stood, there stryked he with his tail and made it smooth with his mouth, that no man should espy it. That learned I there of my false father, and many subtleties that I tofore knew nothing of. Then departed he thence and ran to the village ward for to do his things; and I forgot not, but sprang and leapt to the hole ward, and how well that he had supposed that he had made all fast I was not so much a fool but that I found the hole well, and scratched and scraped with my feet the sand out of the hole, and crept therein. There found I the most plenty of silver and gold that ever I saw. Here is none so old that ever so much saw on one heap in all his life. Tho took I Ermelyne my wife to help, and we rested ne night ne day to bear and carry away, with great labour and pain, this rich treasure in to another place that lay for us better, under an hawe in a deep hole. In the mean while that mine housewife and I thus laboured, my father was with them that would betray the King. Now may ye hear what they did. Bruin the Bear and Isegrim the Wolf sent all the land about if any man would take wages that they should come to Bruin and he would pay them their souldye or wages tofore. My father ran all over the land and bare the letters.

---

hawe, hawthorn or, more probably, hedge.   *souldye*, hire (cf. *soldier*).

He wist little that he was robbed of his treasure; yea though he might have wonnen all the world, he had not conne find a penny thereof.

"When my father had been over all in the land between the Elbe and the Somme, and had gotten many a soldier that should the next summer have comen to help Bruin, tho came he again to the Bear and his fellows, and told them in how great a venture he had be tofore the boroughs in the land of Saxon, and how the hunters daily ridden and hunted with hounds after him in such wise that he unnethes escaped with his life. When he had told this to these four false traitors, then showed he them letters that pleased much. To Bruin therein were written twelve hundred of Isegrim's lineage by name, without the bears, the foxes, the cats, and the dassen, all these had sworn that with the first messenger that should come for them they should be ready, and come for to help the Bear if they had their wages a month tofore. This aspied I, I thank God. After these words my father went to the hole where his treasure was lain, and would look upon it. Tho began he a great sorrow; that he sought he found nothing. He found his hole broken, and his treasure borne away. There did he that I may well sorrow and bewail, for great anger and sorrow he went and hung himself. Thus abode the treason of Bruin by my subtilty after. Now see mine infortune. These traitors Isegrim and Bruin ben now most privy of counsel about the King, and sit by him on the high bench. And I, poor Reynart, have ne thanks ne reward. I have buried mine own father, because the King should have his life. My lord," said the Fox, "where ben they that would so do, that is, to destroy them self for to keep you?"

had not conne, would not be able.

The King and the Queen hoped to win the treasure and without council took to them Reynart and prayed him that he would do so well as to tell them where this treasure was.

Reynart said, "How should I tell the King, or them that would hang me for love of the traitors and murderers which by their flattery would fain bring me to death? Should I tell to them where my good is, then were I out of my wit."

The Queen then spake, "Nay, Reynart, the King shall let you have your life, and shall altogether forgive you, and ye shall be from henceforth wise and true to my lord."

The Fox answered to the Queen, "Dear lady, if the King will believe me, and that he will pardon and forgive me all my old trespasses, there was never King so rich as I shall make him. For the treasure that I shall do him have is right costly and may not be numbered."

The King said, "Ach, Dame, will ye believe the Fox? Save your reverence, he is born to rob, steal, and to lie. This cleaves to his bones, and can not be had out of the flesh."

The Queen said, "Nay, my lord, ye may now well believe him. Though he were tofore fell, he is now changed otherwise than he was. Ye have well heard that he hath impeached his father and the Dasse his nephew, which he might well have laid on other beasts if he would have been false, fell, and a liar."

The King said, "Dame, will ye then have it so, and think ye it best to be don, though I supposed it should hurt me I will take all these trespasses of Reynart upon me and believe his words. But I swear by my crown, if he ever hereafter misdo and trespass, that shall he dear abye and all his lineage unto the ninth degree."

The Fox looked on the King stoundmele, and was glad in his heart, and said, "My lord, I were not wise if I should say things that were not true."

The King took up a straw from the ground, and pardoned and forgave the Fox all the misdeeds and trespasses of his father and of him also.

[*In the remainder of this very long chapter, Reynart convinces the King that the treasure is buried in a place called Krekenpyt and gives directions for finding it. He excuses himself from accompanying him on the ground that he has taken a vow to go on a pilgrimage to Rome and thence to the Holy Land. The King accepts his excuse. In Chapter XVIII, Reynard persuades the Queen to give him a scrip made of a piece of the Bear's hide and four shoes taken from the paws of Isegrim and his wife, Ersewynde.*]

How Isegrim and his wife Ersewynde must suffer their shoes to be plucked off, and how Reynart did on the shoes for to go to Rome with.   Capitulo xix.

. . . The next day, when the sun arose, Reynart then did grease his shoes which he had of Isegrim and Ersewynde his wife, and did them on, and bound them to his feet, and went to the King and to the Queen and said to them with a glad cheer, "Noble Lord and Lady, God give you good morrow, and I desire of your grace that I may have male and staff blessed as belongeth to a pilgrim."

Then the King anon sent for Bellyn the Ram, and when he came he said, 'Sir Bellyn, ye shall do mass tofore Reynart, for he shall go on pilgrimage; and give to him male and staff."

The Ram answered again and said, "My lord, I

stoundmele, for a space of time.   *male,* bag, scrip.

dare not do that, for he hath said that he is in the Pope's curse."

The King said what thereof master Gelys hath said to us, if a man had don as many sins as all the world and he would tho sins forsake, shrive him and receive penance, and do by the priest's counsel, God will forgive them and be merciful unto him. Now will Reynart go over the sea into the Holy Land, and make him clear of all his sins.

Then answered Bellyn to the King, "I will not do little ne much herein but if ye save me harmless in the spiritual court, before the bishop Prendelor and tofore his archdeacon Looswinde and tofore Sir Rapiamus his official."

The King began to wax wroth, and said, "I shall not bid you so much in half a year! I had liever hang you than I should so much pray you for it."

When the Ram saw that the King was angry, he was so sore afraid that he quoke for fear, and went to the altar and sang in his books and read such as him thought good over Reynart, which little set thereby save that he would have the worship thereof.

When Bellyn the Ram had all said his service devoutly, then he hung on the fox's neck a male covered with the skin of Bruin the Bear and a little psalter thereby. Tho was Reynart ready toward his journey. Tho looked he toward the King, as he had been sorrowful to depart; and feigned as he had wept, right as he had yamerde in his heart; but if he had any sorrow it was because all the other that were there were not in the same plight as the Wolf and Bear were brought in by him. Nevertheless he stood and prayed them all to pray for him, like as he would pray for them. The Fox thought that he tarried long and would fain have departed, for he knew himself guilty.

yamerde, grieved.

The King said, "Reynart, I am sorry ye be so hasty, and will no longer tarry."

"Nay, my lord, it is time, for we ought not spare to do well, I pray you to give me leave to depart: I must do my pilgrimage."

The King said, "God be with you," and commanded all them of the court to go and carry Reynart on his way, save the Wolf and the Bear which fast lay bounden. There was none that durst be sorry therefor, and if ye had seen Reynart how personably he went with his male and psalter on his shoulder, and the shoes on his feet, ye should have laughed. He went and showed him outward wisely, but he laughed in his heart that all they brought him forth which had a little tofore been with him so wroth. And also the King, which so much hated him, he had made him such a fool that he brought him to his owne intent. He was a pilgrim of deuce ace.

"My Lord the King," said the Fox, "I pray you to return again. I will not that ye go any further with me. Ye might have harm thereby. Ye have there two murderers arrested. If they escape you ye might be hurt by them. I pray God keep you from misadventure!" With these words he stood upon his afterfeet, and prayed all the beasts, great and small, that would be partners of his pardon, that they should pray for him.

They said that they all would remember him.

Then departed he from the King so heavily that many of them ermed.

Then said he to Cuwart the Hare and to Bellyn the Ram merrily, "Here, friends, shall we now depart? Yea, with a good will accompany me further. Ye

deuce ace, a lucky throw in dice, of a one-spot and a two.
ermed, grieved.

two made me never angry. Ye be good for to walk with, courteous, friendly, and not complained on of any beast. Ye be of good conditions and ghostly of your living; ye live both as I did when I was a recluse. If ye have leaves and grass ye be pleased, ye reck not of bread, of flesh, ne such manner meat."

With such flattering words hath Reynart these two flattered that they went with him till they came tofore his house Maleperduys.

How Cuwart the Hare was slain by the Fox.

Capitulo xx.

[*When Reynard comes to Malperduis, he takes Cuwart into the castle, while he says farewell to his wife. He immediately kills the Hare and serves him for dinner.*]

. . . Now was Bellyn the Ram angry that Cuwart his fellow was so long in the hole, and called loud, "Come out, Cuwart, in the devil's name; how long shall Reynard keep you there? Haste you, and come! Let us go."

When Reynard heard this, he went out and said softly to Bellyn the Ram, "Lief Bellyn, wherefore be ye angry? Cuwart speaketh to his dear Aunt. Methinketh ye ought not to be displeased therefor. He bade me say to you ye might well go tofore, and he shall come after; he is lighter of foot than ye. He must tarry awhile with his Aunt and her children, they weep and cry because I shall go from them."

Bellyn said, "What did Cuwart? Methought he cried after help."

The Fox answered, "What say ye? Ween ye that he should have any harm? Now hark what he then did. When we were comen into mine house, and

Lief, Dear.

Ermelyne my wife understood that I should go over sea, she fell down in a swoon, and when Cuwart saw that, he cried loud, 'Bellyn, come help mine Aunt to bring her out of her swoon.'"

Then said the Ram, "In faith I understood that Cuwart had been in great danger."

The Fox said, "Nay truly, or Cuwart should have any harm in my house I had liever that my wife and children should suffer much hurt."

How the Fox sent the head of Cuwart the Hare to the King by Bellyn the Ram.   *Capitulo xxi.*

The Fox said, "Bellyn, remember ye not that yesterday the King and his council commanded that ere I should depart out of this land I should send him two letters? Dear cousin, I pray you to bear them, they be ready written."

The Ram said, "I wot never. If I wist that your inditing and writing were good, ye might peradventure so much pray me that I would bear them, if I had anything to bear them in."

Reynart said, "Ye shall not fail to have somewhat to bear them in. Rather than they should be unborne I shall rather give you my male that I bear; and put the King's letters therein, and hang them about your neck. Ye shall have of the King great thanks therefor, and be right welcomen to him."

Hereupon Bellyn promised him to bear these letters.

Tho returned Reynart into his house and took the male and put therein Cuwart's head, and brought it to Bellyn for to bring him in danger, and hang it on his neck, and charged him not to look in the male if he would have the King's friendship. "And if ye will that the King take you into his grace and love you, say that ye yourself have made this letter and indited it, and have given the counsel that it is so well made and written. Ye shall have great thanks therefor."

Bellyn the Ram was glad hereof, and thought he should have great thanks, and said, "Reynart, I wot well that ye now do for me. I shall be in the Court greatly praised when it is known that I can indite and make a letter, though I cannot make it. Ofttimes it happeneth that God suffereth some to have worship and thank of the labours and cunning of other men, and so it shall befall me now. Now, what counsel ye, Reynart? Shall Cuwart the Hare come with me to the Court?"

"Nay," said the Fox, "he shall anon follow you. He may not yet come, for he must speak with his Aunt. Now go ye forth tofore. I shall show to Cuwart secret things which ben not yet known."

Bellyn said, "Farewell, Reynart," and went him forth to the Court. And he ran and hasted so fast, that he came tofore midday to the Court, and found the King in his palace with his Barons. The King marvelled when he saw him bring the male again which was made of the Bear's skin. The King said, "Say on, Bellyn, from whence come ye? Where is the Fox? How is it that he hath not the male with him?"

Bellyn said, "My Lord, I shall say you all that I know. I accompanied Reynart unto his house. And when he was ready, he asked me if I that would for your sake bear two letters to you. I said, for to do you pleasure and worship, I would gladly bear to you seven. Tho brought he to me this male wherein the letters be, which ben indited by my cunning, and I gave counsel of the making of them. I trow ye saw never letters better ne craftlier made ne indited."

The King commanded anon Bokart, his secretary, to read the letters, for he understood all manner languages. Tybert the Cat and he took the male off Bellyn's neck, and Bellyn hath so far said and confessed that he therefore was dampned.

The clerk Bokwart undid the male, and drew out Cuwart's head, and said, "Alas, what letters ben these! Certainly, my Lord, this is Cuwart's head."

"Alas," said the King, "that ever I believed so the Fox!" There might men see great heaviness of the King and of the Queen. The King was so angry that he held long down his head, and at last, after many thoughts, he made a great cry, that all the beasts were afraid of the noise.

Tho spake Sir Firapeel the Leopard, which was sybbe somewhat to the King, and said, "Sire King, how make ye such a noise! Ye make sorrow enough though the Queen were dead. Let this sorrow go, and make good cheer. It is great shame. Be ye not a Lord and King of this land? Is it not all under you, that here is?"

The King said, "Sir Firapeel, how should I suffer this? One false shrew and deceiver has betrayed me and brought me so far, that I have forwrought and angered my friends the stout Bruin the Bear and Isegrim the Wolf, which sore me repenteth. And this goeth against my worship, that I have done amiss against my best Barons, and that I trusted and believed so much the false Fox. And my wife is cause thereof. She prayed me so much that I heard her prayer, and that me repenteth, though it be too late."

Bokart (in the Low German, *Botsaert* or *Boekert*) has not been identified as any animal.
dampned, condemned.   *sybbe*, related by blood.
forwrought, done evil to.

"What though, Sir King," said the Leopard. "If there be any thing misdone it shall be amended. We shall give to Bruin the Bear to Isegrim the Wolf and to Ersewynde his wife for the piece of his skin and for their shoes, for to have good peace, Bellyn the Ram. For he hath confessed himself that he gave counsel and consented to Cuwart's death. It is reason that he abyē it. And we shall all go fetch Reynart, and we shall arrest him and hang him by the neck, without law or judgment. And there with all shall be content."

How Bellyn the Ram and all his lineage were given in the hands of Isegrim and Bruin, and how he was slain.

Capitulo xxii.

The King said, "I will do it gladly."

Firapeel the Leopard went tho to the prison and unbound them first, and then he said, "Ye, sirs, I bring to you a fast pardon and my lord's love and friendship. It repenteth him, and is sorry that he ever hath done spoken or trespassed against you, and therefore ye shall have a good appointment. And also amends he shall give to you, Bellyn the Ram and all his lineage fro now forthon to doomsday, in such wise that wheresomever ye find them, in field or in wood, that ye may freely bite and eat them without any forfeit. And also the King granteth to you that ye may hunt and do the worst ye can to Reynart and all his lineage without misdoing. This fair great privilege will the King grant to you ever to hold of him. And the King will that ye swear to him never to misdo, but do him homage and fealty. I counsel you to do this, for ye may do it honourably."

Thus was the peace made by Firapeel the Leopard, friendly and well. And that cost Bellyn the Ram his

tabart and also his life, and the Wolf's lineage hold
these privileges of the King. And in to this day they
devour and eat Bellyn's lineage where that they may
find them. This debate was begun thus in an evil
time, for the peace could never sith be made between
them.

The King did forth with his Court and feast length
twelve days longer for love of the Bear and the Wolf,
so glad was he of the making of this peace.

*Here endeth the First Part of the Historye of Reynard the
Foxe, etc.*

[*The Second Part follows in the main the plan of the
First. The Fox, once more arraigned by the other
Beasts and advised by Grimbart, appears at court. This
time he escapes hanging by challenging Isegrim to mortal
combat and, by a series of ruses devised by his aunt,
Dame Rukenawe the She-Ape, defeats him utterly. He
is once more forgiven and is fully reinstated in the King's
regard.*]

Caxton's Epilogue [1]

Now who that said to you of the ffox more or lesse
than ye haue herd or red, I holde it for lesynge; but
this that ye haue herd or red, that may ye byleue wel.
And who that byleueth it not, is not therfore out of
the right byleue; how be it ther be many yf that they
had seen it they shold haue non the lasse doubte of it.
For ther ben many thynges in the world whiche ben
byleuyd though they were neuer seen: Also ther ben
many fygures, plays, founden that neuer were don ne

---

tabart, tabard, sleeveless coat worn in early times by peasants, and later by
    knights and heralds. The suggestion seems to be that Cuwart had been
    a herald (?).
sith, after, since.   *lasse,* less.

[1] This Epilogue is given in the old spelling.

happed, but for an example to the peple that they may
ther by the better vse and folowe vertue and teschew
synne and vyces.   In lyke wyse may it be by this
booke that who that wyl rede this mater, though it be
of iapes and bourdes, yet he may fynde therin many a
good wysedom and lernynges by whiche he may come
to vertue and worship.   Ther is no good man blamed
herein; hit is spoken generally.   Late euery man take
his owne part as it belongeth and behoueth, and he
that fyndeth hym gylty in ony dele or part therof,
late hym bettre and amende hym.   And he that is
veryly good, I pray God kepe hym therin.   And yf
ony thyng be said or wreten herin that may greue or
dysplease ony man, blame not me but the foxe, for
they be his wordes and not myne.

Prayeng alle them that schal see this lytyl treatis,
to correcte and amende where they shal fynde faute;
For I haue not added ne mynusshed, but haue
folowed as nyghe as I can my copye whiche was in
dutche and by me william Caxton translated in to
this rude and symple englyssh in thabbey of west-
mestre, fynysshed the vj daye of Juyn the yere of our
lord 'M.CCCC.Lxxxj. and the xxj yere of the regne of
kynge Edward the iiijth.

William Caxton, Historye of Reynart the Foxe, from the
    Dutch prose version, Hystorie van Reynaert de Vos,
    printed at Gouda by Gheraert Leeuw, 1479.

iapes and bourdes, gibes and jests.

RENAISSANCE

THE BURGHERS OF CALAIS [1]

c. 1500

After that the frenche kyng was . . . departed fro *Sangate*, they within Calays sawe well howe their socoure fayled them, for the whiche they were in great sorrow.[2] Than they desyred so moche their captayn sir *John* of *Vyen*, that he went to the walles of the towne, and made a sygne to speke with some person of the host. Whan the kyng herde therof, he sende thyder *Gaultier* of *Manny*, and sir *Basset*. Than sir *John* of *Vyen* sayd to them: Sirs, you be right valyant knyghtes in dedes of armes, and you knowe well howe the kyng my maister hath sende me and other to this towne, and commaunded vs to kepe it to his behofe, in suche wyse that we take no blame nor to hym no dammage; and we haue done all that lyeth in oure power. Nowe our socours hath fayled vs, and we be so sore strayned that we haue nat to lyue withall, but that we muste all dye, or els enrage for famyn, without the noble and gentyl kyng of yours woll take mercy on vs; the which to do we requyre you to desyre hym, to haue pytye on vs, and let vs go and depart as we be, and lette hym take the towne and castell and all the goodes that be therin, the whiche is great habundaunce. Than sir *Gaultyer* of *Manny* sayde, Sir, we knowe somwhat of the entencyon of the kynge our maister, for he hath shewed it vnto vs. Surely knowe for trouth it is nat his mynde that ye nor they within the towne shulde depart so, for it is his wyll that ye all shulde put your selfes into

---

[1] This selection is given in the old spelling.

[2] The French king was Philip V, whose defeat at Crécy (1346) made it impossible for him to relieve Calais, which had been now besieged by Edward III of England for a year.

his pure wyll to ransome all suche as pleaseth hym and putte to dethe suche as he lyste, for they of *Calays* hath done hym suche contraryes and despyghtes, and hath caused hym to dyspende soo moche good, and loste many of his menne, that he is sore greued agaynst them. Than the captayne sayde, Sir, this is to harde a mater to vs, we ar here within a small sorte of knyghtes and squyers, who hath trewely serued the kynge our maister, as well as ye serue yours in like case. And we haue endured moche payne and vnease, but we shall yet endure as moche payne as euer knyghtes did rather thanne to consent that the worst ladde in the towne shulde haue any more yuell than the grettest of vs all. Therefore sir we pray you that of your humylite yet that you will go and speke to the kynge of *Englande*, and desyre hym to haue pytie of vs, for we trust in hym so moche gentylnesse, that by the grace of God his purpose shall chaunge. Sir *Gaultier* of *Manny* and sir *Basset* retourned to the kynge, and declared to hym all that hadde ben sayde: the kynge sayde he wolde none other wyse, but that they shulde yelde theym vp symply to his pleasure. Than sir *Gaultyer* sayde, Sir, sauyng your dyspleasure in this, ye may be in the wronge, for ye shall gyue by this an yuell ensample: if ye sende any of vs your servaunts into any fortresse, we will nat be very gladde to go, if ye putte any of theym in the towne to dethe after they be yelded, for in lykewise they will deale with vs, if the case fell lyke: the whiche wordes dyuerse other lordes that were there present sustayned and maynteyned. Than the Kynge sayde, Sirs, I will nat be alone agaynst you all, therefore sir *Gaultyer* of *Manny* ye shall goo and say to the capytayne, that all the grace that they shall fynde nowe in me is, that they lette sixe of the chiefe burgesses of the towne come out bare heded, bare foted, and bare legged, and in their shertes, with haulters about their neckes, with the keyes of the towne and castel in their handes, and lette theym sixe yelde themselfe purely to my wyll, and the resydewe I will take to mercy. Than sir *Gaultyer* retourned and founde sir *John* of *Vyen* styll on the wall abydinge for an answere: than sir *Gaultier* shewed hym all the grace that he culde gette of the kynge. Well, quoth sir *Johan*, Sir, I requyre you to tary here a certayne space tyll I go into the towne and shewe this to the commons of the towne who sent me hyder. Than sir *John* went vnto the market place and sowned the common bell: than incontynent men and women assembled there: than the captayne made reporte of all that he had done, and sayde, Sirs, it wyll be none otherwyse, therfore nowe take aduyse and make a shorte aunswere. Thanne all the people beganne to wepe and to make such sorowe that there was nat so hard a hert if they had sene them but that wolde haue had great pytie on theym: the captayne hymselfe wepte pyteously. At last the moost riche burgesse of all the towne called *Ewstace* of saynt *Peters* rose vp and sayde openly. Sirs, great and small, great myschiefe it shulde be to suffre to dye suche people as be in this towne, other by famyn or otherwyse, whan there is a meane to saue theym. I thynke he or they shulde haue great merytte of our lorde God that myght kepe theym fro suche myschiefe: and for my parte I haue so good truste in our lorde God that if I dye in the quarel to saue the residewe that God wolde pardone me. Wherefore to saue them I wyll be the first to putte my lyfe in ieopardy. Whan he had thus sayde euery man worshypped hym, and dyuers kneled downe at his fete with sore wepyng and sore sighes. Than another honest burgesse rose and sayde I wyll kepe company

with my gossyppe *Eustace*, he was called *John Dayre*.
Than rose up *Jaques* of *Wyssant*, who was riche in
goodes and herytage: he sayd also that he wolde holde
company with his two cosyns in likwyse: so dyd *Peter*
of *Wyssant* his brother, and thanne rose two other:
they sayde they wolde do the same. Thanne they
went and aparelled them as the kynge desyred . . .
Whan sir *Gaultier* presented these burgesses to the
kyng they kneled downe and helde vp their handes
and sayd, Gentyll kyng, beholde here we sixe who were
burgesses of *Calays* and great marchantes, we haue
brought to you the kayes of the towne and of the castell, and we submyt ourselues clerely into your wyll
and pleasure, to saue the resydue of the people of
Calays, who have suffred great payne. Sir, we be-
seche your grace to haue mercy and pytie on us
through your hygh nobles: than all the erles & bar-
ownes, and other that were there wept for pytie. The
kyng loked felly on theym, for greatly he hated the
people of *Calays*, for the gret damages and dyspleas-
ures they had done to hym on the see before. Than he
commaunded their heedes to be stryken off. Than
euery man requyred the kyng for mercy, but he wolde
here no man in that behalfe. Than sir *Gaultier* of
Manny said, A, noble kyng, for Goddes sake refrayn
your courage, ye haue the name of souerayn nobles,
therfore nowe do nat a thyng that shulde blemysshe
your renome, not to gyue cause to some to speke of you
villany, euery man will say it is a great cruelty to put
to deth suche honest persons, who by their owne
wylles putte themselue into your grace to saue their
company. Than the kyng wryed away fro hym, and
commaunded to sende for the hangman, and sayd they
of *Calays* hath caused many of my men to be slayne,
wherfore these shall dye in like wyse. Than the quene

beynge great with chylde, kneled downe & sore wepyng sayd: A, gentyll sir, syth I passed the see in great
perill I haue desyred nothyng of you, therfore nowe I
humbly requyre you in the honour of the son of the
virgyn *Mary* and for the loue of me, that ye will take
mercy of these burgesses. The kyng behelde the
quene & stode styll in a study a space, and than sayd,
A, dame, I wold ye had ben as nowe in some other
place, ye make suche request to me that I can nat
deny you; wherfore I gyue them to you to do your
pleasure with theym. Than the quene caused them
to be brought into her chambre, and made the halters
to be taken fro their neckes and caused them to be
newe clothed, and gaue them their dyner at their
leser. And than she gaue ech of them sixe nobles, and
made them to be brought out of thoost in sauegard &
set at their lyberte.

John Bourchier, Lord Berners' translation of Froissart's
Chronicles of England and France. 1524–25.

WHAT THEY LAUGHED AT IN THE
SIXTEENTH CENTURY
1526

*Of him that said that a woman's tongue was lightest
meat of digestion.*

A certain artificer in London there was which was
sore sick, that could not well digest his meat, to whom
a physician came to give him counsel and said that
he must use to eat meat that be light of digestion, as
small birds, as sparrows or swallows, and especial that
bird that is called a wagtail, whose flesh is marvellous
light of digestion, because that bird is ever moving and
stirring. The sick man, hearing the physician said so,

leser, ease.   *thoost,* the host.

answered him and said: "Sir, if that be the cause that those birds be light of digestion, then I know a meat much lighter of digestion than either sparrow, swallow, or wagtail, and that is my wife's tongue, for it is never in rest but ever moving and stirring."

By this tale ye may learn a good general rule of physic.

Of the woman that followed her fourth husband's hearse and wept.

A woman there was which had had iiii husbands. It fortuned also that this fourth husband died & was brought to church upon the bier, whom this woman followed and made great moan & waxt very sorry. In so much that her neighbors thought she would swoon and die for sorrow, wherefor one of her gossips came to her & spake to her in her ear & bade her for God's sake to comfort her self & refrain that lamentation or else it would hurt her greatly & peradventure put her in jeopardy of her life. To whom this woman answered & said: "Iwis, good gossip, I have great cause to mourn, if ye knew all; for I have buried iii husbands beside this man, but I was never in the case I am now, for there was not one of them but when I followed the corpse to church yet I was sure alway of an other husband before that the corpse came out of my house, & now I am sure of no other husband & therefore ye may be sure I have great cause to be sad and heavy."

By this tale ye may see that the old proverb is true, that it is as great pity to see a woman weep as a goose go barefoot.

Of the man that would have the pot stand there as he would.

A young man late married to a wife thought it was

good policy to get the mastery of her in the beginning. Came to her, the pot seething over the fire, although the meat therein were not enough, suddenly commanded her to take the pot from the fire, which answered and said that the meat was not ready to eat. And he said again, "I will have it taken off for my pleasure." This good woman, loth yet to offend him, set the pot beside the fire as he bade. And anon after he commanded her to set the pot behind the door & she said thereto again, "Ye be not wise therein." But he precisely said it should be so as he bade. And she gently again did his commandment. This man yet not satisfied commanded her to set the pot a-high upon the hen-roost. "What," quoth the wife, "I trow ye be mad." And he fiercely then commanded her to set it there or else he said she should repent. She, somewhat afeared to move his patience, took a ladder and set it to the roost, and went herself up the ladder and took the pot in her hand, praying her husband then to hold the ladder fast for sliding, which so did.

And when the husband looked up and saw the pot stand there on high, he said thus: "Lo now standeth the pot there as I would have it." This wife, hearing that, suddenly poured the hot pottage on his head, and said thus: "And now been the pottage there as I would have them."

By this tale men may see it is no wisdom for a man to attempt a meek woman's patience too far, lest it turn to his own hurt and damage.

Hundred Merry Tales[1]

Came to her, etc., i.e., he came to her, etc.
enough, i.e., boiled enough.

[1] "*Beatrice:* . . . That I had my good wit out of the 'Hundred Merry Tales': — well, this was Signior Benedick that said so." *Much Ado About Nothing*, II, i, 135.

A VERY GODLY LETTER

[ab. 1565]

A very godly letter made unto Philip Sidney, his son, then at school in Shrewsbury,[1] by Sir Henry Sidney, K.G., Lord Deputy of Ireland, and Lord President of Wales.

Son Philip,

I have received two letters from you — one written in Latin, the other in French — which I take in good part; and will you to exercise that practice of learning often: for that will stand you in most stead in that profession of life that you are born to live in.

And now sithence this is my first letter that ever I did write to you, I will not that it be all empty of some advices; which my natural care of you provoketh me to wish you to follow, as documents to you in this your tender age.

Let your first action be the lifting up of your mind to Almighty God by hearty prayer; and feelingly digest the words you speak in prayer, with continual meditation and thinking of Him to whom you pray: and use this as an ordinary act, and at an ordinary hour. Whereby the time itself will put you in remembrance to do that which you are accustomed to do in that time.

Apply your study to such hours as your discreet Master doth assign you, earnestly: and the time, I know, he will so limit; as shall be both sufficient for your learning, and safe for your health. And mark the sense and matter of that you do read as well as the words: so shall you both enrich your tongue with words and your wit with matter; and judgment will grow as years grow in you.

[1] Sidney entered Shrewsbury School on October 17, 1564. He was ten years old.

Be humble and obedient to your Master: for unless you frame yourself to obey others, yea, and feel in yourself what obedience is; you shall never be able to teach others how to obey you. Be courteous of gesture and affable unto all men; with diversity of reverence according to the dignity of the person. There is nothing that winneth so much, with so little cost.

Use moderate diet: so as, after your meal, you may find your wit fresher, and not duller; and your body more lively, and not more heavy. Seldom drink wine: and yet sometimes do; lest being enforced to drink upon the sudden, you should find yourself inflamed.

Use exercise of body, but such as is without peril of your bones or joints. It will increase your force, and enlarge your breath. Delight to be cleanly, as well in all parts of your body, as in your garments. It shall make you grateful in each company: and otherwise loathsome.

Give yourself to be merry: for you degenerate from your father, if you find not yourself most able in wit and body to do anything, when you be most merry. But let your mirth be ever void of all scurrility and biting words to any man: for a wound given by a word is oftentimes harder to be cured than that which is given with a sword.

Be you rather a hearer and bearer away of other men's talk, than a beginner or procurer of speech: otherwise you shall be accounted to delight to hear yourself speak.

Be modest in each assembly, and rather be rebuked of light fellows for maiden-like shamefastness; than of your sad friends, for pert boldness. Think upon every word that you will speak, before you utter it: and remember how Nature hath rampered up, as it were, the

sad, sober, serious.   *rampered*, walled.

tongue with teeth, lips, yea, and hair without the lips; and all, betokening reins or bridles for the loose use of that member.

Above all things, tell no untruth. No, not in trifles. The custom of it is nought: and let it not satisfy you that, for a time, the hearers take it for a truth: yet after it will be known as it is, to your shame. For there cannot be a greater reproach to a Gentleman, than to be accounted a liar.

Study and endeavor yourself to be virtuously occupied: so shall you make such an habit of well doing in you; as you shall not know how to do evil, though you should.

Remember, my son! the noble blood you are descended of by your mother's side: and think that only by virtuous life and good action you may be an ornament to that illustrious family; otherwise, through vice and sloth, you may be counted *labes generis*, "a spot of your kin," one of the greatest curses that can happen to man.

Well! my little Philip! this is enough for me; and too much, I fear, for you. But if I shall find that this light meat of digestion nourish you in anything, the weak stomach of your young capacity; I will, as I find the same grow stronger, feed it with other food.

Commend me most heartily unto Master Justice Corbet, old Master Onslowe, and my cousin his son. Farewell! Your mother and I send our blessings: and Almighty God grant you His! nourish you with His fear! govern you with His grace! and make you a good servant to your Prince and country!

Your loving father,

So long as you live in the fear of God,

H. Sidney.

A Postscript by my Lady Mary Sidney, in the skirts of my Lord President's letter, to her said son Philip.

Your noble and careful father hath taken pains with his own hand to give you in this his letter, so wise, so learned, and most requisite precepts for you to follow with a diligent and humble thankful mind; as I will not withdraw your eyes from beholding and reverent honoring the same: no, not so long time as to read any letter from me. And therefore, at this time, I will write unto you no other letter than this: whereby I first bless you, with my desire to God to plant in you His grace; and secondarily, warn you to have always before the eyes of your mind these excellent counsels of my lord your dear father, and that you fail not continually once in four or five days to read them over.

And for a final leave-taking for this time, see that you show yourself as a loving obedient scholar to your good Master! to govern you yet many years; and that my lord and I may hear that you profit so in your learning as thereby you may increase our loving care of you, and deserve at his hands the continuance of his great joy, to have him often witness with his own hand the hope he hath in your well doing.

Farewell, my little Philip! and once again the Lord bless you!   Your loving mother,

Mary Sidney.

LADY JANE GREY

1570

Before I went into Germany, I came to Brodegate in Leicestershire to take leave of that noble Lady Jane Grey,[1] to whom I was exceeding beholden. Her par-

[1] Lady Jane Grey (c. 1537–54) was great granddaughter of Henry VII. She was made queen when she was seventeen, reigned for only nine days, and was then beheaded in the Tower.

ents, the Duke and Duchess, with all the household, Gentlemen and Gentlewomen, were hunting in the Park: I found her, in her chamber, reading *Phaedon Platonis* in Greek, and that with as much delight, as some gentlemen would read a merry tale in Bocace. After salutation, and duty done, with some other talk, I asked her why she would lose such pastime in the Park? Smiling she answered me: "I wisse, all their sport in the Park is but a shadow to that pleasure, that I find in Plato: Alas, good folk, they never felt what true pleasure meant." "And how came you, Madam," quoth I, "to this deep knowledge of pleasure, and what did chiefly allure you unto it: seeing, not many women, but very few men have attained thereunto?" "I will tell you," quoth she, "and tell you a truth, which perchance ye will marvel at. One of the greatest benefits, that ever God gave me, is that he sent me so sharp and severe parents, and so gentle a schoolmaster. For when I am in presence either of father or mother, whether I speak, keep silence, sit, stand, or go, eat, drink, be merry, or sad, be sewing, playing, dancing, or doing anything else, I must do it, as it were, in such weight, measure, and number, even so perfectly as God made the world, or else I am so sharply taunted, so cruelly threatened, yea presently sometimes with pinches, nips, and bobs, and other ways, which I will not name, for the honour I bear them, so without measure misordered, that I think myself in hell, till time come, that I must go to Mr. Elmer, who teacheth me so gently, so pleasantly, with such fair allurements to learning, that I think all the time nothing, whiles I am with him. And when I am called from him, I fall on weeping, because, what-

Phaedon Platonis, the *Phaedo* of Plato.
bobs, jeers, or, perhaps, blows.

Bocace, Boccaccio.
Elmer, John Aylmer.

soever I do else but learning, is full of grief, trouble, fear, and whole misliking unto me: and thus my book hath been so much my pleasure, and bringeth daily to me more pleasure and more, that in respect of it, all other pleasures, in very deed, be but trifles and troubles unto me." I remember this talk gladly, both because it is so worthy of memory, and because also, it was the last talk that ever I had, and the last time that ever I saw that noble and worthy Lady.

Roger Ascham, The Schoolmaster

THE EXECUTION OF LADY JANE GREY

1563

When she first mounted the scaffold, she spake to the spectators in this manner: "Good people, I am come hither to die, and by a law I am condemned to the same. The fact against the queen's highness was unlawful, and the consenting thereunto by me: but, touching the procurement and desire thereof by me, or on my behalf, I do wash my hands thereof in innocency before God, and the face of you, good christian people, this day:" and therewith she wrung her hands, wherein she had her book. Then she said, "I pray you all, good christian people, to bear me witness that I die a good christian woman, and that I do look to be saved by no other means, but only by the mercy of God in the blood of his only Son Jesus Christ: and I confess, that when I did know the word of God, I neglected the same, loved myself and the world, and therefore this plague and punishment is happily and worthily happened unto me for my sins: and yet I thank God, that of his goodness he hath thus given me a time and a respite to repent: and now, good people, while I am alive, I pray you assist me with your prayers." And then, kneeling down, she turned to Feck-enham,[1] saying, "Shall I say this psalm?" and he said, "Yea." Then she said the Psalm of Miserere mei Deus, in English, in a most devout manner throughout to the end; and then she stood up, and gave to her maid, Mrs. Ellen, her gloves and handkerchief, and her book to Mr. Bruges; and then she untied her gown, and the executioner pressed upon her to help her off with it: but she, desiring him to let her alone, turned toward her two gentlewomen, who helped her off therewith, and also with her frowes, paste, and necker-chief, giving her a fair handkerchief to put about eyes.

Then the executioner kneeled down, and asked her forgiveness, whom she forgave most willingly. Then he desired her to stand upon the straw; which doing, she saw the block. Then she said, "I pray you des-patch me quickly." Then she kneeled down, saying, "Will you take it off before I lay me down?" And the executioner said, "No, madam." Then she tied the handkerchief about her eyes, and feeling for the block, she said, "What shall I do? Where is it? Where is it?" One of the standers-by guiding her thereunto, she laid her head down upon the block, and then stretched forth her body, and said, "Lord, into thy hands I commend my spirit:" and so finished her life, in the year of our Lord 1554, the 12th day of February, about the seventeenth year of her age.

Thus died the Lady Jane: and on the same day the Lord Guildford, her husband, one of the Duke of Northumberland's sons, was likewise beheaded, two innocents in comparison of them that sat upon them. For they were both very young, and ignorantly ac-cepted that which others had contrived, and by open

Psalm 51.   *frowes*, perhaps a wig.
paste, some sort of headdress.   *sat upon*, judged.

[1] John of Feckenham, private chaplain to Queen Mary.

proclamation consented to take from others, and give to them.

Touching the condemnation of this pious lady, it is to be noted, that Judge Morgan who gave sentence against her, soon after he had condemned her, fell mad, and in his raving cried out continually, to have the lady Jane taken away from him, and so he ended his life.

> John Foxe, *Actes and Monuments of these latter and perillous Dayes, touching matters of the Church, etc.* (commonly called *The Book of Martyrs*).

FLOWERS OF RHETORICK

1579

i

A MEDITATION ON THE FOOLISHNESS OF MEN

God hath armed every creature against his enemy: The Lion with paws, the Bull with horns, the Boar with tusks, the Vulture with talons, Harts, Hinds, and such like, with swiftness of feet, because they are fearful, every one of them putting his gift in practice; But man which is Lord of the whole earth, for whose service herbs, trees, roots, plants, fish, fowl, and beasts of the field were first made, is far worse than the brute beasts: for they endued but with sense, do *Appetere salutaria, et declinare noxia,* "seek that which helps them, and forsake that which hurts them."

Man is enriched with reason and knowledge: with knowledge, to serve his maker and govern himself; with reason to distinguish good and ill, and choose the best, neither referring the one to the glory of God, nor using the other to his own profit. Fire and Air mount upwards, Earth and Water sink down, and every in-

Judge Morgan, Sir Richard Morgan (died 1556).

sensible body else, never rests, till it bring itself to his own home. But we which have both sense, reason, wit, and understanding, are ever overlashing, passing our bounds, going beyond our limits, never keeping ourselves within compass, nor once looking after the place from whence we came, and whither we must in spite of our hearts.

Aristotle thinketh that in great winds, the Bees carry little stones in their mouths to peise their bodies, lest they be carried away, or kept from their Hives, unto which they desire to return with the fruits of their labour. The Crane is said to rest upon one leg, and holding up the other, keep a pebble in her claw, which as soon as the senses are bound by approach of sleep, falls to the ground, and with the noise of the knock against the Earth, makes her awake, whereby she is ever ready to prevent her enemies. Geese are foolish birds, yet when they fly over the mount Taurus, they shew great wisdom in their own defence: for they stop their pipes full of gravel to avoid gagling, and so by silence escape the Eagles. Woodcocks, though they lack wit to save themselves, yet they want not will to avoid hurt, when they thrust their heads in a Bush, and think their bodies out of danger. But we, which are so brittle, that we break with every fillip; so weak, that we are drawn with every thread; so light, that we are blown away with every blast; so unsteady, that we slip in every ground; neither peise our bodies against the wind, nor stand on one leg, for sleeping too much: nor close up our lips for betraying ourselves, nor use any wit, to guard our own persons, nor shew ourselves willing to shun our own harms, running most greedily to those places, where we are soonest overthrown.

I cannot liken our affections better than to an Ar-

peise, poise, weight.   *gagling*, cackling, honking.

row, which getting liberty, with wings is carried beyond our reach; kept in the Quiver, it is still at commandment: Or to a Dog, let him slip, he is straight out of sight, hold him in the Leash, he never stirs: Or to a Colt, give him the Bridle, he flings about; rein him hard, and you may rule him: Or a Ship, hoist the sails it runs on ahead; let fall the Anchor, all is well: Or to Pandora's box, lift up the lid, out flies the Devil; shut it up fast, it cannot hurt us ...

Stephen Gosson, The Schoole of Abuse

ii

PURE EUPHUISM

A letter commending his friend, Thomas Watson's *Hecatompathia* (1582).

My good friend, I have read your new passions, and they have renewed mine old pleasures, the which brought me no less delight than they have done to your self-commendations. And certes had not one of mine eyes about serious affairs been watchful, both by being too too busy, had been wanton: such is the nature of persuading pleasure, that it melteth the marrow before it scorch the skin and burneth before it warmeth. Not unlike unto the oil of jet, which rotteth the bone and never rankleth the flesh, or the scarab flies which enter into the root and never touch the fruit.

And whereas you desire to have my opinion, you may imagine that my stomach is rather cloyed than queasy, and therefore mine appetite of less force than my affection, fearing rather a surfeit of sweetness than desiring a satisfying. The repeating of love wrought in me a semblance of liking; but searching the very veins of my heart I could find nothing but a broad scar where I left a deep wound: and loose strings where I tied hard knots: and a table of steel where I framed a plot of wax.

Whereby I noted that young swans are grey, and the old white, young trees tender and the old tough, young men amorous, and, growing in years, either wiser or warier. The coral plant in the water is a soft weed, on the land a hard stone: a sword frieth in the fire like a black eel; but laid in earth like white snow: the heart in love is altogether passionate; but free from desire altogether careless.

But it is not my intent to inveigh against love, which women account but a bare word and men reverence as the best God. Only this I would add without offence to gentlewomen, that were not men more superstitious in their praises than women are constant in their passions love would either be born out of use, or men out of love, or women out of lightness. I can condemn none but by conjecture, nor commend any but by lying, yet suspicion is as free as thought, and as far as I can see as necessary as credulity.

Touching your mistress I must needs think well, seeing you have written so well, but as false glasses shew the fairest faces so fine gloses amend the baddest fancies. Appelles painted the phœnix by hearsay not by sight, and Lysippus engraved Vulcan with a straight leg whom nature framed with a poult foot, which proveth men to be of greater affection their judgment. But in that so aptly you have varied upon women I will not vary from you, so confess I must, and if I should not, yet mought I be compelled, that to love would be the sweetest thing in the earth if women were the faithfullest, and that women would be more constant if men were more wise.

gloses, false shows. *poult foot*, club foot.
their, misprint for *then*, meaning *than?*

And seeing you have used me so friendly as to make me acquainted with your passions, I will shortly make you privy to mine which I would be loth the printer should see, for that my fancies being never so crooked he would put them into straight lines unfit for my humour, necessary for his art, who setteth down blind in as many letters as seeing. — Farewell.

John Lyly

iii

SOME ELIZABETHAN TITLE-PAGES

(*a*) THE SCHOOL OF ABUSE, conteining a plesaunt invective against Poets, Pipers, Pleiers, Iesters, and such like Caterpillers of a Commonwealth; Setting up the Flagge of Defiance to their Mischievous exercise, and overthrowing their Bulwarkes, by Prophane Writers, Naturall reason, and common experience: A discourse as pleasaunt for Gentlemen that favour learning, as profitable for all that wyll follow vertue. By Stephen Gosson. Stud. Oxon. 1579.

(*b*) A BANQUET OF DAINTIE CONCEITS: furnished with verie delicate and choyse Inventions, to delight their Mindes who take Pleasure in Musique; and there-withall to sing sweete Ditties, either to the Lute, Bandora, Verginalles, or anie other instrument. Published at the desire of bothe honorable and worshipful Personages, who have had copies of divers of the Ditties heerin contained. 1588.

(*c*) PAPPE WITH A HATCHET, Alias, A figge for my God sonne. Or Cracke me this nut. Or a Countrie Cuffe, that is, a sound boxe of the eare, for the idiot Martin to hold his peace, seeing the patch will take no warning. Written by one that dares call

---

blind, blinde, with the *e*, according to the old spelling, having six letters, the same number as *seeing*.

a dog, a dog, and made to prevent Martins dog daies.
Imprinted by John Anoke, and John Astile, for the
Baylive of Withernam, cum privilegio perennitatis,
and are to bee sold at the signe of the crab tree cudgell
in thwackcoate lane. 1589.[1]

(d) GREENES NEVER TOO LATE. Or, A
Powder of Experience: Sent to all youthfull Gentlemen;
to roote out the infectious follies, that over-reaching
conceits foster in the springtime of their youth. De-
cyphering in a true English historie, those particular
vanities, that with their frothie vapours nip the blossoms of everie ripe braine, from atteining to his intended perfection. As plesant, as profitable, being
a right pumice-stone, apt to race out idlenesse with
delight, and follie with admonition. 1590.

MENAPHON [2]

A PASTORAL ROMANCE

1589

[*Arcadia having been wasted by a pestilence, Democles,
the king, sent certain nobles to the oracle of Delphos to
ascertain the cause; but the oracle returned so enigmatic
a reply that he decided to take no action but to wait until
time should provide an explanation.*]

Whiles thus *Arcadia* rested in a silent quiet, *Mena-*
phon the Kings Shepheard, a man of high account
among the Swaines of *Arcadie*, loved of the Nymphes,
as the paragon of all their countrey youngsters, walking solitarie downe to the shore, to see if any of his
ewes and lambes were straggled downe to the strond to
brouse on sea ivie, wherfore they take speciall delight
to feede; he found his flockes grazing upon the Pro-

---

[1] This title-page is burlesque: the others are not. The *Pap with a
Hatchet* (ascribed to John Lyly) is one of the most famous of the tracts in
the Martin Marprelate controversy.

[2] *Menaphon* is given in the old spelling.

montorie Mountaines hardlie: whereon resting himselfe on a hill that over-peered the great *Mediterra-
neum*, noting how *Phoebus* fetched his *Lavaltos* on the
purple Plaines of *Neptunus*, as if he had meant to have
courted *Thetis* in the royaltie of his robes: the Dol-
phines (the sweet conceipters of Musicke) fetcht their
carreers on the calmed waves, as if *Arion* had touched
the stringes of his silver sounding instrument: the
Mermaides thrusting their heades from the bosome of
Amphitrite, sate on the mounting bankes of *Neptune*,
drying their waterie tresses in the Sunne beames:
Aeolus forbare to throw abroad his gustes on the
slumbering browes of the Sea God, as giving *Triton*
leave to pleasure his Queene with desired melodie, and
Proteus libertie to followe his flockes without disquiet.

Menaphon looking over the champion of *Arcadie* to
see if the Continent were as full of smiles, as the seas
were of favors, sawe the shrubbes as in a dreame with
delightfull harmonie, and the birdes that chaunted on
their braunches not disturbed with the least breath of
a favourable *Zephirus*.   Seeing this the accord of
the Land and Sea, casting a fresh gaze on the water
Nimphs, he began to consider how *Venus* was feigned
by the Poets to spring of the froathe of the Seas; which
drave him straight into a deepe conjecture of the in-
constacie of Love: that as if *Luna* were his load-starre,
had everie minute ebbes and tides, sometime over-
flowing the banks of Fortune with a gracious look
lightened from the eyes of a favourable lover, other-
whiles ebbing to the dangerous shelfe of despaire, with
the piercing frowne of a froward Mistresse. . . .

And in this Satyricall humor smiling at his owne
conceipts, hee tooke his pipe in his hand, and be-
tweene everie report of his instrument sung a *stanzo* to
this effect.

Lavaltos, lavoltas, lively dances.   *champion*, champaign, level landscape.

MENAPHON'S SONG

Some say Love
Foolish Love
   Doth rule and governe all the Gods,
I say Love,
Inconstant Love,
   Sets mens senses farre at ods.
Some sweare Love
Smooth'd face Love
   Is sweetest sweete that men can have:
I say Love,
Sower Love
   Makes vertue yeeld as beauties slave.
A bitter sweete, a follie worst of all
That forceth wisedome to be follies thrall.

Love is sweete.
Wherein sweete?
   In fading pleasures that doo paine.
Beautie sweete.
Is that sweete
   That yeeldeth sorrow for a gaine?
If Loves sweete
Heerein sweete
   That minutes joyes are monthlie woes.
Tis not sweete,
That is sweete
   Nowhere, but where repentance growes.
Then love who list if beautie be so sower:
Labour for me, Love rest in Princes bower.

Menaphon having ended his roundelay, rising up,
thinking to passe from the mountaine downe to the

Sower, sour.

valley, casting his eye to the sea side, espied certain fragments of a broken ship floating upon the waves, and sundrie persons driven upon the shore with a calme, walking all wet and weary upon the sands. Wondring at this strange sight he stood amazed; yet desirous to see the event of this accident, he shrowded himself to rest unespied til he might perceive what would happen: at last he might descrie it was a woman holding a childe in her armes, and an olde man directing her as it were her guide.

These three (as distressed wrackes) preserved by some further forepoynting fate, coveted to clime the mountaine, the better to use the favor of the Sunne to drie their drenched apparaile; at last crawled up where poor *Menaphon* lay close, and resting them under a bush, the old man did nothing but sende out sighes, and the woman ceased not from streaming foorth rivolets of teares, that hung on her cheekes like the droppes of pearled deaw upon the riches of *Flora*. The poore babe was the touch-stone of his mothers passions; for when he smiled and lay laughing in hir lappe, were her heart never so deeply overcharged with her present sorrowes; yet kissing the pretie infant, shee lightened out smiles from those cheekes that were furrowed with continual sources of teares; but if he cried, then sighes as smokes, and sobbes as thunder-cracks, foreranne those showers, that with redoubled distresse distilled from her eyes: thus with pretie inconstant passions, trimming up her babie, and at last to lull him a sleepe, she warbled out of her wofull breast this dittie.

SEPHESTIA'S SONG TO HER CHILDE

Weepe not my wanton! smile upon my knee!
When thou art olde, ther's grief inough for thee!

Mothers wagge, pretie boy,
Fathers sorrow, fathers joy.
When thy father first did see
Such a boy by him and mee,
He was glad, I was woe.
Fortune changèd made him so,
When he left his pretie boy,
Last his sorowe, first his joy.

Weepe not my wanton! smile upon my knee!
When thou art olde, ther's griefe inough for thee!
  Streaming teares that never stint,
  Like pearle drops from a flint,
  Fell by course from his eyes,
  That one anothers place supplies:
  Thus he grieved in everie part,
  Teares of bloud fell from his hart,
  When he left his pretie boy,
  Fathers sorowe, fathers joy.

Weepe not my wanton! smile upon my knee!
When thou art olde, ther's grief inough for thee!
  The wanton smilde, father wept;
  Mother cride, babie lept:
  More he crowde, more we cride;
  Nature could not sorowe hide.
  He must goe, he must kisse
  Childe and mother, babie blisse:
  For he left his pretie boy,
  Fathers sorowe, fathers joy.

Weepe not my wanton! smile upon my knee!
When thou art olde, ther's grief inough for thee!

stint, stop, cease.   *by course*, in a stream.   *blisse*, bless.

With this lullaby the babie fell a sleepe, and *Sephestia* laying it upon the greene grasse covered it with a mantle, and then leaning her head on her hand, and her elbow on her lap she fell a fresh to poure foorth abundaunce of plaintes, which *Lamedon* the old man espying, although in his face appeared the mappe of discontent, and in everie wrinckle was a catalogue of woes, yet to cheere up *Sephestia*, shrowding his inward sorrow with an outward smile, he began to comfort her in his manner. . . .

All this while *Menaphon* sate amongst the shrubs fixing his eyes on the glorious object of her face, hee noted her tresses, which hee compared to the coloured *Hiacinth* of *Arcadia*, her browes to the mountaine snowes that lie on the hils, her eyes to the gray glister of *Titans* gorgeous mantle, her alabaster necke to the whitenesse of his flockes, her teates to pearle, her face to borders of Lillies interseamed with Roses: to be briefe our Shepheard *Menaphon*, that heeretofore was an Atheist to love, and as the *Thessalian* of *Bacchus*, so hee a contemner of *Venus*, was nowe by the wylie shaft of *Cupid* so intengled in the perfection and beauteous excellence of *Sephestia*; as now he swore no benigne Planet but *Venus*, no God but *Cupide*, nor exquisite deitie but Love. Being thus fettered with the pliant perswasions of fancie, impatient in his newe affections, as the horse that never before felt the spurre, he could not bridle his new conceaved amors, but watching when they shulde depart, perceiving by the gestures of the olde man, and the teares of the Gentlewoman that they were distrest, thought to offer anie helpe that laie within the compasse of his abilitie.

As thus he mused in his new passions, *Lamedon* and *Sephestia* rose up, and resolved to take their course

flockes, i.e., clouds.

which way the winde blew; passing so downe the mountaine to goe seeke out some towne, at last they pacing softlie on, *Lamedon* espied *Menaphon*: desirous therefore to know the course of the countrey, hee saluted him thus.

Shepheard, for so farre thy attire warrants me; courteous, for so much thy countenance imports: if distressed persons whom Fortune hath wronged, and the seas favored, (if we may count it favour to live and want) may without offence crave so farre ayde as to know some place where to rest our wearie and weather-beaten bones, your charges shall be paid, and you have for recompence such thankes as Fortunes outlawes may yeeld to their favourers.

Menaphon hearing him speake so gravelie, but not fitting his eare to his eye, stood staring still on *Sephestias* face, which shee perceiving, flashed out such a blush from her alabaster cheeks that they lookt like the ruddie gates of the Morning: this sweete bashfulnesse amazing *Menaphon*, at last hee began thus to answere.

Strangers, your degree I know not, therefore pardon if I give lesse title than your estates merit: Fortunes frownes are Princes fortunes, and Kings are subject to chance and destinie. Mishap is to be salued with pitie, not scorne: and we that are Fortunes darlings, are bounde to relieve them that are distrest: therefore follow me, and you shal have such succour as a shepheard may afford.

Lamedon and *Sephestia* were passing glad, and *Menaphon* led the way, not content onelie to feed his sight with the beautie of his new Mistres, but thought also to inferre some occasion of parley, to heare whether her voyce were as melodious, as her face beautiful, hee therefore prosecuted his prattle thus.

Gentlewoman, when first I saw you sitting upon the *Arcadian* Promontorie with your babie on your lappe, and this old father by; I thought I had seene *Venus* with *Cupide* on her knee courted by *Anchises* of *Troy*: the excellence of your looks could discover no less than *Mars* his paramour, and the beautie of the childe as much as the dignitie of her wanton: at last perceiving by your teares and your childs shrikes, that ye were passengers distrest, I lent you sighes to partake of your sorrowes, and luke warme drops to signifie how I pitie overcharged persons, in lieu whereof let mee crave your name, countrey, and parentage.

Sephestia seeing by the shepheards passionate lookes, that the swain was halfe in love, replyed thus; Curteous shepheard, if my blubbered cheekes did look like *Venus* at a blush, it was when the woful Goddesse wept for her faire *Adonis*, my boye is no *Cupide* but the sonne of care, Fortunes fondling in his youth, to bee I hope her darling in his age: in that your lookes saw our griefe, and your thoughts pitied our woes, our tongues shal give thanks (the bountie of sorrowes tenants) and our hearts praye that the Gods may be as friendly to your flockes, as you favourable to us. My name is *Samela*, my countrey *Cipres*, my parentage meane, the wife of a poore Gentleman nowe deceased: how we arrived heere by shipwrack, gentle shepheard inquire not, least it be tedious for thee to heare it, and a double griefe for mee to rehearse it.

The shepheard not daring to displease his Mistres, as having loves threates hanging on her lippes, he conveighed them home to his house: as soone as they were arrived there, he began at the dore to entertain them thus.

Faire Mistres the flower of all our Nymphes that

Mars his, Mars's.

live here in *Arcadia*, this is my cotage wherein I live content, and your lodging, where (please it you) ye may rest quiet. I have not rich cloathes of *Aegypt* to cover the walls, nor store of plate to discover anie wealth; for shepheards use neither to be proud nor covetous: you shall find heere cheese and milke for dainties, and wooll for cloathing; in everie corner of the house Content sitting smiling, and tempering everie homelie thing with a welcome: this if ye can brooke and accept of, (as Gods allow the meanest hospitalitie) ye shall have such welcome and fare as *Philemon* and *Baucis* gave to *Jupiter*.

Sephestia thankt him heartelie, and going into his house found what he promist: after that they had sate a little by the fire and were well warmed, they went to supper, where *Sephestia* fedde well, as one whom the sea had made hungrie, and *Lamedon* so plide his teeth, that all supper he spake not one word: after they had taken their repast, *Menaphon*, seeing they were wearie, and that sleepe chimed on to rest, he let them see their lodging, and so gave them the good night.

Lamedon on his flocke bedde, and *Sephestia* on her countrey couch were so wearie, that they slept well: but *Menaphon*, poore *Menaphon* neither asked his swaynes for his sheepe, nor tooke his mole-spade on his necke to see his pastures; but as a man pained with a thousand passions, drenched in distresse, and over-whelmed with a multitude of uncouth cares, he sate like the pictures that *Perseus* tourned with his *Gorgons* head into stones. His sister Carmela kept his house, (for so was the Countrey wench called) and shee seeing her brother sit so malcontented, stept to her cup-boorde and fetched a little beaten spice in an olde bladder, she sparde no evening milke, but went among the cream bowles, and made him a posset. But alas,

Love had so lockt up the shepheards stomacke, that
none would down with *Menaphon*: Carmela seeing her
brother refuse his spicet drinke, thought all was not
well, and therefore sate downe and wept; to be short,
she blubbered and he sightht, and his men that came
in and sawe their master with a kercher on his head
mournde; so that amongst these swaines there was
such melodie, that *Menaphon* tooke his bow and
arrowes and went to bedde: where casting himselfe,
he thought to have beguiled his passions with some
sweete slumbers.   But Love that smiled at his new
interteined champion, sitting on his beddes. head,
prickt him forward with new desires; charging *Morpheus*, *Phobetor*, and *Icolon*, the Gods of sleepe, to
present unto his closed eies the singular beautie and
rare perfections of *Samela*: (for so will we now call her)
in that the *Idea* of her excellence forst him to breath
out scalding sighes smothered within the fornace of his
thoughts into this or the like passion.

I had thought, *Menaphon*, that he which weareth
the bay leafe had been free from lightening, and the
Eagles penne a preservative against thunder; that
labour had been enemie to love, and the eschewing
of idlenesse an *Antidote* against fancie: but I see by
proofe there is no adamant so harde, but the blood of
a Goate will make soft; no fort so wel defenced, but
strong batterie will enter; nor anie hart so pliant to
restlesse labours, but inchantments of love will overcome.   Unfortunate *Menaphon*, that a late thoughtst
Venus a strumpet and her sonne a bastard, now must
thou offer incense at her shrine, and sweare *Cupide* no
lesse than a God: thou hast reason *Menaphon*; for hee
that lives without love, lives without life; presuming
as *Narcissus* to hate all, and being like him at length
despised of all.   Can there bee a sweeter blisse than

beautie, a greater heaven than her heavenly perfections that is mistres of thy thoughts? If the sparkle of her eyes appeare in the night, the starres blush at her brightnesse: if her haire glister in the daye, *Phoebus* puts off his wreath of diamonds, as overcome with the shine of her tresses; if she walke in the fields, *Flora* seeing her face, bids al her glorious flowers close themselves, as being by her beautie disgraced; if her alabaster necke appeere, then *Hiems* covereth his snowe, as surpassed in whitenesse. To be shorte, *Menaphon*, if *Samela* had appeared in *Ida*, *Juno* for majestie, *Pallas* for wisedome, and *Venus* for beautie had let my *Samela* have the supremacie: why shouldest thou not then love, and thinke there is no life to love, seeing the end of love is the possession of such a heavenly Paragon? But what of this, *Menaphon*, hast thou anie hope to enjoy her person, she is a widdow, true, but too high for thy fortunes; she is in distresse, ah, *Menaphon*, if thou hast anie sparke of comfort, this must set thy hope on fire. Want is the load stone of affection, distresse forceth deeper than Fortunes frownes, and such as are poore will rather love than want reliefe, fortunes frownes are whetstones to fancie: and as the horse starteth at the spurre, so love is prickt forward with distresse. *Samela* is shipwrackt, *Menaphon* relieves her; she wants, he supplies with wealth; he sues for love, either must she grant, or buy deniall with perpetuall repentance.

In this hope rested the poore shepheard, and with that *Menaphon* laide his head downe on the pillow and toke a sound nappe, sleeping out fancie, with a good slumber.

As soone as the sunne appeared the shepheard got him up and fed fat with this hope, went merely with his men to the foldes, and there letting foorth his sheepe, after that hee had appointed where they should graze, returned home, and looking when his guests should rise, having supt il the last night went roundly to his breakfast; by that time he had ended his *desiune*, *Lamedon* was gotten up, and so was *Samela*. Against their rising, *Carmela* had showen her cookerie, and *Menaphon* tired in his russet jacket, his redde sleeves of chamlet, his blew bonnet, and his round slop of countrey cloth, bestirred him, as everie joynt had been set to a sundrie office. *Samela* no sooner came out of her chamber, but *Menaphon* as one that claimed pitie for his passions, bad her good morrow with a firme lovers look: *Same a* knowing the fowle by the feather, was able to cast his disease without his water, perceived that *Cupide* had caught the poore shepheard in his net, and unles he sought quickly to break out of the snare would make him a tame foole: faire lookes she gave him, and with a smiling sorow discovered how she grieved at his misfortune, and yet favoured him. Well, to breakfast they went. *Lamedon* and *Samela* fed hard, but *Menaphon* like the *Argive* in the Date gardens of *Arabia*, lived with the contemplation of his Mistres beautie: the Salamander liveth not without the fire, the Herring from the water, the Mole from the earth, nor the Cameleon from the aire, nor coulde *Menaphon* live from the sight of his *Samela*; whose breath was perfumed aire, whose eyes were fire wherein he delighted to dallie, whose heart the earthlie Paradice wherein hee desired to ingraffe the essence of his love and affection: thus did the poore shepheard bathe in a kinde of blisse, whiles his eyes feeding on his mistres face, did surfet with the excellencie of her perfection.

desiune, déjeuné, breakfast.
chamlet, camlet, cloth made of camel's hair or an imitation of such cloth.
round slop, smock.

So long he gazde, that at length breakfast was ended, and he desirous to doo her anie service, first put her childe to nurse, and then led her forth to see his folds; thinking with the sight of his flockes to inveigle her, whose minde had rather have chosen anie misfortune, than have deigned her eyes on the face and feature of so lowe a peasant. Well, abroad they went, *Menaphon* with his sheephooke fringed with cruell, to signifie he was chiefe of the swaynes, *Lamedon* and *Samela* after: plodding thus over the greene fields, at last they came to the mountaines where *Menaphons* flockes grazed, and there he discoursed to *Samela* thus:

I tell thee, faire Nymph, these Plaines that thou seest stretching Southward, are pastures belonging to *Menaphon*: there growes the cintfoyle, and the hyacinth, the cowsloppe, the prinrose, and the violet, which my flockes shall spare for flowers to make thee garlands, the milke of my ewes shall be meate for thy pretie wanton, the wool of the fat weathers that seemes as fine as the fleece that *Iason* fet from *Colchos*, shall serve to make *Samela* webbes withall; the mountaine tops shall be thy mornings walke, and the shadie valleies thy evenings arbour: as much as *Menaphon* owes shall be at *Samelas* command, if she like to live with *Menaphon*.

This was spoken with such deepe effects, that *Samela* could scarce keepe her from smiling, yet she covered her conceipt with a sorrowful countenance, which *Menaphon* espying, to make her merrie, and rather for his own advauntage, seeing *Lamedon* was a sleepe, tooke her by the hand and sate downe, and pulling foorth his pipe, began, after some melodie, to carroll out this roundelay.

cruell, crewel, worsted yarn.   *fet*, fetched.   *owes*, owns.

MENAPHONS ROUNDELAY

When tender ewes brought home with evening Sunne
Wend to their foldes,
And to their holdes
The shepheards trudge when light of day is done.
Upon a tree
The Eagle, *Jove's* faire bird, did pearch,
There resteth hee.
A little flie his harbor then did search,
And did presume (though others laught thereat)
To pearch whereas the princelie Eagle sat.

The Eagle frownd, and shooke her royall wings,
And chargde the Flie
From thence to hie:
Afraid in hast the little creature flings,
Yet seekes againe,
Fearfull, to pearke him by the Eagles side.
With moodie vaine
The speedie post of *Ganimede* replide;
Vassaile avant or with my wings you die,
Ist fit an Eagle seate him with a Flie?

The Flie cravde pitie, still the Eagle frownde,
The sillie Flie
Readie to die
Disgracte, displacte, fell groveling to the ground.
The Eagle sawe
And with a royall minde, said to the Flie,
Be not in awe,
I scorne by me the meanest creature die;
Then seate thee heere: the joyfull Flie up flings,
And sate safe shadowed with the Eagles wings.

post of Ganimede, the eagle had carried Ganymede to Jove.

As soone as *Menaphon* had ended this roundelay, turning to *Samela*, after a countrey blush, he began to court her in this homely fashion; What thinke you, *Samela*, of the Eagle for his royall deede? That he falsified the old Proverbe *Aquila non capit muscas*? But I meane, *Samela*, are you not in opinion, that the Eagle gives instances of a princelie resolution, in preferring the safetie of a Flie before the credit of her royall Majesty?

I thinke, *Menaphon*, that high mindes are the shelters of povertie, and Kings seates are coverts for distressed persons; that the Eagle in shrowding the Flie did well, but a little forgot her honour.

But how thinke you, *Samela*, is not this proportion to be observed in love?

I gesse no, for the Flie did it not for love, but for succour.

Hath love then respect of circumstance?

Els it is not love, but lust; for where the parties have no simpathie of Estates, there can no firme love be fixed; discord is reputed the mother of division, and in nature this is an unrefuted principle, that it falteth which faileth in uniformitie. He that grafteth Jilly-flowers upon the Nettle marreth the smell; who coveteth to tie the Lambe and the Lion in one tedder maketh a brawle; equall fortunes are loves favorites, and therefore shoulde fancie bee alwayes limitted by Geometricall proportion; least if young matching with olde, fire and frost fall at a combate: and if rich with poore there happe manie daungerous and braving objections.

Menaphon halfe nipte in the pate with this replie, yet like a tall souldier stoode to his tackling, and made aunswere; Suppose, gentle *Samela*, that a man of

Aquila, etc., the eagle does not seize the fly.   *falteth*, is at fault.

meane estate, whome disdainefull Fortune had abased, intending to make hir power prodigall in his misfortunes, being feathered with *Cupides* bolt, were snared in the beautie of a Queene, should he rather die than discover his amors?

If Queens (quoth she) were of my mind, I had rather die, than perish in baser fortunes.

Venus loved *Vulcan*, replied *Menaphon*.

Truth, quoth *Samela*, but though he was polt-footed, yet he was a God.

Phaon enjoyed *Sapho*, he a Ferriman that lived by his hands thrifte, she a Princesse that sate invested with a diadem.

The more fortunate, quoth *Samela*, was he in his honours, and she the lesse famous in her honestie.

To leave these instances, replied *Menaphon*, (for love had made him hardie) I, sweete *Samela*, inferre these presupposed premisses, to discover the basenes of my meane birth, and yet the deepnesse of my affection, who ever since I saw the brightnesse of your perfection shining upon the mountaines of *Arcadie*, like the glister of the Sunne upon the topless Promontorie of *Sicilia*, was so snared with your beautie, and so inveigled with the excellence, that love entring my desire, hath mainteined himselfe by force; that unlesse sweete *Samela* grant me favour of her love, and play the princelie Eagle, I shall with the poore Flie perish in my Fortunes. He concluded this period with a deepe sigh, and *Samela* grieving at this follie of the Shepheard, gave him mildelie this aunswere.

Menaphon, my distressed haps are the resolutions of the Destinies, and the wrongs of my youth, are the forerunners of my woes in age; my native home is my worst nurserie, and my friends denie that which

feathered, etc., wounded by Cupid's arrow.   *polt-footed*, club-footed.

strangers prejudiciallie grant: I arrived in *Arcady* shipwrackt, and *Menaphon* favouring my sorrowes hath affoorded me succours, for which *Samela* rests bound, and will proove thankfull: as for love, knowe that *Venus* standeth on the Tortoys, as shewing that *Love* creepeth on by degrees; that affection is like the Snayle, which stealeth to the top of the lance by minutes; the grasse hath his increase, yet never anie sees it augment, the Sonne shadowes, but the motion is not seene; love like those should enter into the eie, and by long gradations passe into the heart; *Cupid* hath wings to flie, not that love should be swift, but that he may soare high to avoyd base thoughts. The Topace being throwne into the fire burneth straight, but no sooner out of the flame but it freezeth; strawe is soone kindled, but it is but a blaze; and love that is caught in a moment, is lost in a minute; give me leave then *Menaphon* first to sorrowe for my fortunes, then to call to minde my husbands late funeralls, then if the Fates have assigned I shall fancie, I will account of thee before anie shepheard in *Arcadie.*

This conclusion of *Samela* drave *Menaphon* into such an exstasie for joy, that he stood as a man metamorphozed; at last, calling his senses together, hee tolde her he rested satisfied with her answere, and thereupon lent her a kisse, such as blushing *Thetis* receaves from her choycest lemman.

At this, *Lamedon* awakte, otherwise *Menaphon* no doubt had replied, but breaking off their talk they went to view their pastures, and so passing downe to the place where the sheepe grazed, they searched the shepheards bagges, and so emptied their bottles as *Samela* mervailed at such an uncouth banquet: at last they returned home, *Menaphon* glorying in the hope

Topace, topaz.　　　*lemman,* paramour, lover.

of his successe, interteining *Samela* still with such courtesie, that shee finding such content in the cotage, began to despise the honors of the Court.

Resting thus in house with the shepheard, to avoide tedious conceipts she framed herself so to countrey labours, that she oft times would lead the flocks to the fieldes herselfe, and being drest in homelie attire, she seemed like *Oenone* that was amorous of *Paris*. . . .

[*As will be seen by these pages of Menaphon, there is very little story. In what follows, however, the plot rapidly becomes complicated and entirely preposterous. Melicertus, a shepherd of the neighborhood, is really Sephestia's husband; but he does not recognize her, and woos her again. Her child, Pleusidippus, is stolen by pirates and carried to Hadrianopolis, where Agenor, king of Thessaly, and Eriphila, his queen, adopt him. In the end, Sephestia (or Samela) is in the peculiar position of being courted by her father, her son, and her husband. All, however, ends as it should. The part I have given is the best. "Like Shakespeare's* As You Like It," *says Professor Arber, "this Romance seems filled with the sunshine of that Golden Age which illuminated the souls of the later Poets of Elizabeth's reign; while, under the disguise of shepherds and shepherdesses on the Mediterranean shores, such works have preserved to us the fine-filed talk of the English Court. So that they are models to us of the cultivated speech of that time.*"]

Robert Greene, Menaphon. *Camillas alarum to slumbering Euphues, in his melancholie Cell at Silexedra, etc.* London, 1589.

THE LAST FIGHT OF THE REVENGE

1591

The Lord Thomas Howard with six of her Majesty's ships, six victualers of London, the bark Raleigh, and two or three other pinnaces riding at anchor near unto Flores, one of the westerly islands of the Azores, the last of August in the afternoon, had intelligence by one Captain Middleton of the approach of the armada. Which Middleton, being a very good sailor, had kept them company three days before, of good purpose both to discover their forces the more, as also to give advice to my Lord Thomas of their approach. He had no sooner delivered the news but the fleet was in sight; many of our ships' companies were on shore in the island, some providing ballast for their ships, others filling of water and refreshing themselves from the land with such things as they could, either for money or by force, recover. By reason whereof, our ships being all pestered and rummaging every thing out of order, very light for want of ballast, and that which was most to our disadvantage, the one half part of the men of every ship sick and utterly unserviceable; for in the Revenge there were ninety diseased, and in the Bonaventure not so many in as could handle her mainsail. For had not twenty men been taken out of a bark of Sir George Carey's, his being commanded to be sunk, and those appointed to her, she had hardly ever recovered England. The rest, for the most part, were in little better state. The names of her Majesty's ships were these, as followeth: the Defiance, which was admiral; the Revenge, viseadmiral; the Bonaventure, commanded by Captain Cross; the

pestered, full of vermin (barnacles?) or overloaded.
rummaging, in confusion.   *recovered*, regained.

Lion by George Fenner; the Foresight by Mr. Thomas Vavasour; and the Crane by Duffield. The Foresight and the Crane being but small ships, only the others were of the middle size; the rest, besides the Raleigh, commanded by Captain Thin, were victualers, and of small force or none. The Spanish fleet, having shrouded their approach by reason of the island, were now so soon at hand as our ships had scarce time to weigh their anchors, but some of them were driven to let slip their cables and set sail. Sir Richard Grenville was the last that weighed, to recover the men that were upon the island, which otherwise had been lost. The Lord Thomas with the rest hardly recovered the wind, which Sir Richard Grenville not being able to do, was persuaded by the master and others to cut his mainsail and cast about, and to trust to the sailing of the ship, for the squadron of Seville were on his weather bow. But Sir Richard utterly refused to turn from the enemy, alleging that he would rather choose to die than to dishonor himself, his country, and her Majesty's ship, persuading his company that he would pass through the two squadrons in despite of them and enforce those of Seville to give him way. Which he performed upon divers of the foremost, who, as the mariners term it, sprang their luff, and fell under the lee of the Revenge. But the other course had been the better, and might right well have been answered in so great an impossibility of prevailing. Notwithstanding, out of the greatness of his mind, he could not be persuaded. In the meanwhile, as he attended those which were nearest him, the great San Philip, being in the wind of him and coming towards him, becalmed his sails in such sort, as the ship could neither make

Grenville (c. 1541–91) was Raleigh's cousin and was vice-admiral of Howard's expedition.
sprang their luff, turned away from the wind.

way nor feel the helm; so huge and high charged was the Spanish ship, being of a thousand and five hundred tons. Who after laid the Revenge aboard. When he was thus bereft of his sails, the ships that were under his lee, luffing up, also laid him aboard, of which the next was the admiral of the Biscayans, a very mighty and puissant ship commanded by Brittandona. The said Philip carried three tiers of ordnance on a side, and eleven pieces in every tier. She shot eight forthright out of her chase, besides those of her stern ports.

After the Revenge was entangled with the Philip, four others boarded her, two on her larboard, and two on her starboard. The fight, thus beginning at three o'clock in the afternoon, continued very terrible all that evening. But the great San Philip, having received the lower tier of the Revenge, discharged with crossbar shot, shifted herself with all diligence from her sides, utterly misliking her first entertainment. Some say that the ship foundered, but we cannot report it for truth, unless we were assured. The Spanish ships were filled with companies of soldiers, — in some two hundred besides the mariners, in some five, in others eight hundred. In ours there were none at all beside the mariners but the servants of the commanders and some few voluntary gentlemen only. After many interchanged volleys of great ordnance and small shot, the Spaniards deliberated whether to enter the Revenge, and made divers attempts, hoping to force her by the multitudes of their armed soldiers and musketeers, but were still repulsed again and again, and at all times beaten back into their own ships, or into the seas. In the beginning of the fight, the George Noble of London, having received some

high charged, built high above the water.
forthright, etc., directly out of her bow guns or forward battery.

shot through her by the armadas, fell under the lee of the Revenge, and asked Sir Richard what he would command him, being but one of the victualers and of small force. Sir Richard bade him save himself, and leave him to his fortune. After the fight had thus, without intermission, continued while the day lasted and some hours of the night, many of our men were slain and hurt, and one of the great galleons of the armada, and the admiral of the hulks both sunk, and in many other of the Spanish ships great slaughter was made. Some write that Sir Richard was very dangerously hurt almost at the beginning of the fight, and lay speechless for a time ere he recovered. But two of the Revenge's own company brought home in a ship of Lima from the islands, affirmed that he was never so wounded as that he forsook the upper deck, till an hour before midnight, then being shot into the body with a musket, as he was dressing was again shot into the head, and withal his surgeon wounded to death. This agreeth also with an examination, taken by Sir Francis Godolphin, of four other mariners of the same ship, being returned, which examination the said Sir Francis sent unto Master William Killigrew, of her Majesty's privy chamber.

But to return to the fight: the Spanish ships which attempted to board the Revenge, as they were wounded and beaten off, so always others came in their places, she having never less than two mighty galleons by her sides and aboard her. So that ere the morning, from three of the clock the day before, there had fifteen several armadas assailed her; and all so ill approved their entertainment as they were by the break of day far more willing to hearken to a composition than hastily to make any more assaults or

armadas, properly fleets, here single great vessels.

entries. But as the day increased, so our men decreased; and as the light grew more and more, by so much more grew our discomforts. For none appeared in sight but enemies, saving one small ship called the Pilgrim, commanded by Jacob Whiddon, who hovered all night to see the success, but in the morning, bearing with the Revenge, was hunted like a hare amongst so many ravenous hounds, but escaped.

All the powder of the Revenge to the last barrel was now spent, all her pikes broken, forty of her best men slain, and the most part of the rest hurt. In the beginning of the fight she had but one hundred free from sickness, and fourscore and ten sick, laid in hold upon the ballast: a small troop to man such a ship, and a weak garrison to resist so mighty an army. By those hundred all was sustained, the volleys, boardings, and enterings of fifteen ships of war, besides those which beat her at large. On the contrary, the Spanish were always supplied with soldiers brought from every squadron, all manner of arms and powder at will. Unto ours there remained no comfort at all, no hope, no supply either of ships, men, or weapons; the masts all beaten overboard, all her tackle cut asunder, her upper work altogether razed, and in effect evened she was with the water, but the very foundation or bottom of a ship, nothing being left overhead, either for flight or defence. Sir Richard, finding himself in this distress, and unable any longer to make resistance, having endured, in this fifteen hours' fight, the assault of fifteen several armadas, all by turns aboard him, and by estimation eight hundred shot of great artillery besides many assaults and entries; and that himself and the ship must needs be possessed by the enemy, who were now all cast in a ring round about him, (the Revenge not able to move one way or other, but as she was moved with the waves and billows of the sea), commanded the master gunner, whom he knew to be a most resolute man, to split and sink the ship, that thereby nothing might remain of glory or victory to the Spaniards, seeing in so many hours' fight, and with so great a navy, they were not able to take her, having had fifteen hours' time, above ten thousand men, and fifty and three sail of men-of-war to perform it withal; and persuaded the company, or as many as he could induce, to yield themselves unto God, and to the mercy of none else; but as they had, like valiant resolute men, repulsed so many enemies, they should not now shorten the honor of their nation by prolonging their own lives for a few hours or a few days. The master gunner readily condescended and divers others; but the captain and the master were of another opinion, and besought Sir Richard to have care of them, alleging that the Spaniard would be as ready to entertain a composition, as they were willing to offer the same, and that there being divers sufficient and valiant men yet living, and whose wounds were not mortal, they might do their country and prince acceptable service hereafter. And whereas Sir Richard had alleged that the Spaniards should never glory to have taken one ship of her Majesty, seeing they had so long and so notably defended themselves; they answered, that the ship had six foot of water in hold, three shot under water, which were so weakly stopped, as with the first working of the sea, she must needs sink, and was besides so crushed and bruised, as she could never be removed out of the place.

And as the matter was thus in dispute, and Sir Richard refusing to hearken to any of those reasons, the master of the Revenge (while the captain won unto him the greater party) was convoyed aboard the

General Don Alfonso Bacan. Who (finding none
over hasty to enter the Revenge again, doubting lest
Sir Richard would have blown them up and himself,
and perceiving by the report of the master of the
Revenge his dangerous disposition) yielded that all
their lives should be saved, the company sent for
England, and the better sort to pay such reasonable
ransom as their estate would bear, and in the mean
season to be free from galley or imprisonment. To
this he so much the rather condescended as well, as I
have said, for fear of further loss and mischief to
themselves, as also for the desire he had to recover Sir
Richard Grenville; whom for his notable valor he
seemed greatly to admire and honor.

When this answer was returned, and that safety of
life was promised, the common sort being now at the
end of their peril, the most drew back from Sir Richard
and the master gunner, being no hard matter to dis-
suade men from death to life. The master gunner,
finding himself and Sir Richard thus prevented and
mastered by the greater number, would have slain
himself with a sword, had he not been by force with-
held and locked into his cabin. Then the General sent
many boats aboard the Revenge, and divers of our
men, fearing Sir Richard's disposition, stole away
aboard the General and other ships. Sir Richard,
thus overmatched, was sent unto by Alfonso Bacan to
remove out of the Revenge, the ship being marvelous
unsavory, filled with blood and bodies of dead, and
wounded men like a slaughter house. Sir Richard
answered that he might do with his body what he list,
for he esteemed it not, and as he was carried out of the
ship he swooned, and reviving again desired the company to pray for him. The General used Sir Richard
with all humanity, and left nothing unattempted that

tended to his recovery, highly commending his valor and worthiness, and greatly bewailing the danger wherein he was, being unto them a rare spectacle, and a resolution seldom approved, to see one ship turn toward so many enemies, to endure the charge and boarding of so many huge armadas, and to resist and repel the assaults and entries of so many soldiers. All which and more is confirmed by a Spanish captain of the same armada, and a present actor in the fight, who being severed from the rest in a storm, was by the Lion of London, a small ship, taken and is now prisoner in London.

The general commander of the Armada, was Don Alphonso Bacan, brother to the Marquis of Santa Cruz. The admiral of the Biscayan squadron was Brittandona. Of the squadron of Seville, the Marquis of Arumburch. The hulks and flyboats were commanded by Luis Coutinho. There were slain and drowned in this fight well near one thousand of the enemies, and two special commanders, Don Luis de Sant John and Don George de Prunaria de Mallaga, as the Spanish captain confesseth, besides divers others of special account, whereof as yet report is not made.

The Admiral of the hulks and the Ascension of Seville were both sunk by the side of the Revenge; one other recovered the road of Saint Michael and sunk also there; a fourth ran herself with the shore to save her men. Sir Richard died, as it is said, the second or third day aboard the General, and was by them greatly bewailed. What became of his body, whether it were buried in the sea or on the land, we know not: the comfort that remaineth to his friends is, that he hath ended his life honorably in respect of the reputation won to his nation and country, and of the same to

his posterity, and that being dead, he hath not outlived his own honor. . . .

> *Sir Walter Raleigh, from A Report of the truth of the fight
> about the isles of Azores, the last of August, 1591, betwixt
> the Revenge, one of her Majesty's ships, and an armada of
> the king of Spain.*

LAWS OF NATURE

1594

Now if nature should intermit her course, and
leave altogether though it were but for a while the
observation of her own laws; if those principal and
mother elements of the world, whereof all things in
this lower world are made, should lose the qualities
which now they have; if the frame of that heavenly
arch erected over our heads should loosen and dissolve
itself; if celestial spheres should forget their wonted
motions, and by irregular volubility turn themselves
any way it might happen; if the prince of the lights of
heaven, which now as a giant doth run his unwearied
course, should as it were through a languishing faint-
ness begin to stand and to rest himself; if the moon
should wander from her beaten way, the times and
seasons of the year blend themselves by disordered
and confused mixture, the winds breathe out their last
gasp, the clouds yield no rain, the earth be defeated of
heavenly influence, the fruits of the earth pine away
as children at the withered breasts of their mother no
longer able to yield them relief: what would become of
man himself, whom these things now do all serve?
See we not plainly that obedience unto the law of
nature is the stay of the whole world?

Richard Hooker, The Laws of Ecclesiasticall Politie

THE SEARCH

Man doth seek a triple perfection: first, a sensual, consisting in those things which very life itself requireth either as necessary supplements, or as beauties and ornaments thereof; then an intellectual, consisting in those things which none underneath man is either capable of or acquainted with; lastly, a spiritual and divine, consisting in those things whereunto we tend by supernatural means here, but here cannot attain unto them. They that make the first of these three the scope of their whole life, are said by the Apostle to have no god but only their belly, to be earthly minded men. Unto the second they bend themselves, who seek especially to excel in all such knowledge and virtue as doth most commend men. To this branch belongeth the law of moral and civil perfection. That there is somewhat higher than either of these two, no other proof doth need than the very process of man's desire, which being natural should be frustrate, if there were not some farther thing wherein it might rest at the length contented, which in the former it cannot do. For man doth not seem to rest satisfied, either with fruition of that wherewith his life is preserved, or with performance of such actions as advance him most deservedly in estimation; but doth further covet, yea oftentimes manifestly pursue with great sedulity and earnestness, that which cannot stand him in any stead for vital use; that which exceedeth the reach of sense; yea somewhat above capacity of reason, somewhat divine and heavenly, which with hidden exultation it rather surmiseth than conceiveth; somewhat it seeketh, and what that is directly it knoweth not, yet very intentive desire thereof doth so incite it, that all other known delights and pleasures are laid aside, they give place to the search of this but only suspected desire.

Richard Hooker, The Laws of Ecclesiasticall Politie

AN ELIZABETHAN WIFE

1597

[*Simon Eyre, an upright and successful shoemaker, hears through one of his apprentices (John the Frenchman) of a rich cargo just come to port, which he can buy for £3,000.*]

Now as soon as John the Frenchman came home, he moved that matter unto his master, desiring him that he would do what he could for the merchant. When his master had heard each circumstance, noting therewith the want of such commodities in the land, cast in his mind as he stood cutting up his work, what were best to be done in this case, saying to his man John, I will think upon it betwixt this and the morning, and then I will tell you my mind: and therewithall casting down his cutting knife, he went out of his shop into his chamber, and therein walked up and down alone very sadly, ruminating hereon: he was so far in his muse, that, his wife sending for him to supper two or three times, he nothing regarded the maids call, hammering this matter in his head.

At last his wife came to him, saying, husband, what mean you that you do not come to supper? why speak you not man? Hear you? good husband; come away, your meat will be cold: but for all her words he stayed walking up and down still, like a man that had sent his wits a wool-gathering, which his wife seeing, puled him by the sleeve, saying, why, husband in the name of God, why come you not? wil you not come to supper to night? I called you a good while ago.

Body of me, wife (said he) I promise thee I did not hear thee.

No faith, it seemeth so (quoth she) I marvel whereupon your mind runneth.

Beleeve me wife (quoth he) I was studying how to make my selfe Lord Maior and thee a lady.

Now God help you (quoth she) I pray God make us able to pay every man his own, that we may live out of debt and danger, and drive the woolf from the doore, and I desire no more.

But wife (said he) I pray thee now tell me, doest thou not think that thou couldest make shift to bear the name of a lady, if it should be put upon thee.

In truth husband (quoth she) Ile not dissemble with you, if your wealth were able to beare it, my mind would beare it well enough.

Well wife (replyed he) I tell thee now in sadnesse, that, if I had money, there is a commodity now to be bought, the gains whereof would be able to make me a gentleman forever.

Alas husband, that dignitie your trade allows you already, being a squire of the Gentle Craft, then how can you be lesse than a gentleman, seeing your sonne is a prince borne?

Tush, wife (quoth he) those titles do onely rest in name, but not in nature: but of that sort had I rather be, whose lands are answerable to their vertues, and whose rents can maintain the greatnesse of their minde.

Then sweet husband, tell me (said his wife) tell me, what commodity is that which you might get so much by? I am sure your self hath some money, and it shall go very hard but Ile procure friends to borrow one forty shillings, and beside that, rather then you should lose so good a bargain, I have a couple of crowns that saw no sun since we were first married, and them also shall you have.

Alasse wife (said Simon) all this comes not neere that matter: I confesse it would do some good in buying some backs of leather, but in this thing it is nothing, for this is merchandise that is precious at this time, and rare to be had; and I hear that whosoever will have it must lay down three thousand pounds ready money. Yea, wife, and yet thereby he might get three and three thousand pounds profit.

His wife hearing him say so was inflamed with the desire thereof, as women are (for the most part) very covetous: that matter running still in her mind, she could scant finde in her heart to spare him time to go to supper, for very eagernesse to animate him on, to take that bargain upon him. Wherefore so soon as they had supt, and given God thanks, she called her husband, saying, I pray you come hither, I would speak a word with you: that man is not alwayes to be blamed that sometimes takes counsell of his wife; though womens wits are not able to comprehend the greatest things, yet in doubtful matters they oft help on a sudden.

Well wife, what mean you by this (said her husband)?

In truth (quoth she) I would have you pluck up a mans heart, and speedily chop up a bargain for these goods you speak of.

Who I? (quoth he), which way should I do it, that am not able for three thousand pounds, to lay down three thousand pence?

Tush man (quoth she) what of that? every man that beholds a man in the face, knows not what he hath in his purse, and whatsoever he be that owes the goods,

owes, owns.

he will no doubt be content to stay a moneth for his money, or three weeks at the least: And, I promise you, to pay a thousand pounds a week is a pretty round payment, and, I may say to you, not much to be misliked of.

Now husband, I would have you in the morning with John the Frenchman to the Grecian merchant, and with good discretion drive a sound bargain with him for the whole fraught of the ship, and thereupon give him halfe a dozen angels in earnest, and eight and twenty dayes after the delivery of the goods, condition to deliver him the rest of the money.

But woman (quoth he) dost thou imagine he would take my word for so weighty a masse of money, and to deliver his goods upon no better security?

Good Lord (quoth she) have you no wit in such a case to make shift? Ile tell you what you shall do: Be not known that you bargain for your own selfe, but tell him that you do it in the behalf of one of the chief aldermen in the city; but beware in any case, that you leave with him your own name in writing; he being a Grecian cannot read English: and you have no need at all to shew John the Frenchman, nor if you should, it were no great matter, for you can tell well enough that he can neither write nor read.

I perceive wife (quoth he) thou wouldest fain be a lady, and worthy thou art to be one, that dost thus imploy thy wits to bring thy husband profit: but tell me, if he should be desirous to see the alderman to confer with him, how shall we do then?

Jesus have mercy upon us (quoth she) you say women are fools, but me seemeth men have need to be taught sometimes. Before you come away in the morn-

angels, coins of value 6s. 8d. to 10s.; so called because the design was of St. Michael killing the dragon.

ing, let John the Frenchman tell him that the alderman himselfe shall come to his lodging in the afternoon: and, receiving a note of all the goods that be in the ship, he shall deliver unto him a bill of his hand for the payment of his money, according to that time. Now sweetheart (quoth she) this alderman shall be thine own selfe, and Ile go borrow for thee all things that shall be necessary against that time.

Tush (quoth her husband) canst thou imagine that he, seeing me in the morning, will not know me again in the afternoon?

O husband (quoth she) he will not know thee, I warrant thee: for in the morning thou shalt go to him in thy doublet of sheeps skins, with a smuched face, and thy apron before thee, thy thumb-leather and hand-leather buckled close to thy wrist, with a foule band about thy neck, and a greasie cap on thy head.

Why woman (quoth he) to go in this sort will be a discredit to me, and make the merchant doubtfull of my dealing: for men of simple attire are (God wot) slenderly esteemed.

Hold your peace good husband (quoth she) it shall not be so with you, for John the Frenchman shall give such good report to the merchant for your honest dealing (as I praise God he can do no lesse) that the Grecian will rather conceive the better of you than otherwise: judging you a prudent discreet man, that will not make a shew of that you are not, but go in your attire agreeable to your trade.   And because none of our folks shall be privy to our intent, to-morrow weel dine at my cousin John Barbers in Saint Clements Lane, which is not far from the George in Lumbard Street, where the merchant strangers lie. Now Ile be sure that all things shall be ready at my cousin Johns that you shall put on in the afternoon.

And there he shall first of all with his scissors snap off all the superfluous hairs, and fashion thy bushy beard after the aldermans grave cut: then he shall wash thee with a sweet camphire ball, and besprinkle thine head and face with the purest rose-water; then shalt thou scoure thy pitchy fingers in a basin of hot water, with an ordinary washing ball; and all this being done, strip thee from these common weeds, and Ile put thee on a very fair doublet of tawny sattin, over the which thou shalt have a cassock of branched damask, furred round about the skirts with the finest foynes, thy breeches of black velvet, and shooes and stockings fit for such array: a band about thy neck as white as the driven snow, and for thy wrists a pretty pair of cuffs, and on thy head a cap of the finest black, then shalt thou put on a fair gown, welted about with velvet, and over-thwart the back thwart it shall be with rich foyne, with a pair of sweet gloves on thy hands, and on thy forefinger a great seale-ring of gold.

Thou being thus attired, Ile entreat my cousin John Barber, because he is a very handsome young man, neat and fine in his apparell (as indeed all barbers are) that he would take the pains to wait upon you unto the merchants, as if he were your man, which he will do at the first, because one of you cannot understand the other, so that it will be sufficient with outward courtesie one to greet another, and he to deliver unto you his notes, and you to give him your bill, and so come home.

It doth my heart good, to see how trimly this ap-parell doth become you, in good faith, husband, me seems in my mind, I see you in it already, and how like an alderman you will look, when you are in this

---

foynes, foins (furs of the beech-martin).
overthwart, etc., across the back breadth.

costly array. At your return from the merchant, you shall put off all these clothes at my cousins again, and come home as you did go forth. Then tell John the Frenchman, that the alderman was with the merchant this afternoon, you may send him to him in the morning, and bid him to command that his ship may be brought down the river: while she is coming about, you may give notice to the linnen drapers, of the commodities you have coming.

Enough wife (quoth he) thou hast said enough; and, by the grace of God, Ile follow thy counsell, and I doubt not but to have good fortune.

[*The ruse is completely successful and by this single stroke Simon becomes a rich man. He and his wife are invited to a banquet at the Lord Mayor's and he behaves with such dignity and discretion that he is appointed sheriff of London. In the end he becomes Lord Mayor himself, builds Leaden Hall and establishes the leather-market there, and dies full of honors.*]

Thomas Deloney, The Gentle Craft

THE WATCH

1598

A street. — Enter Dogberry and Verges[1] with the Watch.

Dog. Are you good men and true?

Verg. Yea, or else it were pity but they should suffer salvation, body and soul.

Dog. Nay, that were a punishment too good for them, if they should have any allegiance in them, being chosen for the prince's watch.

---

[1] Dogberry is a constable; Verges, a headborough, or petty constable.

Verg. Well, give them their charge, neighbour Dogberry.

Dog. First, who think you the most desartless man to be constable?

First Watch. Hugh Oatcake, sir, or George Seacole; for they can write and read.

Dog. Come hither, neighbour Seacole. God hath blessed you with a good name: to be well-favoured man is the gift of fortune; but to write and read comes by nature.

Sec. Watch. Both which, master constable, ——

Dog. You have: I knew it would be your answer. Well, for your favour, sir, why, give God thanks, and make no boast of it; and for your writing and reading, let that appear when there is no need of such vanity. You are thought here to be the most senseless and fit man for the constable of the watch; therefore bear you the lantern. This is your charge: you shall comprehend all vagrom men; you are to bid any man stand, in the prince's name.

Sec. Watch. How if a' will not stand?

Dog. Why, then, take no note of him, but let him go; and presently call the rest of the watch together, and thank God you are rid of a knave.

Verg. If he will not stand when he is bidden, he is none of the prince's subjects.

Dog. True, and they are to meddle with none but the prince's subjects. You shall also make no noise in the streets; for for the watch to babble and to talk is most tolerable and not to be endured.

Watch. We will rather sleep than talk: we know what belongs to a watch.

Dog. Why, you speak like an ancient and most quiet watchman; for I cannot see how sleeping should

bills, pikes or halberds, staffs with hooked and pointed ends.

offend: only, have a care that your bills be not stolen. Well, you are to call at all the alehouses, and bid those that are drunk get them to bed.

Watch. How if they will not?

Dog. Why, then, let them alone till they are sober: if they make you not then the better answer, you may say they are not the men you took them for.

Watch. Well, sir.

Dog. If you meet a thief, you may suspect him, by virtue of your office, to be no true man; and, for such kind of men, the less you meddle or make with them, why, the more is your honesty.

Watch. If we know him to be a thief, shall we not lay hands on him?

Dog. Truly, by your office, you may; but I think they that touch filth will be defiled: the most peaceable way for you, if you do take a thief, is to let him show himself what he is, and steal out of your company.

Verg. You have been always called a merciful man, partner.

Dog. Truly, I would not hang a dog by my will, much more a man who has any honesty in him.

Verg. If you hear a child crying in the night, you must call to the nurse and bid her still it.

Watch. How if the nurse be asleep and will not hear us?

Dog. Why, then, depart in peace, and let the child wake her with crying; for the ewe that will not hear her lamb when it baes will never answer a calf when he bleats.

Verg. 'Tis very true.

Dog. This is the end of the charge: — you, constable, are to present the prince's own person: if you meet the prince in the night, you may stay him.

Verg. Nay, by'r lady, that I think a' cannot.

Dog. Five shillings to one on't, with any man that knows the statues, he may stay him: marry, not without the prince be willing; for, indeed, the watch ought to offend no man; and it is an offence to stay a man against his will.

Verg. By'r Lady, I think it be so.

Dog. Ha, ha, ha! Well, master, good night: an there be any matter of weight chances, call up me: keep your fellows' counsels and your own; and good night. Come, neighbour.

Watch. Well, masters, we hear our charge: let us go sit here upon the church-bench till two, and then all to bed.

William Shakespeare, Much Ado about Nothing, Act III, Scene III.

THE ART OF ACTING

1604

Speak the speech, I pray you, as I pronounced it to you, trippingly on the tongue: but if you mouth it, as many of your players do, I had as lief the town-crier spoke my lines. Nor do not saw the air too much with your hand, thus; but use all gently: for in the very torrent, tempest, and, as I may say, whirlwind of your passion, you must acquire and beget a temperance that may give it smoothness. O, it offends me to the soul to hear a robustious periwig-pated fellow tear a passion to tatters, to very rags, to split the ears of the groundlings, who, for the most part, are capable of nothing but inexplicable dumb-shows and noise: I would have such a fellow whipped for o'erdoing Termagant; it out-herods Herod: pray you, avoid it. . . .

Be not too tame neither, but let your own discre-

Termagant, a common character in the old mystery-plays, apparently a Saracen god, and notable for tyranny and violence.
Out-herods Herod, out-doing in fury Herod, a similar character.

tion be your tutor: suit the action to the word, the
word to the action; with this special observance, that
you o'erstep not the modesty of nature: for anything
so overdone is from the purpose of playing, whose end,
both at the first and now, was and is, to hold, as
'twere, the mirror up to nature; to show virtue her
own feature, scorn her own image, and the very age
and body of the time his form and pressure.   Now
this overdone or come tardy off, though it make the
unskilful laugh, cannot but make the judicious grieve;
the censure of the which one must in your allowance o'erweigh a whole theatre of others.   O, there
be players that I have seen play and heard others
praise, and that highly, not to speak it profanely, that
neither having the accent of Christians nor the gait of
Christian, pagan, nor man, have so strutted and bel-
lowed, that I have thought some of nature's journey-
men had made men, and not made them well, they
imitated humanity so abominably. . . .

And let those that play your clowns speak no more
than is set down for them: for there be of them that
will themselves laugh, to set on some quantity of
barren spectators to laugh too, though in the mean
time some necessary question of the play be then to
be considered: that's villainous, and shows a most
pitiful ambition in the fool that uses it.

*William Shakespeare, The Tragedy of Hamlet, Prince of
Denmark, Act III, Scene II.*

ON THE ART OF CONFERRING [1]

1603

. . . The most fruitfull and naturall exercise of our
spirit, is, in my selfe-pleasing conceit, conference.

pressure, impress, imprint.
conferring, conversation.   [1] This essay is given in the old spelling.

The use whereof, I finde to be more delightsome, then any other action of our life: And that's the reason why, if I were now forced to choose, (being in the minde I now am in) I would rather yeeld to lose my sight, than forgoe my hearing or my speech. The Athenians and also the Romans, did ever hold this exercise in high honour and reputation, namely in their *Academies*. And at this day, the Italians doe yet keepe a kinde of forme and trace of it, to their great profit, as may apparently be discerned by comparing their wits unto ours. The study and plodding on bookes, is a languishing and weake kinde of motion, and which heateth or earnesteth nothing; whereas conference doth both learne, teach and exercise at once. If I conferre with a stubborne wit, and encounter a sturdy wrestler, he toucheth me to the quicke, hits me on the flanks, and pricks me both on the left and right side: his imaginations vanquish and confound mine. Jelousie, glory and contention drive, cast, and raise me above myselfe. And an unison or consent, is a quality altogether tedious and wearisome in conference.

But as our minde is fortified by the communication of regular and vigorous spirits; it cannot well be expressed, how much it loseth and is bastardized, by the continuall commerce and frequentation, we have with base, weake and dull spirits. No contagion spreds it selfe further then that. I know by long experience what an ell of it is worth. I love to contest and discourse, but not with many, and onely for myselfe. For, to serve as a spectacle unto great men, and by way of contention, for one to make a glorious shew of his ready wit and running tongue: I deeme it a profession farre unfitting a man of honour. Sottish-

earnesteth, strengtheneth.   *Sottishness*, stupidity.

nes is an ill quality, but not to be able to endure it, as
hapneth to me, is another kinde of imperfection,
which in importunity is not much behinde sottishnes:
and that's it I will now accuse in my selfe.

I doe with great liberty and facility, enter into conference and disputation: forsomuch as opinion findes
but a hard soile to enter and take any deepe roote in
me. No propositions amaze me, no conceit wound-
eth me, what contrariety soever they have to mine.
There is no fantazie so frivolous or humour so extravagant, that in mine opinion is not sortable to the production of humane wit. Wee others, who debarre our
judgement of the right to make conclusions, regard but
negligently the diverse opinions: and if we lend it not
our judgement, we easily affoord it our eares. Where
one scale of the ballance is altogether empty, I let the
other waver too and fro, under an old wives dreames.
And me seemeth, I may well be excused, if I rather
accept an odde number, than an even: Thursday in
respect of Friday, if I had rather make a twelfth or
fourteenth at a table, then a thirteenth: if when I am
travelling I would rather see a Hare coasting, then
crossing my way; and rather reach my left, then my
right foote, to be shod. All such fond conceits, now
in credit about us, deserve at least to be listend unto.
As for me, they onely beare away inanity, and surely
they do so. Vulgar and casuall opinions are yet of
some waight, which in nature are something els then
nothing. And who wadeth not so far into them, to
avoid the vice of superstition, falleth happily into
the blame of wilfulnesse. The contradictions then of
judgements, doe neither offend nor move, but awaken
and exercise me. We commonly shunne correction
whereas we should rather seeke and present ourselves

sortable, suitable, congenial.

unto it, chiefly when it commeth by the way of conference, and not of regency.   At every opposition, we
consider not whether it be just; but be it right or
wrong, how we may avoide it: In stead of reaching our
armes, we stretch forth our claws unto it.   I should
endure to bee rudely handled and checked by my
friends, though they should call me foole, coxecombe,
or say I raved.   I love a man that doth stoutly ex-
presse himselfe, amongst honest and worthy men, and
whose words answere his thoughts.   We should forti-
fie and harden our hearing, against the tendernesse of
the ceremonious sound of words.   I love a friendly society and a virile and constant familiarity: An amitie,
which in the earnestnesse and vigor of its commerce,
flattereth it selfe: as love in bitings and bloody scratch-
ings.   It is not sufficiently generous or vigorous, except it be contentious and quarrelous: If she be civilised and a skilfull artist: if it feare a shocke or free
encounter,[1] and have hir starting holes or forced by-
wayes.   *Neque enim disputari sine reprehensione potest.*
Disputation cannot be held without reprehension.

When I am impugned or contraried, then is mine
attention and not mine anger, stirred up: I advance
my selfe toward him, that doth gainesay and instruct
me.   *The cause of truth, ought to be the common cause,*
both to one and other: What can he answer?   The passion of choller hath already wounded his judgement;
trouble, before reason hath seized upon it.   It were
both profitable and necessary, that the determining of
our disputations, might be decided by way of wagers;
and that there were a materiall marke of our losses:
that we might better remember and make more ac-

regency, teaching, rule.
Neque enim, etc., Cicero, *De Fin.* 1, 8.

[1] *If she be civilised,* etc.   "If it is tame and artificial, if it fears conflict and
is constrained in its ways." — G. B. Ives's translation.

compt of it: and that my boy might say unto me: Sir, if you call to minde; your contestation, your ignorance and your selfe-wilfulnesse, at severall times, cost you a hundred crownes the last yeare.

I feast, I cherish and I embrace truth, where and in whom soever I finde it, and willingly and merily yeeld my selfe unto her, as soone as I see but her approach, though it be a farre-off, I lay downe my weapon and yeeld myselfe vanquished.   And always provided, one persist not or proceede therein, with an over im-perious stiffnesse or commanding surlinesse; I am well pleased to be reproved.   And I often accomodate my selfe unto my accusers more by reason of civility, then by reason of amendment: loving by the facility of yeelding, to gratifie and foster their libertie, to teach or advertise me.   It is notwithstanding no easie mat-ter to draw men of my times unto it.   They have not the courage to correct, because they want the heart to endure correction: And ever speake with dissimulation in presence one of another.   I take so great a pleasure to be judged and knowne, that it is indifferent to me, in whether of the two formes I be so.   Mine owne imagination doth so often contradict and condemne it selfe, that if another do it, all is one unto me; espe-cially seeing, I give his reprehension no other author-ity then I list.   But I shall breake a straw or fall at ods with him, that keepes himselfe so aloft; as I know some, that will fret and chafe if their opinions be not believed, and who take it as an injury, yea and fall out with their best friends, if they will not follow it.   That *Socrates* ever smiling, made a collection of such con-tradictions as were opposed to his discourse, one might say, his force was cause of it, and that the advantage being assuredly to fall on his side, he tooke them as a

advertise, warn.   *whether,* which.

subject of a new victory; neverthelesse we see on the contrary, that nothing doth so nicely yeeld our sense unto it as the opinion of preheminence and disdaine of the adversary. And that by reason, it rather befits the weakest to accept of opposition in good part, which restore and repaire him. Verily I seeke more the conversation of such as curbe me, then of those that feare me. It is an unsavory and hurtful pleasure, to have to doe with men, who admire and give us place. *Antisthenes* commanded his children, never to be beholding unto, or thanke any that should commend them. I feele my selfe more lusty and cranke for the victory I gaine over my selfe, when in the heate or fury of the debate, I perceive to bend and fall under the power of my adversaries reason, then I am pleased with the victory, I obtaine of him by his weaknesse. To conclude, I receive all blowes and allow all attaints given directly, how weake soever: but am very impatient at such as are strucken at random and without order. I care little for the matter, and with me opinions are all one, and the victory of the subject in a manner indifferent. I shall quietly contest a whole day, if the conduct of the controversie be followed with order and decorum. It is not force nor subtilty, that I so much require, as forme and order. The forme and order dayly seene in the altercations of Shepheards, or contentions of shop-prentise boyes: but never amongst us; If they part or give one another over, it is with incivilitie: and so doe we. But their wrangling, their brawling and impatience, cannot make them to forgoe or forget their theame. Their discourse holds on his course. If they prevent one another, if they stay not for, at least they understand one another. A man

---

Antisthenes, in Plutarch, *Of False Shame.*
attaints, injuries.

cranke, brisk.
prevent, anticipate, interrupt.

doth ever answere sufficiently well for me, if he answere what I say. But when the disputation is confounded and orderlesse, I quit the matter, and betake me to the forme, with spight and indiscreation: and embrace a kinde of debating, teasty, headlong, malicious and imperious, whereat I afterward blush.

It is impossible to treate quietly and dispute orderly with a foole. My judgement is not onely corrupted under the hand of so imperious a maister, but my conscience also. Our disputations ought to be forbidden and punished, as other verball crimes. What vice raise they not, and heape up together, being ever swayed and commanded by choller? First we enter into enmity with the reasons, and then with the men. We learne not to dispute, except it be to contradict: and every man contradicting and being contradicted, it commonly followeth, that the fruit of disputing, is to loose and disanull the trueth. So *Plato,* in his commonwealth, forbiddeth foolish, unapt, and base minded spirits, to undertake that exercise. . . .

John Florio, translation of *The Essayes of Michael, Lord of Montaigne,* Book III, Chapter VIII.

THE SLEEP-WALKER

1606

Dunsinane. Ante-room in the castle.

Enter a Doctor of Physic and a Waiting-Gentlewoman.

Doct. I have two nights watched with you, but can perceive no truth in your report. When was it she last walked?

Gent. Since his majesty went into the field, I have seen her rise from her bed, throw her nightgown upon

teasty, testy, irritable.   *nightgown,* dressing-gown.

her, unlock her closet, take forth paper, write upon 't, read it, afterwards seal it, and again return to bed; yet all this while in a most fast sleep.

Doct. A great perturbation in nature, to receive at once the benefit of sleep and the effects of watching! In this slumbery agitation, besides her walking and other actual performances, what, at any time, have you heard her say?

Gent. That, sir, which I will not report after her.

Doct. You may to me, and 'tis most meet you should.

Gent. Neither to you nor any one, having no witness to confirm my speeches.

Enter Lady Macbeth, with a taper.

Lo you, here she comes! This is her very guise, and, upon my life, fast asleep. Observe her; stand close.

Doct. How came she by that light?

Gent. Why, it stood by her; she has light by her continually; 'tis her command.

Doct. You see, her eyes are open.

Gent. Ay, but their sense is shut.

Doct. What is it she does now? Look, how she rubs her hands.

Gent. It is an accustomed action with her, to seem thus washing her hands: I have known her to continue in this a quarter of an hour.

Lady M. Yet here's a spot.

Doct. Hark! she speaks: I will set down what comes from her, to satisfy my remembrance the more strongly.

Lady M. Out, damned spot! out, I say! One: two: why, then 'tis time to do 't. Hell is murky. Fie, my lord, fie! a soldier, and afeard? What need we fear who knows it, when none can call our power to account? Yet who would have thought the old man to have had so much blood in him?

Doct. Do you mark that?

Lady M. The thane of Fife had a wife; where is she now? What, will these hands ne'er be clean? No more o' that, my lord, no more o' that: you mar all with this starting.

Doct. Go to, go to; you have known what you should not.

Gent. She has spoke what she should not, I am sure of that: heaven knows what she has known.

Lady M. Here's the smell of blood still: all the perfumes of Arabia will not sweeten this little hand. Oh, oh, oh!

Doct. What a sigh is there! The heart is sorely charged.

Gent. I would not have such a heart in my bosom for the dignity of the whole body.

Doct. Well, well, well, ——

Gent. Pray God it be, sir.

Doct. This disease is beyond my practice: yet I have known those which have walked in their sleep who have died holily in their beds.

Lady M. Wash your hands; put on your nightgown; look not so pale: I tell you yet again, Banquo's buried; he cannot come out on's grave.

Doct. Even so?

Lady M. To bed, to bed; there's knocking at the gate: come, come, come, come, give me your hand: what's done cannot be undone: to bed, to bed, to bed.

(Exit.

Doct. Will she go now to bed?

Gent. Directly.

Doct. Foul whisperings are abroad: unnatural deeds

Do breed unnatural troubles: infected minds
To their deaf pillows will discharge their secrets:
More needs she the divine than the physician.
God, God forgive us all! Look after her;
Remove from her the means of all annoyance,
And still keep eyes upon her. So good night:
My mind she has mated and amazed my sight:
I think, but dare not speak.

    Gent. Good night, good doctor.   (*Exeunt.*

    William Shakespeare, Macbeth, Act V, Scene 1

OF PAINTING THE FACE

1614

If that which is most ancient be best, then the face
that one is borne with, is better than it that is borrowed: Nature is more ancient than Art, and Art is
allowed to help Nature, but not to hurt it; to mend it,
but not to mar it; for perfection, but not for perdition:
but this artificiall facing doth corrupt the naturall colour of it. Indeed God hath given a man oil for his
countenance, as He hath done wine for his heart, to
refresh and cheere it; but this is by reflection and not
by plaister-work; by comforting, and not by dawbing
and covering; by mending and helping the naturall
colour, and not by marring or hiding it with an artificiall lit. What a miserable vanity is it a man or
woman beholding in a glasse their borrowed face,
their bought complexion, to please themselves with a
face that is not their owne? And what is the cause
they paint? Without doubt nothing but pride of
heart, disdaining to bee behind their neighbour, dis-
contentment with the worke of God, and vaine glory,
or a foolish affectation of the praise of men. This
kind of people are very hypocrites, seeming one thing

mated, bewildered.   *lit,* dye, stain.

and being another, desiring to bee that in show which
they cannot be in substance, and coveting to be judged
that, they are not: They are very grosse Deceivers;
for they study to delude men with shewes, seeking
hereby to bee counted more lovely creatures than they
are, affecting that men should account that naturall,
which is but artificiall. I may truly say they are deceivers of themselves; for if they thinke they doe well
to paint, they are deceived; if they think it honest and
just to beguile men, and to make them account them
more delicate and amiable, then they are in truth, they
are deceived; if they thinke it meete that that should
bee counted God's worke, which is their owne, they
are deceived: If they thinke that [they] shall not one day
give account unto Christ of idle deeds, such as this, as
well as of idle words, they are deceived; if they thinke
that God regards not such trifles, but leaves them to
their free election herein; they are deceived. Now
they that deceive themselves, who shall they be trusted
with? A man, that is taken of himselfe, is in a worse
taking than he that is caught of another. This self-
deceiver, is a double sinner: he sinnes in that he is deceived, hee sinnes again in that he doth deceive himself. To bee murdered of another is not a sin in him
that is murdered; but for a man to be deceived in what
he is forbidden, is a sinne; it were better to bee murdered, than so to be deceived: For there the body is
but killed, but here the soule herself is endangered.
Now, how unhappy is the danger, how grievous is the
sin, when a man is merely of himself endangered? It
is a misery of miseries for a man to bee slaine with his
owne sword, with his owne hand, and long of his owne
will: Besides, this painting is very scandalous and of
ill report; for any man therefore to use it, is to thwart
the precept of the Holy Ghost in Saint Paul, who saith

unto the Phillippians in this wise, Whatsoever things are true (but a painted face is a false face) whatsoever things are venerable (but who esteems a painted face venerable?) whatsoever things are just (but will any man of judgement say, that to paint the face is a point of justice? Who dare say it is according to the will of God which is the rule of justice?

Doth the law of God command it? Doth true reason teach it? Doth lawes of men enjoyne it?) whatsoever things are (chaste and) pure: (but is painting of the face a point of chastity? Is that pure which proceeds out of the impurity of the soule, and which is of deceipt, and tends unto deceipt? Is that chaste, which is used to wooe mens eyes unto it?) *whatsoever things are lovely* (but will any man out of a well informed judgment say, that this kinde of painting is worthy of love, or that a painted face is worthy to be fancied?) *whatsoever things are of good report: If there bee any vertue, if there bee any praise, think on these things*. But I hope to paint the face, to weare an artificiall colour, or complexion, is no vertue; neither is it of good report amongst the vertuous. I read that Iezabel did practise it, but I find not that any holy Matrone or religious Vergine ever used it: And it may perhaps of some be praised, but doubtlesse not of such as are judicious, but of them rather hated and discommended. A painted face is the devils *Lookingglasse:* there hee stands peering and toying (as an Ape in a looking-glasse) joying to behold himselfe therein; for in it he may reade pride, vanity, and vaine-glory. Painting is an enemy to blushing, which is vertues colour. And indeed how unworthy are they to bee credited in things of moment, that are so false in their haire, or colour, over which age, and sicknesse, and

Philippians, IV, 8.   *Jezabel*, 2 Kings IX, 30.

many accidents doe tyrannize; yea, and where their deceipt is easily discerned? And whereas the passions and conditions of a man, and his age, is something discovered by the face, this painting hindereth a mans judgement herein, so that if they were as well able to colour the eyes, as they are their haire and faces, a man could discerne little or nothing in such kind of people. In briefe, these painters are sometimes injurious to those, that are naturally faire and lovely, and no painters; partly, in that these are thought sometimes to bee painted, because of the common use of painting; and partly, in that these artificiall creatures steal away the praise from the naturall beauty by reason of their Art, when it is not espyed, whereas were it not for their cunning, they would not bee deemed equall to the other. It is a great pity that this outlandish vanity is in so much request and practise with us, as it is.

   T.T., New Essayes, Meditations, and Vowes, including in them the Chiefe Duties of a Christian, both for Faith and Manners. 1614.

SEVENTEENTH CENTURY

THE STORY OF JOSEPH

1604-11

Now the sons of Jacob were twelve:

The sons of Leah; Reuben, Jacob's firstborn, and Simeon, and Levi, and Judah; and Issachar, and Zebulum:

The sons of Rachel; Joseph, and Benjamin:

And the sons of Bilhah, Rachel's handmaid; Dan, and Naphtali:

And the sons of Zilpah, Leah's handmaid; Gad, and Asher: these are the sons of Jacob, which were born to him in Padan-aram.

i

Joseph, being seventeen years old, was feeding the flock with his brethren; and the lad was with the sons of Bilhah, and with the sons of Zilpah, his father's wives: and Joseph brought unto his father their evil report.

Now Israel loved Joseph more than all his children, because he was the son of his old age: and he made him a coat of many colours. And when his brethren saw that their father loved him more than all his brethren, they hated him, and could not speak peaceably unto him.

And Joseph dreamed a dream, and he told it his brethren: and they hated him yet the more. And he said unto them, Hear, I pray you, this dream which I have dreamed: for, behold we were binding sheaves

Padan-aram, Mesopotamia.

brought . . . evil report, i.e., told tales of them.   *Israel*, Jacob.

in the field, and, lo, my sheaf arose, and also stood upright; and, behold, your sheaves stood round about, and made obeisance to my sheaf. And his brethren said unto him, Shalt thou indeed reign over us? or shalt thou indeed have dominion over us? And they hated him yet the more for his dreams, and for his words.

And he dreamed yet another dream, and told it his brethren, and said, Behold I have dreamed a dream more; and behold, the sun and the moon and the eleven stars made obeisance to me. And he told it to his father, and to his brethren: and his father rebuked him, and said unto him, What is this dream that thou hast dreamed? Shall I and thy mother and thy brethren indeed come to bow down ourselves to thee to the earth? And his brethren envied him; but his father observed the saying.

And his brethren went to feed their father's flock in Shechem. And Israel said unto Joseph, Do not thy brethren feed the flock in Shechem? come, and I will send thee unto them. And he said to him, Here am I. And he said to him, Go, I pray thee, see whether it be well with thy brethren, and well with the flocks; and bring me word again. So he sent him out of the vale of Hebron, and he came to Shechem.

And a certain man found him, and, behold, he was wandering in the field: and the man asked him, saying, What seekest thou? And he said, I seek my brethren: tell me, I pray thee, where they feed their flocks. And the man said, They are departed hence; for I heard them say, Let us go to Dothan. And Joseph went after his brethren, and found them in Dothan. And

Shechem, a city and locality in Samaria, in central Palestine. Jacob owned pasture-lands there.
Hebron, or Mamre, in Judæa, southern Palestine.
Dothan, a town near Shechem.

when they saw him afar off, even before he came near unto them, they conspired against him to slay him. And they said one to another, Behold, this dreamer cometh. Come now therefore, and let us slay him, and cast him into some pit, and we will say, Some evil beast hath devoured him: and we shall see what will become of his dreams. And Reuben heard it, and he delivered him out of their hands; and said, Let us not kill him. And Reuben said unto them, Shed no blood, but cast him into this pit that is in the wilderness, and lay no hand upon him; that he might rid him out of their hands to deliver him to his father again.

And it came to pass, when Joseph was come unto his brethren, that they stript Joseph out of his coat, his coat of many colours that was on him; and they took him, and cast him into a pit: and the pit was empty, there was no water in it. And they sat down to eat bread: and they lifted up their eyes and looked, and, behold, a company of Ishmeelites came from Gilead with their camels bearing spicery and balm and myrrh, going to carry it down to Egypt. And Judah said unto his brethren, What profit is it if we slay our brother, and conceal his blood? Come, let us sell him to the Ishmeelites, and let not our hand be upon him; for he is our brother and our flesh. And his brethren were content. Then there passed by Midianites merchantmen; and they drew and lifted up Joseph out of the pit, and sold Joseph to the Ishmeelites for twenty pieces of silver: and they brought Joseph into Egypt.

And Reuben returned unto the pit; and, behold, Joseph was not in the pit; and he rent his clothes. And he returned unto his brethren, and said, The

pit, a well, or cistern.   *Ishmeelites*, Arabians from near Mecca.
Gilead, a district in eastern Palestine, north of the Dead Sea.
Midianites, Arabians.

child is not; and I, whither shall I go? And they took Joseph's coat, and killed a kid of the goats, and dipped the coat in the blood; and they sent the coat of many colours, and they brought it to their father; and said, This have we found: know now whether it be thy son's coat or no. And he knew it, and said, It is my son's coat; an evil beast hath devoured him; Joseph is without doubt rent in pieces. And Jacob rent his clothes, and put sackcloth upon his loins, and mourned for his son many days. And all his sons and all his daughters rose up to comfort him; but he refused to be comforted; and he said, For I will go down into the grave unto my son mourning. Thus his father wept for him. And the Midianites sold him into Egypt unto Potiphar, an officer of Pharaoh's, and captain of the guard.

ii

And Joseph was brought down to Egypt; and Potiphar, an officer of Pharaoh, captain of the guard, an Egyptian, bought him out of the hands of the Ishmeelites, which had brought him down thither. And the Lord was with Joseph, and he was a prosperous man; and he was in the house of his master the Egyptian. And his master saw that the Lord was with him, and that the Lord made all that he did to prosper in his hand. And Joseph found grace in his sight, and he served him: and he made him overseer over his house, and all that he had he put into his hand. And it came to pass from the time that he had made him overseer in his house, and over all that he had, that the Lord blessed the Egyptian's house for Joseph's sake; and the blessing of the Lord was upon all that he

Pharaoh, a title of kingship. Joseph's Pharaoh appears to have been the last of the Hyksos or Shepherd Kings, Apophis II (or Aa-Keneri-Ra), whose reign ended about 1600 B.C.

had in the house, and in the field. And he left all that he had in Joseph's hand; and he knew not ought he had, save the bread which he did eat. And Joseph was a goodly person, and well favoured.

And it came to pass after these things, that his master's wife cast her eyes upon Joseph; and she said, Lie with me. But he refused, and said unto his master's wife, Behold, my master wotteth not what is with me in the house, and he hath committed all that he hath to my hand; there is none greater in his house than I; neither hath he kept back any thing from me but thee, because thou art his wife: how then can I do this great wickedness, and sin against God? And it came to pass, as she spake to Joseph day by day, that he hearkened not unto her, to lie by her, or to be with her. And it came to pass about this time, that Joseph went into the house to do his business; and there was none of the men of the house there within. And she caught him by his garment, saying, Lie with me: and he left his garment in her hand, and fled, and got him out. And it came to pass, when she saw that he had left his garment in her hand, and was fled forth, that she called unto the men of her house, and spake unto them, saying, See, he hath brought in an Hebrew unto us to mock us; he came in unto me to lie with me, and I cried with a loud voice: and it came to pass, when he heard that I lifted up my voice and cried, that he left his garment with me, and fled, and got him out. And she laid up his garment by her, until his lord came home. And she spake unto him, according to these words, saying, The Hebrew servant, which thou hast brought unto us, came in unto me to mock me: and it came to pass, as I lifted up my voice and cried, that he left his garment with me, and fled out. And it came to pass, when his master heard the words of his wife, which she spake unto him, saying, After this manner did thy servant to me; that his wrath was kindled. And Joseph's master took him, and put him into the prison, a place where the king's prisoners were bound: and he was there in prison.

But the Lord was with Joseph, and shewed him mercy, and gave him favour in the sight of the keeper of the prison. And the keeper of the prison committed to Joseph's hand all the prisoners that were in the prison; and whatsoever they did there, he was the doer of it. The keeper of the prison looked not to anything that was under his hand; because the Lord was with him, and that which he did, the Lord made it to prosper.

iii

And it came to pass after these things, that the butler of the king of Egypt and his baker had offended their lord the king of Egypt. And Pharaoh was wroth against two of his officers, against the chief of the butlers, and against the chief of the bakers. And he put them in ward in the house of the captain of the guard, into the prison, the place where Joseph was bound. And the captain of the guard charged Joseph with them, and he served them: and they continued a season in ward.

And they dreamed a dream both of them, each man his dream in one night, each man according to the interpretation of his dream, the butler and the baker of the king of Egypt, which were bound in the prison. And Joseph came in unto them in the morning, and looked upon them, and, behold, they were sad. And he asked Pharaoh's officers that were with him in the ward of his lord's house, saying, Wherefore look ye so sadly to day? And they said unto him, We have dreamed a dream, and there is no interpreter of it. And Joseph said unto them, Do not interpretations belong to God? tell me them, I pray you. And the chief butler told his dream to Joseph, and said to him, In my dream, behold, a vine was before me; and in the vine were three branches: and it was as though it budded, and her blossoms shot forth; and the clusters thereof brought forth ripe grapes: And Pharaoh's cup was in my hand: and I took the grapes, and pressed them into Pharaoh's cup, and I gave the cup into Pharaoh's hand. And Joseph said unto him, This is the interpretation of it: The three branches are three days: yet within three days shall Pharaoh lift up thine head, and restore thee unto thy place: and thou shalt deliver Pharaoh's cup into his hand, after the manner when thou wast his butler. But think on me when it shall be well with thee, and shew kindness, I pray thee, unto me, and make mention of me unto Pharaoh, and bring me out of this house: for indeed I was stolen away out of the land of the Hebrews: and here also have I done nothing that they should put me into the dungeon. When the chief baker saw that the interpretation was good, he said unto Joseph, I also was in my dream, and, behold, I had three white baskets on my head: and in the uppermost basket there was all manner of bakemeats for Pharaoh; and the birds did eat them out of the basket upon my head. And Joseph answered and said, This is the interpretation thereof: The three baskets are three days: yet within three days shall Pharaoh lift up thy head from off thee, and shall hang thee on a tree; and the birds shall eat thy flesh from off thee.

And it came to pass the third day, which was Pharaoh's birthday, that he made a feast unto all his servants: and he lifted up the head of the chief butler

and of the chief baker among his servants. And he
restored the chief butler unto his butlership again; and
he gave the cup into Pharaoh's hand: but he hanged
the chief baker: as Joseph had interpreted to them.
Yet did not the chief butler remember Joseph, but
forgat him.

iv

And it came to pass at the end of two full years, that
Pharaoh dreamed: and, behold, he stood by the river.
And, behold, there came up out of the river seven well
favoured kine and fatfleshed; and they fed in a
meadow. And, behold, seven other kine came up
after them out of the river, ill favoured and leanfleshed; and stood by the other kine upon the brink of
the river. And the ill favoured and leanfleshed kine
did eat up the seven well favoured and fat kine. So
Pharaoh awoke. And he slept and dreamed the second time: and, behold, seven ears of corn came up upon
one stalk, rank and good. And, behold, seven thin
ears and blasted with the east wind sprung up after
them. And the seven thin ears devoured the seven
rank and full ears. And Pharaoh awoke, and, behold,
it was a dream. And it came to pass in the morning
that his spirit was troubled; and he sent and called for
all the magicians of Egypt, and all the wise men
thereof; but there was none that could interpret them
unto Pharaoh.

Then spake the chief butler unto Pharaoh, saying,
I do remember my faults this day: Pharaoh was wroth
with his servants, and put me in ward in the captain
of the guard's house, both me and the chief baker:
and we dreamed a dream in one night, I and he; we
dreamed each man, according to the interpretation of

corn, any grain, such as wheat.

his dream. And there was there with us a young man, an Hebrew, servant to the captain of the guard; and we told him, and he interpreted to us our dreams; to each man according to his dream did he interpret. And it came to pass, as he interpreted to us, so it was; me he restored unto mine office, and him he hanged.

Then Pharaoh sent and called Joseph, and they brought him hastily out of the dungeon: and he shaved himself, and changed his raiment, and came in unto Pharaoh. And Pharaoh said unto Joseph, I have dreamed a dream, and there is none that can interpret it: and I have heard say of thee, that thou canst understand a dream to interpret it. And Joseph answered Pharaoh, saying, It is not in me: God shall give Pharaoh an answer of peace. And Pharaoh said unto Joseph, In my dream, behold, I stood upon the bank of the river: and, behold, there came up out of the river seven kine, fatfleshed and well favoured; and they fed in a meadow: and, behold, seven other kine came up after them, poor and very ill favoured and leanfleshed, such as I never saw in all the land of Egypt for badness: and the lean and the ill favoured kine did eat up the first seven fat kine: and when they had eaten them up, it could not be known that they had eaten them; but they were still ill favoured, as at the beginning. So I awoke. And I saw in my dream, and, behold, seven ears came up in one stalk, full and good: and, behold, seven ears, withered, thin, and blasted with the east wind, sprung up after them: and the thin ears devoured the seven good ears: and I told this unto the magicians; but there was none that could declare it to me.

And Joseph said unto Pharaoh, The dream of Pharaoh is one: God hath shewed Pharaoh what he is about to do. The seven good kine are seven years;

and the seven good ears are seven years: the dream is one. And the seven thin and ill favoured kine that came up after them are seven years; and the seven empty ears blasted with the east wind shall be seven years of famine. This is the thing which I have spoken unto Pharaoh: What God is about to do he sheweth unto Pharaoh. Behold, there come seven years of great plenty throughout the land of Egypt: and there shall arise after them seven years of famine; and all the plenty shall be forgotten in the land of Egypt; and the famine shall consume the land; and the plenty shall not be known in the land by reason of that famine following; for it shall be very grievous. And for that the dream was doubled unto Pharaoh twice; it is because the thing is established by God, and God will shortly bring it to pass. Now therefore let Pharaoh look out a man discreet and wise, and set him over the land of Egypt. Let Pharaoh do this, and let him appoint officers over the land, and take up the fifth part of the land of Egypt in the seven plenteous years. And let him gather all the food of those good years that come, and lay up corn under the hand of Pharaoh, and let them keep food in the cities. And that food shall be for store to the land against the seven years of famine, which shall be in the land of Egypt; that the land perish not through the famine.

And the thing was good in the eyes of Pharaoh, and in the eyes of all his servants. And Pharaoh said unto his servants, Can we find such a one as this is, a man in whom the spirit of God is? And Pharaoh said unto Joseph, Forasmuch as God hath shewed thee all this, there is none so discreet and wise as thou art: thou shalt be over my house, and according unto thy word shall all my people be ruled: only in the throne will I be greater than thou. And Pharaoh said unto Joseph,

See, I have set thee over all the land of Egypt. And
Pharaoh took off his ring from his hand, and put it
upon Joseph's hand, and arrayed him in vestures of
fine linen, and put a gold chain about his neck; and he
made him to ride in the second chariot which he had;
and they cried before him, Bow the knee: and he made
him ruler over all the land of Egypt. And Pharaoh
said unto Joseph, I am Pharaoh, and without thee
shall no man lift up his hand or foot in all the land of
Egypt. And Pharaoh called Joseph's name Zaphnath-
paaneah; and he gave him to wife Asenath the daughter of Poti-pherah priest of On. And Joseph went out
over all the land of Egypt.

And Joseph was thirty years old when he stood before Pharaoh king of Egypt. And Joseph went out
from the presence of Pharaoh, and went throughout
all the land of Egypt. And in the seven plenteous
years the earth brought forth by handfuls. And he
gathered up all the food of the seven years, which were
in the land of Egypt, and laid up the food in the cities:
the food of the field, which was round about every
city, laid he up in the same. And Joseph gathered
corn as the sand of the sea, very much, until he left
numbering; for it was without number. And unto
Joseph were born two sons before the years of famine
came, which Asenath the daughter of Poti-pherah
priest of On bare unto him. And Joseph called the
name of the firstborn Manasseh: For God, said he,
hath made me forget all my toil, and all my father's
house. And the name of the second called he Ephraim: For God hath caused me to be fruitful in the
land of my affliction.

And the seven years of plenteousness, that was in

Zaphnath-paaneah, revealer of secrets, or, more probably, nourisher of
Pharaoh.
Manasseh, forgetting. Ephraim, fruitful.

the land of Egypt, were ended. And the seven years of dearth began to come, according as Joseph had said: and the dearth was in all lands; but in all the land of Egypt there was bread. And when all the land of Egypt was famished, the people cried to Pharaoh for bread: and Pharaoh said unto all the Egyptians, Go unto Joseph; what he saith to you, do. And the famine was over all the face of the earth: and Joseph opened all the storehouses, and sold unto the Egyptians; and the famine waxed sore in the land of Egypt. And all countries came into Egypt to Joseph for to buy corn; because that the famine was so sore in all lands.

V

Now when Jacob saw that there was corn in Egypt, Jacob said unto his sons, Why do ye look one upon another? And he said, Behold, I have heard that there is corn in Egypt; get you down thither, and buy for us from thence; that we may live, and not die.

And Joseph's ten brethren went down to buy corn in Egypt. But Benjamin, Joseph's brother, Jacob sent not with his brethren; for he said, Lest peradventure mischief befall him. And the sons of Israel came to buy corn among those that came: for the famine was in the land of Canaan. And Joseph was governor over the land, and he it was that sold to all the people of the land: and Joseph's brethren came, and bowed themselves before him with their faces to the earth. And Joseph saw his brethren, and he knew them, but made himself strange unto them, and spake roughly unto them; and he said unto them, Whence come ye? And they said, From the land of Canaan to buy food. And Joseph knew his brethren, but they

Canaan, Palestine.

knew not him. And Joseph remembered the dreams which he dreamed of them, and said unto them, Ye are spies; to see the nakedness of the land ye are come. And they said unto him, Nay, my lord, but to buy food are thy servants come. We are all one man's sons; we are true men, thy servants are no spies. And he said unto them, Nay, but to see the nakedness of the land ye are come. And they said, Thy servants are twelve brethren, the sons of one man in the land of Canaan; and, behold, the youngest is this day with our father, and one is not. And Joseph said unto them, That is it that I spake unto you, saying, Ye are spies; hereby ye shall be proved: by the life of Pharaoh ye shall not go forth hence, except your youngest brother come hither. Send one of you, and let him fetch your brother, and ye shall be kept in prison, that your words may be proved, whether there be any truth in you: or else by the life of Pharaoh ye are spies. And he put them all together into ward three days. And Joseph said unto them, the third day, This do, and live; for I fear God: if ye be true men, let one of your brethren be bound in the house of your prison: go ye, carry corn for the famine of your houses: but bring your youngest brother unto me; so shall your words be verified, and ye shall not die. And they did so.

And they said one to another, We are verily guilty concerning our brother, in that we saw the anguish of his soul, when he besought us, and we would not hear; therefore is this distress come upon us. And Reuben answered them, saying, Spake I not unto you, saying, Do not sin against the child; and ye would not hear? therefore, behold, also his blood is required. And they knew not that Joseph understood them; for he spake unto them by an interpreter. And he turned himself about from them, and wept; and returned to them again, and communed with them, and took from them Simeon, and bound him before their eyes.

Then Joseph commanded to fill their sacks with corn, and to restore every man's money into his sack, and to give them provision for the way: and thus he did unto them. And they laded their asses with the corn, and departed thence. And as one of them opened his sack to give his ass provender in the inn, he espied his money; for, behold, it was in his sack's mouth. And he said unto his brethren, My money is restored; and, lo, it is even in my sack: and their heart failed them, and they were afraid, saying one to another, What is this that God hath done unto us?

And they came unto Jacob their father unto the land of Canaan, and told him all that befell unto them, saying, The man, who is the lord of the land, spake roughly to us, and took us for spies of the country. And we said unto him, We are true men; we are no spies: we be twelve brethren, sons of our father; one is not, and the youngest is this day with our father in the land of Canaan. And the man, the lord of the country, said unto us, Hereby shall I know that ye are true men; leave one of your brethren here with me, and take food for the famine of your households, and be gone: and bring your youngest brother unto me: then shall I know that ye are no spies, but that ye are true men: so will I deliver you your brother, and ye shall traffick in the land.

And it came to pass as they emptied their sacks, that, behold, every man's bundle of money was in his sack: and when both they and their father saw the bundles of money, they were afraid. And Jacob their father said unto them, Me have ye bereaved of my children: Joseph is not, and Simeon is not, and ye will take Benjamin away: all these things are against me. And Reuben spake unto his father, saying, Slay my two sons, if I bring him not to thee: deliver him into my hand, and I will bring him to thee again. And he said, My son shall not go down with you; for his brother is dead, and he is left alone: if mischief befall him by the way in the which ye go, then shall ye bring down my gray hairs with sorrow to the grave.

vi

And the famine was sore in the land. And it came to pass, when they had eaten up the corn, which they had brought out of Egypt, their father said unto them, Go again, buy us a little food. And Judah spake unto him, saying, The man did solemnly protest unto us, saying, Ye shall not see my face, except your brother be with you. If thou wilt send our brother with us, we will go down and buy thee food: but if thou wilt not send him, we will not go down: for the man said unto us, Ye shall not see my face, except your brother be with you. And Israel said, Wherefore dealt ye so ill with me, as to tell the man whether ye had yet a brother? And they said, The man asked us straitly of our state, and of our kindred, saying, Is your father yet alive? have ye another brother? and we told him according to the tenor of these words: could we certainly know that he would say, Bring your brother down? And Judah said unto Israel his father, Send the lad with me, and we will arise and go; that we may live, and not die, both we, and thou, and also our little ones. I will be surety for him; of my hand shalt thou require him: if I bring him not unto thee, and set him before thee, then let me bear the blame forever: for except we had lingered, surely now we had returned this second time. And their father Israel said unto them, If it must be so now, do this; take of the best fruits in the land in your vessels, and carry down the man a present, a little balm, and a little honey, spices, and myrrh, nuts, and almonds: and take double money in your hand; and the money that was brought again in the mouth of your sacks, carry it again in your hand; peradventure it was an oversight: take also your brother, and arise, go again unto the man: and God Almighty give you mercy before the man, that he may send away your other brother, and Benjamin. If I be bereaved of my children, I am bereaved.

And the men took that present, and they took double money in their hand, and Benjamin; and rose up, and went down to Egypt, and stood before Joseph. And when Joseph saw Benjamin with them, he said to the ruler of his house, Bring these men home, and slay, and make ready; for these men shall dine with me at noon. And the man did as Joseph bade; and the man brought the men into Joseph's house. And the men were afraid, because they were brought into Joseph's house; and they said, Because of the money that was returned in our sacks at the first time are we brought in; that he may seek occasion against us, and fall upon us, and take us for bondmen, and our asses. And they came near to the steward of Joseph's house, and they communed with him at the door of the house, And said, O sir, we came indeed down at the first time to buy food: and it came to pass, when we came to the inn, that we opened our sacks, and, behold, every man's money was in the mouth of his sack, our money in full weight: and we have brought it again in our hand. And other money have we brought down in our hands to buy food: we cannot tell who put our money in our sacks. And he said,

Peace be to you, fear not: your God, and the God of your father, hath given you treasure in your sacks: I had your money. And he brought Simeon out unto them. And the man brought the men into Joseph's house, and gave them water, and they washed their feet; and he gave their asses provender. And they made ready the present against Joseph came at noon: for they heard that they should eat there.

And when Joseph came home, they brought him the present which was in their hand into the house, and bowed themselves to him to the earth. And he asked of their welfare, and said, Is your father well, the old man of whom ye spake? Is he yet alive? And they answered, Thy servant our father is in good health, he is yet alive. And they bowed down their heads, and made obeisance. And he lifted up his eyes, and saw his brother Benjamin, his mother's son, and said, Is this your younger brother, of whom ye spake unto me? And he said, God be gracious unto thee, my son. And Joseph made haste; for his bowels did yearn upon his brother: and he sought where to weep; and he entered into his chamber, and wept there. And he washed his face, and went out, and refreshed himself, and said Set on bread. And they set on for him by himself, and for them by themselves, and for the Egyptians, which did eat with him, by themselves: because the Egyptians might not eat bread with the Hebrews; for that is an abomination unto the Egyptians. And they sat before him, the firstborn according to his birthright, and the youngest according to his youth: and the men marvelled one at another. And he took and sent messes unto them from before him: but Benjamin's mess was five times so much as any of their's. And they drank, and were merry with him.

vii

And he commanded the steward of his house, saying,
Fill the men's sacks with food, as much as they can
carry, and put every man's money in his sack's mouth.
And put my cup, the silver cup, in the sack's mouth of
the youngest, and his corn money.   And he did according to the word that Joseph had spoken.   As soon
as the morning was light, the men were sent away,
they and their asses.   And when they were gone out
of the city, and not yet far off, Joseph said unto his
steward, Up, follow after the men; and when thou
dost overtake them, say unto them, Wherefore have
ye rewarded evil for good?   Is not this it in which my
lord drinketh, and whereby indeed he divineth? ye
have done evil in so doing.

And he overtook them, and he spake unto them
these same words.   And they said unto him, Wherefore saith my lord these words?   God forbid that thy
servants should do according to this thing: behold,
the money, which we found in our sacks' mouths, we
brought again unto thee out of the land of Canaan:
how then should we steal out of thy lord's house silver
or gold?   With whomsoever of thy servants it be
found, both let him die, and we also will be my lord's
bondmen.   And he said, Now also let it be according
unto your words: he with whom it is found shall be
my servant; and ye shall be blameless.   Then they
speedily took down every man his sack to the ground,
and opened every man his sack.   And he searched,
and began at the eldest, and left at the youngest: and
the cup was found in Benjamin's sack.   Then they
rent their clothes, and laded every man his ass, and
returned to the city.

And Judah and his brethren came to Joseph's
house; for he was yet there: and they fell before him

on the ground. And Joseph said unto them, What deed is this that ye have done? wot ye not that such a man as I can certainly divine? And Judah said, What shall we say unto my lord? what shall we speak? or how shall we clear ourselves? God hath found out the iniquity of thy servants: behold, we are my lord's servants, both we, and he also with whom the cup is found. And he said, God forbid that I should do so: but the man in whose hand the cup is found, he shall be my servant; and as for you, get you up in peace unto your father.

Then Judah came near unto him, and said, Oh my lord, let thy servant, I pray thee, speak a word in my lord's ears, and let not thine anger burn against thy servant: for thou art even as Pharaoh. My lord asked his servants, saying, Have ye a father, or a brother? And we said unto my lord, We have a father, an old man, and a child of his old age, a little one; and his brother is dead, and he alone is left of his mother, and his father loveth him. And thou saidst unto thy servants, Bring him down unto me, that I may set mine eyes upon him. And we said unto my lord, The lad cannot leave his father: for if he should leave his father, his father would die. And thou saidst unto thy servants, Except your youngest brother come down with you, ye shall see my face no more. And it came to pass when we came up unto thy servant my father, we told him the words of my lord. And our father said, Go again, and buy us a little food. And we said, We cannot go down: if our youngest brother be with us, then will we go down: for we may not see the man's face, except our youngest brother be with us. And thy servant my father said unto us, Ye know that my wife bare me two sons: and the one went out from me, and I said, Surely he is torn in pieces; and I saw him not since: and if ye take this also from me, and mischief befall him, ye shall bring down my gray hairs with sorrow to the grave. Now therefore when I come to thy servant my father, and the lad be not with us; seeing that his life is bound up in the lad's life; it shall come to pass, when he seeth that the lad is not with us, that he will die: and thy servants shall bring down the gray hairs of thy servant our father with sorrow to the grave. For thy servant became surety for the lad unto my father, saying, If I bring him not unto thee, then I shall bear the blame to my father for ever. Now therefore, I pray thee, let thy servant abide instead of the lad a bondman to my lord; and let the lad go up with his brethren. For how shall I go up to my father, and the lad be not with me? lest peradventure I see the evil that shall come on my father.

viii

Then Joseph could not refrain himself before all them that stood by him; and he cried, Cause every man to go out from me. And there stood no man with him, while Joseph made himself known unto his brethren. And he wept aloud: and the Egyptians and the house of Pharaoh heard. And Joseph said unto his brethren, I am Joseph; doth my father yet live? And his brethren could not answer him; for they were troubled at his presence. And Joseph said unto his brethren, Come near to me, I pray you. And they came near. And he said, I am Joseph your brother, whom ye sold into Egypt. Now therefore be not grieved, nor angry with yourselves, that ye sold me hither: for God did send me before you to preserve life. For these two years hath the famine been in the land: and yet there are five years, in the which there shall be neither earing nor harvest. And God sent me before you to preserve you a posterity in the earth, and to save your lives by a great deliverance. So now it was not you that sent me hither, but God: and he hath made me a father to Pharaoh, and lord of all his house, and a ruler throughout all the land of Egypt. Haste ye, and go up to my father, and say unto him, Thus saith thy son Joseph, God hath made me lord of all Egypt: come down to me, tarry not. And thou shalt dwell in the land of Goshen, and thou shalt be near unto me, thou, and thy children, and thy children's children, and thy flocks, and thy herds, and all that thou hast: and there will I nourish thee; for yet there are five years of famine: lest thou, and thy household, and all thou hast, come to poverty. And behold, your eyes see, and the eyes of my brother Benjamin, that it is my mouth that speaketh unto you. And ye shall tell my father of all my glory in Egypt, and of all that ye have seen; and ye shall haste and bring down my father hither. And he fell upon his brother Benjamin's neck and wept; and Benjamin wept upon his neck. Moreover he kissed all his brethren, and wept upon them: and after that his brethren talked with him.

And the fame thereof was heard in Pharaoh's house, saying, Joseph's brethren are come: and it pleased Pharaoh well, and his servants. And Pharaoh said unto Joseph, Say unto thy brethren, This do ye; lade your beasts, and go, get you unto the land of Canaan; and take your father and your households, and come unto me: and I will give you the good of the land of Egypt, and ye shall eat the fat of the land. Now thou art commanded, this do ye; take you wagons out

earing, plowing.
Goshen, a district in northern Egypt, in the Nile delta.

of the land of Egypt for your little ones, and for your wives, and bring your father, and come. Also regard not your stuff; for the good of all the land of Egypt is yours. And the children of Israel did so: and Joseph gave them wagons, according to the commandment of Pharaoh, and gave them provision for the way. To all of them he gave each man changes of raiment; but to Benjamin he gave three hundred pieces of silver, and five changes of raiment. And to his father he sent after this manner; ten asses laden with the good things of Egypt, and ten she asses laden with corn and bread and meat for his father by the way. So he sent his brethren away, and they departed: and he said unto them, See that ye fall not out by the way.

And they went up out of Egypt, and came into the land of Canaan, unto Jacob their father, and told him, saying, Joseph is yet alive, and he is governing over all the land of Egypt. And Jacob's heart fainted, for he believed them not. And they told him all the words of Joseph, which he had said unto them: and when he saw the wagons which Joseph had sent to carry him, the spirit of Jacob their father revived: and Israel said, It is enough; Joseph my son is yet alive: I will go and see him before I die.

ix

And Israel took his journey with all that he had, and came to Beer-sheba, and offered sacrifices unto the God of his father Isaac. And God spake unto Israel in the visions of the night, and said, Jacob, Jacob. And he said, Here am I. And he said, I am God, the God of thy father: fear not to go down into Egypt; for I will there make of thee a great nation: I will go down with thee into Egypt; and I will also surely bring

Beer-sheba, on the southern border of Palestine.

thee up again: and Joseph shall put his hand upon thine eyes. And Jacob rose up from Beer-sheba: and the sons of Israel carried Jacob their father, and their little ones, and their wives, in the wagons which Pharaoh had sent to carry him. And they took their cattle, and their goods, which they had gotten in the land of Canaan, and came into Egypt, Jacob, and all his seed with him: his sons, and his sons' sons with him, his daughters, and his sons' daughters, and all his seed brought he with him into Egypt. . . .

And he sent Judah before him unto Joseph, to direct his face unto Goshen; and they came into the land of Goshen. And Joseph made ready his chariot, and went up to meet Israel his father to Goshen, and presented himself unto him; and he fell on his neck, and wept on his neck a good while. And Israel said unto Joseph, Now let me die, since I have seen thy face, because thou art yet alive.

The First Book of Moses, called Genesis, from The Holy Bible, containing the Old and New Testaments, translated out of the original tongues: and with the former translations diligently compared and revised, by His Majesty's special command.

THE PRODIGAL SON

A PARABLE

A certain man had two sons: and the younger of them said to his father, Father, give me the portion of goods that falleth to me. And he divided unto them his living. And not many days after the younger son gathered all together, and took his journey into a far country, and there wasted his substance with riotous living. And when he had spent all, there arose a mighty famine in that land; and he began to be in want. And he went and joined himself to a citizen of that country; and he sent him into his fields to feed swine. And he would fain have filled his belly with the husks that the swine did eat: and no man gave unto him.

And when he came to himself, he said, How many hired servants of my father's have bread enough and to spare, and I perish with hunger I will arise and go to my father, and will say unto him, Father, I have sinned against heaven, and before thee, and am no more worthy to be called thy son: make me as one of thy hired servants. And he arose, and came to his father. But when he was yet a great way off, his father saw him, and had compassion, and ran, and fell on his neck, and kissed him. And the son said unto him, Father, I have sinned against heaven, and in thy sight, and am no more worthy to be called thy son. But the father said to his servants, Bring forth the best robe, and put it on him; and put a ring on his hand, and shoes on his feet: and bring hither the fatted calf, and kill it; and let us eat, and be merry: for this my son was dead, and is alive again; he was lost, and is found. And they began to be merry.

Now his elder son was in the field: and as he came and drew nigh to the house, he heard musick and dancing. And he called one of the servants, and asked what these things meant. And he said unto him, Thy brother is come; and thy father hath killed the fatted calf, because he hath received him safe and sound. And he was angry, and would not go in: therefore came his father out, and entreated him. And he, answering said to his father, Lo, these many years do I serve thee, neither transgressed I at any time thy commandment: and yet thou never gavest me a kid, that I might make merry with my friends: but as soon as this thy son was come, which hath

devoured thy living with harlots, thou hast killed for
him the fatted calf. And he said unto him, Son, thou
art ever with me, and all I have is thine. It was meet
that we should make merry, and be glad: for this thy
brother was dead, and is alive again; and was lost,
and is found.

The Gospel according to Saint Luke, XV, 11–32

DIVES AND LAZARUS

A PARABLE

There was a certain rich man, which was clothed in
purple and fine linen, and fared sumptuously every
day: and there was a certain beggar named Lazarus,
which was laid at his gate, full of sores, and desiring to
be fed with the crumbs which fell from the rich man's
table: moreover the dogs came and licked his sores.

And it came to pass, that the beggar died, and was
carried by the angels into Abraham's bosom: the rich
man also died, and was buried; and in hell he lift up
his eyes, being in torments, and seeth Abraham afar
off, and Lazarus in his bosom. And he cried and said,
Father Abraham, have mercy on me, and send Lazarus, that he may dip the tip of his finger in water, and
cool my tongue; for I am tormented in this flame.
But Abraham said, Son, remember that thou in thy
lifetime receivedst thy good things, and likewise
Lazarus evil things: but now he is comforted, and thou
art tormented. And beside all this, between us and
thou there is a great gulf fixed: so that they which
would pass from hence to you cannot; neither can they
pass to us, that would come from thence.

Then he said, I pray thee therefore, father, that
thou wouldest send him to my father's house: for I

have five brethren; that he may testify unto them, lest they also come into this place of torment. Abraham saith unto him, They have Moses and the prophets; let them hear them. And he said, Nay, father Abraham: but if one went unto them from the dead, they will repent. And he said unto him, If they hear not Moses and the prophets, neither will they be persuaded, though one rose from the dead.

The Gospel according to Saint Luke, XVI, 19–31

CHARITY [1]

1604–11

Though I speake with the tongues of men & of Angels, and have not charity, I am become as sounding brasse or a tinkling cymbal. And though I have the gift of Prophesie, and understand all mysteries and all knowledge: and though I have all faith, so that I could remoove mountaines, and have no charitie, I am nothing. And though I bestowe all my goods to feede the poore, and though I give my body to bee burned, and have not charitie, it profiteth me nothing. Charitie suffereth long, and is kinde: charitie envieth not: charitie vaunteth not itselfe, is not puffed up, Doeth not behave itselfe unseemly, seeketh not her owne, is not easily provoked, thinketh no evill, Rejoyceth not in iniquitie, but rejoyceth in the trueth: Beareth all things, beleeveth all things, hopeth all things, endureth all things. Charitie never faileth: but whether there bee prophesies, they shall faile; whether there bee tongues, they shall cease; whether there bee knowledge, it shall vanish away. For we know in part, and we prophesie in part. But when that which is perfect is come, then that which is in part, shalbe done away.

[1] This passage is given in the original spelling.   *charitie*, love.

When I was a childe, I spake as a childe, I understood as a childe, I thought as a childe: but when I became a man, I put away childish things. For now we see through a glasse, darkly: but then face to face: now I know in part, but then shall I know even as also I am knowen. And now abideth faith, hope, charitie, these three, but the greatest of these is charitie.

1 *Corinthians*, XIII, 1–13

OF STUDIES

1597–98. æt. 37–38

Studies serve for pastimes, for ornaments, and for abilities. Their chief use for pastime is in privateness and retiring; for ornament is in discourse; and for ability is in judgment.

For expert men can execute, but learned men are fittest to judge or censure.

To spend too much time in them is sloth, to use them too much for ornament is affectation: to make judgments wholly by their rules, is the humour of a scholar. They perfect nature, and

1625. æt. 65

Studies serve for delight, for ornament, and for ability. Their chief use for delight is in privateness and retiring; for ornament is in discourse; and for ability is in the judgment and disposition of business. For expert men can execute and perhaps judge of particulars, one by one; but the general counsels and the plots and marshalling of affairs come best from those that are learned. To spend too much time in studies is sloth; to use them too much for ornament is affectation; to make judgment wholly by their rules is the humour of a scholar. They perfect nature, and are perfected by experience.

Crafty men contemn them, simple men admire them, and wise men use them.
For they teach not their own use, but that is a wisdom without them: and above them won by observation.
Read not to contradict, nor to believe, but to weigh and consider.

Some books are to be tasted, others to be swallowed, and some few to be chewed and digested: that is, some books are to be read only in parts; others to be read, but cursorily, and some few to be read wholly and with diligence and attention.

are perfected by experience.
For natural abilities are like natural plants, that need pruning by study: and studies themselves do give forth directions too much at large, except they be bounded in by experience.
Crafty men contemn studies; simple men admire them; and wise men use them.
For they teach not their own use; but that is a wisdom without them, and above them, won by observation.
Read not to contradict, and confute; nor to believe and take for granted; nor to find talk and discourse; but to weigh and consider.
Some books are to be tasted, others to be swallowed, and some few to be chewed and digested: that is, some books are to be read only in parts; others to be read but not curiously; and some few to be read wholly, and with diligence and attention.
Some books also may be read by deputy, and extracts made of them by others; but that would be

only in the less important arguments and the meaner sort of books: else distilled books are like common distilled waters, flashy things.

Reading maketh a full man, conference a ready man, and writing an exact man. And therefore if a man write little, he had need have a great memory, if he confer little he had need have a present wit, and if he read little he had need have much cunning, to seem to know that he doth not. Histories make men wise, poets witty: the mathematics subtle, natural philosophy deep: moral grave, logic and rhetoric able to contend.

Reading maketh a full man; conference a ready man; and writing an exact man. And therefore if a man write little, he had need have a great memory; if he confer little, he had need have a present wit; and if he read little, he had need have much cunning, to seem to know that he doth not. Histories make men wise; poets witty; the mathematics subtil; natural philosophy deep; moral grave; logic and rhetoric able to contend. *Abeunt studia in mores.* Nay, there be no stond or impediment in the wit, but may be wrought out by fit studies: like as diseases of the body may have appropriate exercises. Bowling is good for the stone and reins, shooting for the lungs and breast, gentle walking for the stomach,

---

writing an exact man. The Latin text reads: " writing prints what is read on the mind and fixes it deeper."

Abeunt, etc. Manners are changed through studies. Ovid, *Heroides,* XV, 83.

riding for the head, and the like. So if a man's wit be wandering, let him study the mathematics; for in demonstrations, if his wit be called away never so little, he must begin again. If his wit be not apt to distinguish or find differences, let him study the school-men, for they are *Cymini sectores*. If he be not apt to beat over matters and to call up one thing to prove and illustrate another, let him study the lawyer's cases. So every defect of the mind may have a special receipt.

Sir Francis Bacon, Essays

OF DISCOURSE

1597, 1612, 1625

Some in their discourse desire rather commendation of wit in being able to hold all arguments, than of judgment in discerning what is true; as if it were a praise to know what might be said, and not what should be thought. Some have certain common-places and themes wherein they are good, and want variety; which kind of poverty is for the most part tedious, and when it is once perceived, ridiculous. The honorablest part of talk is to give the occasion, and again to moderate and pass to somewhat else; for then a man leads the dance. It is good in discourse

Cymini sectores, splitters of hairs (*literally of* cumin-seeds). Dio Cassius, LXX, 3.

and speech of conversation to vary and intermingle speech of the present occasion with arguments, tales with reasons, asking of questions with telling of opinions, and jest with earnest: for it is a dull thing to tire, and as we say now, to jade, anything too far. As for jest, there be certain things which ought to be privileged from it — namely, religion, matters of state, great persons, any man's present business of importance, and any case that deserveth pity. Yet there be some that think their wits have been asleep, except they dart out somewhat that is piquant and to the quick; that is a vein which would be bridled.

Parce, puer, stimulis, et fortius utere loris.

And, generally, men ought to find the difference between saltness and bitterness. Certainly he that hath a satirical vein, as he maketh others afraid of his wit, so he had need be afraid of others' memory. He that questioneth much shall learn much, and content much; but especially if he apply his questions to the skill of the persons whom he asketh; for he shall give them occasion to please themselves in speaking, and himself shall continually gather knowledge. But let his questions be not troublesome, for that is fit for a poser; and let him be sure to leave other men their turns to speak. Nay, if there be any that would reign and take up all the time, let him find means to take them off, and to bring others on; as musicians use to do with those that dance too long galliards. If you dissemble sometimes your knowledge of that you are thought to know, you shall be thought another time to know that you know not. Speech of a man's self ought to be seldom, and well chosen. I knew one was wont to say in scorn, *He must needs be a wise man,* he

Parce, etc., Spare, boy, the whip and tighter hold the reins. Ovid, *Metamorphoses*, II, 127.
poser, one who puzzles others intentionally.

speaks so much of himself. And there is but one case wherein a man may commend himself with good grace, and that is in commending virtue in another; especially if it be such a virtue whereunto himself pretendeth. Speech of touch towards others should be sparingly used; for discourse ought to be as a field, without coming home to any man. I knew two noblemen of the west part of England, whereof the one was given to scoff, but kept ever royal cheer in his house; the other would ask of those that had been at the other's table, *Tell truly, was there never a flout or dry blow given?* To which the guest would answer, *Such and such a thing passed.* The lord would say, *I thought he would mar a good dinner.* Discretion of speech is more than eloquence; and to speak agreeably to him with whom we deal is more than to speak in good words or in good order. A good continued speech, without a good speech of elocution, shows slowness; and a good reply or second speech, without a good settled speech, showeth shallowness and weakness. As we see in beasts, that those that are weakest in the course are yet nimblest in the turn; as it is betwixt the greyhound and the hare. To use too many circumstances ere one come to the matter is wearisome; to use none at all, is blunt.

Sir Francis Bacon, Essays

OF PARENTS AND CHILDREN

1625

The joys of parents are secret, and so are their griefs and fears. They cannot utter the one, nor they will not utter the other. Children sweeten labours, but they make misfortunes more bitter. They in-

touch, sensitiveness.   *field,* i.e., a common or public place.

crease the cares of life, but they mitigate the remembrance of death. The perpetuity by generation is common to beasts; but memory, merit, and noble works are proper to men. And surely a man shall see the noblest works and foundations have proceeded from childless men, which have sought to express the images of their minds, where those of their bodies have failed. So the care of posterity is most in them that have no posterity. They that are the first raisers of their houses are most indulgent towards their children, beholding them as the continuance, not only of their kind, but of their work; and so both children and creatures.

The difference in affection of parents towards their several children is many times unequal, and sometimes unworthy, especially in the mother; as Solomon saith, "A wise son rejoiceth the father, but an ungracious son shames the mother." A man shall see where there is a house full of children one or two of the eldest respected, and the youngest made wantons. But in the midst some there are, as it were, forgotten, who many times, nevertheless, prove the best. The illiberality of parents in allowance towards their children is an harmful error, makes them base, acquaints them with shifts, makes them sort with mean company, and makes them surfeit more when they come to plenty. And therefore the proof is best when men keep their authority towards their children, but not their purse. Men have a foolish manner (both parents and schoolmasters and servants) in creating and breeding an emulation between brothers during childhood, which many times sorteth to discord when they are men, and disturbeth families. The Italians make little difference between children and nephews,

A wise son, etc., Proverbs X, 1.

or near kinsfolk; but so they be of the lump they care not, though they pass not through their own body. And to say truth in nature, it is much a like matter, insomuch that we see a nephew sometimes resembleth an uncle, or a kinsman, more than his own parent, as the blood happens. Let parents choose betimes the vocations and courses they mean their children should take, for then they are most flexible. And let them not too much apply themselves to the disposition of their children, as thinking they will take best to that which they have most mind to. It is true, that if the affection or aptness of the children be extraordinary, then it is good not to cross it, but generally the precept is good: *Optimum elige, suave et facile illud faciet consuetudo.* Younger brothers are commonly fortunate, but seldom or never where the elder are disinherited.

Sir Francis Bacon, Essays

OF ADVERSITY

1625

It was an high speech of Seneca (after the manner of the Stoics), that the good things which belong to prosperity are to be wished; but the good things that belong to adversity are to be admired: *Bona rerum secundarum, optabilia; adversarum mirabilia.* Certainly, if miracles be the command over nature, they appear most in adversity. It is yet a higher speech of his than the other (much too high for a heathen): It is true greatness to have in one the frailty of a man and the security of a God, *Vere magnum habere fragilitatem hominis, securitatem Dei.* This would have done bet-

Optimum, etc., Choose the best, habit will easily and pleasantly bring it to pass. A saying of Pythagoras, quoted by Plutarch, *De Exilio*, c. 8.
Bona rerum, etc., *Epistles*, 56.   *Vere magnum*, etc., *ibid.*, 53.

ter in poesy, where transcendences are more allowed. And the poets, indeed, have been busy with it; for it is, in effect, the thing which is figured in that strange fiction of the ancient poets, which seemeth not to be without mystery; nay, and to have some approach to the state of a Christian: that Hercules, when he went to unbind Prometheus, by whom human nature is represented, sailed the length of the great ocean in an earthen pot or pitcher; lively describing Christian resolution, that saileth in the frail bark of the flesh through the waves of the world.   But to speak in a mean, the virtue of prosperity is temperance; the virtue of adversity is fortitude, which in morals is the more heroical virtue.   Prosperity is the blessing of the Old Testament; adversity is the blessing of the New, which carrieth the greater benediction, and the clearer revelation of God's favour.   Yet, even in the Old Testament, if you listen to David's harp, you shall hear as many hearse-like airs as carols; and the pencil of the Holy Ghost hath laboured more in describing the afflictions of Job than the felicities of Salomon. Prosperity is not without many fears and distastes; and adversity is not without comforts and hopes. We see in needleworks and embroideries, it is more pleasing to have a lively work upon a sad and solemn ground, than to have a dark and melancholy work upon a lightsome ground.   Judge, therefore, of the pleasure of the heart by the pleasure of the eye.   Certainly, virtue is like precious odours, most fragrant when they are incensed or crushed; for prosperity doth best discover vice, but adversity doth best discover virtue.

Sir Francis Bacon, Essays

OF TRUTH [1]

1625

What is *Truth*; said jesting *Pilate*; [2] And would not
stay for an Answer. Certainly there be, that delight
in Giddinesse; And count it a Bondage, to fix a Beleefe; Affecting Freewill in Thinking, as well as in
Acting. And though the Sects of Philosophers of that
Kinde be gone, yet there remaine certaine discoursing
Wits, which are of the same veines, though there be
not so much Bloud in them, as was in those of the
Ancients. But it is not onely the Difficultie, and
Labour, which Men take in finding out of *Truth*;
Nor againe, that when it is found, it imposeth upon
mens Thoughts; that doth bring *Lies* in favour: But a
naturall, though corrupt Love, of the *Lie* it selfe.
One of the later Schoole of the Grecians, examineth
the matter, and is at a stand, to thinke what should be
in it, that men should love *Lies*; where neither they
make for Pleasure, as with Poets; Nor for Advantage,
as with the Merchant; but for the *Lies* sake. But I
cannot tell: This same *Truth*, is a Naked, and Open day
light, that doth not shew, the Masques, and Mum-
meries, and Triumphs of the world, halfe so Stately,
and daintily, as Candlelights. *Truth* may perhaps
come to the price of a Pearle, that sheweth best by
day: But it will not rise, to the price of a Diamond, or
Carbuncle, that sheweth best in varied lights.   A
mixture of a *Lie* doth ever adde Pleasure.   Doth any
man doubt, that if there were taken out of Mens
Mindes, Vaine Opinions, Flattering Hopes, False
valuations, Imaginations as one would, and the like;

Sects, the Skeptics (fl. 3d cent. B.C.).
One of the later Schoole, Lucian of Samosata (2d cent. A.D.).

[1] This essay is given in the original spelling.
[2] John XVIII, 38.

but it would leave the Mindes, of a Number of Men, poore shrunken Things; full of Melancholy, and Indisposition, and unpleasing to themselves? One of the Fathers, in great Severity, called Poesie, *Vinum Dæmonum*; because it filleth the Imagination, and yet it is, but with the shadow of a *Lie*. But it is not the *Lie*, that passeth through the Minde, but the Lie that sinketh in, and setleth in it, that doth the hurt, such as we spake of before. But howsoever these things are thus, in mens depraved Judgements, and Affections, yet *Truth*, which onely doth judge it selfe, teacheth, that the Inquirie of *Truth*, which is the Love-making, or Wooing of it; The knowledge of *Truth*, which is the Presence of it; and the Beleefe of *Truth*, which is the Enjoying of it; is the Souveraigne Good of humane Nature. The first Creature of God, in the workes of the Dayes, was the Light of the Sense; The last, was the Light of Reason; And his Sabbath Worke, ever since, is the Illumination of his Spirit. First he breathed Light, upon the Face, of the Matter or Chaos; Then he breathed Light, into the Face of Man; and still breatheth and inspireth Light, into the Face of his Chosen. The Poet, that beautified the Sect, that was otherwise inferiour to the rest, saith yet excellently well: *It is a pleasure to stand upon the shore, and to see ships tost upon the Sea: A pleasure to stand in the window of a Castle, and to see a Battaile, and the Adventures thereof, below: But no pleasure is comparable, to the standing, upon the vantage ground of Truth:* (A hill not to be commanded, and where the Ayre is alwaies cleare and serene;) *And to see the Errours and Wandrings, and Mists, and Tempests, in the vale below:* So alwaies, that this prospect,

One of the Fathers, i.e., of the Church (Jerome or Augustine).
Vinum Dæmonum, devil's wine.
Poet, Lucretius, *De Rerum Natura*, II, 1.   *Sect*, the Epicureans.

be with Pitty, and not Swelling, or Pride.   Certainly, it is Heaven upon Earth, to have a Mans Minde Move in Charitie, Rest in Providence, and Turne upon the Poles of *Truth*.

To passe from Theologicall, and Philosophicall *Truth*, to the *Truth* of civill Businesse; It will be acknowledged, even by those, that practise it not, that Cleare and Round dealing, is the Honour of Mans Nature; And that Mixture of Falshood, is like Allay in Coyne of Gold and Silver; which may make the Metall worke the better, but embaseth it.   For these winding, and crooked courses, are the Goings of the Serpent; which goeth basely upon the belly, and not upon the Feet.   There is no Vice, that doth so cover a Man with Shame, as to be found false, and perfidious.   And therefore Mountaigny [1] saith prettily, when he enquired the reason, why the word of the *Lie*, should be such a Disgrace, and such an Odious Charge?   Saith he, *If it be well weighed, To say that a man lieth, is as much to say, as that he is brave towards God, and a Coward towards men.*   For a *Lie* faces God, and shrinkes from Man.   Surely the Wickednesse of Falsehood, and Breach of Faith, cannot possibly be so highly expressed, as in that it shall be the last Peale, to call the Judgements of God, upon the Generations of Men, It being foretold that when Christ commeth, *He shall not finde Faith upon the Earth.*

   Sir Francis Bacon, *The Essayes or Counsels, Civill and Morall.*

He shall not, etc., Luke XVIII, 8.

   [1] Montaigne, *Essaies*, II, 18. Montaigne borrowed the idea from Plutarch's *Lives*.

ON A CHILD

1628

A child is a man in a small letter, yet the best copy of Adam before he tasted of Eve or the apple; and he is happy whose small practice in the world can only write his character. He is Nature's fresh picture newly drawn in oil, which time and much handling dims and defaces. His soul is yet a white paper unscribbled with observations of the world, wherewith, at length, it becomes a blurred notebook. He is purely happy because he knows no evil, nor hath made means by sin to be acquainted with misery. He arrives not at the mischief of being wise, nor endures evils to come by foreseeing them. He kisses and loves all, and, when the smart of the rod is past, smiles on his beater. Nature and his parents alike dandle him, and tice him on with a bait of sugar to a draught of wormwood. He plays yet, like a young prentice the first day, and is not come to his task of melancholy. His hardest labor is his tongue, as if he were loath to use so deceitful an organ; and he is best company with it when he can but prattle. We laugh at his foolish sports, but his game is our earnest; and his drums, rattles, and hobbyhorses, but the emblems and mocking of man's business. His father hath writ him as his own little story, wherein he reads those days of his life that he cannot remember, and sighs to see what innocence he hath outlived. The elder he grows, he is a stair lower from God; and, like his first father, much worse in his breeches. He is the Christian's example, and the old man's relapse; the one imitates his pureness, and the other falls into his simplicity. Could he put off his body with his little coat, he had got eternity without a burden, and exchanged but one heaven for another.

John Earle, Microcosmography

A YOUNG GENTLEMAN OF THE UNIVERSITY

1628

A young gentleman of the university is one that comes there to wear a gown, and to say hereafter he has been at the university. His father sent him thither because he heard there were the best fencing and dancing schools; from these he has his education, from his tutor the oversight. The first element of his knowledge is to be shown the colleges, and initiated in a tavern by the way, which hereafter he will learn of himself. The two marks of his seniority is the bare velvet of his gown and his proficiency at tennis, where when he can once play a set, he is a freshman no more. His study has commonly handsome shelves, his books neat silk strings, which he shows his father's man, and is loath to untie or take down for fear of misplacing. Upon foul days for recreation he retires thither, and looks over the pretty book his tutor reads to him, which is commonly some short history, or a piece of Euphormio; for which his tutor gives him money to spend next day. His main loitering is at the library, where he studies arms and books of honor, and turns a gentleman critic in pedigrees. Of all things he endures not to be mistaken for a scholar, and hates a black suit, though it be made of satin. His companion is ordinarily some stale fellow, that has been notorious for an ingle to gold hatbands, whom he admires at first, afterwards scorns. If he have spirit or wit he may light of better company, and may learn

strings, holding the books closed tight.
Euphormio, Euphormionis Satyricon, by John Barclay, 1603, 1607. It is a Latin picaresque novel.
ingle, crony.
gold hatbands, wealthy students. The idea is that he is a flatterer or a toady.
light of, light upon.

some flashes of wit, which may do him knight's service in the country hereafter. But he is now gone to the inns-of-court, where he studies to forget what he learned before, his acquaintance and the fashion.

John Earle, Microcosmography

THE GOOD SCHOOLMASTER

1642

There is scarce any profession in the commonwealth more necessary, which is so slightly performed. The reasons whereof I conceive to be these: First, young scholars make this calling their refuge, yea, perchance, before they have taken any degree in the university, commence schoolmasters in the country, as if nothing else were required to set up this profession but only a rod and a ferula. Secondly, others who are able, use it only as a passage to better preferment, to patch the rents in their present fortune, till they can provide a new one, and betake themselves to some more gainful calling. Thirdly, they are disheartened from doing their best with the miserable reward which in some places they receive, being masters to the children and slaves to their parents. Fourthly, being grown rich, they grow negligent, and scorn to touch the school, but by the proxy of an usher. But see how well our schoolmaster behaves himself.

1. *His genius inclines him with delight to his profession.* Some men had as lief be schoolboys as schoolmasters, to be tied to the school as Cooper's Dictionary and Scapula's Lexicon are chained to the desk therein; and though great scholars, and skilful in other arts, are bunglers in this: but God of his goodness hath fitted several men for several callings, that

inns-of-court, the community of lawyers.   *usher*, assistant teacher.

the necessity of church and state, in all conditions, may be provided for. So that he who beholds the fabric thereof may say, God hewed out this stone, and appointed it to lie in this very place, for it would fit none other so well, and here it doth most excellent. And thus God mouldeth some for a schoolmaster's life, undertaking it with desire and delight, and discharging it with dexterity and happy success.

2. *He studieth his scholars' natures as carefully as they their books;* and ranks their dispositions into several forms. And though it may seem difficult for him in a great school to descend to all particulars, yet experienced schoolmasters may quickly make a grammar of boys' natures, and reduce them all, saving some few exceptions, to these general rules:

(*a*) Those that are ingenious and industrious. The conjunction of two such planets in a youth presage much good unto him. To such a lad a frown may be a whipping, and a whipping a death; yea, where their master whips them once, shame whips them all the week after. Such natures he useth with all gentleness.

(*b*) Those that are ingenious and idle. These think, with the hare in the fable, that, running with snails (so they count the rest of their schoolfellows), they shall come soon enough to the post, though sleeping a good while before their starting. Oh, a good rod would finely take them napping!

(*c*) Those that are dull and diligent. Wines, the stronger they be, the more lees they have when they are new. Many boys are muddy-headed till they be clarified with age, and such afterwards prove the best. Bristol diamonds are both bright, and squared and

forms, classes or grades. *ingenious,* bright or intelligent by nature.
Bristol diamonds, a kind of quartz or rock crystal found near Bristol.

pointed by nature, and yet are soft and worthless; whereas orient ones in India are rough and rugged naturally. Hard, rugged, and dull natures of youth acquit themselves afterwards the jewels of the country, and therefore their dullness at first is to be borne with, if they be diligent. That schoolmaster deserves to be beaten himself, who beats nature in a boy for a fault. And I question whether all the whipping in the world can make their parts, which are naturally sluggish, rise one minute before the hour nature hath appointed.

(*d*) Those that are invincibly dull and negligent also. Correction may reform the latter, not amend the former. All the whetting in the world can never set a razor's edge on that which hath no steel in it. Such boys he consigneth over to other professions. Shipwrights and boatmakers will choose those crooked pieces of timber which other carpenters refuse. Those may make excellent merchants and mechanics who will not serve for scholars.

3. *He is able, diligent, and methodical in his teaching;* not leading them rather in a circle than forwards. He minces his precepts for children to swallow, hanging clogs on the nimbleness of his own soul, that his scholars may go along with him.

4. *He is and will be known to be an absolute monarch in his school.* If cockering mothers proffer him money to purchase their sons an exemption from his rod (to live as it were in a peculiar, out of their master's jurisdiction), with disdain he refuseth it, and scorns the late custom, in some places, of commuting whipping into money, and ransoming boys from the rod at a set price. If he hath a stubborn youth, correction-proof, he debaseth not his authority by contesting

cockering, coddling.   *peculiar*, special privilege.

with him, but fairly, if he can, puts him away before his obstinacy hath infected others.

5. *He is moderate in inflicting deserved correction.* Many a schoolmaster better answereth the name *paidotribes* than *paidogogos*, rather tearing his scholars' flesh with whipping, than giving them good education. No wonder if his scholars hate the muses, being presented unto them in the shapes of fiends and furies. Junius complains *de insolenti carnificina* of his schoolmaster, by whom *conscindebatur flagris septies aut octies in dies singulos*. Yea, hear the lamentable verses of poor Tusser,[1] in his own Life:

> From Paul's I went to Eton sent,
> To learn straightways the Latin phrase,
> Where fifty-three stripes given to me
> At once I had.
> For fault but small, or none at all,
> It came to pass thus beat I was;
> See, Udal,[2] see the mercy of thee
> To me, poor lad.

Such an Orbilius[3] mars more scholars than he makes: their tyranny hath caused many tongues to stammer, which spake plain by nature, and whose stuttering at first was nothing else but fears quavering on their speech at their master's presence; and whose mauling them about their heads hath dulled those who in quickness exceeded their master.

6. *He makes his school free to him who sues to him in*

paidotribes, teacher of wrestling; *paidogogos*, teacher of arts and sciences.
Junius, probably Franciscus Junius, a French theologian of the 16th century.
de insolenti, etc., of harsh brutality.
conscindebatur, etc., He was scourged seven or eight times a day.
sues ... in forma pauperis, appeals because of poverty.

[1] Thomas Tusser (1527–80), an English bucolic poet.

[2] Nicholas Udall (1506–56), famous schoolmaster, author of *Ralph Roister Doister*.

[3] Orbilius, the master of Horace, the poet. See Horace, *Epistles*, II, i, 71.

forma pauperis. And surely learning is the greatest alms that can be given. But he is a beast who, because the poor scholar cannot pay him wages, pays the scholar in his whipping. Rather are diligent lads to be encouraged with all excitements to learning. This minds me of what I have heard concerning Mr. Bust, that worthy late schoolmaster of Eton, who would never suffer any wandering begging scholar, such as justly the statute hath ranked in the forefront of rogues, to come into his school, but would thrust him out with earnestness (however privately charitable unto him) lest his schoolboys should be disheartened from their books, by seeing some scholars, after their studying in the university, preferred to beggary.

7. *He spoils not a good school to make thereof a bad college,* therein to teach his scholars logic. For besides that logic may have an action of trespass against grammar for encroaching on her liberties, syllogisms are solecisms taught in the school, and oftentimes they are forced afterwards in the university to unlearn the fumbling skill they had before.

8. *Out of his school he is no wit pedantical in carriage or discourse;* contenting himself to be rich in Latin, though he doth not jingle with it in every company wherein he comes.

To conclude, let this amongst other motives make schoolmasters careful in their place, that the eminencies of their scholars have commended the memories of their schoolmasters to posterity, who otherwise in obscurity had altogether been forgotten. Who had ever heard of R. Bond in Lancashire, but for the breeding of learned Ascham [1] his scholar; or of Hartgrave in Brundley school, in the same county, but because he

---

preferred to, promoted to (humorously used in the ecclesiastical sense).

[1] Ascham, see p. 72.

was the first did teach worthy Dr. Whitaker? [1] Nor do
I honor the memory of Mulcaster [2] for anything so
much as for his scholar, that gulf of learning, Bishop
Andrews. [3] This made the Athenians, the day before
the great feast of Theseus, their founder, to sacrifice a
ram to the memory of Conidas his schoolmaster that
first instructed him.

> *Thomas Fuller, The Holy State and the Profane State,*
>   Book II, chap. XVI.

LIFE, SLEEP, AND DREAMS

1633–35

Now for my life, it is a miracle of thirty years, which
to relate, were not a history, but a piece of poetry, and
would sound to common ears like a fable. For the
world, I count it not an inn, but an hospital; and a
place not to live, but to die in. The world that I regard is myself; it is the microcosm of my own frame
that I cast mine eye on: for the other, I use it but like
my globe, and turn it round sometimes for my recreation. Men that look upon my outside, perusing only
my condition and fortunes, do err in my altitude; for
I am above Atlas's shoulders. The earth is a point
not only in respect of the heavens above us, but of
that heavenly and celestial part within us. That
mass of flesh that circumscribes me limits not my
mind. That surface that tells the heavens it hath an
end cannot persuade me I have any. I take my circle
to be above three hundred and sixty. Though the
number of the arc do measure my body, it compre-
hendeth not my mind. Whilst I study how I am a

I am above Atlas's shoulders, I am a world.

[1] Jeremiah Whitaker (1599–1654), a Puritan preacher.

[2] Richard Mulcaster, first head-master of Merchant Taylors' School.

[3] Lancelot Andrewes (1555–1626), Bishop of Winchester and famous
preacher.

microcosm, or little world, I find myself something more than the great. There is surely a piece of divinity in us; something that was before the elements, and owes no homage unto the sun. Nature tells me, I am the image of God, as well as Scripture. He that understands not thus much hath not his introduction or first lesson, and is yet to begin the alphabet of man. Let me not injure the felicity of others, if I say I am as happy as any. *Ruat coelum, fiat voluntas tua*, salveth all; so that, whatsoever happens, it is but what our daily prayers desire. In brief, I am content; and what should providence add more? Surely this is it we call happiness, and this do I enjoy; with this I am happy in a dream, and as content to enjoy a happiness in a fancy, as others in a more apparent truth and reality. There is surely a nearer apprehension of any thing that delights us, in our dreams, than in our waked senses. Without this I were unhappy; for my waked judgement discontents me, ever whispering unto me that I am from my friend, but my friendly dreams in the night requite me, and make me think I am within his arms. I thank God for my happy dreams, as I do for my good rest; for there is a satisfaction in them unto reasonable desires, and such as can be content with a fit of happiness. And surely it is not a melancholy conceit to think we are all asleep in this world, and that the conceits of this life are as mere dreams, to those of the next, as the phantasms of the night, to the conceit of the day. There is an equal delusion in both; and the one doth but seem to be the emblem or picture of the other. We are somewhat more than ourselves in our sleeps; and the slumber of the body seems to be but the waking of the soul. It is the ligation of

Ruat coelum, etc., Let the heavens perish, so thy will be done.
ligation, binding, tying up.

sense, but the liberty of reason; and our waking conceptions do not match the fancies of our sleeps. At
my nativity, my ascendant was the earthly sign of
Scorpio. I was born in the planetary hour of *Saturn*,
and I think I have a piece of that leaden planet in me.
I am no way facetious, nor disposed for the mirth and
galliardise of company; yet in one dream I can compose a whole comedy, behold the action, apprehend
the jests, and laugh myself awake at the conceits
thereof. Were my memory as faithful as my reason
is then fruitful, I would never study but in my dreams,
and this time also would I choose for my devotions:
but our grosser memories have then so little hold of
our abstracted understandings, that they forget the
story, and can only relate to our awaked souls a confused and broken tale of that which hath passed.
Aristotle, who hath written a singular tract of sleep,
hath not methinks thoroughly defined it; nor yet
Galen, though he seem to have corrected it; for those
noctambulos and night-walkers, though in their sleep,
do yet enjoy the action of their senses. We must therefore say that there is something in us that is not in the
jurisdiction of Morpheus; and that those abstracted
and ecstatick souls do walk about in their own corpses,
as spirits with the bodies they assume, wherein they
seem to hear, see, and feel, though indeed the organs
are destitute of sense, and their natures of those faculties that should inform them. Thus it is observed,
that men sometimes, upon the hour of their departure,
do speak and reason above themselves. For then the
soul begins to be freed from the ligaments of the

Scorpio, the eighth sign of the Zodiac, and the second of Autumn.
Saturn, children born under this planet were, in astrology, destined to mel-
    ancholy or misfortune.
galliardise, merriment.
departure, falling asleep(?) or dying(?).

body, begins to reason like herself, and to discourse in a strain above mortality.

We term sleep a death; and yet it is waking that kills us, and destroys those spirits that are the house of life. 'Tis indeed a part of life that best expresseth death; for every man truly lives, so long as he acts his nature, or some way makes good the faculties of himself. Themistocles therefore, that slew his soldier in his sleep, was a merciful executioner: 'tis a kind of punishment the mildness of no law hath invented; I wonder the fancy of Lucan and Seneca did not discover it. It is that death by which we may be literally said to die daily; a death which Adam died before his mortality; a death whereby we live a middle and moderating point between life and death. In fine, so like death, I dare not trust it without my prayers, and an half adieu unto the world, and take my farewell in a colloquy with God:

The night is come, like to the day;
Depart not thou, great God, away.
Let not my sins, black as the night,
Eclipse the lustre of thy light.
Keep still in my horizon; for to me
The sun makes not the day, but thee.
Thou whose nature cannot sleep,
On my temples sentry keep;
Guard me 'gainst those watchful foes,
Whose eyes are open while mine close.
Let no dreams my head infest,
But such as Jacob's temples blest.
While I do rest, my soul advance;
Make my sleep a holy trance:

sleep a death. The early editions read *death a sleep.*
die daily, cf. 1 Corinthians XV, 22 and 31.

That I may, my rest being wrought,
Awake into some holy thought.
And with as active vigour run
My course as doth the nimble sun.
Sleep is a death; — O make me try,
By sleeping, what it is to die!
And as gently lay my head
On my grave, as now my bed.
Howe'er I rest, great God, let me
Awake again at last with thee.
And thus assur'd, behold I lie
Securely, or to wake or die.
These are my drowsy days; in vain
I do now wake to sleep again:
O come that hour, when I shall never
Sleep again, but wake for ever!

This is the dormitive I take to bedward; I need no other *laudanum* than this to make me sleep; after which I close mine eyes in security, content to take my leave of the sun, and sleep unto the resurrection.

Sir Thomas Browne, Religio Medici, sects. XI–XII

ON MUMMIES [1]

Date?

Wise Egypt, prodigal of her embalmments, wrapped up her princes and great commanders in aromatical folds, and, studiously extracting from corruptible bodies their corruption, ambitiously looked forward to immortality; from which vainglory we have become acquainted with many remnants of the old world, who

[1] Simon Wilkin, in his edition of Browne (1835), gives this fragment, but says that he has never seen the original, supposed to be in the British Museum.

could discourse unto us of the great things of yore, and
tell us strange tales of the sons of Misraim, and ancient
braveries of Egypt.   Wonderful indeed are the preserves of time, which openeth unto us mummies from
crypts and pyramids, and mammoth bones from cav-
erns and excavations; whereof man hath found the
best preservation, appearing unto us in some sort
fleshly, while beasts must be fain of an osseous continuance.

In what original this practice of the Egyptians had
root, divers authors dispute; while some place the
origin hereof in the desire to prevent the separation of
the soul, by keeping the body untabified, and alluring
the spiritual part to remain by sweet and precious
odours.   But all this was but fond inconsideration.
The soul, having broken its [tenement], is not stayed
by bands and cerecloths, nor to be recalled by Sabæan
odours, but fleeth to the place of invisibles, the *ubi* of
spirits, and needeth a surer than Hermes's seal to imprison it to its medicated trunk, which yet subsists
anomalously in its indestructible case, and, like a
widow looking for her husband, anxiously awaits its
return.

.   .   .   .

That mummy is medicinal, the Arabian doctor Haly
delivereth and divers confirm; but of the particular
uses thereof, there is much discrepancy of opinion.
While Hofmannus prescribes the same to epileptics,
Johan de Muralto commends the use thereof to gouty
persons; Bacon likewise extols it as a stiptic: and
Junkenius considers it of efficacy to resolve coagulated
blood.   Meanwhile, we hardly applaud Francis the
First, of France, who always carried mummies with

Mizraim, Hebrew name for Egypt.   *untabified*, undissolved.
Sabæan, Arabian.   *ubi*, the where, whereabouts.
Hermes's seal, cf. "hermetically sealed."

him as a panacea against all disorders; and were the efficacy thereof more clearly made out, scarce conceive the use thereof allowable in physic, exceeding the barbarities of Cambyses, and turning old heroes unto unworthy potions. Shall Egypt lend out her ancients unto chirurgeons and apothecaries, and Cheops and Psammitticus be weighed unto us for drugs? Shall we eat of Chamnes and Amosis in electuaries and pills, and be cured by cannibal mixtures? Surely such diet is dismal vampirism; and exceeds in horror the black banquet of Domitian, not to be paralleled except in those Arabian feasts, wherein Ghoules feed horribly.

Radzivil hath a strange story of some mummies which he had stowed in seven chests, and was carrying on ship board from Egypt, when a priest on the mission, while at his prayers, was tormented by two ethnic spectres or devils, a man and a woman, both black and horrible; and at the same time a great storm at sea, which threatened shipwreck, till at last they were enforced to pacify the enraged sea, and put those demons to flight by throwing their mummy freight overboard, and so with difficulty escaped. What credit the relation of the worthy person deserves, we leave unto others. Surely, if true, these demons were Satan's emissaries, appearing in forms answerable unto Horus and Mompta, the old deities of Egypt, to delude unhappy men. For those dark caves and mummy repositories are Satan's abodes, wherein he speculates and rejoices on human vain-glory, and keeps those kings and conquerors, whom alive he be-

Cambyses, Cheops, etc., names of Egyptian kings or conquerors (mentioned by Herodotus).
Domitian, Roman emperor, infamous for unnatural practices.
ethnic, probably pagan or heathen.

witched, whole for that great day, when he will claim his own, and marshal the kings of Nilus and Thebes in sad procession unto the pit.

Death, that fatal necessity which so many would overlook, or blinkingly survey, the old Egyptians held continually before their eyes. Their embalmed ancestors they carried about at their banquets, as holding them still a part of their families, and not thrusting them from their places at feasts. They wanted not likewise a sad preacher at their tables to admonish them daily of death, surely an unnecessary discourse while they banqueted in sepulchres. Whether this were not making too much of death, as tending to assuefaction, some reason there is no doubt, but certain it is that such practices would hardly be embraced by our modern gourmands who like not to look on faces of *morta*, or be elbowed by mummies.

Yet in those huge structures and pyramidal immensities, of the builders whereof so little is known, they seemed not so much to raise sepulchres or temples to death, as to contemn and disdain it, astonishing heaven with their audacities, and looking forward with delight to their interment in those eternal piles. Of their living habitations they made little account, conceiving of them but as *hospitia*, or inns, while they adorned the sepulchres of the dead, and planting thereon lasting bases, defied the crumbling touches of time and the misty vaporousness of oblivion. Yet all were but Babel vanities. Time sadly overcometh all things, and is now dominant, and sitteth upon a sphinx, and looketh unto Memphis and old Thebes, while her sister Oblivion reclineth semi-somnous on a pyramid, gloriously triumphing, making puzzles of Titanian erections, and turning old glories into dreams.

assuefaction, habituation.   *morta*, dead bodies.

History sinketh beneath her cloud. The traveller as he paceth amazedly through these deserts asketh of her, who builded them? and she mumbleth something, but what it is he heareth not.

Egypt itself is now become the land of obliviousness and doteth. Her ancient civility is gone, and her glory hath vanished as a phantasma. Her youthful days are over, and her face hath become wrinkled and tetrick. She poreth not upon the heavens, astronomy is dead unto her, and knowledge maketh other cycles. Canopus is afar off, Memnon resoundeth not to the sun, and Nilus heareth strange voices. Her monuments are but hieroglyphically sempiternal. Osiris and Anubis, her averruncous deities, have departed, while Orus yet remains dimly shadowing the principle of vicissitude and the effluxion of things, but receiveth little oblation.

Sir Thomas Browne, Fragment on Mummies

OF MYSELF

1668

It is a hard and nice subject for a man to write of himself; it grates his own heart to say anything of disparagement and the reader's ears to hear anything of praise for him. There is no danger from me of offending him in this kind; neither my mind, nor my body, nor my fortune allow me any materials for that vanity. It is sufficient for my own contentment that they have preserved me from being scandalous or remarkable on the defective side. But besides that, I shall here speak of myself only in relation to the sub-

civility, civilization. *tetrick*, harsh, austere.
Canopus, a city of ancient Egypt.
Memnon, a reference to the singing statue at Thebes (in Egypt).
averruncous, averted (no longer propitious).
Orus (Horus), was the sun-god, symbolized as a falcon.

ject of these precedent discourses, and shall likelier thereby to fall into the contempt than rise up to the estimation of most people. As far as my memory can return back into my past life, before I knew or was capable of guessing what the world, or glories, or business of it were, the natural affections of my soul gave me a secret bent of aversion from them, as some plants are said to turn away from others by an antipathy imperceptible to themselves and inscrutable to man's understanding. Even when I was a very young boy at school, instead of running about on holidays and playing with my fellows, I was wont to steal from them and walk into the fields, either alone with a book, or with some one companion, if I could find any of the same temper. I was then, too, so much an enemy to all constraint, that my masters could never prevail on me, by any persuasions or encouragements, to learn without book the common rules of grammar, in which they dispensed with me alone, because they found I made a shift to do the usual exercises out of my own reading and observation. That I was then of the same mind as I now am (which, I confess, I wonder at myself) may appear by the latter end of an ode which I made when I was but thirteen years old, and which was then printed with many other verses. The beginning of it is boyish, but of this part which I here set down, if a very little were corrected, I should hardly now be much ashamed.

IX

This only grant me, that my means may lie
Too low for envy, for contempt too high.
　　Some honor I would have,
Not from great deeds, but good alone;
The unknown are better than ill-known:

Rumor can ope the grave.
Acquaintance I would have, but when 't depends
Not on the number, but the choice of friends.

X

Books should, not business, entertain the light,
And sleep, as undisturbed as death, the night.
    My house a cottage more
  Than palace; and should fitting be
    For all my use, no luxury.
    My garden painted o'er
  With Nature's hand, not Art's; and pleasures yield,
Horace might envy in his Sabine field.

XI

Thus would I double my life's fading space;
For he that runs it well twice runs his race.
    And in this true delight,
  These unbought sports, this happy state,
    I would not fear, nor wish, my fate;
    But boldly say each night,
"To-morrow let my sun his beams display,
Or in clouds hide them, — I have lived to-day."

You may see by it I was even then acquainted with
the poets (for the conclusion is taken out of Horace),
and perhaps it was the immature and immoderate
love of them, which stamped first, or rather engraved,
these characters in me. They were like letters cut
into the bark of a young tree, which with the tree still
grow proportionably. But how this love came to be
produced in me so easily is a hard question. I believe I can tell the particular little chance that filled
my head first with such chimes of verse as have never

"*To-morrow let,*" etc., Horace, *Odes*, XXIX, 41.

since left ringing there.   For I remember when I began to read, and to take some pleasure in it, there was wont to lie in my mother's parlor (I know not by what accident, for she herself never in her life read any book but one of devotion), but there was wont to lie Spenser's works; this I happened to fall upon, and was infinitely delighted with the stories of the knights, and giants, and monsters, and brave houses, which I found everywhere there (though my understanding had little to do with all this); and by degrees with the tinkling of the rhyme and dance of the numbers; so that I think I had read him all over before I was twelve years old, and was thus made a poet as irremediably as a child is made a eunuch.   With these affections in mind, I went to the university, but was soon torn from thence by that violent public storm which would suffer nothing to stand where it did, but rooted up every plant, even from the princely cedars to me, the hyssop.   Yet I had as good fortune as could have befallen me in such a tempest; for I was cast by it into the family of one of the best persons, and into the court of one of the best princesses of the world.   Now, though I was here engaged in ways most contrary to the original design of my life, that is, into much company, and no small business, and into a daily sight of greatness, both militant and triumphant, for that was the state then of the English and French courts: yet all this was so far from altering my opinion, that it only added the confirmation of reason to that which was before but natural inclination.   I saw plainly all the paint of that kind of life the nearer I came to it; and that beauty which I did not fall in love with when,

tempest, the wars of the Great Rebellion, in which Cowley was a Royalist.
persons . . . princesses, Henry Jermyn, afterwards Earl of St. Albans, and Henrietta Maria, Queen Consort of Charles I.
courts, Cowley as secretary to Lord Jermyn, advisor of Queen Henrietta Maria, lived in Paris between 1644 and 1660.

for aught I knew, it was real, was not like to bewitch
or entice me when I saw that it was adulterate. I met
with several great persons whom I liked very well, but
could not perceive that any part of their greatness was
to be liked or desired, no more than I would be glad
or content to be in a storm, though I saw many ships
which rid safely and bravely in it. A storm would
not agree with my stomach, if it did with my courage.
Though I was in a crowd of as good company as could
be found anywhere, though I was in business of great
and honourable trust, though I ate at the best table,
and enjoyed the best conveniences for present sub-
sistance that ought to be desired by a man of my
condition in banishment and public distresses, yet I
could not abstain from renewing my old schoolday's
wish in a copy of verses to the same effect:

> Well then; I now do plainly see
> This busy world and I shall ne'er agree, &c.[1]

And I never then proposed to myself any other advantage from his Majesty's happy Restoration but the
getting into some moderately convenient retreat in the
country, which I thought in that case I might easily
have compassed, as well as some others, who, with no
greater probabilities or pretenses, have arrived to extraordinary fortunes. But I had before written a
shrewd prophecy against myself, and I think Apollo
inspired me in the truth, though not in the elegance of
it:

Thou, neither great at court, nor in the war,
Nor at th' exchange shall be, nor at the wrangling bar;
Content thyself with the small barren praise,
Which neglected verse does raise, &c.

[1] See *College Book of Verse*, p. 197.

However, by the failing of the forces which I had expected, I did not quit the design which I had resolved on; I cast myself into it *à corps perdu*, without making capitulations or taking counsel of fortune. But God laughs at a man who says to his soul, "Take thy ease." I met presently not only with many little incumbrances and impediments, but with so much sickness (a new misfortune to me) as would have spoiled the happiness of an emperor as well as mine. Yet I do neither repent nor alter my course. *Non ego perfidum dixi sacramentum.* Nothing shall separate me from a mistress which I have loved so long, and have now at last married, though she neither has brought me a rich portion, nor lived yet so quietly with me as I hoped from her.

"*Nec vos, dulcissima mundi*
Nomina, vos, Musae, libertas, otia, libri,
Hortique sylvaeque, anima remanente, reliquam."
    (Nor by me e'er shall you,
You, of all names the sweetest and the best,
You, Muses, books, and liberty, and rest;
You, gardens, fields, and woods, forsaken be,
As long as life itself forsakes not me.)

But this is a very pretty ejaculation. Because I have concluded all the other chapters with a copy of verses, I will maintain the humour to the last.

[*The Essay concludes with translations of two Epistles of Martial: Lib. 10, Ep. 47 and 96.*]

Abraham Cowley, Several Discourses by Way of Essays in Prose and Verse. 1688.

à corps perdu, head foremost.
Non ego, etc., I have not sworn a faithless oath. — Horace, *Odes* II, XVII, 10.
mistress, i.e., solitude and a country life.
Nec vos, etc. Apparently of Cowley's own composition.

TABLE-TALK

1666–1680

EQUITY

Equity in Law, is the same that the Spirit is in Religion, what every one pleases to make it. Sometimes they go according to Conscience, sometimes according to Law, sometimes according to the Rule of Court.

2. Equity is a Roguish thing: for Law we have a measure, know what to trust to; Equity is according to the Conscience of him that is Chancellor, and as that is larger or narrower, so is Equity. 'Tis all one as if they should make the Standard for the measure, we call a Foot, a Chancellor's Foot; what an uncertain Measure would this be? One Chancellor has a long Foot, another a short Foot, a Third an indifferent Foot: 'Tis the same thing in the Chancellor's Conscience.

3. That saying, "Do as you would be done to," is often misunderstood, for 'tis not thus meant, that I a private Man should do to you a private Man, as I would have you to me, but do, as we have agreed to do one to another by public Agreement. If the Prisoner should ask the Judge, whether he would be content to be hanged, were he in his case, he would answer no. Then says the Prisoner, do as you would be done to. Neither of them must do as private Men, but the Judge must do by him as they have publicly agreed; that is, both Judge and Prisoner have consented to a Law, that if either of them steal, they shall be hanged.

MEASURE OF THINGS

We measure from ourselves; and as things are for our use and purpose, so we approve them. Bring a Pear to the Table that is rotten we cry it down, 'tis naught; but bring a Medlar that is rotten, and 'tis a fine thing; and yet I'll warrant you the Pear thinks as well of itself as the Medlar does.

We measure the Excellency of other Men by some Excellency we conceive to be in ourselves. Nashe, a Poet, poor enough (as Poets used to be), seeing an Alderman with his Gold Chain, upon his great Horse, by way of scorn, said to one of his Companions, "Do you see yon fellow, how goodly, how big he looks? Why that fellow cannot make a blank Verse."

Nay we measure the goodness of God from ourselves; we measure his Goodness, his Justice, his Wisdom, by something we call Just, Good, or Wise in ourselves; and in so doing, we judge proportionably to the Country-fellow in the Play, who said if he were a King, he would live like a Lord, and have Peas and Bacon every day, and a Whip that cried Slash.

OPINION

Opinion and Affection extremely differ. I may affect a Woman best, but it does not follow I must think her the handsomest Woman in the World. I love Apples best of any Fruit, but it does not follow, I must think Apples to be the best Fruit. Opinion is something wherein I go about to give reason why all the World should think as I think. Affection is a thing wherein I look after the pleasing of myself.

'Twas a good fancy of an old Platonic: the Gods which are above Men, had something whereof Man did partake, an Intellect, Knowledge, and the Gods kept on their courses quietly. The Beasts, which are below Man, has something whereof Man did partake, Sense and Growth, and the Beasts lived quietly in their way. But Man had something in him, whereof neither Gods nor Beasts did partake, which gave him all the Trouble, and made all the Confusion in the World; and that is Opinion.

'Tis a vain thing to talk of a Heretic, for a Man for his heart can think no otherwise than he does think. In the Primitive Times there were many opinions, nothing scarce but some or other held. One of these Opinions being embraced by some Prince, and received into his Kingdom, the rest were condemned as Heresies; and his Religion, which was but one of several Opinions, first is said to be Orthodox, and so have continued ever since the Apostles.

STRAY REFLECTIONS

Patience is the chiefest fruit of Study. A man that strives to make himself a different thing from other men by much reading, gains this chiefest good, that in all Fortunes, he hath something to entertain and comfort himself withal.

Wise men say nothing in dangerous times. The Lion you know called the Sheep to ask her if his Breath smelt: she said, Aye; he bit her Head off for a Fool. He called the Wolf and asked him: he said no; he tore him in pieces for a Flatterer. At last he called the Fox and asked him: truly he had got a Cold and could not smell.

.   .   .   .

Wit must grow like Fingers. If it be taken from others, 'tis like Plums stuck upon black Thorns. there they are for a while, but they come to nothing;

.   .   .   .

Of all Actions of a Man's Life, his Marriage does

least concern other people, yet of all Actions of our
Life 'tis most meddled with by other People.

Table-Talk: being the Discourses of John Seldon, Esq. 1689.
(Collected by the Rev. Richard Milward, Seldon's
amanuensis.)

SHAKESPEARE

1665, 1684

He was the man of all Modern, and perhaps Ancient
Poets, had the largest and most comprehensive soul.
All the Images of Nature were still present to him, and
he drew them, not laboriously, but luckily; when he
describes anything you more than see it, you feel it
too.   Those who accuse him to have wanted learning
give him the greater commendation: he was naturally
learned; he needed not the spectacles of Books to read
Nature; he looked inwards, and found her there.   I
cannot say he is everywhere alike; were he so, I should
do him injury to compare him with the greatest of
Mankind.   He is many times flat, insipid; his Com-
ick wit degenerating into clenches, his serious swelling
into Bombast.   But he is always great when some
great occasion is presented to him; no man can say he
ever had a fit subject for his wit and did not then raise
himself as high above the rest of poets,

Quantum lenta solent inter viburna cupressi.

The consideration of this made Mr. Hales of Eton
say, that there was no other subject of which any poet
ever writ but he would produce it much better treated
of in Shakespeare.

John Dryden, An Essay of Dramatic Poesy

clenches, puns.
Quantum, etc., As the cypresses are among the pliant shrubs.   Virgil,
Eclogues, I, 26.

CHAUCER

1699

In the first place, as he is the father of English poetry, so I hold him in the same degree of veneration as the Grecians held Homer, or the Romans Virgil. He is a perpetual fountain of good sense; learned in all sciences; and, therefore, speaks properly on all subjects. As he knew what to say, so he knows also when to leave off; a continence which is practised by few writers, and scarcely by any of the ancients, except Virgil and Homer. . . .

He must have been a Man of a most wonderful comprehensive Nature, because, as it has been truly observed of him, he has taken into the compass of his *Canterbury Tales* the various Manners and Humours (as we now call them) of the whole English Nation, in his Age. Not a single Character has escaped him. All his Pilgrims are severally distinguished from each other; and not only in their inclinations, but in their very physiognomies and persons. Baptista Porta could not have described their natures better than by the marks which the Poet gives them. The Matter and Manner of their Tales, and of their Telling, are so suited to their different Educations, Humours, and Calling, that each of them would be improper in any other mouth. Even the grave and serious Characters are distinguished by their several sorts of Gravity: their Discourses are such as belong to their Age, their Calling, and their Breeding; such as are becoming of them, and of them only. Some of his Persons are Vicious, and some Vertuous; some are unlearned or (as Chaucer calls them) lewd, and some are learned. Even the ribaldry of the Low Characters is different:

Baptista Porta, Neapolitan physicist (1540–1615), inventor of the camera obscura.

the Reeve, the Miller, and the Cook, are several men,
and distinguished from each other as much as the
mincing Lady-Prioress and the broad-speaking, gap-
toothed Wife of Bath.   But enough of this; there is
such a variety of Game springing up before me, that I
am distracted in my Choice, and know not which to
follow.   'Tis sufficient to say, according to the Proverb, that *here is God's plenty*.

John Dryden, Preface to the Fables

SENTENCES AND PARAGRAPHS

1617–18

O eloquent, just, and mighty Death! whom none
could advise thou hast persuaded; what none hath
dared thou hast done; and whom all the world hath
flattered, thou only hast cast out of the world and despised: thou hast drawn together all the far-stretched
greatness, all the pride, cruelty, and ambition of man,
and covered it all over with these two narrow words,
Hic jacet.

Sir Walter Raleigh, A History of the World

1644

I cannot praise a fugitive and cloistered virtue, un-
exercised and unbreathed, that never sallies out and
sees her adversary, but slinks out of the race, where
that immortal garland is to be run for not without
dust and heat.

John Milton, Areopagitica

1653

Turn out of the way a little, good Scholar, towards
yonder high honeysuckle hedge: there we'll sit and
sing whilst this shower falls so gently upon the teem-
ing earth, and gives yet a sweeter smell to the lovely
flowers that adorn these verdant meadows.

Look, under that broad Beech-tree, I sat down, when I was last this way a-fishing, and the little birds in the adjoining grove seemed to have a friendly contention with an Echo, whose dead voice seemed to live in a hollow cave, near to the brow of that Primrose-hill; there I sat viewing the silver streams glide silently towards their centre, the tempestuous sea; yet, sometimes opposed by rugged roots, and pebble stones, which broke their waves, and turned them into foam: and sometimes I beguiled time by viewing the harmless Lambs, some leaping securely in the cool shade, while others sported themselves in the cheerful Sun: and saw others were craving comfort from the swollen udders of their bleating Dams. As I thus sat, these and other sights had so fully possessed my soul with content, that I thought as the Poet has happily expressed it:

I was for that time lifted above earth;
And possessed joys not promised in my birth.

As I left this place, and entered into the next field, a second pleasure entertained me, 'twas a handsome Milkmaid that had not yet attained so much age and wisdom as to load her mind with any fears of many things that will never be (as too many men too often do), but she cast away all care, and sung like a Nightingale: her voice was good, and the Ditty fitted for it; 'twas that smooth song, which was made by Kit. Marlowe, now at least fifty years ago: and the Milkmaid's Mother sung an answer to it, which was made by Sir Walter Rawleigh in his younger days.[1]

They were old-fashioned Poetry, but choicely good, I think much better than the strong lines that are now

[1] The songs are "The Passionate Shepherd to His Love" and "The Nymph's Reply." See *College Book of Verse*, pp. 85, 86.

in fashion in this critical age. Look yonder! on my word, yonder they both be a-milking again, I will give her the Chub, and persuade them to sing those two songs to us.

God speed you good woman, I have been a-fishing, and am going to Bleak-hall to my bed, and having caught more fish than will sup myself and my friend, I will bestow this upon you and your daughter, for I use to sell none.

Milkwoman. Marry God requite you Sir, and we'll eat it cheerfully, and if you come this way a-fishing two months hence, a grace of God I'll give you a silly-bub of new verjuice, in a new made haycock, for it, and my Maudlin shall sing you one of her best Ballads; for she and I both love all Anglers, they be such honest, civil, quiet men.

Izaak Walton, The Compleat Angler

1655

So have I seen a lark rising from his bed of grass, and soaring upwards, singing as he rises, and hopes to get to heaven, and climb above the clouds; but the poor bird was beaten back with the loud sighings of an eastern wind, and his motion made irregular and inconstant, descending more at every breath of the tempest, than it could recover by the liberation and frequent weighing of his wings; till the little creature was forced to sit down and pant, and stay till the storm was over; and then it made a prosperous flight, and did rise and sing, as if it had learned music and motion from an angel, as he passed through the air, about his ministries here below: so is the prayer of a good man.

Jeremy Taylor, Sermons

Chub, a fish that he has just caught.
sillibub, milk curdled with crab-apple juice or other fruit-juice (verjuice) and sweetened and flavored.

1661

[Death] comes equally to us all, and makes us all equal when it comes.   The ashes of an Oak in the Chimney are no Epitaph of that Oak to tell me how high or how large that was; it tells me not what flocks it sheltered while it stood, nor what men it hurt when it fell.   The dust of great persons' graves is speechless too, it says nothing, it distinguishes nothing: as soon the dust of a wretch whom thou wouldest not, as of a Prince thou couldest not look upon, will trouble thine eyes, if the wind blow it thither; and when a whirlwind hath blown the dust of the Churchyard into the Church, and the man sweeps out the dust of the Church into the Churchyard, who will undertake to sift those dusts again, and to pronounce, This is the Patrician, this is the noble flour, and this the yeomanly, this the Plebeian bran?   So is the death of Jesabel (Jesabel was a Queen) expressed: *They shall not say, this is Jesabel;* not only not wonder that it is, nor pity that it should be, but they will not say, they shall not know, This is Jesabel.

John Donne, Sermons

1678–84

Now as they were going along and talking, they espied a Boy feeding his Father's Sheep.   The Boy was in very mean Cloathes, but of a very fresh and well-favoured Countenance, and as he sat by himself he sung.   Hark, said Mr. Greatheart, to what the Shepherd's Boy saith.   So they hearkened, and he said,

> *He that is down, need fear no fall,*
> *He that is low, no Pride:*
> *He that is humble, ever shall*
> *Have God to be his Guide.*
> *I am content with what I have,*

> *Little be it, or much:*
> *And, Lord, contentment still I crave,*
> *Because thou savest such.*
> *Fullness to such a burden is*
> *That go on Pilgrimage:*
> *Here little, and hereafter Bliss,*
> *Is best from Age to Age.*

Then said the Guide, Do you hear him? I will dare
say, that this Boy lives a merrier life, and wears more
of that Herb called Heart's-ease in his Bosom, than he
that is clad in Silk and Velvet.

John Bunyan, The Pilgrim's Progress

EIGHTEENTH CENTURY

NED SOFTLY THE POET

April 25, 1710

Idem inficeto est inficetior rure,
Simul poemata attigit; neque idem unquam
Aeque est beatus, ac poema quum scribit:
Tam gaudet in se, tamque se ipse miratur.
Nimirum idem omnes fallimur; neque est quisquam
Quem non in aliqua re videre Suffenum
Possis . . .

CATULLUS

Will's Coffee-house, April 24

I yesterday came hither about two hours before the company generally make their appearance, with a design to read over all the newspapers; but upon my sitting down, I was accosted by Ned Softly, who saw me from a corner in the other end of the room, where I found he had been writing something. "Mr. Bickerstaff," says he, "I observe by a late paper of yours, that you and I are just of a humour; for you must know, of all impertinences, there is nothing which I so much hate as news. I never read a gazette in my life; and never trouble my head about our armies, whether they win or lose; or in what part of the world they lie encamped." Without giving me time to reply, he drew a paper of verses out of his pocket, telling me, That he had something which would entertain me more agreeably; and that he would desire my judgment upon

Idem inficeto, etc. Suffenus has no more wit than a mere clown when he attempts to write verses; and yet he is never happier than when he is scribbling: so much does he admire himself and his compositions. And, indeed, this is the foible of every one of us; for there is no man living who is not a Suffenus in one thing or other. Catullus, *De Suffeno*, XX, 14.

every line, for that we had time enough before us until
the company came in.

Ned Softly is a very pretty poet, and a great ad-
mirer of easy lines. Waller is his favorite; and as that
admirable writer has the best and worst verses of any
among our great English poets, Ned Softly has got all
the bad ones without book; which he repeats upon
occasion, to shew his reading, and garnish his conversation. Ned is indeed a true *English* reader, incapable
of relishing the great and masterly strokes of this art;
but wonderfully pleased with the little Gothic ornaments of epigrammatical conceits, turns, points, and
quibbles, which are so frequent in the most admired of
our English poets, and practised by those who want
genius and strength to represent, after the manner
of the ancients, simplicity in its natural beauty and
perfection.

Finding myself unavoidably engaged in such a conversation, I was resolved to turn my pain into a pleasure, and to divert myself as well as I could with so
very odd a fellow. "You must understand," says
Ned, "that the sonnet I am going to read to you was
written upon a lady who shewed me some verses of her
own making, and is, perhaps, the best poet of our age.
But you shall hear it." Upon which he began to read
as follows:

TO MIRA, ON HER INCOMPARABLE POEMS

i

When dress'd in laurel wreaths you shine,
    And tune your soft melodious notes,
You seem a sister of the Nine,
    Or Phoebus' self in petticoats.

sonnet, a little song.

ii

> I fancy, when your song you sing
>   (Your song you sing with so much **art**),
> Your pen was pluck'd from Cupid's wing;
>   For, ah! it wounds me like his dart.

"Why," says I, "this is a little nosegay of conceits,
a very lump of salt: every verse hath something in it
that piques; and then the Dart in the last line is certainly as pretty a sting in the tail of an epigram (for so
I think your critics call it) as ever entered into the
thought of a poet." — "Dear Mr. Bickerstaff," says
he, shaking me by the hand, "everybody knows you
to be a judge of these things; and to tell you truly, I
read over Roscommon's translation of Horace's Art of
Poetry three several times, before I sat down to write
the sonnet which I have shewn you. But you shall
hear it again, and pray observe every line of it, for
not one of them shall pass without your approbation.

> When dress'd in laurel wreaths you shine.

"This is," says he, "when you have your garland
on; when you are writing verses." To which I replied,
"I know your meaning: A metaphor!" — "The
same," said he, and went on.

> And tune your soft melodious notes.

"Pray observe the gliding of that verse; there is
scarce a consonant in it: I took care to make it run
upon liquids. Give me your opinion of it." —
"Truly," said I, "I think it as good as the former." —
"I am very glad to hear you say so," says he; "but
mind the next:

You seem a sister of the Nine.

"That is," says he, "you seem a sister of the Muses; for, if you look into ancient authors, you will find it was their opinion that there were nine of them." — "I remember it very well," said I: "but pray proceed."

Or Phoebus' self in petticoats.

"Phoebus," says he, "was the god of poetry. These little instances, Mr. Bickerstaff, shew a gentleman's reading. Then to take off from the air of learning, which Phoebus and the Muses have given to this first stanza, you may observe how it falls, all of a sudden into the familiar — 'in petticoats!'"

Or Phoebus' self in petticoats.

"Let us now," says I, "enter upon the second stanza; I find the first line is still a continuation of the metaphor."

I fancy, when your song you sing.

"It is very right," says he; "but pray observe the turn of words in those two lines. I was a whole hour in adjusting of them, and have still a doubt upon me whether, in the second line it should be — 'Your song you sing,' or, 'You sing your song.' You shall hear them both: —

> I fancy, when your song you sing
> (Your song you sing with so much art);

or,

> I fancy, when your song you sing
> (You sing your song with so much art)."

"Truly," said I, "the turn is so natural either way,

that you have made me almost giddy with it." — "Dear Sir," said he, grasping me by the hand, "you have a great deal of patience; but pray what do you think of the next verse? —

Your pen was pluck'd from Cupid's wing."

"Think!" says I; "I think you have made Cupid look like a little goose." — "That was my meaning," says he; "I think the ridicule is well enough hit off. But we come now to the last, which sums up the whole matter.

For, Ah! it wounds me like his dart.

"Pray how do you like that *Ah!* doth it not make a pretty figure in that place? *Ah!* — it looks as if I felt the dart, and cried out at being pricked with it.

For, Ah! it wounds me like his dart.

"My friend Dick Easy," continued he, "assured me he would rather have written that *Ah!* than to have been the author of the Æneid. He indeed objected, that I made Mira's pen like a quill in one of the lines, and like a dart in the other. But as to that" — "Oh! as to that," says I, "it is but supposing Cupid to be like a porcupine, and his quills and darts will be the same thing." He was going to embrace me for the hint; but half-a-dozen critics coming into the room, whose faces he did not like, he conveyed the sonnet into his pocket, and whispered me in the ear, he would shew it me again as soon as his man had written it over fair.

Joseph Addison, The Tatler

THE VISION OF MIRZA

Sept. 1, 1711

Omnem, quae nunc obducta tuenti
Mortales hebetat visus tibi, et humida circum
Caligat, numbem eripiam.

VIRGIL, *Æneid*, II, 604

When I was at Grand Cairo, I picked up several Oriental manuscripts, which I have still by me. Among others I met with one entitled, "The Vision of Mirza," which I have read over with great pleasure. I intend to give it to the public when I have no other entertainment for them; and shall begin with the first Vision, which I have translated word for word as follows:

"On the fifth day of the moon, which, according to the custom of my forefathers, I always keep holy, after having washed myself, and offered up my morning devotions, I ascended the high hills of Bagdad, in order to pass the rest of the day in meditation and prayer. As I was here airing myself on the tops of the mountains, I fell into a profound contemplation on the vanity of human life; and passing from one thought to another, 'Surely,' said I, 'man is but a shadow, and life but a dream.' Whilst I was thus musing, I cast my eyes towards the summit of a rock that was not far from me, where I discovered one in the habit of a shepherd, with a musical instrument in his hand. As I looked upon him he applied it to his lips, and began to play upon it. The sound of it was exceeding sweet, and wrought into a variety of tunes that were inexpressibly melodious, and altogether different from anything I had ever heard. They put me in mind of

Omnem, etc.
        The cloud, which, intercepting the clear light,
        Hangs o'er thy eyes, and blunts thy mortal sight,
        I will remove.

those heavenly airs that are played to the departed
souls of good men upon their first arrival in Paradise,
to wear out the impressions of their last agonies, and
qualify them for the pleasures of that happy place.
My heart melted away in secret raptures.

"I had been often told that the rock before me was
the haunt of a genius, and that several had been entertained with music who had passed by it, but never
heard that the musician had before made himself
visible. When he had raised my thoughts by those
transporting airs which he played, to taste the pleasures of his conversation, as I looked upon him like one
astonished, he beckoned to me, and, by the waving of
his hand directed me to approach the place where he
sat. I drew near with that reverence which is due to
a superior nature; and, as my heart was entirely subdued by the captivating strains I had heard, I fell
down at his feet and wept. The genius smiled upon
me with a look of compassion and affability that
familiarized him to my imagination, and at once dis-
pelled all the fears and apprehensions with which I
approached him. He lifted me from the ground, and,
taking me by the hand, 'Mirza,' said he, 'I have heard
thee in thy soliloquies; follow me.'

"He then led me to the highest pinnacle of the rock,
and, placing me on the top of it, 'Cast thy eyes eastward,' said he, 'and tell me what thou seest.' 'I see,'
said I, 'a huge valley, and a prodigious tide of water
rolling through it.' 'The valley that thou seest,' said
he, 'is the Vale of Misery, and the tide of water that
thou seest is part of the great tide of Eternity.'
'What is the reason,' said I, 'that the tide I see rises
out of a thick mist at one end, and again loses itself in
a thick mist at the other?' 'What thou seest,' said

genius, a genie or jinn, nature spirit.

he, 'is that portion of Eternity which is called Time, measured out by the sun, and reaching from the beginning of the world to its consummation. Examine now,' said he, 'this sea that is bounded with darkness at both ends, and tell me what thou discoverest in it.' 'I see a bridge,' said I, 'standing in the midst of the tide.' 'The bridge thou seest,' said he, 'is Human Life; consider it attentively.' Upon a more leisurely survey of it, I found that it consisted of threescore and ten entire arches, with several broken arches, which, added to those that were entire, made up the number about a hundred. As I was counting the arches, the genius told me that this bridge consisted at first of a thousand arches; but that a great flood swept away the rest, and left the bridge in the ruinous condition I now beheld it. 'But tell me further,' said he, 'what thou discoverest on it.' 'I see multitudes of people passing over it,' said I, 'and a black cloud hanging on each end of it.' As I looked more attentively I saw several of the passengers dropping through the bridge into the great tide that flowed underneath it; and, upon further examination, perceived there were innumerable trap-doors that lay concealed in the bridge, which the passengers no sooner trod upon, but they fell through them into the tide, and immediately disappeared. These hidden pitfalls were set very thick at the entrance of the bridge, so that throngs of people no sooner broke through the cloud, but many of them fell into them. They grew thinner towards the middle, but multiplied and lay closer together towards the end of the arches that were entire.

"There were indeed some persons, but their number was very small, that continued a kind of hobbling march on the broken arches, but fell through one after another, being quite tired and spent with so long a walk.

"I passed some time in the contemplation of this wonderful structure, and the great variety of objects which it presented. My heart was filled with a deep melancholy to see several dropping unexpectedly in the midst of mirth and jollity, and catching at everything that stood by them to save themselves. Some were looking up towards the heavens in a thoughtful posture, and in the midst of a speculation stumbled and fell out of sight. Multitudes were busy in the pursuit of bubbles that glittered in their eyes and danced before them; but often when they thought themselves within the reach of them, their footing failed and down they sunk. In this confusion of objects I observed some with scimitars in their hands, who ran to and fro from the bridge, thrusting several persons on trap-doors, which did not seem to lie in their way, and which they might have escaped had they not been thus forced upon them.

"The genius, seeing me indulge myself on this melancholy prospect, told me I had dwelt long enough upon it. 'Take thine eyes off the bridge,' said he, 'and tell me if thou yet seest anything thou dost not comprehend.' Upon looking up, 'What mean,' said I, 'those great flights of birds that are perpetually hovering about the bridge, and settling upon it from time to time? I see vultures, harpies, ravens, cormorants, and, among many other feathered creatures, several little winged boys that perch in great numbers upon the middle arches.' 'These,' said the genius, 'are Envy, Avarice, Superstition, Despair, Love, with the like cares and passions that infest human life.'

"I here fetched a deep sigh. 'Alas,' said I, 'man was made in vain! how is he given away to misery and mortality! tortured in life, and swallowed up in death!' The genius, being moved with compassion toward me, bade me quit so uncomfortable a prospect. 'Look no more,' said he, 'on man in the first stage of his existence, in his setting out for Eternity; but cast thine eye on that thick mist into which the tide bears the several generations of mortals that fall into it.' I directed my sight as I was ordered, and, whether or no the good genius strengthened it with any supernatural force, or dissipated part of the mist that was before too thick for the eye to penetrate, I saw the valley opening at the further end, and spreading forth into an immense ocean, that had a huge rock of adamant running through the midst of it, and dividing it into two equal parts. The clouds still rested on one half of it, insomuch that I could discover nothing in it; but the other appeared to me a vast ocean planted with innumerable islands, that were covered with fruits and flowers, and interwoven with a thousand little shining seas that ran among them. I could see persons dressed in glorious habits, with garlands upon their heads, passing among the trees, lying down by the sides of fountains, or resting on beds of flowers; and could hear a confused harmony of singing birds, falling waters, human voices, and musical instruments. Gladness grew in me upon the discovery of so delightful a scene. I wished for the wings of an eagle that I might fly away to those happy seats; but the genius told me there was no passage to them except through the gates of death that I saw opening every moment upon the bridge. 'The islands,' said he, 'that lie so fresh and green before thee, and with which the whole face of the ocean appears spotted as far as thou canst see, are more in number than the sands on the sea-shore: there are myriads of islands behind those which thou here discoverest, reaching further than thine eye, or even thine imagination, can extend itself. These are the mansions of good men after death, who, according to the degree and kinds of virtue in which they excelled, are distributed among those several islands, which abound with pleasures of different kinds and degrees, suitable to the relishes and perfections of those who are settled in them; every island is a paradise accommodated to its respective inhabitants. Are not these, O Mirza, habitations worth contending for? Does life appear miserable that gives thee opportunities of earning such a reward? Is death to be feared that will convey thee to so happy an existence? Think not man was made in vain, who has such an Eternity reserved for him.' I gazed with inexpressible pleasure on these happy islands. At length, said I, 'Show me now, I beseech thee, the secrets that lie hid under those dark clouds which cover the ocean on the other side of the rock of adamant.' The genius making me no answer, I turned about to address myself to him a second time, but I found that he had left me. I turned again to the vision which I had been so long contemplating; but instead of the rolling tide, the arched bridge, and the happy islands, I saw nothing but the long hollow valley of Bagdad, with oxen, sheep, and camels grazing upon the sides of it."

Joseph Addison, The Spectator

A DAY'S RAMBLE IN LONDON

Aug. 11, 1712

It is an inexpressible pleasure to know a little of the world, and be of no character or significancy in it.

To be ever unconcerned, and ever looking on new objects with an endless curiosity, is a delight known only to those who are turned for speculation: nay, they who enjoy it, must value things only as they are the objects of speculation, without drawing any worldly advantage to themselves from them, but just as they are what contribute to their amusements, or the improvement of the mind. I lay one night last week at Richmond; and being restless, not out of dissatisfaction, but a certain busy inclination one sometimes has, I rose at four in the morning, and took boat for London, with a resolution to rove by boat and coach for the next four and twenty hours, until the many different objects I must needs meet with should tire my imagination, and give me an inclination to a repose more profound than I was at that time capable of. I beg people's pardon for an odd humour I am guilty of, and was often that day, which is saluting any person whom I like, whether I know him or not. This is a particularity would be tolerated in me, if they considered that the greatest pleasure I know I receive at my eyes, and that I am obliged to an agreeable person for coming abroad into my view, as another is for a visit of conversation at their own houses.

The hours of day and night are taken up in the different cities of London and Westminster, by people as different from each other as those who are born in different centuries. Men of six a-clock give way to those of nine, they of nine to the generation of twelve, and they of twelve disappear, and make room for the fashionable world who have made two a-clock the noon of the day.

When we first put off from shore, we soon fell in with a fleet of gardeners bound for the several market-ports of London; and it was the most pleasing scene imaginable to see the cheerfulness with which those industrious people plied their way to a certain sale of their goods. The banks on each side are as well peopled, and beautified with as agreeable plantations as any spot on earth; but the Thames itself, loaded with the product of each shore, added very much to the landscape. It was very easy to observe by their sailing, and the countenances of the ruddy virgins, who were supercargoes, the parts of the town to which they were bound. There was an air in the purveyors for Covent Garden, who frequently converse with the morning rakes, very unlike the seemly sobriety of those bound for Stocks Market.

Nothing remarkable happened in our voyage; but I landed with ten sail of apricot boats at Strand Bridge, after having put in at Nine-Elms, and taken in melons, consigned by Mr. Cuffe of that place, to Sarah Sewell and company, at their stall in Covent Garden. We arrived at Strand-Bridge at six of the clock, and were unloading, when the hackney-coachman of the foregoing night took their leave of each other at the Darkhouse, to go to bed before the day was too far spent. Chimney-sweepers passed by us as we made up to the market, and some raillery happened between one of the fruit-wenches and those black men, about the Devil and Eve, with allusions to their several professions. I could not believe any place more entertaining than Covent Garden; where I strolled from one fruit shop to another, with crowds of agreeable young women around me, who were purchasing fruit for their respective families. It was almost eight of the clock before I could leave that variety of objects. I took coach and followed a young lady, who tripped into another just before me, attended by her maid. I saw immediately she was of the family of the Vain-

Vain-loves. Vain-love is a character in Congreve's comedy, *The Old Bachelor.*

loves. There are a set of these who of all things affect the play of Blindman's-buff, and leading men into love for they know not whom, who are fled they know not where. This sort of woman is usually a jaunty slattern; she hangs on her clothes, plays her head, varies her posture, and changes places incessantly; and all with an appearance of striving at the same time to hide herself, and yet give you to understand she is in humour to laugh at you. You must have often seen the coachmen make signs with their fingers as they drive by each other, to intimate how much they have got that day. They can carry on that language to give intelligence where they are driving. In an instant my coachman took the wink to pursue, and the lady's driver gave the hint that he was going through Long-Acre, towards St. James's. While he whipped up James-Street, we drove for King-Street, to save the pass at St. Martin's-Lane. The coachmen took care to meet, jostle, and threaten each other for way, and be entangled at the end of Newport-Street and Long-Acre. The fright, you must believe, brought down the lady's coach-door, and obliged her, with her mask off, to enquire into the bustle, when she sees the man she would avoid. The tackle of the coach-window is so bad she cannot draw it up again, and she drives on sometimes wholly discovered, and sometimes half escaped, according to the accident of carriages in her way. One of these ladies keeps her seat in a hackney-coach, as well as the best rider does on a managed horse. The laced shoe of her left foot, with a careless gesture, just appearing on the opposite cushion, held her both firm, and in a proper attitude to receive the next jolt.

As she was an excellent coach-woman, many were the glances at each other which we had for an hour and a half, in all parts of the town, by the skill of our drivers; until at last my lady was conveniently lost with notice from her coachman to ours to make off, and he should hear where she went.   This chase was now at an end, and the fellow who drove her came to us, and discovered that he was ordered to come again in an hour, for that she was a Silkworm.   I was surprised with this phrase, but found it was a cant among the hackney fraternity for their best customers, women who ramble twice or thrice a week from shop to shop, to turn over all the goods in town without buying anything.   The Silkworms are, it seems, indulged by the tradesmen; for though they never buy, they are ever talking of new silks, laces, and ribbons, and serve the owners, in getting them customers as their common dunners do in making them pay.

The day of people of fashion began now to break, and carts and hacks were mingled with equipages of show and vanity; when I resolved to walk it out of cheapness; but my unhappy curiosity is such, that I find it always my interest to take coach, for some odd adventure among beggars, ballad-singers, or the like, detains and throws me into expense.   It happened so immediately; for at the corner of Warwick Street, as I was listening to a new ballad, a ragged rascal, a beggar who knew me, came up to me, and began to turn the eyes of the good company upon me, by telling me he was extreme poor, and should die in the street for want of drink, except I immediately would have the charity to give him sixpence to go into the next alehouse and save his life.   He urged, with a melancholy face, that all his family had died of thirst.   All the mob have humour, and two or three began to take the jest; by which Mr. Sturdy carried his point, and let me sneak off to a coach.   As I drove along, it was a pleasing reflection to see the world so prettily checkered since I left Richmond, and the scene still filling with children of a new hour. This satisfaction increased as I moved towards the city, and gay signs, well disposed streets, magnificent public structures, and wealthy shops, adorned with contented faces, made the joy still rising till we came into the centre of the city, and centre of the world of trade, the Exchange of London. As other men in the crowds about me were pleased with their hopes and bargains, I found my account in observing them, in attention to their several interests. I, indeed, looked upon myself as the richest man that walked the Exchange that day; for my benevolence made me share the gains of every bargain that was made. It was not the least of my satisfactions in my survey, to go up stairs, and pass the shops of agreeable females; to observe so many pretty hands busy in the folding of ribbons, and the utmost eagerness of agreeable faces in the sale of patches, pins, and wares, on each side of the counters, was an amusement in which I should longer have indulged myself, had not the dear creatures called to me to ask what I wanted, when I could not answer, only "To look at you." I went to one of the windows which opened to the area below, where all the several voices lost their distinction, and rose up in a confused humming, which created in me a reflection that could not come into the mind of any but of one a little too studious; for I said to myself, with a kind of pun in thought — "What nonsense is all the hurry of this world to those who are above it?" In these, or not much wiser thoughts, I had like to have lost my place at the chop-house, where every man, according to the natural bashfulness or sullenness of our nation, eats in a public room a mess of broth, or chop of meat, in dumb silence, as if they had no pretence to speak to each other on the foot of being men, except they were of each other's acquaintance.

I went afterwards to Robin's, and saw people who had dined with me at the fivepenny ordinary just before, give bills for the value of large estates; and could not but behold with great pleasure, property lodged in, and transferred in a moment from such as would never be masters of half as much as is seemingly in them, and given from them every day they live. But before five in the afternoon I left the city, came to my common scene of Covent Garden, and passed the evening at Will's, in attending the discourses of several sets of people, who relieved each other within my hearing on the subject of cards, dice, love, learning, and politics. The last subject kept me until I heard the streets in the possession of the bellman, who had now the world to himself, and cried — "Past two of the clock." This roused me from my seat, and I went to my lodging, led by a light, whom I put into the discourse of his private economy, and made him give me an account of the charge, hazard, profit, and loss of a family that depended upon a link, with a design to end my trivial day with the generosity of sixpence, instead of a third part of that sum. When I came to my chambers I writ down these minutes; but was at a loss what instruction I should propose to my reader from the enumeration of so many insignificant matters and occurrences; and I thought it of great use, if they could learn with me to keep their minds open to gratification, and ready to receive it from anything it meets with. This one circumstance will make every face

Robin's, a coffee-house, frequented by brokers.
Will's, famous coffee-house at the corner of Bow and Russell Streets. A favorite of Dryden.
link, torch.

you see give you the satisfaction you now take in beholding that of a friend; will make every object a pleasing one; will make all the good which arrives to any man, an increase of happiness to yourself.

Sir Richard Steele, The Spectator, No. 454

THE FINE LADY'S JOURNAL

March 11, 1712

... Modo vir, modo foemina ...

VIRGIL

The journal with which I presented my reader on Tuesday last, has brought me in several letters, with accounts of many private lives cast into that form. I have the Rake's Journal, the Sot's Journal, and among several others a very curious piece, entitled — "The Journal of a Mohock." By these instances I find that the intention of my last Tuesday's paper has been mistaken by many of my readers. I did not design so much to expose vice as idleness, and aimed at those persons who pass away their time rather in trifle and impertinence, than in crimes and immoralities. Offences of this latter kind are not to be dallied with, or treated in so ludicrous a manner. In short, my journal only holds up folly to the light, and shews the disagreeableness of such actions as are indifferent in themselves, and blameable only as they proceed from creatures endowed with reason.

My following correspondent, who calls herself *Clarinda,* is such a journalist as I require: she seems by her letter to be placed in a modish state of indifference between vice and virtue, and to be susceptible of

Modo vir, etc. Sometimes a man, sometimes a woman.
journal, the journal of a man-about-town — a satire similar to this one.
Mohock, one of a class of aristocratic ruffians of the time.

either, were there proper pains taken with her. Had her journal been filled with gallantries, or such occurrences as had shewn her wholly divested of her natural innocence, notwithstanding it might have been more pleasing to the generality of readers, I should not have published it; but as it is only the picture of a life filled with a fashionable kind of gaiety and laziness, I shall set down five days of it, as I have received it from the hand of my fair correspondent.

Dear Mr. Spectator,

You having set your readers an exercise in one of your last week's papers, I have performed mine according to your orders, and herewith send it you inclosed. You must know, Mr. Spectator, that I am a maiden lady of a good fortune, who have had several matches offered me for these ten years past, and have at present warm applications made to me by a very pretty fellow. As I am at my own disposal, I come up to town every winter, and pass my time in it after the manner you will find in the following journal, which I began to write upon the very day after your Spectator upon that subject.

Tuesday night. Could not go to sleep till one in the morning for thinking of my journal.

Wednesday. From eight till ten. Drank two dishes of chocolate in bed, and fell asleep after them.

From ten to eleven. Eat a slice of bread and butter, drank a dish of bohea, read the Spectator.

From eleven to one. At my toilette, tried a new head. Gave orders for Veny to be combed and washed. Mem. I look best in blue.

From one till half an hour after two. Drove to the Change. Cheapened a couple of fans.

Veny, a lap-dog.

Till four. At dinner. Mem. Mr. Froth passed by in his new liveries.

From four to six. Dressed, paid a visit to old Lady Blithe and her sister, having heard they were gone out of town that day.

From six to eleven. At Basset. Mem. Never set again upon the ace of diamonds.

Thursday. From eleven at night to eight in the morning. Dreamed that I punted to Mr. Froth.

From eight to ten. Chocolate. Read two acts in Aureng-zebe a-bed.

From ten to eleven. Tea-table. Read the playbills. Received a letter from Mr. Froth. Mem. Locked it up in my strong box.

Rest of the morning. Fontange,[1] the tire-woman, her account of my Lady Blithe's wash. Broke a tooth in my little tortoise-shell comb. Sent Frank to know how my Lady Hectic rested after her monkey's leaping out at window. Looked pale. Fontange tells me my glass is not true. Dressed by three.

From three to four. Dinner cold before I sat down.

From four to eleven. Saw company. Mr. Froth's opinion of Milton. His account of the Mohocks. His fancy for a pincushion. Picture in the lid of his snuff-box. Old Lady Faddle promises me her woman to cut my hair. Lost five guineas at crimp.

Twelve a'clock at night. Went to bed.

Friday. Eight in the morning. A-bed. Read over all Mr. Froth's letters.

Ten a'clock. Staid within all day, not at home.

From ten to twelve. In conference with my mantua-maker. Sorted a suit of ribbons. Broke my blue china cup.

From twelve to one. Shut myself up in my chamber, practised Lady Betty Modely's skuttle.

One in the afternoon. Called for my flowered handker-

Basset, a card game.
punted, laid a stake against the bank, in faro, ombre, or other card game.
Aurengzebe, heroic play by Dryden, 1675.
crimp, a card game.
skuttle, "a pace of affected precipitation." — Chalmers's note.

[1] Mlle. de Fontange introduced a fashionable head-dress.

chief. Worked half a violet-leaf in it. Eyes ached and head out of order. Threw by my work, and read over the remaining part of Aurengzebe.

From three to four. Dined.

From four to twelve. Changed my mind, dressed, went abroad, and played at crimp till midnight. Found Mrs. Spitely at home. Conversation: Mrs. Brilliant's necklace false stones. Old Lady Loveday going to be married to a young fellow that is not worth a groat. Miss Prue gone into the country. Tom Townley has red hair. Mem. Mrs. Spitely whispered in my ear that she had something to tell me about Mr. Froth, I am sure it is not true.

Between twelve and one. Dreamed that Mr. Froth lay at my feet, and called me Indamora.

Saturday. Rose at eight a'clock in the morning. Sat down to my toilette.

From eight to nine. Shifted a patch for half an hour before I could determine it. Fixed it above my left eyebrow.

From nine to twelve. Drank my tea, and dressed.

From twelve to two. At chapel. A great deal of good company. Mem. The third air in the new opera. Lady Blithe dressed frightfully.

From three to four. Dined. Miss Kitty called upon me to go to the opera before I was risen from table.

From dinner to six. Drank tea. Turned off a footman for being rude to Veny.

Six a'clock. Went to the opera. I did not see Mr. Froth till the beginning of the second act. Mr. Froth talked to a gentleman in a black wig. Bowed to a lady in the front box. Mr. Froth and his friend clapped Nicolini [1] in the third act. Mr. Froth cried out Ancora. Mr. Froth led me to my chair. I think he squeezed my hand.

Eleven at night. Went to bed. Melancholy dreams. Methought Nicolini said he was Mr. Froth.

Sunday. Indisposed.

Monday. Eight a'clock. Waked by Miss Kitty. Aurengzebe lay upon the chair by me. Kitty repeated without

Indamora, the heroine of *Aurengzebe*.

[1] Nicolino Grimaldi, an Italian singer, who came to London in 1708.

book the eight best lines in the play. Went in our mobs to the dumb man according to appointment. Told me that my lover's name began with a G. Mem. The conjurer was within a letter of Mr. Froth's name, &c.

Upon looking back into this my journal, I find that I am at a loss to know whether I pass my time well or ill; and indeed never thought of considering how I did it before I perused your speculation upon that subject. I scarce find a single action in these five days that I can thoroughly approve of, except the working upon the violet-leaf, which I am resolved to finish the first day I am at leisure. As for Mr. Froth and Veny, I did not think they took up so much of my time and thoughts as I find they do upon my journal. The latter of them I will turn off, if you insist upon it; and if Mr. Froth does not bring matters to a conclusion very suddenly, I will not let my life run away in a dream. Your humble servant,

Clarinda.

To resume one of the morals of my first paper, and to confirm Clarinda in her good inclinations, I would have her consider what a pretty figure she would make among posterity, were the history of her whole life published like these five days of it. I shall conclude my paper with an epitaph written by an uncertain author on Sir Philip Sidney's sister, a lady, who seems to have been of a temper very much different from that of Clarinda. The last thought of it is so very noble, that I dare say my reader will pardon me the quotation.

IN THE COUNTESS DOWAGER OF PEMBROKE

Underneath this marble hearse
Lies the subject of all verse,

mobs, large caps covering the entire head.
the dumb man, Duncan Campbell, a fashionable fortune-teller in Drury Lane.

> Sidney's sister, Pembroke's mother:
> Death, ere thou hast kill'd another,
> Fair, and learned, and good as she,
> Time shall throw a dart at thee.[1]

> Joseph Addison, The Spectator, No. 322

POPE RIDES WITH HIS BOOKSELLER

(*Alexander Pope to the Earl of Burlington*)

1716

My Lord — If your mare could speak, she would give an account of what extraordinary company she had on the road; which, since she cannot do, I will.

It was the enterprising Mr. Lintot,[2] the redoubtable rival of Mr. Tonson, who, mounted on a stone-horse (no disagreeable companion to your Lordship's mare), overtook me in Windsor Forest. He said he heard I designed for Oxford, the seat of the muses, and would, as my bookseller, by all means accompany me thither.

I asked him where he got his horse? He answered he got it of his publisher. "For that rogue, my printer," said he, "disappointed me; I hoped to put him in good humor by a treat at the tavern, of a brown fricassee of rabbits, which cost two shillings, with two quarts of wine, besides my conversation. I thought myself cocksure of his horse, which he readily promised me, but said that Mr. Tonson had just such another design of going to Cambridge, expecting there the copy of a new kind of Horace from Dr. Bentley,[3]

---

stone-horse, a stallion.

[1] This epitaph is usually ascribed to William Browne of Tavistock, though some have claimed it for Ben Jonson.

[2] Barnaby Bernard Lintot (1675–1736); published Pope's *Iliad* and *Odyssey*. Later, satirized in the *Dunciad*.

[3] Richard Bentley (1662–1742), Master of Trinity, famous classical scholar.

and if Mr. Tonson [1] went, he was pre-engaged to attend him, being to have the printing of the said copy.

"So, in short, I borrowed this stone-horse of my publisher, which he had of Mr. Oldmixon [2] for a debt. He lent me, too, the pretty boy you see after me; he was a smutty dog yesterday, and cost me near two hours to wash the ink off his face; but the devil is a well-conditioned devil, and very forward in his catechise; if you have any more bags, he shall carry them."

I thought Mr. Lintot's civility not to be neglected, so gave the boy a small bag containing three shirts and an Elzavir Virgil; and, mounting in an instant, proceeded on the road, with my man before, my courteous stationer beside, and the aforesaid devil behind.

Mr. Lintot began in this manner: "Now, damn them! what if they should put it into the newspaper how you and I went together to Oxford? what would I care? If I should go down into Sussex, they would say I had gone to the Speaker. But what of that? If my son were but big enough to go on with the business, by G—d I would keep as good company as old Jacob."

Hereupon I inquired of his son. "The lad," says he, "has fine parts, but is somewhat sickly, much as you are — I spare for nothing in his education at Westminster. Pray, don't you think Westminster to be the best school in England? most of the late ministry came out of it, so did many of this ministry; I hope the boy will make his fortune." Don't you design to let him pass a year at Oxford? "To what purpose?" said

Speaker, Spencer Compton, Earl of Wilmington, Speaker of the House of Commons. He was a member of the Kit-Kat Club.
old Jacob, Jacob Tonson (1656–1736), publisher, and founder of the Kit-Cat Club.
[1] Mr. Tonson. See above.
[2] John Oldmixon, pamphleteer and minor poet, one of Pope's victims in the *Dunciad*.

he, "the universities do but make pedants, and I intend to breed him a man of business."

As Mr. Lintot was talking, I observed he sat uneasy on his saddle, for which I expressed some solicitude. "Nothing," says he, "I can bear it well enough; but since we have the day before us, methinks it would be very pleasant for you to rest awhile under the woods." When we were alighted, "See here, what a mighty pretty Horace I have in my pocket! what if you amused yourself in turning an ode, till we mount again? Lord! if you pleased, what a clever miscellany might you make at leisure hours." Perhaps I may, said I, if we ride on; the motion is an aid to my fancy, a round trot very much awakens my spirits; then jog on apace, and I'll think as hard as I can.

Silence ensued for a full hour; after which Mr. Lintot lugged the reins, stopped short, and broke out: "Well, sir, how far have you gone?" I answered, seven miles. "Zounds, sir," said Lintot, "I thought you had done seven stanzas. Oldsworth, in a ramble round Wimbleton Hill, would translate a whole ode in half this time. I'll say that for Oldsworth [1] (though I lost by his Timothy's [2]), he translates an ode of Horace the quickest of any man in England. I remember Dr. King [3] would write verses in a tavern three hours after he could not speak; and there's Sir Richard,[4] in that rumbling old chariot of his, between Fleetditch and St. Giles's pond, shall make you half a job.

Pray, Mr. Lintot, said I, now you talk of translators, what is your method of managing them? "Sir," replied he, "those are the saddest pack of rogues in the

---

[1] Oldsworth, William Oldisworth (1680–1734), translator and pamphleteer.

[2] Timothy's, *A Dialogue between Timothy and Philatheus.* It was published in three parts, at intervals.

[3] Dr. King, William King (1663–1712), scholar and translator.

[4] Sir Richard Blackmore, physician and poet. Died 1729.

world; in a hungry fit, they'll swear they understand all the languages in the universe; I have known one of them to take down a Greek book upon my counter and cry, Ay, this is Hebrew, I must read it from the latter end. By g—d, I can never be sure in these fellows, for I neither understand Greek, Latin, French, nor Italian myself. But this is my way: I agree with them for ten shillings per sheet, with a proviso that I will have their doings corrected by whom I please; so by one or the other they are led at last to the true sense of an author; my judgment giving the negative to all my translators." But how are you secure those correctors may not impose upon you? "Why, I get any civil gentleman (especially any Scotchman) that comes into my shop, to read the original to me in English; by this I know whether my first translator be deficient, and whether my corrector merits his money or not.

"I'll tell you what happened to me last month: I bargained with S—— for a new version of Lucretius to publish against Tonson's; agreeing to pay the author so many shillings at his producing so many lines. He made a great progress in a very short time, and I gave it to the corrector to compare with the Latin, but he went directly to Creech's [1] translation, and found it the same, word for word, all but the first page. Now, what d'ye think I did? I arrested the translator for a cheat; nay, and I stopped the corrector's pay, too, upon this proof, that he had made use of Creech instead of the original."

Pray, tell me next how you deal with the critics? "Sir," said he, "nothing more easy. I can silence the most formidable of them; the rich ones for a sheet

---

[1] Thomas Creech (1659–1700). His *Lucretius* (1682) inaugurated a new epoch in translation.

apiece of the blotted manuscript, which costs me
nothing; they'll go about with it to their acquaintance,
and pretend they had it from the author, who submitted it to their correction; this has given some of
them such an air, that in time they come to be con-
sulted with, and dedicated to as the top critics of the
town.   As for the poor critics, I'll give you one instance of my management, by which you may guess
at the rest.   A lean man, that looked like a very good
scholar, came to me t'other day; he turned over your
Homer, shook his head, shrugged up his shoulders, and
pished at every line of it.   One would wonder (says
he) at the strange presumption of some men; Homer is
no such easy task, that every stripling, every versifier
—— He was going on, when my wife called to dinner.
Sir, said I, will you please to eat a piece of beef with
me?   Mr. Lintot (said he), I am sorry you should be
at the expense of this great book; I am really concerned on your account —— Sir, I am obliged to you;
if you can dine upon a piece of beef, together with a
slice of pudding —— Mr. Lintot, I do not say but
Mr. Pope, if he would condescend to advise with men
of learning —— Sir, the pudding is on the table, if you
please to go in —— My critic complies, he comes to a
taste of your poetry, and tells me in the same breath
that the book is commendable, and the pudding excellent.   "Now, sir," concluded Mr. Lintot, "in return
to the frankness I have shown, pray tell me, is it the
opinion of your friends at Court that my Lord Lansdowne will be brought to the bar or not?" [1]   I told
him I heard he would not, and I hoped it, my Lord
being one I had particular obligations to.   "That may
be," replied Mr. Lintot, "but, by G—d, if he should
not, I shall lose the printing of a very good trial."

[1] George Granville, Lord Lansdowne (1667–1735) was a patron of Pope's.

These, my Lord, are a few traits by which you may discern the genius of Mr. Lintot, which I have chosen for the subject of a letter. I dropped him as soon as I got to Oxford, and paid a visit to my Lord Carleton at Middleton.

The conversations I enjoy here are not prejudiced by my pen, and the pleasures from them only to be equalled when I meet your Lordship. I hope in a few days to cast myself from my horse at your feet.

I am, etc.

Alexander Pope, Letters

THE EUROPEAN YAHOOS

1720–26

[*Lemuel Gulliver, a respectable middle-class Englishman, after visiting the countries of Lilliput, Brobdingnag, Laputa, Balnibarbi, Glubbdubdrib, Luggnagg, and Japan, has arrived in the land of the Houyhnhnms, of which the ruling inhabitants are horses and the domestic animals Yahoos — a peculiarly loathsome kind of men. He is looked upon as a superior Yahoo, and in the passage below gives his master, who is of course a horse, a description of the manners and customs of Europe.*]

The reader may please to observe that the following extract of many conversations I had with my master, contains a summary of the most material points which were discoursed at several times, for above two years, his Honor often desiring fuller satisfaction, as I farther improved in the Houyhnhnm tongue. I laid before him, as well as I could, the whole state of Europe; I discoursed of trade and manufactures, of arts and sciences; and the answers I gave to all the questions he made, as they arose upon several subjects, were a fund of conversation not to be exhausted. But I shall here only set down the substance of what passed between us concerning my own country, reducing it into order as well as I can, without any regard to time, or other circumstances, while I strictly adhere to truth. My only concern is, that I shall hardly be able to do justice to my master's arguments and expressions, which must needs suffer by my want of capacity, as well as by a translation into our barbarous English.

In obedience, therefore, to his Honor's commands, I related to him the revolution under the Prince of Orange; the long war with France entered into by the said Prince, and renewed by his successor the present Queen, wherein the greatest powers of Christendom were engaged, and which still continued; I computed, at his request, that about a million Yahoos might have been killed in the whole progress of it, and perhaps a hundred or more cities taken, and five times as many ships burnt or sunk.

He asked me what were the usual causes or motives that made one country go to war with another. I answered they were innumerable; but I should only mention a few of the chief. Sometimes the ambition of princes, who never think they have land or people enough to govern; sometimes the corruption of ministers, who engage their master in war in order to stifle or divert the clamor of the subjects against their evil administration. Difference in opinion hath cost many millions of lives: for instance, whether flesh be bread, or bread be flesh; whether the juice of a certain berry be blood or wine; whether whistling be a vice or virtue; whether it be better to kiss a post, or throw it into the fire; what is the best color for a coat — whether black, white, red, or gray; and whether it should be long or short, narrow or wide, dirty or clean; with many more.

Neither are any wars so furious and bloody, or of so long continuance, as those occasioned by difference in opinion, especially if it be in things indifferent.

Sometimes the quarrel between two princes is to decide which of them shall dispossess a third of his dominions, where neither of them pretend to any right. Sometimes one prince quarreleth with another, for fear the other should quarrel with him. Sometimes a war is entered upon, because the enemy is too strong; and sometimes because he is too weak. Sometimes our neighbours want the things which we have, or have the things which we want; and we both fight, till they take ours, or give us theirs. It is a very justifiable cause of a war, to invade a country, after the people have been wasted by famine, destroyed by pestilence, or embroiled by factions among themselves. It is justifiable to enter into war against our nearest ally, when one of his towns lies convenient for us, or a territory of land, that would render our dominions round and complete. If a prince sends forces into a nation where the people are poor and ignorant, he may lawfully put half of them to death, and make slaves of the rest, in order to civilize and reduce them from their barbarous way of living. It is a very kingly, honourable, and frequent practice, when one prince desires the assistance of another to secure him against invasion, that the assistant, when he hath driven out the invader, should seize on the dominions himself, and kill, imprison, or banish the prince he came to relieve. Alliance by blood or marriage is a frequent cause of war between princes; and the nearer the kindred is, the greater is their disposition to quarrel. Poor nations are hungry, and rich nations are proud; and pride and hunger will ever be at variance. For these reasons, the trade of a soldier is held the most honourable of all others; because a soldier is a Yahoo hired to kill in cold blood as many of his own species, who had never offended him, as possibly he can.

There is likewise a kind of beggarly princes in Europe, not able to make war by themselves, who hire out their troops to richer nations, for so much a day to each man; of which they keep three-fourths to themselves, and it is the best part of their maintenance; such are those in Germany and other northern parts of Europe.

"What you have told me," said my master, "upon the subject of war, does, indeed, discover most admirably the effects of that reason you pretend to; however, it is happy that the shame is greater than the danger, and that Nature hath left you utterly incapable of doing much mischief. For, your mouths lying flat with your faces, you can hardly bite each other to any purpose, unless by consent. Then, as to the claws upon your feet before and behind, they are so short and tender, that one of our Yahoos would drive a dozen of yours before him. And therefore, in recounting the numbers of those who have been killed in battle, I cannot but think that you have said the thing which is not."

I could not forbear shaking my head, and smiling a little at his ignorance. And, being no stranger to the art of war, I gave him a description of cannons, culverins, muskets, carbines, pistols, bullets, powder, swords, bayonets, battles, sieges, retreats, attacks; undermines, countermines, bombardments, sea-fights, ships sunk with a thousand men; twenty thousand killed on each side; dying groans, limbs flying in the air; smoke, noise, confusion; trampling to death under horses' feet; flight, pursuit, victory; fields strewed with carcases, left for food to dogs and wolves and birds of prey; plundering, stripping, ravishing, burning, destroying. And, to set forth the valour of my own dear countrymen, I assured him that I had seen them blow up a hundred enemies at once in a siege, and as many of them in a ship; and beheld the dead bodies come down in pieces from the clouds, to the great diversion of the spectators.

I was going on to more particulars when my master commanded me silence. He said, whoever understood the nature of Yahoos might easily believe it possible for so vile an animal to be capable of every action I had named, if their strength and cunning equaled their malice. But as my discourse had increased his abhorrence of the whole species, so he found it gave him a disturbance in his mind, to which he was wholly a stranger before. He thought his ears, being used to such abominable words, might, by degrees, admit them with less detestation. That, although he hated the Yahoos of this country, yet he no more blamed them for their odious qualities than he did a *gnnayh* (a bird of prey) for its cruelty, or a sharp stone for cutting his hoof. But when a creature pretending to reason could be capable of such enormities, he dreaded lest the corruption of that faculty might be worse than brutality itself. He seemed therefore confident that, instead of reason, we were only possessed of some quality fitted to increase our natural vices, as the reflection from a troubled stream returns the image of an ill-shapen body, not only larger, but more distorted.

He added that he had heard too much upon the subject of war, both in this and some former discourses. There was another point which a little perplexed him at present. I had informed him that some of our crew left their country on account of being ruined by law; that I had already explained the meaning of the word, but he was at a loss how it should come to pass that the law, which was intended for every man's preservation, should be any man's ruin. Therefore he desired to be further satisfied what I meant by law, and the dispensers thereof, according to the present practice in my own country; because he thought Nature and reason were sufficient guides for a reasonable animal, as we pretended to be, in showing us what we ought to do and what to avoid.

I assured his Honor that law was a science in which I had not much conversed, further than by employing advocates in vain, upon some injustices that had been done me; however, I would give him all the satisfaction I was able.

I said, there was a society of men among us, bred up from their youth in the art of proving, by words multiplied for the purpose, that white is black, and black is white, according as they are paid. To this society all the rest of the people are slaves. For example, if my neighbour hath a mind to my cow, he hires a lawyer to prove that he ought to have my cow from me. I must then hire another to defend my right, it being against all rules of law that any man should be allowed to speak for himself. Now in this case I, who am the right owner, lie under two disadvantages; first, my lawyer, being practiced almost from his cradle in defending falsehood, is quite out of his element when he would be an advocate for justice — which, as an office unnatural, he always attempts with great awkwardness, if not with ill-will. The second disadvantage is, that my lawyer must proceed with great caution, or else he will be reprimanded by the judges, and abhorred by his brethren, as one that would lessen the practice of the law. And therefore I have but two methods to preserve my cow. The first is, to gain over my adversary's lawyer with a double fee; who will then betray his client, by insinuating that he hath justice on his side. The second way is for my lawyer to make my cause appear as unjust as he can, by allowing the cow to belong to my adversary; and this, if it be skillfully done, will certainly bespeak the favour of the bench. Now, your Honor is to know that these judges are persons appointed to decide all controversies of property, as well as for the trial of criminals, and picked out from the most dexterous lawyers, who are grown old or lazy, and, having been biassed all their lives against truth and equity, are under such a fatal necessity of favouring fraud, perjury, and oppression, that I have known several of them refuse a large bribe from the side where justice lay, rather than injure the faculty by doing anything unbecoming their nature or their office.

It is a maxim among these lawyers that whatever hath been done before may legally be done again; and therefore they take special care to record all the decisions formerly made against common justice and the general reason of mankind. These, under the name of precedents, they produce as authorities, to justify the most iniquitous opinions, and the judges never fail of directing accordingly.

In pleading, they studiously avoid entering into the merits of the cause, but are loud, violent, and tedious, in dwelling upon all circumstances which are not to the purpose. For instance, in the case already mentioned, they never desire to know what claim or title my adversary hath to my cow, but whether the said cow were red or black, her horns long or short — whether the field I graze her in be round or square — whether she was milked at home or abroad — what diseases she is subject to, and the like; after which they consult precedents, adjourn the cause from time to time, and in ten, twenty, or thirty years, come to an issue.

It is likewise to be observed that this society hath a peculiar cant and jargon of their own, that no other mortal can understand, and wherein all their laws are written, which they take special care to multiply; whereby they have wholly confounded the very essence of truth and falsehood, of right and wrong; so that it will take thirty years to decide whether the field left me by ancestors for six generations, belongs to me, or to a stranger three hundred miles off. . . .

My master was yet wholly at a loss to understand what motives could incite this race of lawyers to perplex, disquiet, and weary themselves, and engage in a confederacy of injustice, merely for the sake of injuring their fellow-animals; neither could he comprehend what I meant in saying they did it for hire. Whereupon I was at much pains to describe to him the use of money, the materials it was made of, and the value of the metals; that, when a Yahoo had got a great store of this precious substance, he was able to purchase whatever he had a mind to — the finest clothing, the noblest houses, great tracts of land, the most costly meats and drinks, and have his choice of the most beautiful females. Therefore, since money alone was able to perform all these feats, our Yahoos thought they could never have enough of it to spend, or to save, as they found themselves inclined, from their natural bent, either to profusion or avarice. That the rich man enjoyed the fruit of the poor man's labour, and the latter were a thousand to one in proportion to the former. That the bulk of our people were forced to live miserably, by labouring every day for small wages, to make a few live plentifully. I enlarged my-self much on these and many other particulars, to the same purpose, but his Honor was still to seek; for he went upon a supposition that all animals had a title to their share in the productions of the earth, and es-pecially those who presided over the rest. Therefore he desired I would let him know what these costly meats were, and how any of us happened to want them. Whereupon I enumerated as many sorts as came into my head, with the various methods of dress-ing them, which could not be done without sending vessels by sea to every port of the world, as well for liquors to drink, as for sauces, and innumerable other conveniences. I assured him that this whole globe must be at least three times gone round, before one of our better female Yahoos could get her breakfast, or a cup to put it in. He said that must needs be a miserable country which cannot furnish food for its own inhabitants. But what he chiefly wondered at, was how such vast tracts of ground as I described should be wholly without fresh water, and the people put to the necessity of sending over the sea for drink. I replied that England (the dear place of my nativity) was computed to produce three times the quantity of food more than its inhabitants are able to consume, as well as liquors extracted from grain, or pressed out of the fruit of certain trees, which made excellent drink; and the same proportion in every other convenience of life. But in order to feed the luxury and intemperance of the males, and the vanity of the females, we sent away the greatest part of our necessary things to other countries, from whence, in return, we brought the materials of diseases, folly, and vice, to spend among ourselves. Hence it follows of necessity that vast numbers of our people are compelled to seek their livelihood by begging, robbing, stealing, cheating, pimping, forswearing, flattering, suborning, forging, gaming, lying, fawning, hectoring, voting, scribbling, star-gazing, poisoning, whoring, canting, libeling, free-thinking, and the like occupations; every one of which terms I was at much pains to make him understand.

That wine was not imported among us from foreign countries to supply the want of water, or other drinks, but because it was a sort of liquid which made us merry, by putting us out of our senses; diverted all melancholy thoughts, begat wild extravagant imaginations in the brain, raised our hopes, and banished our fears; suspended every office of reason for a time, and deprived us of the use of our limbs, till we fell into a profound sleep; although it must be confessed that we always awaked sick and dispirited, and that the use of this liquor filled us with diseases which made our lives uncomfortable and short.

But, besides all this, the bulk of our people supported themselves by furnishing the necessities or conveniences of life to the rich, and to each other. For instance, when I am at home, and dressed as I ought to be, I carry on my body the workmanship of an hundred tradesmen; the building and furniture of my house employ as many more, and five times the number to adorn my wife.

I was going on to tell him of another sort of people, who get their livelihood by attending the sick, having upon some occasions informed his Honor that many of my crew had died of diseases. But here it was with the utmost difficulty that I brought him to comprehend what I meant. He could easily conceive that a Houyhnhnm grew weak and heavy a few days before his death; or, by some accident, might hurt a limb. But that Nature, who works all things to perfection,

should suffer any pains to breed in our bodies, he
thought impossible, and desired to know the reason of
so unaccountable an evil. I told him, we fed on a
thousand things, which operated contrary to each
other; that we ate when we were not hungry, and
drank without the provocation of thirst; that we sat
whole nights drinking strong liquors, without eating a
bit, which disposed us to sloth, inflamed our bodies,
and precipitated or prevented digestion. That it
would be endless to give him a catalogue of all diseases
incident to human bodies, for they could not be fewer
than five or six hundred, spread over every limb and
joint; in short, every part, external and intestine,
having diseases appropriated to each. To remedy
which, there was a sort of people bred up among us,
in the profession, or pretence, of curing the sick.
And, because I had some skill in the faculty, I would
in gratitude to his Honor, let him know the whole
mystery and method by which they proceed.

Their fundamental idea is, that all diseases arise
from repletion; from whence they conclude that a
great evacuation of the body is necessary. Their next
business is, from herbs, minerals, gums, oils, shells,
salts, juices, seaweed, excrements, barks of trees,
serpents, toads, frogs, spiders, dead men's flesh and
bones, birds, beasts, and fishes, to form a composition
for smell and taste the most abominable, nauseous,
and detestable they can possibly contrive, which the
stomach immediately rejects with loathing; and this
they call a vomit. Or else, from the same storehouse,
with some other poisonous additions, they command
us to take medicine equally annoying and disgustful
to the bowels. . . .

But, besides real diseases, we are subject to many
that are only imaginary, for which the physicians

have invented imaginary cures; these have their several names, and so have the drugs that are proper for them; and with these our female Yahoos are always infested. . . .

Jonathan Swift, Travels into Several Remote Nations of the World. In Four Parts. By Lemuel Gulliver. 1726.

THE BURDEN OF MUCH TALKING

Pub. 1726

The Wise Man observes, that there is a time to speak, and a time to keep silence.[1] One meets with people in the world, who seem never to have made the last of these observations. And yet these great talkers do not at all speak from their having anything to say, as every sentence shows, but only from their inclination to be talking. Their conversation is merely an exercise of the tongue: no other human faculty has any share in it. It is strange these persons can help reflecting, that unless they have in truth a superior capacity, and are in an extraordinary manner furnished for conversation; if they are entertaining, it is at their own expense. Is it possible, that it should never come into people's thoughts to suspect, whether or no it be to their advantage to show so very much of themselves? Oh that you would altogether hold your peace, and it should be your wisdom. Remember likewise there are persons who love fewer words, an inoffensive sort of people, and who deserve some regard, though of too still and composed tempers for you. Of this number was the son of Sirach: for he plainly speaks from experience, when he says, As hills

[1] *Ecclesiastes*, III, 7.
Sirach, author of *Ecclesiasticus, or the Wisdom of the Son of Sirach*, in the *Apochrypha*.

of sand are to the steps of the aged, so is one of many words to a quiet man. But one would think it should be obvious to every one, that when they are in company with their superiors of any kind, in years, knowledge, and experience, when proper and useful subjects are discoursed of, which they cannot bear a part in; that these are times of silence: when they should learn to hear, and be attentive; at least in their turn. It is indeed a very unhappy way these people are in: they in a manner cut themselves out from all advantage of conversation, except that of being entertained with their own talk: their business in coming into company not being at all to be informed, to hear, to learn; but to display themselves; or rather to exert their faculty and talk without any design at all. And if we consider conversation as an entertainment, as somewhat to unbend the mind: as a diversion from the cares, the business, and the sorrows of life; it is of the very nature of it, that the discourse be mutual. This I say, is implied in the very notion of what we distinguish as conversation, or being in company. Attention to the continued discourse of one alone grows more painful often, than the cares and business we come to be diverted from. He therefore who imposes this upon us is guilty of a double offence; arbitrarily enjoining silence upon all the rest, and likewise obliging them to this painful attention.

Bishop Joseph Butler, sermon *On the Government of the Tongue.*

OF AVARICE

1741–42

It is easy to observe, that comic writers exaggerate every character, and draw their fop or coward with stronger features than are anywhere to be met with in nature. This moral kind of painting for the stage has been often compared to the painting for cupolas and ceilings, where the colours are overcharged, and every part is drawn excessively large, and beyond nature. The figures seem monstrous and disproportioned, when seen too nigh; but become natural and regular, when set at a distance, and placed in that point of view, in which they are intended to be surveyed. For a like reason, when characters are exhibited in theatrical representations, the want of reality removes, in a manner, the personages; and rendering them more cold and unentertaining, makes it necessary to compensate, by the force of colouring, what they want in substance. Thus we find in common life, that when a man once allows himself to depart from truth in his narrations, he never can keep within bounds of probability but adds still some new circumstance to render his stories more marvellous, and to satisfy his imagination. Two men in buckram suits became eleven to Sir John Falstaff, before the end of the story.[1]

There is only one vice, which may be found in life with as strong features, and as high a colouring as need be employed by any satirist or comic poet; and that is Avarice. Every day we meet with men of immense fortunes, without heirs, and on the very brink of the grave, who refuse themselves the most common necessaries of life, and go on heaping possessions on possessions under the real pressures of the severest poverty. An old usurer, says the story, lying in his last agonies, was presented by the priest with the crucifix to worship. He opens his eyes a moment before he expires, considers the crucifix, and cries, *These jewels are not true; I can only lend ten pistoles upon such*

[1] *I Henry IV*, II, iv.

a pledge. This was probably the invention of some epigrammatist; and yet every one, from his own experience, may be able to recollect almost as strong instances of perseverance in avarice. It is commonly reported of a famous miser in this city, that finding himself near death, he sent for some of the magistrates, and gave them a bill of an hundred pounds, payable after his decease, which sum he intended should be disposed of in charitable uses; but scarce were they gone, when he orders them to be called back, and offers them ready money if they would abate five pounds of the sum. Another noted miser in the north, intending to defraud his heirs, and leave his fortune to the building an hospital, protracted the drawing of his will from day to day; and it is thought, that if those interested in it had not paid for the drawing of it, he would have died intestate. In short, none of the most furious excesses of love and ambition are, in any respect, to be compared to the extremes of avarice.

The best excuse that can be made for avarice is, that it generally prevails in old men, or in men of cold tempers, where all the other affections are extinct; and the mind being incapable of remaining without some passion or pursuit, at last finds out this monstrously absurd one, which suits the coldness and inactivity of its temper. At the same time, it seems very extraordinary, that so frosty, spiritless a passion should be able to carry us further than all the warmth of youth and pleasure. But if we look more narrowly into the matter, we shall find, that this very circumstance renders the explication of the case more easy. When the temper is warm and full of vigor, it naturally shoots out more ways than one, and produces inferior passions to counterbalance, in some degree, its predominant inclination. It is impossible for a person of that temper, however bent on any pursuit, to be deprived of all sense of shame, or all regard to sentiments of mankind. His friends must have some influence over him; and other considerations are apt to have their weight. All this serves to restrain him within some bounds. But it is no wonder that the avaricious man, being, from the coldness of his temper, without regard to reputation, to friendship, or to pleasure, should be carried so far by his prevailing inclination, and should display his passion in such surprising instances.

Accordingly, we find no vice so irreclaimable as avarice; and though there scarcely has been a moralist or philosopher, from the beginning of the world to this day, who has not levelled a stroke at it, we hardly find a single instance of any person's being cured of it. For this reason, I am more apt to approve of those who attack it with wit and humour, than of those who treat it in a serious manner. There being so little hopes of doing good to the people infected with this vice, I would have the rest of mankind at least, diverted by our manner of exposing it; as indeed there is no kind of diversion, of which they seem so willing to partake.

Among the fables of Monsieur de la Motte,[1] there is one levelled against avarice, which seems to me more natural and easy than most of the fables of that ingenious author. A miser, says he, being dead, and fairly interred, came to the banks of the Styx, desiring to be ferried over along with the other ghosts. Charon demands his fare, and is surprised to see the miser, rather than pay it, throw himself into the river, and swim over to the other side, notwithstanding all the clamor and opposition that could be made to him. All

[1] Antoine de La Motte (1672–1731), French dramatist and fabulist.

hell was in an uproar; and each of the judges was meditating some punishment suitable to a crime of such dangerous consequence to the infernal revenues. Shall he be chained to the rock with Prometheus? or tremble below the precipice in company with the Danaides? or assist Sisyphus in rolling his stone? No, says Minos, none of these. We must invent some severer punishment. Let him be sent back to the earth, to see the use his heirs are making of his riches.

I hope it will not be interpreted as a design of setting myself in opposition to this celebrated author, if I proceed to deliver a fable of my own, which is intended to expose the same vice of avarice. The hint of it was taken from these lines of Mr. Pope:

> Damn'd to the mines, an equal fate betides
> The slave that digs it, and the slave that hides.[1]

Our old mother Earth once lodged an indictment against Avarice before the courts of heaven, for her wicked and malicious counsel and advice in tempting, inducing, persuading, and traitorously seducing the children of the plaintiff to commit the detestable crime of parricide upon her, and, mangling the body, ransack her very bowels for hidden treasure. The indictment was very long and verbose; but we must omit a great part of the repetitions and synonymous terms, not to tire our readers too much with our tale. Avarice, being called before Jupiter to answer to this charge, had not much to say in her own defence. The injury was clearly proved upon her. The fact, indeed, was notorious, and the injury had been frequently repeated. When, therefore, the plaintiff demanded justice, Jupiter very readily gave sentence in her

---

[1] *Moral Essays*, Epistle III, ll. 110-11.

favour; and his decree was to this purpose — That, since dame Avarice, the defendant, had thus grievously injured dame Earth, the plaintiff, she was hereby ordered to take that treasure, of which she had feloniously robbed the said plaintiff by ransacking her bosom, and restore it back to her without diminution or retention.   From this sentence it will follow, says Jupiter to the by-standers, that in all future ages, the retainers of Avarice shall bury and conceal their riches, and thereby restore to the earth what they take from her.

David Hume, Essays Moral, Political, and Literary

THE MAKING OF A MERCHANT

SELECTIONS FROM A DIARY [1]

1741–56

1741. What the mind is bent upon obtaining, the hand seldom fails in accomplishing.   I detested the frame, as totally unsuitable to my temper; therefore I produced no more profit than necessity demanded. I made shift, however, with a little overwork and a little credit, to raise a genteel suit of clothes, fully adequate to the sphere in which I moved.   The girls eyed me with some attention; nay I eyed myself as much as any of them.

1743. At Whitsuntide I went to see my father, and was favourably received by my acquaintance.   One of them played upon a bell-harp.   I was charmed with the sound, and agreed for the price, when I could raise the sum, half-a-crown.

At Michaelmas I went to Derby, to pay for and

frame, stocking-frame, a loom for knitting stockings.
bell-harp, a box-like stringed instrument, swung to and fro when played.
[1] These selections from Hutton's autobiography were made by Leigh Hunt and published in *A Book for a Corner,* 1849.

bring back my bell-harp, whose sound I thought seraphic. This opened a scene of pleasure which continued many years. Music was my daily delight and study. But, perhaps, I laboured under greater difficulties than any one had done before me. I could not afford an instructor. I had no books, nor could I borrow, or buy; neither had I a friend to give me the least hint, or put my instrument in tune.

Thus I was in the situation of the first inventor, left to grope in the dark to find something. I had first my ear to bring into tune, before I could tune the instrument; for the ear is the foundation of all music. That is the best tune which best pleases the ear, and he keeps the best time who draws the most music from his tune.

For six months did I use every effort to bring a tune out of an instrument which was so dreadfully out, it had no tune in it. Assiduity never forsook me. I was encouraged by a couplet in Dyce's Spelling-book:

"Despair of nothing that you would attain,
    Unwearied diligence your point will gain!"

When I was able to lay a foundation, the improvement and the pleasure were progressive. Wishing to rise, I borrowed a dulcimer, made one by it, then learned to play upon it. But in the fabrication of this instrument, I had neither timber to work upon, tools to work with, nor money to purchase either. It is said "necessity is the mother of invention." I pulled a large trunk to pieces, one of the relics of my family, but formerly the property of Thomas Parker, the first Earl of Macclesfield. And as to tools, I considered

---

dulcimer, a stringed instrument, somewhat like a zither, played with little hammers.
Earl of Macclesfield (1666?–1732), a prominent though unpopular jurist.

that the hammer-key and the plyers belonging to the stocking-frame, would supply the place of hammer and pincers.   My pocket-knife was all the edge-tools I could raise; a fork, with one limb, was made to act in the double capacity of spring-awl and gimlet.

I quickly was master of this piece of music; for if a man can play upon one instrument he can soon learn upon any.

A young man, apprentice to a baker, happening to see the dulcimer, asked if I could perform upon it. Struck with the sound, and with seeing me play with what he thought great ease, he asked if I would part with the instrument, and at what price?   I answered in the affirmative, and, for sixteen shillings.   He gave it.   I told him, "If he wanted advice, or his instrument wanted tuning, I would assist him."   "Oh no, there's not a doubt but I shall do."   I bought a coat with the money, and constructed a better instrument. . . .

1746. An inclination for books began to expand; but here, as in music and dress, money was wanting. The first article of purchase was three volumes of the *Gentleman's Magazine*, 1742, 3, and 4.   As I could not afford to pay for binding, I fastened them together in a most cobbled style.   These afforded me a treat.

I could only raise books of small value, and these in worn-out bindings. I learned to patch, procured paste, varnish, &c., and brought them into tolerable order; erected shelves, and arranged them in the best manner I was able.

If I purchased shabby books, it is no wonder that I dealt with a shabby bookseller who kept his working apparatus in his shop.   It is no wonder, too, if by repeated visits I became acquainted with this shabby bookseller, and often saw him at work; but it is a wonder and a fact, that I never saw him perform one act but I could perform it myself; so strong was the desire to attain the art.

I made no secret of my progress, and the bookseller rather encouraged me, and for two reasons: I bought such rubbish as nobody else would; and he had often an opportunity of selling me a cast-off book for a shilling, not worth a penny. As I was below every degree of opposition, a rivalship was out of the question.

The first book I bound was a very small one, Shakspeare's *Venus and Adonis.* I showed it to the bookseller. He seemed surprised. I could see jealousy in his eye. However, he recovered in a moment. He had no doubt but I should break.

He offered me a worn-out press for two shillings, which no man could use, and which was laid by for the fire. I considered the nature of its construction, bought it, and paid the two shillings. I then asked him to favor me with a hammer and a pin, which he brought with half a conquering smile, and half a sneer. I drove out the garter-pin, which, being galled, prevented the press from working, and turned another square, which perfectly cured the press. He said in anger, "If I had known, you should not have had it." However, I could see he consoled himself with the idea that all must return in the end. This proved for forty-two years my best binding press.

I now purchased a tolerably genteel suit of clothes and was so careful of them, lest I should not be able to procure another, that they continued my best for five years.

The stocking-frame being my own, and trade being

garter-pin, the (wooden) pin which works in the groove of a screw to raise and lower the upper plate of a press.
galled, abraded, worn-down.

dead, the hosiers would not employ me; they could hardly employ their own frames. I was advised to try Leicester, and took with me half-a-dozen pair of stockings to sell. I visited several warehouses; but, alas! all proved blank. They would neither employ me, nor give my goods anything near prime cost. As I stood like a culprit before a gentleman of the name of Bennet, I was so affected, that I burst into tears, to think that I should have served seven years to a trade at which I could not get bread.

My sister took a house, and to soften the rent, my brother and I lodged with her.

1747. It had been the pride of my life, ever since pride commenced, to wear a watch. I bought a silver one for thirty-five shillings. It went ill. I kept it for four years, then gave *that* and a guinea for another, which went as ill. I afterwards exchanged this for a brass one, which going no better, I sold it for five shillings; and to complete the watch farce, I gave the five shillings away, and went without a watch thirty years.

I had promised to visit my father on Whitsun eve, at Derby. Business detained me till it was eleven at night before I arrived. Expectation had for some time been on the stretch, and was now giving way. My father being elevated with liquor, and by my arrival, rose in ecstasy, and gave me the first kiss, and, I believe, the last, he ever gave me.

This year I began to dip into rhyme. The stream was pleasant, though I doubt whether it flowed from Helicon. Many little pieces were the produce of my pen, which, perhaps, pleased; however, they gave no offence, for they slept on my shelf till the rioters burnt them in 1791.[1]

---

[1] In the Birmingham Riots, a Tory mob attacked the leaders of Liberal and Unitarian principles, burning Hutton's house and library and the house and laboratory of Priestley, the scientist.

1748.   Every soul who knew me scoffed at the idea
of my book-binding, except my sister, who encouraged
and aided me; otherwise I must have sunk under it.
I considered that I was naturally of a frugal temper;
that I could watch every penny, live upon a little;
that I hated stocking-making, but not book-binding;
that if I continued at the frame, I was certain to be
poor; and if I ventured to leave it, I could not be so.
My only fear was lest I should draw in my friends; for
I had nothing of my own.

I had frequently heard that every man had, some
time or other in his life, an opportunity of rising. As
this was a received opinion, I would not contradict it.
I had, however, watched many years for the high tide
of my affairs, but thought it had never yet reached me.

I still pursued the two trades. Hurt to see my
three volumes of magazines in so degraded a state, I
took them to pieces, and clothed them in a superior
dress.

1749.   It was now time to look out for a future place
of residence.   A large town must be the mark, or there
would be no room for exertion.   London was thought
of, between my sister and me, for I had no soul else to
consult.   This was rejected for two reasons.   I could
not venture into such a place without a capital, and
my work was not likely to pass among a crowd of
judges.

My plan was to fix upon some market town, within
a stage of Nottingham, and open shop there on the
market day, till I should be better prepared to begin
the world at Birmingham.

I fixed upon Southwell, as the first step of elevation.
It was fourteen miles distant, and the town as despica-
ble as the road to it.   I went over at Michaelmas, took

draw in, involve.

a shop at the rate of twenty shillings a-year, sent a few boards for shelves, a few tools, and about two hundred-weight of *trash*, which might be dignified with the name of *books*, and worth, perhaps, a year's rent of my shop.   I was my own joiner, put up the shelves and their furniture, and in one day became the most eminent bookseller in the place.

During this rainy winter, I set out at five every Saturday morning, carried a burden of from three pounds weight to thirty, opened shop at ten, starved in it all day upon bread, cheese, and half a pint of ale, took from one to six shillings, shut up shop at four, and by trudging through the solitary night and the deep roads five hours more, I arrived at Nottingham by nine; where I always found a mess of milk porridge by the fire, prepared by my valuable sister.

Nothing short of a surprising resolution and rigid economy could have carried me through this scene.

1750.   Returning to Nottingham, I gave warning to quit Southwell, and prepared for a total change of life.

On the 10th of April I entered Birmingham, for the third time, to try if I could be accommodated with a small shop.   If I could procure any situation, I should be in the way of procuring a better.   On the 11th I travelled the streets of Birmingham, agreed with Mrs. Dix for the lesser half of her shop, No. 6 in Bull Street, at one shilling a-week; and slept at Lichfield in my way back to Nottingham.

On May 13th, Mr. Rudsdall, a dissenting minister of Gainsborough, with whom my sister had lived as a servant, travelling from Nottingham to Stamford, requested my company, and offered to pay my expenses, and give me eighteenpence a day for my time.   The afternoon was wet in the extreme.   He asked why I did not bring my greatcoat.   Shame forbade an answer, or I could have said I had none. The water completely soaked through my clothes, but not being able to penetrate the skin, it filled my boots. Arriving at the inn, every traveller, I found, was wet; and every one produced a change of apparel but me. I was left out because the house could produce no more. I was obliged to sit the whole evening in my drenched garments, and to put them on nearly as wet on my return next morning! What could I expect but destruction? Fortunately I sustained no injury.

It happened that Mr. Rudsdall, now declined housekeeping, his wife being dead. He told my sister that he should part with the refuse of his library, and would sell it to me. She replied, "He has no money." "We will not differ about that. Let him come to Gainsborough; he shall have the books at his own price." I walked to Gainsborough on the 15th of May, stayed there the 16th, and came back on the 17th.

The books were about two hundred pounds' weight. Mr. Rudsdall gave me his corn chest for their deposit; and for payment, drew the following note, which I signed: "I promise to pay to Ambrose Rudsdall, one pound seven shillings, when I am able." Mr. Rudsdall observed, "You shall never need pay this note if you only say you are not able." The books made a better show, and were more valuable than all I possessed beside.

I had now a most severe trial to undergo; parting with my friends, and residing wholly among strangers. May 23rd, I left Nottingham, and I arrived at Birmingham on the 25th. Having little to do but look into the street, it seemed singular to see thousands of faces pass, and not one that I knew. I had entered the world, in which I led a melancholy life, a life of silence and tears. Though a young man, and of rather a cheerful turn, it was remarked "that I was never seen to smile."

The rude family into which I was cast added to the load of melancholy.

My brother came to see me about six weeks after my arrival, to whom I observed, that the trade fully supported me. Five shillings a-week covered every expense; as food, rent, washing, lodging, &c. Thus a solitary year rolled round, when a few young men of elevated character and sense took notice of me. I had saved about twenty pounds, and was become more reconciled to my situation. The first who took a fancy to me was Samuel Salte, a mercer's apprentice, who five years after, resided in London, where he acquired £100,000. He died in 1797. Our intimacy lasted his life. . . .[1]

Among others who wished to serve me, I had two friends, Mr. Dowler, a surgeon, who resided opposite me, and Mr. Grace, a hosier at the Gateway, in the High-street. Great consequences often rise from small things. The house adjoining that of Mr. Grace's was to be let. My friends both urged me to take it. I was frightened at the rent, eight pounds. However, one drew, and the other pushed, till they placed me there. A small house is too large for a man without furniture, and a small rent may be too large for an income which has nothing certain in it but its smallness. Having felt the extreme of poverty, I dreaded nothing so much; but I believed I had seized the tide, and I was unwilling to stop.

Here I pursued business in a more elevated style, and with more success.

No event in a man's life is more consequential than

---

[1] Samuel Salte is apparently not the Samual Salt immortalized by Lamb in "Old Benches of the Inner Temple."

marriage; nor is any more uncertain. Upon this die his sum of happiness depends. Pleasing views arise, which vanish as the cloud; because, like that, they have no foundation. Circumstances change, and tempers with them. Let a man's prior judgment be ever so sound, he cannot foresee a change; therefore he is liable to deception. I was deceived myself, but, thanks to my kind fate, it was on the right side. I found in my wife more than I ever expected to find in woman. Just in proportion as I loved her, I must regret her loss. If my father, with whom I only lived fourteen years, who loved me less, and has been gone forty, never is a day out of my thoughts, what must be my thoughts towards her, who loved me as herself, and with whom I resided an age!

1756. My dear wife brought me a little daughter, who has been the pleasure of my life to this day. We had now a delightful plaything for both.

Robert Bage,[1] an old and intimate friend, and a paper-maker, took me to his inn, where we spent the evening. He proposed that I should sell paper for him, which I might either buy on my own account, or sell on his commission. As I could spare one or two hundred pounds, I chose to purchase; therefore appropriated room for the reception of goods, and hung out a sign — *The Paper Warehouse*. From this small hint I followed the stroke forty years, and acquired an ample fortune.

The Life of William Hutton

[1] Robert Bage, novelist, author of *Man as He Is*, *Hermsprong*.

THE PHILOSOPHIC COBBLER

(*A Letter from Lien Chu Altangi, a Chinese Traveller in England, to Fum Hoam, First President of the Ceremonial
Academy at Pekin.*)

1760

Though not very fond of seeing a pageant myself,
yet I am generally pleased with being in the crowd
which sees it; it is amusing to observe the effect which
such a spectacle has upon the variety of faces; the
pleasure it excites in some, the envy in others, and the
wishes it raises in all. With this design, I lately went
to see the entry of a foreign ambassador, resolved to
make one in the mob, to shout as they shouted, to fix
with earnestness upon the same frivolous objects, and
participate for a while the pleasures and the wishes of
the vulgar.

Struggling here for some time, in order to be first to
see the cavalcade as it passed, some one of the crowd
unluckily happened to tread upon my shoe, and tore
it in such a manner, that I was utterly unqualified to
march forward with the main body, and obliged to fall
back in the rear. Thus rendered incapable of being
a spectator of the show myself, I was at least willing
to observe the spectators, and limped behind like one
of the invalids which follow the march of an army.

In this plight, as I was considering the eagerness
that appeared on every face, how some bustled to get
foremost and others contented themselves with taking
a transient peep when they could; how some praised
the four black servants that were stuck behind one of
the equipages, and some the ribbons that decorated
the horses' necks in another; my attention was called
off to an object more extraordinary than any I had yet
seen: a poor cobbler sat in his stall by the wayside,
and continued to work while the crowd passed by,

without testifying the smallest share of curiosity. I own his want of attention excited mine; and as I stood in need of his assistance, I thought it best to employ a philosophic cobbler on this occasion. Perceiving my business, therefore, he desired me to enter and sit down, took my shoe in his lap, and began to mend it with his usual indifference and taciturnity.

"How, my friend," said I to him, "can you continue to work, while all those fine things are passing by your door?" "Very fine they are, master," returned the cobbler, "for those that like them, to be sure; but what are all those fine things to me? You don't know what it is to be a cobbler, and so much the better for yourself. Your bread is baked; you may go and see sights the whole day, and eat a warm supper when you come home at night; but for me, if I should run hunting after all these fine folk, what should I get by my journey but an appetite, and, God help me! I have too much of that at home already, without stirring out for it. Your people who may eat four meals a day, and a supper at night, are but a bad example to such a one as I. No, master, as God has called me into this world in order to mend old shoes, I have no business with fine folk, and they no business with me." I here interrupted him with a smile. "See this last, master," continues he, "and this hammer; this last and hammer are the two best friends I have in this world; nobody else will be my friend, because I want a friend. The great folks you saw pass by just now have five hundred friends, because they have no occasion for them: now while I stick to my good friends here, I am very contented; but when I ever so little run after sights and fine things, I begin to hate my work, I grow sad, and have no heart to mend shoes any longer."

This discourse only served to raise my curiosity to

know more of a man whom nature had thus formed into a philosopher. I therefore insensibly led him into a history of his adventures. "I have lived," said he, "a wandering sort of a life now five and fifty years; here to-day, and gone to-morrow; for it was my misfortune, when I was young, to be fond of changing." "You have been a traveller, then, I presume?" interrupted I. "I cannot boast much of travelling," continued he, "for I have never left the parish in which I was born but three times in my life, that I can remember; but then there is not a street in the whole neighborhood that I have not lived in, at some time or another. When I began to settle, and to take to my business in one street, some unforeseen misfortune, or a desire of trying my luck elsewhere, has removed me perhaps a whole mile away from my former customers, while some more lucky cobbler would come into my place, and make a handsome fortune among friends of my making; there was one who actually died in a stall that I had left, worth seven pounds seven shillings, all in hard gold, which he had quilted into the waistband of his breeches."

I could not but smile at these migrations of a man by the fireside, and continued to ask if he had ever been married. "Aye, that I have, master," replied he, "for sixteen long years, and a weary life I had of it, Heaven knows. My wife took it into her head that the only way to thrive in this world was to save money; so, though our comings-in was but about three shillings a week, all that ever she could lay her hands upon she used to hide away from me, though we were obliged to starve the whole week after for it.

"The first three years we used to quarrel about this every day, and I always got the better; but she had a hard spirit, and still continued to hide as usual; so that

I was at last tired of quarrelling and getting the better, and she scraped and scraped at pleasure, till I was almost starved to death. Her conduct drove me at last to the ale-house; here I used to sit with people who hated home like myself, drank while I had money left, and ran in score when anybody would trust me; till at last the landlady, coming one day with a long bill when I was from home, and putting it into my wife's hands, the length of it effectually broke her heart. I searched the whole stall after she was dead for money, but she had hidden it so effectually, that with all my pains I could never find a farthing."

By this time my shoe was mended, and satisfying the poor artist for his trouble, and rewarding him besides for his information, I took my leave, and returned home to lengthen out the amusement his conversation afforded, by communicating it to my friend.

Oliver Goldsmith, The Citizen of the World, 1762. (First published in Newbery's *Public Ledger,* 1760.)

A KING'S LEVEE AND A KING'S FUNERAL

(*Horace Walpole to George Montagu*)

Arlington Street, Nov. 13, 1760

Dear George. — Even the honeymoon of a new raign don't produce events every day. There is nothing but the common saying of addresses and kissing hands. The chief difficulty is settled; Lord Gower yields the mastership of the horse to Lord Huntington, and removes to the great wardrobe, from whence Sir Thomas Robinson was to have gone into Ellis's place, but he is saved. The city, however, have a mind to be out of humor; a paper has been fixed on the Royal Exchange, with these words, "No petticoat government, no Scotch minister, no Lord George Sackville;" two hints totally unfounded, and the other scarce true. No petticoat ever governed less; it is left to Leicester House; Lord George's breeches are as little concerned; and, except Lady Susan Stuart and Sir Harry Erskine, nothing has yet been done for any Scots. For the King himself, he seems all good nature, and wishing to satisfy everybody: all his speeches are obliging. I saw him again yesterday, and was surprised to find the levee-room had lost so entirely the air of the lion's den. This sovereign don't stand in one spot, with his eyes fixed royally on the ground, and dropping bits of German news; he walks about, and speaks to everybody. I saw him afterwards on the throne, where he is graceful and genteel, sits with dignity, and reads his answers to addresses well; it was the Cambridge address, carried by the Duke of Newcastle in his doctor's hood, and looking like the *médecin malgré lui*. He had been vehemently solicitous for attendance, for fear my Lord Westmorland, who vouchsafes himself to bring the address from Oxford, should outnumber him. Lord Litchfield and several other Jacobites have kissed hands; George Selwyn says, "They go to St. James's, because now there are so many *Stuarts* there."[1]

Do you know I had the curiosity to go to the burying t'other night. I had never seen a royal funeral; nay, I walked as a rag of quality, which I found would be, and so it was, the easiest way of seeing it. It is absolutely a noble sight. The Prince's chamber, hung with purple, and a quantity of silver lamps, the coffin under a canopy of purple velvet, and six vast chandeliers of silver, on high stands, had a very good effect. The ambassador from Tripoli and his son were carried to see that chamber. The procession, through a line

King, George III.   *funeral*, of George II.

[1] The drift here is that Lord Bute, George III's first prime minister (1760–63) was of the Stuart family.

of footguards, every seventh man bearing a torch, the horse-guards lining the outside, their officers, with drawn sabres and crape sashes, on horseback, the drums muffled, the fifes, bells tolling, and minute guns; all this was very solemn. But the charm was the entrance of the abbey, where we were received by the dean and chapter in rich robes, the choir and almsmen bearing torches, the whole abbey so illuminated, that one saw it to greater advantage than by day; the tombs, long aisles, and fretted roof, all appearing distinctly, and with the happiest *chiara scuro*. There wanted nothing but incense, and little chapels, here and there, with priests saying mass for the repose of the defunct; yet one could not complain of its not being Catholic enough. I had been in dread of being coupled with some boy of ten years old; but the heralds were not very accurate, and I walked with George Grenville, taller and older, to keep me in countenance. When we came to the chapel of Henry the Seventh, all solemnity and decorum ceased; no order was observed, people sat or stood where they could or would; the yeomen of the guard crying out for help, oppressed by the immense weight of the coffin; the bishop read sadly, and blundered in the prayers; the fine chapter, *Man that is born of woman*, was chanted, not read; and the anthem, besides being immeasurably tedious, would have served as well for a nuptial. The real serious part was the figure of the Duke of Cumberland, heightened by a thousand melancholy circumstances. He had a dark brown adonis, and a cloak of black cloth, with a train of five yards. Attending the funeral of a father could not be pleasant; his leg extremely bad, yet forced to stand upon it near two hours; his face bloated and distorted with his late

Duke of Cumberland, George III's uncle.   *adonis*, a kind of wig.

paralytic stroke, which has affected too one of his eyes; and placed over the mouth of the vault, into which, in all probability, he must himself so soon descend; think how unpleasant a situation! He bore it all with a firm and unaffected countenance. This grave scene was fully contrasted by the burlesque Duke of Newcastle. He fell into a fit of crying the moment he came into the chapel, and flung himself back in a stall, the archbishop hovering over him with a smelling-bottle; but in two minutes his curiosity got the better of his hypocrisy, and he ran about the chapel with his glass, to spy who was or was not there, spying with one hand, and mopping his eyes with the other. Then returned the fear of catching cold; and the Duke of Cumberland, who was sinking with heat, felt himself weighed down, and turning round, found it was the Duke of Newcastle standing upon his train, to avoid the chill of the marble. It was very theatric to look down into the vault, where the coffin lay, attended by mourners with lights. Clavering, the groom of the bedchamber, refused to sit up with the body, and was dismissed by the King's order.

I have nothing more to tell you but a trifle, a very trifle. The King of Prussia has totally defeated Marshal Daun.[1] This, which would have been prodigious news a month ago, is nothing to-day; it only takes its turn among the questions, "Who is to be groom of the bedchamber? What is Sir T. Robinson to have?" I have been to Leicester Fields to-day; the crowd was immoderate; I don't believe it will continue so. Good-night. Yours ever.

Horace Walpole, Letters

Leicester Fields. Leicester House was the residence of the Prince of Wales.

[1] In the battle of Torgau, in Saxony, Frederick the Great defeated the Austrians under Marshal Daun (Seven Years' War). The battle was fought Nov. 3, 1760.

THE STORY OF LE FEVER

1762

i

It was some time in the summer of that year in which *Dendermond* was taken by the allies — which was about seven years before my father came into the country — and about as many, after that time, that my uncle *Toby* and *Trim* had privately decamped from my father's house in town, in order to lay some of the finest sieges to some of the finest fortified cities in *Europe* —— when my uncle *Toby* [1] was one evening getting his supper, with *Trim* sitting behind him at a small sideboard — I say, sitting — for in consideration of the corporal's lame knee (which sometimes gave him exquisite pain) — when my uncle *Toby* dined or supped alone, he would never suffer the corporal to stand; and the poor fellow's veneration for his master was such, that, with a proper artillery, my uncle *Toby* could have taken *Dendermond* itself, with less trouble than he was able to gain this point over him; for many a time when my uncle *Toby* supposed the corporal's leg was at rest, he would look back, and detect him standing behind him with the most dutiful respect: this bred more little squabbles betwixt them, than all other causes for five-and-twenty years together. —— But this is neither here nor there — why do I mention it? —— Ask my pen — it governs me — I govern not it.

He was one evening sitting thus at his supper, when the landlord of the little inn in the village came into the parlor, with an empty phial in his hand, to beg a glass or two of sack; 'Tis for a poor gentleman — I

Dendermond, a town in Belgium.

[1] Uncle Toby and Corporal Trim, his servant, were retired soldiers, who made a hobby of miniature warfare, played in a garden with toy soldiers.

think, of the army, said the landlord, who has been
taken ill at my house four days ago, and has never held
up his head since, or had a desire to taste any thing
till just now, that he has a fancy for a glass of sack and
a thin toast, —— *I think*, says he, taking his hand
from his forehead, *it would comfort me* ——

—— If I could neither beg, borrow, or buy such a
thing — added the landlord — I would almost steal it
for the poor gentleman, he is so ill. —— I hope in God
he will still mend, continued he — we are all of us concerned for him.

Thou art a good-natured soul, I will answer for thee,
cried my uncle *Toby;* and thou shalt drink the poor
gentleman's health in a glass of sack thyself — and
take a couple of bottles with my service, and tell him
he is heartily welcome to them, and to a dozen more if
they will do him good.

Though I am persuaded, said my uncle *Toby*, as the
landlord shut the door, he is a very compassionate
fellow — *Trim* — yet I cannot help entertaining a
high opinion of his guest too; there must be something
more than common in him, that in so short a time
should win so much upon the affections of his host;
—— And of his whole family, added the corporal, for
they all are concerned for him. — Step after him, said
my uncle *Toby* — do, *Trim* — and ask if he knows his
name.

—— I have quite forgot it truly, said the landlord,
coming back into the parlour with the corporal — but
I can ask his son again:—— Has he a son with him
then? said my uncle *Toby*. — A boy, replied the landlord, of about eleven or twelve years of age; — but the
poor creature has tasted almost as little as his father;
he does nothing but mourn and lament for him night
and day: —— He has not stirred from the bed-side
these two days.

My uncle *Toby* laid down his knife and fork, and thrust his plate from before him, as the landlord gave him the account; and *Trim*, without being ordered, took away, without saying one word, and in a few minutes after brought him his pipe and tobacco.

—— Stay in the room a little, said my uncle *Toby*.

Trim! —— said my uncle *Toby*, after he lighted his pipe, and smoak'd about a dozen whiffs. —— *Trim* came in front of his master, and made his bow — my uncle *Toby* smoak'd on, and said no more. —— Corporal! said my uncle *Toby* —— the corporal made his bow. —— My uncle *Toby* proceeded no farther, but finished his pipe.

Trim! said my uncle Toby, I have a project in my head, as it is a bad night, of wrapping myself up warm in my roquelaure, and paying a visit to this poor gentleman. —— Your honour's roquelaure, replied the corporal, has not once been had on, since the night before your honour received your wound, when we mounted guard in the trenches before the gate of St. *Nicholas;* —— and besides, it is so cold and rainy a night, that what with the roquelaure, and what with the weather, 'twill be enough to give your honour your death, and bring on your honour's trouble in your groin. I fear so, replied my uncle *Toby;* but I am not at rest in my mind, *Trim*, since the account the landlord has given me. —— I wish I had not known so much of this affair — added my uncle *Toby* — or that I had known more of it: —— How shall we manage it? Leave it, an't please your honour, to me, quoth the corporal; —— I'll take my hat and stick and go to the house and reconnoitre, and act accordingly; and I will bring your honour a full account in an hour. —— Thou shalt go, *Trim*, said my uncle *Toby*, and here's a shilling for thee to drink with his servant. —— I shall

get it all out of him, said the corporal shutting the
door.

My uncle *Toby* filled his second pipe; and had it not
been, that he now and then wandered from the point,
with considering whether it was not full as well to
have the curtain of the tenaille a straight line, as a
crooked one — he might be said to have thought of
nothing else but poor *Le Fever* and his boy the whole
time he smoaked it.

ii

It was not till my uncle *Toby* had knocked the ashes
out of his third pipe, that corporal *Trim* returned from
the inn, and gave him the following account.

I despaired, at first, said the corporal, of being able
to bring back your honour any kind of intelligence concerning the poor sick lieutenant — Is he in the army,
then? said my uncle *Toby* —— He is, said the corporal —— And in what regiment? said my uncle *Toby*
—— I'll tell your honour, replied the corporal, every
thing straight forwards, as I learnt it. — Then, *Trim*,
I'll find another pipe, said my uncle *Toby*, and not interrupt thee till thou hast done; so sit down at thy
ease, *Trim*, in the window-seat, and begin thy story
again. The corporal made his old bow, which generally spoke as plain as a bow could speak it — *Your
honour is good:* —— And having done that, he sat
down, as he was ordered — and begun the story to
my uncle *Toby* over again in pretty near the same
words.

I despaired at first, said the corporal, of being able
to bring back any intelligence to your honour, about
the lieutenant and his son; for when I asked where his
servant was, from whom I made myself sure of knowing every thing which was proper to be asked — That's

a right distinction, *Trim,* said my uncle *Toby* — I was answered, an' please your honour, that he had no servant with him; —— that he had come to the inn with hired horses, which, upon finding himself unable to proceed (to join, I suppose, the regiment), he had dismissed the morning after he came. —— If I get better, my dear, said he, as he gave his purse to his son to pay the man — we can hire horses from hence. —— But alas! the poor gentleman will never get from hence, said the landlady to me — for I heard the death-watch all night long; —— and when he dies, the youth, his son, will certainly die with him; for he is broken-hearted already.

I was hearing this account, continued the corporal, when the youth came into the kitchen, to order the thin toast the landlord spoke of; —— but I will do it for my father myself, said the youth. —— Pray let me save you the trouble, young gentleman, said I, taking up a fork for the purpose, and offering him a chair to sit down upon by the fire, whilst I did it. —— I believe, Sir, said he, very modestly, I can please him best myself. —— I am sure, said I, his honour will not like the toast the worse for being toasted by an old soldier. —— The youth took hold of my hand, and instantly burst into tears. —— Poor youth! said my uncle *Toby* — he has been bred up from an infant in the army, and the name of a soldier, *Trim,* sounded in his ears like the name of a friend; — I wish I had him here.

—— I never, in the longest march, said the corporal, had so great a mind to my dinner, as I had to cry with him for company: — What could be the matter with me, an' please your honour? Nothing in the world, *Trim,* said my uncle *Toby,* blowing his nose — but that thou art a good-natured fellow.

When I gave him the toast, continued the corporal, I thought it was proper to tell him I was captain *Shandy's* servant, and that your honour (though a stranger) was extremely concerned for his father; — and that if there was any thing in your house or cellar —— (And thou might'st have added my purse too, said my uncle *Toby*) —— he was heartily welcome to it: —— He made a very low bow (which was meant for your honour), but no answer — for his heart was full — so he went upstairs with the toast; — I warrant you, my dear, said I, as I opened the kitchen-door, your father will be well again. —— Mr. *Yorick's* curate was smoaking a pipe by the kitchen fire — but said not a word good or bad to comfort the youth. —— I thought it wrong; added the corporal —— I think so too, said my uncle *Toby*.

When the lieutenant had taken his glass of sack and toast, he felt himself a little revived, and sent down into the kitchen, to let me know, that in about ten minutes he should be glad if I would step up stairs. —— I believe, said the landlord, he is going to say his prayers —— for there was a book laid upon the chair by his bedside, and as I shut the door, I saw his son take up a cushion. ——

I thought, said the curate, that you gentlemen of the army, Mr. *Trim*, never said your prayers at all. —— I heard the poor gentleman say his prayers last night, said the landlady, very devoutly, and with my own ears, or I could not have believed it. —— Are you sure of it? replied the curate. —— A soldier, an' please your reverence, said I, prays as often (of his own accord) as a parson —— and when he is fighting for his king, and for his own life, and for his honour too, he has the most reason to pray to God of any one in the

Mr. Yorick, Sterne's name for himself.

whole world. —— 'Twas well said of thee, *Trim*, said my
uncle *Toby*. —— But when a soldier, said I, an' please
your reverence, has been standing for twelve hours together in the trenches, up to his knees in cold water —
or engaged, said I, for months together in long and
dangerous marches; — harassed, perhaps, in his rear
to-day; — harassing others to-morrow; — detached
here; — countermanded there; — resting this night
out upon his arms; — beat up in his shirt the next; —
benumbed in his joints; — perhaps without straw in
his tent to kneel on; — must say his prayers *how* and
when he can. —— I believe, said I — for I was piqued,
quoth the corporal, for the reputation of the army —
I believe, an' please your reverence, said I, that when
a soldier gets time to pray — he prays as heartily as a
parson — though not with all his fuss and hypocrisy.
—— Thou shouldst not have said that, *Trim*, said my
uncle *Toby* — for God only knows who is a hypocrite,
and who is not; —— At the great and general review
of us all, corporal, at the day of judgment (and not till
then) — it will be seen who has done their duties in
this world — and who has not; and we shall be advanced, *Trim*, accordingly. —— I hope we shall, said
Trim. —— It is in the Scripture, said my uncle *Toby;*
and I will shew it thee to-morrow: — In the mean
time we may depend upon it, *Trim*, for our comfort,
said my uncle *Toby*, that God Almighty is so good and
just a governor of the world, that if we have but done
our duties in it — it will never be enquired into,
whether we have done them in a red coat or a black
one: —— I hope not, said the corporal. —— But go
on, *Trim*, said my uncle *Toby*, with thy story.

When I went up, continued the corporal, into the
lieutenant's room, which I did not do till the expira-
tion of the ten minutes — he was lying in his bed with

his head raised upon his hand, with his elbow upon the pillow, and a clean white cambric handkerchief beside it: —— The youth was just stooping to take up the cushion, upon which I supposed he had been kneeling — the book was laid upon the bed — and, as he rose, in taking up the cushion with one hand, he reached out his other to take it away at the same time —— Let it remain there, my dear, said the lieutenant.

He did not offer to speak to me, till I had walked up close to his bed-side: — If you are captain *Shandy's* servant, said he, you must present my thanks to your master, with my little boy's thanks along with them, for his courtesy to me; — if he was of *Leven's* — said the lieutenant. — I told him your honour was — Then, said he, I served three campaigns with him in *Flanders*, and remember him — but 'tis most likely, as I had not the honour of any acquaintance with him, that he knows nothing of me. —— You will tell him, however, that the person his good-nature has laid under obligations to him, is one *Le Fever*, a lieutenant of *Angus's* —— but he knows me not — said he, a second time, musing; —— possibly he may my story — added he — pray tell the captain, I was the ensign at *Breda*, whose wife was most unfortunately killed with a musket-shot, as she lay in my arms in my tent. —— I remember the story, an't please your honour, said I, very well. —— Do you so? said he, wiping his eyes with his handkerchief — then well may I. — In saying this, he drew a little ring out of his bosom, which seemed tied with a black ribband about his neck, and kiss'd it twice. —— Here, *Billy*, said he —— the boy flew across the room to the bed-side — and falling down upon his knee, took the ring in his hand, and

Breda, a town in the Netherlands.

kissed it too — then kissed his father, and sat down upon the bed and wept.

I wish, said my uncle *Toby*, with a deep sigh — I wish, *Trim*, I was asleep.

Your honour, replied the corporal, is too much concerned; — shall I pour your honour out a glass of sack to your pipe? —— Do, *Trim*, said my uncle *Toby*.

I remember, said my uncle *Toby*, sighing again, the story of the ensign and his wife, with a circumstance his modesty omitted; — and particularly well that he, as well as she, upon some account or other (I forget what) was universally pitied by the whole regiment; — but finish the story thou art upon: — 'Tis finished already, said the corporal — for I could stay no longer — so wished his honour a good night; young *Le Fever* rose from off the bed, and saw me to the bottom of the stairs; and as we went down together, told me, they had come from *Ireland*, and were on their route to join the regiment in *Flanders*. —— But alas! said the corporal — the lieutenant's last day's march is over. — Then what is to become of the poor boy? cried my uncle *Toby*.

iii

It was to my uncle *Toby's* eternal honour —— though I tell it only for the sake of those, who, when coop'd in betwixt a natural and a positive law, know not, for their souls, which way in the world to turn themselves —— That notwithstanding my uncle *Toby* was warmly engaged at that time in carrying on the siege of *Dendermond*, parallel with the allies, who pressed theirs on so vigorously, that they scarce allowed him time to get his dinner —— that nevertheless he gave up *Dendermond*, though he had already made a lodgment upon the counterscarp; — and bent his whole thoughts towards the private distresses at the inn; and except that he ordered the garden gate to be bolted up, by which he might be said to have turned the siege of *Dendermond* into a blockade — he left *Dendermond* to itself — to be relieved or not by the *French* king, as the *French* king thought good; and only considered how he himself should relieve the poor lieutenant and his son.

—— That kind BEING, who is a friend to the friendless, shall recompence thee for this.

Thou hast left the matter short, said my uncle *Toby*, to the corporal, as he was putting him to bed —— and I will tell thee in what, *Trim*. —— In the first place, when thou madest an offer of my services to *Le Fever* —— as sickness and travelling are both expensive, and thou knowest he was but a poor lieutenant, with a son to subsist as well as himself out of his pay — that thou didst not make an offer to him of my purse; because, had he stood in need, thou knowest, *Trim*, he had been as welcome to it as myself. —— Your honour knows, said the corporal, I had no orders; —— True, quoth my uncle *Toby* — thou didst very right, *Trim*, as a soldier — but certainly very wrong as a man.

In the second place, for which, indeed, thou hast the same excuse, continued my uncle *Toby* —— when thou offeredst him whatever was in my house —— thou shouldst have offered him my house too: —— A sick brother officer should have the best quarters, *Trim*, and if we had him with us — we could tend and look to him: —— Thou art an excellent nurse thyself, *Trim* — and what with thy care of him, and the old woman's and his boy's, and mine together, we might recruit him again at once, and set him upon his legs. ——

—— In a fortnight or three weeks, added my uncle

Toby, smiling —— he might march. —— He will never march; an' please your honour, in this world, said the corporal: —— He will march; said my uncle *Toby*, rising up from the side of the bed, with one shoe off: —— An' please your honour, said the corporal, he will never march but to his grave: —— He shall march, cried my uncle *Toby*, marching the foot which had a shoe on, though without advancing an inch — he shall march to his regiment. —— He cannot stand it, said the corporal; —— He shall be supported, said my uncle *Toby;* —— He'll drop at last, said the corporal, and what will become of his boy? —— He shall not drop, said my uncle *Toby*, firmly. —— A-well-o'day — do what we can for him, said *Trim*, maintaining his point — the poor soul will die: —— He shall not die, by G——, cried my uncle *Toby*.

— The ACCUSING SPIRIT, which flew up to heaven's chancery with the oath, blush'd as he gave it in; — and the RECORDING ANGEL, as he wrote it down, dropp'd a tear upon the word, and blotted it out for ever.

iv

—— My uncle *Toby* went to his bureau — put his purse into his breeches pocket, and having ordered the corporal to go early in the morning for a physician — he went to bed, and fell asleep.

v

The sun looked bright the morning after, to every eye in the village but *Le Fever's* and his afflicted son's; the hand of death press'd heavy upon his eye-lids —— and hardly could the wheel at the cistern turn round its circle — when my uncle *Toby*, who had rose up an hour before his wonted time, entered the lieutenant's room, and without preface or apology, sat himself down upon the chair by the bed-side, and, independently of all modes and customs, opened the curtain in the manner an old friend and brother officer would have done it, and asked him how he did — how he had rested in the night — what was his complaint — where was his pain — and what he could do to help him: —— and without giving him time to answer any one of the enquiries, went on, and told him of the little plan which he had been concerting with the corporal the night before for him. ——

—— You shall go home directly, *Le Fever*, said my uncle *Toby*, to my house — and we'll send for a doctor to see what's the matter — and we'll have an apothecary — and the corporal shall be your nurse; —— and I'll be your servant, *Le Fever*.

There was a frankness in my uncle *Toby* — not the *effect* of familiarity — but the *cause* of it — which let you at once into his soul, and shewed you the goodness of his nature; to this, there was something in his looks, and voice, and manner, superadded, which eternally beckoned to the unfortunate to come and take shelter under him; so that before my uncle *Toby* had half finished the kind offers he was making to the father, had the son insensibly pressed up close to his knees, and had taken hold of the breast of his coat, and was pulling it towards him. —— The blood and spirits of *Le Fever*, which were waxing cold and slow within him, and were retreating to their last citadel, the heart — rallied back — the film forsook his eyes for a moment — he looked up wistfully in my uncle *Toby's* face — then cast a look upon his boy —— and that *ligament*, fine as it was — was never broken. ——

Nature instantly ebb'd again — the film returned to its place —— the pulse fluttered —— stopp'd ——

went on —— throbb'd —— stopp'd again —— moved
—— stopp'd —— shall I go on? —— No.

    *Laurence Sterne, The Life and Opinions of Tristram Shandy,
    Gentleman.* Book VI, Chaps. VI–X.

[*Uncle Toby adopts young Le Fever, educates him,
procures a place for him in the army, and, after he
has met with reverses, persuades Mr. Shandy to appoint him tutor to Tristram.*]

THE TORTOISE

April 12, 1772

While I was in Sussex last autumn my residence was
at the village near Lewes. . . . On the 1st of November
I remarked that the old tortoise . . . began first to dig
the ground in order to the forming of its hybernacu-
lum, which it had fixed on just beside a great tuft of
hepaticas. It scrapes out the ground with its fore-
feet, and throws it up over its back with its hind; but
the motion of its legs is ridiculously slow, little exceeding the hour-hand of a clock. Nothing can be more
assiduous than this creature night and day in scooping
the earth, and forcing its great body into the cavity;
but, as the noons of that season proved unusually
warm and sunny, it was continually interrupted, and
called forth by the heat in the middle of the day; and
though I continued there till the 13th of November,
yet the work remained unfinished. Harsher weather,
and frosty mornings, would have quickened its opera-
tions.

No part of its behaviour ever struck me more than
the extreme timidity it always expresses with regard
to rain; for, though it has a shell that would secure it
against the wheel of a loaded cart, yet does it discover

as much solicitude about rain as a lady dressed in all her best attire, shuffling away on the first sprinklings, and running its head up in a corner. If attended to, it becomes an excellent weather-glass; for as sure as it walks elate, and as it were on tiptoe, feeding with great earnestness in a morning, so sure will it rain before night. It is totally a diurnal animal, and never pretends to stir after it becomes dark. . . . I was much taken with its sagacity in discerning those that do it kind offices; for, as soon as the good lady comes in sight who has waited on it for more than thirty years, it hobbles towards its benefactress with awkward alacrity, but remains inattentive to strangers. Thus not only the "ox knoweth his owner, and the ass his master's crib,"[1] but the most abject reptile and torpid of beings distinguishes the hand that feeds it, and is touched with the feelings of gratitude.

In about three days after I left Sussex, the tortoise retired into the ground under the hepatica.

April 21, 1780

The old Sussex tortoise . . . is become my property. I dug it out of its winter dormitory in March last, when it was awakened enough to express its resentment by hissing; and, packing it in a box with earth, carried it eighty miles in post-chaises. The rattle and hurry of the journey so perfectly roused it that, when I turned it out on a border, it walked twice down to the bottom of my garden. However, in the evening, the weather being cold, it buried itself in the loose mould, and continues still concealed. As it will be under my eye, I shall now have an opportunity of enlarging my observations on its mode of life; and already perceive that, towards the time of coming forth,

[1] Isaiah, I, 3.

it opens a breathing place in the ground near its head — requiring, I conclude, a freer respiration as it becomes more alive. This creature not only goes under the earth from the middle of November to the middle of April, but sleeps great part of the summer, and often does not stir in the morning till late. Besides, it retires to rest for every shower, and does not move at all in wet days.

When one reflects on the state of this strange being, it is a matter of wonder to find that Providence should bestow such a profusion of days, such a seeming waste of longevity, on a reptile that appears to relish it so little as to squander more than two-thirds of its existence in a joyless stupor, and be lost to all sensation for months together in the profoundest of slumbers.

While I was writing this letter, a moist and warm afternoon, with the thermometer at 50°, brought forth troops of shell-snails; and at the same juncture the tortoise heaved up the mould and put out its head, and the next morning came forth, as it were, raised from the dead, and walked about till four in the afternoon. This was a curious coincidence, a very amusing occurrence! to see such a similarity of feeling between the two φερέοικοι — for so the Greeks call both the shell-snail and the tortoise. . . .

Because we call this creature an abject reptile, we are too apt to undervalue his abilities and depreciate his powers of instinct. Yet he is, as Mr. Pope says of his lord —

Much too wise to walk into a well,[1]

and has so much discernment as not to fall down a haha, but to stop and withdraw from the brink with

[1] Satires, VI, 191.

the readiest precaution. Though he loves warm weather, he avoids the hot sun, because his thick shell, when once heated, would, as the poet says of solid armour, "scald with safety." He therefore spends the more sultry hours under the umbrella of a large cabbage leaf, or amidst the waving forests of an asparagus bed. But, as he avoids heat in summer, so, in the decline of the year, he improves the faint autumnal beams by getting within the reflection of a fruit-wall; and though he never has read that planes inclining to the horizon receive a greater share of warmth, he inclines his shell, by tilting it against the wall, to collect and admit every feeble ray.

Pitiable seems the condition of this poor embarrassed reptile — to be cased in a suit of ponderous armour, which he cannot lay aside; to be imprisoned, as it were, within his own shell, must preclude, we should suppose, all activity and disposition for enterprise. Yet there is a season of the year (usually the beginning of June) when his exertions are remarkable. He then walks on tiptoe, and is stirring by five in the morning; and, traversing the garden, examines every wicket and interstice in the fences, through which he will escape if possible; and often has eluded the care of the gardener, and wandered to some distant field. The motives that impel him to undertake these rambles seem to be of the amorous kind; his fancy then becomes intent on attachments, which transport him beyond his usual gravity, and induce him to forget for a time his ordinary solemn deportment.

Gilbert White, The Natural History and Antiquities of Selbourne. 1789.

BOSWELL AS BEAR-LEADER

1776

I am now to record a very curious incident in Dr. Johnson's life which fell under my own observation; of which *pars magna fui*, and which I am persuaded will, with the liberal-minded, be much to his credit.

My desire of being acquainted with celebrated men of every description had made me, much about the same time, obtain an introduction to Dr. Samuel Johnson and to John Wilkes, Esq.[1] Two men more different could perhaps not be selected out of all mankind. They had even attacked one another with some asperity in their writings; yet I lived in habits of friendship with both. I could fully relish the excellence of each; for I have ever delighted in that intellectual chemistry which can separate good qualities from evil in the same person.

Sir John Pringle,[2] "mine own friend, and my father's friend," between whom and Dr. Johnson I in vain wished to establish an acquaintance, as I respected and lived in intimacy with both of them, observed to me once, very ingeniously, "It is not in friendship as in mathematics, where two things, each equal to a third, are equal between themselves. You agree with Johnson as a middle quality, and you agree with me as a middle quality; but Johnson and I should not agree." Sir John was not sufficiently flexible; so I desisted; knowing, indeed, that the repulsion was equally strong on the part of Johnson; who, I know not from what cause, unless his being a Scotchman, had formed a very erroneous opinion of Sir John. But I conceived

pars magna fui, a great part was.

[1] John Wilkes (1727–97), a politician, whose stormy history made him one of the best-known men of his time.

[2] Sir John Pringle (1707–82), an eminent physician, who reformed the medical service of the army.

an irresistible wish, if possible, to bring Dr. Johnson and Mr. Wilkes together. How to manage it, was a nice and difficult matter.

My worthy booksellers and friends, Messieurs Dilly, in the Poultry, at whose hospitable and well-covered table I have seen a greater number of literary men than at any other, except that of Sir Joshua Reynolds, had invited me to meet Mr. Wilkes and some more gentlemen on Wednesday, May 15. "Pray," said I, "let us have Dr. Johnson." "What with Mr. Wilkes? not for the world," said Mr. Edward Dilly: "Dr. Johnson would never forgive me." "Come," said I, "if you'll let me negotiate for you, I will be answerable that all shall go well." Dilly: "Nay, if you will take it upon you, I am sure I shall be very happy to see them both here."

Notwithstanding the high veneration which I entertained for Dr. Johnson, I was sensible that he was sometimes a little actuated by the spirit of contradiction, and by means of that I hoped I should gain my point. I was persuaded that if I had come upon him with a direct proposal: "Sir, will you dine in company with Jack Wilkes?" he would have flown into a passion, and would probably have answered, "Dine with Jack Wilkes, Sir! I'd as soon dine with Jack Ketch." I therefore, while we were sitting quietly by ourselves at his house in an evening, took occasion to open my plan thus: "Mr. Dilly, Sir, sends his respectful compliments to you, and would be happy if you would do him the honour to dine with him on Wednesday next along with me, as I must go soon to Scotland." Johnson. "Sir, I am obliged to Mr. Dilly. I will wait upon him." Boswell. "Provided, Sir, I suppose, that the

Messrs. Dilly, three brothers, John, Edward, and Charles. Their firm published Boswell's *Johnson*.
Jack Ketch, a hangman.

company which he is to have is agreeable to you?" Johnson. "What do you mean, Sir? What do you take me for? Do you think I am so ignorant of the world as to imagine that I am to prescribe to a gentleman what company he is to have at his table?" Boswell. "I beg your pardon, Sir, for wishing to prevent you from meeting people whom you may not like. Perhaps he may have some of what he calls his patriotic friends with him." Johnson. "Well, Sir, and what then? What care *I* for his patriotic friends? Poh!" Boswell. "I should not be surprised to find Jack Wilkes there." Johnson. "And if Jack Wilkes *should* be there, what is that to me, Sir? My dear friend, let us have no more of this. I am sorry to be angry with you; but really it is treating me strangely to talk to me as if I could not meet any company whatever, occasionally." Boswell. "Pray forgive me, Sir: I meant well. But you shall meet whoever comes, for me." Thus I secured him, and told Dilly that he would find him very well pleased to be one of his guests on the day appointed.

Upon the much expected Wednesday, I called upon him about half an hour before dinner, as I often did when we were both to dine out together, to see that he was ready in time, and to accompany him. I found him buffeting his books as upon a former occasion, covered with dust, and making no preparation for going abroad. "How is this, Sir?" said I. "Don't you recollect that you are to dine at Mr. Dilly's?" Johnson. "Sir, I did not think of going to Dilly's; it went out of my head. I have ordered dinner at home with Mrs. Williams." [1] Boswell. "But, my dear Sir, you know you were engaged to Mr. Dilly, and I told him so. He will expect you, and will be much disappointed if

[1] Mrs. Williams, a protégé of Johnson's, who lived in his house.

you don't come." Johnson. "You must talk to Mrs. Williams about this."

Here was a sad dilemma. I feared that what I was so confident I had secured would yet be frustrated. He had accustomed himself to show Mrs. Williams such a degree of humane attention as frequently imposed some restraint upon him; and I knew that if she should be obstinate, he would not stir. I hastened downstairs to the blind lady's room, and told her I was in great uneasiness, for Dr. Johnson had engaged to me to dine this day at Mr. Dilly's, but that he had forgotten the engagement, and had ordered dinner at home. "Yes, Sir," said she, pretty peevishly, "Dr. Johnson is to dine at home." "Madam," said I, "his respect for you is such that I know he will not leave you, unless you absolutely desire it. But as you have so much of his company, I hope you will be good enough to forego it for a day, as Mr. Dilly is a very worthy man, has frequently had agreeable parties at his house for Dr. Johnson, and will be vexed if the Doctor neglects him to-day. And then, Madam, be pleased to consider my situation; I carried the message, and I assured Mr. Dilly that Dr. Johnson was to come; and no doubt he has made a dinner, and invited a company, and boasted of the honour he expected to have. I shall be quite disgraced if the Doctor is not there." She gradually softened to my solicitations, which were certainly as earnest as most entreaties to ladies upon any occasion, and was graciously pleased to empower me to tell Dr. Johnson, "that all things considered, she thought he should certainly go." I flew back to him, still in dust, and careless of what should be the event, "indifferent in his choice to go or stay:" but as soon as I announced to him Mrs. Williams's consent, he roared, "Frank, a

clean shirt," and was very soon dressed. When I had
him fairly seated in a hackney-coach with me, I exulted as much as a fortune-hunter who has got an
heiress into a postchaise with him to set out for Gretna
Green.[1]

When we entered Mr. Dilly's drawing-room, he
found himself in the midst of a company he did not
know. I kept myself snug and silent, watching how
he would conduct himself. I observed him whispering to Mr. Dilly, "Who is that gentleman, Sir?" —
"Mr. Arthur Lee."[2]   Johnson: "Too, too, too"
(under his breath) which was one of his habitual mut-
terings. Mr. Arthur Lee could not but be very obnox-
ious to Johnson, for he was not only a patriot, but
an American. He was afterwards minister from the
United States at the Court of Madrid.   "And who is
the gentleman in lace?" — "Mr. Wilkes, Sir."   This
information confounded him still more; he had some
difficulty to restrain himself, and taking up a book, sat
down upon a window-seat and read, or at least kept
his eye upon it for some time, till he composed himself.
His feelings, I dare say, were awkward enough.   But
he no doubt recollected having rated me for supposing
that he could be at all disconcerted by any company,
and he, therefore, resolutely set himself to behave
quite as an easy man of the world, who could adapt
himself at once to the disposition and manners of those
whom he might chance to meet.

The cheering sound of "Dinner is upon the table,"
dissolved his reverie, and we *all* sat down without any
symptom of ill-humour.   There were present, beside
Mr. Wilkes, and Mr. Arthur Lee, who was an old
companion of mine when he studied physic at Edin-

[1] Gretna Green, a village in Scotland, a former scene of runaway marriages.

[2] Arthur Lee, American diplomatist and statesman.

burgh, Mr. (now Sir John) Miller, Dr. Lettsom, and Mr. Slater, the druggist.[1] Mr. Wilkes placed himself next to Dr. Johnson, and behaved to him with so much attention and politeness that he gained upon him insensibly. No man ate more heartily than Johnson, or loved better what was nice and delicate. Mr. Wilkes was very assiduous in helping him to some fine veal. "Pray give me leave, sir — It is better here — A little of the brown — Some fat, sir — A little of the stuffing — Some gravy — Let me have the pleasure of giving you some butter — Allow me to recommend a squeeze of this orange; or the lemon, perhaps, may have more zest." "Sir, sir, I am obliged to you, sir," cried Johnson, bowing and turning his head to him with a look for some time of "surly virtue," but, in a short while, of complacency.

Foote[2] being mentioned, Johnson said, "He is not a good mimic." One of the company added, "A merryandrew, a buffoon." Johnson: "But he has wit too, and is not deficient in ideas, and not empty of reading; he has knowledge enough to fill up his part. One species of wit he has in an eminent degree, that of escape. You drive him into a corner with both hands; but he's gone, sir, when you think you have got him — like an animal that jumps over your head. Then he has a great range for wit; he never lets truth stand between him and a jest, and he is sometimes mighty coarse. Garrick is under many restraints from which Foote is free." Wilkes: "Garrick's wit is more like Lord Chesterfield's." Johnson: "The first time I was in company with Foote was at Fitzherbert's. Having no good opinion of the fellow, I was resolved not to be

"surly virtue," Johnson's London, a Poem, 145.

[1] Of these only Dr. John Coakley Lettsom is remembered. He was a Quaker physician and philanthropist.

[2] Samuel Foote, a famous wit and entertainer.

pleased; and it is very difficult to please a man against his will. I went on eating my dinner pretty sullenly, affecting not to mind him. But the dog was so very comical that I was obliged to lay down my knife and fork, throw myself back upon my chair, and fairly laugh it out.[1] No, sir, he was irresistible. He upon one occasion experienced in an extraordinary degree, the efficacy of his powers of entertaining. Amongst the many and various modes which he tried of getting money, he became a partner with a small-beer brewer, and he was to have a share of the profits for procuring customers amongst his numerous acquaintance. Fitzherbert was one who took his small-beer; but it was so bad that the servants resolved not to drink it. They were at some loss how to notify their resolution, being afraid of offending their master, who they knew liked Foote much as a companion. At last they fixed upon a little black boy, who was rather a favorite, to be their deputy, and deliver their remonstrance; and having invested him with the whole authority of the kitchen, he was to inform Mr. Fitzherbert, in all their names, upon a certain day, that they would drink Mr. Foote's small-beer no longer. On that day Foote happened to dine at Fitzherbert's, and this boy served at table; he was so delighted with Foote's stories, and merriment, and grimace, that when he went downstairs, he told them, 'This is the finest man I have ever seen. I will not deliver your message. I will drink his small-beer.'"

Somebody observed that Garrick could not have done this. Wilkes: "Garrick would have made the small-beer still smaller. He is now leaving the stage; but he will play *Scrub* all his life." I knew that John-

Scrub, a servant of Lady Bountiful's, in Farquhar's *The Beaux' Stratagem.*

[1] Foote told me that Johnson said of him, "For loud obstreperous broad-faced mirth I know not his equal." — *Boswell's note.*

son would let nobody attack Garrick but himself, as Garrick said to me, and I had heard him praise his liberality; so to bring out his commendation of his celebrated pupil, I said loudly, "I have heard Garrick is liberal." Johnson: "Yes, sir, I know that Garrick has given away more money than any man in England that I am acquainted with, and that not from ostentatious views. Garrick was very poor when he began life; so when he came to have money, he probably was very unskilful in giving away, and saved when he should not. But Garrick began to be liberal as soon as he could; and I am of opinion, the reputation of avarice which he has had has been very lucky for him, and prevented his having many enemies. You despise a man for avarice, but do not hate him. Garrick might have been much better attacked for living with more splendour than is suitable to a player: if they had had the wit to have assaulted him in that quarter, they might have galled him more. But they have kept clamouring about his avarice, which has rescued him from much obloquy and envy."

Talking of the great difficulty of obtaining authentic information for biography, Johnson told us, "When I was a young fellow I wanted to write the 'Life of Dryden,' and in order to get materials, I applied to the only two persons then alive who had seen him; these were old Swinney and old Cibber.[1] Swinney's information was no more than this, 'That at Will's coffee-house Dryden had a particular chair for himself, which was set by the fire in winter, and was then called his winter-chair; and that it was carried out for him to the balcony in summer, and was then called his summer-chair.' Cibber could tell no more but 'that he

---

[1] Owen MacSwinney (d. 1754) playwright and theatrical manager. Colley Cibber (1671–1757) actor and dramatist — "old Cibber" to distinguish him from his son, Theophilus, also an actor and dramatist.

remembered him a decent old man, arbiter of critical disputes at Will's.' You are to consider that Cibber was then at a great distance from Dryden, had perhaps one leg only in the room, and durst not draw in the other." Boswell: "But Cibber was a man of observation?" Johnson: "I think not." Boswell: "You will allow his *Apology* to be well done." Johnson: "Very well done, to be sure, sir. That book is a striking proof of the justice of Pope's remark:

'Each might his sev'ral province well command,
  Would all but stoop to what they understand.'" [1]

Boswell: "And his plays are good." Johnson: "Yes; but that was his trade; *l'esprit de corps;* he had been all his life among players and playwriters. I wondered that he had so little to say in conversation, for he had kept the best company, and learnt all that can be got by the ear. He abused Pindar to me, and then showed me an ode of his own, with an absurd couplet, making a linnet soar on an eagle's wing. I told him that when the ancients made a simile they always made it like something real."

Mr. Wilkes remarked, that "among all the bold flights of Shakespeare's imagination, the boldest was making Birnam wood march to Dunsinane; creating a wood where there never was a shrub; a wood in Scotland! — ha! ha! ha!" And he also observed, that "the clannish slavery of the Highlands of Scotland was the single exception to Milton's remark of 'The Mountain Nymph, sweet Liberty,' being worshipped in all hilly countries." "When I was at Inverary (said he), on a visit to my old friend Archibald, Duke of Argyll, his dependents congratulated me on being such a

Apology, Cibber's autobiography.
[1] *Essay on Criticism*, l. 67.

favorite of his Grace. I said, 'It is then, gentlemen, truly lucky for me; for if I had displeased the Duke, and he had wished it, there is not a Campbell among you but would have been ready to bring John Wilkes's head to him in a charger. It would have been only

" Off with his head! So much for *Aylesbury.*" [1]

I was then member for Aylesbury."

Dr. Johnson and Mr. Wilkes talked of the contested passage in Horace's Art of Poetry, " *Difficile est proprie communia dicere.*" Mr. Wilkes, according to my note, gave the interpretation thus: "It is difficult to speak with propriety of common things; as, if a poet had to speak of Queen Caroline drinking tea, he must endeavour to avoid the vulgarity of cups and saucers." But upon reading my note, he tells me that he meant to say, that "the word *communia* being a Roman law-term, signifies here things *communis juris,* that is to say, what have never yet been treated by anybody; and this appears clearly from what followed,

"tuque
Rectius Iliacum carmen deducisi in actus,
Quam si proferres ignota indictaque primus."

You will easier make a tragedy out of the *Iliad* than on any subject not handled before. [2] Johnson: "He means that it is difficult to appropriate to particular persons qualities which are common to all mankind, as Homer has done."

Wilkes: "We have no city poet now; that is an office which has gone into disuse. The last was Elkanah

---

[1] *Richard III,* by Colley Cibber (altered from Shakespeare). — "Off with his head! so much for Buckingham!"

[2] Boswell has here a very long footnote — a little essay on the disputed line quoted in the text. I have omitted it, because he arrives at no conclusion except that the passage in which it occurs is "a *crux* for the critics of Horace."

Settle.[1] There is something in *names* which one cannot help feeling. Now *Elkanah Settle* sounds so *queer*, who can expect much from that name? We should have no hesitation to give it for John Dryden, in preference to Elkanah Settle, from the names only, without knowing their different merits." Johnson: "I suppose, sir, Settle did as well for aldermen in his time, as John Home[2] could do now. Where did Beckford and Trecothick learn English?"

Mr. Arthur Lee mentioned some Scotch who had taken possession of a barren part of America, and wondered why they should choose it. Johnson: "Why, sir, all barrenness is comparative. The *Scotch* would not know it to be barren." Boswell: "Come, come, he is flattering the English. You have now been in Scotland, sir, and say if you did not see meat and drink enough there." Johnson: "Why yes, sir; meat and drink enough to give the inhabitants sufficient strength to run away from home." All these quick and lively sallies were said sportively, quite in jest, and with a smile, which showed that he meant only wit. Upon this topic, he and Mr. Wilkes could perfectly assimilate; here was a bond of union between them, and I was conscious that as both of them had visited Caledonia, both were fully satisfied of the strange, narrow ignorance of those who imagine that it is a land of famine. But they amused themselves with persevering in the old jokes. When I claimed a superiority for Scotland over England in one respect, that no one can be arrested there for debt, merely because another swears it against him; but there must

---

[1] Elkanah Settle (1648–1724), poet and playwright, satirized by Dryden and Pope.
[2] John Home (1722–1808), Scotch dramatist, whose *Douglas* was immensely popular. — Johnson, who is sneering at Home here, had declared that there were not ten good lines in *Douglas*. Beckford and Trecothick are mentioned merely as aldermen who had attained some reputation.

first be the judgment of a court of law ascertaining its justice; and that a seizure of the person, before judgment is obtained, can take place only if his creditor should swear that he is about to fly from the country, or, as it is technically expressed, is *in meditatione fugae*. Wilkes: "That, I should think, may be safely sworn of all the Scotch nation." Johnson (to Mr. Wilkes): "You must know, sir, I lately took my friend Boswell, and showed him genuine civilised life in an English provincial town. I turned him loose at Lichfield, my native city, that he might see for once real civility: for you know he lives among savages in Scotland, and among rakes in London." Wilkes: "Except when he is with grave, sober, decent people, like you and me." Johnson (smiling): "And we ashamed of him."

They were quite frank and easy. Johnson told the story of his asking Mrs. Macaulay to allow her footman to sit down with them, to prove the ridiculousness of the argument for the equality of mankind; and he said to me afterwards, with a nod of satisfaction, "You saw Mr. Wilkes acquiesced." Wilkes talked with all imaginable freedom of the ludicrous title given to the Attorney-General, *Diabolus Regis*; adding, "I have reason to know something about that officer; for I was prosecuted for a libel." Johnson, who many people would have supposed must have been furiously angry at hearing this talked of so lightly, said not a word. He was now, *indeed*, "a good-humoured fellow."

After dinner, we had an accession of Mrs. Knowles,[1] the Quaker lady, well known for her various talents, and of Mr. Alderman Lee. Amidst some patriotic groans, somebody (I think the alderman) said, "Poor

Diabolus Regis, King's devil (but here *diabolus* means *accuser* or *prosecutor*).
[1] Mrs. Mary Knowles (1733–1807), a witty and beautiful poet and writer on religious topics.

old England is lost." Johnson: "Sir, it is not so much to be lamented that Old England is lost, as that the Scotch have found it."[1] Wilkes: "Had Lord Bute governed Scotland only, I should not have taken the trouble to write his eulogy, and dedicate my *Mortimer* to him."

Mr. Wilkes held a candle to show a fine print of a beautiful female figure which hung in the room, and pointed out the elegant contour of the bosom, with the finger of an arch connoisseur. He afterwards, in a conversation with me, waggishly insisted, that all the time Johnson showed visible signs of a fervent admiration of the corresponding charms of the fair Quaker.

This record, though by no means as perfect as I could wish, will serve to give a notion of a very curious interview, which was not only pleasing at the time, but had the agreeable and benignant effect of reconciling any animosity, and sweetening any acidity, which in the various bustle of political contest, had been produced in the minds of two men, who, though widely different, had so many things in common — classical learning, modern literature, wit and humour, and ready repartee — that it would have been much to be regretted if they had been for ever at a distance from each other.

Mr. Burke gave me much credit for this successful *negotiation*; and pleasantly said, "that there was nothing equal to it in the whole history of the *Corps Diplomatique*."

I attended Dr. Johnson home, and had the satisfaction to hear him tell Mrs. Williams how much he

---

[1] It would not become me to expatiate on this strong and pointed remark, in which a very great deal of meaning is condensed. — *Boswell's note.* Boswell, as a Scotchman, feels that he can make no defense of Bute, his extremely unpopular countryman.

had been pleased with Mr. Wilkes's company, and what an agreeable day he had passed.

James Boswell, The Life of Samuel Johnson, LL.D.

JOHNSON AGAINST GARRICK

Printed 1815

A BURLESQUE

Dr. Samuel Johnson and Sir Joshua Reynolds

Reynolds. Let me alone, I'll bring him out (*Aside*). I have been thinking, Dr. Johnson, this morning, on a matter that has puzzled me very much; it is a subject that I daresay has often passed in your thoughts, and though *I* cannot, I dare say *you* have made up your mind upon it.

Johnson. Tilly fally! what is all this preparation, what is all this mighty matter?

Reynolds. Why, it is a very weighty matter. The subject I have been thinking upon is, predestination and freewill, two things I cannot reconcile together for the life of me; in my opinion, Dr. Johnson, freewill and foreknowledge cannot be reconciled.

Johns. Sir, it is not of very great importance what your opinion is upon such a question.

Reyn. But I meant only, Dr. J., to know your opinion.

Johns. No, sir, you meant no such thing; you meant only to show these gentlemen that you are not the man they took you to be, but that you think of high matters sometimes, and that you may have the credit of having it said that you held an argument with Sam Johnson on predestination and freewill; a subject of that magnitude as to have engaged the attention of the world, to have perplexed the wisdom of man for these two thousand years; a subject on which the fallen angels, who *had not yet lost their original bright-ness,*[1] find themselves *in wandering mazes lost.* That such a subject would be discussed in the levity of convivial conversation, is a degree of absurdity beyond what is easily conceivable.

Reyn. It is so, as you say, to be sure; I talked once to our friend Garrick upon this subject, but I remember we could make nothing of it.

Johns. O noble pair!

Reyn. Garrick was a clever fellow, Dr. J.: Garrick, take him altogether, was certainly a very great man.

Johns. Garrick, sir, may be a great man in your opinion, so far as I know, but he is not in mine; little things are great to little men.

Reyn. I have heard you say, Dr. Johnson ——

Johns. Sir, you never heard me say that David Garrick was a great man; you may have heard me say that Garrick was a good repeater — of other men's words — words put into his mouth by other men: this makes but a faint approach towards being a great man.

Reyn. But take Garrick upon the whole, now, in regard to conversation ——

Johns. Well, sir, in regard to conversation, I never discovered in the conversation of David Garrick any intellectual energy, any wide grasp of thought, any extensive comprehension of mind, or that he possessed any of those powers to which *great* could, in any degree of propriety, be applied.

Reyn. But still ——

Johns. Hold, sir, I have not done — there are, to be sure, in the laxity of colloquial speech, various kinds of greatness; a man may be a great tobacconist, a man may be a great painter, he may be likewise a great

[1] *Paradise Lost*, Book I, 591; Book II, 561.

mimic: now you may be the one, and Garrick the other, and yet neither of you be great men.

Reyn. But, Dr. Johnson ——

Johns. Hold, sir, I have often lamented how dangerous it is to investigate and to discriminate character, to men who have no discriminative powers.

Reyn. But Garrick as a companion, I heard you say — no longer ago than last Wednesday, at Mr. Thrale's table ——

Johns. You tease me, sir. Whatever you may have heard me say, no longer ago than last Wednesday, at Mr. Thrale's table, I tell you I do not say so now: besides, as I said before, you may not have understood me, you misapprehended me, you may not have heard me.

Reyn. I am very sure I heard you.

Johns. Besides, besides, sir, besides — do you not know — are you so ignorant as not to know, that it is the highest degree of rudeness to quote a man against himself?

Reyn. But if you differ from yourself, and give one opinion to-day ——

Johns. Have done, sir: the company you see are tired, as well as myself.

Sir Joshua Reynolds, Dialogues in Imitation of Dr. Johnson's Conversation.

THE EPHEMERA:

AN EMBLEM OF HUMAN LIFE

(*To Madame Brillon, of Passy*)

1778

You may remember, my dear friend, that when we lately spent that happy day in the delightful garden

---

Henry Thrale, a wealthy friend of Johnson's.

and sweet society of the Moulin Joly, I stopped a little in one of our walks, and stayed some time behind the company. We had been shown numberless skeletons of a kind of little fly, called an ephemera, whose successive generations, we are told, were bred and expired within the day. I happened to see a living company of them on a leaf, who appeared to be engaged in conversation. You know I understand all the inferior animal tongues. My too great application to the study of them is the best excuse I can give for the little progress I have made in your charming language. I listened through curiosity to the discourse of these little creatures; but as they, in their natural vivacity, spoke three or four together, I could make but little of their conversation. I found, however, by some broken expressions that I heard now and then, they were disputing warmly on the merit of two foreign musicians, one a *cousin*, the other a *moscheto*; in which dispute they spent their time, seemingly as regardless of the shortness of life as if they had been sure of living a month. Happy people! thought I; you are certainly under a wise, just, and mild government, since you have no public grievances to complain of, nor any subject of contention but the perfections and imperfections of foreign music. I turned my head from them to an old gray-headed one, who was single on another leaf, and talking to himself. Being amused with his soliloquy, I put it down in writing, in hopes it will likewise amuse her to whom I am so much indebted for the most pleasing of all amusements, her delicious company and heavenly harmony.

"It was," said he, "the opinion of learned philos-

Moulin Joly, a little island in the Seine, near Paris.   *cousin*, a gnat
spent their time. "At the time the letter was written, all conversations a
Paris were filled with disputes about the music of Gluck" (*cousin*) "an
Picini" (*mosquito*), "a German and Italian musician." — *Franklin.*

ophers of our race, who lived and flourished long before my time, that this vast world, the Moulin Joly,
could not itself subsist more than eighteen hours; and
I think there was some foundation for that opinion,
since, by the apparent motion of the great luminary
that gives life to all nature, and which in my time has
evidently declined considerably towards the ocean at
the end of our earth, it must then finish its course, be
extinguished in the waters that surround us, and leave
the world in cold and darkness, necessarily producing
universal death and destruction. I have lived seven
of those hours, a great age, being no less than four
hundred and twenty minutes of time. How very few
of us continue so long! I have seen generations born,
flourish, and expire. My present friends are the children and grandchildren of the friends of my youth,
who are now, alas, no more! And I must soon follow
them; for, by the course of nature, though still in
health, I cannot expect to live above seven or eight
minutes longer. What now avails all my toil and
labor, in amassing honeydew on this leaf, which I cannot live to enjoy! What the political struggles I have
been engaged in, for the good of my compatriot inhabitants of this bush, or my philosophical studies for
the benefit of our race in general! for, in politics, what
can laws do without morals? Our present race of
ephemeræ will, in a course of minutes, become corrupt, like those of other and older bushes, and consequently as wretched. And in philosophy how small
our progress! Alas! art is long, and life is short! My
friends would comfort me with the idea of a name,
they say, I shall leave behind me; and they tell me I
have lived long enough to nature and to glory. But
what will fame be to an ephemera who no longer
exists? And what will become of all history in the

eighteenth hour, when the world itself, even the whole Moulin Joly, shall come to its end, and be buried in universal ruin?

To me, after all my eager pursuits, no solid pleasures now remain, but the reflection of a long life spent in meaning well, the sensible conversation of a few good lady ephemeræ, and now and then a kind smile and a tune from the ever-amiable *Brillante*.

Benjamin Franklin, Bagatelles, published 1818

MR. PUFF

A SATIRIC PORTRAIT

1779

The scene is a room in the house of MR. DANGLE, *a gentleman passionately devoted to actors and stage-plays.* MR. SNEER, *a critic, is calling, when a servant announces* MR. PUFF.

Enter PUFF.

Dang. My dear Puff!

Puff. My dear Dangle, how is it with you?

Dang. Mr. Sneer, give me leave to introduce Mr. Puff to you.

Puff. Mr. Sneer is this? — Sir, he is a gentleman whom I have long panted for the honour of knowing — a gentleman whose critical talents and transcendent judgement ——

Sneer. Dear sir ——

Dang. Nay, don't be so modest, Sneer; my friend Puff only talks to you in the style of his profession.

Sneer. His profession.

Puff. Yes, sir; I make no secret of the trade I follow: among friends and brother authors, Dangle knows I

Brillante, Mme. Brillon.

love to be frank on the subject, and to advertise myself
viva voce! — I am, sir, a practitioner in panegyric, or,
to speak more plainly, a professor of the art of puffing,
at your service — or anybody else's.

Sneer. Sir, you are very obliging! — I believe, Mr.
Puff, I have often admired your talents in the daily
prints.

Puff. Yes, sir, I flatter myself I do as much business
that way as any six of the fraternity in town. —
Devilish hard work all the summer, friend Dangle —
never worked harder! But harke'e — the winter
managers were a little sore, I believe.

Dang. No; I believe they took it all in good part.

Puff. Ay! then that must have been affectation in
them: for, egad, there were some of the attacks which
there was no laughing at!

Sneer. Ay, the humorous ones. — But I should
think, Mr. Puff, that authors would in general be able
to do this sort of work for themselves.

Puff. Why, yes — but in a clumsy way. Besides,
we look on that as an encroachment, and so take the
opposite side. I dare say, now, you conceive half the
very civil paragraphs and advertisements you see to
be written by the parties concerned, or their friends?
No such thing: nine out of ten manufactured by me in
the way of business.

Sneer. Indeed!

Puff. Even the auctioneers now — the auctioneers,
I say — though the rogues have lately got some credit
for their language — not an article of the merit theirs:
take them out of their pulpits, and they are as dull as
catalogues! — No, sir; 'twas I first enriched their style
— 'twas I first taught them to crowd their advertisements with panegyrical superlatives, each epithet
rising above the other, like the bidders in their own

auction rooms! From me they learned to inlay their phraseology with variegated chips of exotic metaphor: by me too their inventive faculties were called forth: — yes, sir, by me they were instructed to clothe ideal walls with gratuitous fruits — to insinuate obsequious rivulets into visionary groves — to teach courteous shrubs to nod their approbation of the grateful soil; or on emergencies to raise upstart oaks, where there never had been an acorn; to create a delightful vicinage without the assistance of a neighbour; or fix the temple of Hygeia in the fens of Lincolnshire!

Dang. I am sure you have done them infinite service; for now, when a gentleman is ruined, he parts with his house with some credit.

Sneer. Service! if they had any gratitude, they would erect a statue to him; they would figure him as a presiding Mercury, the god of traffic and fiction, with a hammer in his hand instead of a caduceus. — But pray, Mr. Puff, what first put you on exercising your talents in this way?

Puff. Egad, sir, sheer necessity! — the proper parent of an art so nearly allied to invention. You must know, Mr. Sneer, that from the first time I tried my hand at an advertisement, my success was such, that for some time after I led a most extraordinary life indeed!

Sneer. How, pray?

Puff. Sir, I supported myself two years entirely by my misfortunes.

Sneer. Your misfortunes!

Puff. Yes, sir, assisted by long sickness, and other occasional disorders: and a very comfortable living I had of it.

Sneer. From sickness and misfortune! You practised as a doctor and an attorney at once?

Puff. No, egad; both maladies and miseries were my own.

Sneer. Hey! what the plague!

Dang. 'Tis true, i'faith.

Puff. Hark'ee! — By advertisements — *To the charitable and humane!* and *To those whom Providence hath blessed with affluence!*

Sneer. Oh, I understand you.

Puff. And, in truth, I deserved what I got! for, I suppose never man went through such a series of calamities in the same space of time. Sir, I was five times made a bankrupt, and reduced from a state of affluence, by a train of unavoidable misfortunes: then, sir, though a very industrious tradesman, I was twice burned out, and lost my little all both times: I lived upon those fires a month. I soon after was confined by a most excruciating disorder, and lost the use of my limbs: that told very well; for I had the case strongly attested, and went about to collect the subscriptions myself.

Dang. Egad, I believe that was when you first called on me.

Puff. In November last? — O no; I was at that time a close prisoner in the Marshalsea, for a debt benevolently contracted to serve a friend. I was afterwards twice tapped for a dropsy, which declined into a very profitable consumption. I was then reduced to — O no — then, I became a widow with six helpless children, and being left every time eight months gone with child, and without money to get me into an hospital!

Sneer. And you bore all with patience, I make no doubt?

Puff. Why yes; though I made some occasional attempts at *felo de se*; but as I did not find those rash

felo de se, suicide.

actions answer, I left off killing myself very soon. Well, sir, at last, what with bankruptcies, fires, gout, dropsies, imprisonments, and other valuable calamities, having got together a pretty handsome sum, I determined to quit a business which had always gone rather against my conscience, and in a more liberal way still to indulge my talents for fiction and embellishment, through my favourite channels of diurnal communication — and so, sir, you have my history.

Sneer. Most obligingly communicative indeed! and your confession, if published, might certainly serve the cause of true charity, by rescuing the most useful channels of benevolence from the cant of imposition. But surely, Mr. Puff, there is no great mystery in your present profession?

Puff. Mystery, sir! I will take upon me to say the matter was never scientifically treated nor reduced to rule before.

Sneer. Reduced to rule!

Puff. O Lud, sir, you are very ignorant, I am afraid! — Yes, sir, puffing is of various sorts; the principal are, the puff direct, the puff preliminary, the puff collateral, the puff collusive, and the puff oblique, or puff by implication. These all assume, as circumstances require, the various forms of Letter to the Editor, Occasional Anecdote, Impartial Critique, Observation from Correspondent, or Advertisement from the Party.

Sneer. The puff direct, I can conceive ——

Puff. O yes, that's simple enough! For instance — a new comedy or farce is to be produced at one of the theatres (though by-the-by they don't bring out half what they ought to do) — the author, suppose Mr. Smatter, or Mr. Dapper, or any particular friend of mine — very well; the day before it is to be per-

formed, I write an account of the manner in which it
was received; I have the plot from the author, and
only add — "Characters strongly drawn — highly
coloured — hand of a master — fund of genuine
humour — mine of invention — neat dialogue —
Attic salt." Then for the performance — "Mr. Dodd
was astonishingly great in the character of Sir Harry.
That universal and judicious actor, Mr. Palmer, perhaps never appeared to more advantage than in the
colonel; — but it is not in the power of language to do
justice to Mr. King: indeed he more than merited
those repeated bursts of applause which he drew from
a most brilliant and judicious audience. As to the
scenery — the miraculous powers of Mr. De Loutherbourg's [1] pencil are universally acknowledged. In
short, we are at a loss which to admire most, the un-
rivalled genius of the author, the great attention and
liberality of the managers, the wonderful abilities of the
painter, or the incredible exertions of the performers."

Sneer. That's pretty well indeed, sir.

Puff. Oh, cool! — quite cool! — to what I sometimes do.

Sneer. And do you think there are any who are influenced by this?

Puff. O Lud, yes, sir! the number of those who
undergo the fatigue of judging for themselves is very
small indeed.

Sneer. Well, sir, the puff preliminary.

Puff. O, that, sir, does well in the form of a caution.
In a matter of gallantry now — Sir Flimsy Gossamer
wishes to be well with Lady Fanny Fête — he applies
to me — I open trenches for him with a paragraph
in the *Morning Post.* — "It is recommended to the

---

[1] Philip James De Loutherbourg, R.A., noted for the elaborate stage-
settings which he designed. The others were noted actors.

beautiful and accomplished Lady F four stars F dash
E to be on her guard against that dangerous character,
Sir F dash G; who, however pleasing and insinuating
his manners may be, is certainly not remarkable for
the *constancy of his attachments!*" — in italics. Here,
you see, Sir Flimsy Gossamer is introduced to the
particular notice of Lady Fanny, who perhaps never
thought of him before — she finds herself publicly
cautioned to avoid him, which naturally makes her
desirous of seeing him; the observation of their acquaintance causes a pretty kind of mutual embarrassment; this produces a sort of sympathy of interest,
which if Sir Flimsy is unable to improve effectually,
he at least gains the credit of having their names
mentioned together, by a particular set, and in a
particular way — which nine times out of ten is the
full accomplishment of modern gallantry.

Dang. Egad, Sneer, you will be quite an adept in
the business.

Puff. Now, sir, the puff collateral is much used as
an appendage to advertisements, and may take the
form of anecdote. — "Yesterday, as the celebrated
George Bonmot was sauntering down St. James's
Street, he met the lively Lady Mary Myrtle coming
out of the park: — 'Good God, Lady Mary, I'm
surprised to meet you in a white jacket — for I expected never to have seen you, but in a full-trimmed
uniform and a light horseman's cap!' — 'Heavens,
George, where could you have learned that?' —
'Why,' replied the wit, 'I just saw a print of you, in
a new publication called the Camp Magazine; which
by the by, is a devilish clever thing, and is sold at No
3, on the right hand of the way, two doors from the
printing-office, the corner of Ivy Lane, Paternoster
Row, price only one shilling.'"

Sneer. Very ingenious indeed!

Puff. But the puff collusive is the newest of any; for it acts in the disguise of determined hostility. It is much used by bold booksellers and enterprising poets. — "An indignant correspondent observes, that the new poem called *Beelzebub's Cotillon, or Proserpine's Fête Champètre*, is one of the most unjustifiable performances he ever read. The severity with which certain characters are handled is quite shocking: and as there are many descriptions in it too warmly coloured for female delicacy, the shameful avidity with which this piece is bought by all people of fashion is a reproach of the taste of the times, and a disgrace to the delicacy of the age." Here you see the two strongest inducements are held forth; first, that nobody ought to read it; and, secondly, that everybody buys it: on the strength of which the publisher boldly prints the tenth edition, before he has sold ten of the first; and then establishes it by threatening himself with the pillory, or absolutely indicting himself for *scan. mag.*

Dang. Ha! Ha! Ha! — 'gad, I know it is so.

Puff. As to the puff oblique, or puff by implication, it is too various and extensive to be illustrated by an instance: it attracts in titles and presumes in patents; it lurks in the limitation of a subscription, and invites in the assurance of crowd and incommodation at public places; it delights to draw forth concealed merit, with a most disinterested assiduity; and sometimes wears a countenance of smiling censure and tender reproach. It has a wonderful memory for parliamentary debates, and will often give the whole speech of a favoured member with the most flattering accuracy. But, above all, it is a great dealer in reports and sup-

---

scan. mag., scandalum magnatum, offense of defaming magnates of the realm.

positions. It has the earliest intelligence of intended preferments that will reflect honour on the patrons; and embryo promotions of modest gentlemen, who know nothing of the matter themselves. It can hint a ribbon for implied service in the air of common report; and with the carelessness of a casual paragraph, suggest officers into commands, to which they have no pretension but their wishes. This, sir, is the last principal class of the art of puffing — an art which I hope you will now agree with me is of the highest dignity, yielding a tablature of benevolence and public spirit; befriending equally trade, gallantry, criticism, and politics: the applause of genius — the register of charity — the triumph of heroism — the self-defence of contractors — the fame of orators — and the gazette of ministers.

Sneer. Sir, I am completely a convert both to the importance and ingenuity of your profession; and now, sir, there is but one thing which can possibly increase my respect for you, and that is, your permitting me to be present this morning at the rehearsal of your new trag——

Puff. Hush, for heaven's sake! — *My* tragedy! — Egad, Dangle, I take this very ill: you know how apprehensive I am of being known to be the author.

Dang. I'faith I would not have told — but it's in the papers, and your name at length in the *Morning Chronicle.*

Puff. Ah! those damned editors can never keep a secret! —— Well, Mr. Sneer, no doubt you will do me great honour — I shall be infinitely happy — highly flattered ——

Dang. I believe it must be near the time — shall we go together?

---

tablature, mental picture, graphic description.

Puff. No; it will not be yet this hour, for they are always late at the theatre: besides, I must meet you there, for I have some little matters here to send to the papers, and a few paragraphs to scribble before I go. — *Looking at memorandums.* Here is *A conscientious Baker, on the subject of the Army Bread; and a Detester of visible Brickwork, in favour of the new invented Stucco;* both in the style of Junius, and promised for to-morrow. The Thames navigation too is at a stand. Misomud or Anti-shoal must go to work again directly. — Here too are some political memorandums — I see; ay — *To take Paul Jones and get the Indiamen out of the Shannon — reinforce Byron — compel the Dutch to* — so! — I must do that in the evening papers, or reserve it for the *Morning Herald;* for I know that I have undertaken to-morrow, besides, to establish the unanimity of the fleet in the *Public Advertiser,* and to shoot Charles Fox in the *Morning Post.* — So, egad, I ha'n't a moment to lose.

Dang. Well, we'll meet in the Green Room.

[*Exeunt severally.*

Richard Brinsley Sheridan, *The Critic; or, A Tragedy Rehearsed,* Act I. (First acted at Drury Lane Theatre in 1779.)

Junius. The *Letters of Junius* (probably by Sir Philip Francis), noted for their bitterness and sardonic irony.
Misomud, Anti-shoal, names Puff uses when advocating the dredging of the river.
John Paul Jones's flagship, Bonhomme Richard, was a refitted Indiaman. The Shannon is the principal river in Ireland. The Hon. John Byron, vice-admiral, was in 1779 engaged in an expedition against the French. (He was the poet Byron's grandfather.)
Charles James Fox (1749–1806), was an intimate friend of Sheridan. He was wounded in a duel a month after the first production of *The Critic.*

A POET RECEIVES A COMMISSION

(*William Cowper to Lady Hesketh*)

The Lodge, Nov. 27, 1787

It is the part of wisdom, my dearest Cousin, to sit down contented under the demands of necessity, because they are such. I am sensible that you cannot, in my uncle's present infirm state, and of which it is not possible to expect any considerable amendment, indulge either us or yourself with a journey to Weston. Yourself, I say, because I know it will give you pleasure to see *Causidice mi* once more, especially in the comfortable abode where you have placed him, and because after so long imprisonment in London, you, who love the country, and have a taste for it, would of course be glad to return to it. For my own part, to me it is ever new, and though I have now been an inhabitant of this village a twelvemonth, and have during the half of that time been at liberty to expatiate and make discoveries, I am daily finding out fresh scenes and walks, which you would never be satisfied with enjoying — some of them unapproachable by you either on foot or in your carriage. Had you twenty toes (whereas I suppose you have but ten) you could not reach them; and coach-wheels have never been seen there since the flood. Before it indeed, (as Burnet [1] says that the earth was then perfectly free from all inequalities in its surface) they might have been seen there every day. We have other walks, both upon hill tops and in valleys beneath, some of which, by the help of your carriage, and many of them without its help, would be always at your command.

Causidice mi, advocate, barrister. "The appellation which Sir Thomas Hesketh used to give him in jest, when he was of the Temple." — Southey.
[1] Dr. Thomas Burnet (1635–1715), author of *The Sacred Theory of the Earth*.

On Monday morning last, Sam brought me word that there was a man in the kitchen who desired to speak to me. I ordered him in. A plain, decent, elderly figure made its appearance, and, being desired to sit, spoke as follows: "Sir, I am clerk of the parish of All-saints in Northampton; brother of Mr. Cox, the upholsterer. It is customary for the person in my office to annex to a bill of mortality, which he publishes at Christmas, a copy of verses. You will do me a great favour, Sir, if you would furnish me with one." To this I replied, "Mr. Cox, you have several men of genius in your town, why have you not applied to some of them? There is a namesake of yours in particular, Cox, the statuary, who, every body knows, is a first-rate maker of verses. He surely is the man of all the world for your purpose." — "Alas! Sir, I have heretofore borrowed help from him, but he is a gentleman of so much reading that the people of our town cannot understand him." I confess to you, my dear, I felt all the force of the compliment implied in this speech, and was almost ready to answer, "Perhaps, my good friend, they may find me unintelligible too for the same reason." But, on asking him whether he had walked over to Weston on purpose to implore the assistance of my muse, I felt my mortified vanity a little consoled, and, pitying the poor man's distress, which appeared to be considerable, promised to supply him. The waggon has accordingly gone this day to Northampton loaded in part with my effusions in the mortuary style. A fig for poets who write epitaphs upon individuals! I have written *one*, that serves *two hundred* persons.[1]

---

[1] Here is an example:
    Like crowded forest trees we stand,
      And some are marked to fall;
    The axe will smite at God's command,
      And soon shall smite us all.

A few days since I received a second very obliging letter from Mr. Mackenzie.[1] He tells me that his own papers, which are by far (he is sorry to say it) the most numerous, are marked V.I.Z. Accordingly, my dear, I am happy to find that I am engaged in a correspondence with Mr. Viz., a gentleman for whom I have always entertained the profoundest veneration. But the serious fact is, that the papers distinguished by those signatures have ever pleased me most, and struck me as the work of a sensible man, who knows the world well, and has more of Addison's delicate humour than any body.

A poor man begged food at the Hall lately. The cook gave him some vermicelli soup. He ladled it about some time with the spoon, and then returned it to her, saying, "I am a poor man it is true, and I am very hungry, but yet I cannot eat broth with maggots in it." Once more, my dear, a thousand thanks for your box full of good things, useful things, and beautiful things.

Yours ever,

W. C.

Cowper's Private Correspondence, ed. by The Rev. T. S. Grimshawe, A.M. 1835.

[1] Henry Mackenzie (1745–1831), essayist (*The Lounger*) and novelist (*The Man of Feeling*).

NINETEENTH CENTURY 310

NINETEENTH CENTURY

PROVERBS

Before 1827

In seed time learn, in harvest teach, in winter enjoy.

Drive your cart and your plough over the bones of the dead.

Prudence is a rich ugly old maid courted by Incapacity.

A fool sees not the same tree that a wise man sees.

The busy bee has no time for sorrow.

The hours of Folly are measured by the clock, but of Wisdom no clock can measure.

The most sublime act is to set another before you.

If the fool would persist in his folly he would become wise.

What is now proved was once only imagined.

One thought fills immensity.

Always be ready to speak your mind, and a base man will avoid you.

The eagle never lost so much time as when he submitted to learn of the crow.

You never know what is enough, unless you know what is more than enough.

If others had not been foolish we should be so.

One law for the lion and ox is oppression.

To create a little flower is the labour of ages.

Damn braces. Bless relaxes.

When thou seest an eagle thou seest a portion of genius: lift up thy head!

The crow wished everything was black, the owl that everything was white.

Improvement makes straight road, but the crooked roads without improvement are roads of genius.

He who has suffered you to impose on him knows you.

William Blake

POETRY

1800

Aristotle, I have been told, has said that poetry is the most philosophic of all writing:[1] it is so: its object is truth, not individual and local, but general and operative; not standing upon external testimony, but carried alive into the heart by passion; truth which is its own testimony, which gives competence and confidence to the tribunal to which it appeals, and receives them from the same tribunal. Poetry is the image of man and nature. . . . Poetry is the breath and finer spirit of all knowledge; it is the impassioned expression which is in the countenance of all science. Emphatically may it be said of the poet, as Shakespeare hath said of man, "that he looks before and after."[2] He is the rock of defense for human nature; an upholder and preserver, carrying everywhere with him relationship and love. In spite of difference of soil and climate, of language and manners, of laws and customs: in spite of things silently gone out of mind, and things violently destroyed; the poet binds together by passion and knowledge the vast empire of human society, as it is spread over the whole earth, and over all time. The objects of the poet's thoughts are everywhere; though the eyes and senses of man are, it is true, his favorite guides, yet he will follow whereso-

---

[1] *Poetics*, 9:3. — "Poetry is more philosophical and more serious than history."

[2] *Hamlet*, IV, iv, 37.

ever he can find an atmosphere of sensation in which to move his wings. Poetry is the first and last of all knowledge — it is as immortal as the heart of man. . . . Poetry is the spontaneous overflow of powerful feelings; it takes its origin from emotion recollected in tranquillity; the emotion is contemplated till, by a species of reaction, the tranquillity gradually disappears, and an emotion, kindred to that which was before the subject of contemplation, is gradually produced, and does itself actually exist in the mind.

William Wordsworth, Preface to the . . . *Lyrical Ballads*, 1800.

1817

A poem is that species of composition, which is opposed to works of science, by proposing for its immediate object pleasure, not truth; and from all other species (having this object in common with it) it is discriminated by proposing to itself such delight from the whole, as is compatible with a distinct gratification from each component part. . . .

If a man chooses to call every composition a poem, which is rhyme, or measure, or both, I must leave his opinion uncontroverted. The distinction is at least competent to characterize the writer's intention. If it were subjoined, that the whole is likewise entertaining or affecting, as a tale, or as a series of interesting reflections, I of course admit this as another fit ingredient of a poem, and an additional merit. But if the definition sought for be that of a legitimate poem, I answer, it must be one the parts of which mutually support and explain each other; all in their proportion harmonizing with, and supporting the purpose and known influences of metrical arrangement. The philosophic critics of all ages coincide with the ultimate judgment of all countries, in equally denying the praises of a just poem, on the one hand, to a series of striking lines or distichs, each of which, absorbing the whole attention of the reader to itself, disjoins it from its context, and makes it a separate whole, instead of a harmonizing part; and on the other hand, to an un-sustained composition, from which the reader collects rapidly the general result unattracted by the component parts. The reader should be carried forward, not merely or chiefly by the mechanical impulse of curiosity, or by a restless desire to arrive at the final solution; but by the attractions of the journey itself. Like the motion of a serpent, which the Egyptians made the emblem of intellectual power; or like the path of sound through the air; at every step he pauses and half recedes, and from the retrogressive movement collects the force which again carries him onward. *Praecipitandus est liber spiritus*, says Petronius Arbiter most happily. The epithet *liber*, here balances the preceding verb; and it is not easy to conceive more meaning condensed in fewer words. . . .

The poet, described in ideal perfection, brings the whole soul of man into activity, with the subordination of its faculties to each other according to their relative worth and dignity. He diffuses a tone and spirit of unity, that blends, and (as it were) fuses, each into each, by that synthetic and magical power, to which I would exclusively appropriate the name of imagination. This power, first put in action by the will and understanding, and retained under their irremissive, though gentle and unnoticed control (*laxis effertur habenis*) reveals itself in the balance or reconcilement of opposite or discordant qualities: of sameness, with difference; of the general, with the concrete; the idea,

Praecipitandus, etc., The free spirit ought to be urged onward. *Satyric.*, p. 63.
laxis, etc., is borne along with loose reins.

with the image; the individual, with the representative; the sense of novelty and freshness, with old and
familiar objects; a more than usual state of emotion,
with a more than usual order; judgment ever awake
and steady self-possession, with enthusiasm and feeling
profound or vehement; and while it blends and harmo-
nizes the natural and the artificial, still subordinates
art to nature; the manner to the matter; and our admiration of the poet to our sympathy with the poetry.

Finally, good sense is the body of poetic genius,
fancy its drapery, motion its life, and imagination the
soul that is everywhere, and in each; and forms all into
one graceful and intelligent whole.

Samuel Taylor Coleridge, Biographia Literaria, chap. xiv

1821

Poetry is the record of the best and happiest moments of the happiest and best minds. . . . Poetry turns
all things to loveliness; it exalts the beauty of that
which is most beautiful, and it adds beauty to that
which is most deformed; it marries exultation and
horror, grief and pleasure, eternity and change; it sub-
dues to union under its light yoke all irreconcilable
things. It transmutes all that it touches, and every
form moving within the radiance of its presence is
changed by wondrous sympathy to an incarnation of
the spirit which it breathes; its secret alchemy turns to
potable gold the poisonous waters which flow from
death through life; it strips the veil of familiarity from
the world, and lays bare the naked and sleeping beauty
which is the spirit of its forms.

All things exist as they are perceived: at least in relation to the percipient.

The mind is its own place, and in itself
Can make a Heaven of Hell, a Hell of Heaven.[1]

[1] *Paradise Lost*, I, 254–55.

But poetry defeats the curse which binds us to be subjected to the accident of surrounding impressions. And whether it spreads its own figured curtain, or withdraws life's dark veil from before the scene of things, it equally creates for us a being within our being. It makes us the inhabitant of a world to which the familiar world is a chaos. It reproduces the common universe of which we are portions and percipients, and it purges from our inward sight the film of familiarity which obscures from us the wonder of our being. It compels us to feel that which we perceive, and to imagine that which we know. It creates anew the universe, after it has been annihilated in our minds by the recurrence of impressions blunted by reiteration. It justifies the bold and true words of Tasso: *Non merita nome di creatore, se non Iddio ed il Poeta.*

Percy Bysshe Shelley, A Defense of Poetry, 1821

● 1818

In poetry I have a few axioms, and you will see how far I am from their centre.

1st. I think poetry should surprise by a fine excess, and not by singularity; It should strike the reader as a wording of his own highest thoughts, and appear almost a remembrance.

2nd. Its touches of beauty should never be halfway, thereby making the reader breathless, instead of content. The rise, the progress, the setting of imagery should, like the sun, come natural to him, shine over him, and set soberly, although in magnificence, leaving him in the luxury of twilight. But it is easier to think what poetry should be than to write it — And this leads me to

Another axiom — That if poetry comes not as

Non merita, etc., "None merits the name of creator, except God and the Poet."

naturally as the leaves to a tree, it had better not come
at all.

John Keats, Letters: To John Taylor, Feb. 27, 1818

1829

Shepherd.[1] In this season o' the year, especially
when the flowers are a' seen again in lauchin' flocks
ower the braes, like children returnin' to school after a
lang snaw, I can wi' truth avoo, that the sight of a
primrose is to me like the soun' o' a prayer, and that I
seldom walk alone by myself for half a mile, without
thochts sae calm and sae serene, and sae humble and
sae grateful, that I houp I'm not deceivin' myself noo
when I venture to ca' them — religious.

North. No, James, you are not self-deceived.
Poetry melts into religion.

Shepherd. It is religion, sir, for what is religion but
a clear — often a sudden — insicht, accompanied wi'
emotion, into the dependence o' a' beauty and a' glory
on the Divine Mind? A wee dew-wat gowany, as it
makes a scarcely perceptible sound and stir, which it
often does, amang the grass that loves to shelter but
not hide the bonnie earth-born star, glintin' up sae
kindly wi' its face into mine, while by good fortune my
feet touched it not, has hundreds o' times affected me
as profoundly as ever did the Sun himsell setting in a'
his glory — as profoundly — and, oh! far mair tenderly,
for a thing that grows and grows, and becomes every
hour mair and mair beautifu', and then hangs fixed for
a season in the perfection o' its lovely delicht, and
then — wae is me — begins to be a little dim — and
then dimmer and dimmer, till we feel that it is indeed

dew-wat gowany, dew-wet daisy.
[1] *Shepherd,* James Hogg (1772–1835), who was known as the Ettrick
Shepherd. Christopher North is the pseudonym of John Wilson (1785–
1854).

— in very truth, there's nae denyin 't — fading — fading — faded — gone — dead — buried. Oh! sir, sic an existence as that has an overwhelmin' analogy to our ain life — and *that* I hae felt — nor doubt I that you, my dear sir, hae felt it too — when on some saft, sweet, silent, incense-breathing morning o' spring — far awa', perhaps, frae the smoke o' ony human dwellin' and walkin' ye cared na, kent na whither — sae early that the ground-bees were but beginnin' to hum out o' their bikes — when, I say, some flower suddenly attracted the licht within your ee, wi' a power like that o' the loadstone, and though, perhaps, the commonest o' the flowers that beautify the braes o' Scotland — only, as I said, a bit ordinary gowan — yet, what a sudden rush o' thochts and feelings overflowed your soul at the simple sicht! while a' nature becam for a moment overspread wi' a tender haze belongin' not to hersell, for there was naething there to bedim her brightness, but existin' only in your ain two silly een, sheddin' in the solitude a few holy tears!

North. James, I will trouble you for the red-herrings.

  John Wilson ("*Christopher North*"), *Noctes Ambrosianae,*
    No. XLII, April, 1829.

                                            1844

If a young reader should ask, after all, What is the quickest way of knowing bad poets from good, the best poets from the next best, and so on? the answer is, the only and twofold way: first, the perusal of the best poets with the greatest attention; and second, the cultivation of that love of truth and beauty which made them what they are. Every true reader of poetry partakes a more than ordinary portion of the poetic nature; and no one can be completely such, who

  bikes, hives.

does not love, or take an interest in, everything that interests the poet, from the firmament to the daisy — from the highest heart of man to the most pitiable of the low. It is a good practice to read with pen in hand, marking what is liked or doubted. It rivets the attention, realizes the greatest amount of enjoyment and facilitates reference. It enables the reader also, from time to time, to see what progress he makes with his own mind, and how it grows up towards the stature of its exalter. . . .

Leigh Hunt, An Answer to the Question, "What is Poetry?"
1844.

MY FIRST PLAY

At the north end of Cross Court there yet stands a portal, of some architectural pretensions, though reduced to humble use, serving at present for an entrance to a printing-office. This old door-way, if you are young, reader, you may not know was the identical pit entrance to Old Drury — Garrick's Drury — all of it that is left. I never pass it without shaking some forty years from off my shoulders, recurring to the evening when I passed through it to see *my first play*. The afternoon had been wet, and the condition of our going (the elder folks and myself) was, that the rain should cease. With what a beating heart did I watch from the window the puddles, from the stillness of which I was taught to prognosticate the desired cessation! I seem to remember the last spurt, and the glee with which I ran to announce it.

We went with orders, which my godfather F. had sent us. He kept the oil shop (now Davies's) at the corner of Featherstone Building, in Holborn. F. was

orders, passes.   *F.*, Francis Fielde.

a tall grave person, lofty in speech, and had pretensions above his rank. He associated in those days
with John Palmer, the comedian, whose gait and bearing he seemed to copy; if John (which is quite as
likely) did not rather borrow somewhat of his manner
from my godfather. He was also known to, and visited
by, Sheridan. It was to his house in Holborn that
young Brinsley brought his first wife on her elopement
with him from a boarding-school at Bath — the beautiful Maria Linley. My parents were present (over a
quadrille table) when he arrived in the evening with
his harmonious charge. — From either of these con-
nexions it may be inferred that my godfather could
command an order for the then Drury Lane theatre at
pleasure — and, indeed, a pretty liberal issue of those
cheap billets, in Brinsley's easy autograph, I have
heard him say was the sole remuneration which he had
received for many years' nightly illumination of the
orchestra and various avenues of that theatre — and
he was content it should be so. The honour of Sheridan's familiarity — or supposed familiarity — was
better to my godfather than money.

F. was the most gentlemanly of oilmen: grandilo-
quent, yet courteous. His delivery of the commonest
matters of fact was Ciceronian. He had two Latin
words almost constantly in his mouth (how odd sounds
Latin from an oilman's lips!), which my better knowledge since has enabled me to correct. In strict pronunciation they should have been sounded *vice versa* —
but in those young years they impressed me with more
awe than they would now do, read from Seneca or
Varro — in his own peculiar pronunciation monosyl-
labically elaborated, or Anglicised, into something like
verse verse. By an imposing manner, and the help of
these distorted syllables, he climbed (but that was

little) to the highest parochial honours which St. Andrew's has to bestow.

He is dead — and thus much I thought due to his memory, both for my first orders (little wondrous talismans! — slight keys, and insignificant to outward sight, but opening to me more than Arabian paradises!) and moreover, that by his testamentary beneficence I came into possession of the only landed property which I could ever call my own — situate near the road-way village of pleasant Puckeridge, in Hertfordshire. When I journeyed down to take possession, and planted foot on my own ground, the stately habits of the donor descended upon me, and I strode (shall I confess the vanity?) with larger paces over my allotment of three-quarters of an acre, with its commodious mansion in the midst, with the feeling of an English freeholder that all betwixt sky and centre was my own. The estate has passed into more prudent hands, and nothing but an agrarian can restore it.

In those days were pit orders. Beshrew the uncomfortable manager who abolished them! — with one of these we went. I remember waiting at the door — not that which is left — but between that and an inner door in shelter — O when shall I be such an expectant again! — with the cry of nonpareils, an indispensable play-house accompaniment in those days. As near as I can recollect, the fashionable pronunciation of the theatrical fruiteresses then was, "Chase some oranges, chase some numparels, chase a bill of the play;" — chase *pro* chuse. But when we got in, and I beheld the green curtain that veiled a heaven to my imagination, which was soon to be disclosed — the breathless anticipations I endured! I had seen something like it

St. Andrew's, a London parish.
nonpareils, a kind of sweetmeat or candy.

in the plate prefixed to Troilus and Cressida, in Rowe's[1] Shakespeare — the tent scene with Diomede — and a sight of that plate can always bring back in a measure the feeling of that evening. — The boxes at that time, full of well-dressed women of quality, projected over the pit; and the pilasters reaching down were adorned with a glistering substance (I know not what) under glass (as it seemed), resembling — a homely fancy — but I judged it to be sugar-candy — yet, to my raised imagination, divested of its homelier qualities, it appeared a glorified candy! — The orchestra lights at length arose, those "fair Auroras!" Once the bell sounded. It was to ring out yet once again — and, incapable of the anticipation, I reposed my shut eyes in a sort of resignation upon the maternal lap. It rang the second time. The curtain drew up — I was not past six years old — and the play was Artaxerxes!

I had dabbled a little in the Universal History — the ancient part of it — and, here was the court of Persia. I was being admitted to a sight of the past. I took no proper interest in the action going on, for I understood not its import — but I heard the word Darius, and I was in the midst of Daniel. All feeling was absorbed in vision. Gorgeous vests, gardens, palaces, princesses, passed before me. I knew not players. I was in Persepolis for the time; and the burning idol of their devotion almost converted me into a worshipper. I was awe-struck, and believed those significations to be something more than elemental fires. It was all enchantment and a dream. No such pleasure has since visited me but in dreams. — Harlequin's invasion followed; where, I remember,

Artaxerxes, an opera adapted from Metastasio, with music by Dr. Arne (first prod. 1762).
Harlequin, a stock character in pantomime. Harlequin's Invasion was a pantomime.

[1] Nicholas Rowe (1674–1718). His edition of Shakespeare was published in 1709.

the transformations of the magistrates into reverend beldams seemed to me a piece of grave historical justice, and the tailor carrying his own head to be as sober a verity as the legend of St. Denys.

The next play to which I was taken was the Lady of the Manor, of which, with the exception of some scenery, very faint traces are left in my memory. It was followed by a pantomime, called Lun's Ghost — a satiric touch, I apprehend, upon Rich, not long since dead — but to my apprehension (too sincere for satire), Lun was as remote a piece of antiquity as Lud — the father of a line of Harlequins — transmitting his dagger of lath (the wooden sceptre) through countless ages. I saw the primeval Motley come from his silent tomb in a ghastly vest of white patch-work, like the apparition of a dead rainbow. So Harlequins (thought I) look when they are dead.

My third play followed in quick succession. It was the Way of the World. I think I must have sat at it as grave as a judge; for, I remember, the hysteric affectations of good Lady Wishfort affected me like some solemn tragic passion. Robinson Crusoe followed; in which Crusoe, man Friday, and the parrot, were as good and authentic as in the story. — The clownery and pantaloonery of these pantomimes have clean passed out of my head. I believe, I no more laughed at them, than at the same age I should have been disposed to laugh at the grotesque Gothic heads (seeming to me then replete with devout meaning) that gape, and grin, in stone around the inside of the old Round Church (my church) of the Templars.

I saw these plays in the season 1781–2, when I was

Lady of the Manor, a comic opera by Wm. Kenrick.
Rich, John, a famous harlequin, who used the name Lun, in the part.
Lud, a mythical king of Britain.
Lady Wishfort, in Congreve's *The Way of the World* (1700).

from six to seven years old. After the intervention of six or seven other years (for at school all play-going was inhibited) I again entered the doors of a theatre. That old Artaxerxes evening had never done ringing in my fancy. I expected the same feelings to come again with the same occasion. But we differ from ourselves less at sixty and sixteen, than the latter does from six. In that interval what had I not lost! At the first period I knew nothing, understood nothing, discriminated nothing. I felt all, loved all, wondered all —

Was nourished, I could not tell how —

I had left the temple a devotee, and was returned a rationalist. The same things were there materially; but the emblem, the reference, was gone! — The green curtain was no longer a veil, drawn between two worlds, the unfolding of which was to bring back past ages, to present "a royal ghost" — but a certain quantity of green baize, which was to separate the audience for a given time from certain of their fellow-men who were to come forward and pretend those parts. The lights — the orchestra lights — came up a clumsy machinery. The first ring, and the second ring, was now but a trick of the prompter's bell — which had been, like the note of the cuckoo, a phantom of a voice, no hand seen or guessed at which ministered to its warning. The actors were men and women painted. I thought the fault was in them; but it was in myself, and the alteration which those many centuries — of six short twelvemonths — had wrought in me. — Perhaps it was fortunate for me that the play of the evening was but an indifferent comedy, as it gave me time to crop some unreasonable expectations, which might have interfered with the genuine emotions, with which

I was soon after enabled to enter upon the first appearance to me of Mrs. Siddons in Isabella. Comparison and retrospection soon yielded to the present attraction of the scene; and the theatre became to me, upon a new stock, the most delightful of recreations.

Charles Lamb, The Essays of Elia, 1823

POOR RELATIONS

1823

A poor Relation — is the most irrelevant thing in nature — a piece of impertinent correspondency — an odious approximation — a haunting conscience — a preposterous shadow, lengthening in the noontide of our prosperity — an unwelcome remembrancer — a perpetually recurring mortification — a drain on your purse — a more intolerable dun upon your pride — a drawback upon success — a rebuke to your rising — a stain in your blood — a blot on your 'scutcheon — a rent in your garment — a death's head at your banquet — Agathocles' pot — a Mordecai in your gate — a Lazarus at your door — a lion in your path — a frog in your chamber — a fly in your ointment — a mote in your eye — a triumph to your enemy, an apology to your friends — the one thing not needful — the hail in harvest — the ounce of sour in a pound of sweet.

He is known by his knock.   Your heart telleth you "That is Mr. ———."   A rap, between familiarity and respect; that demands, and at the same time, seems to despair of entertainment.   He entereth smiling and —

Isabella, heroine of Shakespeare's *Measure for Measure*.
Agathocles' pot, an unpleasant reminder.   Agathocles, tyrant of Sicily, in the third century, B.C., was son of a potter.
Mordecai, see *Esther*, III, 1–2.   *Lazarus*, see above, p. 156.
lion . . . frog . . . fly . . . mote . . . thing . . . needful, all Biblical phrases.

embarrassed. He holdeth out his hand to you to shake, and — draweth it back again. He casually looketh in about dinner-time — when the table is full. He offereth to go away, seeing you have company, but is induced to stay. He filleth a chair, and your visitor's two children are accommodated at a side table. He never cometh upon open days, when your wife says with some complacency, "My dear, perhaps Mr. —— will drop in to-day." He remembreth birthdays — and professeth he is fortunate to have stumbled upon one. He declareth against fish, the turbot being small — yet suffereth himself to be importuned into a slice against his first resolution. He sticketh by the port — yet will be prevailed upon to empty the remainder glass of claret, if a stranger press it upon him. He is a puzzle to the servants, who are fearful of being too obsequious, or not civil enough to him. The guests think "they have seen him before." Every one speculateth upon his condition; and the most part take him to be — a tide waiter. He calleth you by your Christian name, to imply that his other is the same with your own. He is too familiar by half, yet you wish he had less diffidence. With half the familiarity he might pass for a casual dependent; with more boldness he would be in no danger of being taken for what he is. He is too humble for a friend, yet taketh on him more state than befits a client. He is a worse guest than a country tenant, inasmuch as he bringeth up no rent — yet 'tis odds, from his garb and demeanor, that your guests take him for one. He is asked to make one at the whist table; refuseth on the score of poverty, and — resents being left out. When the company break up he proffereth to go for a coach — and lets the

---

tide waiter (literally a customs officer), one who waits for a lucky turn of events.

servant go. He recollects your grandfather; and will thrust in some mean and quite unimportant anecdote of — the family. He knew it when it was not quite so flourishing as "he is blest in seeing it now." He reviveth past situations to institute what he calleth — favorable comparisons. With a reflecting sort of congratulation, he will inquire the price of your furniture: and insults you with a special commendation of your window-curtains. He is of opinion that the urn is the more elegant shape, but, after all, there was something comfortable about the old tea-kettle — which you must remember. He dare say you must find a great convenience in having a carriage of your own, and appealeth to your lady if it is not so. Inquireth if you have had your arms done on vellum yet; and did not know, till lately, that such-and-such had been the crest of the family. His memory is unseasonable; his compliments perverse; his talk a trouble; his stay pertinacious; and when he goeth away, you dismiss his chair into a corner, as precipitately as possible, and feel fairly rid of two nuisances.

There is a worse evil under the sun, and that is — a female Poor Relation. You may do something with the other; you may pass him off tolerably well; but your indigent she-relative is hopeless. "He is an old humorist," you may say, "and affects to go threadbare. His circumstances are better than folks would take them to be. You are fond of having a Character at your table, and truly he is one." But in the indications of female poverty there can be no disguise. No woman dresses below herself from caprice. The truth must out without shuffling. "She is plainly related to the L——s; or what does she at their house?" She is, in all probability, your wife's cousin. Nine times out of ten, at least, this is the case. Her garb is something between a gentlewoman and a beggar, yet the former evidently predominates. She is most provokingly humble, and ostentatiously sensible to her inferiority. He may require to be repressed sometimes — *aliquando sufflaminandus erat* — but there is no raising her. You send her soup at dinner, and she begs to be helped — after the gentlemen. Mr. —— requests the honor of taking wine with her; she hesitates between port and Madeira, and chooses the former — because he does. She calls the servant *Sir;* and insists on not troubling him to hold her plate. The housekeeper patronizes her. The children's governess takes upon her to correct her, when she has mistaken the piano for a harpsichord.

Richard Amlet, Esq., in the play, is a notable instance of the disadvantages to which this chimerical notion of *affinity constituting a claim to acquaintance*, may subject the spirit of a gentleman. A little foolish blood is all that is betwixt him and a lady of great estate. His stars are perpetually crossed by the malignant maternity of an old woman, who persists in calling him "her son Dick." But she has wherewithal in the end to recompense his indignities, and float him again upon the brilliant surface, under which it had been her seeming business all along to sink him. All men, besides, are not of Dick's temperament. I know an Amlet in real life, who, wanting Dick's buoyancy, sank indeed. Poor W—— was of my own standing at Christ's, a fine classic, and a youth of promise. If he had a blemish, it was too much pride; but its quality was inoffensive; it was not of that sort which hardens the heart, and serves to keep inferiors at a distance; it

aliquando, etc., sometimes he had to be checked.
Richard Amlet, in *The Confederacy,* by John Vanbrugh (1664–1726).
W——, a young man named Favell. See Lamb's *Christ's Hospital Five-and-Thirty Years Ago.*

only sought to ward off derogation from itself.   It was
the principle of self-respect carried as far as it could go,
without infringing upon that respect, which he would
have every one else equally maintain for himself.   He
would have you to think alike with him on this topic.
Many a quarrel have I had with him, when we were
rather older boys, and our tallness made us more ob-
noxious in the blue clothes, because I would not thread
the alleys and blind ways of the town with him to elude
notice, when we have been out together on a holiday
in the streets of this sneering and prying metropolis.
W—— went, sore with these notions, to Oxford, where
the dignity and sweetness of a scholar's life, meeting
with the alloy of a humble introduction, wrought in
him a passionate devotion to the place, with a profound aversion from the society.   The servitor's gown
(worse than his school array) clung to him with Nessian
venom.   He thought himself ridiculous in a garb,
under which Latimer would have walked erect; and in
which Hooker, in his young days, possibly flaunted in
a vein of no discommendable vanity.   In the depth of
college shades, or in his lonely chamber, the poor
student shrunk from observation.   He found shelter
among books, which insult not; and studies, that ask
no questions of a youth's finances.   He was lord of his
library, and seldom cared for looking out beyond his
domains.   The healing influence of studious pursuits
was upon him, to soothe and to abstract.   He was almost a healthy man; when the waywardness of his fate
broke out against him with a second and worse malignity.   The father of W—— had hitherto exercised the
humble profession of house-painter at N——, near

servitor, an undergraduate who received aid from the university and who
    waited on table at the Commons.
Nessian, a reference to the robe of Nessus, in the myth of Hercules.
Latimer and *Hooker* were both sizers or servitors at Cambridge and Oxford,
    respectively.

Oxford. A supposed interest with some of the heads of the colleges had now induced him to take up his abode in that city, with the hope of being employed upon some public works which were talked of. From that moment I read in the countenance of the young man, the determination which at length tore him from academic pursuits forever. To a person unacquainted with our universities, the distance between the gownsmen and the townsmen, as they are called — the trading part of the latter especially — is carried to an excess that would appear harsh and incredible. The temperament of W——'s father was diametrically the reverse of his own. Old W—— was a little, busy, cringing tradesman, who with his son upon his arm, would stand bowing and scraping, cap in hand, to anything that wore the semblance of a gown — insensible to the winks and opener remonstrances of the young man, to whose chamber-fellow, or equal in standing, perhaps, he was thus obsequiously and gratuitously ducking. Such a state of things could not last. W—— must change the air of Oxford or be suffocated. He chose the former; and let the sturdy moralist, who strains the point of filial duties as high as they can bear, censure the dereliction; he cannot estimate the struggle. I stood with W——, the last afternoon I ever saw him, under the eaves of his paternal dwelling. It was in the fine lane leading from the High-street to the back of —— College, where W—— kept his rooms. He seemed thoughtful, and more reconciled. I ventured to rally him — finding him in a better mood — upon a representation of the Artist Evangelist, which the old man, whose affairs were beginning to flourish, had caused to be set up in a splendid sort of frame over his really handsome shop,

Artist Evangelist, St. Luke, by tradition a painter as well as a physician.

either as a token of prosperity, or badge of gratitude to his saint. W—— looked up at the Luke, and, like Satan, "knew his mounted sign — and fled." [1] A letter on his father's table the next morning, announced that he had accepted a commission in a regiment about to embark for Portugal. He was among the first who perished before the walls of St. Sebastian.

I do not know how, upon a subject which I began with treating half-seriously, I should have fallen upon a recital so eminently painful; but this theme of poor relations is replete with so much matter for tragic as well as comic associations, that it is difficult to keep the account distinct without blending. The earliest impressions which I received on this matter are certainly not attended with anything painful, or very humiliating, in the recalling. At my father's table (no very splendid one) was to be found, every Saturday, the mysterious figure of an aged gentleman, clothed in neat black, of a sad yet comely appearance. His deportment was of the essence of gravity; his words few or none; and I was not to make a noise in his presence. I had little inclination to have done so — for my cue was to admire in silence. A particular elbow chair was appropriated to him, which was in no case to be violated. A peculiar sort of sweet pudding, which appeared on no other occasion, distinguished the days of his coming. I used to think him a prodigiously rich man. All I could make out of him was, that he and my father had been school-fellows a world ago at Lincoln, and that he came from the Mint.[2] The Mint I knew to be a place where all the money was coined — and I thought he was the owner of all that money. Awful ideas of the Tower twined themselves

[1] *Paradise Lost*, IV, 1013.
[2] The Mint was on Tower Hill near the Tower of London.

about his presence. He seemed above all human in-
firmities and passions. A sort of melancholy grandeur
invested him. From some inexplicable doom I
fancied him obliged to go about in an eternal suit of
mourning; a captive — a stately being, let out of the
Tower on Saturdays. Often have I wondered at the
temerity of my father, who, in spite of an habitual
general respect which we all in common manifested
towards him, would venture now and then to stand up
against him in some argument, touching their youthful
days. The houses of the ancient city of Lincoln are
divided (as most of my readers know) between dwellers on the hill, and in the valley. This marked distinction formed an obvious division between the boys who
lived above (however brought together in a common
school) and the boys whose paternal residence was on
the plain; a sufficient cause of hostility in the code of
these young Grotiuses.[1] My father had been a leading
Mountaineer; and would still maintain the general
superiority, in skill and hardihood, of the *Above Boys*
(his own faction) over the *Below Boys* (so they were
called), of which party his contemporary had been a
chieftain. Many and hot were the skirmishes on this
topic — the only one upon which the old gentleman
was ever brought out — and bad blood bred; even
sometimes almost to the recommencement (so I expected) of actual hostilities. But my father, who
scorned to insist upon advantages, generally contrived
to turn the conversation upon some adroit by-com-
mendation of the old Minster, in the general preference of which, before all other cathedrals in the island,
the dweller on the hill, and the plain-born, could meet
on a conciliating level, and lay down their less impor-

---

[1] Hugo Grotius (1583–1645) was a great Dutch authority on international
law.

tant differences.   Once only I saw the old gentleman
really ruffled, and I remember with anguish the
thought that came over me: "Perhaps he will never
come here again."   He had been pressed to take another plate of the viand, which I have already mentioned as the indispensable concomitant of his visits.
He had refused, with a resistance amounting to rigor
— when my aunt, an old Lincolnian, but who had
something of this, in common with my cousin Bridget,
that she would sometimes press civility out of season
— uttered the following memorable application —
"Do take another slice, Mr. Billet, for you do not
get pudding every day."   The old gentleman said
nothing at the time — but he took occasion in the
course of the evening, when some argument had inter-
vened between them, to utter with an emphasis which
chilled the company and which chills me now as I
write it — "Woman, you are superannuated."   John
Billet did not survive long, after the digesting of this
affront; but he survived long enough to assure me that
peace was actually restored! and, if I remember aright,
another pudding was discreetly substituted in the
place of that which had occasioned the offence.   He
died at the Mint (Anno 1781) where he had long held,
what he accounted, a comfortable independence; and
with five pounds, fourteen shillings, and a penny,
which were found in his escritoire after his decease,
left the world, blessing God that he had enough to
bury him, and that he had never been obliged to any
man for a sixpence.   This was — a Poor Relation.

Charles Lamb, Last Essays of Elia, 1833

cousin Bridget, is Lamb's name, in the *Essays,* for his sister Mary.   The
officious Aunt was Sarah Lamb, known as Aunt Hetty.

ON GOING A JOURNEY

1821

One of the pleasantest things in the world is going a journey; but I like to go by myself. I can enjoy society in a room; but out of doors, nature is company enough for me. I am then never less alone than when alone.

"The fields his study, nature was his book." [1]

I cannot see the wit of walking and talking at the same time. When I am in the country, I wish to vegetate like the country. I am not for criticising hedge-rows and black cattle. I go out of town in order to forget the town and all that is in it. There are those who for this purpose go to watering-places, and carry the metropolis with them. I like more elbow-room, and fewer incumbrances. I like solitude, when I give myself up to it, for the sake of solitude; nor do I ask for

"—— a friend in my retreat,
Whom I may whisper, solitude is sweet." [2]

The soul of a journey is liberty, perfect liberty, to think, feel, do, just as one pleases. We go a journey chiefly to be free of all impediments and all inconveniences; to leave ourselves behind much more than to get rid of others. It is because I want a little breathing-space to muse on indifferent matters, where Contemplation

"May plume her feathers and let grow her wings,
That in the various bustle of resort
Were all too ruffled, and sometimes impaired," [3]

that I absent myself from the town for a while, without

---

[1] *The Farmer's Boy*, by Robert Bloomfield.
[2] *Retirement*, by William Cowper.   [3] *Comus*, by Milton.

feeling at a loss the moment I am left by myself. Instead of a friend in a post-chaise or a Tilbury, to exchange good things with and vary the same stale topics over again, for once let me have a truce with impertinence. Give me the clear blue sky over my head, and the green turf beneath my feet, a winding road before me, and a three hours' march to dinner — and then to thinking! It is hard if I cannot start some game on these lone heaths. I laugh, I run, I leap, I sing for joy. From the point of yonder rolling cloud, I plunge into my past being, and revel there, as the sunburnt Indian plunges headlong into the wave that wafts him to his native shore. Then long-forgotten things, like "sunken wrack and sumless treasuries," [1] burst upon my eager sight, and I begin to feel, think, and be myself again. Instead of an awkward silence, broken by attempts at wit or dull commonplaces, mine is that undisturbed silence of the heart which alone is perfect eloquence. No one likes puns, alliterations, antitheses, argument, and analysis better than I do; but sometimes I had rather be without them. "Leave, oh, leave me to my repose!" [2] I have just now other business in hand, which would seem idle to you, but is with me "very stuff o' the conscience." [3] Is not this wild rose sweet without a comment? Does not this daisy leap to my heart set in its coat of emerald? Yet if I were to explain to you the circumstance that has so endeared it to me, you would only smile. Had I not better then keep it to myself, and let it serve me to brood over, from here to yonder craggy point, and from thence onward to the far-distant horizon? I should be but bad company all that way, and therefore prefer being alone. I have heard it said that you

[1] *Henry V*, I, ii, 165. [2] *The Descent of Odin*, by Gray.
[3] *Othello*, I, ii, 2.

may, when the moody fit comes on, walk or ride on by
yourself, and indulge your reveries. But this looks
like a breach of manners, a neglect of others, and you
are thinking all the time that you ought to rejoin your
party. "Out upon such a half-faced fellowship," [1] say
I. I like to be either entirely to myself, or entirely at
the disposal of others; to talk or be silent, to walk or sit
still, to be sociable or solitary. I was pleased with an
observation of Mr. Cobbett's, [2] that, "he thought it a
bad French custom to drink our wine with our meals,
and that an Englishman ought to do only one thing at
a time." So I cannot talk and think, or indulge in
melancholy musing and lively conversation by fits and
starts. "Let me have a companion of my way," says
Sterne, "were it but to remark how the shadows
lengthen as the sun declines." [3] It is beautifully said;
but in my opinion, this continual comparing of notes
interferes with the involuntary impression of things
upon the mind, and hurts the sentiment. If you only
hint what you feel in a kind of dumb show, it is insipid: if you have to explain it, it is making a toil of
pleasure. You cannot read the book of nature without
being continually put to the trouble of translating it
for the benefit of others. I am for this synthetical
method on a journey in preference to the analytical. I
am content to lay in a stock of ideas then, and to
examine and anatomise them afterwards. I want to
see my vague notions float like the down of the thistle
before the breeze, and not to have them entangled in
the briars and thorns of controversy. For once, I like
to have it all my own way; and this is impossible unless you are alone, or in such company as I do not
covet. I have no objection to argue a point with any

[1] *I Henry IV*, I, III, 208.
[2] William Cobbett (1762–1835), economist and reformer.
[3] *Sermons*, by Laurence Sterne.

one for twenty miles of measured road, but not for pleasure. If you remark the scent of a bean-field crossing the road, perhaps your fellow-traveller has no smell. If you point to a distant object, perhaps he is short-sighted, and has to take out his glass to look at it. There is a feeling in the air, a tone in the colour of a cloud which hits your fancy, but the effect of which you are unable to account for. There is then no sympathy, but an uneasy craving after it, and a dissatisfaction which pursues you on the way, and in the end probably produces ill-humour. Now, I never quarrel with myself, and take all my conclusions for granted, till I find it necessary to defend them against objections. It is not merely that you may not be of accord on the objects and circumstances that present themselves before you — these may recall a number of objects, and lead to associations too delicate and refined to be possibly communicated to others. Yet these I love to cherish, and sometimes still fondly clutch them, when I escape from the throng to do so. To give way to our feelings before company seems extravagance or affectation; and, on the other hand, to have to unravel this mystery of our being at every turn, and to make others take an equal interest in it (otherwise the end is not answered), is a task to which few are competent. We must "give it an understanding, but no tongue." [1] My old friend Coleridge, however, could do both. He could go on in the most delightful explanatory way over hill and dale a summer's day, and convert a landscape into a didactic poem or a Pindaric ode. "He talked far above singing." [2] If I could so clothe my ideas in sounding and flowing words, I might perhaps wish to have some one with

[1] *Hamlet*, I, II, 250.
[2] Beaumont and Fletcher, *Philaster*, V, v, 165.

me to admire the swelling theme; or I could be more content, were it possible for me still to hear his echoing voice in the woods of All-Foxden. They had "that fine madness in them which our first poets had;" [1] and if they could have been caught by some rare instrument, would have breathed such strains as the following:

> "——— Here be woods as green
> As any, air likewise as fresh and sweet
> As where smooth Zephyrus plays on the fleet
> Face of the curled streams, with flow'rs as many
> As the young spring gives, and as choice as any;
> Here be all new delights, cool streams and wells;
> Arbours o'ergrown with woodbines; caves, and dells:
> Choose where thou wilt, whilst I sit by and sing,
> Or gather rushes, to make many a ring
> For thy long fingers; tell thee tales of love;
> How the pale Phoebe, hunting in a grove,
> First saw the boy Endymion, from whose eyes
> She took eternal fire that never dies;
> How she conveyed him softly in a sleep,
> His temples bound with poppy, to the steep
> Head of old Latmos, where she stoops each night,
> Gilding the mountains with her brother's light,
> To kiss her sweetest." [2]

Had I words and images at command like these, I would attempt to wake the thoughts that lie slumbering on golden ridges in the evening clouds: but at the sight of nature my fancy, poor as it is, droops and closes up its leaves, like flowers at sunset. I can make nothing out on the spot — I must have time to collect myself. In general, a good thing spoils out-of-door prospects

---

[1] Michael Drayton, *To Henry Reynolds — Of Poets and Poesie.*.
[2] Fletcher's *The Faithful Shepherdess*, I, III, 26 *ff.*

it should be reserved for Table-Talk. Lamb is for this reason, I take it, the worst company in the world out of doors; because he is the best within. I grant there is one subject on which it is pleasant to talk on a journey; and that is, what one shall have for supper when we get to our inn at night. The open air improves this sort of conversation or friendly altercation, by setting a keener edge on appetite. Every mile of the road heightens the flavour of the viands we expect at the end of it. How fine it is to enter some old town, walled and turreted, just at approach of nightfall, or to come to some straggling village, with the lights streaming through the surrounding gloom; and then, after inquiring for the best entertainment that the place affords, to "take one's ease at one's inn!" [1] These eventful moments in our lives' history are too precious, too full of solid, heartful happiness to be frittered and dribbled away in imperfect sympathy. I would have them all to myself, and drain them to the last drop: they will do to talk of or to write about afterwards. What a delicate speculation it is, after drinking whole goblets of tea,

"The cups that cheer, but not inebriate," [2]

and letting the fumes ascend into the brain, to sit considering what we shall have for supper — eggs and a rasher, a rabbit smothered in onions, or an excellent veal cutlet! Sancho in such a situation once fixed on cow-heel; [3] and his choice, though he could not help it, is not to be disparaged. Then, in the intervals of pictured scenery and Shandean contemplation, to catch the preparation and the stir in the kitchen. *Procul, O procul este profani!* [4] (Avaunt! avaunt! ye

[1] *I Henry IV*, III, iii, 92–93. [2] Cowper's *Task*, IV, 39–40.
[3] *Don Quixote*, Part II, chap. lix. [4] *Æneid*, VI, 258.

unhallowed.)   These hours are sacred to silence and to musing, to be treasured up in the memory, and to feed the source of smiling thoughts hereafter.   I would not waste them in idle talk; or if I must have the integrity of fancy broken in upon, I would rather it were by a stranger than a friend.   A stranger takes his hue and character from the time and place; he is a part of the furniture and costume of an inn.   If he is a Quaker, or from the West Riding of Yorkshire, so much the better. I do not even try to sympathize with him, and he breaks no squares.   I associate nothing with my travelling companion but present objects and passing events.   In his ignorance of me and my affairs, I in a manner forget myself.   But a friend reminds one of other things, rips up old grievances, and destroys the abstraction of the scene.   He comes in ungraciously between us and our imaginary character.   Something is dropped in the course of conversation that gives a hint of your profession and pursuits; or from having some one with you that knows the less sublime portions of your history, it seems that other people do. You are no longer a citizen of the world; but your "unhoused free condition is put into circumspection and confine." [1]   The *incognito* of an inn is one of its striking privileges — "lord of one's self, uncumbered with a name." [2]   Oh! it is great to shake off the trammels of the world and of public opinion — to lose our importunate, tormenting, everlasting personal identity in the elements of nature, and become the creature of the moment, clear of all ties — to hold to the universe only by a dish of sweetbreads, and to owe nothing but the score of the evening — and no longer seeking for applause and meeting with contempt, to be known by

[1] *Othello*, I, II, 26–27.
[2] Dryden, *To my Honoured Kinsman John Driden.*

no other title than *the Gentleman in the parlour!* One
may take one's choice of all characters in this romantic
state of uncertainty as to one's real pretensions, and
become indefinitely respectable and negatively right-
worshipful. We baffle prejudice and disappoint conjecture; and from being so to others, begin to be objects of curiosity and wonder even to ourselves. We
are no more those hackneyed commonplaces that we
appear in the world; an inn restores us to the level of
nature, and quits scores with society! I have certainly
spent some enviable hours at inns — sometimes when
I have been left entirely to myself, and have tried to
solve some metaphysical problem, as once at Witham
Common, where I found out the proof that likeness is
not a case of the association of ideas — at other times,
when there have been pictures in the room, as at St.
Neot's (I think it was), where I first met with Gribe-
lin's engravings of the Cartoons, into which I entered
at once, and at a little inn on the borders of Wales,
where there happened to be hanging some of Westall's[1]
drawings, which I compared triumphantly (for a
theory that I had, not for the admired artist) with the
figure of a girl who had ferried me over the Severn,
standing up in a boat between me and the twilight
— at other times I might mention luxuriating in
books, with a peculiar interest in this way, as I remember sitting up half the night to read *Paul and
Virginia*, which I picked up at an inn at Bridgewater,
after being drenched in the rain all day; and at the
same place I got through two volumes of Madame
D'Arblay's[2] *Camilla*. It was on the 10th of August
1798 that I sat down to a volume of the *New Eloise*, at

artoons, i.e., of Raphael. A cartoon is a full-sized drawing for a painting.
..ul and Virginia, by B. de Saint-Pierre, French romancer.
..ew Eloïse, by J. J. Rousseau (1712–78).
[1] Richard Westall (1765–1836), English painter.
[2] Mme. D'Arblay, i.e., Fanny Burney (1752–1840), novelist.

the inn at Llangollen, over a bottle of sherry and a cold chicken. The letter I chose was that in which St. Preux describes his feelings as he first caught a glimpse from the heights of the Jura of the Pays de Vaud, which I had brought with me as a *bon bouche* to crown the evening with. It was my birthday, and I had for the first time come from a place in the neighborhood to visit this delightful spot. The road to Llangollen turns off between Chirk and Wrexham; and on passing a certain point, you come all at once upon the valley, which opens like an amphitheatre, broad, barren hills rising in majestic state on either side, with "green upland swells that echo to the bleat of flocks" [1] below, and the river Dee babbling over its stony bed in the midst of them. The valley at this time "glittered green with sunny showers," [2] and a budding ash-tree dipped its tender branches in the chiding stream. How proud, how glad I was to walk along the high road that overlooks the delicious prospect, repeating the lines which I have just quoted from Mr. Coleridge's poems! But besides the prospect which opened beneath my feet, another also opened to my inward sight, a heavenly vision, on which were written, in letters large as Hope could make them, these four words, LIBERTY, GENIUS, LOVE, VIRTUE; which have since faded into the light of common day, or mock my idle gaze.

"The beautiful is vanished, and returns not." [3]

Still I would return some time or other to this enchanted spot; but I would return to it alone. What other self could I find to share that influx of thoughts of regret, and delight, the fragments of which I could hardly conjure up to myself, so much have they been

[1] Coleridge's *Ode on the Departing Year.*   [2] *Idem.*
[3] Coleridge's translation of Schiller's *Death of Wallenstein*, V, i, 68.

broken and defaced. I could stand on some tall rock and overlook the precipice of years that separates me from what I then was. I was at that time going shortly to visit [1] the poet whom I have above named. Where is he now? Not only I myself have changed; the world, which was then new to me, has become old and incorrigible. Yet will I turn to thee in thought, O sylvan Dee, in joy, in youth and gladness as thou then wert; and thou shalt always be to me the river of Paradise, where I will drink of the waters of life freely!

There is hardly anything that shows the short-sightedness or capriciousness of the imagination more than travelling does. With change of place we change our ideas; nay, our opinions and feelings. We can by an effort indeed transport ourselves to old and long-forgotten scenes, and then the picture of the mind revives again; but we forget those that we have just left. It seems that we can think but of one place at a time. The canvas of the fancy is but of a certain extent, and if we paint one set of objects upon it, they immediately efface every other. We cannot enlarge our conceptions, we only shift our point of view. The landscape bares its bosom to the enraptured eye, we take our fill of it, and seem as if we could form no other image of beauty or grandeur. We pass on, and think no more of it; the horizon that shuts it from our sight also blots it from our memory like a dream. In travelling through a wild, barren country, I can form no idea of a woody and cultivated one. It appears to me that all the world must be barren, like what I see of it. In the country we forget the town, and in town we despise the country. "Beyond Hyde Park," says Sir Fopling Flutter, "all is a desert." [2] All that part of

---

[1] This visit is described in Hazlitt's fine essay, *My First Acquaintance with Poets.*

[2] Etherege's *The Man of Mode*, V, II.

the map that we do not see before us is blank. The world in our conceit of it is not much bigger than a nutshell. It is not one prospect expanded into another, country joined to country, kingdom to kingdom, land to seas, making an image voluminous and vast; — the mind can form no larger idea of space than the eye can take in at a single glance. The rest is a name written in a map, a calculation of arithmetic. For instance, what is the true signification of that immense mass of territory and population, known by the name of China to us? An inch of pasteboard on a wooden globe, of no more account than a China orange! Things near us are seen of the size of life: things at a distance are diminished to the size of the understanding. We measure the universe by ourselves, and even comprehend the texture of our own being only piecemeal. In this way, however, we remember an infinity of things and places. The mind is like a mechanical instrument that plays a great variety of tunes, but it must play them in succession. One idea recalls another, but it at the same time excludes all others. In trying to renew old recollections, we cannot as it were unfold the whole web of our existence; we must pick out the single threads. So in coming to a place where we have formerly lived, and with which we have intimate associations, every one must have found that the feeling grows more vivid the nearer we approach the spot, from the mere anticipation of the actual impression: we remember circumstances, feelings, persons, faces, names that we had not thought of for years; but for the time all the rest of the world is forgotten! — To return to the question I have quitted above: —

I have no objection to go to see ruins, aqueducts, pictures, in company with a friend or a party, but rather the contrary, for the former reason reversed.

They are intelligible matters, and will bear talking about. The sentiment here is not tacit, but communicable and overt. Salisbury Plain is barren of criticism, but Stonehenge will bear a discussion antiquarian, picturesque, and philosophical. In setting out on a party of pleasure, the first consideration always is where we shall go to: in taking a solitary ramble, the question is what shall we meet by the way. "The mind is its own place;" [1] nor are we anxious to arrive at the end of our journey. I can myself do the honours indifferently well to works of art and curiosity. I once took a party to Oxford with no mean *éclat* — showed them that seat of the Muses at a distance,

"With glistering spires and pinnacles adorn'd" — [2]

descanted on the learned air that breathes from the grassy quadrangles and stone walls of halls and cottages — was at home in the Bodleian; and at Blenheim quite superseded the powdered Cicerone that attended us, and that pointed in vain with his wand to commonplace beauties in matchless pictures. As another exception to the above reasoning, I should not feel confident in venturing on a journey in a foreign country without a companion. I should want at intervals to hear the sound of my own language. There is an involuntary antipathy in the mind of an Englishman to foreign manners and notions that requires the assistance of social sympathy to carry it off. As the distance from home increases, this relief, which was at first a luxury, becomes a passion and an appetite. A person would almost feel stifled to find himself in the deserts of Arabia without friends and countrymen: there must be allowed to be something in the view of

[1] *Paradise Lost*, I, 254.   [2] *Idem*, III, 550.

Athens or old Rome that claims the utterance of speech; and I own that the Pyramids are too mighty for any single contemplation. In such situations, so opposite to all one's ordinary train of ideas, one seems a species by one's-self, a limb torn off from society, unless one can meet with instant fellowship and support. Yet I did not feel this want or craving very pressing once, when I first set my foot on the laughing shores of France. Calais was peopled with novelty and delight. The confused, busy murmur of the place was like oil and wine poured into my ears; nor did the Mariners' Hymn, which was sung from the top of an old crazy vessel in the harbour, as the sun went down, send an alien sound into my soul. I only breathed the air of general humanity. I walked over "the vine-covered hills and gay regions of France," [1] erect and satisfied; for the image of man was not cast down and chained at the foot of arbitrary thrones: I was at no loss for language, for that of all the great schools of painting was open to me. The whole is vanished like a shade. Pictures, heroes, glory, freedom, all are fled: nothing remains but the Bourbons and the French people! — There is undoubtedly a sensation in travelling into foreign parts that is to be had nowhere else: but it is more pleasing at the time than lasting. It is too remote from our habitual associations to be a common topic of discourse or reference, and, like a dream or another state of existence, does not piece into our daily modes of life. It is an animated but a momentary hallucination. It demands an effort to exchange our actual for our ideal identity; and to feel the pulse of our old transports revive very keenly, we must "jump" all our present comforts and connections. Our romantic and itinerant character is not to be domesticated. Dr.

[1] From a song by William Roscoe.

Johnson remarked how little foreign travel added to
the facilities of conversation in those who had been
abroad. In fact, the time we have spent there is
both delightful, and, in one sense, instructive; but it
appears to be cut out of our substantial, downright
existence, and never to join kindly on to it. We are
not the same, but another, and perhaps more enviable individual, all the time we are out of our own
country. We are lost to ourselves, as well as our
friends. So the poet somewhat quaintly sings,

"Out of my country and myself I go." [1]

Those who wish to forget painful thoughts, do well to
absent themselves for a while from the ties and objects that recall them: but we can be said only to fulfill
our destiny in the place that gave us birth. I should
on this account like well enough to spend the whole of
my life in travelling abroad, if I could anywhere borrow another life to spend afterwards at home!

   William Hazlitt, Table Talk; or *Original Essays on Men and
   Manners,* 1821–22.

NATURAL SUPERNATURALISM

1828–29

   "Deep has been, and is, the significance of Miracles,"
thus quietly begins the Professor; [2] "far deeper perhaps than we imagine. Meanwhile, the question of
questions were: What specially is a Miracle? To that
Dutch King of Siam, an icicle had been a miracle;
whoso had carried with him an air-pump, and vial of
vitriolic ether, might have worked a miracle. To my
Horse, again, who unhappily is still more unscientific,

[1] Perhaps by Hazlitt himself.

[2] *Professor,* Diogenes Teufelsdroeckh, the ostensible author of the work
of which *Sartor Resartus* is a pretended translation.

do not I work a miracle, and magical '*Open sesame!*' every time I please to pay twopence, and open for him an impassable *Schlagbaum*, or shut Turnpike?

"'But is not a real Miracle simply a violation of the Laws of Nature?' ask several. Whom I may answer by this new question: What are the Laws of Nature? To me perhaps the rising of one from the dead were no violation of these Laws, but a confirmation; were some far deeper Law, now first penetrated into, and by Spiritual Force, even as the rest have all been, brought to bear on us with its Material Force.

"Here too may some inquire, not without astonishment: On what ground shall one, that can make Iron swim,[1] come and declare that therefore he can teach Religion? To us, truly, of the Nineteenth Century, such declaration were inept enough; which nevertheless to our fathers, of the First Century, was full of meaning.

"'But is it not the deepest Law of Nature that she be constant?' cries an illuminated class: 'Is not the Machine of the Universe fixed to move by unalterable rules?' Probable enough, good friends: nay I, too, must believe that the God, whom ancient inspired men assert to be 'without variableness or shadow of turning,'[2] does indeed never change; that Nature, that the Universe, which no one whom it so pleases can be prevented from calling a Machine, does move by the most unalterable rules. And now of you, too, I make the old inquiry: What those same unalterable rules, forming the complete Statute-Book of Nature, may possibly be?

"They stand written in our Works of Science, say you; in the accumulated records of Man's Experience? — Was Man with his Experience present at the Crea

<hr />

[1] Cf. 2 *Kings*, VI, 6.   [2] *James*, I, 17.

tion, then, to see how it all went on? Have any deepest scientific individuals yet dived-down to the foundations of the Universe, and gauged everything there? Did the Maker take them into His counsel; that they read His groundplan of the incomprehensible All; and can say, This stands marked therein, and no more than this? Alas, not in anywise! These scientific individuals have been nowhere but where we also are; have seen some handbreadths deeper than we see into the Deep that is infinite, without bottom as without shore.

"Laplace's Book on the Stars, wherein he exhibits that certain Planets, with their Satellites, gyrate round our worthy Sun, at a rate and in a course, which, by greatest good fortune, he and the like of him have succeeded in detecting — is to me as precious as to another. But is this what thou namest 'Mechanism of the Heavens' and 'System of the World'; [1] this, wherein Sirius and the Pleiades, and all Herschel's Fifteen thousand Suns per minute, being left out, some paltry handful of Moons, and inert Balls, had been — looked at, nicknamed, and marked in the Zodiacal Way-bill; so that we can now prate of their Whereabouts; their How, their Why, their What, being hid from us, as in the signless Inane?

"System of Nature! To the wisest man, wise as is his vision, Nature remains of quite *infinite* depth, of quite infinite expansion; and all Experience thereof limits itself to some few computed centuries and measured square-miles. The course of Nature's phases, on this our little fraction of a Planet, is partially known to us: but who knows what deeper courses these depend on; what infinitely larger Cycle (of causes) our little Epicycle revolves on? To the

[1] Laplace's work was entitled *Méchanique Celeste*.

Minnow every cranny and pebble, and quality and accident, of its little native Creek may have become familiar: but does the Minnow understand the Ocean Tides and periodic Currents, the Trade-winds, and Monsoons, and Moon's Eclipses; by all which the condition of its little Creek is regulated, and may, from time to time (*un*miraculously enough), be quite over-set and reversed? Such a Minnow is Man; his Creek this Planet Earth; his Ocean the immeasurable All; his Monsoons and periodic Currents the mysterious Course of Providence through Æons of Æons.

"We speak of the Volume of Nature: and truly a Volume it is — whose Author and Writer is God. To read it! Dost thou, does man, so much as well know the Alphabet thereof? With its Words, Sentences, and grand descriptive Pages, poetical and philo-sophical, spread out through Solar Systems, and Thousands of Years, we shall not try thee. It is a Volume written in celestial hieroglyphs, in the true Sacred-writing; of which even Prophets are happy that they can read here a line and there a line. As for your Institutes, and Academies of Science, they strive bravely; and, from amid the thick-crowded, inextri-cably intertwisted hieroglyphic writing, pick-out, by dexterous combination, some Letter in the vulgar Character, and therefrom put together this and the other economic Recipe, of high avail in Practice. That Nature is more than some boundless Volume of such Recipes, or huge, well-nigh inexhaustible Do-mestic-Cookery Book, of which the whole secret will in this manner one day evolve itself, the fewest dream

"Custom," continues the Professor, "doth make dotards of us all. Consider well, thou wilt find that Custom is the greatest of Weavers; and weaves air raiment for all the Spirits of the Universe; whereby these dwell with us visibly, as ministering servants, in our houses and workshops; but their spiritual nature becomes, to the most, forever hidden. Philosophy complains that Custom has hoodwinked us, from the first; that we do everything by Custom, even Believe by it; that our very Axioms, let us boast of Free-thinking as we may, are oftenest simply such Beliefs as we have never heard questioned. Nay, what is Philosophy throughout but a continual battle against Custom; an ever-renewed effort to *transcend* the sphere of blind Custom, and so become Transcendental?

"Innumerable are the illusions and legerdemain-tricks of Custom: but of all these, perhaps the clever-est is her knack of persuading us that the Miraculous, by simple repetition, ceases to be Miraculous. True, it is by this means we live; for man must work as well as wonder: and herein is Custom so far a kind nurse, guiding him to his true benefit. But she is a fond fool-ish nurse, or rather we are false foolish nurslings, when, in our resting and reflecting hours, we prolong the same deception. Am I to view the Stupendous with stupid indifference, because I have seen it twice, or two-hundred, or two-million times? There is no reason in Nature or in Art why I should: unless, in-deed, I am a mere Work-Machine, for whom the divine gift of Thought were no other than the terrestrial gift of Steam is to the Steam-engine; a power whereby Cot-ton might be spun, and money and money's worth realised.

"Notable enough too, here as elsewhere, wilt thou find the potency of Names; which indeed are but one of such custom-woven, wonder-hiding Garments. Witch-craft, and all manner of Spectre-work, and Demon-ology, we have now named Madness and Disease of the Nerves. Seldom reflecting that still the new question comes upon us: What is Madness, what are Nerves? Ever, as before, does Madness remain a mysterious-terrific, altogether *infernal* boiling-up of the Nether Chaotic Deep, through this fair-painted vision of Creation, which swims thereon, which we name the Real. Was Luther's picture of the Devil less a Reality whether it were formed within the bodily eye, or without it? In every wisest Soul lies a whole world of internal Madness, an authentic Demon Empire; out of which, indeed, his world of Wisdom has been creatively built together, and now rests there, as on its dark foundations does a habitable flowery Earth-rind.

"But the deepest of all illusory Appearances, for hiding Wonder, as for many other ends, are your two grand fundamental world-enveloping Appearances, SPACE and TIME. These, as spun and woven for us before Birth itself, to clothe our celestial ME for dwelling here, and yet to blind it — lie all embracing, as the universal canvas, or warp and woof, whereby all minor Illusions, in this Phantasm Existence, weave and paint themselves. In vain, while here on Earth, shall you endeavor to strip them off; you can, at best, but rend them asunder for moments, and look through.

"Fortunatus had a wishing Hat, which when he put on, and wished himself Anywhere, behold he was There. By this means had Fortunatus triumphed over Space, he had annihilated Space; for him there was no Where, but all was Here. Were a Hatter to establish himself, in the Wahngasse of Weissnichtwo,[1] and make felts of this sort for all mankind, what a world we should have of it! Still stranger, should, on the opposite side of the street, another Hatter estab-

[1] *Weissnichtwo* (Know-not-where) is the imaginary German city in which Teufelsdroeckh lives; *Wahngasse* (Street of Illusion), the street where he resides.

lish himself; and as his fellow-craftsman made Space-annihilating Hats, make Time-annihilating! Of both would I purchase, were it with my last groschen; but chiefly of this latter. To clap-on your felt, and, simply by wishing that you were Any*where*, straightway to be *There!* Next to clap on your other felt, and simply by wishing that you were Any*when*, straightway to be *Then!* This were indeed the grander: shooting at will from the Fire-Creation of the World to its Fire-Consummation; here historically present in the First Century, conversing face to face with Paul and Seneca; there prophetically in the Thirty-first, conversing also face to face with other Pauls and Senecas, who as yet stand hidden in the depth of that late Time!

"Or thinkest thou it were impossible, unimaginable? Is the Past annihilated, then, or only past; is the Future non-existent, or only future? Those mystic faculties of thine, Memory and Hope, already answer: already through those mystic avenues, thou the Earth-blinded summonest both Past and Future, and communest with them, though as yet darkly, and with mute beckonings. The curtains of Yesterday drop down, the curtains of Tomorrow roll up; but Yesterday and Tomorrow both *are*. Pierce through the Time-element, glance into the Eternal. Believe what thou findest written in the sanctuaries of Man's Soul, even as all Thinkers, in all ages, have devoutly read it there: that Time and Space are not God, but creations of God; that with God as it is a universal HERE, so it is an everlasting NOW.

"And seest thou therein any glimpse of IM-MORTALITY? — O Heaven! Is the white Tomb of our Loved One, who died from our arms, and had to be left behind us there, which rises in the distance, like a pale, mournfully receding Milestone, to tell how many toilsome uncheered miles we have journeyed on alone — but a pale spectral Illusion! Is the lost Friend still mysteriously Here, even as we are Here mysteriously, with God! — Know of a truth that only the Time-shadows have perished, or are perishable; that the real Being of whatever was, and whatever is, and whatever will be, *is* even now and forever. This, should it unhappily seem new, thou mayest ponder at thy leisure; for the next twenty years, or the next twenty centuries: believe it thou must; understand it thou canst not.

"That the Thought-forms, Space and Time, wherein, once for all, we are sent into this Earth to live, should condition and determine our whole Practical reasonings, conceptions, and imagings or imaginings — seems altogether fit, just, and unavoidable. But that they should, furthermore, usurp such sway over pure spiritual Meditation, and blind us to the wonder everywhere lying close on us, seems nowise so. Admit Space and Time to their due rank as Forms of Thought; nay even, if thou wilt, to their quite undue rank of Realities: and consider, then, with thyself how their thin disguises hide from us the brightest God-effulgences! Thus, were it not miraculous, could I stretch forth my hand and clutch the Sun? Yet thou seest me daily stretch forth my hand and therewith clutch many a thing, and swing it hither and thither. Art thou a grown baby, then, to fancy that the Miracle lies in miles of distance, or in pounds avoirdupois of weight; and not to see that the true inexplicable God-revealing Miracle lies in this, that I can stretch forth my hand at all; that I had free Force to clutch aught therewith? Innumerable other of this sort are the deceptions, and wonder-hiding stupefactions, which Space practises on us.

"Still worse is it with regard to Time. Your grand

anti-magician, and universal wonder-hider, is this same lying Time. Had we but the Time-annihilating Hat, to put on for once only, we should see ourselves in a World of Miracles, wherein all fabled or authentic Thaumaturgy, and feats of Magic, were outdone. But unhappily we have not such a Hat; and man, poor fool that he is, can seldom and scantily help himself without one.

"Were it not wonderful, for instance, had Orpheus, or Amphion, built the walls of Thebes by the mere sound of his Lyre? Yet tell me, Who built these walls of Weissnichtwo; summoning-out all the sandstone rocks, to dance along from the *Steinbruch* (now a huge Troglodyte Chasm, with frightful green-mantled pools); and shape themselves into Doric and Ionic pillars, squared ashlar houses and noble streets? Was it not the still higher Orpheus, or Orpheuses, who, in past centuries, by the divine Music of Wisdom, succeeded in civilizing Man? Our highest Orpheus walked in Judea, eighteen hundred years ago: his sphere-melody, flowing in wild native tones, took captive the ravished souls of men; and, being of a truth sphere-melody, still flows and sounds, though now with thousandfold accompaniments, and rich symphonies, through all our hearts; and modulates, and divinely leads them. Is that a wonder, which happens in two hours; and does it cease to be wonderful if happening in two million? Not only was Thebes built by the music of an Orpheus; but without the music of some inspired Orpheus was no city ever built, no work that man glories-in ever done.

"Sweep away the Illusion of Time; glance, if thou hast eyes, from the near moving-cause to its far-distant Mover: The stroke that came transmitted through a whole galaxy of elastic balls, was it less a stroke than if the last ball only had been struck, and set flying? O, could I (with the Time-annihilating Hat) transport thee direct from the Beginnings to the Endings, how were thy eyesight unsealed, and thy heart set flaming in the Light-sea of celestial wonder! Then sawest thou that this fair Universe, were it in the meanest province thereof, is in very deed the star-domed City of God; that through every star, through every grass-blade, and most through every Living Soul, the glory of a present God still beams. But Nature, which is the Time-vesture of God, and reveals Him to the wise, hides Him from the foolish.

"Again, could anything be more miraculous than an actual authentic Ghost? The English Johnson longed, all his life, to see one; but could not, though he went to Cock Lane,[1] and thence to the church-vaults, and tapped on coffins. Foolish Doctor! Did he never, with the mind's eye as well as the body's look round him into that full tide of human Life he so loved; did he never so much as look into Himself? The good Doctor was a Ghost, as actual and authentic as heart could wish; well-nigh a million of Ghosts were travelling the streets by his side. Once more I say, sweep away the illusion of Time; compress the threescore years into three minutes: what else was he, what else are we? Are we not Spirits, that are shaped into a body, into an Appearance; and that fade-away again into air and Invisibility? This is no metaphor, it is a simple scientific *fact*: we start out of Nothingness, take figure, and are Apparitions; round us, as round the veriest spectre, is Eternity; and to Eternity minutes are as years and æons. Come there not tones of Love and Faith, as from celestial harp-strings, like the Song

---

[1] *Cock Lane.* The Cock Lane or Stockwell Ghost set all London agog in 1762. Its manifestations proved to be the trickery of a servant-girl.

of beautified Souls?   And again, do not we squeak and
jibber (in our discordant, screech-owlish debatings and
recriminatings); and glide bodeful, and feeble, and
fearful; or uproar (*poltern*), and revel in our mad Dance
of the Dead — till the scent of the morning air summons us to our still Home; and dreamy Night becomes
awake and Day?   Where now is Alexander of Macedon:
does the steel Host, that yelled in fierce battle-shouts
at Issus and Arbela, remain behind him; or have they
all vanished utterly, even as perturbed Goblins must?
Napoleon too, and his Moscow Retreats and Austerlitz
Campaigns!   Was it all other than the veriest Spectre-
hunt; which has now, with its howling tumult that
made Night hideous, flitted away? — Ghosts!   There
are nigh a thousand-million walking the Earth openly
at noontide; some half-hundred have vanished from it,
some half-hundred have arisen in it, ere thy watch
ticks once.

"O Heaven, it is mysterious, it is awful to consider
that we not only carry each a future Ghost within him;
but are, in very deed, Ghosts!   These Limbs, whence
had we them; this stormy Force; this life-blood with
its burning Passion?   They are dust and shadow; a
Shadow-system gathered round our Me; wherein,
through some moments or years, the Divine Essence
is to be revealed in the Flesh.   That warrior on his
strong war-horse, fire flashes through his eyes; force
dwells in his arm and heart: but warrior and war-horse
are a vision; a revealed Force, nothing more.   Stately
they tread the Earth, as if it were a firm substance:
fool! the earth is but a film; it cracks in twain, and
warrior and war-horse sink beyond plummet's sounding.   Plummet's?   Fantasy herself will not follow
them.   A little while ago, they were not; a little while,
and they are not, their very ashes are not.

"So it has been from the beginning, so will it be to the end. Generation after generation takes to itself the Form of a Body; and forth-issuing from Cimmerian Night, on Heaven's mission APPEARS. What Force and Fire is in each he expends: one grinding in the mill of Industry; one hunter-like climbing the giddy Alpine heights of Science; one madly dashed in pieces on the rocks of Strife, in war with his fellow: — and then the Heaven-sent is recalled; his earthly Vesture falls away, and soon even to Sense becomes a vanished Shadow. Thus, like some wild-flaming, wild-thundering train of Heaven's Artillery, does this mysterious MANKIND thunder and flame, in long-drawn, quick-succeeding grandeur, through the unknown Deep. Thus, like a God-created, fire-breathing Spirit-host, we emerge from the Inane; haste stormfully across the astonished Earth; then plunge again into the Inane. Earth's mountains are levelled, and her seas filled up, in our passage: can the Earth, which is but dead and a vision, resist Spirits which are reality and are alive? On the hardest adamant some footprint of us is stamped-in; the last Rear of the host will read traces of the earliest Van. But whence? — O Heaven, whither Sense knows not; Faith knows not; only that it is through Mystery to Mystery, from God and to God.

"We are *such stuff*
As Dreams are made of, and our little Life
Is rounded with a sleep!" [1]

Thomas Carlyle, Sartor Resartus, Book III, chap. VIII, 1833

SHADOW — A PARABLE

1835

Ye who read are still among the living; but I who write shall have long since gone my way into the region

[1] *The Tempest*, IV, I, 166–68.

of shadows. For indeed strange things shall happen, and secret things be known, and many centuries shall pass away, ere these memorials be seen of men. And, when seen, there will be some to disbelieve and some to doubt, and yet a few who will find much to ponder upon in the characters here graven with a stylus of iron.

The year had been a year of terror, and of feelings more intense than terror for which there is no name upon the earth. For many prodigies and signs had taken place, and far and wide, over sea and land, the black wings of the Pestilence were spread abroad. To those, nevertheless, cunning in the stars, it was not unknown that the heavens wore an aspect of ill; and to me, the Greek Oinos, among others, it was evident that now had arrived the alternation of that seven hundred and ninety-fourth year when, at the entrance of Aries, the planet Jupiter is conjoined with the red ring of the terrible Saturnus. The peculiar spirit of the skies, if I mistake not greatly, made itself manifest, not only in the physical orb of the earth, but in the souls, imaginations, and meditations of mankind.

Over some flasks of the red Chian wine, within the walls of a noble hall in a dim city called Ptolemais, we sat at night, a company of seven. And to our chamber there was no entrance save by a lofty door of brass; and the door was fashioned by the artisan Corinnos, and, being of rare workmanship, was fastened from within. Black draperies likewise, in the gloomy room, shut out from our view the moon, the lurid stars, and the peopleless streets — but the boding and the memory of Evil, they would not be so excluded. There were things around us and about of which I could render no distinct account — things material and spiritual: heaviness in the atmosphere, a sense of suffocation, anxiety — and, above all, that terrible state of existence which the nervous experience when the senses are keenly living and awake, and meanwhile the powers of thought lie dormant. A dead weight hung upon us. It hung upon our limbs, upon the household furniture, upon the goblets from which we drank; and all things were depressed, and borne down thereby — all things save only the flames of the seven iron lamps which illumined our revel. Uprearing themselves in tall slender lines of light, they thus remained burning, all pallid and motionless; and in the mirror which their lustre formed upon the round table of ebony at which we sat, each of us there assembled beheld the pallor of his own countenance, and the unquiet glare in the downcast eyes of his companions. Yet we laughed and were merry in our proper way — which was hysterical; and sang the songs of Anacreon — which were madness; and drank deeply — although the purple wine reminded us of blood. For there was yet another tenant of our chamber in the person of young Zoilus. Dead and at full length he lay, enshrouded: the genius and the demon of the scene. Alas! he bore no portion in our mirth, save that his countenance, distorted with the plague, and his eyes in which Death had but half extinguished the fire of the pestilence, seemed to take such interest in our merriment as the dead may haply take in the merriment of those who are to die. But although I, Oinos, felt that the eyes of the departed were upon me, still I forced myself not to perceive the bitterness of their expression, and, gazing down steadily into the depths of the ebony mirror, sang with a loud and sonorous voice the songs of the son of Teios. But gradually my songs they ceased, and their echoes, rolling afar off among the sable draperies of the chamber, became weak, and undistinguishable, and so faded away. And lo! from among those sable draper-

ies where the sound of the song departed, there came
forth a dark and undefined shadow — a shadow such
as the moon, when low in heaven, might fashion from
the figure of a man; but it was the shadow neither of
man, nor of God, nor of any familiar thing.   And
quivering there awhile among the draperies of the
room, it at length rested in full view upon the surface
of the door of brass.   But the shadow was vague, and
formless, and indefinite, and was the shadow neither of
man nor of God — neither God of Greece, nor God of
Chaldæa, nor any Egyptian God.   And the shadow
rested upon the brazen doorway, and under the arch of
the entablature of the door, and moved not, nor spoke
any word, but there became stationary and remained.
And the door whereupon the shadow rested was, if I
remember aright, over against the feet of the young
Zoilus enshrouded.   But we, the seven there assembled, having seen the shadow as it came out from
among the draperies, dared not steadily behold it, but
cast down our eyes, and gazed continually into the
depths of the mirror of ebony.   And at length I,
Oinos, speaking some low words, demanded of the
shadow its dwelling and its appellation.   And the
shadow answered, "I am SHADOW, and my dwelling
is near to the catacombs of Ptolemais, and hard by
those dim plains of Helusion which border upon the
foul Charonian canal."   And then did we, the seven,
start from our seats in horror, and stand trembling,
and shuddering, and aghast: for the tones in the voice
of the shadow were not the tones of any one being, but
of a multitude of beings, and, varying in their cadences
from syllable to syllable, fell duskily upon our ears in
the well-remembered and familiar accents of many
thousand departed friends.

Edgar Allan Poe

Charonian canal, the river Styx.

GIFTS

1841

Gifts of one who loved me —
'Twas high time they came;
When he ceased to love me,
Time they stopped for shame.

It is said that the world is in a state of bankruptcy, that the world owes the world more than the world can pay, and ought to go into chancery, and be sold. I do not think this general insolvency, which involves in some sort all the population, to be the reason of the difficulty experienced at Christmas and New Year, and other times, in bestowing gifts; since it is always so pleasant to be generous, though very vexatious to pay debts. But the impediment lies in the choosing. If, at any time, it comes into my head that a present is due from me to somebody, I am puzzled what to give until the opportunity is gone. Flowers and fruits are always fit presents; flowers, because they are a proud assertion that a ray of beauty outvalues all the utilities of the world. These gay natures contrast with the somewhat stern countenance of ordinary nature; they are like music heard out of a workhouse. Nature does not cocker us: we are children, not pets: she is not fond: everything is dealt to us without fear or favor, after severe universal laws. Yet these delicate flowers look like the frolic and interference of love and beauty. Men used to tell us that we love flattery, even though we are not deceived by it, because it shows that we are of importance enough to be courted. Something like that pleasure, the flowers give us: what am I to whom these sweet hints are addressed? Fruits are acceptable gifts, because they are the flower of commodities, and admit of fantastic values being attached to them. If a man should send to me to come a hundred miles to visit him, and should set before me a basket of fine summer fruit, I should think there was some proportion between the labour and the reward.

For common gifts, necessity makes pertinences and beauty every day, and one is glad when an imperative leaves him no option, since if the man at the door has no shoes you have not to consider whether you could procure him a paint-box. And as it is always pleasing to see a man eat bread, or drink water, in the house or out of doors, so it is always a great satisfaction to supply these first wants. Necessity does everything well. In our condition of universal dependence, it seems heroic to let the petitioner be the judge of his necessity, and to give all that is asked, though at great inconvenience. If it be a fantastic desire, it is better to leave to others the office of punishing him. I can think of many parts I should prefer playing to that of the Furies. Next to things of necessity, the rule for a gift, which one of my friends prescribed, is, that we might convey to some person that which properly belonged to his character, and was easily associated with him in thought. But our tokens of compliment and love are for the most part barbarous. Rings and other jewels are not gifts, but apologies for gifts. The only gift is a portion of thyself. Thou must bleed for me. Therefore the poet brings his poem; the shepherd, his lamb; the farmer, corn; the miner, a gem; the sailor, coral and shells; the painter, his picture; the girl, a handkerchief of her own sewing. This is right and pleasing, for it restores society in so far to its primary basis, when a man's biography is conveyed in his gift, and every man's wealth is an index of his merit. But it is a cold, lifeless business when you go to the shops to buy me something, which does not represent your life and talent, but a goldsmith's. This is fit for kings, and rich men who represent kings, and a false state of property, to make presents of gold and silver stuffs, as a kind of symbolical sin-offering, or payment of black-mail.

The law of benefits is a difficult channel, which requires careful sailing, or rude boats. It is not the office of a man to receive gifts. How dare you give them? We wish to be self-sustained. We do not quite forgive a giver. The hand that feeds us is in some danger of being bitten. We can receive anything from love, for that is a way of receiving it from ourselves; but not from any one who assumes to bestow. We sometimes hate the meat which we eat, because there seems something of degrading dependence in living by it.

"Brother, if Jove to thee a present make,
    Take heed that from his hands thou nothing take." [1]

We ask the whole. Nothing less will content us. We arraign society if it do not give us besides earth, and fire, and water, opportunity, love, reverence, and objects of veneration.

He is a good man who can receive a gift well. We are either glad or sorry at a gift, and both emotions are unbecoming. Some violence, I think, is done, some degradation borne, when I rejoice or grieve at a gift. I am sorry when my independence is invaded, or when a gift comes from such as do not know my spirit, and so the act is not supported; and if the gift pleases me overmuch, then I should be ashamed that the donor should read my heart, and see that I love his commodity and not him. The gift, to be true, must be the flowing of the giver unto me, correspondent to my flowing unto him. When the waters are at a level,

[1] Hesiod, *Works and Days*, VIII, 5–8.

then my goods pass to him, and his to me. All his are mine, all mine his. I say to him, "How can you give me this pot of oil, or this flagon of wine, when all your oil and wine is mine?" which belief of mine this gift seems to deny. Hence the fitness of beautiful, not useful things for gifts. This giving is flat usurpation, and therefore when the beneficiary is ungrateful, as all beneficiaries hate all Timons, not at all considering the value of the gift, but looking back to the greater store it was taken from, I rather sympathize with the beneficiary than with the anger of my lord Timon. For, the expectation of gratitude is mean, and is continually punished by the total insensibility of the obliged person. It is a great happiness to get off without injury and heart-burning from one who has had the ill luck to be served by you. It is a very onerous business, this of being served, and the debtor naturally wishes to give you a slap. A golden text for these gentlemen is that which I so admire in the Buddhist, who never thanks, and who says, "Do not flatter your benefactors."

The reason of these discords I conceive to be, that there is no commensurability between a man and any gift. You cannot give anything to a magnanimous person. After you have served him, he at once puts you in debt by his magnanimity. The service a man renders his friend is trivial and selfish, compared with the service he knows his friend stood in readiness to yield him, alike before he had begun to serve his friend, and now also. Compared with that goodwill I bear my friend, the benefit it is in my power to render him seems small. Besides, our action on each other, good as well as evil, is so incidental and at random, that

---

Timon of Athens (cf. Shakespeare's play of that title) was foolishly generous.

we can seldom hear the acknowledgements of any person who would thank us for a benefit without some shame and humiliation. We can rarely strike a direct stroke, but must be content with an oblique one; we seldom have the satisfaction of yielding a direct benefit, which is directly received. But rectitude scatters favors on every side without knowing it, and receives with wonder the thanks of all people.

I fear to breathe any treason against the majesty of love, which is the genius and god of gifts, and to whom we must not affect to prescribe. Let him give kingdoms or flower-leaves indifferently. There are persons from whom we always expect fairy-tokens; let us not cease to expect them. This is prerogative, and not to be limited by our municipal rules. For the rest, I like to see that we cannot be bought and sold. The best of hospitality and of generosity is also not in the will, but in fate. I find that I am not much to you; you do not need me; you do not feel me; then am I thrust out of doors, though you proffer me house and lands. No services are of any value, but only likeness. When I have attempted to join myself to others by services, it proved an intellectual trick — no more. They eat your service like apples, and leave you out. But love them, and they feel you, and delight in you all the time.

Ralph Waldo Emerson, Essays: Second Series, 1844 (first published in *The Dial,* 1841).

LITERATURE OF KNOWLEDGE AND LITERATURE OF POWER

1848

What is it that we mean by *literature?* Popularly, and amongst the thoughtless, it is held to include everything that is printed in a book. Little logic is required to disturb *that* definition. The most thoughtless person is easily made aware that in the idea of *literature* one essential element is — some relation to a general and common interest of man, so that what applies only to a local or professional or merely personal interest, even though presenting itself in the shape of a book, will not belong to literature. So far the definition is easily narrowed; and it is as easily expanded. For not only is much that takes a station in books not literature, but, inversely, much that really *is* literature never reaches a station in books. The weekly sermons of Christendom, that vast pulpit literature which acts so extensively upon the popular mind — to warn, to uphold, to renew, to comfort, to alarm — does not attain the sanctuary of libraries in the ten-thousandth part of its extent. The drama, again, as for instance the finest of Shakespeare's plays in England and all leading Athenian plays in the noontide of the Attic stage, operated as a literature on the public mind, and were (according to the strictest letter of that term) *published* [1] through the audiences that witnessed their representation, some time before they were published as things to be read; and they were published in this scenical mode of publication with much more effect than they could have had as books during ages of costly copying or of costly printing.

Books, therefore, do not suggest an idea co-extensive and interchangeable with the idea of literature, since much literature, scenic, forensic, or didactic (as from lectures and public orators), may never come into books, and much that *does* come into books may con-

[1] "Charles I, for example, when Prince of Wales, and many others in his father's court, gained their known familiarity with Shakspeare — not through the original quartos, so slenderly diffused, nor through the first folio of 1623, but through the court representations of his chief dramas at Whitehall." — De Quincey's note.

nect itself with no literary interest. But a far more important correction, applicable to the common vague idea of literature, is to be sought, not so much in a better definition of literature, as in a sharper distinction of the two functions which it fulfills. In that great social organ which, collectively, we call literature, there may be distinguished two separate offices, that may blend and often *do* so, but capable, severally, of a severe insulation, and naturally fitted for reciprocal repulsion. There is, first, the literature of *knowledge*, and, secondly, the literature of *power*. The function of the first is to *teach*; the function of the second is to *move*: the first is a rudder; the second an oar or a sail. The first speaks to the *mere* discursive understanding; the second speaks ultimately, it may happen, to the higher understanding, or reason, but always *through* affections of pleasure and sympathy. Remotely it may travel towards an object seated in what Lord Bacon calls *dry* light; but proximately it does and must operate — else it ceases to be a literature of *power* — on and through that *humid* light which clothes itself in the mists and glittering *iris* of human passions, desires, and genial emotions. Men have so little reflected on the higher functions of literature as to find it a paradox if one should describe it as a mean or subordinate purpose of books to give information. But this is a paradox only in the sense which makes it honourable to be paradoxical. Whenever we talk in ordinary language of seeking information or gaining knowledge, we understand the words as connected with something of absolute novelty. But it is the grandeur of all truth which *can* occupy a very high place in human interests that i

Lord Bacon is an incorrect title. He was Baron Verulam and Viscount S
 Albans, but Sir Francis Bacon.
dry light, the reference by Bacon (in his *Apothegms New and Old*) is t
 Heracleitus, who said, "The dry light was the best soul"; meanin
 apparently, the rational understanding unaffected by the emotions.

is never absolutely novel to the meanest of minds: it exists eternally, by way of germ or latent principle, in the lowest as in the highest, needing to be developed but never to be planted. To be capable of transplantation is the immediate criterion of a truth that ranges on a lower scale. Besides which, there is a rarer thing than truth, namely, *power*, or deep sympathy with truth. What is the effect, for instance, upon society, of children? By the pity, by the tenderness, and by the peculiar modes of admiration, which connect themselves with the helplessness, with the innocence, and with the simplicity of children, not only are the primal affections strengthened and continually renewed, but the qualities which are dearest in the sight of heaven — the frailty, for instance, which appeals to forbearance, the innocence which symbolizes the heavenly, and the simplicity which is most alien from the worldly — are kept up in perpetual remembrance, and their ideals are continually refreshed. A purpose of the same nature is answered by the higher literature, *viz.*, the literature of power. What do you learn from *Paradise Lost*? Nothing at all. What do you learn from a cookery-book? Something new, something that you do not know before, in every paragraph. But would you therefore put the wretched cookery-book on a higher level of estimation than the divine poem? What you owe to Milton is not any knowledge, of which a million separate items are still but a million of advancing steps on the same earthly level; what you owe is *power*, that is, exercise, and expansion to your own latent capacity of sympathy with the infinite, where every pulse and each separate influx is a step upwards, a step ascending as upon a Jacob's ladder from earth to mysterious altitudes above the earth. *All* the steps of knowledge, from first to last, carry you further on the same plane, but could never raise you one foot above your ancient level of earth; whereas the very *first* step in power is a flight, is an ascending movement into another element where earth is forgotten.

Were it not that human sensibilities are ventilated and continually called out into exercise by the great phenomena of infancy, or of real life as it moves through chance and change, or of literature as it recombines these elements in the mimicries of poetry, romance, etc., it is certain that, like any animal power or muscular energy falling into disuse, all such sensibilities would gradually droop and dwindle. It is in relation to these great *moral* capacities of man that the literature of *power*, as contra-distinguished from that of knowledge, lives and has its field of action. It is concerned with what is highest in man; for the Scriptures themselves never condescended to deal by suggestion or co-operation with the mere discursive understanding: when speaking of man in his intellectual capacity, the Scriptures speak, not of the understanding, but of "the understanding heart," [1] making the heart — that is, the great *intuitive* (or non-discursive) organ, to be the interchangeable formula for man in his highest state of capacity for the infinite. Tragedy, romance, fairy tale, or epopee, all alike restore to man's mind the ideals of justice, of hope, of truth, of mercy, of retribution, which else (left to the support of daily life in its realities) would languish for want of sufficient illustration. What is meant, for instance, by *poetic justice?* It does not mean a justice that differs by its object from the ordinary justice of human jurisprudence, for then it must be confessedly a very bad kind of justice; but it means a justice that differs from common forensic justice by the degree in which it *attains*

[1] 1 *Kings,* III, 9, 12.

its object, a justice that is more omnipotent over its own ends, as dealing, not with the refractory elements of earthly life, but with elements of its own creation and with materials flexible to its own purest preconceptions. It is certain that, were it not for the literature of power, these ideals would often remain amongst us as mere notional forms; whereas, by the creative forces of man put forth in literature, they gain a vernal life of restoration and germinate into vital activities. The commonest novel, by moving in alliance with human fears and hopes, with human instincts of wrong and right, sustains and quickens those affections. Calling them into action, it rescues them from torpor. And hence the pre-eminency, over all authors that merely *teach*, of the meanest that moves, or that teaches, if at all, indirectly *by* moving. The very highest work that has ever existed in the literature of knowledge is but a provisional work, a book upon trial and sufferance, and *quamdiu bene se gesserit*. Let its teaching be even partially revised, let it be but placed in a better order, and instantly it is superseded. Whereas the feeblest works in the literature of power, surviving at all, survive as finished and unalterable among men. For instance, the *Principia* [1] of Sir Isaac Newton was a book *militant* on earth from the first. In all stages of its progress it would have to fight for its existence: first, as regards absolute truth; secondly, when that combat was over, as regards its form, or mode of presenting the truth. And as soon as a La Place, or anybody else, builds higher upon the foundations laid by this book, effectually he throws it out of the sunshine into decay and darkness; by weapons won from this book he superannuates and destroys this book, so that soon the

quamdiu, etc., as long as it bore itself well.

[1] *Philosophiae Naturalis Principia Mathematica* (*The Mathematical Principles of Natural Philosophy*), published 1687.

name of Newton remains a mere *nominis umbra*, but his book, as a living power, has transmigrated into other forms. Now, on the contrary, the *Iliad*, the *Prometheus* of Æschylus, the *Othello* or *King Lear*, the *Hamlet* or *Macbeth*, and the *Paradise Lost* are not militant but triumphant forever, as long as the languages exist in which they speak or can be taught to speak. They never *can* transmigrate into new incarnations. To reproduce these in new forms or variations, even if in some things they should be improved, would be to plagiarize. A good steam-engine is properly superseded by a better. But one lovely pastoral valley is not superseded by another, nor a statue of Praxiteles by a statue by Michael Angelo. These things are separated, not by imparity, but by disparity. They are not thought of as unequal under the same standard, but as different in *kind*, and, if otherwise unequal, as equal under a different standard. Human works of immortal beauty and works of nature in one respect stand on the same footing: they never approach so near as not to differ; and they differ not as better and worse, or simply by more and less; they differ by undecipherable and incommunicable differences, that cannot be caught by mimicries, that cannot be reflected in the mirror of copies, that cannot become ponderable in the scales of vulgar comparison.

Thomas De Quincey, The Poetry of Pope, 1848

THE SEEING EYE

1843-60

THE SKY

It is a strange thing how little in general people know about the sky. It is the part of creation in which

nominis umbra, shadow of a name.

nature has done more for the sake of pleasing man, more for the sole and evident purpose of talking to him and teaching him, than in any other part of her works, and it is just the part in which we least attend to her. There are not many of her other works in which some more material or essential purpose than the mere pleasing of man is not answered by every part of their organisation; but every essential purpose of the sky might, so far as we know, be answered if once in three days, or thereabouts, a great ugly, black rain-cloud were brought up over the blue, and everything well watered, and so all left blue again till next time, with perhaps a film of morning and evening mist for dew. And instead of this there is not a moment of any day of our lives when nature is not producing scene after scene, picture after picture, glory after glory, and working still upon such exquisite and constant principles of the most perfect beauty that it is quite certain it is all done for us and intended for our perpetual pleasure. And every man, wherever placed, however far from other sources of interest or of beauty, has this doing for him constantly. The noblest scenes of the earth can be seen and known but by few; it is not intended that man should live always in the midst of them; he injures them by his presence, he ceases to feel them if he be always with them: but the sky is for all; bright as it is, it is not

> "Too bright or good
> For human nature's daily food;" [1]

it is fitted in all its functions for the perpetual comfort and exalting of the heart, for soothing it and purifying it from its dross and dust. Sometimes gentle, sometimes capricious, sometimes awful, never the same for two minutes together, almost human in its passions, al-

---

[1] Wordsworth, *She was a phantom of delight.*

most spiritual in its tenderness, almost divine in its infinity, its appeal to what is immortal in us is as distinct as its ministry of chastisement or of blessing to what is mortal is essential. And yet we never attend to it, we never make it a subject of thought, but as it has to do with our animal sensations: we look upon all by which it speaks to us more clearly than to brutes, upon all which bears witness to the intention of the Supreme that we are to receive more from the covering vault than the light and the dew which we share with the weed and the worm, only as a succession of meaningless and monotonous accident, too common and too vain to be worthy of a moment of watchfulness or a glance of admiration. If in our moments of utter idleness and insipidity we turn to the sky as a last resource, which of its phenomena do we speak of? One says it has been wet; and another, it has been windy; and another, it has been warm. Who, among the whole chattering crowd, can tell me of the forms and the precipices of the chain of tall white mountains that girded the horizon at noon yesterday? Who saw the narrow sunbeam that came out of the south and smote upon their summits until they melted and mouldered away in a dust of blue rain? Who saw the dance of the dead clouds when the sunlight left them last night and the west wind blew them before it like withered leaves? All has passed, unregretted as unseen; or if the apathy be ever shaken off, even for an instant, it is only by what is gross or what is extraordinary; and yet it is not in the broad and fierce manifestations of the elemental energies, not in the clash of the hail nor the drift of the whirlwind, that the highest characters of the sublime are developed. God is not in the earthquake nor in the fire, but in the still, small voice.[1] They are but the

[1] 1 *Kings*, XIX, 11–12.

blunt and the low faculties of our nature which can
only be addressed through lampblack and lightning.
It is in quiet and subdued passages of unobtrusive
majesty, the deep and the calm and the perpetual; that
which must be sought ere it is seen, and loved ere it is
understood; things which the angels work out for us
daily and yet vary eternally, which are never wanting
and never repeated, which are to be found always yet
each found but once; it is through these that the lesson
of devotion is chiefly taught, and the blessing of beauty
given. These are what the artist of highest aim must
study; it is these, by the combination of which his ideal
is to be created; these, of which so little notice is ordinarily taken by common observers that I fully believe,
little as people in general are concerned with art, more
of their ideas of sky are derived from pictures than
from reality, and that if we could examine the conception formed in the minds of most educated persons
when we talk of clouds, it would frequently be found
composed of fragments of blue and white reminiscences of the old masters. — *Modern Painters*, Pt. II,
sect. III, chap. I.

RUNNING WATER

When water, not in very great body, runs in a rocky
bed much interrupted by hollows, so that it can rest
every now and then in a pool as it goes along, it does
not acquire a continuous velocity of motion. It
pauses after every leap, and curdles about, and rests a
little, and then goes on again; and if in this comparatively tranquil and rational state of mind it meets with
any obstacle, as a rock or stone, it parts on each side of
it with a little bubbling foam, and goes round; if it
comes to a step in its bed, it leaps it lightly, and then,

after a little splashing at the bottom, stops again to take breath. But if its bed be on a continuous slope, not much interrupted by hollows, so that it cannot rest, or if its own mass be so increased by flood that its usual resting-places are not sufficient for it but that it is perpetually pushed out of them by the following current before it has time to tranquillize itself, it of course gains velocity with every yard that it runs; the impetus got at one leap is carried to the credit of the next, until the whole stream becomes one mass of un-checked, accelerating motion. Now, when water in this state comes to an obstacle, it does not part at it, but clears it like a race-horse; and when it comes to a hollow, it does not fill it up and run out leisurely at the other side, but it rushes down into it and comes up again on the other side, as a ship into the hollow of the sea. Hence the whole appearance of the bed of the stream is changed, and all the lines of the water altered in their nature. The quiet stream is a succession of leaps and pools; the leaps are light and springy and parabolic, and make a great deal of splashing when they tumble into the pools; then we have a space of quiet curdling water and another similar leap below. But the stream when it has gained an impetus *takes the shape* of its bed, goes down into every hollow, not with a leap, but with a swing, not foaming nor splashing, but in the bending line of a strong sea-wave, and comes up again on the other side, over rock and ridge, with the ease of a bounding leopard; if it meet a rock three or four feet above the level of its bed, it will often neither part nor foam, nor express any concern about the matter, but clear it in a smooth dome of water, with-out apparent exertion, the whole surface of the surge being drawn into parallel lines by its extreme velocity; so that the whole river has the appearance of a deep and raging sea, with this only difference, that the torrent-waves always break backwards, and sea-waves forwards. Thus, then, in the water which has gained an impetus, we have the most exquisite arrangements of curved lines, perpetually changing from convex to concave, and *vice versa*, following every swell and hollow of the bed with their modulating grace, and all in unison of motion, presenting perhaps the most beautiful series of inorganic forms which nature can possibly produce; for the sea runs too much into similar and concave curves with sharp edges, but every motion of the torrent is united, and all its curves are modifications of beautiful line. — *Modern Painters*, Pt. II, sect. v, chap. iii.

MOUNTAINS

Inferior hills ordinarily interrupt, in some degree, the richness of the valleys at their feet; the grey downs of southern England, and treeless coteaux of central France, and grey swells of Scottish moor, whatever peculiar charm they may possess in themselves, are at least destitute of those which belong to the woods and fields of the lowlands. But the great mountains *lift* the lowlands *on their sides*. Let the reader imagine, first, the appearance of the most varied plain of some richly cultivated country; let him imagine it dark with graceful woods and soft with deepest pastures; let him fill the space of it, to the utmost horizon, with innumerable and changeful incidents of scenery and life, leading pleasant streamlets through its meadows, strewing clusters of cottages beside their banks, tracing sweet footpaths through its avenues, and animating its fields with happy flocks and slow spots of wandering cattle:

coteaux, slopes, declivities.

and when he has wearied himself with endless imagining, and left no space without some loveliness of its own, let him conceive all this great plain, with its infinite treasures of natural beauty and happy human life, gathered up in God's hands from one edge of the horizon to the other, like a woven garment; and shaken into deep, falling folds, as the robes droop from a king's shoulders; all its bright rivers leaping into cataracts along the hollows of its slopes, as a rider rears himself back when his horse plunges; and all its villages nestling themselves into the new windings of its glens; and all its pastures thrown into steep waves of greensward, dashed with dew along the edges of their folds, and sweeping down into endless slopes, with a cloud here and there lying quietly, half on the grass, half in the air; and he will have as yet, in all this lifted world, only the foundation of one of the great Alps. And whatever is lovely in the lowland scenery becomes lovelier in this change: the trees which grew heavily and stiffly from the level line of plain assume strange curves of strength and grace as they bend themselves against the mountain side; they breathe more freely and toss their branches more carelessly, as each climbs higher, looking to the clear light above the topmost leaves of its brother tree; the flowers which on the arable plain fell before the plough now find out for themselves unapproachable places, where year by year they gather into happier fellowship and fear no evil; and the streams which in the level land crept in dark eddies by unwholesome banks now move in showers of silver, and are clothed with rainbows, and bring health and life wherever the glance of their waves can reach. — *Modern Painters*, Pt. V, chap. VII.

LEAVES, LICHENS, AND MOSSES

Leaves motionless. The strong pines wave above them, and the weak grasses tremble beside them; but the blue stars rest upon the earth with a peace as of heaven; and far along the ridges of iron rock, moveless as they, the rubied crests of Alpine rose flush in the low rays of morning. Nor these yet the stillest leaves. Others there are, subdued to a deeper quietness, the mute slaves of the earth, to whom we owe, perhaps, thanks and tenderness the most profound of all we have to render for the leaf-ministries.

It is strange to think of the gradually diminished power and withdrawn freedom among the orders of leaves — from the sweep of the chestnut and gadding of the vine, down to the close-shrinking trefoil and contented daisy, pressed on earth; and, at last, to the leaves that are not merely close to earth but themselves a part of it, fastened down to it by their sides, here and there only a wrinkled edge rising from the granite crystals. We have found beauty in the tree yielding fruit and in the herb yielding seed. How of the herb yielding *no* seed, the fruitless, flowerless lichen of the rock?

Lichen and mosses (though these last in their luxuriance are deep and rich as herbage, yet both for the most part humblest of the green things that live), how of these? Meek creatures! the first mercy of the earth, veiling with hushed softness its dintless rocks; creatures full of pity, covering with strange and tender honour the scarred disgrace of ruin, laying quiet finger on the trembling stones to teach them rest. No words that I know will say what these mosses are. None are delicate enough, none perfect enough, none rich

blue star, Alpine rose, characteristic flowers of the Alps, the one a columbine, the other a rhododendron (?).

enough. How is one to tell of the rounded bosses of furred and beaming green; the starred divisions of rubied bloom, fine-filmed as if the Rock Spirits could spin porphyry as we do glass; the traceries of intricate silver, and fringes of amber, lustrous, arborescent, burnished through every fibre into fitful brightness and glossy traverses of silken change, yet all subdued and pensive, and framed for simplest, sweetest offices of grace. They will not be gathered, like the flowers, for chaplet or love-token; but of these the wild bird will make its nest, and the wearied child his pillow.

And, as the earth's first mercy, so they are its last gift to us. When all other service is vain, from plant and tree, the soft mosses and gray lichen take up their watch by the headstone. The woods, the blossoms, the gift-bearing grasses have done their parts for a time, but these do service forever. Trees for the builder's yard, flowers for the bride's chamber, corn for the granary, moss for the grave.

Yet, as in one sense the humblest, in another they are the most honoured, of the earth-children. Unfading as motionless, the worm frets them not, and the autumn wastes not. Strong in lowliness, they neither blanch in heat nor pine in frost. To them, slow-fingered, constant-hearted, is entrusted the weaving of the dark, eternal tapestries of the hills; to them, slow-pencilled, iris-dyed, the tender framing of their endless imagery. Sharing the stillness of the unimpassioned rock, they share also its endurance; and while the winds of departing spring scatter the white hawthorn blossom like drifted snow, and summer dims on the parched meadow the drooping of its cowslip-gold, far above, among the mountains, the silver lichen-spots rest, star-like, on the stone, and the gathering orange stain upon the edge of yonder western peak reflects the

sunsets of a thousand years. — *Modern Painters*, Pt.
VI, chap. x.

John Ruskin

THE WIND ON THE HEATH

Pub. 1851

"What is your opinion of death, Mr. Petulengro?"
said I, as I sat down beside him.

"My opinion of death, brother, is much the same as
that in the old song of Pharaoh, which I have heard my
grandam sing: —

'Cana marel o manus chivios andé puv,
Ta rovel pa leste o chavo ta romi.' [1]

When a man dies, he is cast into the earth, and his wife
and child sorrow over him. If he has neither wife nor
child, then his father and mother, I suppose; and if he
is quite alone in the world, why, then, he is cast into the
earth, and there is an end of the matter."

"And do you think that is the end of a man?"

"There's an end of him, brother, more's the pity."

"Why do you say so?"

"Life is sweet, brother."

"Do you think so?"

"Think so! There's night and day, brother, both
sweet things; sun, moon, and stars, brother, all sweet
things; there's likewise the wind on the heath. Life
is very sweet, brother; who would wish to die?"

"I would wish to die —— "

"You talk like a gorgio — which is the same as talk-

Jasper Petulengro (his name means a master-smith) is a gypsy.
gorgio, a Gentile, non-gypsy.

[1] *Cana marel*, etc. The Romany words are translated in the next
sentence.

ing like a fool — were you a Rommany Chal you would talk wiser. Wish to die, indeed! A Rommany Chal would wish to live for ever!"

"In sickness, Jasper?"

"There's still the sun and stars, brother."

"In blindness, Jasper?"

"There's the wind on the heath, brother; if I could only feel that, I would gladly live for ever. Dosta, we'll now go to the tents and put on the gloves; and I'll try to make you feel what a sweet thing it is to be alive, brother!"

George Borrow, Lavengro: The Scholar, the Gypsy, the Priest, chap. xxv.

OLIVER GOLDSMITH

1853

"Jeté sur cette boule,
    Laid, chétif et souffrant;
Etouffé dans la foule,
    Faute d'être assez grand:

"Une plainte touchante
    De ma bouche sortit.
Le bon Dieu me dit: Chante,
    Chante, pauvre petit!

"Chanter ou je m'abuse,
    Est ma tâche ici-bas.
Tous ceux qu'ainsi j'amuse
    Ne m'aimeront-ils pas?" [1]

Rommany Chal, gipsy lad or man.   *Dosta,* enough!

[1] "Cast upon this ball, ugly, suffering, suffocated in the crowd because am not great enough, a touching plaint issues from my mouth. The goo God says to me, 'Sing, sing, poor little one!' Unless I deceive myself, t sing is my task here below. All those whom I thus amuse, will they n love me?" — Béranger, French lyric poet (1780–1857).

In those charming lines of Béranger one may fancy
described the career, the sufferings, the genius, the
gentle nature of Goldsmith, and the esteem in which
we hold him. Who, of the millions whom he has
amused, doesn't love him? To be the most beloved of
English writers, what a title that is for a man! A wild
youth, wayward but full of tenderness and affection,
quits the country village where his boyhood has been
passed in happy musing, in idle shelter, in fond longing
to see the great world out of doors, and achieve name
and fortune: and after years of dire struggle and neglect
and poverty, his heart turning back as fondly to his
native place as it had longed eagerly for change when
sheltered there, he writes a book and a poem, full of the
recollections and feelings of home; he paints the friends
and scenes of his youth, and peoples Auburn and
Wakefield with remembrances of Lissoy. Wander he
must, but he carries away a home-relic with him and
dies with it on his breast. His nature is truant; in repose it longs for change, as on the journey it looks back
for friends and quiet. He passes to-day in building
an air-castle for to-morrow or in writing yesterday's
elegy; and he would fly away this hour but that a cage
and necessity keep him. What is the charm of his
verse, of his style, and humor? His sweet regrets, his
delicate compassion, his soft smile, his tremulous
sympathy, the weakness which he owns? Your love
for him is half pity. You come hot and tired from the
day's battle, and this sweet minstrel sings to you.
Who could harm the kind vagrant harper? Whom did
he ever hurt? He carries no weapon — save the harp
on which he plays to you, and with which he delights
great and humble, young and old, the captains in the

Auburn, described in *The Deserted Village*; *Wakefield*, in *The Vicar of Wakefield*; *Lissoy*, see p. 382.

tents, or the soldiers round the fire, or the women and children in the villages, at whose porches he stops and sings his simple songs of love and beauty. With that sweet story of *The Vicar of Wakefield* he has found entry into every castle and every hamlet in Europe. Not one of us, however busy or hard, but once or twice in our lives has passed an evening with him and undergone the charm of his delightful music.

Goldsmith's father was no doubt the good Doctor Primrose, whom we all of us know. Swift was yet alive when the little Oliver was born at Pallas, or Pallasmore, in the county of Longford, in Ireland. In 1730, two years after the child's birth, Charles Goldsmith removed his family to Lissoy, in the county of Westmeath, that sweet "Auburn" which every person who hears me has seen in fancy. Here the kind parson brought up his eight children; and loving all the world, as his son says, fancied all the world loved him. He had a crowd of poor dependents besides those hungry children. He kept an open table, round which sat flatterers and poor friends, who laughed at the poor rector's many jokes and ate the produce of his seventy acres of farm. Those who have seen an Irish house in the present day can fancy that one of Lissoy. The old beggar still has his allotted corner by the kitchen turf; the maimed soldier still gets his potatoes and buttermilk; the poor cottier still asks his Honor's charity, and prays God bless his Reverence for the sixpence; the ragged pensioner still takes his place by right and sufferance. There's still a crowd in the kitchen, and a crowd round the parlour table; profusion, confusion, kindness, poverty. If an Irishman comes to London to make his fortune, he has a half-dozen of Irish dependents who take a percentage of his earnings. The good Charles Goldsmith left but little provision for his hungry race when death summoned him; and one of his daughters being engaged to a squire of rather superior dignity, Charles Goldsmith impoverished the rest of his family to provide the girl with a dowry.

The small-pox, which scourged all Europe at that time, and ravaged the roses off the cheeks of half the world, fell foul of poor little Oliver's family, when the child was eight years old, and left him scarred and disfigured for his life. An old woman in his father's village taught him his letters, and pronounced him a dunce: Paddy Byrne, the hedge-schoolmaster, took him in hand: and from Paddy Byrne he was transmitted to a clergyman at Elphin. When a child was sent to school in those days the classic phrase was that he was placed under Mr. So-and-So's *ferule*. Poor little ancestors! It is hard to think how ruthlessly you were birched, and how much of needless whipping and tears our small forefathers had to undergo! A relative, kind Uncle Contarine, took the main charge of little Noll, who went through his school-days righteously doing as little work as he could, robbing orchards, playing at ball, and making his pocket-money fly about whenever fortune sent it to him. Everybody knows the story of that famous "Mistakes of a Night," [1] when the young schoolboy, provided with a guinea and a nag, rode up to the "best house" in Ardagh, called for the landlord's company over a bottle of wine at supper, and for a hot cake for breakfast in the morning; and found, when he asked for the bill, that the best house was Squire Featherstone's, and not the inn for which he mistook it. Who does not know every story about Goldsmith? That is a delightful and fantastic picture of the child dancing and capering about in the kitchen at home, when the old fiddler gibed at

[1] The sub-title of *She Stoops to Conquer*.

him for his ugliness and called him Æsop; and little
Noll made his repartee of "Heralds proclaim aloud
this saying — See Æsop dancing and his monkey
playing." One can fancy a queer, pitiful look of
humor and appeal upon that little scarred face — the
funny little dancing figure, the funny little brogue. In
his life, and his writings, which are the honest expression of it, he is constantly bewailing that homely face
and person; anon he surveys them in the glass ruefully; and presently assumes the most comical dignity.
He likes to deck out his little person in splendor and
fine colors. He presented himself to be examined for
ordination in a pair of scarlet breeches; and said honestly that he did not like to go into the Church, because he was fond of colored clothes. When he tried to
practise as a doctor, he got by hook or by crook a black
velvet suit, and looked as big and grand as he could, and
kept his hat over a patch on the old coat: in better days
he bloomed out in plum-color, in blue silk, and in new
velvet. For some of these splendors the heirs and
assignees of Mr. Filby, the tailor, have never been paid
to this day: perhaps the kind tailor and his creditor
have met and settled their little account in Hades.

They showed until lately a window at Trinity College, Dublin, on which the name of "O. Goldsmith"
was engraved with a diamond. Whose diamond was
it? Not the young sizar's, who made but a poor figure
in that place of learning. He was idle, penniless, and
fond of pleasure: he learned his way early to the pawnbroker's shop. He wrote ballads, they say, for the
street-singers, who paid him a crown for a poem; and
his pleasure was to steal out at night and hear his
verses sung. He was chastised by his tutor for giving

sizar, a student whose fees are paid out of the funds of the university and
  who usually works for his board.

a dance in his rooms, and took the box on the ear so much to heart that he packed up his all, pawned his books and little property, and disappeared from college and family. He said he intended to go to America; but when his money was spent, the young prodigal came home ruefully, and the good folks there killed their calf — it was a lean one — and welcomed him back.

After college, he hung about his mother's house, and lived for some years the life of a buckeen — passed a month with this relation and that, a year with one patron, a great deal of time at the public-house. Tired of this life, it was resolved that he should go to London and study at the Temple; but he got no farther on the road to London and the woolsack than Dublin, where he gambled away the fifty pounds given to him for his outfit, and whence he returned to the indefatigable forgiveness of home. Then he determined to be a doctor, and Uncle Contarine helped him to a couple of years at Edinburgh. Then from Edinburgh he felt that he ought to hear the famous professors of Leyden and Paris, and wrote most amusing pompous letters to his uncle about the great Farheim, Du Petit, and Duhamel du Monceau, whose lectures he proposed to follow. If Uncle Contarine believed those letters; if Oliver's mother believed that story which the youth related of his going to Cork, with the purpose of embarking to America, of his having paid his passage-money and having sent his kit on board; of the anonymous captain sailing away with Oliver's valuable luggage in a nameless ship, never to return — if Uncle Contarine and the mother at Ballymahon believed his stories, they must have been a very simple pair, as it was a

---

buckeen, a younger son of the poorer aristocracy, who aped the manners of the gentry.

very simple rogue indeed who cheated them. When the lad, after failing in his clerical examination, after failing in his plan for studying law, took leave of these projects and of his parents, and set out for Edinburgh, he saw mother and uncle and lazy Ballymahon and green native turf and sparkling river for the last time. He was never to look on old Ireland more, and only in fancy revisit her.

"But me, not destined such delights to share,
My prime of life in wandering spent and care;
Impelled, with steps unceasing, to pursue
Some fleeting good that mocks me with the view;
That, like the circle bounding earth and skies,
Allures from far, yet, as I follow, flies;
My fortune leads to traverse realms alone,
And find no spot of all the world my own." [1]

I spoke in a former lecture of that high courage which enabled Fielding, in spite of disease, remorse, and poverty, always to retain a cheerful spirit, and to keep his manly benevolence and love of truth intact, as if these treasures had been confided to him for the public benefit, and he was accountable to posterity for their honorable employ; and a constancy equally happy and admirable, I think, was shown by Goldsmith, whose sweet and friendly nature bloomed kindly always in the midst of a life's storm and rain and bitter weather. The poor fellow was never so friendless but he could befriend some one, never so pinched and wretched but he could give of his crust and speak his word of compassion. If he had but his flute left, he could give that, and make the children happy in the dreary London court. He could give the coals in that queer coal-scuttle we read of to his poor neighbor; he

---

[1] *The Traveller*, ll. 23–30.

could pawn his coat to save his landlord from jail; when he was a school-usher, he spent his earnings in treats for the boys, and the good-natured school-master's wife said justly that she ought to keep Mr. Goldsmith's money as well as the young gentlemen's. When he met his pupils in later life, nothing would satisfy the Doctor but he must treat them still. "Have you seen the print of me after Sir Joshua Reynolds?" he asked of one of his old pupils. "Not seen it? not bought it? Sure, Jack, if your picture had been published, I'd not have been without it half-an-hour." His purse and his heart were everybody's, and his friends' as much as his own. When he was at the height of his reputation, and the Earl of Northumberland, going as Lord Lieutenant to Ireland, asked if he could be of any service to Doctor Goldsmith, Goldsmith recommended his brother, and not himself, to the great man. "My patrons," he gallantly said, "are the booksellers, and I want no others." Hard patrons they were, and hard work he did; but he did not complain much: if in his early writings some bitter words escaped him, some allusions to neglect and poverty, he withdrew these expressions when his works were republished, and better days seemed to open for him; and he did not care to complain that printer or publisher had overlooked his merit or left him poor. The Court face was turned from honest Oliver — the Court patronised Beattie. The fashion did not shine on him — fashion adored Sterne. Fashion pronounced Kelly to be the great writer of comedy of his day. A little — not ill-humor, but plaintiveness, a little betrayal of wounded pride which he showed, render him not the less amiable. The

James Beattie (1735–1803), a Scotch poet.
Hugh Kelly (1739–77), whose *False Delicacy* was written with the intention of rivalling Goldsmith's *Good-natured Man*.

author of *The Vicar of Wakefield* had a right to protest
when Newbery kept back the manuscript for two
years; had a right to be a little peevish with Sterne; a
little angry when Colman's actors declined their parts
in his delightful comedy, when the manager refused to
have a scene painted for it, and pronounced its damna-
tion before hearing.[1] He had not the great public
with him; but he had the noble Johnson and the admirable Reynolds and the great Gibbon and the great
Burke and the great Fox — friends and admirers illustrious indeed; as famous as those who, fifty years
before, sat round Pope's table.

Nobody knows, and I dare say Goldsmith's buoyant
temper kept no account of, all the pains which he endured during the early period of his literary career.
Should any man of letters in our day have to bear up
against such, Heaven grant he may come out of the
period of misfortune with such a pure, kind heart as
that which Goldsmith obstinately bore in his breast.
The insults to which he had to submit are shocking to
read of — slander, contumely, vulgar satire, brutal
malignity perverting his commonest motives and actions; he had his share of these, and one's anger is
roused at reading of them, as it is at seeing a woman in-
sulted or a child assaulted, at the notion that a creature
so very gentle and weak and full of love should have
had to suffer so.   And he had worse than insult to
undergo — to own to fault and deprecate the anger of
ruffians.   There is a letter of his extant to one Griffiths,
a bookseller, in which poor Goldsmith is forced to confess that certain books sent by Griffiths are in the
hands of a friend from whom Goldsmith had been
forced to borrow money.   "He was wild, sir," Johnson

John Newbery, English bookseller and publisher.
    [1] The comedy was *She Stoops to Conquer*; Colman was the manager of
Covent Garden Theatre.

said, speaking of Goldsmith to Boswell with his great, wise benevolence and noble mercifulness of heart, "Dr. Goldsmith was wild, sir; but he is so no more." Ah! if we pity the good and weak man who suffers undeservedly, let us deal very gently with him from whom misery extorts not only tears but shame; let us think humbly and charitably of the human nature that suffers so sadly and falls so low. Whose turn may it be to-morrow? What weak heart, confident before trial, may not succumb under temptation invincible? Cover the good man who has been vanquished — cover his face and pass on.

For the last half-dozen years of his life, Goldsmith was far removed from the pressure of any ignoble necessity, and in the receipt, indeed, of a pretty large income from the booksellers, his patrons. Had he lived but a few years more, his public fame would have been as great as his private reputation, and he might have enjoyed alive a part of that esteem which his country has ever since paid to the vivid and versatile genius who has touched on almost every subject of literature, and touched nothing that he did not adorn. Except in rare instances, a man is known in our profession and esteemed as a skilful workman, years before the lucky hit which trebles his usual gains and stamps him a popular author. In the strength of his age and the dawn of his reputation, having for backers and friends the most illustrious literary men of his time, fame and prosperity might have been in store for Goldsmith, had fate so willed it, and, at forty-six, had not sudden disease carried him off. I say prosperity rather than competence, for it is probable that no sum could have put order into his affairs or sufficed for his irreclaimable habits of dissipation. It must be remembered that he owed £2000 when he died. "Was ever poet," John-

son asked, "so trusted before?" As has been the case
with many another good fellow of his nation, his life
was tracked and his substance wasted by crowds of
hungry beggars and lazy dependents. If they came at
a lucky time (and be sure they knew his affairs better
than he did himself, and watched his pay-day), he gave
them of his money; if they begged on empty-purse
days, he gave them his promissory bills; or he treated
them to a tavern where he had credit; or he obliged
them with an order upon honest Mr. Filby for coats,
for which he paid as long as he could earn and until the
shears of Filby were to cut for him no more. Stagger-
ing under a load of debt and labor; tracked by bailiffs
and reproachful creditors; running from a hundred poor
dependents, whose appealing looks were the hardest of
all pains for him to bear; devising fevered plans for the
morrow, new histories, new comedies, all sorts of new
literary schemes; flying from all these into seclusion,
and out of seclusion into pleasure — at last, at five-
and-forty, death seized him and closed his career. I
have been many times in the chambers in the Temple
which were his, and passed up the staircase which
Johnson and Burke and Reynolds trod to see their
friend, their poet, their kind Goldsmith — the stair on
which the poor women sat weeping bitterly when they
heard that the greatest and most generous of men was
dead within the black oak door. Ah, it was a different
lot from that for which the poor fellow sighed when he
wrote, with heart yearning for home, those most charming of all fond verses, in which he fancies he revisits
Auburn:

"Here as I take my solitary rounds,
   Amidst thy tangling walks and ruined grounds,
   And, many a year elapsed, return to view

Where once the cottage stood, the hawthorn grew,
Remembrance wakes, with all her busy train,
Swells at my breast, and turns the past to pain.

    In all my wanderings round this world of care,
In all my griefs — and God has given my share —
I still had hopes, my latest hours to crown,
Amidst these humble bowers to lay me down;
To husband out life's taper at the close,
And keep the flame from wasting by repose:
I still had hopes — for pride attends us still —
Amidst the swains to show my book-learned skill,
Around my fire an evening group to draw,
And tell of all I felt and all I saw;
And as a hare whom hounds and horns pursue
Pants to the place from whence at first she flew —
I still had hopes, my long vexations past,
Here to return — and die at home at last.

    O blest retirement, friend to life's decline,
Retreats from care that never must be mine,
How blest is he who crowns, in shades like these,
A youth of labor with an age of ease;
Who quits a world where strong temptations try,
And, since 'tis hard to combat, learns to fly!
For him no wretches born to work and weep
Explore the mine or tempt the dangerous deep;
Nor surly porter stands in guilty state
To spurn imploring famine from the gate:
But on he moves to meet his latter end,
Angels around befriending virtue's friend;
Sinks to the grave with unperceived decay,
Whilst resignation gently slopes the way;
And, all his prospects brightening to the last,
His heaven commences ere the world be past." [1]

[1] *The Deserted Village*, ll. 77-112.

In these verses, I need not say with what melody, with what touching truth, with what exquisite beauty of comparison — as indeed in hundreds more pages of the writings of this honest soul — the whole character of the man is told — his humble confession of faults and weakness; his pleasant little vanity, and desire that his village should admire him; his simple scheme of good in which everybody was to be happy — no beggar was to be refused his dinner — nobody in fact was to work much, and he to be the harmless chief of the Utopia, and the monarch of the Irish Yvetot. He would have told again, and without fear of their failing, those famous jokes which had hung fire in London; he would have talked of his great friends of the Club — of my Lord Clare and my Lord Bishop, my Lord Nugent — sure he knew them intimately, and was hand and glove with some of the best men in town — and he would have spoken of Johnson and of Burke, and of Sir Joshua, who had painted him — and he would have told wonderful sly stories of Ranelagh and the Pantheon, and the masquerades of Madame Cornelys; and he would have toasted, with a sigh, the Jessamy Bride — the lovely Mary Horneck.

The figure of that charming young lady forms one of the prettiest recollections of Goldsmith's life. She and her beautiful sister, who married Bunbury, the graceful and humorous amateur artist of those days, when Gilray had but just begun to try his powers, were among the kindest and dearest of Goldsmith's many friends; cheered and pitied him, travelled abroad with him, made him welcome at their home, and gave him

---

Yvetot, a town in Normandy.   The reference is to the King of Yvetot (subject of a famous song by Béranger), who "rose late, went to bed early, ate four meals a day, rode on an ass through his domains, and made pleasure his only code."

Ranelagh and the Pantheon, pleasure grounds.   *Madame Cornelys*, the manager of public social assemblies in London.

many a pleasant holiday. He bought his finest clothes
to figure at their country-house at Barton — he wrote
them droll verses. They loved him, laughed at him,
played him tricks, and made him happy. He asked for
a loan from Garrick, and Garrick kindly supplied him,
to enable him to go to Barton; but there were to be no
more holidays and only one brief struggle for poor
Goldsmith. A lock of his hair was taken from the
coffin and given to the Jessamy Bride. She lived quite
into our time. Hazlitt saw her, an old lady but beautiful still, in Northcote's painting-room, who told the
eager critic how proud she always was that Goldsmith
had admired her.[1]

The younger Colman has left a touching reminiscence of him: "I was only five years old," he says,
"when Goldsmith took me on his knee one evening
whilst he was drinking coffee with my father, and began
to play with me, which amiable act I returned, with
the ingratitude of a peevish brat, by giving him a very
smart slap on the face: it must have been a tingler, for
it left the marks of my spiteful paw on his cheek. This
infantile outrage was followed by summary justice, and
I was locked up by my indignant father in an adjoining
room to undergo solitary imprisonment in the dark.
Here I began to howl and scream most abominably,
which was no bad step towards my liberation, since
those who were not inclined to pity me might be likely
to set me free for the purpose of abating a nuisance.
At length a generous friend appeared to extricate me
from jeopardy, and that generous friend was no other
than the man I had so wantonly molested by assault

George Colman, the Younger (1762–1836), dramatist.
[1] The story of Goldsmith and Mary Horneck is the subject of *The
Jessamy Bride*, a novel by Frankfort Moore. *Jessamy* was a popular form
of *jessamine*, *jasmine*, a flower of exquisite perfume. It was used by Goldsmith as a compliment to Mary's sweetness.

and battery — it was the tender-hearted Doctor himself, with a lighted candle in his hand, and a smile upon his countenance, which was still partially red from the effects of my petulance. I sulked and sobbed as he fondled and soothed, till I began to brighten. Goldsmith seized the propitious moment of returning good-humor when he put down the candle and began to conjure. He placed three hats, which happened to be in the room, and a shilling under each. The shillings he told me were England, France, and Spain. 'Hey presto cockalorum!' cried the Doctor, and lo, on uncovering the shillings, which had been dispersed each beneath a separate hat, they were all found congregated under one. I was no politician at five years old, and therefore might not have wondered at the sudden revolution which brought England, France, and Spain all under one crown; but as also I was no conjuror, it amazed me beyond measure. . . . From that time, whenever the Doctor came to visit my father, 'I plucked his gown to share the good man's smile';[1] a game at romps constantly ensued, and we were always cordial friends, and merry playfellows. Our unequal companionship varied somewhat as to sports as I grew older; but it did not last long: my senior playmate died in his forty-fifth year, when I had attained my eleventh. . . . In all the numerous accounts of his virtues and foibles, his genius and absurdities, his knowledge of nature and ignorance of the world, his 'compassion for another's woe' was always predominant; and my trivial story of his humoring a froward child weighs but as a feather in the recorded scale of his benevolence."

Think of him as reckless, thriftless, vain, if you like — but merciful, gentle, generous, full of love and pity.

[1] *Deserted Village*, l. 173.

He passes out of our life, and goes to render his account beyond it.   Think of the poor pensioners weeping at his grave; think of the noble spirits that admired and deplored him; think of the righteous pen that wrote his epitaph — and of the wonderful and unanimous response of affection with which the world has paid back the love he gave it.   His humor delighting us still, his song fresh and beautiful as when first he charmed with it, his words in all our mouths, his very weaknesses beloved and familiar — his benevolent spirit seems still to smile upon us, to do gentle kindnesses, to succor with sweet charity, to soothe, caress, and forgive, to plead with the fortunate for the unhappy and the poor.

William Makepeace Thackeray, The English Humorists of the Eighteenth Century (delivered as a lecture, in England and America, 1852–53).

WALKING, AND THE WILD [1]

Pub. 1862

I wish to speak a word for Nature, for absolute freedom and wildness, as contrasted with a freedom and culture merely civil — to regard man as an inhabitant, or a part and parcel of Nature, rather than a member of society.   I wish to make an extreme statement, if so I may make an emphatic one, for there are enough champions of civilization: the minister and the school committee, and every one of you will take care of that.

I have met with but one or two persons in the course of my life who understand the art of Walking, that is, of taking walks — who had a genius, so to speak, for *sauntering*: which word is beautifully derived "from idle people who roved about the country, in the Middle Ages, and asked charity, under pretence of going *à la*

righteous pen, Dr. Johnson's.   [1] This essay has been abridged.

Sainte Terre," [1] to the Holy Land, till the children exclaimed, "There goes a *Sainte-Terrer*," a Saunterer — a
Holy-Lander. They who never go to the Holy Land
in their walks, as they pretend, are indeed mere idlers
and vagabonds; but they who do go there are saunter-
ers in the good sense, such as I mean. Some, however,
would derive the word from *sans terre*, without land or
a home, which therefore, in the good sense, will mean,
having no particular home, but equally at home everywhere. For this is the secret of successful sauntering.
He who sits still in a house all the time may be the
greatest vagrant of all; but the saunterer, in the good
sense, is no more vagrant than the meandering river,
which is all the while sedulously seeking the shortest
course to the sea. But I prefer the first, which indeed
is the most probable derivation. For every walk is a
sort of crusade, preached by some Peter the Hermit in
us, to go forth and reconquer this Holy Land from the
hands of the Infidels.

It is true that we are but faint-hearted crusaders,
even the walkers, nowadays, who undertake no persevering, never-ending enterprises. Our expeditions
are but tours, and come round again at evening to the
old hearth-side from which we set out. Half the walk
is but retracing our steps. We should go forth on the
shortest walk, perchance, in the spirit of undying adventure, never to return — prepared to send back our
embalmed hearts only as relics to our desolate kingdoms. If you are ready to leave father and mother,
and brother and sister, and wife and child and friends,
and never see them again — if you have paid your
debts, and made your will, and settled all your affairs,
and are a free man, then you are ready for a walk.

---

[1] This derivation is fanciful. *Saunter* is probably from the Old French
s'aventurer. Cf. *adventure*.

To come down to my own experience, my companion and I, for I sometimes have a companion, take pleasure in fancying ourselves knights of a new, or rather an old, order — not Equestrians or Chevaliers, not Ritters or Riders, but Walkers, a still more ancient and honourable class, I trust.   The chivalric and heroic spirit which once belonged to the Rider seems now to reside in, or perchance to have subsided into, the Walker — not the Knight, but Walker Errant. He is a sort of fourth estate, outside of Church and State and People.

We have felt that we almost alone hereabouts practised this noble art; though, to tell the truth, at least if their own assertions are to be received, most of my townsmen would fain walk sometimes, as I do, but they cannot.   No wealth can buy the requisite leisure, freedom, and independence, which are the capital of this profession.   It comes only by the grace of God. It requires a direct dispensation from Heaven to become a walker.   You must be born into the family of the Walkers.   *Ambulator nascitur, non fit.*   Some of my townsmen, it is true, can remember and have described to me some walks which they took ten years ago, in which they were so blessed as to lose themselves for half-an-hour in the woods; but I know very well that they have confined themselves to the highway ever since, whatever pretensions they may make to belong to this select class.   No doubt they were elevated for a moment as by the reminiscence of a previous state of existence, when even they were foresters and outlaws.

"When he came to grene wode,
In a mery mornynge,

Ambulator, etc., The walker is born, not made.

> There he herde the notes small
> Of byrdes mery syngynge.
>
> "It is ferre gone, sayd Robyn,
>   That I was last here;
> Me lyste a lytell for to shote
>   At the donne dere."

I think that I cannot preserve my health and spirits unless I spend four hours a day at least — and it is commonly more than that — sauntering through the woods and over the hills and fields, absolutely free from all worldly engagements. You may safely say, A penny for your thoughts, and a thousand pounds. When sometimes I am reminded that the mechanics and shopkeepers stay in their shops not only all the forenoon, but all the afternoon too, sitting with crossed legs, so many of them — as if the legs were made to sit upon, and not to stand or walk upon — I think that they deserve some credit for not having all committed suicide long ago.

I, who cannot stay in my chamber for a single day without acquiring some rust, and when sometimes I have stolen forth for a walk at the eleventh hour of four o'clock in the afternoon, too late to redeem the day, when the shades of night were already beginning to be mingled with the daylight, have felt as if I had committed some sin to be atoned for — I confess that I am astonished at the power of endurance, to say nothing of the moral insensibility, of my neighbours who confine themselves to shops and offices the whole day for weeks and months, ay, and years almost together. I know not what manner of stuff they are of — sitting there now at three o'clock in the afternoon, as if it were three o'clock in the morning. Bonaparte may talk of the three-o'clock-in-the-morning courage, but it is nothing to the courage which can sit down cheerfully at this hour in the afternoon over against one's self whom you have known all the morning, to starve out a garrison to whom you are bound by such strong ties of sympathy. I wonder that about this time, or say between four and five o'clock in the afternoon, too late for the morning papers and too early for the evening ones, there is not a general explosion heard up and down the street, scattering a legion of antiquated and house-bred notions and whims to the four winds for an airing — and so the evil cure itself. . . .

No doubt temperament, and, above all, age, have a good deal to do with it. As a man grows older, his ability to sit still and follow indoor occupations increases. He grows vespertinal in his habits as the evening of life approaches, till at last he comes forth only just before sundown, and gets all the walk that he requires in half-an-hour.

But the walking of which I speak has nothing in it akin to taking exercise, as it is called, as the sick take medicine at stated hours — as the swinging of dumbbells or chairs; but is itself the enterprise and adventure of the day. If you would get exercise, go in search of the springs of life. Think of a man's swinging dumbbells for his health, when those springs are bubbling up in far-off pastures unsought by him!

Moreover, you must walk like a camel, which is said to be the only beast which ruminates when walking. When a traveller asked Wordsworth's servant to show him her master's study, she answered, "here is his library, but his study is out of doors."

Living much out of doors, in the sun and wind, will no doubt produce a certain roughness of character — will cause a thicker cuticle to grow over some of the finer qualities of our nature, as on the face and hands, or as severe manual labour robs the hands of some of their delicacy of touch. So staying in the house, on the other hand, may produce a softness and smoothness, not to say thinness of skin, accompanied by an increased sensibility to certain impressions. Perhaps we should be more susceptible to some influences important to our intellectual and moral growth if the sun had shone and the wind blown on us a little less; and no doubt it is a nice matter to proportion rightly the thick and thin skin. But methinks that is a scurf that will fall off fast enough — that the natural remedy is to be found in the proportion which the night bears to the day, the winter to the summer, thought to experience. There will be so much the more air and sunshine in our thoughts. The callous palms of the labourer are conversant with finer tissues of self-respect and heroism, whose touch thrills the heart, than the languid fingers of idleness. That is mere sentimentality that lies abed by day and thinks itself white, far from the tan and callus of experience.

When we walk, we naturally go to the fields and woods: what would become of us if we walked only in a garden or a mall? Even some sects of philosophers have felt the necessity of importing the woods to themselves, since they did not go to the woods. "They planted groves and walks of Platanes," where they took *subdiales ambulationes* in porticos open to the air. Of course it is of no use to direct our steps to the woods if they do not carry us thither. I am alarmed when it happens that I have walked a mile into the woods bodily without getting there in spirit. In my afternoon walk I would fain forget all my morning occupations and my obligations to society. But it sometimes

Platanes, plane-trees.   *subdiales*, etc., open-air walks.

happens that I cannot easily shake off the village.
The thought of some work will run in my head, and I
am not where my body is — I am out of my senses.
In my walks I would fain return to my senses. What
business have I in the woods, if I am thinking of something out of the woods? I suspect myself, and cannot
help a shudder, when I find myself so implicated in
what are called good works — for this may sometimes
happen.

My vicinity affords many good walks; and though
for so many years I have walked almost every day, and
sometimes for several days together, I have not yet exhausted them. An absolutely new prospect is a great
happiness, and I can still get this any afternoon. Two
or three hours' walking will carry me to as strange a
country as I expect ever to see. A single farmhouse
which I had not seen before is sometimes as good as the
dominions of the King of Dahomey. There is in fact a
sort of harmony discoverable between the capabilities
of the landscape within a circle of ten miles' radius, or
the limits of an afternoon walk, and the three-score
years and ten of human life. It will never become
quite familiar to you.

Nowadays almost all man's improvements, so
called, as the building of houses, and the cutting down
of the forest and of all large trees, simply deform the
landscape, and make it more and more tame and
cheap. A people who would begin by burning the
fences and let the forest stand! I saw the fences half
consumed, their ends lost in the middle of the prai-
rie, and some worldly miser with a surveyor looking
after his bounds, while heaven had taken place around
him, and he did not see the angels going to and fro, but
was looking for an old posthole in the midst of paradise.
I looked again, and saw him standing in the middle of

a boggy, stygian fen, surrounded by devils, and he had found his bounds without a doubt, three little stones, where a stake had been driven, and looking nearer, I saw that the Prince of Darkness was his surveyor.

I can easily walk ten, fifteen, twenty, any number of miles, commencing at my own door, without going by any house, without crossing a road except where the fox and the mink do: first along by the river, and then the brook, and then the meadow and the wood-side. There are square miles in my vicinity which have no inhabitant. From many a hill I can see civilization and the abodes of men afar. The farmers and their works are scarcely more obvious than woodchucks and their burrows. Man and his affairs, church and state and school, trade and commerce, and manufactures and agriculture, even politics, the most alarming of them all — I am pleased to see how little space they occupy in the landscape. Politics is but a narrow field, and that still narrower highway yonder leads to it. I sometimes direct the traveller thither. If you would go to the political world, follow the great road — follow that market-man, keep his dust in your eyes, and it will lead you straight to it; for it, too, has its place merely, and does not occupy all space. I pass from it as from a bean-field into the forest, and it is forgotten. In one half-hour I can walk off to some portion of the earth's surface, where a man does not stand from one year's end to another and there, consequently, politics are not, for they are but as the cigar-smoke of a man.

The village is the place to which the roads tend, a sort of expansion of the highway, as a lake of a river. It is the body of which roads are the arms and legs — a trivial or quadrivial place, the thoroughfare and ordinary of travellers. The word is from the Latin *villa*, which, together with *via*, a way, or more anciently *ved* and *vella*, Varro derives from *veho*, to carry, because the villa is the place to and from which things are carried. They who get their living by teaming were said *vellaturam facere*. Hence, too, apparently, the Latin word *vilis* and our vile; also *villain*. This suggests what kind of degeneracy villagers are liable to. They are wayworn by travel that goes by and over them, without travelling themselves.

Some do not walk at all; others walk in the highways; a few walk across lots. Roads are made for horses and men of business. I do not travel in them much, comparatively, because I am not in a hurry to get to any tavern or grocery or livery-stable or depot to which they lead. I am a good horse to travel, but not from choice a roadster. The landscape-painter uses the figures of men to mark a road. He would not make that use of my figure. I walk out into a Nature such as the old prophets and poets, Menu, Moses, Homer, Chaucer, walked in. You may name it America, but it is not America: neither Americus Vespucius, nor Columbus, nor the rest were the discoverers of it. There is a truer account of it in mythology than in any history of America, so called, that I have seen. . . .

Above all, we cannot afford not to live in the present. He is blessed over all mortals who loses no moment of the passing life in remembering the past. Unless our philosophy hears the cock crow in every barn-yard within our horizon, it is belated. That sound commonly reminds us that we are growing rusty and antique in our employments and habits of thought. His philosophy comes down to a more recent time than ours. There is something suggested by it that is a newer testament — the gospel according to this moment. He has not fallen astern; he has got up early and kept up early, and to be where he is to be in season, in the foremost rank of time. It is an expression of the health and soundness of Nature, a brag for all the world — healthiness as of a spring burst forth, a new fountain of the Muses, to celebrate this last instant of time. Where he lives no fugitive slave laws are passed. Who has not betrayed his master many times since last he heard that note?

The merit of this bird's strain is in its freedom from all plaintiveness. The singer can easily move us to tears or to laughter, but where is he who can excite in us a pure morning joy? When, in doleful dumps, breaking the awful stillness of our wooden sidewalk on a Sunday, or, perchance, a watcher in the house of mourning, I hear a cockerel crow far or near, I think to myself, "There is one of us well, at any rate" — and with a sudden gush return to my senses.

We had a remarkable sunset one day last November. I was walking in a meadow, the source of a small brook, when the sun at last, just before setting, after a cold gray day, reached a clear stratum in the horizon, and the softest, brightest morning sunlight fell on the dry grass and on the stems of the trees in the opposite horizon, and on the leaves of the shrub-oaks on the hill-side, while our shadows stretched long over the meadow eastward, as if we were the only motes in its beams. It was such a light as we could not have imagined a moment before, and the air also was so warm and serene that nothing was wanting to make a paradise of that meadow. When we reflected that this was not a solitary phenomenon, never to happen again, but that it would happen for ever and ever an infinite number of evenings, and cheer and reassure the latest child that walked there, it was more glorious still.

The sun sets on some retired meadow, where no house is visible, with all the glory and splendour that it lavishes on cities, and, perchance, as it has never set before — where there is but a solitary marsh-hawk to have his wings gilded by it, or only a musquash looks out from his cabin, and there is some little black-veined brook in the midst of the marsh, just beginning to meander, winding slowly round a decaying stump. We walked in so pure and bright a light, gilding the withered grass and leaves, so softly and serenely bright, I thought I had never bathed in such a golden flood, without a ripple or a murmur to it. The west side of every wood and rising ground gleamed like the boundary of Elysium, and the sun on our backs seemed like a gentle herdsman driving us home at evening.

So we saunter toward the Holy Land, till one day the sun shall shine more brightly than ever he has done, shall perchance shine into our minds and hearts, and light up our whole lives with a great awakening light, as warm and serene and golden as on a bank-side in autumn.

Henry David Thoreau, Excursions, 1863 (first published in The Atlantic Monthly in 1862)

IN THE MEDITERRANEAN

1854

The first sight of a shore so historical as that of Europe gives an American a strange thrill. What we always feel the artistic want of at home is background. It is all idle to say we are Englishmen, and that English history is ours too. It is precisely in this that we are *not* Englishmen, inasmuch as we only possess their history through our minds, and not by life-long association with a spot and an idea we call England. History without the soil it grew in is more instructive than inspiring — an acquisition, and not an inheritance. It is laid away in our memories, and does not run in our veins. Surely, in all that concerns æsthetics, Europeans have us at an immense advantage. They start at a point which we arrive at after weary years, for literature is not shut up in books, nor art in galleries: both are taken in by unconscious absorption through the finer pores of mind and character in the atmosphere of society. We are not yet out of our Crusoehood, and must make our own tools as best we may. Yet I think we shall find the good of it one of these days, in being thrown back more wholly on nature; and our literature, when we have learned to feel our strength, and to respect our own thought because it is ours, and not because the European Mrs. Grundy agrees with it, will have a fresh flavor and a strong body that will recommend it, especially as what we import is watered more and more liberally with every vintage.

My first glimpse of Europe was the shore of Spain. Since we got into the Mediterranean, we have been becalmed for some days within easy view of it. All along are fine mountains, brown all day, and with a bloom on them at sunset like that of a ripe plum. Here and there at their feet little white towns are sprinkled along the edge of the water, like grains of rice dropped by the princess in the story. Sometimes we see larger buildings on the mountain slopes, probably convents. I sit and wonder whether the farther peaks may not be the Sierra Morena (the rusty saw) of Don Quixote. I resolve that they shall be, and am content. Surely latitude and longitude never showed me any particular respect, that I should be over-scrupulous with them.

But, after all, Nature, though she may be more beautiful, is nowhere so entertaining as in man, and the best thing I have seen and learned at sea is our Chief Mate. My first acquaintance with him was made over my knife, which he asked to look at, and, after a critical examination, handed back to me, saying, "I shouldn't wonder if that 'ere was a good piece o' stuff." Since then he has transferred a part of his regard for my knife to its owner. I like folks who like an honest piece of steel, and take no interest whatever in "your Raphaels, Correggios, and stuff." There is always more than the average human nature in a man who has a hearty sympathy with iron. It is a manly metal, with no sordid associations like gold and silver. My sailor fully came up to my expectation on further acquaintance. He might well be called an old salt who had been wrecked on Spitzbergen before I was born. He was not an American, but I should never have guessed it by his speech, which was the purest Cape Cod, and I reckon myself a good taster of dialects. Nor was he less Americanized in all his thoughts and feelings, a singular proof of the ease with which our omnivorous country assimilates foreign matter, provided it be Protestant, for he was a man ere he became an American citizen. He used to walk the deck with his hands in his pockets, in seeming abstraction, but nothing escaped his eye. *How* he saw, I could never make out, though I had a theory that it was with his elbows. After he had taken me (or my knife) into his confidence, he took care that I should see whatever he deemed of interest to a landsman. Without looking up, he would say suddenly, "There's a whale blowin' clearn up to win'ard," or, "Them's porpises to leeward: that means change o' wind." He is as impervious to cold as the polar bear, and paces the deck during his watch much as one of those yellow hummocks goes slumping up and down his cage. On the Atlantic, if the wind blew a gale from the north-east, and it was cold as an English summer, he was sure to turn out in a calico shirt and trousers, his furzy brown chest half bare, and slippers, without stockings. But lest you might fancy this to have chanced by defect of wardrobe, he comes out in a monstrous pea-jacket here in the Mediterranean when the evening is so hot that Adam would have been glad to leave off his fig-leaves. "It's a kind o' damp and unwholesome in these 'ere waters," he says evidently regarding the Midland Sea as a vile standing pool, in comparison with the bluff ocean. At meals he is superb, not only for his strengths, but his weaknesses. He has somehow or other come to think me a wag, and if I ask him to pass the butter, detects an occult joke, and laughs as much as is proper for a mate. For you must know that our social hierarchy on shipboard is precise, and the second mate, were he present, would only laugh half as much as the first. Mr. X. always combs his hair and works himself into a black frock-coat (on Sundays he adds a waistcoat) before he comes to meals, sacrificing himself nobly and painfully to the social proprieties. The second mate, on the other hand, who eats after us, enjoys the privilege of shirt-sleeves, and is, I think, the happier man of the two. We do not have seats above and below the salt, as in old time, but above and below the white sugar. Mr. X. always takes brown sugar, and it is delightful to see how he ignores the existence of certain delicates which he considers above his grade, tipping his head on one side with an air of abstraction, so that he may seem not to deny himself, but to omit helping himself from inadvertence or absence of mind. At such times he wrinkles his forehead in a peculiar manner, inscrutable at first as a cuneiform inscription, but as easily read after you once get the key. The sense of it is something like this: "I, X., know my place, a height of wisdom attained by few. Whatever you may think, I do *not* see that currant jelly, nor that preserved grape. Especially, a kind Providence has made me blind to bowls of white sugar, and deaf to the pop of champagne corks. It is much that a merciful compensation gives me a sense of the dingier hue of Havanna, and the muddier gurgle of beer. Are there potted meats? My physician has ordered me three pounds of minced salt-junk at every meal." There is such a thing, you know, as a ship's husband: X. is the ship's poor relation.

As I have said, he takes also a below-the-white-sugar interest in the jokes, laughing by precise point of compass, just as he would lay the ship's course, all *yawing* being out of the question with his scrupulous decorum at the helm. Once or twice I have got the better of him, and touched him off into a kind of compromised explosion, like that of damp fireworks, that splutter and simmer a little, and then go out with painful slowness and occasional relapses. But his fuse is always of the unwillingest, and you must blow your match, and touch him off again and again with the same joke. Or rather, you must magnetize him many times to get him *en rapport* with a jest. This once accomplished, you have him, and one bit of fun will last the whole voyage. He prefers those of one syllable, the *a-b abs* of humor. The gradual fattening of the steward, a benevolent mulatto with whiskers and earrings, who looks as if he had been meant for a woman, and had become a man by accident, as in some of those stories of the elder physiologists, is an abiding topic of

ship's husband, an agent who has charge of a ship in port.

humorous comment with Mr. X. "That 'ere stooard," he says, with a brown grin like what you might fancy on the face of a serious and aged seal, "'s a gittin' as fat's a porpis. He was as thin's a shingle when he come aboord last v'yge. Them trousers'll bust yit. He don't darst take 'em off nights, for the whole ship's company couldn't git him into 'em agin." And then he turns aside to enjoy the intensity of his emotion by himself, and you hear at intervals low rumblings, an indigestion of laughter. He tells me of St. Elmo's fires, Marvell's *corposants*, though with him the original *corpos santos* has suffered a sea change, and turned to *comepleasants*, pledges of fine weather. I shall not soon find a pleasanter companion. It is so delightful to meet a man who knows just what you do *not*. Nay, I think the tired mind finds something in plump ignorance like what the body finds in cushiony moss. Talk of the sympathy of kindred pursuits! It is the sympathy of the upper and nether millstones, both for ever grinding the same grist, and wearing each other smooth. One has not far to seek for book-nature, artist-nature, every variety of superinduced nature, in short, but genuine human-nature is hard to find. And how good it is! Wholesome as a potato, fit company for any dish. The freemasonry of cultivated men is agreeable, but artificial, and I like better the natural grip with which manhood recognizes manhood.

X. has one good story, and with that I leave him, wishing him with all my heart that little inland farm at last which is his calenture as he paces the windy deck. One evening, when the clouds looked wild and whirling, I asked X. if it was coming on to blow. "No, I guess

corposants, same as St. Elmo's fires; balls of fire sometimes seen on ships. Mentioned by Andrew Marvell, in a poem, *First Anniversary*, l. 270 (1655).

not," said he; "bumby the moon'll be up, and scoff away that 'ere loose stuff." His intonation set the phrase "scoff away" in quotation marks as plain as print. So I put a query in each eye, and he went on. "Ther' was a Dutch cappen onct, an' his mate come to him in the cabin, where he sot takin' his schnapps, an' says, 'Cappen, it's agittin' thick, an' looks kin' o' squally; hedn't we's good's shorten sail?' 'Gimmy my alminick,' says the cappen. So he looks at it a spell, an' says he, 'The moon's due in less 'n half an hour, an' she'll scoff away ev'ythin' clare agin.' So the mate he goes, an' bumby down he comes agin, an' says, 'Cappen, this 'ere's the allfiredest, powerfullest moon't ever you *did* see. She's scoffed away the mainto'-gallants'l, an' she's to work on the foretops'l now. Guess you'd better look in the alminick agin, an' fin' out when *this* moon sets.' So the cappen thought 'twas 'bout time to go on deck. Dreadful slow them Dutch cappens be." And X. walked away, rumbling inwardly like the rote of the sea heard afar.

And so we arrived at Malta. Did you ever hear of one of those eating-houses where, for a certain fee, the guest has the right to make one thrust with a fork into a huge pot, in which the whole dinner is bubbling, getting perhaps a bit of boiled meat, or a potato, or else nothing? Well, when the great cauldron of war is seething, and the nations stand around it striving to fish out something to their purpose from the mess, Britannia always has a great advantage with her trident. Malta is one of the tit-bits she has impaled with that awful implement. I was not sorry for it, when I reached my clean inn, with its kindly English landlady.

James Russell Lowell, Leaves from My Journal, Sect. II

schnapps, Holland gin.   *rote*, repetition (as of a song learned by heart).

PAGAN AND MEDIÆVAL RELIGIOUS
SENTIMENT

1865

. . . It happened that lately, after I had been thinking much of Marcus Aurelius and his times, I took down the *Dictionnaire des Origines du Christianisme*, to see what it had to say about paganism and pagans. I found much what I expected. I read the article, *Révélation Evangélique, sa Nécessité.* There I found what a sink of iniquity was the whole pagan world; how one Roman fed his oysters on his slaves, how another put a slave to death that a curious friend might see what dying was like; how Galen's mother tore and bit her waiting-women when she was in a passion with them. I found this account of the religion of paganism: "Paganism invented a mob of divinities with the most hateful character, and attributed to them the most monstrous and abominable crimes. It personified in them drunkenness, incest, kidnapping, adultery, sensuality, knavery, cruelty, and rage." And I found that from this religion there followed such practices as was to be expected: "What must naturally have been the state of morals under the influence of such a religion, which penetrated with its own spirit the public life, the family life, and the individual life of antiquity?"

The colours in this picture are laid on very thick, and I for my part cannot believe that any human societies, with a religion and practice such as those just described, could ever have endured as the societies of Greece and Rome endured, still less have done what the societies of Greece and Rome did. We are not brought far by descriptions of the vices of great cities, or even of individuals driven mad by unbounded means of self-indulgence. Feudal and aristocratic life in Christendom has produced horrors of selfish ness and cruelty, not surpassed by the grandee of pagan Rome; and then, again, in antiquity there is Marcus Aurelius's mother to set against Galen's. Eminent examples of vice and virtue in individuals prove little as to the state of societies. What, under the first emperors, was the condition of the Roman poor upon the Aventine compared with that of our poor in Spitalfields and Bethnal Green? What, in comfort, morals, and happiness, were the rural population of the Sabine country under Augustus's rule, compared with the rural population of Hertfordshire and Buckinghamshire under the rule of Queen Victoria?

But these great questions are not now for me. Without trying to answer them, I ask myself, when I read such declamation as the foregoing, if I can find anything that will give me a near, distinct sense of the real difference in spirit and sentiment between paganism and Christianity, and of the natural effect of this difference upon people in general. I take a representative religious poem of paganism — of the paganism which all the world has in its mind when it speaks of paganism. To be a representative poem, it must be one for popular use, one that the multitude listens to. Such a religious poem may be found at the end of one of the best and happiest of Theocritus's idylls, the fifteenth. In order that the reader may the better go along with me in the line of thought I am following, I will translate it; and, that he may see the medium in which religious poetry of this sort is found existing, the society out of which it grows, the people who form it and are formed by it, I will translate the whole, or nearly the whole, of the idyll (it is not long) in which the poem occurs.

The idyll is dramatic. Somewhere about two hundred and eighty years before the Christian era, a couple of Syracusan women, staying at Alexandria, agreed on the occasion of a great religious solemnity — the feast of Adonis — to go together to the palace of King Ptolemy Philadelphus, to see the image of Adonis, which the queen Arsinoe, Ptolemy's wife, had had decorated with peculiar magnificence. A hymn, by a celebrated performer, was to be recited over the image. The names of the two women are Gorgo and Praxinoe; their maids, who are mentioned in the poem, are called Eunoe and Eutychis. Gorgo comes by appointment to Praxinoe's house to fetch her, and there the dialogue begins: —

Gorgo. Is Praxinoe at home?

Praxinoe. My dear Gorgo, at last! Yes, here I am. Eunoe, find a chair — get a cushion for it.

Gorgo. It will do beautifully as it is.

Praxinoe. Do sit down.

Gorgo. Oh, this gad-about spirit! I could hardly get to you, Praxinoe, through all the crowd and all the carriages. Nothing but heavy boots, nothing but men in uniform. And what a journey it is. My dear child, you really live *too* far off.

Praxinoe. It is all that insane husband of mine. He has chosen to come out here to the end of the world, and take a hole of a place — for a house it is not — on purpose that you and I might not be neighbours. He is always just the same; — anything to quarrel with one! anything for spite!

Gorgo. My dear, don't talk so of your husband before the little fellow. Just see how astonished he looks at you. Never mind, Zopyrio, my pet, she is not talking about papa.

Praxinoe. Good heavens! the child does really understand.

Gorgo. Pretty papa!

Praxinoe. That pretty papa of his the other day (though I told him beforehand to mind what he was about), when I sent him to a shop to buy soap and rouge, brought me home salt instead; — stupid, great, big, interminable animal!

Gorgo. Mine is just the fellow to him [a perfect spendthrift — Diocleides! Yesterday he got what he meant for five fleeces, and paid seven shillings a piece for — what do you suppose? — dogskins, shreds of old leather wallets, mere trash — trouble on trouble.] [1] But never mind now, get on your things and let us be off to the palace to see the Adonis. I hear the Queen's decorations are splendid.

Praxinoe. In grand people's houses everything is grand. What things you have seen in Alexandria! What a deal you will have to tell anybody who has never been here!

Gorgo. Come, we ought to be going.

Praxinoe. Every day is holiday to people who have nothing to do. Eunoe, pick up your work; and take care, lazy girls, how you leave it lying about again; the cats find it just the bed they like. Come, stir yourself, fetch me some water, quick! I wanted the water first, and the girl brings me the soap. Never mind; give it me. Not all that, extravagant! Now pour out the water; — stupid! why don't you take care of my dress? That will do. I have got my hands washed as it pleased God. Where is the key of the large wardrobe? Bring it here; — quick!

Gorgo. Praxinoe, you can't think how well that dress, made full, as you have got it, suits you. Tell me, how much did it cost? — the dress by itself, I mean.

Praxinoe. Don't talk of it, Gorgo: more than eight

---

[1] Arnold's omission is supplied from Lang's translation.

guineas of good hard money. And about the work on it I have almost worn my life out.

Gorgo. Well, you couldn't have done better.

Praxinoe. Thank you. Bring me my shawl, and put my hat properly on my head; — properly. No, child (*to her little boy*), I am not going to take you; there's a bogy on horseback, who bites. Cry as much as you like; I'm not going to have you lamed for life. Now we'll start. Nurse, take the little one and amuse him; call the dog in, and shut the street-door. (*They go out*). Good heavens! what a crowd of people! How on earth are we ever to get through all this? They are like ants: you can't count them. My dearest Gorgo, what will become of us? here are the royal Horse Guards. My good man, don't ride over me! Look at that bay horse rearing bolt upright; what a vicious one! Eunoe, you mad girl, do take care! — that horse will certainly be the death of the man on his back. How glad I am now, that I left the child safe at home!

Gorgo. All right, Praxinoe, we are safe behind them; and they have gone on to where they are stationed.

Praxinoe. Well, yes, I begin to revive again. From the time I was a little girl I have had more horror of horses and snakes than of anything in the world. Let us get on; here's a great crowd coming this way upon us.

Gorgo (*to an old woman*). Mother, are you from the palace?

Old Woman. Yes, my dears.

Gorgo. Has one a tolerable chance of getting there?

Old Woman. My pretty young lady, the Greeks got to Troy by dint of trying hard; trying will do anything in this world.

Gorgo. The old creature has delivered herself of an oracle and departed.

Praxinoe. Women can tell you everything about everything, Jupiter's marriage with Juno not excepted.

Gorgo. Look, Praxinoe, what a squeeze at the palace gates!

Praxinoe. Tremendous! Take hold of me, Gorgo; and you, Eunoe, take hold of Eutychis! — tight hold, or you'll be lost. Here we go in all together. Hold tight to us, Eunoe! Oh, dear! Oh, dear! Gorgo, there's my scarf torn right in two. For heaven's sake, my good man, as you hope to be saved, take care of my dress.

Stranger. I'll do what I can, but it doesn't depend upon me.

Praxinoe. What heaps of people! They push like a drove of pigs.

Stranger. Don't be frightened, ma'am, we are all right.

Praxinoe. May you be all right, my dear sir, to the last day you live, for the care you have taken of us! What a kind, considerate man! There is Eunoe jammed in a squeeze. Push, you goose, push! Capital! We are all of us the right side of the door, as the bridegroom said when he had locked himself in with the bride.

Gorgo. Praxinoe, come this way. Do but look at that work, how delicate it is! — how exquisite! Why, they might wear it in heaven.

Praxinoe. Heavenly patroness of needlewomen,[1] what hands were hired to do that work! Who designed those beautiful patterns? They seem to stand up and move about, as if they were real; — as if they were living things, and not needlework. Well, man is

[1] Athene.

a wonderful creature! And look, look, how charming he lies there on his silver couch, with just a soft down on his cheeks, that beloved Adonis — Adonis, whom one loves though he is dead!

Another Stranger. You wretched women, do stop your incessant chatter! Like turtles, you go on for ever. They are enough to kill one with their broad lingo — nothing but *a, a, a.*

Gorgo. Lord, where does the man come from? What is it to you if we *are* chatterboxes? Order about your own servants! Do you give orders to Syracusan women? If you want to know, we came originally from Corinth, as Bellerophon did; we speak Peloponnesian. I suppose Dorian women may be allowed to have a Dorian accent.

Praxinoe. Oh, honey-sweet Proserpine, let us have no more masters than the one we've got! We don't the least care for *you;* pray don't trouble yourself about nothing.

Gorgo. Be quiet, Praxinoe! That first-rate singer, the Argive woman's daughter, is going to sing the *Adonis* hymn. She is the same who was chosen to sing the dirge last year.[1] We are sure to have something first-rate from *her.* She is going through her airs and graces ready to begin. —

So far the dialogue; and, as it stands in the original, it can hardly be praised too highly. It is a page torn fresh out of the book of human life. What freedom! What gaiety! What naturalness! It is said that Theocritus, in composing this poem, borrowed from a work of Sophron,[2] a poet of an earlier and better time;

---

[1] Bion's *Lament for Adonis,* which served as a model for part of Shelley's *Adonais,* and for other English elegies, is an example of such a dirge. It has been translated by Andrew Lang, in his *Theocritus, Bion, and Moschus.*

[2] Sophron's idyl, the *Isthmiazusae,* is said to have represented two ladies at the Isthmian games.

but, even if this is so, the form is still Theocritus's own, and how excellent that form, how masterly! And this in a Greek poem of the decadence! — for Theocritus's poetry, after all, is poetry of the decadence. When such is Greek poetry of the decadence, what must be Greek poetry of the prime?

Then the singer begins her hymn:

"Mistress, who loveth the haunts of Golgi, and Idalium, and high-peaked Eryx, Aphrodite that playest with gold! how have the delicate-footed Hours, after twelve months, brought thy Adonis back to thee from the ever-flowing Acheron! Tardiest of the immortals are the boon Hours, but all mankind wait their approach with longing, for they ever bring something with them. O Cypris, Dione's child! thou didst change — so is the story among men — Berenice from mortal to immortal, by dropping ambrosia into her fair bosom; and in gratitude to thee for this, O thou of many names and many temples! Berenice's daughter, Arsinoe, lovely Helen's counterpart, makes much of Adonis with all manner of braveries.

"All fruits that the tree bears are laid before him, all treasures of the garden in silver baskets, and alabaster boxes, gold-inlaid, of Syrian ointment; and all confectionery that cunning women make on their kneading-tray, kneading up every sort of flowers with white meal, and all that they make of sweet honey and delicate oil, and all winged and creeping things are here set before him.[1] And there are built for him green bowers with wealth of tender anise, and little boy-loves flutter about over them, like young nightingales trying their new wings on the tree, from bough to bough. Oh, the ebony, the gold, the eagle of white

Cypris, Aphrodite (from Cyprus, where she was worshipped).

[1] "All cakes fashioned in the semblance of things that fly, and of things that creep, lo, here are set," etc. — Lang's translation.

ivory that bears aloft his cup-bearer to Cronos-born
Zeus! And up there, see! a second couch strewn for
lovely Adonis, scarlet coverlets softer than sleep itself
(so Miletus and the Samian wool-grower will say);
Cypris has hers, and the rosy-armed Adonis has his,
that eighteen or nineteen-year-old bridegroom. His
kisses will not wound, the hair on his lip is yet light.

"Now, Cypris, good-night, we leave thee with thy
bridegroom; but to-morrow morning with the earliest
dew, we will one and all bear him forth to where the
waves splash upon the sea-strand, and letting loose our
locks, and letting fall our robes, with bosoms bare, we
will set up this, our melodious strain:

"'Beloved Adonis, alone of the demigods (so men
say) thou art permitted to visit both us and Acheron!
This lot had neither Agamemnon, nor the mighty
moon-struck hero Ajax, nor Hector the first-born of
Hecuba's twenty children, nor Patroclus, nor Pyrrhus
who came home from Troy, nor those yet earlier Lapi-
thæ and the sons of Deucalion, nor the Pelasgians, the
root of Argos and of Pelops' isle. Be gracious to us
now, loved Adonis, and be favourable to us for the
year to come! Dear to us hast thou been at this coming, dear to us shalt thou be when thou comest
again.'"

The poem concludes with a characteristic speech
from Gorgo: —

"Praxinoe, certainly women are wonderful things.
That lucky woman to know all that! and luckier still to
have such a splendid voice! And now we must see
about getting home. My husband has not had his
dinner. That man is all vinegar, and nothing else; and

cup-bearer, Ganymede.
alone . . . thou art permitted, etc. Adonis (see p. 421) represented the sun,
  which visited both this world and Hades.
Acheron, one of the rivers of the lower world.

if you keep him waiting for his dinner, he's dangerous
to go near. Adieu, precious Adonis, and may you find
us all well when you come next year!"

So, with the hymn still in her ears, says the incorrigible Gorgo.

But what a hymn that is! Of religious emotion, in
our acceptation of the words, not a particle. And yet
many elements of religious emotion are contained in
the beautiful story of Adonis. Symbolically treated,
as the thoughtful man might treat it, as the Greek
mysteries undoubtedly treated it, this story was capable of a noble and touching application, and could
lead the soul to elevating and consoling thoughts.
Adonis was the sun in his summer and in his winter
course, in his time of triumph and his time of defeat;
but in his time of triumph still moving towards his defeat, in his time of defeat still returning towards his
triumph. Thus he became an emblem of the power of
human life and the bloom of human beauty, hastening
inevitably to diminution and decay, yet in that very
decay finding

"Hope, and a renovation without end." [1]

But nothing of this appears in the story as prepared for
popular religious use, as presented to the multitude in
a popular religious ceremony. Its treatment is not
devoid of a certain grace and beauty, but it has nothing
whatever that is elevating, nothing that is consoling,
nothing that is in our sense of the word religious. The
religious ceremonies of Christendom, even on occasion
of the most joyful and mundane matters, present the
multitude with strains of profoundly religious character, such as the *Kyrie eleison* and the *Te Deum*. But

Kyrie eleison (Lord, have mercy); *Te Deum laudamus* (We praise thee,
O Lord), great hymns of the Catholic church.

[1] Wordsworth, *Address to My Infant Daughter*, l. 65.

this Greek hymn to Adonis adapts itself exactly to the tone and temper of a gay and pleasure-loving multitude — of light-hearted people, like Gorgo and Praxinoe, whose moral nature is much of the same calibre as that of Phillina in Goethe's *Wilhelm Meister*, people who seem never made to be serious, never made to be sick or sorry. And, if they happen to be sick or sorry, what will they do then? But that we have no right to ask. Phillina, within the enchanted bounds of Goethe's novel, Gorgo and Praxinoe, within the enchanted bounds of Theocritus's poem, never will be sick and sorry, never can be sick and sorry. The ideal, cheerful, sensuous, pagan life is not sick or sorry. No; yet its natural end is in the sort of life which Pompeii and Herculaneum bring so vividly before us — a life which by no means suggests the thought of horror and misery, which even, in many ways, gratifies the senses and the understanding; but by the very intensity and unremittingness of its appeal to the senses and the understanding, by its stimulating a single side of us too absolutely, ends by fatiguing and revolting us; ends by leaving us with a sense of confinement, of oppression — with a desire for an utter change, for clouds, storms, effusion, and relief.

In the beginning of the thirteenth century, when the clouds and storms had come, when the gay sensuous pagan life was gone, when men were not living by the senses and understanding, when they were looking for the speedy coming of Antichrist, there appeared in Italy, to the north of Rome, in the beautiful Umbrian country at the foot of the Apennines, a figure of the most magical power and charm, St. Francis. His century is, I think, the most interesting in the history of Christianity after its primitive age, more interesting than even the century of the Reformation; and one of the chief figures, perhaps the very chief, to which this interest attaches itself, is St. Francis. And why? Because of the profound popular instinct which enabled him, more than any man since the primitive age, to fit religion for popular use. He brought religion to the people. He founded the most popular body of ministers of religion that has ever existed in the Church. He transformed monachism by uprooting the stationary monk, delivering him from the bondage of property, and sending him, as a mendicant friar, to be a stranger and sojourner, not in the wilderness, but in the most crowded haunts of men, to console them and to do them good. This popular instinct of his is at the bottom of his famous marriage with poverty. Poverty and suffering are the condition of the people, the multitude, the immense majority of mankind; and it was towards this *people* that his soul yearned. "He listens," it was said of him, "to those to whom God himself will not listen."

So in return, as no other man he was listened to. When an Umbrian town or village heard of his approach, the whole population went out in joyful procession to meet him, with green boughs, flags, music, and songs of gladness. The master, who began with two disciples, could in his own lifetime (and he died at forty-four) collect to keep Whitsuntide with him, in presence of an immense multitude, five thousand of his Minorites. And thus he found fulfillment to his prophetic cry: "I hear in my ears the sound of the tongues of all the nations who shall come unto us; Frenchmen, Spaniards, Germans, Englishmen. The Lord will make of us a great people, even unto the ends of the earth."

Prose could not satisfy this ardent soul, and he

Minorites, Franciscans, from *Fratres Minores*, or Lesser Brethren.

made poetry. Latin was too learned for this simple, popular nature, and he composed in his mother tongue, in Italian. The beginnings of the mundane poetry of the Italians are in Sicily, at the court of kings; the beginnings of their religious poetry are in Umbria, with St. Francis. His are the humble upper waters of a mighty stream; at the beginning of the thirteenth century it is St. Francis, at the end, Dante. Now it happens that St. Francis, too, like the Alexandrian songstress, has his hymn for the sun, for Adonis. *Canticle of the Sun, Canticle of the Creatures* — the poem goes by both names. Like the Alexandrian hymn, it is designed for popular use, but not for use by King Ptolemy's people; artless in language, irregular in rhythm, it matches with the childlike genius that produced it, and the simple natures that loved and repeated it: —

"O most high, almighty, good Lord God, to thee belong praise, glory, honour, and all blessing!

"Praised be my Lord God with all his creatures; and specially our brother the sun, who brings us the day, and who brings us the light; fair is he, and shining with a very great splendour: O Lord, he signifies to us thee!

"Praised be my Lord for our sister the moon, and for the stars the which he has set clear and lovely in heaven.

"Praised be my Lord for our brother the wind, and for air and cloud, calms and all weather, by the which thou upholdest in life all creatures.

"Praised be my Lord for our sister water, who is very serviceable unto us, and humble, and precious, and clean.

"Praised be my Lord for our brother fire, through whom thou givest us light in the darkness; and he is bright, and pleasant, and very mighty, and strong.

"Praised be my Lord for our mother the earth, the which doth sustain us and keep us, and bringeth forth divers fruits, and flowers of many colours, and grass.

"Praised be my Lord for all those who pardon one another for his love's sake, and who endure weakness and tribulation; blessed are they who peaceably shall endure, for thou, O most Highest, shalt give them a crown!

"Praised be my Lord for our sister, the death of the body, from whom no man escapeth. Woe to him who dieth in mortal sin! Blessed are they who are found walking by thy most holy will, for the second death shall have no power to do them harm.

"Praise ye, and bless ye the Lord, and give thanks unto him, and serve him with great humility."

It is natural that man should take pleasure in his senses. But it is natural, also, that he should take refuge in his heart and imagination from his misery. And when one thinks what human life is for the vast majority of mankind, how little of a feast for their senses it can possibly be, one understands the charm for them of a refuge offered in the heart and imagination. Above all, when one thinks what human life was in the Middle Ages, one understands the charm of such a refuge.

Now, the poetry of Theocritus's hymn is poetry treating the world according to the demand of the senses; the poetry of St. Francis's hymn is poetry treating the world according to the demand of the heart and imagination. The first takes the world by its outward, sensible side; the second by its inward, symbolical side. The first admits as much of the world as is pleasure-giving; the second admits the whole world, rough and smooth, painful and pleasure-giving, all alike, but transfigured by the power of a

spiritual emotion, all brought under the law of super-
sensual love, having its seat in the soul. It can thus
even say: "Praised be my Lord for *our sister, the death
of the body.*"

But these very words are, perhaps, an indication
that we are touching upon an extreme. When we see
Pompeii, we can put our finger upon the pagan sentiment in its extreme. And when we read of Monte
Alverno and the *stigmata*; [1] when we read of the repulsive, because self-caused, sufferings of the end of St.
Francis's life; when we find him saying, "I have sinned
against my brother the ass," meaning by these words
that he had been too hard upon his own body; when we
find him assailed, even himself, by the doubt "whether
he who had destroyed himself by the severity of his
penances could find mercy in eternity," we can put our
finger on the mediæval Christian sentiment in its
extreme. Human nature is neither all senses and understanding, nor all heart and imagination. Pompeii
was a sign that for humanity at large the measure of
sensualism had been overpassed; St. Francis's doubt
was a sign that for humanity at large the measure of
spiritualism had been overpassed. Humanity, in its
violent rebound from one extreme, had swung from
Pompeii to Monte Alverno; but it was sure not to stay
there.

The Renascence is, in part, a return towards the
pagan spirit, in the special sense in which I have been
using the word pagan; a return towards the life of the
senses and the understanding. The Reformation, on
the other hand, is the very opposite to this; in Luther
there is nothing Greek or pagan; vehemently as he

[1] In 1224, St. Francis went up Mount Alverno, where, after forty days
of fasting and prayer, he had an angelic vision. When the vision had
passed, he found upon his body the "Stigmata of the Crucified" — that
is, marks corresponding to the seven wounds of Christ. The Stigmata are
generally represented in paintings of the saint.

attacked the adoration of St. Francis, Luther had himself something of St. Francis in him; he was a thousand
times more akin to St. Francis than to Theocritus or to
Voltaire. The Reformation — I do not mean the inferior piece given under that name, by Henry the
Eighth and a second-rate company, in this island,
but the real Reformation, the German Reformation,
Luther's Reformation — was a reaction of the moral
and spiritual sense against the carnal and pagan sense;
it was a religious revival like St. Francis's, but this
time against the Church of Rome, not within her; for
the carnal and pagan sense had now, in the government of the Church of Rome herself, its prime representative. But the grand reaction against the rule of
the heart and imagination, the strong return towards
the rule of the senses and understanding, is in the
eighteenth century. And this reaction has had no
more brilliant champion than a man of the nineteenth,
of whom I have already spoken; [1] a man who could feel
not only the pleasurableness but the poetry of the life
of the senses (and the life of the senses has its deep
poetry); a man who, in his very last poem, divided the
whole world into "barbarians and Greeks" — Heinrich Heine. No man has reached the Monte Alverno,
the Christian extreme, the heart and imagination sub-
jugating the senses and understanding, more bitterly
than Heine; no man has extolled the Pompeii extreme,
the pagan extreme, more rapturously.

"All through the Middle Age these sufferings, this
fever, this over-tension lasted; and we moderns still
feel in all our limbs the pain and weakness from them.
Even those of us who are cured have still to live with a
hospital-atmosphere all around us, and find ourselves
as wretched in it as a strong man among the sick.

[1] In the essay, "Heinrich Heine," in *Essays in Criticism, First Series.*

Some day or other, when humanity shall have got quite well again, when the body and soul have made their peace together, the fictitious quarrel which Christianity has cooked up between them will appear something hardly comprehensible. The fairer and happier generations, offspring of unfettered unions, that will rise up and bloom in the atmosphere of a religion of pleasure, will smile sadly when they think of their poor ancestors, whose life was passed in melancholy abstinence from the joys of this beautiful earth, and who faded away into spectres, from the mortal compression which they put upon the warm and glowing emotions of sense. Yes, with assurance I say it, our descendants will be fairer and happier than we are; for I am a believer in progress, and I hold God to be a kind being who has intended man to be happy."

That is Heine's sentiment, in the prime of life, in the glow of activity, amid the brilliant whirl of Paris. I will no more blame it than I blamed the sentiment of the Greek hymn to Adonis. I wish to decide nothing as of my own authority; the great art of criticism is to get oneself out of the way and to let humanity decide. Well, the sentiment of the "religion of pleasure" has much that is natural in it; humanity will gladly accept it if it can live by it; to live by it one must never be sick or sorry, and the old, ideal, limited, pagan world never, I have said, *was* sick or sorry, never at least shows itself to us sick or sorry:

"What pipes and timbrels! what wild ecstasy!" [1]

For our imagination, Gorgo and Praxinoe cross the human stage chattering their blithe Doric — *like turtles*, as the cross stranger said — and keep gaily chattering on till they disappear. But in the new,

[1] Keats, *Ode on a Grecian Urn*.

real, immense, post-pagan world — in the barbarian world — the shock of accident is unceasing, the serenity of existence is perpetually troubled, not even a Greek like Heine can get across the mortal stage without bitter calamity. How does the sentiment of the "religion of pleasure" serve then? does it help, does it console? Can a man live by it? Heine again shall answer; Heine just twenty years older, stricken with incurable disease, waiting for death:

"The great pot stands smoking before me, but I have no spoon to help myself. What does it profit me that my health is drunk at banquets out of gold cups and in most exquisite wines, if I myself, while these ovations are going on, lonely and cut off from the pleasures of the world, can only just wet my lips with barley-water? What good does it to me that all the roses of Shiraz open their leaves and burn for me with passionate tenderness? Alas! Shiraz is some two thousand leagues from the Rue d'Amsterdam, where in the solitude of my sick chamber all the perfume I smell is that of hot towels. Alas! the mockery of God is heavy upon me! The great author of the universe, the Aristophanes of Heaven, has determined to make the petty earthly author, the so-called Aristophanes of Germany, feel to his heart's core what pitiful needle-pricks his cleverest sarcasms have been, compared with the thunderbolts which his divine humour can launch against feeble mortals! . . .

"In the year 1340, says the Chronicle of Limburg, all over Germany everybody was strumming and humming certain songs more lovely and delightful than any which had ever yet been known in German countries; and all people, old and young, the women particularly, were perfectly mad about them, so that from morning till night you heard nothing else. Only, the

Chronicle adds, the author of these songs happened to be a young clerk, afflicted with leprosy, and living apart from all the world in a desolate place. The excellent reader does not require to be told how horrible a complaint was leprosy in the Middle Ages, and how the poor wretches who had this incurable plague were banished from society, and had to keep at a distance from every human being. Like living corpses, in a gray gown reaching down to the feet, and with the hood brought over their face, they went about, carrying in their hands an enormous rattle, called Saint Lazarus's rattle. With this rattle they gave notice of their approach, that every one might have time to get out of their way. This poor clerk, then, whose poetical gift the Limburg Chronicle extols, was a leper, and he sate moping in the dismal deserts of his misery, whilst all Germany, gay and tuneful, was praising his songs.

"Sometimes, in my sombre visions of the night, I imagine that I see before me the poor leprosy-stricken clerk of the Limburg Chronicle, and then from under his gray hood his distressed eyes look out upon me in a fixed and strange fashion; but the next instant he disappears, and I hear dying away in the distance, like the echo of a dream, the dull creak of Saint Lazarus's rattle."

We have come a long way from Theocritus there; the expression of that has nothing of the clear, positive, happy, pagan character; it has much more the character of one of the indeterminate grotesques of the suffering Middle Age. Profoundness and power it has, though at the same time it is not truly poetical; it is not natural enough for that, there is too much waywardness in it, too much bravado. But as a condition of sentiment to be popular — to be a comfort for the mass of mankind, under the pressure of calamity, to live by — what a manifest failure is this last word of the religion of pleasure! One man in many millions, a Heine, may console himself, and keep himself erect in suffering, by a colossal irony of this sort, by covering himself and the universe with the red fire of this sinister mockery; but the many millions cannot — cannot if they would. That is where the sentiment of a religion of sorrow has such a vast advantage over the sentiment of a religion of pleasure; in its power to be a general, popular, religious sentiment, a stay for the mass of mankind, whose lives are full of hardship. It really succeeds in conveying far more joy, far more of what the mass of mankind are so much without, than its rival. I do not mean joy in prospect only, but joy in possession, actual enjoyment of the world. Mediæval Christianity is reproached with its gloom and austerities; it assigns the material world, says Heine, to the devil. But yet what a fulness of delight does St. Francis manage to draw from this material world itself, and from its commonest and most universally enjoyed elements — sun, air, earth, water, plants! His hymn expresses a far more cordial sense of happiness, even in the material world, than the hymn of Theocritus. It is this which made the fortune of Christianity — its gladness, not its sorrow; not its assigning the spiritual world to Christ, and the material world to the devil, but its drawing from the spiritual world a source of joy so abundant that it ran over upon the material world and transfigured it.

I have said a great deal of harm of paganism; and, taking paganism to mean a state of things which it is commonly taken to mean, and which did really exist, no more harm than it well deserved. Yet I must not end without reminding the reader, that before this state of things appeared, there was an epoch in Greek life — in pagan life — of the highest possible beauty and value. That epoch by itself goes far towards making Greece the Greece we mean when we speak of Greece — a country hardly less important to mankind than Judæa. The poetry of later paganism lived by the senses and understanding; the poetry of mediæval Christianity lived by the heart and imagination. But the main element of the modern spirit's life is neither senses and understanding, nor the heart and imagination; it is imaginative reason. And there is a century in Greek life — the century preceding the Peloponnesian War, from about the year 530 to the year 430 B.C. — in which poetry made, it seems to me, the noblest, the most successful effort she has ever made as the priestess of the imaginative reason, of the element by which the modern spirit, if it would live right, has chiefly to live. Of this effort, of which the four great names are Simonides, Pindar, Æschylus, Sophocles, I must not now attempt more than the bare mention; but it is right, it is necessary, after all I have said, to indicate it. No doubt that effort was imperfect. Perhaps everything, take it at what point of its existence you will, carries within itself the fatal law of its own ulterior development. Perhaps, even of the life in Pindar's time, Pompeii was the inevitable bourne. Perhaps the life of their beautiful Greece could not afford to its poets all that fulness of varied experience, all that power of emotion, which

> "... the heavy and the weary weight
> Of all this unintelligible world" [1]

affords the poet of after-times. Perhaps in Sophocles the thinking-power a little overbalances the religious

[1] Wordsworth, *Tintern Abbey.*

sense, as in Dante the religious sense overbalances the thinking-power. The present has to make its own poetry, and not even Sophocles and his compeers, any more than Dante and Shakespeare, are enough for it. That I will not dispute; nor will I set up the Greek poets, from Pindar to Sophocles, as objects of blind worship. But no other poets so well show to the poetry of the present the way it must take; no other poets have lived so much by the imaginative reason; no other poets have made their work so well balanced; no other poets, who have so well satisfied the thinking-power, have so well satisfied the religious sense:

"Oh! that my lot may lead me in the path of holy innocence of word and deed, the path which august laws ordain, laws that in the highest empyrean had their birth, of which Heaven is the father alone, neither did the race of mortal men beget them, nor shall oblivion ever put them to sleep. The power of God is mighty in them, and groweth not old." [1]

Let St. Francis — nay, or Luther either — beat that!

Matthew Arnold, Essays in Criticism: First Series, 1865

A CYNIC'S APOLOGY

1869

There are certain outcasts of humanity — pariahs to whom the most benevolent of mankind refuse to extend a helping hand — misshapen cripples in soul, who are displayed by some cruel demonstrator, like specimens in bottles at a medical museum, to illustrate the disastrous consequences of grievous moral disease; — and of these unfortunates I confess myself to be one. I seldom enter a church, or attend a public meeting,

[1] Sophocles, *Œdipus the King*.

without hearing myself held up to execration — not by name, but by reputation — as the heartless cynic, the man who sits in the seat of the scorner, or the rightful owner of some other opprobrious title drawn from profane or sacred sources. In short, I am a person given to rather dyspeptic views of things, inclined to look at the seamy side of the world, and much more ready to laugh at a new actor than to go wild with enthusiasm over his performance. Now I freely admit that for the most part the preachers are perfectly right. Undoubtedly enthusiasm is the most essential of all qualities, if not the one thing needful. It prevents the world from sinking into a stagnant and putrefying pool. We could not improve, not even remain in a stationary position without it. And, what is more, the preachers are justified in giving a rather exaggerated prominence to the enthusiastic view of life; for mankind is much more in want of the spur than of the curb. Let them encourage any number of young St. Georges to mount and ride forth in search of a dragon; for though in real life the dragon breed is probably extinct since the days of the pterodactyle, it will be some time before we shall want game-laws to protect dragons of the metaphysical kind, or be able to dispense with the services of any St. George that may enlist. Yet, after all, there is another side of things which we may sometimes remember when we are beyond the charmed circle of pulpit eloquence. A clergyman does well to insist chiefly upon the necessity of self-denial; but it does not follow that we should never have a taste of cakes and ale. As, indeed, we are ready enough for the most part to take our meals regularly without special encouragement, our teachers do not insist upon the necessity of our eating and drinking and indulging in an occasional festivity. They trust to the unaided propensities of our nature to secure the proper discharge of these functions, and are content to throw their whole weight upon the side of restraining our excesses. For a similar reason, I presume, we are never told that we ought sometimes to laugh at our neighbors, to throw cold water upon their zeal, and to pick holes in their favorite little projects for the reform of humanity. It is imagined that that duty may be safely left to the unprompted malevolence of our nature, of which it is presumed that there will be a sufficient crop after every diligence has been used in pruning it down. Now here, I venture to suggest, there is an omission in the common run of exhortation. There is, as I shall try to prove, a certain useful piece of work to be done, and if we are content simply to denounce those who do it, it will, of course, be done in a bad spirit and from malevolent motives. I claim no lofty mission for the cynic; and I merely suggest that, like mosquitoes, they are part of the economy of nature. One of Lincoln's apologues — of which the original application matters little — told how he and his brother were once ploughing on a Kentucky farm: the horse was going at an unusually good pace, when Lincoln knocked off a huge "chin-fly" that was fastened to his hide. "What did you do that for?" exclaimed his brother. "That's all that made him go." The whole of my claim for cynics is that they act at times the part of "chin-fly," on the pachydermatous population of the world. If we rashly attempt to crush them out of existence, we only make them more spiteful than before, and may not improbably discover that, like other vermin, they do some dirty work, which is not the less essential to our comfort. The most ingenious of the socialist theorizers maintained that men who did particularly unpleasant services to mankind, should be rewarded by being held in special honor, instead of being shunned as is usual in our imperfect society. Scavengers and chimney sweeps, for example, would have some compensation for groping in filth by occupying at other times the best seats in public places. I do not go so far as this. I am content to be trodden under foot (in spirit only) by innumerable preachers — and perhaps it does not want much courage to bear the satire of ordinary sermons; they may spit upon my gaberdine, and call me misbeliever, cut-throat dog, as much as they like. I shall never desire to cut off a pound of their flesh; I would, at most, retaliate, like poor old Shylock, by some harmless abuse, and invite them, not (as I might) to be grateful, but to remember that I too, like venomous reptiles, have a certain place in the world. To explain this a little more in detail, let us consider one or two particular cases. Thus, for example, every one who has reached a certain time of life has been annoyed by a peculiar race, known amongst its own members as the "earnest," and to the rest of mankind as prigs. It is notoriously difficult even for naturalists to trace out the identity of certain creatures who vary much at different stages of their development. A man who remembers the companions of his university career is sometimes amazed at the number of enthusiastic clergymen and respectable lawyers who at a later period claim to have been among his contemporaries, and wonders from what new material this finished product has been constructed. Gradually he finds that a stout boating-man, whose talk was of bumping and whose food was of bleeding beefsteak, has fined down into an ascetic priest; or that a cadaverous mathematical student has blossomed into a rubicund lawyer. Now the case of the prig is the reverse of this. He is a specimen of arrested development. In stead of being modified by the atmosphere of the outside world, he has carried into it all the simplicity characteristic of his earliest manhood. There is something refreshing and even elevating about the spectacle of these harmless enthusiasts. They carry us back to the time when the sight of our names in a class-list produced a feeling of ineffable pride, and a fellowship seemed more glorious than a seat in the Cabinet. There is upon this earth no person who surveys mankind "from China to Peru" [1] with a more exquisite sense of perfect complacency than the young gentleman who has just put on his bachelor's hood. Early donhood, if I may so call it, is the time of life at which nature assists us by throwing out an abnormal development of self-esteem, as the marmot grows fat to strengthen him against the approach of winter. The Union [2] is still to our minds an assembly whose debates reverberate throughout the empire; to row in the university eight is an honour worth the sacrifice certainly of learning, and possibly even of health; to be a first-class man is to have won a decisive success in the battle of life. In the little world to which our ambition has hitherto been confined, we have risen to the summit of all things; for tutors, professors, and other authorities are nothing but contemptible old fogies hide-bound with useless pedantry. So imposing, indeed, is the position of the youth who has just won honours, that I confess that I have never been able to meet as an equal those who attained that position when I was a freshman. Thackeray speaks of the old gentleman of seventy who still shuddered at the dream of being flogged by the terrible head-master of his youth. In my imagination, the lads who held sway in

first-class man, a student in the highest group in an examination.
[1] Johnson, *The Vanity of Human Wishes*, ll. 1-2.
[2] *Union*, a debating society at Oxford University.

the university when I first had the honour of a gown, and who, as we fondly believed, rivalled, in different departments, Porson, and Sir Isaac Newton, and Pitt, and Coleridge, and Byron, are still surrounded by a glory exceeding that of any of the sons of men. But a cynical freshmen would be an impossible creature.

Most men soon part with their university bloom: the world demolishes their splendid ideal, and even Oxford and Cambridge sink to provincial towns with a large proportion of cultivated men and promising lads; but not enchanted palaces of virtue and learning. The senior wrangler himself walks down the Strand without attracting a crowd; and a benighted metropolis has rather hazy notions of the precise meaning of triposes and littlegoes. Yet there are a happy few who carry about with them to later life the rose-coloured atmosphere which first gathered round them in the walks of Trinity or Christ church, and retain the estimate then formed of the outer world of barbarians. These are the genuine prigs; and as live and let live is a very good, though very trite, motto, I have no objection to their existence. They would not voluntarily hurt my feelings; and indeed the really irritating things about them is their invariable condescension. They have the art of posing themselves like monumental statues on invisible pedestals which they carry about with them. They smile benevolently at any little criticisms which we may hazard, as one smiles at the infantile prattle of children. They have a mission, of which they are perfectly conscious, and they move in a light not vouchsafed to the horny eyes of a cynic. But they feel deeply that their ineffable superiority does not

senior wrangler, first student in the first class when it was arranged in order of merit.
triposes (Cambridge university), lists of successful candidates in honour examination.
littlegoes, first examinations for B.A. degree at Cambridge.

entitle them to be harsh with us. They have even
been known to approve an occasional joke, though
never condescending to make one themselves; they
deal gently but firmly with us; and after we have
amused ourselves with our playthings, bring us back to
the discussion of a serious subject. If the conversation
strays, for example, to some mere personal gossip, they
take advantage of the first accidental loophole to ask
our opinion of the merits of female suffrage, or the
prospects of trades-unionism. On woman's rights they
are especially strong — it may be from a natural sense
of gratitude; for women, as natural haters of cynicism
and inclined to sentiment, are generally far more
tolerant of priggishness than men. Perhaps, too,
there is something pleasant to the feminine imagination in the air of infallibility which these excellent beings affect; for they are apt to gather into cliques, and
round private prophets, of whom to confess ignorance
is to confess yourself one of the prophane. This gives
them that great advantage which belongs to the eso-
teric disciples of a narrow sect — the power of forming
mutual admiration societies. A great, though unin-
tentional, service has been done them by an eloquent
writer, as far as possible removed from their weaknesses, in popularizing the nickname Philistine. Like
other nicknames, that word has degenerated in common use, till it is sometimes a mere shibboleth, employed by the genuine prig to designate all who are not
prigs. Not but that the two characters may be sometimes reconciled in that truly portentous variety of the
prig who founds his claim to superiority on the exclusive possession of the true doctrine about the currency,
or the checks and balances of the British constitution.
But, as a rule, to do him justice, the prig chooses for

eloquent writer. Matthew Arnold, in his *Culture and Anarchy.*

his pet doctrine some less husky and indigestible fragments of truth.

To object to such persons in their youth would be morose; though even then the phase is not without its dangers. It implies a consciousness — which may frequently be well founded — of great powers, and a rather overweening estimate of their importance. It is useful, we may say, as the yolk which surrounds a bird before it has left the egg — on condition that it is thoroughly absorbed. When the daydreams of the youth begin to turn into the settled delusion of the man, they first show their enervating influence. To eradicate these delusions requires that treatment with some biting social acids which cynics are destined by nature to secrete. The youthful enthusiast who has not undergone some such hardening process suffers from a sort of fatty degeneration of the moral nature. He exhibits that insipid flabby sentimentalism which does more than anything to disgust reasonable men with philanthropy. It is, doubtless, a thousand pities that any one should be disgusted with so essential a virtue: but how is it to be avoided? A man who is capable of deep emotion at the mass of misery which still stagnates in the world, who is anxious for stern and sharp remedies well considered and vigorously carried into execution, is thrust aside by the crowd of amiable quacks who are occupied in puffing themselves and their pet nostrums. The cliques — each of which possesses, in its own estimation, the one panacea for curing all our evils — form, as it were, a series of social hothouses, in which philanthropists are forced, like early peas, to an unhealthy precocity of growth. They shoot up into prize specimens, intensely admired by those who have carefully cultivated them, and manured them with compliment and applause, but o

weak fibre and feeble constitution. If you venture to
criticise one of these gushing and feminine creatures,
you are accused of harshness, brutality, and indifference to the finer feelings of our nature. You are a
coarse cynic, and probably a sceptic into the bargain;
your impatience of schemes that won't work, and of
feeble attempts to varnish decayed places instead of
curing them, is considered to imply indifference to the
end desired. It is easy to set down the contempt of
practical men for half the charitable schemes of the
day to a grovelling selfishness. Much of it may be so;
but it only needs a glance at the chaotic muddle of the
London charities, to see the advantage that would result if people would look before they leap, and take a
lesson or two from the scorners and sneerers. Doing
good requires forethought as well as other things; and
the fashionable denunciation of cynicism has tended to
deprive us of the benefits of all criticism. People are
so charmed with the romantic aspect of things that
they won't look at the prosaic, commonplace aspect of
the evils to be encountered. To say the truth, one is
occasionally inclined to regret that martyrdom has
gone out of fashion. Doubtless it was wrong to saw an
apostle in two; but the practice had its advantages.
It forced social reformers into a sterner temper, and
a more thorough-going policy, and discouraged the
crowd of thoughtless volunteers, who hinder the work
they profess to help. The word, indeed, remains, but
its whole signification is altered. Two of the most desirable events in life are, to be suppressed by Act of
Parliament or to become a martyr. In one case, you
are left with a good income and nothing to do; in the
other, you are the object of universal sympathy, and
may very probably receive even pecuniary compensation. When stakes and faggots were in vogue, there

were objections to the honour; but now it would be hard to show a man a more delicate attention than to prosecute him for heresy, whether theological, political, or even scientific, for he is certain to become a "lion," and not improbably the pet of some enthusiastic clique.

As this moral tonic has gone out of use, the critic's sneer is, perhaps, the best substitute left. It may do something to clear the atmosphere of cant, and to strip the prig of his inordinate affectations. By itself it can, indeed, do nothing; but it gets rid of some of the constantly accumulating masses of humbug, and allows us at least to see things as they are. To the objection that it is cruel, the answer is that it can hardly hold the existing evils in check. The unfounded superstition that brutal critics of a former day slew Keats by their abuse has long since been worn out, and is scarcely even quoted more than once a week or so. We may say, in Rosalind's words, "men have died, and worms have eaten them" [1] — but not of criticism. Persons who talk of the ferocity of the most fabulous creature known as the slashing critic, must indulge in some very erroneous estimates of the amount of genius in this country. A hasty calculation may be easily made. Compare the number of novelists of established reputation with the swarms of aspirants, whose first efforts are criticized in nearly every paper we take up, and then compare the number of favourable and unfavourable judgments. A rule of three will result, which would prove either that we are now turning out rivals to Fielding, or Scott, or Thackeray with unprecedented rapidity, or that many respectable writers are being welcomed with an excess of compliment. It is only too easy to say which is the most probable alterna-

[1] *As You Like It*, IV, i, 105.

tive. Or we may compare the number of living authors of recognized ability, who struggled against critics in their youth — if any can be named — with the number who have been hopelessly spoilt by undue praise. At every turn we find really clever novelists, poets, and artists who have made a hit on their first attempt, and have ever since been their own servile imitators. It is of the rarest occurrence now to find one who has been exposed to the opposite and less searching trial of hostility, or even want of recognition. Unless a man willfully plunges into some abstruse branch of inquiry, some thorny byway of metaphysical or historical inquiry, he is in especially greater danger from the excess than the deficiency of sympathy. A patron, we know, in Dr. Johnson's time, was "one who looked with unconcern on a man struggling for life in the water, and when he had reached ground, encumbered him with help." [1] The public, we are told, has taken the place of patron and discharges it in very different fashion. It has innumerable critics placed, like the Humane Society's men on the Serpentine, with ample provision of hooks, ropes, and grapples. On the first appearance of a swimmer of any buoyancy, he is seized, hauled on shore, patted on the back, applauded, petted, treated to drinks, supplied with funds, and generally made into an idol with all the questionable advantages of such a position. If some poor critic comes by and says, "Really that young man is an impostor," he is hooted at as a cynic whose only motive must be an unworthy jealousy. And yet there are imposters — if we may imitate Galileo's [2] profession of faith. Nay, so far is

---

[1] Johnson's letter to Lord Chesterfield, February, 1755.

[2] Galileo "at the age of seventy was obliged to abjure his system in order to gain his liberty. After pronouncing his abjuration, he said, in a ʻage whisper, *E pur si muove* (It does move, though)." — *Dictionary of Phrase and Fable.* The story is apocryphal.

criticism from damaging genuine talent, that even an impostor, if endowed with sufficient impudence, can thrive and wax fat and sell innumerable editions in the teeth of his scorners. All that the critic can hope to do is to keep alive the belief that there is some distinction between good writing and bad, and to encourage public opinion occasionally to assert its independence. It is an encouraging fact that by incessantly hammering at the point, sensation novelists have been forced to put forward a defence. Critics are totally unable to crush the faults of which they complain, but they can maintain a certain sensibility to blame. It is still known by tradition that there are some canons of good taste, which a man may indeed safely defy so far as his bookseller's account is concerned, but which will avenge themselves on his future fame. If the tradition does not quite expire, it is due to a few faithful critics — much reviled by the enthusiastic part of mankind — who go about smiting pretenders right and left; and, it may be, sometimes administering a random blow to some one who does not deserve it.

The enthusiasts, who think that revolutions are to be made with rosewater, that the world is to be awed by patting all the good boys on the head without administering the birch to the bad ones, may possibly object to this doctrine. It sounds plausible to say, praise the good and let the bad find its own path to decay. Yet even they will perhaps admit some force in the next claim which I venture to put forward. There are in this world certain persons known by the good old English name of fools. Although we shrink from applying the name to any individual, we know that, in the aggregate, they form a vast and almost impenetrable phalanx. Like other men, they have their uses; they serve, perhaps, as ballast, and prevent the ma-

chinery of the world from moving too fast. Certainly
they do it effectually. There is something portentous
about the huge masses of dogged stupidity which en-
viron us on every side. There are noodles alive who
repeat with infinite variations the oration composed
for them by Sydney Smith,[1] and repeat their little saws
about the wisdom of our ancestors, the contrast
between theory and practice, and other profound
considerations leading up to the grand conclusion,
Nolumus leges Angliae mutari. It may be that some of
the finest specimens of the tribe were those who lately
engaged in the defense of the worst abuses in work-
houses, and happily compared all who denounced them
to persons with a morbid appetite for "putrid oysters."
The force of the analogy may not be very obvious, but
it had a certain currency at the time from the happy
confusion of ideas which it indicated. Vestrymen, as
this scrap of their eloquence implies, are frequently
dull; and it may even be that their education gives
them a dullness of a peculiarly fine flavour. But we
cannot flatter ourselves that dullness is confined to
Bumbledom, nor to its unfortunate subjects. There
is, we may venture to imagine, some stupidity in high
places; and if any doubts be entertained on the subject, we might ask Mr. Mill for his opinion of Conservative members of Parliament, or Mr. Bright for his
views of bishops. Assuming that those eminent men
cannot be speaking entirely without book, and noting,
for our private edification, the singular resemblance
between the two sides of the House of Commons, and
the fact that lawn sleeves do not naturally change

Nolumus, etc. We do not wish the laws of England to be changed....
    [*The concluding sentence of "Noodle's Oration."*]
Bumbledom, parish beadles in general, from Bumble, in *Oliver Twist.*
lawn sleeves, the sleeves of bishops.
    [1] "Noodle's Oration," a burlesque, was published in the *Edinburgh
Review* in 1825. It consists entirely of rhetorical questions, platitudes, and
appeals to prejudice.

human nature, we may venture to hazard a conjecture that there is probably a good deal of stupidity up and down the country. How is it to be assaulted with any prospect of success? The thick armour which Providence has bestowed upon this class of mankind is proverbial. Take it for a rule, as the poet observes,

"No creature smarts so little as a fool." [1]

But if anything is to be done, he must be made to smart. Some one must do for him that kind office which had to be done for the mediæval knight who had been tumbled over in his impregnable suit of armour, and force open the rivets. Where is this vulnerable place? Preaching, however eloquent, passes over him like a distant pleasant murmur. He plants himself more firmly in his seat, and refuses to budge. He is like a huge wrestler whom I have seen wearing down his active antagonist by sheer weight. If he moved, he was thrown in an instant; but so long as he stood stolidly stockstill no efforts were of the slightest use. We want some one to stir him up as the Spanish bull is excited by a firework or two planted in his neck. Now, fortunately, the very dullest of mortals is more or less accessible to contempt. He dislikes being written down an ass. He throws off his mantle of sevenfold indifference under a few judicious taunts, and brings his clumsy strength into the arena. It is curious to remark how, in a political contest, the loftiest eloquence loses its effect after a day or two; and some little epigram thrown out in the heat of the contest remains fizzing and sparkling unquenchably, in spite of all efforts to stamp it out, and keeps up the spirit of the weary combatants. Keen, scornful common sense, compressed into a few pungent words, piercing through

---

[1] Pope, *Epistle to Arbuthnot*, l. 84.

the buncombe and the flummery, should be welcomed even by those it attacks. It is the signal that the parade of the fencer with blunted foils is over, and that real work with sharp steel is beginning.

But it may be urged this is, after all, a debasing view of things. Even if the hero laughs at them, the popular mind is prejudiced. If, in those old days of dragons and martyrs, there had been such things as newspaper reporters and weekly essayists, what kind of criticism would have greeted men who died in the discharge of the noblest of duties? Or suppose that even now some gallant missionary has been devoured in the Cannibal Islands, and that the court journalist of that country has managed to catch something of the European tone. "The news which has just come to us," he would perhaps say, "is certainly to be lamented. Cannibalism, as a custom, is undoubtedly doomed, though we may regret the sentimentality which has finally suppressed so picturesque and harmless a custom. Be that as it may, we have become too dainty to eat our enemies, though not too dainty to kill them; we have sacrificed to morbid prejudices a savoury and nutritious article of diet; and, of course, laws, however unsatisfactory in point of reason, must be obeyed. Even missionaries who land upon our shores must be protected. But we would ask them, if they still retain any gleams of common sense, what it is that they expect to gain? Mumbo Jumbo may not be in all respects a satisfactory object of worship; but what known doctrine is thoroughly satisfactory? His worshippers believe that if they knock each other on the head, or marry more than a dozen wives, or eat human flesh out of season, they will suffer for it; it is a rough creed containing, it may

---

Mumbo Jumbo, a devil worshipped and greatly feared by the natives of West Africa.

be, some errors; but, on the whole, it is excellently adapted to the state of civilization, and any more refined doctrines would simply fly over the people's heads. Mumbo Jumbo's priests are not men of any high polish, but they have a great influence over the vulgar, and save some expense in police arrangements. The man who upsets such a state of things, incurs a heavy responsibility, and it ought to be perfectly clear that his teaching will be better adapted to the minds of his audience. If he is fool enough for the sake of so doubtful a good, to run the risk of being made into chops, we are of course bound, as far as may be, to frustrate his excellent intention, and to prevent him from obtaining the object of his foolish wishes. So far as we can secure it by reasonable precautions, his friends shall not boast that he has been converted into meat, roast, boiled, or baked; but if we unluckily fail, they must also thoroughly understand that we hold him to be simply an idiot whose folly has met with its natural, if not its lawful reward.''

In some such tone, I imagine, we should greet many martyrdoms nowadays: and I fully admit that it is only within narrow bounds, only when acting as a strictly subordinate check, that cynicism is desirable or pardonable. Mustard is a good thing, but we cannot dine off it; and there are, undoubtedly, limits to the use of vitriol. When chivalry is sneered away, there is a fearful loss to the people whose powers of reverence are injured; only at present I fear it is in equal danger of being stifled by injudicious praise, and lost from sight in a mass of Brummagem imitations. A little supply of cynicism should be kept on hand to test the genuine nature of the article. Let us only reflect, to

---

Brummagem, corruption of *Birmingham*, cheap, showy, in allusion to counterfeit groats made there in the seventeenth century, and to its plated goods.

use one obvious illustration, how much good would be
done if in every church there came in at sermon-time
the cynic who is so often denounced in his absence; if
he was accommodated with a seat, and allowed to put
the clergyman a few questions afterwards in private:
would not the logic to which we are treated be generally
sounder, the eloquence more severe, and a little more
care be shown not to shelter sheer nonsense under the
respect due to sacred things?   We should, I fancy,
more frequently enjoy what, in spite of all that is said
against sermons, is really one of the most elevating of
all possible influences, the eloquence of a man who has
put the whole powers of his mind to enforce doctrines
of whose truth and vital importance he is even passionately convinced, and who further remembers that
he is talking to men as well as to children.

Sir Leslie Stephen (first published in The Cornhill Magazine, May, 1869).

THE DEATH OF SOCRATES

Pub. 1871

[Socrates is in prison, taking farewell of his friends and
disciples. He has been discoursing on the grounds for
belief in immortality, after having refused to consider plans
of escape proposed by Crito. The narrative is given in the
words of Phaedo, the "beloved disciple," as delivered by
him to Echecrates and others. The incident took place
399 B.C.]

"Wherefore, Simmias, seeing all these things, what
ought not we to do in order to obtain virtue and wisdom in this life?   Fair is the prize, and the hope great.

"I do not mean to affirm that the description which I
have given of the soul and her mansions is exactly true
— a man of sense ought hardly to say that.   But I do
say that, inasmuch as the soul is shown to be immortal,
he may venture to think, not improperly or unworthily,

that something of the kind is true. The venture is a glorious one, and he ought to comfort himself with words like these, which is the reason why I lengthen out the tale. Wherefore, I say, let a man be of good cheer about his soul, who has cast away the pleasures and ornaments of the body as alien to him, and rather hurtful in their effects, and has followed after the pleasures of knowledge in this life; who has adorned the soul in her own proper jewels, which are temperance, and justice, and courage, and nobility, and truth — in these she is ready to go on her journey to the world below, when her time comes. You, Simmias and Cebes, and all other men, will depart at some time or other. Me already, as the tragic poet would say, the voice of fate calls. Soon I must drink the poison; and I think I had better repair to the bath first, in order that the women may not have the trouble of washing my body, after I am dead."

When he had done speaking, Crito said: "And have you any commands for us, Socrates — anything to say about your children, or any other matter in which we can serve you?"

"Nothing particular," he said: "only, as I always told you, I would have you look to yourselves; that is a service which you may always be doing to me and mine as well as to yourselves. And you need not make professions; for if you take no thought for yourselves, and walk not according to the precepts which I have given you, not now for the first time, the warmth of your professions will be of no avail."

"We will do our best," said Crito. "But in what way would you have us bury you?"

"In any way that you like; only you must get hold of me, and take care that I do not walk away from you." Then he turned to us, and added with a smile:

"I cannot make Crito believe that I am the same Socrates who have been talking and conducting the argument; he fancies that I am the other Socrates whom he will soon see, a dead body — and he asks, How shall he bury me? And though I have spoken many words in the endeavor to show that when I have drunk the poison I shall leave you and go to the joys of the blessed — these words of mine, with which I comforted you and myself, have had, as I perceive, no effect upon Crito. And therefore I want you to be surety for me now, as he was surety for me at the trial: but let the promise be of another sort; for he was my surety to the judges that I would remain, but you are my surety to him that I shall not remain, but go away and depart; and then he will suffer less at my death, and not be grieved when he sees my body being burned or buried. I would not have him sorrow at my hard lot, or say at the burial, Thus we lay out Socrates, or, Thus we follow him to the grave and bury him; for false words are not only evil in themselves, but they infect the soul with evil. Be of good cheer then, my dear Crito, and say that you are burying my body only, and do with that as is usual, and as you think best."

When he had spoken these words, he arose and went into the bath-chamber with Crito, who bid us wait; and we waited, talking and thinking of the subject of the discourse, and also of the greatness of our sorrow; he was like a father of whom we were being bereaved, and we were about to pass the rest of our lives as orphans. When he had taken the bath his children were brought to him — (he had two young sons and an elder one); and the women of his family also came, and he talked with them and gave them a few directions in the presence of Crito; and he then dismissed them and returned to us.

Now the hour of sunset was near, for a good deal of time had passed while he was within. When he came out, he sat down with us again after his bath, but not much was said. Soon the jailer, who was the servant of the Eleven, entered and stood by him, saying: "To you, Socrates, whom I know to be the noblest and gentlest and best of all who ever came to this place, I will not impute the angry feelings of other men, who rage and swear at me when, in obedience to the authorities, I bid them drink the poison — indeed I am sure that you will not be angry with me; for others, as you are aware, and not I, are the guilty cause. And so fare you well, and try to bear lightly what must needs be; you know my errand." Then bursting into tears he turned and went out.

Socrates looked at him and said, "I return your good wishes, and will do as you bid." Then turning to us, he said, "How charming the man is: since I have been in prison he has always been coming to see me, and at times he would talk to me, and was as good as could be to me, and now see how generously he sorrows for me. But we must do as he says, Crito; let the cup be brought, if the poison is prepared: if not, let the attendant prepare some."

"Yet," said Crito, "the sun is still upon the hilltops, and many a one has taken the draught late, and after the announcement has been made to him, he has eaten and drunk, and indulged in sensual delights; do not hasten then, there is still time."

Socrates said: "Yes, Crito, and they of whom you speak are right in doing thus, for they think that they will gain by the delay; but I am right in not doing thus, for I do not think that I should gain anything by drink-

---

Eleven, a police-board under whose supervision capital penalties were carried out.

ing the poison a little later; I should be sparing and saving a life which is already gone: I could only laugh at myself for this. Please then to do as I say, and not to refuse me."

Crito, when he heard this, made a sign to the servant; and the servant went in, and remained for some time, and then returned with the jailer carrying the cup of poison. Socrates said: "You, my good friend, who are experienced in these matters, shall give me directions how I am to proceed." The man answered: "You have only to walk about until your legs are heavy, and then to lie down, and the poison will act." At the same time he handed the cup to Socrates, who in the easiest and gentlest manner, without the least fear or change of colour or feature, looking at the man with all his eyes, Echecrates, as his manner was, took the cup and said: "What do you say about making a libation out of this cup to any god? May I, or not?" The man answered: "We only prepare, Socrates, just so much as we deem enough." "I understand," he said: "yet I may and must pray to the gods to prosper my journey from this to that other world — may this then, which is my prayer, be granted to me." Then holding the cup to his lips, quite readily and cheerfully he drank off the poison. And hitherto most of us had been able to control our sorrow; but now when we saw him drinking, and saw too that he had finished the draught, we could not longer forbear, and in spite of myself my own tears were flowing fast; so that I covered my face and wept over myself, for certainly I was not weeping over him, but at the thought of my own calamity in having lost such a companion. Nor was I the first, for Crito, when he found himself unable to restrain his tears, had got up and moved away, and I followed; and at that moment, Apollodorus, who had been weeping all the time, broke out into a loud cry which made cowards of us all. Socrates alone retained his calmness. "What is this strange outcry?" he said. "I sent away the women mainly in order that they might not offend in this way, for I have heard that a man should die in peace. Be quiet then, and have patience." When we heard that, we were ashamed, and refrained our tears; and he walked about until, as he said, his legs began to fail, and then he lay on his back, according to the directions, and the man who gave him the poison now and then looked at his feet and legs; and after a while he pressed his foot hard and asked if he could feel; and he said, No; and then his leg, and so upwards, and showed us that he was cold and stiff. And he felt them himself, and said: "When the poison reaches the heart, that will be the end." He was beginning to grow cold about the groin, when he uncovered his face, for he had covered himself up, and said (they were his last words) — he said: "Crito, I owe a cock to Asclepius; will you remember to pay the debt?" "The debt shall be paid," said Crito; "is there anything else?" There was no answer to this question; but in a minute or two a movement was heard, and the attendants uncovered him; his eyes were set, and Crito closed his eyes and mouth.

Such was the end, Echecrates, of our friend; whom I may truly call the wisest, and justest, and best of all the men whom I have known.

Benjamin Jowett, translation of the *Phaedo* of Plato

THE ASCENT OF MAN

Pub. 1871

Animals of many kinds are social; we find even distinct species living together, as with some American monkeys, and with the united flocks of rooks, jackdaws, and starlings. Man shows the same feeling in his strong love for the dog, which the dog returns with interest. Every one must have noticed how miserable horses, dogs, and sheep are when separated from their companions; and what affection the two former kinds show on their reunion. It is curious to speculate on the feelings of a dog, who will rest peacefully for hours in a room with his master or any of the family, without the least notice being taken of him; but if left for a short time by himself, barks or howls dismally.

The most common service which the higher animals perform for each other is the warning each other of danger by means of the united senses of all. Every sportsman knows how difficult it is to approach animals in a herd or troop. Wild horses and cattle do not, I believe, make any danger-signal; but the attitude of any one who first discovers an enemy, warns the others. Rabbits stamp loudly on the ground with their hind-feet as a signal: sheep and chamois do the same, but with their fore-feet, uttering likewise a whistle. Many birds and some mammals post sentinels, which in the case of seals are said generally to be females. The leader of a troop of monkeys acts as the sentinel, and utters cries expressive both of danger and of safety.

Animals also render more important services to each other; thus wolves and some other beasts of prey hunt in packs, and aid each other in attacking their victims. The Hamadryas baboons turn over stones to find insects; and when they come to a large stone, as many as can stand round turn it over together and share the booty. Social animals mutually defend each other. The males of some ruminants come to the front when there is danger and defend the herd with their horns. Brehm encountered in Abyssinia a great troop of baboons which were crossing a valley; some had already ascended the opposite mountain, and some were still in the valley; the latter were attacked by the dogs, but the old males immediately hurried down from the rocks, and with mouths widely opened roared so fearfully, that the dogs precipitately retreated. They were again encouraged to the attack; but by this time all the baboons had re-ascended the heights, excepting a young one, about six months old, who, loudly calling for aid, climbed on a block of rock and was surrounded. Now one of the largest males, a true hero, came down again from the mountain, slowly went to the young one, coaxed him, and triumphantly led him away — the dogs being too much astonished to make an attack. I cannot resist giving another scene which was witnessed by this same naturalist; an eagle seized a young Ceropithecus, which, by clinging to a branch, was not at once carried off; it cried loudly for assistance, upon which the other members of the troop with much uproar rushed to the rescue, surrounded the eagle, and pulled out so many feathers, that he no longer thought of his prey, but only how to escape. The eagle assuredly would never again attack a monkey in a troop.

It is certain that associated animals have a feeling of love for each other which is not felt by adult and non-social animals. How far in most cases they actually sympathize with each other's pains and pleasures is more doubtful, especially with respect to the latter. Mr. Buxton, however, states that his macaws, which lived free in Norfolk, took "an extravagant interest" in a pair with a nest, and whenever the female left it, she was surrounded by a troop "screaming horrible acclamations in her honour." It is often difficult to judge whether animals have any feeling for each other's

Ceropithecus, a monkey of the same family with the baboons.

sufferings. Who can say what cows feel, when they surround and stare intently on a dead or dying companion? That animals sometimes are far from feeling any sympathy is too certain; for they will expel a wounded animal from the herd, or gore or worry it to death. This is almost the blackest fact in natural history, unless indeed the explanation which has been suggested is true, that their instinct or reason leads them to expel an injured companion, lest beasts of prey, including man, should be tempted to follow the troop. In this case their conduct is not much worse than that of the North American Indians, who leave their feeble comrades to perish on the plains, or the Fijians, who, when their parents get old or fall ill, bury them alive.

Many animals, however, certainly sympathize with each other's distress or danger. This is the case even with birds; Captain Stansbury found on a salt lake in Utah an old and completely blind pelican, which was very fat, and must have been long and well fed by his companions. Mr. Blyth, as he informs me, saw Indian crows feeding two or three of their companions which were blind. We may, if we choose, call these actions instinctive; but such cases are much too rare for the development of any special instinct. I have myself seen a dog, who never passed a great friend of his, a cat which lay sick in a basket, without giving her a few licks of his tongue, the surest sign of kind feeling in a dog.

It must be called sympathy that leads a courageous dog to fly at any one who strikes his master, as he certainly will. I saw a person pretending to beat a lady who had a very timid little dog on her lap, and the trial had never before been made. The little creature instantly jumped away, but after the pretended beating

was over, it was really pathetic to see how persever-
ingly he tried to lick his mistress's face and comfort
her. Brehm states that when a baboon in confinement
was pursued to be punished, the others tried to protect
him. It must have been sympathy in the cases above
given which led the baboons and Ceropitheci to defend
their young comrades from the dogs and the eagle. I
will give only one other instance of sympathetic and
heroic conduct in a little American monkey. Several
years ago a keeper at the Zoölogical Gardens, showed
me some deep and scarcely healed wounds on the nape
of his neck, inflicted on him whilst kneeling on the floor
by a fierce baboon. The little American monkey, who
was a warm friend of this keeper, lived in the same
large compartment, and was dreadfully afraid of the
great baboon. Nevertheless, as soon as he saw his
friend the keeper in peril, he rushed to the rescue, and
by screams and bites so distracted the baboon that the
man was able to escape, after running great risk, as the
surgeon who attended him thought, of his life.

Besides love and sympathy, animals exhibit other
qualities which in us would be called moral; and I
agree with Agassiz that dogs possess something very
like a conscience. They certainly possess some power
of self-command, and this does not appear to be wholly
the result of fear. As Braubach remarks, a dog will refrain from stealing food in the absence of his master.
Dogs have long been accepted as the very type of fidel-
ity and obedience. All animals living in a body which
defend each other or attack their enemies in concert,
must be in some degree faithful to each other; and
those that follow a leader must be in some degree obedient. When the baboons in Abyssinia plunder a
garden, they silently follow their leader; and if an im-
prudent young animal makes a noise, he receives a slap

from the others to teach him silence and obedience;
but as soon as they are sure that there is no danger, all
show their joy by much clamour.

The main conclusion arrived at in this work, and
now held by many naturalists who are well competent
to form a sound judgment, is that man is descended
from some less highly organized form. The ground
upon which this conclusion rests will never be shaken,
for the close similarity between man and the lower
animals in embryonic development, as well as in innumerable points of structure and constitution, the
rudiments which he retains, and the abnormal rever-
sions to which he is occasionally liable, are facts which
cannot be disputed. They have long been known, but
until recently they told us nothing with respect to the
origin of man. Now, when viewed by the light of our
knowledge of the whole organic world their meaning is
unmistakable. The great principle of evolution stands
up clear and firm, when these groups of facts are considered in connexion with others, such as the mutual
affinities of the members of the same group, their geo-
graphical distribution in past and present times, and
their geological succession. It is incredible that all
these facts should speak falsely. He who is not content to look, like a savage, at the phenomena of nature
as disconnected, cannot any longer believe that man is
the work of a separate act of creation.

The greatest difficulty which presents itself, when
we are driven to the above conclusion on the origin of
man, is the high standard of intellectual power and of
moral disposition which he has attained. But every
one who admits the general principle of evolution,
must see that the mental powers of the higher animals,
which are the same in kind with those of mankind,

though so different in degree, are capable of advancement. Thus the interval between the mental powers of one of the higher apes and of a fish, or between those of an ant and a scale-insect, is immense. The development of these powers in animals does not offer any special difficulty; for with our domesticated animals the mental faculties are certainly variable, and the variations are inherited. No one doubts that these faculties are of the utmost importance to animals in a state of nature. Therefore the conditions are favourable for their development through natural selection. The same conclusion may be extended to man; the intellect must have been all-important to him, even at a very remote period, enabling him to use language, to invent and make weapons, tools and traps; by which means, in combination with his social habits, he long ago became the most dominant of all living creatures.

A great stride in the development of the intellect will have followed as soon as, through a previous considerable advance, the half-art and half-instinct of language came into use; for the continued use of language will have reacted on the brain, and produced an inherited effect; and this again will have reacted on the improvement of language. The large size of the brain in man, in comparison with that of the lower animals, relatively to the size of their bodies, may be attributed in chief part to the early use of some simple form of language, that wonderful engine which affixes signs to all sorts of objects and qualities, and excites trains of thought which would never arise from the mere impressions of the senses, and if they did arise would not be followed out.

The development of the moral qualities is a more interesting and difficult problem. Their foundation lies in the social instincts, including in this term the family ties. These instincts are of a highly complex nature, and in the case of the lower animals give special tendencies towards certain definite actions; but the more important elements for us are love, and the distinct emotion of sympathy. Animals endowed with the social instincts take pleasure in each other's company, warn each other of danger, defend and aid each other in many ways. These instincts are not extended to all the individuals of the species, but only to those of the same community. As they are highly beneficial to the species, they have in all probability been acquired through natural selection.

A moral being is one who is capable of comparing his past and future actions and motives; of approving of some and disapproving of others; and the fact that man is the one being who with certainty can be thus designated makes the greatest of all distinctions between him and the lower animals. But in our third chapter I have endeavoured to show that the moral sense follows, firstly, from the enduring and always present nature of the social instincts, in which respect man agrees with the lower animals; and secondly, from his mental faculties being highly active, and his impressions of past events extremely vivid, in which respects he differs from the lower animals. Owing to this condition of mind, man cannot avoid looking backwards and comparing the impressions of past events and actions. He also continually looks forward. Hence after some temporary desire or passion has mastered his social instincts, he will reflect and compare the now weakened impression of such past impulses, with the ever present social instinct; and he will then feel that sense of dissatisfaction which all unsatisfied instincts leave behind them. Consequently he resolves to act differently for the future . . . and this is conscience. Any instinct which is permanently stronger or more enduring than another gives rise to a feeling which we express by saying that it ought to be obeyed. A pointer dog, if able to reflect on his past conduct, would say to himself, I ought to have pointed at that hare and not have yielded to the passing temptation of hunting it.

Social animals are partly impelled by a wish to aid the members of the same community in a general manner, but more commonly to perform certain definite actions. Man is impelled by the same general wish to aid his fellows, but has few or no special instincts. He differs also from the lower animals in being able to express his desires by words, which thus become the guide to the aid required or bestowed. The motive to give aid is likewise somewhat modified in man; it no longer consists solely of a blind instinctive impulse, but is largely influenced by the praise or blame of his fellow men. Both the appreciation and the bestowal of praise and blame rest on sympathy; and this emotion, as we have seen, is one of the most important elements of the social instincts. Sympathy, though gained as an instinct, is also much strengthened by exercise or habit. As all men desire their own happiness, praise or blame is bestowed on actions and motives, according as they lead to this end; and as happiness is an essential part of the general good, the greatest-happiness principle indirectly serves as a nearly safe standard of right and wrong. As the reasoning powers advance and experience is gained, the more remote effects of certain lines of conduct on the character of the individual, and on the general good, are perceived; and then the self-regarding virtues, from coming within the scope of public opinion, receive praise, and their opposites receive blame.

But with the less civilized nations reason often errs, and many bad customs and base superstitions come within the same scope, and consequently are esteemed as high virtues, and their breach as heavy crimes.

The moral faculties are generally esteemed, and with justice, as of higher value than the intellectual powers. But we should always bear in mind that the activity of the mind in vividly recalling past impressions is one of the fundamental though secondary bases of conscience. This fact affords the strongest argument for educating and stimulating in all possible ways the intellectual faculties of every human being. No doubt a man with a torpid mind, if his social affections and sympathies are well developed, will be led to good actions, and may have a fairly sensitive conscience. But whatever renders the imagination of men more vivid and strengthens the habit of recalling and comparing past impressions, will make the conscience more sensitive, and may even compensate to a certain extent for weak social affections and sympathies.

The moral nature of man has reached the highest standard yet attained, partly through the advancement of the reasoning powers and consequently of a just public opinion, but especially through the sympathies being rendered more tender and widely diffused through the effects of habit, example, instruction, and reflection. It is not improbable that virtuous tendencies may through long practice be inherited. With the more civilized races, the conviction of the existence of an all-seeing Deity has had a potent influence on the advancement of morality. Ultimately man no longer accepts the praise or blame of his fellows as his chief guide, though few escape this influence, but his habitual convictions controlled by reason afford him the safest rule. His conscience then becomes his supreme judge and monitor. Nevertheless the first foundation or origin of the moral sense lies in the social instincts, including sympathy; and these instincts no doubt were primarily gained as in the case of the lower animals, through natural selection.

The main conclusion arrived at in this work, namely, that man is descended from some lowly-organized form, will, I regret to think, be highly distasteful to many persons. But there can hardly be a doubt that we are descended from barbarians. The astonishment which I felt on first seeing a party of Fuegians on a wild and broken shore will never be forgotten by me, for the reflection at once rushed into my mind — such were my ancestors. These men were absolutely naked and bedaubed with paint, their long hair was tangled, their mouths frothed with excitement, and their expression was wild, startled, and distrustful. They possessed hardly any arts, and like wild animals lived on what they could catch; they had no government, and were merciless to every one not of their own small tribe. He who has seen a savage in his native land will not feel much shame if forced to acknowledge that the blood of some more humble creature flows in his veins. For my own part I would as soon be descended from that heroic little monkey who braved his dreaded enemy in order to save the life of his keeper; or from that old baboon who, descending from the mountains, carried away in triumph his young comrade from a crowd of astonished dogs, as from a savage who delights to torture his enemies, offers up bloody sacrifices, practises infanticide, without remorse treats his wives like

natural selection, survival of the fittest; i.e., "the process whereby individual variations or peculiarities that are of advantage in a certain environment tend to become perpetuated in the race." — Standard Dictionary.

slaves, knows no decency, and is haunted by the grossest superstitions.

Man may be excused for feeling some pride in having risen, though not through his own exertions, to the very summit of the organic scale; and the fact of his having thus risen, instead of having been aboriginally placed there, may give him hopes for a still higher destiny in the distant future. But we are not here concerned with hopes or fears, only with the truth as far as our reason allows us to discover it. I have given the evidence to the best of my ability; and we must acknowledge, as it seems to me, that man with all his noble qualities, with sympathy which feels for the most debased, with benevolence which extends not only to other men but to the humblest living creature, with his god-like intellect which has penetrated into the movements and constitution of the solar system — with all these exalted powers — Man still bears in his bodily frame the indelible stamp of his lowly origin.

Charles Darwin, The Descent of Man, 1871

A CRISIS IN MY MENTAL HISTORY

1874

From the winter of 1821, when I first read Bentham,[1] and especially from the commencement of the Westminster Review,[2] I had what might truly be called an object in life; to be a reformer of the world. My conception of my own happiness was entirely identified with this object. The personal sympathies I wished for were those of fellow labourers in this enterprise. I endeavoured to pick up as many flowers as I could by

---

[1] Jeremy Bentham (1784–1832), from whom Mill derived his first conceptions of Utilitarianism.

[2] First published April, 1824. Mill was a contributor and the magazine represented principles with which he was in sympathy.

the way; but as a serious and permanent personal satisfaction to rest upon, my whole reliance was placed on this; and I was accustomed to felicitate myself on the certainty of a happy life which I enjoyed, through placing my happiness in something durable and distant, in which some progress might be always making, while it could never be exhausted by complete attainment. This did very well for several years, during which the general improvement going on in the world and the idea of myself as engaged with others in struggling to promote it, seemed enough to fill up an interesting and animated existence. But the time came when I awakened from this as from a dream. It was in the autumn of 1826.[1] I was in a dull state of nerves, such as everybody is occasionally liable to; unsusceptible to enjoyment or pleasurable excitement; one of those moods when what is pleasure at other times, becomes insipid or indifferent; the state, I should think, in which converts to Methodism usually are, when smitten by their first "conviction of sin." In this frame of mind it occurred to me to put the question directly to myself: "Suppose that all your objects in life were realised; that all the changes in institutions and opinions which you are looking forward to, could be completely effected at this very instant: would this be a great joy and happiness to you?" And an irrepressible self-consciousness distinctly answered, "No!" At this my heart sank within me: the whole foundation on which my life was constructed fell down. All my happiness was to have been found in the continual pursuit of this end. The end had ceased to charm, and how could there ever again be any interest in the means? I seemed to have nothing left to live for.

At first I hoped that the cloud would pass away of itself; but it did not. A night's sleep, the sovereign

[1] In 1826, Mill was twenty years old.

remedy for the smaller vexations of life, had no effect on it. I awoke to a renewed consciousness of the woful fact. I carried it with me into all companies, into all occupations. Hardly anything had power to cause me even a few minutes' oblivion of it. For some months the cloud seemed to grow thicker and thicker. The lines in Coleridge's "Dejection" — I was not then acquainted with them — exactly describe my case:

> "A grief without a pang, void, dark, and drear,
>   A drowsy, stifled, unimpassioned grief,
>   Which finds no natural outlet or relief
>   In word, or sigh, or tear."

In vain I sought relief from my favorite books; those memorials of past nobleness and greatness from which I had always hitherto drawn strength and animation. I read them now without feeling, or with the accustomed feeling *minus* all its charm; and I became persuaded, that my love of mankind, and of excellence for its own sake, had worn itself out. I sought no comfort by speaking to others of what I felt. If I had loved any one sufficiently to make confiding my griefs a necessity, I should not have been in the condition I was. I felt, too, that mine was not an interesting, or in any way respectable distress. Advice, if I had known where to seek it, would have been most precious. The words of Macbeth to the physician often occurred to my thoughts. But there was no one on whom I could build the faintest hope of such assistance. My father, to whom it would have been natural for me to have recourse in any practical difficulties, was the last person to whom, in such a case as this, I looked for help. Everything convinced me that he had no knowledge of any such mental state as I was suffering from, and that even if he could be made to understand it, he was not the physician who could heal it. My education, which was wholly his work, had been conducted without any regard to the possibility of its ending in this result; and I saw no use in giving him the pain of thinking that his plans had failed when the failure was probably irremediable, and, at all events, beyond the power of *his* remedies. Of other friends, I had at that time none to whom I had any hope of making my condition intelligible. It was, however, abundantly intelligible to myself; and the more I dwelt upon it, the more hopeless it appeared.

My course of study had led me to believe, that all mental and moral feelings and qualities, whether of a good or of a bad kind, were the results of association; that we love one thing, and hate another, take pleasure in one sort of action or contemplation, and pain in another sort, through the clinging of pleasurable or painful ideas to those things, from the effect of education or of experience. As a corollary from this, I had always heard it maintained by my father, and was myself convinced, that the object of education should be to form the strongest possible associations of the salutary class; associations of pleasure with all things beneficial to the great whole, and of pain with all things hurtful to it. This doctrine appeared inexpugnable; but it now seemed to me, on retrospect, that my teachers had occupied themselves but superficially with the means of forming and keeping up these salutary associations. They seemed to have trusted altogether to the old familiar instruments, praise and blame, reward and punishment. Now, I did not doubt that by these means, begun early, and applied unremittingly, intense associations of pain and pleasure especially of pain, might be created, and might produce desires and aversions capable of lasting undiminished to the end of life. But there must always be something artificial and casual in associations thus produced. The pains and pleasures thus forcibly associated with things, are not connected with them by any natural tie; and it is therefore, I thought, essential to the durability of these associations, that they should have become so intense and inveterate as to be practically indissoluble, before the habitual exercise of the power of analysis had commenced. For I now saw, or thought I saw, what I had always before received with incredulity — that the habit of analysis has a tendency to wear away the feelings: as indeed it has, when no other mental habit is cultivated, and the analysing spirit remains without its natural complements and correctives. The very excellence of analysis (I argued) is that it tends to weaken and undermine whatever is the result of prejudice; that it enables us mentally to separate ideas which have only casually clung together: and no associations whatever could ultimately resist this dissolving force, were it not that we owe to analysis our clearest knowledge of the permanent sequences in nature; the real connections between Things, not dependent on our will and feelings; natural laws, by virtue of which, in many cases, one thing is inseparable from another in fact; which laws, in proportion as they are clearly perceived and imaginatively realised, cause our ideas of things which are always joined together in Nature, to cohere more and more closely in our thoughts. Analytic habits may thus even strengthen the associations between causes and effects, means and ends, but tend altogether to weaken those which are, to speak familiarly, a *mere* matter of feeling. They are therefore (I thought) favourable to prudence and clear-sightedness, but a perpetual worm at the root both of the passions and of the virtues; and, above all, fearfully undermine all desires, and all pleasures, which are the effects of association, that is, according to the theory I held, all except the purely physical and organic; of the entire insufficiency of which to make life desirable, no one had a stronger conviction than I. These were the laws of human nature, by which, as it seemed to me, I had been brought to my present state. All those to whom I looked up, were of opinion that the pleasure of sympathy with human beings, and the feelings which made the good of others, and especially of mankind on a large scale, the object of existence, were the greatest and surest sources of happiness. Of the truth of this I was convinced, but to know that a feeling would make me happy if I had it, did not give me the feeling. My education, I thought, had failed to create these feelings in sufficient strength to resist the dissolving influence of analysis, while the whole course of my intellectual cultivation had made precocious and premature analysis the inveterate habit of my mind. I was thus, as I said to myself, left stranded at the commencement of my voyage, with a well-equipped ship and a rudder, but no sail; without any real desire for the ends which I had been so carefully fitted out to work for: no delight in virtue, or the general good, but also just as little in anything else. The fountains of vanity and ambition seemed to have dried up within me, as completely as those of benevolence. I had had (as I reflected) some gratification of vanity at too early an age: I had obtained some distinction, and felt myself of some importance, before the desire of distinction and of importance had grown into a passion: and little as it was which I had attained, yet having been attained too early, like all pleasures enjoyed too soon, it had made me *blasé* and indifferent to the pursuit. Thus neither selfish nor unselfish pleasures were pleasures to me. And there seemed no power in nature sufficient to begin the formation of my character anew, and create in a mind now irretrievably analytic, fresh associations of pleasure with any of the objects of human desire.

These were the thoughts which mingled with the dry heavy dejection of the melancholy winter of 1826–7. During this time I was not incapable of my usual occupations. I went on with them mechanically, by the mere force of habit. I had been so drilled in a certain sort of mental exercise, that I could still carry it on when all the spirit had gone out of it. I even composed, and spoke several speeches at the debating society,[1] how, or with what degree of success, I know not. Of four years' continual speaking at that society, this is the only year of which I remember next to nothing. Two lines of Coleridge, in whom alone of all writers I have found a true description of what I felt, were often in my thoughts, not at this time (for I had never read them), but in a later period of the same mental malady:

"Work without hope draws nectar in a sieve,
"And hope without an object cannot live."[2]

In all probability my case was by no means so peculiar as I fancied it, and I doubt not that many others have passed through a similar state; but the idiosyncrasies of my education had given to the general phenomenon a special character, which made it seem the natural effect of causes that it was hardly possible for time to remove. I frequently asked myself, if I could, or if I

[1] The Speculative Debating Society. Of Mill's early connection with it, William Minto says: "His . . . reception at the Speculative Debating Society, where he first measured his strength in public conflict, was calculated to produce self-distrust. He found himself looked upon with curiosity as a precocious phenomenon, a 'made man,' an intellectual machine set to grind out certain tunes."

[2] Work without Hope. ll. 13–14. (1825).

was bound to go on living, when life must be passed in this manner. I generally answered to myself, that I did not think I could possibly bear it beyond a year. When, however, not more than half that duration of time had elapsed, a small ray of light broke in upon my gloom. I was reading, accidentally, Marmontel's "Memoires,"[1] and came to the passage which relates his father's death, the distressed position of the family, and the sudden inspiration by which he, then a mere boy, felt and made them feel that he would be everything to them — would supply the place of all that they had lost. A vivid conception of the scene and its feelings came over me, and I was moved to tears. From this moment my burden grew lighter. The oppression of the thought that all feeling was dead within me, was gone. I was no longer hopeless: I was not a stock or a stone. I had still, it seemed, some of the material out of which all worth of character, and all capacity for happiness, are made. Relieved from my ever present sense of irremediable wretchedness, I gradually found that the ordinary incidents of life could again give me some pleasure; that I could again find enjoyment, not intense, but sufficient for cheerfulness, in sunshine and sky, in books, in conversation, in public affairs; and that there was, once more, excitement, though of a moderate kind, in exerting myself for my opinions, and for the public good. Thus the cloud gradually drew off, and I again enjoyed life: and though I had several relapses, some of which lasted many months, I never again was as miserable as I had been.

The experiences of this period had two very marked effects on my opinions and character. In the first

---

[1] Jean François Marmontel (1723–99), author of *Contes moraux* and *Mémoires d'un père.*

place, they led me to adopt a theory of life, very unlike that on which I had before acted, and having much in common with what at that time I certainly had never heard of, the anti-self-consciousness theory of Carlyle. I never, indeed, wavered in the conviction that happiness is the test of all rules of conduct, and the end of life. But I now thought that this end was only to be attained by not making it the direct end. Those only are happy (I thought) who have their minds fixed on some object other than their own happiness; on the happiness of others, on the improvement of mankind, even on some art or pursuit, followed not as a means, but as itself an ideal end. Aiming thus at something else, they find happiness by the way. The enjoyments of life (such was now my theory) are sufficient to make it a pleasant thing, when they are taken *en passant*, without being made a principal object. Once make them so, and they are immediately felt to be insufficient. They will not bear a scrutinising examination. Ask yourself whether you are happy, and you cease to be so. The only chance is to treat, not happiness, but some end external to it, as the purpose of life. Let your self-consciousness, your scrutiny, your self-interrogation, exhaust themselves on that; and if otherwise fortunately circumstanced you will inhale happiness with the air you breathe, without dwelling on it or thinking about it, without either forestalling it in imagination, or putting it to flight by fatal questioning. This theory now became the basis of my philosophy of life. And I still hold to it as the best theory for all those who have but a moderate degree of sensibility and of capacity for enjoyment, that is, for the great majority of mankind.

The other important change which my opinions at this time underwent, was that I, for the first time, gave its proper place, among the prime necessities of human well-being, to the internal culture of the individual. I ceased to attach almost exclusive importance to the ordering of outward circumstances, and the training of the human being for speculation and for action.

I had now learnt by experience that the passive susceptibilities needed to be cultivated as well as the active capabilities, and required to be nourished and enriched as well as guided. I did not, for an instant, lose sight of, or undervalue, that part of the truth, which I had seen before; I never turned recreant to intellectual culture, or ceased to consider the power and practice of analysis as an essential condition both of individual and of social improvement. But I thought that it had consequences which required to be corrected, by joining other kinds of cultivation with it. The maintenance of a due balance among the faculties, now seemed to me of primary importance. The cultivation of the feelings became one of the cardinal points in my ethical and philosophical creed. And my thoughts and inclinations turned in an increasing degree toward whatever seemed capable of being instrumental to that object.

I now began to find meaning in the things which I had read or heard about the importance of poetry and art as instruments of human culture. But it was some time longer before I began to know this by personal experience. The only one of the imaginative arts in which I had from childhood taken great pleasure, was music; the best effect of which (and in this it surpasses perhaps every other art) consists in exciting enthusiasm; in winding up to a high pitch those feeling of an elevated kind which are already in the character but to which this excitement gives a glow and a fervour, which, though transitory at its utmost height, is precious for sustaining them at other times. This effect of music I had often experienced; but like all my pleasurable susceptibilities it was suspended during the gloomy period. I had sought relief again and again from this quarter, but found none. After the tide had turned, and I was in process of recovery, I had been helped forward by music, but in a much less elevated manner. I at this time first became acquainted with Weber's Oberon, and the extreme pleasure which I drew from its delicious melodies did me good, by showing me a source of pleasure to which I was as susceptible as ever. The good, however, was much impaired by the thought, that the pleasure of music (as is quite true of such pleasure as this was, that of mere tune) fades with familiarity, and requires either to be revived by intermittance, or fed by continual novelty. And it is very characteristic, both of my then state, and of the general tone of my mind at this period of my life, that I was seriously tormented by the thought of the exhaustibility of musical combinations. The octave consists of only five tones and two semi-tones, which can be put together in only a limited number of ways, of which but a small proportion are beautiful: most of these, it seemed to me, must have been already discovered, and there could not be room for a long succession of Mozarts and Webers, to strike out, as these had done, entirely new and surpassingly rich veins of musical beauty. This source of anxiety may, perhaps, be thought to resemble that of the philosophers of Laputa, who feared lest the sun should be burnt out. It was, however, connected with the best feature of my character, and the only good point to be found in my very unromantic and in no way honourable distress. For though my dejection,

Laputa, in Swift's *Gulliver's Travels*.

honestly looked at, could not be called other than egotistical, produced by the ruin, as I thought, of my fabric of happiness, yet the destiny of mankind in general was ever in my thoughts, and could not be separated from my own. I felt that the flaw in my life, must be a flaw in life itself; that the question was, whether, if the reformers of society and government could succeed in their objects, and every person in the community were free and in a state of physical comfort, the pleasures of life, being no longer kept up by struggle and privation, would cease to be pleasures. And I felt that unless I could see my way to some better hope than this for human happiness in general my dejection must continue; but that if I could see such an outlet, I should then look on the world with pleasure; content as far as I was myself concerned, with any fair share of the general lot.

This state of my thoughts and feelings made the fact of my reading Wordsworth for the first time (in the autumn of 1828), an important event in my life. I took up the collection of his poems from curiosity, with no expectation of mental relief from it, though I had before resorted to poetry with that hope. In the worst period of my depression, I had read through the whole of Byron (then new to me), to try whether a poet, whose peculiar department was supposed to be that of the intenser feelings, could rouse any feeling in me. As might be expected, I got no good from this reading, but the reverse. The poet's state of mind was too like my own. His was the lament of a man who had worn out all pleasures, and who seemed to think that life, to all who possess the good things of it, must necessarily be the vapid, uninteresting thing which I found it. His Harold and Manfred had the same burden on them which I had; and I was not in a fram of mind to desire any comfort from the vehement sensual passions of his Giaours, or the sullenness of his Laras. But while Byron was exactly what did not suit my condition, Wordsworth was exactly what did. I had looked into the "Excursion" two or three years before, and found little in it; and I should probably have found as little, had I read it at this time. But the miscellaneous poems, in the two-volume edition of 1815 (to which little of value was added in the latter part of the author's life), proved to be the precise thing for my mental wants at that particular juncture.

In the first place, these poems addressed themselves powerfully to one of the strongest of my pleasurable susceptibilities, the love of rural objects and natural scenery; to which I had been indebted not only for much of the pleasure of my life, but quite recently for relief from one of my longest lapses into depression. In this power of rural beauty over me, there was a foundation laid for taking pleasure in Wordsworth's poetry; the more so, as his scenery lies mostly among mountains, which, owing to my early Pyrenean excursion, were my ideal of natural beauty. But Wordsworth would never have had any great effect on me, if he had merely placed before me beautiful pictures of natural scenery. Scott does this still better than Wordsworth, and a very second-rate landscape does it more effectually than any poet. What made Wordsworth's poems a medicine for my state of mind, was that they expressed, not mere outward beauty, but states of feeling, and of thought coloured by feeling, under the excitement of beauty. They seemed to be the very culture of the feelings which I was in quest of. In them I seemed to draw from a source of inward joy, of sympathetic and imaginative pleasures, which could be shared in by all human beings; which had no con-

nection with struggle or imperfection, but would be
made richer by every improvement in the physical or
social condition of mankind. From them I seemed to
learn what would be the perennial sources of happiness, when all the greater evils of life should have been
removed. And I felt myself at once better and happier as I came under their influence. There have
certainly been, even in our own age, greater poets than
Wordsworth; but poetry of deeper and loftier feeling
could not have done for me at that time what his did.
I needed to be made to feel that there was real, permanent happiness in tranquil contemplation. Wordsworth taught me this, not only without turning away
from, but with a greatly increased interest in the common feelings and common destiny of human beings.
And the delight which these poems gave me, proved
that with culture of this sort, there was nothing to
dread from the most confirmed habit of analysis. At
the conclusion of the Poems came the famous Ode,
falsely called Platonic, "Intimations of Immortality":
in which, along with more than his usual sweetness of
melody and rhythm, and along with the two passages
of grand imagery but bad philosophy so often quoted,
I found that he too had had similar experience to mine;
that he also had felt that the first freshness of youthful
enjoyment of life was not lasting; but that he had
sought for compensation, and found it, in the way in
which he was now teaching me to find it. The result
was that I gradually, but completely, emerged from
my habitual depression, and was never again subject
to it. I long continued to value Wordsworth less according to his intrinsic merits, than by the measure of
what he had done for me. Compared with the greatest
poets, he may be said to be the poet of unpoetical
natures, possessed of quiet and contemplative tastes.

But unpoetical natures are precisely those which require poetic cultivation.   This cultivation Wordsworth is much more fitted to give, than poets who are intrinsically far more poets than he.

John Stuart Mill, Autobiography, chap. v

CLASSIC AND ROMANTIC [1]

1876

The words, *classical* and *romantic*, although, like many other critical expressions, sometimes abused by those who have understood them too vaguely or too absolutely, yet define two real tendencies in the history of art and literature.   Used in an exaggerated sense, to express a greater opposition between those tendencies than really exists, they have at times tended to divide people of taste into opposite camps. But in that *House Beautiful*, which the creative minds of all generations — the artists and those who have treated life in the spirit of art — are always building together, for the refreshment of the human spirit, these oppositions cease; and the *Interpreter* of the *House Beautiful*, the true æsthetic critic, uses these divisions, only so far as they enable him to enter into the peculiarities of the objects with which he has to do. The term *classical*, fixed, as it is, to a well-defined literature, and a well-defined group in art, is clear, indeed; but then it has often been used in a hard, and merely scholastic sense, by the praisers of what is old and accustomed, at the expense of what is new, by critics who would never have discovered for themselves the charm of any work, whether new or old, who value what is old, in art or literature, for its acces-

House Beautiful, see *Pilgrim's Progress*.
[1] This essay is abridged.

sories, and chiefly for the conventional authority that has gathered about it — people who would never really have been made glad by any Venus fresh-risen from the sea, and who praise the Venus of old Greece and Rome, only because they fancy her grown now into something staid and tame.

And as the term, *classical*, has been used in a too absolute and therefore in a misleading sense, so the term, *romantic*, has been used much too vaguely, in various accidental senses. The sense in which Scott is called a romantic writer is chiefly this; that, in opposition to the literary tradition of the last century, he loved strange adventure, and sought it in the Middle Age. Much later, in a Yorkshire village, the spirit of romanticism bore a more really characteristic fruit in the work of a young girl, Emily Brontë, the romance of *Wuthering Heights*; the figures of Hareton Earnshaw, of Catherine Linton, and of Heathcliffe — tearing open Catherine's grave, removing one side of her coffin, that he may really lie beside her in death — figures so passionate, yet woven on a background of delicately beautiful, moorland scenery, being typical examples of that spirit. In Germany, again, that spirit is shown less in Tieck,[1] its professional representative, than in Meinhold, the author of *Sidonia the Sorceress* and the *Amber-Witch*. In Germany and France, within the last hundred years, the term has been used to describe a particular school of writers; and, consequently, when Heine [2] criticises the *Romantic School* in Germany — that movement which culminated in Goethe's *Goetz von Berlichingen*; or when Theophile Gautier [3] criticises the romantic movement in France, where, indeed, it

[1] Johann Ludwig Tieck (1773–1853), German poet and novelist.
[2] Heinrich Heine (1799–1856), German poet and satirist.
[3] Théophile Gautier (1811–72), French novelist.

bore its most characteristic fruits, and its play is
hardly yet over — where, by a certain audacity, or *bi-
zarrerie* of motive, united with faultless literary execution, it still shows itself in imaginative literature,
they use the word, with an exact sense of special artistic qualities, indeed; but use it, nevertheless, with a
limited application to the manifestation of those
qualities at a particular period.   But the romantic
spirit is, in reality, an ever-present, an enduring principle, in the artistic temperament; and the qualities of
thought and style which that, and other similar uses
of the word *romantic* really indicate, are indeed but
symptoms of a very continuous and widely working
influence.

Though the words *classical* and *romantic*, then, have
acquired an almost technical meaning, in application
to certain developments of German and French taste,
yet this is but one variation of an old opposition,
which may be traced from the very beginning of the
formation of European art and literature.   From the
first formation of anything like a standard of taste in
these things, the restless curiosity of their more eager
lovers necessarily made itself felt, in the craving for
new motives, new subjects of interest, new modifications of style.   Hence, the opposition between the
classicists and the romanticists — between the ad-
herents, in the culture of beauty, of the principles of
liberty, and authority, respectively — of strength, and
order or what the Greeks called κοσμιότης.[1]

Sainte-Beuve,[2] in the third volume of the *Causeries
du Lundi*, has discussed the question, *What is meant by
a classic?*   It was a question he was well fitted to an-
wer, having himself lived through many phases of

---

[1] decorum.

[2] Charles Augustine Sainte-Beuve (1804–69), foremost French critic.

taste, and having been in earlier life an enthusiastic member of the romantic school: he was also a great master of that sort of "philosophy of literature," which delights in tracing traditions in it, and the way in which various phases of thought and sentiment maintain themselves, through successive modifications, from epoch to epoch. His aim, then, is to give the word *classic* a wider and, as he says, a more generous sense than it commonly bears, to make it expressly *grandiose et flottant*; and, in doing this, he develops, in a masterly manner, those qualities of measure, purity, temperance, of which it is the especial function of classical art and literature, whatever meaning, narrower or wider, we attach to the term, to take care.

The charm, therefore, of what is classical, in art or literature, is that of the well-known tale, to which we can, nevertheless, listen over and over again, because it is told so well. To the absolute beauty of its artistic form, is added the accidental, tranquil, charm of familiarity. There are times, indeed, at which these charms fail to work on our spirits at all, because they fail to excite us. "*Romanticism*," says Stendhal, "is the art of presenting to people the literary works which, in the actual state of their habits and beliefs, are capable of giving them the greatest possible pleasure; *classicism*, on the contrary, of presenting them with that which gave the greatest possible pleasure to their grandfathers." But then, beneath all changes of habits and beliefs, our love of that mere abstract proportion — of music — which what is classical in literature possesses, still maintains itself in the best of us, and what pleased our grandparents may at least tranquillise us. The "classic" comes to us out of the cool and quiet of other times, as the measure of what a long experience has shown will at least never displease us. And in the classical literature of Greece and Rome, as in the classics of the last century, the essentially classical element is that quality of order in beauty, which they possess, indeed, in a pre-eminent degree, and which impresses some minds to the exclusion of everything else in them.

It is the addition of strangeness to beauty, that constitutes the romantic character in art; and the desire of beauty being a fixed element in every artistic organization, it is the addition of curiosity to this desire of beauty, that constitutes the romantic temper. Curiosity and the desire of beauty have each their place in art, as in all true criticism. When one's curiosity is deficient, when one is not eager enough for new impressions, and new pleasures, one is liable to value mere academical proprieties too highly, to be satisfied with worn-out or conventional types, with the insipid ornament of Racine, or the prettiness of that later Greek sculpture, which passed so long for true Hellenic work; to miss those places·where the handiwork of nature, or of the artist, has been most cunning; to find the most stimulating products of art a mere irritation. And when one's curiosity is in excess, when it overbalances the desire of beauty, then one is liable to value in works of art what is inartistic in them; to be satisfied with what is exaggerated in art, with productions like some of those of the romantic school in Germany; not to distinguish, jealously enough, between what is admirably done, and what is done not quite so well, in the writing, for instance, of Jean Paul. And if I had to give instances of these defects, then I

---

strangeness ... beauty, cf. Bacon, *Essays*, "Of Beauty": "That is the best part of Beauty which a picture cannot express; no, not the first sight of the life. There is no excellent beauty that hath not some strangeness in the proportion."

Johann ("Jean") Paul Friedrich Richter (1763-1825), German romancer and humorist.

should say, that Pope, in common with the age of literature to which he belonged, had too little curiosity, so that there is always a certain insipidity in the effect of his work, exquisite as it is; and, coming down to our own time, that Balzac had an excess of curiosity — curiosity not duly tempered with the desire of beauty.

But, however falsely those two tendencies may be opposed by critics, or exaggerated by artists themselves, they are tendencies really at work at all times in art, moulding it, with the balance sometimes a little on one side, sometimes a little on the other, generating, respectively, as the balance inclines on this side or that, two principles, two traditions, in art, and in literature so far as it partakes of the spirit of art. If there is a great overbalance of curiosity, then, we have the grotesque in art: if the union of strangeness and beauty, under very difficult and complex conditions, be a successful one, if the union be entire, then the resultant beauty is very exquisite, very attractive. With a passionate care for beauty, the romantic spirit refuses to have it unless the condition of strangeness be first fulfilled. Its desire is for a beauty born of unlikely elements, by a profound alchemy, by a difficult initiation, by the charm which wrings it even out of terrible things; and a trace of distortion, of the grotesque, may perhaps linger, as an additional element of expression, about its ultimate grace. Its eager, excited spirit will have strength, the grotesque, first of all — the trees shrieking as you tear off the leaves; for Jean Valjean, the long years of convict life; for Redgauntlet, the quicksands of Solway Moss; then, incorporate with this strangeness, and intensified by restraint, as much

trees shrieking, in Dante's *The Inferno*, canto XIII.
Jean Valjean, the hero of Hugo's *Les Misérables*.
Redgauntlet, in Scott's novel of the same name.

sweetness, as much beauty, as is compatible with that. *Energique, frais, et dispos* — these, according to Sainte-Beuve, are the characteristics of a genuine classic — *les ouvrages anciens ne sont pas classiques parcequ'ils sont vieux, mais parcequ'ils sont énergique, frais, et dispos.* Energy, freshness, intelligent and masterly disposition: — there are characteristics of Victor Hugo when his alchemy is complete, in certain figures, like Marius and Cosette, in certain scenes, like that in the opening of *Les Travailleurs de la Mer*, where Déruchette writes the name of *Gilliatt* in the snow, on Christmas morning; but always there is a certain note of strangeness discernible there, as well.

The essential elements, then, of the romantic spirit are curiosity and the love of beauty; and it is only as an illustration of these qualities, that it seeks the Middle Age, because, in the overcharged atmosphere of the Middle Age, there are unworked sources of romantic effect, of a strange beauty, to be won, by strong imagination, out of things unlikely or remote. . . .

Stendhal, a writer whom I have already quoted, and of whom English readers might well know much more than they do, stands between the earlier and later growths of the romantic spirit. His novels are rich in romantic quality; and his other writings — partly criticism, partly personal reminiscences — are a very curious and interesting illustration of the needs out of which romanticism arose. In his book on *Racine and Shakespeare*, Stendhal argues that all good art was romantic in its day; and this is perhaps true in Stendhal's

---

les ouvrages, etc., the ancient works are not classics because they are old, but because they are strong, fresh, and cheerful. (*Dispos* usually means, *nimble, brisk, cheerful*).

Marius and Cosette, characters in *Les Misérables*.

De Stendhal, the pseudonym of Henri Beyle (1783–1842), French novelist, usually looked upon as the founder of modern realism or naturalism in fiction. *La Chartreuse de Parme, Le Rouge et le Noir, etc.*

sense. That little treatise, full of "dry light" and
fertile ideas, was published in the year 1823, and its
object is to defend an entire independence and liberty
in the choice and treatment of subject, both in art and
literature, against those who upheld the exclusive authority of precedent. In pleading the cause of romanticism, therefore, it is the novelty, both of form
and of motive, in writings like the *Hernani* of Victor
Hugo (which soon followed it, raising a storm of
criticism) that he is chiefly concerned to justify. To
be interesting and really stimulating, to keep us from
yawning even, art and literature must follow the
subtle movements of that nimbly-shifting *Time-Spirit*,
or *Zeit-Geist*, understood by French not less than
German criticism, which is always modifying men's
taste, as it modifies their manners and their pleasures.
This, he contends, is what all great workmen had always understood. Dante, Shakespeare, Molière, had
exercised an absolute independence in their choice of
subject and treatment. To turn always with that
ever-changing spirit, yet to retain the flavour of what
was admirably done in past generations, in the classics,
as we say — is the problem of true romanticism.
"Dante," he observes, "was pre-eminently the romantic poet. He adored Virgil, yet he wrote the
Divine Comedy, with the episode of Ugolino, which is as
unlike the *Æneid* as can possibly be. And those who
thus obey the fundamental principle of romanticism,
one by one become classical, and are joined to that
ever-increasing common league, formed by men of all
countries to approach nearer and nearer to perfection."
    Romanticism, then, although it has its epochs, is in

"*dry light*," Bacon's phrase; see *ante* De Quincey's *Literature of Knowledge*
    and Literature of Power.
Hernani, ou l'Honneur Castillan, acted Feb. 25, 1830.
Ugolino della Gherardesca, Inferno XXXIII, 1–90.

its essential characteristics rather a spirit which shows itself at all times, in various degrees, in individual workmen and their work, and the amount of which criticism has to estimate in them taken one by one, than the peculiarity of a time or a school. Depending on the varying proportion of curiosity and the desire of beauty, natural tendencies of the artistic spirit at all times, it must always be partly a matter of individual temperament. The eighteenth century in England has been regarded as almost exclusively a classical period; yet William Blake, a type of so much which breaks through what are conventionally thought the influences of that century, is still a noticeable phenomenon in it, and the reaction in favour of naturalism in poetry begins in that century, early. There are, thus, the born romanticists and the born classicists. There are the born classicists who start with *form*, to whose minds the comeliness of the old, immemorial, well-recognized types in art and literature, have revealed themselves impressively; who will entertain no matter which will not go easily and flexibly into them; whose work aspires only to be a variation upon, or study from, the older masters. "'Tis art's decline, my son!" they are always saying, to the progressive element in their own generation; to those who care for that which in fifty years' time every one will be caring for. On the other hand, there are the born romanticists, who start with an original, untried *matter*, still in fusion; who conceive this vividly, and hold by it as the essence of their work; who, by the very vividness and heat of their conception, purge away, sooner or later, all that is not organically appropriate to it, till the whole effect adjusts itself in clear, orderly, proportionate form; which form, after a very little time, becomes classical in its turn.

The romantic or classical character of a picture, a poem, a literary work, depends, then, on the balance of qualities in it; and in this sense, a very real distinction may be drawn between good classical and good romantic work. But all critical terms are relative; and there is at least a valuable suggestion in that theory of Stendhal's, that all good art was romantic in its day. In the beauties of Homer and Pheidias, quiet as they now seem, there must have been, for those who confronted them for the first time, excitement and surprise, the sudden, unforeseen satisfaction of the desire of beauty. Yet the *Odyssey*, with its marvellous adventure, is more romantic than the *Iliad*, which nevertheless contains, among many other romantic episodes, that of the immortal horses of Achilles, who weep at the death of Patroclus. Æschylus is more romantic than Sophocles, whose *Philoctetes*, were it written now, might figure, for the strangeness of its motive and the perfectness of its execution, as typically romantic; while, of Euripides, it may be said, that his method in writing his plays is to sacrifice readily almost everything else, so that he may attain the fulness of a single romantic effect. These two tendencies, indeed, might be applied as a measure or standard, all through Greek and Roman art and poetry, with very illuminating results; and for an analysis of the romantic principle in art, no exercise would be more profitable, than to walk through the collection of classical antiquities at the Louvre, or the British Museum, or to examine some representative collection of Greek coins, and note how the element of curiosity, of the love of strangeness, insinuates itself into classical design, and record the effects of the romantic spirit there, the traces of struggle, of the grotesque even, though over-balanced here by sweet ness; as in the sculpture of Chartres and Rheims, the real sweetness of mind in the sculptor is often overbalanced by the grotesque, by the rudeness of his strength.

Classicism, then, means for Stendhal, for that younger enthusiastic band of French writers whose unconscious method he formulated into principles, the reign of what is pedantic, conventional, and narrowly academic in art; for him, all good art is romantic. To Sainte-Beuve, who understands the term in a more liberal sense, it is the characteristic of certain epochs, of certain spirits in every epoch, not given to the exercise of original imagination, but rather to the working out of refinements of manner on some authorised matter; and who bring to their perfection, in this way, the elements of sanity, of order and beauty in manner. In general criticism, again, it means the spirit of Greece and Rome, of some phases in literature and art that may seem of equal authority with Greece and Rome, the age of Louis the Fourteenth, the age of Johnson; though this is at its best an uncritical use of the term, because in Greek and Roman work there are typical examples of the romantic spirit. But explain the terms as we may, in application to particular epochs, there are these two elements always recognisable; united in perfect art — in Sophocles, in Dante, in the highest work of Goethe, though not always absolutely balanced there; and these two elements may be not inappropriately termed the classical and romantic tendencies.

Material for the artist, motives of inspiration, are not yet exhausted: our curious, complex, aspiring age still abounds in subjects for æsthetic manipulation by the literary as well as by other forms of art. For the literary art, at all events, the problem just now is, to induce order upon the contorted, proportionless accumulation of our knowledge and experience, our science and history, our hopes and disillusion, and, in effecting this, to do consciously what has been done hitherto for the most part unconsciously, to write our English language as the Latins wrote theirs, as the French write, as scholars should write. Appealing, as he may, to precedent in this matter, the scholar will still remember that if "the style is the man" it is also the age: that the nineteenth century will be found to have had its style, justified by necessity — a style very different, alike from the baldness of an impossible "Queen Anne" revival, and an incorrect, incondite exuberance, after the mode of Elizabeth: that we can only return to either at the price of an impoverishment of form or matter, or both, although, an intellectually rich age such as ours being necessarily an eclectic one, we may well cultivate some of the excellences of literary types as different as those: that in literature as in other matters it is well to unite as many diverse elements as may be: that the individual writer or artist, certainly, is to be estimated by the number of graces he combines, and his power of interpenetrating them in a given work. To discriminate schools, of art, of literature, is, of course, part of the obvious business of literary criticism: but, in the work of literary production, it is easy to be overmuch occupied concerning them. For, in truth, the legitimate contention is, not of one age or school of literary art against another, but of all successive schools alike, against the stupidity which is dead to the substance, and the vulgarity which is dead to form.

Walter Pater, "Postscript" to *Appreciations*, 1889 (first published in *Macmillan's Magazine*, November, 1876).

EL DORADO

1878

It seems as if a great deal were attainable in a world where there are so many marriages and decisive battles, and where we all, at certain hours of the day, and with great gusto and dispatch, stow a portion of victuals finally and irretrievably into the bag which contains us. And it would seem also, on a hasty view, that the attainment of as much as possible was the one goal of man's contentious life. And yet, as regards the spirit, this is but a semblance. We live in an ascending scale when we live happily, one thing leading to another in an endless series. There is always a new horizon for onward-looking men, and although we dwell on a small planet, immersed in petty business and not enduring beyond a brief period of years, we are so constituted that our hopes are inaccessible, like stars, and the term of hoping is prolonged until the term of life. To be truly happy is a question of how we begin and not of how we end, of what we want and not of what we have. An aspiration is a joy forever, a possession as solid as a landed estate, a fortune which we can never exhaust and which gives us year by year a revenue of pleasurable activity. To have many of these is to be spiritually rich. Life is only a very dull and ill-directed theatre unless we have some interests in the piece; and to those who have neither art nor science, the world is a mere arrangement of colours, or a rough footway where they may very well break their shins. It is in virtue of his own desires and curiosities that any man continues to exist with even patience, that he is charmed by the look of things and people, and that he wakens every morning with a renewed appetite for work and pleasure. Desire and curiosity are the two eyes through which he sees the world in the most enchanted colours: it is they that make women beautiful or fossils interesting: and the man may squander his estate and come to beggary, but if he keeps these two amulets he is still rich in the possibilities of pleasure. Suppose he could take one meal so compact and comprehensive that he should never hunger any more; suppose him, at a glance, to take in all the features of the world and allay the desire for knowledge; suppose him to do the like in any province of experience — would not that man be in a poor way for amusement ever after?

One who goes touring on foot with a single volume in his knapsack reads with circumspection, pausing often to reflect, and often laying the book down to contemplate the landscape or the prints in the inn parlour; for he fears to come to an end of his entertainment, and be left companionless on the last stages of his journey. A young fellow recently finished the works of Thomas Carlyle, winding up, if we remember aright, with the ten note-books upon Frederick the Great. "What!" cried the young fellow, in consternation, "is there no more Carlyle? Am I left to the daily papers?" A more celebrated instance is that of Alexander, who wept bitterly because he had no more worlds to subdue. And when Gibbon had finished the *Decline and Fall*, he had only a few moments of joy; and it was with a "sober melancholy" that he parted from his labours.

Happily we all shoot at the moon with ineffectual arrows; our hopes are set on inaccessible El Dorado; we come to an end of nothing here below. Interests are only plucked up to sow themselves again, like mustard. You would think, when the child was born, there would be an end to trouble; and yet it is only the beginning of fresh anxieties; and when you have seen it through its teething and its education, and at last its marriage, alas! it is only to have new fears, new quivering sensibilities, with every day; and the health of your children's children grows as touching a concern as that of your own. Again, when you have married your wife, you would think you were got upon a hilltop, and might begin to go downward by an easy slope. But you have only ended courting to begin marriage. Falling in love and winning love are often difficult tasks to overbearing and rebellious spirits; but to keep in love is also a business of some importance, to which both man and wife must bring kindness and goodwill. The true love story commences at the altar, when there lies before the married pair a most beautiful contest of wisdom and generosity, and a lifelong struggle towards an unattainable ideal. Unattainable? Ay, surely unattainable, from the very fact that they are two instead of one.

"Of making books there is no end,"[1] complained the Preacher; and did not perceive how highly he was praising letters as an occupation. There is no end, indeed, to making books or experiments, or to travel, or to gathering wealth. Problem gives rise to problem. We may study forever, and we are never as learned as we would. We have never made a statue worthy of our dreams. And when we have discovered a continent, or crossed a chain of mountains, it is only to find another ocean or another plain upon the further side. In the infinite universe there is room for our swiftest diligence and to spare. It is not like the works of Carlyle, which can be read to an end. Even in a corner of it, in a private park, or in the neighbourhood of a single hamlet, the weather and the seasons keep so deftly changing that although we walk there for a

[1] *Eccles.* XII, 12.

lifetime there will be always something new to startle and delight us.

There is only one wish realisable on the earth; only one thing that can be perfectly attained: Death. And from a variety of circumstances we have no one to tell us whether it be worth attaining.

A strange picture we make on our way to our chimæras, ceaselessly marching, grudging ourselves the time for rest; indefatigable, adventurous pioneers. It is true that we shall never reach the goal; it is even more than probable that there is no such place; and if we lived for centuries and were endowed with the powers of a god, we should find ourselves not much nearer what we wanted at the end. O toiling hands of mortals! O unwearied feet, travelling ye know not whither! soon, soon, it seems to you, you must come forth on some conspicuous hilltop, and but a little way further, against the setting sun, descry the spires of El Dorado. Little do ye know your own blessedness; for to travel hopefully is a better thing than to arrive, and the true success is to labour.

Robert Louis Stevenson, Virginibus Puerisque and Other Papers, 1881.

FAME'S LITTLE DAY

CHAPTER I

Nobody ever knew, except himself, what made a foolish young newspaper reporter, who happened into a small old-fashioned hotel in New York, observe Mr. Abel Pinkham with deep interest, listen to his talk, ask a question or two of the clerk, and then go away and make up an effective personal paragraph for one of the morning papers. He must have had a heart full of fun, this young reporter, and something honestly rustic and pleasing must have struck him in the guest's demeanor, for there was a flavor in the few lines he wrote that made some of his fellows seize upon the little paragraph, and copy it, and add to it, and keep it moving. Nobody knows what starts such a thing in journalism, or keeps it alive after it is started, but on a certain Thursday morning the fact was made known to the world that among the notabilities then in the city, Abel Pinkham, Esquire, a distinguished citizen of Wetherford, Vermont, was visiting New York on important affairs connected with the maple-sugar industry of his native State. Mr. Pinkham had expected to keep his visit unannounced, but it was likely to occasion much interest in business and civic circles. This was something like the way that the paragraph started; but here and there a kindred spirit of the original journalist caught it up and added discreet lines about Mr. Pinkham's probable stay in town, his occupation of an apartment on the fourth floor of the Ethan Allen Hotel, and other circumstances so uninteresting to the reading public in general that presently in the next evening edition, one city editor after another threw out the item, and the young journalists, having had their day of pleasure, passed on to other things.

Mr. and Mrs. Pinkham had set forth from home with many forebodings, in spite of having talked all winter about this journey as soon as the spring opened. They would have caught at any reasonable excuse for giving it up altogether, because when the time arrived it seemed so much easier to stay at home. Mrs. Abel Pinkham had never seen New York; her husband himself had not been to the city for a great many years; in fact, his reminiscences of the former visit were not altogether pleasant, since he had foolishly fallen into

many snares, and been much gulled in his character of
honest young countryman. There was a tarnished and
worthless counterfeit of a large gold watch still concealed between the outer boarding and inner lath and
plaster of the lean-to bedroom which Mr. Abel Pinkham had occupied as a bachelor; it was not the only
witness of his being taken in by city sharpers, and he
had winced ever since at the thought of their wiles.
But he was now a man of sixty, well-to-do, and of authority in town affairs; his children were all well married and settled in homes of their own, except a
widowed daughter, who lived at home with her young
son, and was her mother's lieutenant in household
affairs.

The boy was almost grown, and at this season, when
the maple sugar was all made and shipped, and it was
still too early for spring work on the land, Mr. Pinkham could leave home as well as not, and here he was in
New York, feeling himself to be a stranger and for-
eigner to city ways. If it had not been for that desire
to appear well in his wife's eyes, which had buoyed
him over the bar of many difficulties, he could have
found it in his heart to take the next train back to
Wetherford, Vermont, to be rid there of his best
clothes and the stiff rim of his heavy felt hat. He
could not let his wife discover that the noise and confusion of Broadway had the least power to make him
flinch: he cared no more for it than for the woods in
snow-time. He was as good as anybody, and she was
better. They owed nobody a cent; and they had come
on purpose to see the city of New York.

They were sitting at the breakfast-table in the
Ethan Allen Hotel, having arrived at nightfall the day
before. Mrs. Pinkham looked a little pale about the
mouth. She had been kept awake nearly all night by

the noise, and had enjoyed but little the evening she had spent in the stuffy parlor of the hotel, looking down out of the window at what seemed to her but garish scenes, and keeping a reproachful and suspicious eye upon some unpleasantly noisy young women of forward behavior who were her only companions. Abel himself was by no means so poorly entertained in the hotel office and smoking-room. He felt much more at home than she did, being better used to meeting strange men than she was to strange women, and he found two or three companions who had seen more than he of New York life. It was there, indeed, that the young reporter had found him, hearty and country-fed, and loved the appearance of his best clothes, and the way Mr. Abel Pinkham brushed his hair, and loved the way he spoke in a loud and manful voice the belief and experience of his honest heart.

In the morning at breakfast-time the Pinkhams were depressed. They missed their good bed at home; they were troubled by the roar and noise of the streets that hardly stopped over night before it began again in the morning. The waiter did not put what mind he may have had to the business of serving them; and Mrs. Abel Pinkham, whose cooking was the triumph of parish festivals at home, had her own opinion about the beefsteak. She was a woman of imagination, and now that she was fairly here, spectacles and all, it really pained her to find that the New York of her dreams, the metropolis of dignity and distinction, of wealth and elegance, did not seem to exist. These poor streets, these unlovely people, were the end of a great illusion. They did not like to meet each other's eyes, this worthy pair. The man began to put on an unbecoming air of assertion, and Mrs. Pinkham's face was full of lofty protest.

"My gracious me, Mary Ann! I *am* glad I happened to get the 'Tribune' this mornin'," said Mr. Pinkham, with sudden excitement. "Just you look here! I'd like well to know how they found out about our comin'!" and he handed the paper to his wife across the table. "There — there 'tis; right by my thumb," he insisted. "Can't you see it?" and he smiled like a boy as she finally brought her large spectacles to bear upon the important paragraph.

"I guess they think somethin' of us, if you don't think much o' them," continued Mr. Pinkham, grandly. "Oh, they know how to keep the run o' folks who are somebody to home! Draper and Fitch knew we was comin' this week; you know I sent word I was comin' to settle with them myself. I suppose they send folks round to the hotels, these newspapers, but I shouldn't thought there'd been time. Anyway, they've thought 'twas worth while to put us in!"

Mrs. Pinkham did not take the trouble to make a mystery out of the unexpected pleasure. "I want to cut it out an' send it right up home to daughter Sarah," she said, beaming with pride, and looking at the printed names as if they were flattering photographs. "I think 'twas most too strong to say we was among the notables. But there! 'tis their business to dress up things, and they have to print somethin' every day. I guess I shall go up and put on my best dress," she added inconsequently; "this one's kind of dusty; it's the same I rode in."

"Le' me see that paper again," said Mr. Pinkham jealously. "I didn't more'n half sense it, I was so taken aback. Well, Mary Ann, you didn't expect you was goin' to get into the papers when you came away. *'Abel Pinkham, Esquire, of Wetherford, Vermont.'* It looks well, don't it? But you might have knocked me down with a feather when I first caught sight of them words."

"I guess I shall put on my other dress," said Mrs. Pinkham, rising, with quite a different air from that with which she had sat down to her morning meal. "This one looks a little out o' style, as Sarah said, but when I got up this mornin' I was so homesick it didn't seem to make any kind o' difference. I expect that saucy girl last night took us to be nobodies. I'd like to leave the paper round where she couldn't help seein' it."

"Don't take any notice of her," said Abel, in a dignified tone. "If she can't do what you want an' be civil, we'll go somewheres else. I wish I'd done what we talked of at first an' gone to the Astor House, but that young man in the cars told me 'twas remote from the things we should want to see. The Astor House was the top o' everything when I was here last, but I expected to find some changes. I want you to have the best there is," he said, smiling at his wife as if they were just making their wedding journey. "Come, let's be stirrin'; 'tis long past eight o'clock," and he ushered her to the door, newspaper in hand.

CHAPTER II

Later that day the guests walked up Broadway, holding themselves erect, and feeling as if every eye was upon them. Abel Pinkham had settled with his correspondents for the spring consignments of maple sugar, and a round sum in bank bills was stowed away in his breast pocket. One of the partners had been a Wetherford boy, so when there came a renewal of interest in maple sugar, and the best confectioners were ready to do it honor, the finest quality being at a large premium, this partner remembered that there never was any sugar made in Wetherford of such melting and delicious flavor as from the trees on the old Pinkham farm. He had now made a good bit of money for himself on this private venture, and was ready that morning to pay Mr. Abel Pinkham cash down, and to give him a handsome order for the next season for all he could make. Mr. Fitch was also generous in the matter of such details as freight and packing; he was immensely polite and kind to his old friends, and begged them to come out and stay with him and his wife, where they lived now, in a not far distant New Jersey town.

"No, no, sir," said Mr. Pinkham promptly. "My wife has come to see the city, and our time is short. Your folks'll be up this summer, won't they? We'll wait an' visit then."

"You must certainly take Mrs. Pinkham up to the Park," said the commission merchant. "I wish I had time to show you round myself. I suppose you've been seeing some things already, haven't you? I noticed your arrival in the 'Herald.'"

"The 'Tribune' it was," said Mr. Pinkham, blushing through a smile and looking round at his wife.

"Oh, no; I never read the 'Tribune,'" said Mr. Fitch. "There was quite an extended notice in my paper. They must have put you and Mrs. Pinkham into the 'Herald' too." And so the friends parted, laughing. "I am quite pleased to have a call from such distinguished guests," said Mr. Fitch, by way of final farewell, and Mr. Pinkham waved his hand grandly in reply.

"Let's get the 'Herald,' then," he said, as they started up the street. "We can go an' sit in that little square that we passed as we came along, and rest an

talk things over about what we'd better do this afternoon. I'm tired out a-trampin' and standin'. I'd
rather have set still while we were there, but he
wanted us to see his store. Done very well, Joe Fitch
has, but 'taint a business I should like."

There was a lofty look and sense of behavior about
Mr. Pinkham of Wetherford. You might have thought
him a great politician as he marched up Broadway,
looking neither to right hand nor left. He felt himself
to be a person of great responsibilities.

"I begin to feel sort of at home myself," said his
wife, who always had a certain touch of simple dignity
about her. "When we was comin' yesterday New York
seemed to be all strange, and there wasn't nobody ex-
pectin' us. I feel now just as if I'd been here before."

They were now on the edge of the better-looking
part of the town; it was still noisy and crowded, but
noisy with fine carriages instead of drays, and crowded
with well dressed people. The hours for shopping and
visiting were beginning, and more than one person
looked with appreciative and friendly eyes at the
comfortable pleased-looking elderly man and woman
who went their easily beguiled and loitering way. The
pavement peddlers detained them, but the cabmen
beckoned them in vain; their eyes were busy with the
immediate foreground. Mrs. Pinkham was embarrassed by the recurring reflection of herself in the great
windows.

"I wish I had seen about a new bonnet before we
came," she lamented. "They seem to be havin' some
o' their spring things."

"Don't you worry, Mary Ann. I don't see anybody
hat looks any better than you do," said Abel, with
oyish and reassuring pride.

Mr. Pinkham had now bought the "Herald," and

also the "Sun," well recommended by an able news-
boy, and presently they crossed over from that corner
by the Fifth Avenue Hotel which seems like the very
heart of New York, and found a place to sit down on
the Square — an empty bench, where they could sit
side by side and look the papers through, reading over
each other's shoulder, and being impatient from page
to page. The paragraph was indeed repeated, with
trifling additions. Ederton of the "Sun" had followed the "Tribune" man's lead, and fabricated a
brief interview, a marvel of art and discretion, but so
general in its allusions that it could create no suspicion;
it almost deceived Mr. Pinkham himself, so that he
found unaffected pleasure in the fictitious occasion,
and felt as if he had easily covered himself with glory.
Except for the bare fact of the interview's being
imaginary, there was no discredit to be cast upon Mr.
Abel Pinkham's having said that he thought the country near Wetherford looked well for the time of year,
and promised a fair hay crop, and that his income was
augmented one-half to three-fifths by his belief in the
future of maple sugar. It was likely to be the great
coming crop of the Green Mountain State. Ederton
suggested that there was talk of Mr. Pinkham's
presence in the matter of a great maple-sugar trust, in
which much of the capital of Wall Street would be
involved.

"How they do hatch up these things, don't they?"
said the worthy man at this point. "Well, it all
sounds well, Mary Ann."

"It says here that you are a very personable man,"
smiled his wife, "and have filled some of the most responsible town offices" (this was the turn taken by
Goffey of the "Herald"). "Oh, and that you are going to attend the performance at Barnum's this even-

ing, and occupy reserved seats. Why, I didn't know — who have you told about that? — who was you talkin' to last night, Abel?"

"I never spoke o' goin' to Barnum's to any livin' soul," insisted Abel, flushing. "I only thought of it two or three times to myself that perhaps I might go an' take you. Now that is singular; perhaps they put that in just to advertize the show."

"Ain't it a kind of a low place for folks like us to be seen in?" suggested Mrs. Pinkham timidly. "People seem to be payin' us all this attention, an' I don't know's 't would be dignified for us to go to one o' them circus places."

"I don't care; we shan't live but once. I ain't comin' to New York an' confine myself to evenin' meetin's," answered Abel, throwing away discretion and morality together. "I tell you I'm goin' to spend this sugar-money just as we've a mind to. You've worked hard, an' counted a good while on comin', and so've I; an' I ain't goin' to mince my steps an' pinch an' screw for nobody. I'm goin' to hire one o' them hacks an' ride up to the Park."

"Joe Fitch said we could go right up in one o' the elevated railroads for five cents, an' return when we was ready," protested Mary Ann, who had a thriftier inclination than her husband; but Mr. Pinkham was not to be let or hindered, and they presently found themselves going up Fifth Avenue in a somewhat battered open landau. The spring sun shone upon them, and the spring breeze fluttered the black ostrich tip on Mrs. Pinkham's durable winter bonnet, and brought the pretty color to her faded cheeks.

"There! this is something like. Such people as we are can't go meechin' round; it ain't expected. Don't it pay for a lot o' hard work?" said Abel; and his wife gave him a pleased look for her only answer. They were both thinking of their gray farm-house high on a long western slope, with the afternoon sun full in its face, the old red barn, the pasture, the shaggy woods that stretched far up the mountain-side.

"I wish Sarah an' little Abel was here to see us ride by," said Mary Ann Pinkham, presently. "I can't seem to wait to have 'em get that newspaper. I'm so glad we sent it right off before we started this mornin'. If Abel goes to the post-office comin' from school, as he always does, they'll have it to read to-morrow before supper-time."

CHAPTER III

This happy day in two plain lives ended, as might have been expected, with the great Barnum show. Mr. and Mrs. Pinkham found themselves in possession of countless advertising cards and circulars next morning, and these added somewhat to their sense of responsibility. Mrs. Pinkham became afraid that the hotel-keeper would charge them double. "We've got to pay for it some way; there. I don't know but I'm more'n willin'," said the good soul. "I never did have such a splendid time in all my life. Findin' you so respected 'way off here is the best of anything; an' then seein' them dear little babies in their nice carriages, all along the streets and up to the Central Park! I never shall forget them beautiful little creatur's. And then the houses, an' the hosses, an' the store windows, an' all the rest of it! Well, I can't make any country pitcher hold no more, an' I want to get home an' think it over, goin' about my housework."

They were just entering the door of the Ethan Allen Hotel for the last time, when a young man met them and bowed cordially. He was the original reporter of their arrival, but they did not know it, and the impulse was strong within him to formally invite Mr. Pinkham to make an address before the members of the Produce Exchange on the following morning; but he had been a country boy himself, and their look of seriousness and self-consciousness appealed to him unexpectedly. He wondered what effect this great experience would have upon their after-life. The best fun, after all, would be to send marked copies of his paper and Ederton's to all the weekly newspapers in that part of Vermont. He saw before him the evidence of their happy increase of self-respect, and he would make all their neighborhood agree to do them honor. Such is the dominion of the press.

"Who was that young man? — he kind of bowed to you," asked the lady from Wetherford, after the journalist had meekly passed; but Abel Pinkham, Esquire, could only tell her that he looked like a young fellow who was sitting in the office the evening that they came to the hotel. The reporter did not seem to these distinguished persons to be a young man of any consequence.

Sarah Orne Jewett, The Life of Nancy, 1890

ON THE STAIRS

1894

The house had been "genteel." When trade was prospering in the East End, and the ship-fitter or block-maker thought it no shame to live in the parish where his workshop lay, such a master had lived here. Now, it was a tall, solid, well-bricked, ugly house, grimy and paintless in the joinery, cracked and patched in the windows: where the front door stood open all day long; and the womankind sat on the steps, talking of sickness and deaths and the cost of things; and treacherous holes lurked in the carpet of road-soil on the stairs and in the passage. For when eight families live in a house, nobody buys a door-mat, and the street was one of those streets that are always muddy. It smelt, too, of many things, none of them pleasant (one was fried fish); but for all that it was not a slum.

Three flights up, a gaunt woman with bare forearms stayed on her way to listen at a door which, opening, let out a warm, fetid waft from a close sick-room. A bent and tottering old woman stood on the threshold, holding the door behind her.

"An' is 'e no better now, Mrs. Curtis?" the gaunt woman asked, with a nod at the opening.

The old woman shook her head, and pulled the door closer. Her jaw wagged loosely in her withered chaps: "Nor won't be; till 'e's gone." Then after a certain pause, "'E's goin'," she said.

"Don't doctor give no 'ope?"

"Lor' bless ye, I don't want to ast no doctors," Mrs. Curtis replied, with something not unlike a chuckle. "I've seed too many on 'em. The boy's a-goin', fast; I can see that. An' then" — she gave the handle another tug, and whispered — "he's been called." She nodded again. "Three seprit knocks at the bed-head las' night; an' I know what *that* means!"

The gaunt woman raised her brows, and nodded. "Ah, well," she said, "we all on us comes to it some day, sooner or later. An' it's often a 'appy release."

The two looked into space beyond each other, the elder with a nod and a croak. Presently the other pursued, "'E's been a very good son, ain't 'e?"

"Ay, ay, well enough son to me," responded the old woman, a little peevishly; "an' I'll 'ave 'im put away decent, though there's on'y the Union for me after. I can do that, thank Gawd!" she added, meditatively, as chin on fist she stared into the thickening dark over the stairs.

"When I lost my pore 'usband," said the gaunt woman, with a certain brightening, "I give 'im a 'ansome funeral. 'E was a Oddfeller, an' I got twelve pound. I 'ad a oak caufin an' a open 'earse. There was a kerridge for the fam'ly an' one for 'is mates — two 'orses each, an' feathers, an' mutes; an' it went the furthest way round to the cimitry. 'Wotever 'appens, Mrs. Manders,' says the undertaker, 'you'll feel as you've treated 'im proper; nobody can't reproach you over that.' An' they couldn't. 'E was a good 'usband to me, an' I buried 'im respectable."

The gaunt woman exulted. The old, old story of Manders's funeral fell upon the other one's ears with a freshened interest, and she mumbled her gums ruminantly. "Bob'll 'ave a 'ansome buryin', too," she said. "I can make it up, with the insurance money, an' this an' that. On'y I donno about mutes. It's a expense."

In the East End, when a woman has not enough money to buy a thing much desired, she does not say so in plain words; she says the thing is an "expense," or a "great expense." It means the same thing, but it sounds better. Mrs. Curtis had reckoned her resources, and found that mutes would be an "expense." At a cheap funeral mutes cost half-a-sovereign and their liquor. Mrs. Manders said as much.

"Yus, yus, 'arf-a-sovereign," the old woman assented. Within, the sick man feebly beat the floor with a stick. "I'm a-comin'," she cried shrilly; "yus, 'arf-a-sovereign, but it's a lot, an' I don't see 'ow I'm to do it — not at present." She reached for the door-handle again, but stopped and added, by afterthought, "Unless I don't 'ave no plooms."

"It 'ud be a pity not to 'ave plooms. I 'ad ——"

There were footsteps on the stairs: then a stumble and a testy word. Mrs. Curtis peered over into the gathering dark. "Is it the doctor, sir?" she asked. It was the doctor's assistant; and Mrs. Manders tramped up to the next landing as the door of the sick-room took him in.

For five minutes the stairs were darker than ever. Then the assistant, a very young man, came out again, followed by the old woman with a candle. Mrs. Manders listened in the upper dark. "He's sinking fast," said the assistant. "He *must* have a stimulant. Dr. Mansell ordered port wine. Where is it?" Mrs. Curtis mumbled dolorously. "I tell you he *must* have it," he averred with unprofessional emphasis (his qualification was only a month old). "The man can't take solid food, and his strength must be kept up somehow. Another day may make all the difference. Is it because you can't afford it?" "It's a expense — sich a expense, doctor," the old woman pleaded. "An' wot with 'arf-pints o' milk an' ——" She grew inarticulate, and mumbled dismally.

"But he must have it, Mrs. Curtis, if it's your last shilling: it's the only way. If you mean you absolutely haven't the money ——" and he paused a little awkwardly. He was not a wealthy young man — wealthy young men do not devil for East End doctors — but he was conscious of a certain haul of sixpences at nap the night before; and, being inexperienced, he did not foresee the career of persecution whereon he was entering at his own expense and of his own motion. He produced five shillings: "If you absolutely haven' the money, why — take this and get a bottle — good not at a public-house. But mind, *at once*. He shoul' have had it before."

nap (abbr. of *Napoleon*), a card game.

It would have interested him, as a matter of coincidence, to know that his principal had been guilty of the selfsame indiscretion — even the amount was identical — on that landing the day before. But, as Mrs. Curtis said nothing of this, he floundered down the stairs and out into the wetter mud, pondering whether or not the beloved son of a Congregational minister might take full credit for a deed of charity on the proceeds of sixpenny nap. But Mrs. Curtis puffed her wrinkles, and shook her head sagaciously as she carried in her candle. From the room came a clink as of money falling into a teapot. And Mrs. Manders went about her business.

The door was shut, and the stair a pit of blackness. Twice a lodger passed down, and up and down, and still it did not open. Men and women walked on the lower flights, and out at the door, and in again. From the street a shout or a snatch of laughter floated up the pit. On the pavement footsteps rang crisper and fewer, and from the bottom passage there were sounds of stagger and sprawl. A demented old clock buzzed divers hours at random, and was rebuked every twenty minutes by the regular tread of a policeman on his beat. Finally, somebody shut the street-door with a great bang, and the street was muffled. A key turned inside the door on the landing, but that was all. A feeble light shone for hours along the crack below, and then went out. The crazy old clock went buzzing on, but nothing left that room all night. Nothing that opened the door. . . .

When next the key turned, it was to Mrs. Manders's knock, in the full morning; and soon the two women came out on the landing, together, Mrs. Curtis with a shapeless clump of bonnet. "Ah, 'e's a lovely corpse," said Mrs. Manders. "Like wax. So was my 'usband."

"I must be stirrin'," croaked the old woman, "an' go about the insurance an' the measurin' an' that. There's lots to do."

"Ah, there is. 'Oo are you goin' to 'ave — Wilkins? I 'ad Wilkins. Better than Kedge, I think: Kedge's mutes dresses rusty, an' their trousis is frayed. If you was thinkin' of 'avin' mutes ——"

"Yus, yus," — with a palsied nodding — "I'm a-goin' to 'ave mutes: I can do it respectable, thank Gawd!"

"And the plooms?"

"Ay, yus, an' the plooms too. They ain't sich a great expense, after all."

Arthur Morrison, Tales of Mean Streets

THE SONG OF THE MINSTER

1898?

When John of Fulda became Prior of Hethholme, says the old chronicle, he brought with him to the Abbey many rare and costly books — beautiful illuminated missals and psalters and portions of the Old and New Testament. And he presented rich vestments to the Minster; albs of fine linen, and copes embroidered with flowers of gold. In the west front he built two great arched windows filled with marvellous storied glass. The shrine of Sr. Egwin he repaired at vast outlay, adorning it with garlands in gold and silver, but the colour of the flowers was in coloured gems, and in like fashion the little birds in the nooks of the foliage. Stalls and benches of carved oak he placed in the choir; and many other noble works he had brought in his zeal for the glory of God's house.

In all the western land was there no more fair o

stately Minster than this of the Black Monks, with the peaceful township on one side, and on the other the sweet meadows and the acres of wheat and barley sloping down to the slow river, and beyond the river the clearings in the ancient forest.

But Thomas the Sub-prior was grieved and troubled in his mind by the richness and the beauty of all he saw about him, and by the Prior's eagerness to be ever adding some new work in stone, or oak, or metal, or jewels.

"Surely," he said to himself, "these things are unprofitable — less to the honour of God than to the pleasure of the eye and the pride of life and the luxury of our house! Had so much treasure not been wasted on these vanities of bright colour and carved stone, our dole to the poor of Christ might have been fourfold, and they filled with good things. But now let our almoner do what best he may, I doubt not many a leper sleeps cold, and many a poor man goes lean with hunger."

This the Sub-prior said, not because his heart was quick with fellowship for the poor, but because he was of a narrow and gloomy and grudging nature, and he could conceive no true service of God which was not one of fasting and praying, of joylessness and mortification.

Now you must know that the greatest of the monks and the hermits and the holy men were not of this kind. In their love of God they were blithe of heart, and filled with a rare sweetness and tranquillity of soul, and they looked on the goodly earth with deep joy, and they had a tender care for the wild creatures of wood and water. But Thomas had yet much to learn of the beauty of holiness.

Often in the bleak dark hours of the night he would

leave his cell and steal into the Minster, to fling himself on the cold stones before the high altar; and there he would remain, shivering and praying, till his strength failed him.

It happened one winter night, when the thoughts I have spoken of had grown very bitter in his mind, Thomas guided his steps by the glimmer of the sanctuary lamp to his accustomed place in the choir. Falling on his knees, he laid himself on his face with the palms of his outstretched hands flat on the icy pavement. And as he lay there, taking a cruel joy in the freezing cold and the torture of his body, he became gradually aware of a sound of far-away yet most heavenly music.

He raised himself to his knees to listen, and to his amazement he perceived that the whole Minster was pervaded by a faint mysterious light, which was every instant growing brighter and clearer. And as the light increased the music grew louder and sweeter, and he knew that it was within the sacred walls. But it was no mortal melody.

The strains he heard were the minglings of angelic instruments, and the cadences of voices of unearthly loveliness. They seemed to proceed from the choir about him, and from the nave and transept and aisles; from the pictured windows and from the clerestory and from the vaulted roofs. Under his knees he felt that the crypt was throbbing and droning like a huge organ. Sometimes the song came from one part of the Minster, and then all the rest of the vast building was silent; then the music was taken up, as it were in response, in another part; and yet again voices and instruments would blend in one indescribable volume of harmony, which made the huge pile thrill and vibrate from roof to pavement.

As Thomas listened, his eyes became accustomed to the celestial light, which encompassed him, and he saw — he could scarce credit his senses that he saw — the little carved angels of the oak stalls in the choir clashing their cymbals and playing their psalteries.

He rose to his feet, bewildered and half terrified. At that moment the mighty roll of unison ceased, and from many parts of the church there came a concord of clear high voices, like a warbling of silver trumpets, and Thomas heard the words they sang. And the words were these:

Tibi omnes Angeli.
To Thee all Angels cry aloud.

So close to him were two of these voices that Thomas looked up to the spandrels in the choir, and he saw that it was the carved angels leaning out of the spandrels that were singing. And as they sang the breath came from their stone lips white and vaporous into the frosty air.

He trembled with awe and astonishment, but the wonder of what was happening drew him towards the altar. The beautiful tabernacle work of the altar screen contained a double range of niches filled with the statues of saints and kings; and these, he saw, were singing. He passed slowly onward with his arms outstretched, like a blind man who does not know the way he is treading.

The figures on the painted glass of the lancets were singing.

The winged heads of the baby angels over the marble memorial slabs were singing.

The lions and griffons and mythical beasts of the finials were singing.

The effigies of dead abbots and priors were singing on their tombs in bay and chantry.

The figures in the frescoes on the walls were singing.

On the painted ceiling westward of the tower the verses of the Te Deum, inscribed in letters of gold above the shields of kings and princes and barons, were visible in the divine light, and the very words of these verses were singing, like living things.

And the breath of all these as they sang turned to a smoke as of incense in the wintry air, and floated about the high pillars of the Minster.

Suddenly the music ceased, all save the deep organ-drone.

Then Thomas heard the marvellous antiphon repeated in the bitter darkness outside; and that music, he knew, must be the response of the galleries of stone kings and queens, of abbots and virgin martyrs, over the western portals, and of monstrous gargoyles along the eaves.

When the music ceased in the outer darkness, it was taken up again in the interior of the Minster.

At last there came one stupendous united cry of all the singers, and in that cry even the organ-drone of the crypt, and the clamour of the brute stones of pavement and pillar, of wall and roof, broke into words articulate. And the words were these:

Per singulos dies, benedicimus Te.
Day by day; we magnify Thee,
And we worship Thy name; ever world without end.

As the wind of summer changes into the sorrowful wail of the yellowing woods, so the strains of joyous worship changed into a wail of supplication; and as he caught the words, Thomas too raised his voice in wild entreaty:

Miserere nostri, Domine, miserere nostri.
O Lord, have mercy upon us; have mercy upon us.

And then his senses failed him, and he sank to the ground in a long swoon.

When he came to himself all was still, and all was dark save for the little yellow flower of light in the sanctuary lamp.

As he crept back to his cell he saw with unsealed eyes how churlishly he had grudged God the glory of man's genius and the service of His dumb creatures, the metal of the hills, and the stone of the quarry, and the timber of the forest; for now he knew that at all seasons, and whether men heard the music or not, the ear of God was filled by day and by night with an ever-lasting song from each stone of the vast Minster:

We magnify Thee,
And we worship Thy name; ever world without end.

William Canton, A Child's Book of Saints

TWENTIETH CENTURY
ON BEING ORIGINAL

1908

There has been a radical change during the last hundred years in the world's attitude toward originality. An age of conformity has given way to an age of self-assertion; so that nowadays a man makes a bid for fame by launching a paradox, much as he might have done in the time of Pope by polishing a commonplace. Then, even a person of genuine originality was in danger of being accounted freakish. Now, many a man passes for original who is in reality only freakish. Boileau, speaking for the old criticism, says that Perrault was "bizarre"; Sainte-Beuve, speaking for the new, says that Perrault had genius. From the outset, the neo-classic critics stifled free initiative in the name of the "rules," and opposed to every attempt at innovation the authority of Aristotle and the ancients. The relation of the literary aspirant to the "models" during this period is not unfairly summed up in the words of the comic opera:

> "Of course you can never be like us,
> But be as like us as you're able to be."

Later, under French influence, the tyranny of etiquette was added to the tyranny of classical imitation. Aristotle was reinforced by the dancing master. Social convention so entwined itself about the whole nature of a Frenchman of the Old Régime that it finally became almost as hard for him as we may suppose it is for a Chinaman to disengage his originality from the coils of custom. The very word original was

often used as a term of ridicule and disparagement.
Brossette writes of the Oriental traveler Tavernier
that he is "brutal and even a bit original." "When it
is desired to turn any one to ridicule," writes Boursault
about the same time, "he is said to be an *original sans
copie.*" Anything in literature or art that departed
from the conventional type was pronounced "monstrous." La Harpe applies this epithet to the *Divine
Comedy*, and points out how inferior the occasional
felicities of this "absurd and shapeless rhapsody" are
to the correct beauties of a true epic like Voltaire's
Henriade.

And so we might go on, as Mr. Saintsbury, for example, does for scores of pages in his *History of Criticism*, exposing the neo-classic narrowness, and setting
forth in contrast the glories of our modern emancipation. But this is to give one's self the pleasure, as the
French would say, of smashing in open doors. Instead of engaging in this exhilarating pastime, we
might, perhaps, find more profit in inquiring, first, into
the definite historical reasons that led to the triumph of
the so-called school of good sense over the school of
genius and originality; and second, in seeking for the
element of truth that lurked beneath even the most
arid and unpromising of the neo-classic conventions.
For if, like Mr. Saintsbury and many other romanticists, we reject the truth along with the convention, we
shall simply fall from one extreme into another.

The whole subject of originality is closely bound up
with what is rather vaguely known as individualism.
We must recollect that before the disciplinary classicism of the later Renaissance there was an earlier
Renaissance which was in a high degree favorable to
originality. At the very beginning of this earlier
period, Petrarch made his famous plea for originality,

in a letter to Boccaccio, and established his claim, in this as in other respects, to be considered the first modern man. "Every one," says Petrarch, "has not only in his countenance and gestures, but also in his voice and language, something peculiarly his own (*quiddam suum ac proprium*), which it is both easier and wiser to cultivate and correct than it is to alter." And so many of the Italians who followed Petrarch set out to cultivate the *quiddam suum ac proprium*, often showing real ardor for self-expression, and still oftener, perhaps, using the new liberty merely as a cloak for license. Society finally took alarm, not only at the license, but at the clash of rival originalities, each man indulging in his own individual sense without much reference to the general or common sense of mankind. We need not, however, repeat what we have already said in our first essay about the reaction of the later Renaissance against an excessive individualism. This reaction, especially in France and Italy, soon ran into excesses of its own. Yet we must not forget that, at the moment when the neo-classic disciplinarian appeared on the scene, the great creative impulse of the early Renaissance was already dying out or degenerating into affectation. The various forms of bad taste that spread like an epidemic over Europe at the end of the sixteenth century and beginning of the seventeenth (cultism, Marinism, euphuism, préciosité, etc.), have their common source in a straining to be original in defiance of sound reason. We may say of the writers of these different schools as a class that, in spite of occasional lyrical felicities, they have "all the nodosities of the oak without its strength and all the contortions of the Sibyl without the inspiration."

The school of good sense was the natural and legitimate protest against this pseudo-originality. But this school can be justified on higher grounds than simply as a reaction from a previous excess. It tried to apply, however imperfectly, the profound doctrine of Aristotle that the final test of art is not its originality, but its truth to the universal. The question is one of special interest because we are living in an age that comes at the end of a great era of expansion, comparable in some ways to that of the Renaissance. Now, as then, there is a riot of so-called originality. In the name of this originality art is becoming more and more centrifugal and eccentric. As the result of our loss of standards, the classicist would complain, we are inbreeding personal and national peculiarities and getting farther and farther away from what is universally human.

In other words, the chief ambition of our modern art, which resembles in this respect some of the art of the later Renaissance, is to be original. The first aim of both classic and neo-classic art, on the other hand, was to be representative. Aristotle had said that it is not enough to render a thing as it is in this or that particular case, but as it is in general; and he goes on to say that the superiority of poetry over history lies in the fact that it has more of this universality, that it is more concerned with the essentials and less with the accidents of human nature. The weakness of neo-classic art was that it substituted the rule of thumb and servile imitation for direct observation in deciding what were accidents and what were essentials. It was ready to proscribe a thing as "monstrous" — that is, as outside of nature — when in reality it was simply outside the bounds set by certain commentators on Aristotle. The artist had to conform to the conventional types established in this way, even if he sacrificed to them poignancy and directness of emotion.

He was limited by the type not only in dealing with any particular literary form — tragedy, epic, and so forth — but even in his creating of individual characters. For example, he must be careful not to paint a particular soldier, but the typical soldier, and of course he was not to depart too far from the classical models in deciding what the traits of the typical soldier are. Thus Rymer condemns Iago because he is not true to the "character constantly worn by soldiers for some thousands of years in the world." According to Rymer, again, the queen in one of Beaumont and Fletcher's plays oversteps the bounds of decorum. Some particular queen, Rymer admits, may have acted in this way; but she must be rid of all her "accidental historical impudence" before she can become an orthodox, typical queen, entitled to "stalk in tragedy on her high shoes."

The attempt of the neo-classicists to tyrannize over originality and restrict the creative impulse in the name of the type was bound in the long run to provoke a reaction. To carry through the difficult and delicate task of breaking with convention some man of more than Socratic wisdom was needed; instead, this task was undertaken by the "self-torturing sophist, wild Rousseau." In almost the opening sentence of his *Confessions*, Rousseau strikes the note that is heard throughout the nineteenth century, from the early romanticists to Ibsen and Sudermann: "If I am not better than other men, at least I am different." By this gloating sense of his own departure from the type Rousseau became the father of eccentric individualists. By his insistence on the rights and legitimacy of unrestrained emotion he inaugurated the age of storm and stress, not only in Germany, but throughout Europe. Our modern impressionists, who would make of their own sensibility the measure of all things, are only his late-born disciples.

Emotion, insists the classicist, must be disciplined and subdued to what is typical; else it will be eccentric and not true to the human heart. "The human heart of whom?" cries Alfred de Musset, like a true disciple of Jean-Jacques. "The human heart of what? Even though the devil be in it, I have my human heart of my own — *j'ai mon cœur humain, moi*." The whole of French romanticism is in that *moi*. Away with stale authority, usage, and tradition, that would come between a man and his own spontaneity, and keep him from immediate contact with "nature." Let him once more see the world bathed in the fresh wonder of the dawn. To this end let him discard books ("a dull and endless strife") and live as if "none had lived before him."

Every man, in short, is to be an original genius. It was the assumption of this attitude by Rousseau's followers in Germany that gave its name to a whole literary period (*Geniezeit*). Germany sought its emancipation from convention, not, as Lessing would have wished, through the discipline of reason, but through "genius" and "originality," which meant in practice the opening of the floodgates of sentiment. We can imagine the disgust with which Lessing looked on the Rousseauism of the youthful Goethe. In *Werther*, critics are accused of being in a conspiracy against originality. Their rules are compared to a system of dams and trenches with which the critics protect their own little cabbage-patches against genius, whose impetuous waves would otherwise burst forth and overwhelm them, and at the same time astound the world. One thinks of Lessing's admirable defense of criticism, of the passage in which he confesses that he owes all he has, not to genius and originality, but to a patient assimilation of the wisdom of the past. "Without criticism I should be poor, cold, short-sighted. I am, therefore, always ashamed or annoyed when I hear or read anything in disparagement of criticism. It is said to suppress genius, and I flattered myself that I had gained from it something very nearly approaching genius. I am a lame man who cannot possibly be edified by abuse of his crutch."

We are still inclined to side with original genius against what Lessing calls criticism. Criticism itself has come to mean nowadays mere appreciativeness, instead of meaning, as it did for Lessing, the application of standards of judgment. It may, however, appear some day how much the great romantic leaders, Shelley for example, suffered from the absence of just what Lessing called criticism. Men may then grow weary of a genius and originality that are at bottom only an outpouring of undisciplined emotion. One whole side of our American transcendental school is only a belated echo of German romanticism, which itself continues the age of original genius. There is special danger even in Emerson's conception of originality, and the unbounded deference with which it fills him for the untrained individual. Every man, to become great, merely needs, it would appear, to plant himself indomitably on his instincts; but it is not safe for the average person to trust so blindly to what Rymer would have called his own "maggot." Hawthorne, the best observer of the group, has left an account of some of the nightmare originalities that were developed under the Concord influence.

We read of a certain character in one of Marivaux's plays: "He is a man whose first impulse is to ask, not, 'Do you esteem me?' but, 'Are you surprised at me?'"

His purpose is not to convince us that he is better than other people, but that he resembles himself alone." The comedy in which this eighteenth-century Bernard Shaw figures was written a number of years before Rousseau assumed the Armenian costume and began to agitate Europe with his paradoxes. Since Rousseau the world has become increasingly familiar with the man who poses and attitudinizes before it and is not satisfied until he can draw its attention to the traits that establish his own uniqueness. The eccentric individualist not only rejoices in his own singularity, but is usually eager to thrust it on other people. His aim is to startle, or, as the French would say, to *épater le bourgeois*, to make the plain citizen "stare and gasp." Dr. Johnson said of Lord Monboddo that if he had had a tail he would have been as proud of it as a squirrel. Perhaps Rousseau was never more deeply hurt than by the lady who said, on breaking with him, "You're just like other men." This, as a French critic remarks, was a home thrust that one of Molière's soubrettes could not have improved upon. The claim of Rousseau and his earlier followers was to be not simply unique, but unique in feeling. This sentiment of uniqueness in feeling speedily became that of uniqueness in suffering — on the familiar principle, no doubt, that life, which is a comedy for those who think, is a tragedy for those who feel. Hence arose in the romantic school a somewhat theatrical affectation of grief. Byron was far from being the first who paraded before the public "the pageant of his bleeding heart." Chateaubriand especially nourished in himself the sense of fated and preëminent sorrow, and was ready to exclaim at the most ordinary mischance: "Such things happen only to me!" Sainte-Beuve makes an interesting comparison between Chateaubriand and another native of Brittany, the author of *Gil Blas*. "A book like *René*," says Sainte-Beuve, "encourages a subtle spiritual pride. A man seeks in his imagination some unique misfortune to which he may abandon himself and which he may fold about him in solitude. He says to himself that a great soul must contain more sorrow than a little one; and adds in a whisper that he himself may be this great soul. *Gil Blas*, on the other hand, is a book that brings you into full contact with life and the throng of your fellow creatures. When you are very gloomy and believe in fatality and imagine that certain extraordinary things happen to you alone, read *Gil Blas*, and you will find that he had that very misfortune or one just like it, and that he took it as a simple mishap and got over it."

The same contrast might be brought out by comparing Montaigne and Rousseau, the two writers who, in a broad sense, are the masters respectively of Lesage and Chateaubriand. This contrast is easily missed, because at first glance Montaigne seems an arch-egotist like Rousseau, and is almost equally ready to bestow his own idiosyncrasies on the reader. Yet in the final analysis Montaigne is interested in Montaigne because he is a human being; Rousseau is interested in Rousseau because he is Jean-Jacques. Montaigne observes himself impartially as a normal specimen of the genus homo. Rousseau, as we have seen, positively gloats over his own otherwiseness. Montaigne aims to be the average, or, it would be less misleading to say, the representative man; Rousseau's aim is to be the extraordinary man, or original genius. Rousseau is an eccentric, Montaigne a concentric individualist. The sentence of Montaigne that sums him up is, "Every man bears within him the entire image of the human lot." Rousseau is rather summed up in his phrase

"There are souls that are too privileged to follow the common path," with its corollary that he is himself one of these privileged souls.

The nineteenth century saw the rise of a race of eccentric individualists, especially in art and literature, who, like Rousseau, scorned the common path and strove to distinguish themselves from the bourgeois and philistine in everything, from the details of their dress to the refinements of their sensations. In this quest of the rare and the original they attained to a departure from the norm that was not only eccentric, but pathological. Every man was to have the right to express not only his own particular vision of life, but his own particular nightmare. We finally come to a writer like Baudelaire, who builds himself a "little strangely scented and strangely colored kiosk on the extreme tip of the romantic Kamchatka" and "cultivates his hysteria with delight and terror;" who, instead of being true to the human heart, as the old-fashioned classicist would say, makes it his ambition to create a "new shudder." All the modern writer cares for, says M. Anatole France, is to be thought original. In his fear of becoming commonplace he prides himself, like Victor Hugo, on reading only those books that other men do not read, or else he does not read at all, and so comes to resemble that eighteenth-century Frenchwoman who was said to have "respected in her ignorance the active principle of her originality." The danger of the man who is too assimilative, who possesses too perfectly the riches of tradition, is to feel that originality is henceforth impossible. It is related of a French critic that he used to turn away wearily from every new volume of poetry that was submitted to him, with the remark: "All the verses are written."

Genuine originality, however, is a hardy growth, and usually gains more than it loses by striking deep root into the literature of the past. La Bruyère begins his *Characters* by observing that "Everything has been said," and then goes on to write one of the most original books in French. Montaigne wrote a still more original book which often impresses the reader as a mere cento of quotations. An excessive respect for the past is less harmful than the excess from which we are now suffering. For example, one of our younger writers is praised in a review for his "stark freedom from tradition . . . as though he came into the world of letters without ever a predecessor. He is the expression in literary art of certain enormous repudiations." It is precisely this notion of originality that explains the immense insignificance of so much of our contemporary writing. The man who breaks with the past in this way will think that he is original when he is in reality merely ignorant and presumptuous. He is apt to imagine himself about a century ahead of his age when he is at least four or five centuries behind it. "He comes to you," as Bagehot puts it, "with a notion that Noah discarded in the ark, and attracts attention to it as if it were a stupendous novelty of his own."

We may be sure that the more enlightened of the Cave Dwellers had already made deeper discoveries in human nature than many of our modern radicals. Goethe said that if as a young man he had known of the masterpieces that already existed in Greek he would never have written a line. Goethe carries his modesty too far; but how grateful just a touch of it would be in the average author of to-day! With even a small part of Goethe's knowledge and insight, he would no longer go on serving up to us the dregs and last muddy lees of the romantic and naturalistic movements as originality and genius. He would see that his very paradoxes were stale. Instead of being a half-baked author, he would become a modest and at the same time judicious reader; or, if he continued to write, he would be less anxious to create and more anxious to humanize his creations. Sooner or later every author, as well as the characters he conceives, will have to answer the question that was the first addressed to any one who designed to enter the Buddhist church: "Are you a human being?" The world's suffrage will go in the long run to the writer or artist who dwells habitually in the centre and not on the remote periphery of human nature. Gautier paid a doubtful compliment to Victor Hugo when he said that Hugo's works seemed to proceed not from a man, but an element, that they were Cyclopean, "as it were, the works of Polyphemus." Hugo remained the original genius to the end, in contrast with Goethe, who attained humane restraint after having begun as a Rousseauist.

Romanticism from the very beginning tended to become eccentric through over-anxiety to be original; and romanticism is now running to seed. Many of our contemporary writers are as plainly in an extreme as the most extreme of the neo-classicists. They think that to be original they need merely to arrive at self-expression without any effort to be representative. The neo-classicist, on the other hand, strove so hard to be representative that he often lost the personal flavor entirely and fell into colorless abstraction. Both extremes fail equally of being humane. For, to revert to our fundamental principle, the humanist must combine opposite extremes and occupy all the space between them. Genuine originality is so immensely difficult because it imposes the task of achieving work that is of general human truth and at the same time intensely individual. Perhaps the best examples of this union of qualities are found in Greek. The original man for the Greek was the one who could create in the very act of imitating the past. Greek literature at its best is to a remarkable degree a creative imitation of Homer.

The modern does not, like the Greek, hope to become original by assimilating tradition, but rather by ignoring it, or, if he is a scholar, by trying to prove that it is mistaken. We have been discussing thus far almost entirely the originality of the Rousseauist or sentimental naturalist; but we should not fail to note the curious points of contact here as elsewhere between sentimental and scientific naturalism. The Baconian aims less at the assimilation of past wisdom than at the advancement of learning. With him too the prime stress is on the new and the original. Formerly there was a pedantry of authority and prescription. As a result of the working together of Rousseauist and Baconian there has arisen a veritable pedantry of originality. The scientific pedant who is entirely absorbed in his own bit of research is first cousin to the artistic and literary pedant who is entirely absorbed in his own sensation. The hero of modern scholarship is not the humanist, but the investigator. The man who digs up an unpublished document from some musty archive outranks the man who can deal judiciously with the documents already in print. His glory will be all the greater if he can make a new document a pretext for writing a book, for attempting a rehabilitation. The love of truth shades imperceptibly into the love of paradox; and Rousseauist and Baconian often coexist in the same person.

A royal road to a reputation for originality is to impugn the verdicts of the past, — to whitewash what is traditionally black or to blackwash what is traditionally white. Only the other day one of the English reviews published the "Blackwashing of Dante." A still better example is Renan's blackwashing of King David, which concludes as follows: "Pious souls, when they take delight in the sentiments filled with resignation and tender melancholy contained in the most beautiful of the liturgical books, will imagine that they are in communion with this bandit. Humanity will believe in final justice on the testimony of David, who never gave it a thought, and of the Sibyl, who never existed," etc. The whitewashings have been still more numerous. Rehabilitations have appeared of Tiberius, the Borgias, and Robespierre. A book has also been written to prove that the first Napoleon was a man of an eminently peace-loving disposition. Mr. Stephen Phillips undertakes to throw a poetical glamour over the character of Nero, that amiable youth, who, as the versifier in "Punch" observes:

> "would have doubtless made his mark,
> Had he not, in a mad, mad, boyish lark,
> Murdered his mother!"

If this whitewashing and blackwashing goes on, the time will soon come when the only way left to be original will be to make a modest plea for the traditional good sense of the world. This traditional good sense was never treated with an easier contempt than at present. A writer named Bax, who recently published a volume rehabilitating the revolutionary monster Marat, says in his preface: "It is in fact a fairly safe rule to ascertain for oneself what most people think on such questions" (i.e., as the character of Marat), "and then assume the exact opposite to be true." Of most books of this kind we may say what FitzGerald said when Henry Irving made himself up in the rôle of Shylock to look like the Saviour: "It is an attempt to strike out an original idea in the teeth of common sense and tradition." Of course there are in every age and individual, as we have said elsewhere, elements that run counter to the main tendency. One of the regular recipes for writing German doctors' theses is to seize on one of these elements, exaggerate it, and take it as a point of departure for refuting the traditional view. Thus Rousseau says in one place that he had always detested political agitators. We may be sure in advance that some German will start from this to prove that Rousseau has been cruelly maligned in being looked on as a revolutionist.

Even our more serious scholars are finding it hard to resist that something in the spirit of the age which demands that their results be not only just, but novel. Even our older universities are becoming familiar with the professor who combines in about equal measure his love of research and his love of the limelight. In public opinion, the perfection of the type is the Chicago professor whose originality has become the jest of the cheap newspapers. Here are a few Chicago "discoveries," selected almost at random from the many that have been announced from time to time in the daily press:

Kissing causes lockjaw.

The Pennsylvanians are turning into Indians.

A man does not need to take exercise after the age of thirty-five.

Music is antiseptic.

A dog will not follow an uneducated man.

Marriage is a form of insanity.

Americans are incapable of friendship.

Boccaccio was a Swede.

John D. Rockefeller is as great a man as Shakespeare.

Some day a wounded or even worn-out heart of a human being may be replaced by a healthy heart from a living monkey, etc.

The Chicago professors would say, and no doubt rightly, that they are misrepresented by these newspaper statements.[1] But we are only giving the general impression. Even the utterance of Dr. Osler that at once gave him such a start over all his academic rivals in the race for notoriety becomes comparatively unsensational when read in its context. The professor with an itch for the limelight has only to pattern himself on Rousseau, the great master of paradox. Rousseau's method has been compared to that of a man who fires off a pistol in the street to attract a crowd. When Rousseau has once drawn his crowd, he may proceed to attenuate his paradox, until sometimes it is in danger of dwindling into a commonplace.

Most good observers would probably agree that contemporary scholarship and literature are becoming too eccentric and centrifugal; they would agree that some unifying principle is needed to counteract this excessive striving after originality. For example, Professor Gummere, who is one of the most distinguished representatives of the scholarly tradition that ultimately goes back to Herder and the Grimm brothers, diagnoses our present malady with great clearness in a recent article on "Originality and Convention in Literature." [2] The higher forms of poetry and

Chicago instructors have told me that the University is the victim of a
plot of conspiracy on the part of certain newspapers. — Author's note.
Quarterly Review, January, 1906. — Author's note.

creative art, he says, are being made impossible by the disintegrating influences at work in modern life, and by an excess of analysis. He suggests as remedy that we jettison this intellectual and analytical element, and seek to restore once more the bond of communal sympathy. This remedy betrays at once its romantic origin. It is only one form of Rousseau's assumption that an unaided sympathy will do more to draw men together than the naked forces of egoism and self-assertion will do to drive them asunder. Even in his studies of the beginnings of poetry Professor Gummere should, perhaps, have insisted more on communal discipline as a needful preliminary to communal sympathy. However that may be, our present hope does not seem to lie in the romanticist's attempt to revert to the unity of instinct and feeling that he supposes to have existed in primitive life. We need to commune and unite in what is above rather than in what is below our ordinary selves, and the pathway to this higher unity is not through sympathy, communal or otherwise, but through restraint. If we have got so far apart, it is because of the lack, not of sympathy, but of humane standards.

Without trying to enter fully into so large a topic as the impressionism of our modern society, its loss of traditional standards, and its failure as yet to find new, we may at least point out that education should be less infected than it is with a pedantic straining after originality. In general, education should represent the conservative and unifying element in our national life. The college especially must maintain humane standards, if it is to have any reason at all for existing as something distinct from university and preparatory school. Its function is not, as is so often assumed, merely to help its students to self-expression but even more to help them to become humane. In the words of Cardinal Newman, the college is "the great ordinary means to a great but ordinary end"; this end is to supply principles of taste and judgment and train in sanity and centrality of view; to give background and perspective, and inspire, if not the spirit of conformity, at least a proper respect for the past experience of the world. Most of us have heard of Mrs. Shelley's reply when advised to send her boy to a school where he would be taught to think for himself: "My God! teach him rather to think like other people." Mrs. Shelley had lived with a man who was not only a real genius, but also an original genius in the German sense, and knew whereof she spoke. Now the college should not necessarily teach its students to think like other people, but it should teach them to distinguish between what is original and what is merely odd and eccentric, both in themselves and others. According to Lowell, this is a distinction that Wordsworth could never make, and Wordsworth is not alone in this respect among the romantic leaders. We must insist, at the risk of causing scandal, that the college is not primarily intended to encourage originality and independence of thought as these terms are often understood. The story is told of a professor in one of our Eastern colleges that he invariably gave a high mark to the undergraduates who contradicted the received opinions in his subject; but the highest mark he reserved for the undergraduate who in addition to contradicting the traditional view set up a new view of his own. As this fact became known, the professor was gratified by a rapid growth among his students of independent and original thinking.

The college should guard against an undue stress on self-expression and an insufficient stress on humane assimilation. This danger is especially plain in the teaching of English composition. A father once said to me of a "daily theme" course that it had at least set his son's wits to working. But what if it set them to working in the void? The most that can be expected of youths who are put to writing with little or no background of humane assimilation is a clever impressionism. They will be fitted, not to render serious service to literature, but at most to shine in the more superficial kinds of journalism. It is still an open question whether any direct method of teaching English really takes the place of the drill in the niceties of style that can be derived from translation, especially the translation of Latin; whether a student, for example, who rendered Cicero with due regard for the delicate shades of meaning would not gain more mastery of English (to say nothing of Latin) than a student who devoted the same amount of time to daily themes and original composition. We must, however, be fair to our departments of English. They have to cope with conditions not entirely of their own making, of which the most serious is something approaching illiteracy in many of the students that are forced upon them from the preparatory schools. In practice they have to devote most of their time to imparting, not the elegancies, but the simplest decencies of the English language. Ultimately a great deal of what goes on in the more elementary college courses in English may well be relegated to the lower schools — and the home — and the work that is done in the advanced course in composition will probably either be omitted entirely, or else done, as it is in France, in connection with the reading and detailed study of great writers. Assimilation will then keep pace as it should with expression.

Spinoza says that a man should constantly keep before his eyes a sort of exemplar of human nature (*idea hominis, tamquam naturæ humanæ exemplar*). He should, in other words, have a humane standard to which he may defer, and which will not proscribe originality, but will help him to discriminate between what is original and what is merely freakish and abnormal in himself and others. Now this humane standard may be gained by a few through philosophic insight, but in most cases it will be attained, if at all, by a knowledge of good literature — by a familiarity with that golden chain of masterpieces which links together into a single tradition the more permanent experience of the race; books which so agree in essentials that they seem, as Emerson puts it, to be the work of one all-seeing, all-hearing gentleman. In short, the most practical way of promoting humanism is to work for a revival of the almost lost art of reading. As a general rule, the humane man will be the one who has a memory richly stored with what is best in literature, with the sound sense perfectly expressed that is found only in the masters. Conversely, the decline of humanism and the growth of Rousseauism has been marked by a steady decay in the higher uses of the memory. For the Greeks the Muses were not the daughters of Inspiration or of Genius, as they would be for a modern, but the daughters of Memory. Sainte-Beuve says that "from time to time we should raise our eyes to the hill-tops, to the group of revered mortals, and ask ourselves: What would they say of us?" No one whose memory is not enriched in the way we have described can profit by this advice. Sainte-Beuve himself in giving it was probably only remembering Longinus.

Irving Babbitt, Literature and the American College

ON LYING IN BED

1909

Lying in bed would be an altogether perfect and supreme experience if only one had a coloured pencil long enough to draw on the ceiling. This, however, is not generally a part of the domestic apparatus on the premises. I think myself that the thing might be managed with several pails of Aspinall and a broom. Only if one worked in a really sweeping and masterly way, and laid on the colour in great washes, it might drip down again on one's face in floods of rich and mingled colour like some strange fairy rain; and that would have its disadvantages. I am afraid it would be necessary to stick to black and white in this form of artistic composition. To that purpose, indeed, the white ceiling would be of the greatest possible use; in fact it is the only use I think of a white ceiling being put to.

But for the beautiful experiment of lying in bed I might never have discovered it. For years I have been looking for some blank spaces in a modern house to draw on. Paper is much too small for any really allegorical design; as Cyrano de Bergerac says: "Il me faut des géants." But when I tried to find these fine clear spaces in modern rooms such as we all live in I was continually disappointed. I found an endless pattern and complication of small objects hung like a curtain of fine links between me and my desire. I examined the walls; I found them to my surprise to be already covered with wall paper, and I found the wall paper to be already covered with very uninteresting images, all bearing a ridiculous resemblance to each other. I could not understand why one arbitrary

Aspinall, a kind of paint.
Il me faut des géants, I must have giants.

symbol — a symbol apparently devoid of any religious or philosophical significance — should thus be sprinkled all over my nice walls like a sort of smallpox. The Bible must be referring to wall papers, I think, when it says, "Use not vain repetitions, as the Gentiles do." I found the Turkey carpet a mass of unmeaning colours, rather like the Turkish Empire, or like the sweet-meat called Turkish delight. I do not exactly know what Turkish delight really is; but I suppose it is Macedonian massacres. Everywhere that I went forlornly, with my pencil or my paint brush, I found that others had unaccountably been before me, spoiling the walls, the curtains, and the furniture with their childish and barbaric designs.

Nowhere did I find a really clear place for sketching until this occasion when I prolonged beyond the proper limit the process of lying on my back in bed. Then the light of that white heaven broke upon my vision, that breath of mere white which is indeed almost the definition of Paradise, since it means purity and also means freedom. But alas! like all heavens, now that it is seen it is found to be unattainable; it looks more austere and more distant than the sky outside the window. For my proposal to paint on it with the bristly end of a broom has been discouraged — never mind by whom; by a person debarred from all political rights — and even my minor proposal to put the other end of the broom into the kitchen fire and turn it into charcoal has not been conceded. Yet I am certain that it was from persons in my position that all the original inspiration came for covering the ceilings of palaces and cathedrals with a riot of fallen angels or victorious gods. I am sure that it was only because Michael Angelo was engaged in the ancient and honourable occupation of lying in bed that he ever realised how the roof of the Sistine Chapel might be made into an awful imitation of a divine drama that could only be acted in the heavens.

The tone now commonly taken toward the practice of lying in bed is hypocritical and unhealthy. Of all the marks of modernity that seem to mean a kind of decadence, there is none more menacing and dangerous than the exaltation of very small and secondary matters of conduct at the expense of very great and primary ones, at the expense of eternal public and tragic human morality. If there is one thing worse than the modern weakening of major morals it is the modern strengthening of minor morals. Thus it is considered more withering to accuse a man of bad taste than of bad ethics. Cleanliness is not next to godliness nowadays, for cleanliness is made an essential and godliness is regarded as an offense. A playwright may attack the institution of marriage so long as he does not misrepresent the manners of society; and I have met Ibsenite pessimists who thought it wrong to take beer, but right to take prussic acid. Especially this is so in matters of hygiene — notably such matters as lying in bed. Instead of being regarded, as it ought to be, as a matter of personal convenience and adjustment, it has come to be regarded by many as it if were a part of essential morals to get up early in the morning. It is, upon the whole, the part of practical wisdom; but there is nothing good about it or bad about its opposite.

Misers get up early in the morning; and burglars, I am informed, get up the night before. It is the great peril of our society that all its mechanism may grow more fixed while it grows more fickle. A man's minor actions and arrangements ought to be free, flexible creative; the things that should be unchangeable are his principles, his ideals. But with us the reverse is true: our views change constantly, but our lunch does not change. Now I shall like men to have strong and rooted conceptions, but as for their lunch, let them have it sometimes in the garden, sometimes in bed, sometimes on the roof, sometimes in the top of a tree. Let them argue from the same first principles, but let them do it in a bed, or a boat, or a balloon. This alarming growth of good habits really means a too great emphasis on those virtues which mere custom can misuse; it means too little emphasis on those virtues which gusto can never quite ensure, sudden and splendid virtues of inspired pity or of inspired candour. If ever that abrupt appeal is made to us, we may fail. A man can get used to getting up at five o'clock in the morning. A man cannot very well get used to being burned for his opinions; the first experiment is commonly fatal. Let us pay a little more attention to these possibilities of the heroic and the unexpected. I daresay that when I get out of this bed I shall do some deed of an almost terrible virtue.

For those who study the great art of lying in bed, there is one emphatic caution to be added. Even for those who can do their work in bed — like journalists — still more for those whose work cannot be done in bed — as, for example, the professional harpooner of whales — it is obvious that the indulgence must be very occasional. But that is not the caution I mean. The caution is this: if you do lie in bed, be sure you do it without any reason or justification at all. I do not speak, of course, of the seriously sick. But if a healthy man lies in bed, let him do it without a rag of excuse; then he will get up a healthy man. If he does it for some secondary hygienic reason, if he has some scientific explanation, he may get up a hypochondriac.

G. K. Chesterton, Tremendous Trifles

ZULEIKA DOBSON

1911

I

That old bell, presage of a train, had just sounded through Oxford station; and the undergraduates who were waiting there, gay figures in tweed or flannel, moved to the margin of the platform and gazed idly up the line. Young and careless, in the glow of the afternoon sunshine, they struck a sharp note of incongruity with the worn boards they stood on, with the fading signals and grey eternal walls of that antique station, which, familiar to them and insignificant, does yet whisper to the tourist the last enchantments of the Middle Age.

At the door of the first-class waiting-room, aloof and venerable, stood the Warden of Judas. An ebon pillar of tradition seemed he, in his garb of old-fashioned cleric. Aloft, between the wide brim of his silk hat and the white extent of his shirt-front, appeared those eyes which hawks, that nose which eagles, had often envied. He supported his years on an ebon stick. He alone was worthy of the background.

Came a whistle from the distance. The breast of an engine was descried, and a long train curving after it, under a flight of smoke. It grew and grew. Louder and louder, its noise foreran it. It became a furious, enormous monster, and, with an instinct for safety, all men receded from the platform's margin. (Yet came there with it, unknown to them, a danger far more terrible than itself.) Into the station it came blustering, with cloud and clangour. Ere it had yet stopped, the door of one carriage flew open, and from it, in a white travelling dress, in a toque a-twinkle with fine diamonds, a lithe and radiant creature slipped nimbly down to the platform.

A cynosure indeed! A hundred eyes were fixed on her, and half as many hearts were lost to her. The Warden of Judas himself had mounted on his nose a pair of black-rimmed glasses. Him espying, the nymph darted in his direction. The throng made way for her. She was at his side.

"Grandpa!" she cried, and kissed the old man on either cheek. (Not a youth there but would have bartered fifty years of his future for that salute.)

"My dear Zuleika," he said, "welcome to Oxford! Have you no luggage?"

"Heaps!" she answered. "And a maid who will find it."

"Then," said the Warden, "let us drive straight to the College." He offered her his arm, and they proceeded slowly to the entrance. She chatted gaily, blushing not in the long avenue of eyes she passed through. All the youths, under her spell, were now quite oblivious of the relatives they had come to meet. Parents, sisters, cousins, ran unclaimed about the platform. Undutiful, all the youths were forming a serried suite for their enchantress. In silence they followed her. They saw her leap into the Warden's landau, they saw the Warden seat himself upon her left. Nor was it until the landau was lost to sight that they turned — how slowly, and with how bad a grace! — to look for their relatives. . . .

The landau was rolling into "the Broad," over that ground which had once blackened under the fagots lit for Latimer and Ridley. It rolled past the portals of Balliol and Trinity, past the Ashmolean. From those pedestals which intersperse the railing of the Sheldonian, the high grim busts of the Roman Emperors stared down at the fair stranger in the equipage. Zuleika returned their stare with but a casual glance. The inanimate had little charm for her.

A moment later, a certain old don emerged from Blackwell's, where he had been buying books. Looking across the road, he saw, to his amazement, great beads of perspiration glistening on the brows of those Emperors. He trembled, and hurried away. That evening, in Common Room, he told what he had seen; and no amount of polite scepticism would convince him that it was but the hallucination of one who had been reading too much Mommsen. He persisted that he had seen what he described. It was not until two days had elapsed that some credence was accorded him.

Yes, as the landau rolled by, sweat started from the brows of the Emperors. They, at least, foresaw the peril that was overhanging Oxford, and they gave such warning as they could. Let that be remembered to their credit. Let that incline us to think more gently of them. In their lives, we know, they were infamous, some of them — "nihil non commiserunt stupri, saevitiae, impietatis." But are they too little punished, after all? Here in Oxford, exposed eternally and inexorably to heat and frost, to the four winds that lash them and the rains that wear them away, they are expiating, in effigy, the abominations of their

nihil, etc., there was nothing of the foul, savage, impious that they had not committed.

pride and cruelty and lust. Who were lechers, they
are without bodies; who were tyrants, they are
crowned never but with crowns of snow; who made
themselves even with the gods, they are by American
visitors frequently mistaken for the Twelve Apostles.
It is but a little way down the road that the two
Bishops perished for their faith, and even now we
do never pass the spot without a tear for them.
Yet how quickly they died in the flames! To these
Emperors, for whom none weeps, time will give no
surcease. . . .

II

The sun streamed through the bay-window of a
"best" bedroom in the Warden's house, and glorified
the pale crayon-portraits on the walls, the dimity
curtains, the old fresh chintz. He invaded the many
trunks which — all painted Z. D. — gaped, in various
stages of excavation, around the room. The doors of
the huge wardrobe stood, like the doors of Janus'
temple in time of war, majestically open; and the sun
seized this opportunity of exploring the mahogany re-
cesses. But the carpet, which had faded under his
immemorial visitations, was now almost *entirely* hidden from him, hidden under layers of fair fine linen,
layers of silk, brocade, satin, chiffon, muslin. All the
colours of the rainbow, materialized by modistes, were
there. Stacked on chairs were I know not what of
sachets, glove-cases, fan-cases. There were innumerable packages in silver-paper and pink ribands. There
was a pyramid of bandboxes. There was a virgin
forest of boot-trees. And rustling quickly hither and
thither, in and out of this profusion, with armfuls of
finery, was an obviously French maid. Alert, un-
erring, like a swallow she dipped and darted. Nothing

escaped her, and she never rested. She had the air of
the born unpacker — swift and firm, yet withal tender. Scarce had her arms been laden but their loads
were lying lightly between shelves or tightly in drawers. To calculate, catch, distribute, seemed in her but
a single process. She was one of those who are born to
make chaos cosmic.

Insomuch that ere the loud chapel-clock tolled another hour all the trunks had been sent empty away.
The carpet was unflecked by any scrap of silver-paper.
From the mantelpiece, photographs of Zuleika surveyed the room with a possessive air. Zuleika's pincushion, a-bristle with new pins, lay on the dimity-
flounced toilet-table, and round it stood a multitude
of multiform glass vessels, domed, all of them, with
dull gold, on which Z. D., in zianites and diamonds,
was encrusted. On a small table stood a great casket
of malachite, initialled in like fashion. On another
small table stood Zuleika's library. Both books
were in covers of dull gold. On the back of one cover
BRADSHAW, in beryls, was encrusted; on the back
of the other, A.B.C. GUIDE, in amethysts, beryls,
chrysoprases, and garnets. And Zuleika's great
cheval-glass stood ready to reflect her. Always it
travelled with her, in a great case specially made for
it. It was framed in ivory, and of fluted ivory were
the slim columns it swung between. Of gold were its
twin sconces, and four tall tapers stood in each of
them.

The door opened, and the Warden, with hospitable
words, left his grand-daughter at the threshold.

Zuleika wandered to her mirror. "Undress me,
Melisande," she said. Like all who are wont to appear by night before the public, she had the habit of
resting towards sunset.

Presently Melisande withdrew. Her mistress, in a white peignoir tied with a blue sash, lay in a great chintz chair, gazing out of the bay-window. The quadrangle below was very beautiful, with its walls of rugged grey, its cloisters, its grass carpet. But to her it was of no more interest than if it had been the rattling court-yard to one of those hotels in which she spent her life. She saw it, but heeded it not. She seemed to be thinking of herself, or of something she desired, or of some one she had never met. There was ennui, and there was wistfulness, in her gaze. Yet one would have guessed these things to be transient — to be no more than the little shadows that sometimes pass between a bright mirror and the brightness it reflects.

Zuleika was not strictly beautiful. Her eyes were a trifle large, and their lashes longer than they need have been. An anarchy of small curls was her chevelure, a dark upland of misrule, every hair asserting its rights over a not discreditable brow. For the rest, her features were not at all original. They seemed to have been derived rather from a gallimaufry of familiar models. From Madame la Marquise de Saint-Ouen came the shapely tilt of the nose. The mouth was a mere replica of Cupid's bow, lacquered scarlet and strung with the littlest pearls. No appletree, no wall of peaches, had not been robbed, nor any Tyrian rose-garden, for the glory of Miss Dobson's cheeks. Her neck was imitation-marble. Her hands and feet were of very mean proportions. She had no waist to speak of.

Yet, though a Greek would have railed at her asymmetry, and an Elizabethan have called her "gipsy," Miss Dobson now, in the midst of the Edvardian Era, was the toast of two hemispheres. . . .

Zuleika, on a desert island, would have spent her

time in looking for a man's foot-print. . . . As she sat
here in the bay-window of her room, she was not re-
viewing the splendid pageant of her past. She was a
young person whose reveries were never in retrospect.
For her the past was no treasury of distinct memories,
all horded and classified, some brighter than others,
and more highly valued. All memories were for her
but as the motes in one fused radiance that followed
her and made more luminous the pathway of her
future. She was always looking forward. She was
looking forward now — that shade of ennui had passed
from her face — to the week she was to spend in Oxford. A new city was a new toy to her, and — for it
was youth's homage that she loved best — this city of
youths was a toy after her own heart.

Aye, and it was youths who gave homage to her
most freely. She was of that high-stepping and flam-
boyant type that captivates youth most surely. Old
men and men of middle age admired her, but she had
not that flower-like quality of shyness and helplessness, that look of innocence, so dear to men who carry
life's secrets in their heads. Yet Zuleika *was* very
innocent, really. She was as pure as that young
shepherdess Marcella, who, all unguarded, roved the
mountains and was by all the shepherds adored. Like
Marcella, she had given her heart to no man, had preferred none. Youths were reputed to have died for
love of her, as Chrysostum died for love of the shepherdess; and she, like the shepherdess, had shed no
tear. When Chrysostum was lying on his bier in the
valley, and Marcella looked down from the high rock,
Ambrosio, the dead man's comrade, cried out on her,
upbraiding her with bitter words — "Oh, basilisk of
our mountains!" Nor do I think Ambrosio spoke too
strongly. Marcella cared nothing for men's admira-

tion, and yet, instead of retiring to one of those nun-
neries which are founded for her kind, she chose to
rove the mountains, causing despair to all the shepherds.[1] Zuleika, with her peculiar temperament,
would have gone mad in a nunnery. "But," you may
argue, "ought not she to have taken the veil, even at
the cost of her reason, rather than cause so much despair in the world? If Marcella was a basilisk, as you
seem to think, what about Miss Dobson?" Ah, but
Marcella knew quite well, boasted even, that she never
would or could love a man. Zuleika, on the other
hand, was a woman of really passionate fibre. She
may not have had that conscious, separate, and quite
explicit desire to be a mother with which modern play-
wrights credit every unmated member of her sex. But
she did know that she could love. And, surely, no
woman who knows that of herself can be rightly cen-
sured for not recluding herself from the world: it is
only women without the power to love who have no
right to provoke men's love.

Though Zuleika had never given her heart, strong in
her were the desire and the need that it should be
given. Withersoever she had fared, she had seen nothing but youths fatuously prostrate to her — not one
upright figure which she could respect. There were
the middle-aged men, the old men, who did not bow
down to her; but from middle-age, as from eld, she had
a sanguine aversion. She could love none but a youth.
Nor — though she herself, womanly, would utterly
base herself before her ideal — could she love one
who fell prone before her. And before her all youths
always did fall prone. She was an empress, and all
youths were her slaves. Their bondage delighted her,
as I have said. But no empress who has any pride

[1] Marcella and Chrysostum. The story is in *Don Quixote*.

could adore one of her slaves. Whom, then, could proud Zuleika adore? It was a question which sometimes troubled her. There were even moments when, looking into her cheval-glass, she cried out against that arrangement in comely lines and tints which got for her the dulia she delighted in. To be able to love once — would not that be better than all the homage in the world? But would she ever meet whom, looking up to him, she could love — she, the omnisubjugant? Would she ever, ever meet him? . . .

She gave a little laugh of coquetry. She laughed, and, long after, her lips were still parted in a smile.

So did she sit, smiling, wondering, with the fringes of her sash between her fingers, while the sun sank behind the opposite wall of the quadrangle, and the shadows crept out across the grass, thirsty for the dew.

Max Beerbohm, Zuleika Dobson, Chapters I and II

AN OLD WOMAN OF THE ROADS [1]

1912

The road was winding like a ribbon in and out of the mountains. On either side there were hedges and bushes. Little, stiff trees which held their foliage in their hands and dared the winds snatch a leaf from that grip. The hills were swelling and sinking, folding and soaring on every view. Now the silence was startled by the falling tinkle of a stream. Far away a cow lowed, a long, deep monotone, or a goat's call trembled from nowhere to nowhere. But mostly there was a silence which buzzed with a multitude of small, winged life. Going up the hills the Philosopher bent

dulia, reverence.

[1] From The Crock of Gold, by James Stephens. Copyright, 1912, by The Macmillan Company. Reprinted by permission.

forward to the gradient, stamping vigorously as he trod, almost snorting like a bull in the pride of successful energy. Coming down the slope he braced back and let his legs loose to do as they pleased. Didn't they know their business? — Good luck to them, and away!

As he walked along he saw an old woman hobbling in front of him. She was leaning on a stick and her hand was red and swollen with rheumatism. She hobbled by reason of the fact that there were stones in her shapeless boots. She was draped in the sorriest, miscellaneous rags that could be imagined, and these were knotted together so intricately that her clothing, having once been attached to her body, could never again be detached from it. As she walked she was mumbling and grumbling to herself, so that her mouth moved round and round in an india-rubber fashion.

The Philosopher soon caught up on her.

"Good morrow, ma'am," said he.

But she did not hear him: she seemed to be listening to the pain which the stones in her boots gave her.

"Good morrow, ma'am," said the Philosopher again.

This time she heard him and replied, turning her old, bleared eyes slowly in his direction —

"Good morrow to yourself, sir," said she, and the Philosopher thought her old face was a very kindly one.

"What is it that is wrong with you, ma'am?" said he.

"It's my boots, sir," she replied. "Full of stones they are, the way I can hardly walk at all, God help me!"

"Why don't you shake them out?"

"Ah, sure, I couldn't be bothered, sir, for there are so many holes in the boots that more would get in before I could take two steps, and an old woman can't be always fidgeting, God help her!"

There was a little house on one side of the road, and when the old woman saw this place she brightened a little.

"Do you know who lives in that house?" said the Philosopher.

"I do not," she replied, "but it's a real nice house with clean windows and a shiny knocker on the door, and smoke in the chimney — I wonder would herself give me a cup of tea now if I asked her — A poor old woman walking the roads on a stick! and maybe a bit of meat, or an egg perhaps . . .'

"You could ask," suggested the Philosopher gently.

"Maybe I will, too," said she, and she sat down by the road just outside the house and the Philosopher also sat down.

A little puppy dog came from behind the house and approached them cautiously. Its intentions were friendly, but it had already found that amicable advances are sometimes indifferently received, for, as it drew near, it wagged its dubious tail and rolled humbly on the ground. But very soon the dog discovered that here there was no evil, for it trotted to the old woman, and without any more preparation jumped into her lap.

The old woman grinned at the dog —

"Ah, you thing you!" said she, and she gave it her finger to bite. The delighted puppy chewed her bony finger, and then instituted a mimic warfare against a piece of rag that fluttered from her breast, barking and growling in joyous excitement, while the old woman fondled and hugged it.

The door of the house opposite opened quickly, and a woman with a frost-bitten face came out.

"Leave that dog down," said she.

The old woman grinned humbly at her.

"Sure, ma'am, I wouldn't hurt the little dog, the thing!"

"Put down that dog," said the woman, "and go about your business — the likes of you ought to be arrested."

A man in shirt sleeves appeared behind her, and at him the old woman grinned even more humbly.

"Let me sit here for a while and play with the little dog, sir," said she, "sure the roads do be lonesome ——"

The man stalked close and grabbed the dog by the scruff of the neck. It hung between his finger and thumb with its tail tucked between its legs, and its eyes screwed round on one side in amazement.

"Be off with you out of that, you old strap!" said the man in a terrible voice.

So the old woman rose painfully to her feet again, and as she went hobbling along the dusty road she began to cry.

The Philosopher also arose, he was very indignant, but did not know what to do. A singular lassitude also prevented him from interfering. As they paced along his companion began mumbling, more to herself than to him —

"Ah, God be with me," said she, "an old woman on a stick, that hasn't a place in the wide world to go to or a neighbor itself . . . I wish I could get a cup of tea, so I do, I wish to God I could get a cup of tea. . . . Me sitting down in my own little house, with the white tablecloth on the table, and the butter in the dish, and the strong, red tea in the teacup; and me pouring cream into it, and, maybe, telling the children not to be wasting the sugar, the things! and himself saying he'd got to mow the big field to-day, or that the red cow was going to calve, the poor thing! and that if the boys went to school, who was going to weed the turnips — and me sitting drinking my strong cup of tea, and telling him where that old trapesing hen was laying. . . . Ah, God be with me! an old creature hobbling along the roads on a stick. I wish I was a young girl again, so I do, and himself coming courting me, and him saying that I was a real nice little girl surely, and that nothing would make him happy or easy at all but me to be loving him — Ah, the kind man that he was, to be sure, the kind, decent man. . . . And Sorca Reilly to be trying to get him from me, and Kate Finnegan with her bold eyes looking after him in the Chapel; and him to be saying that along with me they were only a pair of old nanny goats . . . And then me to be getting married and going home to my own little house with my man — ah, God be with me! And him kissing me, and laughing, and frightening me with his goings on. Ah, the kind man, with his soft eyes, and his nice voice, and his jokes and laughing, and him thinking the world and all of me — ay, indeed. . . . And the neighbors to be coming in and sitting round the fire in the night time, putting the world through each-other, and talking about France and Russia and them other queer places, and him holding up the discourse like a learned man, and them all listening to him and nodding their heads at each other, and wondering at his education and all: or, maybe, the neighbors to be singing, or him making me sing the Coulin, and him to be proud of me . . . and then him to be killed on me with a cold on his chest. . . . Ah then, God be with me, a lone, old creature on a stick and the sun shining into her eyes and her thirsty — I wish I had a cup of tea, so I do. I wish to God had a cup of tea and a bit of meat . . . or, maybe, an egg. A nice fresh egg laid by the speckledy hen that used to be giving me all the trouble, the thing! . . . Sixteen hens I had, and they were the ones for laying, surely. . . . It's the queer world, so it is, the queer world — and the things that do happen for no reason at all . . . Ah, God be with me! I wish there weren't stones in my boots, so I do, and I wish to God I had a cup of tea and a fresh egg. Ah, glory be, my old legs are getting tireder every day, so they are. Wisha, one time — when himself was in it — I could go about the house all day long, cleaning the place, and feeding the pigs, and the hens and all, and then dance half the night, so I could: and himself proud of me. . . ."

The old woman turned up a little rambling road and went on still talking to herself, and the Philosopher watched her go up that road for a long time. He was very glad she had gone away, and as he tramped forward he banished her sad image so that in a little time he was happy again. The sun was still shining, the birds were flying on every side, and the wide hillside above him smiled gaily.

James Stephens, The Crock of Gold, Chapter XI

THE LOST SILK HAT [1]

1913

The Caller stands on a doorstep, "faultlessly dressed," but without a hat. At first he shows despair, then a new thought engrosses him.

Enter the Laborer.

The Caller. Excuse me a moment. Excuse me — but — I'd be greatly obliged to you if — if you could see your way — in fact, you can be of great service to me if ——

The Laborer. Glad to do what I can, sir.

The Caller. Well, all I really want you to do is just to ring that bell and go up and say — er — say that you've come to see to the drains, or anything like that, you know, and get hold of my hat for me.

Laborer. Get hold of your 'at!

Caller. Yes. You see, I left my hat behind most unfortunately. It's in the drawing-room (*points to window*), that room there, half under the long sofa, the far end of the room. And if you could possibly go and get it, why I'd be (*the Laborer's expression changes*) — Why, what's the matter?

Laborer (*firmly*). I don't like this job.

Caller. Don't like this job! But my dear fellow, don't be silly, what possible harm ——?

Laborer. Ah-h. That's what I don't know.

Caller. But what harm can there possibly be in so simple a request? What harm does there seem to be?

Laborer. Oh, it seems all right.

Caller. *Well,* then.

Laborer. All these crack jobs seem all right.

Caller. But I'm not asking you to rob the house.

Laborer. Don't seem as if you are, certainly, but I don't like the looks of it; what if there's things what I can't 'elp taking when I gets inside?

Caller. I only want my hat —— Here, I say, please don't go away — here's a sovereign, it will only take you a minute.

Laborer. *What I want to know ——*

Caller. Yes?

Laborer. — Is what's *in* that hat?

Caller. What's *in* the hat?

Laborer. Yes; that's what I want to know.

Caller. What's *in* the hat?

Laborer. Yes, you aren't going to give me a sovereign ———?

Caller. I'll give you two sovereigns.

Laborer. You aren't going to give me a sovereign, and rise it to two sovereigns, for an *empty* hat.

Caller. But I must have my hat. I can't be seen in the streets like this. There's nothing *in* the hat. What do you think's in the hat?

Laborer. Ah, I'M not clever enough to say *that*, but it looks as if the papers was in that hat.

Caller. The papers?

Laborer. Yes, the papers proving, if you can get them, that you're the heir to that big house, and some poor innocent will be defrauded.

Caller. Look here, the hat's absolutely empty. I *must* have my hat. If there's anything in it you shall have it yourself as well as the two pounds, only get me my hat.

Laborer. Well, that seems all right.

Caller. That's right, then you'll run up and get it?

Laborer. Seems all right to me, and seems all right to you. But it's the police what you and I have got to think of. Will it seem all right to them?

Caller. Oh, for heaven's sake ———

Laborer. Ah!

Caller. What a hopeless fool you are.

Laborer. Ah!

Caller. Look here.

Laborer. Ah, I got you there, mister.

Caller. Look here, for goodness sake, don't go.

Laborer. Ah!   (*Exit.*)

Enter the Clerk.

Caller. Excuse me, sir. Excuse my asking you, but,

as you see, I am without a hat. I shall be extra-ordinarily obliged to you if you would be so very good as to get it for me. Pretend you have come to wind the clocks, you know. I left it in the drawing-room of this house, half under the long sofa, the far end.

Clerk. Oh, er — all right, only ——

Caller. Thanks so much, I am immensely indebted to you. Just say you've come to wind the clocks, you know.

Clerk. I — er — don't think I'm very good at winding clocks, you know.

Caller. Oh, that's all right, just stand in front of the clock and fool about with it. That's all they ever do. I must warn you there's a lady in the room.

Clerk. Oh!

Caller. But that's all right, you know. Just walk past up to the clock.

Clerk. But I think, if you don't mind, as there's some one there ——

Caller. Oh, but she's quite young and very, very beautiful and ——

Clerk. Why don't you get it yourself?

Caller. That is impossible.

Clerk. Impossible?

Caller. Yes, I have sprained my ankle.

Clerk. Oh! Is it bad?

Caller. Yes, very bad indeed.

Clerk. I don't mind trying to carry you up.

Caller. No, that would be worse. My foot has to be kept on the ground.

Clerk. But how will you get home?

Caller. I can walk all right on the flat.

Clerk. I'm afraid I have to be going. It's rather later than I thought.

Caller. But for goodness sake don't leave me. You can't leave me here like this without a hat.

Clerk. I'm afraid I must, it's later than I thought.

                          (*Exit.*)

Enter the Poet.

Caller. Excuse me, sir. Excuse my stopping you. But I should be immensely obliged to you if you would do me a very great favor. I have unfortunately left my hat behind while calling at this house. It is half under the long sofa, at the far end. If you could possibly be so kind as to pretend you have come to tune the piano and fetch my hat for me I should be enormously grateful to you.

Poet. But why cannot you get it for yourself?

Caller. I cannot.

Poet. If you would tell me the reason perhaps I could help you.

Caller. I cannot. I can never enter that house again.

Poet. If you have committed a murder, by all means tell me. I am not sufficiently interested in ethics to wish to have you hanged for it.

Caller. Do I look like a murderer?

Poet. No, of course not. I am only saying that you can safely trust me, for not only does the statute book and its penalties rather tend to bore me, but murder itself has always had a certain fascination for me. I write delicate and fastidious lyrics, yet, strange as it may appear, I read every murder trial, and my sympathies are always with the prisoner.

Caller. But I tell you I am not a murderer.

Poet. Then what have you done?

Caller. I have quarrelled with a lady in that house and have sworn to join the Bosnians and die in Africa.

Poet. But this is beautiful.

Caller. Unfortunately I forgot my hat.

Poet. You go to die for a hopeless love, and in a far country; it was the wont of the troubadours.

Caller. But you will get my hat for me?

Poet. That I will gladly do for you. But we must find an adequate reason for entering the house.

Caller. You pretend to tune the piano.

Poet. That, unfortunately, is impossible. The sound of a piano being unskilfully handled is to me what the continual drop of cold water on the same part of the head is said to be in countries where that interesting torture is practised. There is ———

Caller. But what are you to do?

Poet. There is a house where kind friends of mine have given me that security and comfort that are a poet's necessity. But there was a governess there and a piano. It is years and years since I was able even to see the faces of those friends without an awkward shudder.

Caller. Well, we'll have to think of something else.

Poet. You are bringing back to these unhappy days the romance of an age of which the ballads tell us that kings sometimes fought in no other armor than their lady's nightshirt.

Caller. Yes, but you know first of all I must get my hat.

Poet. But why?

Caller. I cannot possibly be seen in the streets without a hat.

Poet. Why not?

Caller. It can't be done.

Poet. But you confuse externals with essentials.

Caller. I don't know what you call essentials, but being decently dressed in London seems pretty essential to me.

Poet. A hat is not one of the essential things of life.

Caller. I don't want to appear rude, but my hat isn't quite like yours.

Poet. Let us sit down and talk of things that matter, things that will be remembered after a hundred years. (*They sit.*) Regarded in this light one sees at once the triviality of hats. But to die, and die beautifully for a hopeless love, that is a thing one could make a lyric about. That is the test of essential things — try and imagine them in a lyric. One could not write a lyric about a hat.

Caller. I don't care whether you could write a lyric about my hat or whether you couldn't. All I know is that I am not going to make myself absolutely ridiculous by walking about in London without a hat. Will you get it for me or will you not?

Poet. To take any part in the tuning of a piano is impossible to me.

Caller. Well, pretend you've come to look at the radiator. They have one under the window, and I happen to know it leaks.

Poet. I suppose it has an artistic decoration on it.

Caller. Yes, I think so.

Poet. Then I decline to look at it or to go near it. I know these decorations in cast iron. I once saw a pot-bellied Egyptian god, named Bēs, and he was *meant* to be ugly, but he wasn't as ugly as these decorations that the twentieth century can make with machinery. What has a plumber got to do with art that he should dare to attempt decoration?

Caller. Then you won't help me?

Poet. I won't look at ugly things and I won't listen to ugly noises, but if you can think of any reasonable plan I don't mind helping you.

Caller. I can think of nothing else. You don't

look like a plumber or a clock-winder. I can think of nothing more. I have had a terrible ordeal and I am not in the condition to think calmly.

Poet. Then you will have to leave your hat to its altered destiny.

Caller. Why can't you think of a plan? If you're a poet, thinking's rather in your line.

Poet. If I could bring my thoughts to contemplate so absurd a thing as a hat for any length of time no doubt I could think of a plan, but the very triviality of the theme seems to scare them away.

Caller (*rising*). Then I must get it myself.

Poet. For Heaven's sake, don't do that! Think what it means!

Caller. I know it will seem absurd, but not so absurd as walking through London without it.

Poet. I don't mean that. But you will make it up. You will forgive each other, and you will marry her and have a family of noisy, pimply children like everyone else, and Romance will be dead. No, don't ring that bell. Go and buy a bayonet, or whatever one does buy, and join the Bosnians.

Caller. I tell you I can't without a hat.

Poet. What is a hat! Will you sacrifice for it a beautiful doom? Think of your bones, neglected and forgotten, lying forlornly because of hopeless love on endless golden sands. "Lying forlorn!" as Keats said. What a word! Forlorn in Africa. The careless Bedouins going past by day, at night the lion's roar, the grievous voice of the desert.

Caller. As a matter of fact, I don't think you're right in speaking of it as desert. The Bosnians, I believe, are only taking it because it is supposed to be the most fertile land in the world.

Poet. What of that? You will not be remembered

by geography and statistics, but by golden-mouthed Romance. And that is how Romance sees Africa.

Caller. Well, I'm going to get my hat.

Poet. Think! Think! If you enter that door you will never fall among the foremost Bosnians. You will never die in a far-off, lonely land to lie by immense Sahara. And she will never weep for your beautiful doom and call herself cruel in vain.

Caller. Hark! She is playing the piano. It seems to me that she might be unhappy about it for years. I don't see much good in that.

Poet. No. *I* will comfort her.

Caller. I'm damned if you do! Look here! I don't mind saying, I'm damned if you do.

Poet. Calm yourself. Calm yourself. I do not mean in that way.

Caller. Then what on earth do you mean?

Poet. I will make songs about your beautiful death, glad songs and sad songs. They shall be glad because they tell again the noble tradition of the troubadours, and sad because they tell of your sorrowful destiny and of your hopeless love. I shall make legends also about your lonely bones, telling perhaps how some Arabian men, finding them in the desert by some oasis, memorable in war, wonder who loved them. And then as I read them to her, she weeps perhaps a little, and I read instead of the glory of the soldier, how it overtops our transitory ——

Caller. Look here, I'm not aware that you've ever been introduced to her.

Poet. A trifle, a trifle.

Caller. It seems to me that you're in rather an undue hurry for me to get a Jubu spear in me; but I'm going to get my hat first.

Poet. I appeal to you. I appeal to you in the name

of beautiful battles, high deeds, and lost causes; in the name of love-tales told to cruel maidens and told in vain. In the name of stricken hearts broken like beautiful harp-strings, I appeal to you. I appeal in the ancient holy name of Romance: *do not ring that bell.*

(Caller rings the bell.)

Poet (sits down, abject). You will marry. You will sometimes take a ticket with your wife as far as Paris. Perhaps as far as Cannes. Then the family will come: a large sprawling family as far as the eye can see (I speak in hyperbole). You'll earn money and feed it and be like all the rest. No monument will ever be set up to your memory but ——

(Servant answers bell. Caller says something inaudible. Exit through door.)

But let there be graven in brass upon this house: Romance was born again here out of due time and died young.   *(He sits down.)*

Enter Laborer and Clerk with Policeman. The music stops.

Policeman. Anything wrong here?

Poet. Everything's wrong. They're going to kill Romance.

Policeman (to Laborer). This gentleman doesn't seem quite right somehow.

Laborer. They're none of them quite right to-day.

(Music starts again.)

Poet. My God! It is a duet.

Policeman. He seems a bit wrong somehow.

Laborer. You should'a seen the other one.

CURTAIN

Lord Dunsany, Five Plays, 1917

THE PLACE OF SCIENCE IN A LIBERAL EDUCATION

1913

I

Science, to the ordinary reader of newspapers, is represented by a varying selection of sensational triumphs, such as wireless telegraphy and aeroplanes, radio-activity and the marvels of modern alchemy. It is not of this aspect of science that I wish to speak. Science, in this respect, consists of detached up-to-date fragments, interesting only until they are replaced by something newer and more up-to-date, displaying nothing of the systems of patiently constructed knowledge out of which, almost as a casual incident, have come the practically useful results which interest the man in the street. The increased command over the forces of nature which is derived from science is undoubtedly an amply sufficient reason for encouraging scientific research, but this reason has been so often urged and is so easily appreciated that other reasons, to my mind quite as important, are apt to be overlooked. It is with these other reasons, especially with the intrinsic value of a scientific habit of mind in forming our outlook on the world, that I shall be concerned in what follows.

The instance of wireless telegraphy will serve to illustrate the difference between the two points of view. Almost all the serious intellectual labour required for the possibility of this invention is due to three men — Faraday, Maxwell, and Hertz.[1] In alternating layers of experiment and theory these three men built up the modern theory of electro-magnetism,

[1] Michael Faraday (1791–1867), English chemist and physicist; James Clerk Maxwell (1831–1879), Scottish physicist; Heinrich Hertz (1857–1894), German physicist.

and demonstrated the identity of light with electro-magnetic waves. The system which they discovered is one of profound intellectual interest, bringing together and unifying an endless variety of apparently detached phenomena, and displaying a cumulative mental power which cannot but afford delight to every generous spirit. The mechanical details which remained to be adjusted in order to utilize their discoveries for a practical system of telegraphy demanded, no doubt, very considerable ingenuity, but had not that broad sweep and that universality which could give them intrinsic interest as an object of disinterested contemplation.

From the point of view of training the mind, of giving that well-informed, impersonal outlook which constitutes culture in the good sense of this much-abused word, it seems to be generally held indisputable that a literary education is superior to one based on science. Even the warmest advocates of science are apt to rest their claims on the contention that culture ought to be sacrificed to utility. Those men of science who respect culture, when they associate with men learned in the classics, are apt to admit, not merely politely, but sincerely, a certain inferiority on their side, compensated doubtless by the services which science renders to humanity, but none the less real. And so long as this attitude exists among men of science, it tends to verify itself: the intrinsically valuable aspects of science tend to be sacrificed to the merely useful, and little attempt is made to preserve that leisurely, systematic survey by which the finer quality of the mind is formed and nourished.

But even if there be, in present fact, any such inferiority as is supposed in the educational value of science, this is, I believe, not the fault of science, itself but the fault of the spirit in which science is taught. If its full possibilities were realised by those who teach it, I believe that its capacity of producing those habits of mind which constitute the highest mental excellence would be at least as great as that of literature, and more particularly of Greek and Latin literature. In saying this I have no wish whatever to disparage a classical education. I have not myself enjoyed its benefits, and my knowledge of Greek and Latin authors is derived almost wholly from translations. But I am firmly persuaded that the Greeks fully deserve all the admiration that is bestowed upon them, and that it is a very great and serious loss to be unacquainted with their writings. It is not by attacking them, but by drawing attention to neglected excellences in science, that I wish to conduct my argument.

One defect, however, does seem inherent in a purely classical education — namely, a too exclusive emphasis on the past. By the study of what is absolutely ended and can never be renewed, a habit of criticism towards the present and the future is engendered. The qualities in which the present excels are qualities to which the study of the past does not direct attention, and to which, therefore, the student of Greek civilisation may easily become blind. In what is new and growing there is apt to be something crude, insolent, even a little vulgar, which is shocking to the man of sensitive taste; quivering from the rough contact, he retires to the trim gardens of a polished past, forgetting that they were reclaimed from the wilderness by men as rough and earth-soiled as those from whom he shrinks in his own day. The habit of being unable to recognise merit until it is dead is too apt to be the result of a purely bookish life, and a culture based wholly on the past will seldom be able to pierce through everyday surroundings to the essential splendour of contemporary things, or to the hope of still greater splendour in the future.

> "My eyes saw not the men of old;
> And now their age away has rolled.
> I weep — to think I shall not see
> The heroes of posterity."

So says the Chinese poet; but such impartiality is rare in the more pugnacious atmosphere of the West, where the champions of the past and future fight a never-ending battle, instead of combining to seek out the merits of both.

This consideration, which militates not only against the exclusive study of the classics, but against every form of culture which has become static, traditional, and academic, leads inevitably to the fundamental question: What is the true end of education? But before attempting to answer this question it will be well to define the sense in which we are to use the word "education." For this purpose I shall distinguish the sense in which I mean to use it from two others, both perfectly legitimate, the one broader and the other narrower than the sense in which I mean to use the word.

In the broader sense, education will include not only what we learn through instruction, but all that we learn through personal experience — the formation of character through the education of life. Of this aspect of education, vitally important as it is, I will say nothing, since its consideration would introduce topics quite foreign to the question with which we are concerned.

In the narrower sense, education may be confined to

instruction, the imparting of definite information on various subjects, because such information, in and for itself, is useful in daily life. Elementary education — reading, writing, and arithmetic — is almost wholly of this kind. But instruction, necessary as it is, does not *per se* constitute education in the sense in which I wish to consider it.

Education, in the sense in which I mean it, may be defined as *the formation, by means of instruction, of certain mental habits and a certain outlook on life and the world.* It remains to ask ourselves, what mental habits, and what sort of outlook, can be hoped for as the result of instruction? When we have answered this question we can attempt to decide what science has to contribute to the formation of the habits and outlook which we desire.

Our whole life is built about a certain number — not a very small number — of primary instincts and impulses. Only what is in some way connected with these instincts and impulses appears to us desirable or important; there is no faculty, whether "reason" or "virtue" or whatever it may be called, that can take our active life and our hopes and fears outside the region controlled by these first movers of all desire. Each of them is like a queen-bee, aided by a hive of workers gathering honey; but when the queen is gone the workers languish and die, and the cells remain empty of their expected sweetness. So with each primary impulse in civilised man: it is surrounded and protected by a busy swarm of attendant derivative desires, which store up in its service whatever honey the surrounding world affords. But if the queen-impulse dies, the death-dealing influence, though retarded a little by habit, spreads slowly through all the subsidiary impulses, and a whole tract of life becomes inexplicably colourless. What was formerly full of zest, and so obviously worth doing that it raised no questions, has now grown dreary and purposeless: with a sense of disillusion we inquire the meaning of life, and decide, perhaps, that all is vanity. The search for an outside meaning that can *compel* an inner response must always be disappointed: all "meaning" must be at bottom related to our primary desires, and when they are extinct no miracle can restore to the world that value which they reflected upon it.

The purpose of education, therefore, cannot be to create any primary impulse which is lacking in the uneducated; the purpose can only be to enlarge the scope of those that human nature provides, by increasing the number and variety of attendant thoughts, and by showing where the most permanent satisfaction is to be found. Under the impulse of a Calvinistic horror of the "natural man," this obvious truth has been too often misconceived in the training of the young; "nature" has been falsely regarded as excluding all that is best in what is natural, and the endeavour to teach virtue has led to the production of stunted and contorted hypocrites instead of full-grown human beings. From such mistakes in education a better psychology or a kinder heart is beginning to preserve the present generation; we need, therefore, waste no more words on the theory that the purpose of education is to thwart or eradicate nature.

But although nature must supply the initial force of desire, nature is not, in the civilised man, the spasmodic, fragmentary, and yet violent set of impulses that it is in the savage. Each impulse has its constitutional ministry of thought and knowledge and reflection, through which possible conflicts of impulses are foreseen, and temporary impulses are controlled by the unifying impulse which may be called wisdom. In this way education destroys the crudity of instinct, and increases through knowledge the wealth and variety of the individual's contacts with the outside world, making him no longer an isolated fighting unit, but a citizen of the universe, embracing distant countries, remote regions of space, and vast stretches of past and future within the circle of his interests. It is this simultaneous softening in the insistence of desire and enlargement of its scope that is the chief moral end of education.

Closely connected with this moral end is the more purely intellectual aim of education, the endeavour to make us see and imagine the world in an objective manner, as far as possible as it is in itself, and not merely through the distorting medium of personal desire. The complete attainment of such an objective view is no doubt an ideal, indefinitely approachable, but not actually and fully realisable. Education, considered as a process of forming our mental habits and our outlook on the world, is to be judged successful in proportion as its outcome approximates to this ideal; in proportion, that is to say, as it gives us a true view of our place in society, of the relation of the whole human society to its non-human environment, and of the nature of the non-human world as it is in itself apart from our desires and interests. If this standard is admitted, we can return to the consideration of science, inquiring how far science contributes to such an aim, and whether it is in any way superior to its rivals in educational practice.

II

Two opposite and at first sight conflicting merits belong to science as against literature and art. The one, which is not inherently necessary, but is certainly true at the present day, is hopefulness as to the future of human achievement, and in particular as to the useful work that may be accomplished by an intelligent student. This merit and the cheerful outlook which it engenders prevent what might otherwise be the depressing effect of another aspect of science, to my mind also a merit, and perhaps its greatest merit — I mean the irrelevance of human passions and of the whole subjective apparatus where scientific truth is concerned. Each of these reasons for preferring the study of science requires some amplification. Let us begin with the first.

In the study of literature or art our attention is perpetually riveted upon the past: the men of Greece or of the Renaissance did better than any men do now; the triumphs of former ages, so far from facilitating fresh triumphs in our own age, actually increase the difficulty of fresh triumphs by rendering originality harder of attainment; not only is artistic achievement not cumulative, but it seems even to depend upon a certain freshness and *naïveté* of impulse and vision which civilisation tends to destroy. Hence comes, to those who have been nourished on the literary and artistic productions of former ages, a certain peevishness and undue fastidiousness towards the present, from which there seems no escape except into the deliberate vandalism which ignores tradition and in the search after originality achieves only the eccentric. But in such vandalism there is none of the simplicity and spontaneity out of which great art springs: theory is still the canker in its core, and insincerity destroys the advantages of a merely pretended ignorance.

The despair thus arising from an education which suggests no pre-eminent mental activity except that of artistic creation is wholly absent from an education which gives the knowledge of scientific method. The discovery of scientific method, except in pure mathematics, is a thing of yesterday; speaking broadly, we may say that it dates from Galileo.[1] Yet already it has transformed the world, and its success proceeds with ever-accelerating velocity. In science men have discovered an activity of the very highest value in which they are no longer, as in art, dependent for progress upon the appearance of continually greater genius, for in science the successors stand upon the shoulders of their predecessors; where one man of supreme genius has invented a method, a thousand lesser men can apply it. No transcendent ability is required in order to make useful discoveries in science; the edifice of science needs its masons, bricklayers, and common labourers as well as its foremen, master-builders, and architects. In art nothing worth doing can be done without genius; in science even a very moderate capacity can contribute to a supreme achievement.

In science the man of real genius is the man who invents a new method. The notable discoveries are often made by his successors, who can apply the method with fresh vigour, unimpaired by the previous labour of perfecting it; but the mental calibre of the thought required for their work, however brilliant, is not so great as that required by the first inventor of the method. There are in science immense numbers of different methods, appropriate to different classes of problems; but over and above them all, there is something not easily definable, which may be called *the* method of science. It was formerly customary to identify this with the inductive method, and to asso-

[1] Galileo Galilei (1564–1642), Italian astronomer and physicist.

ciate it with the name of Bacon. But the true inductive method was not discovered by Bacon, and the true method of science is something which includes deduction as much as induction, logic and mathematics as much as botany and geology. I shall not attempt the difficult task of stating what the scientific method is, but I will try to indicate the temper of mind out of which the scientific method grows, which is the second of the two merits that were mentioned above as belonging to a scientific education.

The kernel of the scientific outlook is a thing so simple, so obvious, so seemingly trivial, that the mention of it may almost excite derision. The kernel of the scientific outlook is the refusal to regard our own desires, tastes, and interests as affording a key to the understanding of the world. Stated thus baldly, this may seem no more than a trite truism. But to remember it consistently in matters arousing our passionate partisanship is by no means easy, especially where the available evidence is uncertain and inclusive. A few illustrations will make this clear.

Aristotle, I understand, considered that the stars must move in circles because the circle is the most perfect curve. In the absence of evidence to the contrary, he allowed himself to decide a question of fact by an appeal to æsthetico-moral considerations. In such a case it is at once obvious to us that this appeal was unjustifiable. We know now how to ascertain as a fact the way in which the heavenly bodies move, and we know that they do not move in circles, or even in accurate eclipses, or in any other kind of simply describable curve. This may be painful to a certain hankering after simplicity of pattern in the universe, but we know that in astronomy such feelings are irrelevant. Easy as this knowledge seems now, we owe it to the courage and insight of the first inventors of scientific method, and more especially of Galileo.

We may take as another illustration Malthus's [1] doctrine of population. This illustration is all the better for the fact that his actual doctrine is now known to be largely erroneous. It is not his conclusions that are valuable, but the temper and method of his inquiry. As everyone knows, it was to him that Darwin owed an essential part of his theory of natural selection, and this was only possible because Malthus's outlook was truly scientific. His great merit lies in considering man not as the object of praise or blame, but as a part of nature, a thing with a certain characteristic behaviour from which certain consequences must follow. If the behaviour is not quite what Malthus supposed, if the consequences are not quite what he inferred, that may falsify his conclusions, but does not impair the value of his method. The objections which were made when his doctrine was new — that it was horrible and depressing, that people ought not to act as he said they did, and so on — were all such as implied an unscientific attitude of mind; as against all of them, his calm determination to treat man as a natural phenomenon marks an important advance over the reformers of the eighteenth century and the Revolution.

Under the influence of Darwinism the scientific attitude towards man has now become fairly common, and is to some people quite natural, though to most it is still a difficult and artificial intellectual contortion. There is, however, one study which is as yet almost wholly untouched by the scientific spirit — I mean the

[1] Thomas Robert Malthus (1766–1834), English economist. The doctrine referred to was the proposition that "population increases in a geometrical, food in an arithmetical ratio."

study of philosophy. Philosophers and the public imagine that the scientific spirit must pervade pages that bristle with allusions to ions, germ plasms, and the eyes of shell-fish. But as the devil can quote Scripture, so the philosopher can quote science. The scientific spirit is not an affair of quotation, of externally acquired information, any more than manners are an affair of the etiquette-book. The scientific attitude of mind involves a sweeping away of all other desires in the interests of the desire to know — it involves suppression of hopes and fears, loves and hates, and the whole subjective emotional life, until we become subdued to the material, able to see it frankly, without preconceptions, without bias, without any wish except to see it as it is, and without any belief that what it is must be determined by some relation, positive or negative, to what we should like it to be, or to what we can easily imagine it to be.

Now in philosophy this attitude of mind has not as yet been achieved. A certain self-absorption, not personal, but human, has marked almost all attempts to conceive the universe as a whole. Mind, or some aspect of it — thought or will or sentience — has been regarded as the pattern after which the universe is to be conceived, for no better reason, at bottom, than that such a universe would not seem strange, and would give us the cosy feeling that every place is like home. To conceive the universe as essentially progressive or essentially deteriorating, for example, is to give our hopes and fears a cosmic importance which *may*, of course, be justified, but which we have as yet no reason to suppose justified. Until we have learnt to think of it in ethically neutral terms, we have not arrived at a scientific attitude in philosophy; and until we have arrived at such an attitude, it is hardly to be hoped that philosophy will achieve any solid results.

I have spoken so far largely of the negative aspect of the scientific spirit, but it is from the positive aspect that its value is derived. The instinct of constructiveness, which is one of the chief incentives to artistic creation, can find in scientific systems a satisfaction more massive than any epic poem. Disinterested curiosity, which is the source of almost all intellectual effort, finds with astonished delight that science can unveil secrets which might well have seemed for ever undiscoverable. The desire for a larger life and wider interests, for an escape from private circumstances, and even from the whole recurring human cycle of birth and death, is fulfilled by the impersonal cosmic outlook of science as by nothing else. To all these must be added, as contributing to the happiness of the man of science, the admiration of splendid achievement, and the consciousness of inestimable utility to the human race. A life devoted to science is therefore a happy life, and its happiness is derived from the very best sources that are open to dwellers on this troubled and passionate planet.

  Bertrand Russell, Mysticism and Logic, 1925 (first published in *The New Statesman,* May, 1913).

THE STORY OF FANNY PRICE

1915

When he arrived in Paris Philip had his luggage put on a cab and trundled off slowly through the gay streets, over the bridge, and along the narrow ways of the Latin Quarter. He had taken a room at the Hotel des Deux Écoles, which was in a shabby street off the Boulevard du Montparnasse; it was convenient for Amitrano's School at which he was going to work. A waiter took his box up five flights of stairs, and Philip was shown into a tiny room, fusty from unopened windows, the greater part of which was taken up by a large wooden bed with a canopy over it of red rep; there were heavy curtains on the windows of the same dingy material; the chest of drawers served also as a washing-stand; and there was a massive wardrobe of the style which is connected with the good King Louis Philippe. The wall-paper was discolored with age; it was dark gray, and there could be vaguely seen on it garlands of brown leaves. To Philip the room seemed quaint and charming.

Though it was late he felt too excited to sleep and, going out, made his way into the boulevard and walked towards the light. This led him to the station; and the square in front of it, vivid with arc-lamps, noisy with the yellow trams that seemed to cross it in all directions, made him laugh aloud with joy. There were cafés all round, and by chance, thirsty and eager to get a nearer sight of the crowd, Philip installed himself at a little table outside the Café de Versailles. Every other table was taken, for it was a fine night; and Philip looked curiously at the people, here little family groups, there a knot of men with odd-shaped hats and beards talking loudly and gesticulating; next to him were two men who looked like painters with women who Philip hoped were not their lawful wives; behind him he heard Americans loudly arguing on art. His soul was thrilled. He sat very late, tired out but too happy to move, and when at last he went to bed he was wide awake; he listened to the manifold noise of Paris.

II

Next morning at the stroke of nine, trying to seem self-assured, he presented himself at the school. Mrs. Otter [1] was already there, and she came forward with a friendly smile. He had been anxious about the reception he would have as a *nouveau*, for he had read a good deal of the rough joking to which a newcomer was exposed at some of the studios; but Mrs. Otter had reassured him.

"Oh, there's nothing like that here," she said. "You see, about half of our students are ladies, and they set a tone to the place."

The studio was large and bare, with gray walls, on which were pinned the studies that had received prizes. A model was sitting in a chair with a loose wrap thrown over her, and about a dozen men and women were standing about, some talking and others still working on their sketch. It was the first rest of the model.

"You'd better not try anything too difficult at first," said Mrs. Otter. "Put your easel here. You'll find that's the easiest pose."

Philip placed an easel where she indicated, and Mrs. Otter introduced him to a young woman who sat next to him.

"Mr. Carey — Miss Price. Mr. Carey's never studied before; you won't mind helping him a little just at first, will you?" Then she turned to the model. "*La Pose.*"

The model threw aside the paper she had been reading, *La Petite République*, and sulkily, throwing off her gown, got on to the stand. She stood, squarely on both feet, with her hands clasped behind her head.

[1] Mrs. Otter was an older student to whom he had a letter of introduction. She was also manager of the studio.

'It's a stupid pose,' said Miss Price. "I can't imagine why they chose it."

When Philip entered, the people in the studio had looked at him curiously, and the model gave him an indifferent glance, but now they ceased to pay attention to him. Philip, with his beautiful sheet of paper in front of him, stared awkwardly at the model. He did not know how to begin. He had never seen a naked woman before. She was not young and her breasts were shriveled. She had colorless fair hair that fell over her forehead untidily, and her face was covered with freckles. He glanced at Miss Price's work. She had only been working on it two days and it looked as though she had had trouble; her paper was in a mess from constant rubbing out, and to Philip's eyes the figure looked strangely distorted.

"I should have thought I could do as well as that," he said to himself.

He began on the head, thinking that he would work slowly downwards, but, he could not understand why, he found it infinitely more difficult to draw a head from the model than to draw one from his imagination. He got into difficulties. He glanced at Miss Price. She was working with vehement gravity. Her brow was wrinkled with eagerness, and there was an anxious look in her eyes. It was hot in the studio, and drops of sweat stood on her forehead. She was a girl of twenty-six, with a great deal of dull gold hair; it was handsome hair, but it was carelessly done, dragged back from her forehead and tied in a hurried knot. She had a large face, with broad, flat features and small eyes; her skin was pasty, with a singular unhealthiness of tone, and there was no color in the cheeks. She had an unwashed air, and you could not help wondering if she slept in her clothes. She was serious and silent. When the next pause came, she stepped back to look at her work.

"I don't know why I'm having so much bother," she said. "But I mean to get it right." She turned to Philip. "How are you getting on?"

"Not at all," he answered, with a rueful smile.

She looked at what he had done.

"You can't expect to do anything that way. You must take measurements. And you must square out your paper."

She showed him rapidly how to set about the business. Philip was impressed by her earnestness, but repelled by her want of charm. He was grateful for the hints she gave him and set to work again. Meanwhile other people had come in, mostly men, for the women always arrived first, and the studio for the time of year (it was early yet) was fairly full. Presently there came in a young man with thin, black hair, an enormous nose, and a face so long that it reminded you of a horse. He sat down next to Philip and nodded across him to Miss Price.

"You're very late," she said. "Are you only just up?"

"It was such a beautiful day, I thought I'd lie in bed and think how beautiful it was out."

Philip smiled, but Miss Price took the remark seriously.

"That seems a funny thing to do. I should have thought it would be more to the point to get up and enjoy it."

"The way of the humorist is very hard," said the young man gravely.

He did not seem inclined to work. He looked at his canvas; he was working in color, and had sketched in the day before the model who was posing. He turned to Philip.

"Have you just come out from England?"

"Yes."

"How did you find your way to Amitrano's?"

"It was the only school I knew of."

"I hope you haven't come with the idea that you will learn anything here which will be of the smallest use to you."

"It's the best school in Paris," said Miss Price. "It's the only one where they take art seriously."

"Should art be taken seriously?" the young man asked; and since Miss Price replied only with a scornful shrug, he added: "But the point is, all schools are bad. They are academical, obviously. Why this is less injurious than most is that the teaching is more incompetent than elsewhere. Because you learn nothing . . .'

"But why d'you come here then?" interrupted Philip.

"I see the better course, but do not follow it. Miss Price, who is cultured, will remember the Latin of that."

"I wish you would leave me out of your conversation, Mr. Clutton," said Miss Price brusquely.

"The only way to learn to paint," he went on, imperturbable, "is to take a studio, hire a model, and just fight it out for yourself."

"That seems a simple thing to do," said Philip.

"It only needs money," replied Clutton.

He began to paint, and Philip looked at him from the corner of his eye. He was long and desperately thin; his huge bones seemed to protrude from his body; his elbows were so sharp that they appeared to jut out through the arms of his shabby coat. His trousers were frayed at the bottom, and on each of his boots was a clumsy patch. Miss Price got up and went over to Philip's easel.

"If Mr. Clutton will hold his tongue for a moment, I'll just help you a little," she said.

"Miss Price dislikes me because I have humor," said Clutton, looking meditatively at his canvas, "but she detests me because I have genius."

He spoke with solemnity, and his colossal, misshapen nose made what he said very quaint. Philip was obliged to laugh, but Miss Price grew darkly red with anger.

"You're the only person who has ever accused you of genius."

"Also I am the only person whose opinion is of the slightest value to me."

Miss Price began to criticize what Philip had done. She talked glibly of anatomy and construction, planes and lines, and of much else, which Philip did not understand. She had been at the studio a long time and knew the main points which the masters insisted upon, but though she could show what was wrong with Philip's work she could not tell him how to put it right.

"It's awfully kind of you to take so much trouble with me," said Philip.

"Oh, it's nothing," she answered, flushing awkwardly. "People did the same for me when I first came. I'd do it for any one."

"Miss Price wants to indicate that she is giving you the advantage of her knowledge from a sense of duty rather than on account of any charms of your person," said Clutton.

Miss Price gave him a furious look, and went back to her own drawing. The clock struck twelve, and the model with a cry of relief stepped down from the stand.

Miss Price gathered up her things.

"Some of us go to Gravier's for lunch," she said to Philip, with a look at Clutton. "I always go home myself."

"I'll take you to Gravier's if you like," said Clutton.

Philip thanked him and made ready to go. On his way out Mrs. Otter asked him how he had been getting on.

"Did Fanny Price help you?" she asked. "I put you there because I know she can do it if she likes. She's a disagreeable, ill-natured girl, and she can't draw herself at all, but she knows the ropes and she can be useful to a newcomer if she cares to take the trouble."

On their way down the street Clutton said to him:

"You've made an impression on Fanny Price. You'd better look out."

Philip laughed. He had never seen any one on whom he wished less to make an impression. They came to the cheap little restaurant at which several of the students ate, and Clutton sat down at a table at which three or four men were already seated. For a franc, they got an egg, a plate of meat, cheese, and a small bottle of wine. Coffee was extra. They sat on the pavement, and yellow trams passed up and down the boulevard with a ceaseless ringing of bells.

"By the way, what's your name?" said Clutton, as they took their seats.

"Carey."

"Allow me to introduce an old and trusted friend, Carey by name," said Clutton gravely. "Mr. Flanagan, Mr. Lawson."

They laughed and went on with their conversation.

They talked of a thousand things, and they all talked at once. No one paid the smallest attention to any one else. They talked of the places they had been to in the summer, of studios, of the various schools; they mentioned names which were unfamiliar to Philip: Monet, Manet, Renoir, Pizarro, Degas. Philip listened with all his ears, and though he felt a little out of it, his heart leaped with exultation. The time flew. When Clutton got up he said:

"I expect you'll find me here this evening if you care to come. You'll find this about the best place for getting dyspepsia at the lowest cost in the Quarter."

III

Philip walked down the Boulevard du Montparnasse. It was not at all like the Paris he had seen in the spring . . . but reminded him of what he thought a provincial town must be. There was an easy-going air about it, and a sunny spaciousness which invited the mind to day-dreaming. The trimness of the trees, the vivid whiteness of the houses, the breadth, were very agreeable; and he felt himself already thoroughly at home. He sauntered along, staring at the people; there seemed an elegance about the most ordinary, workmen with their broad red sashes and their wide trousers, little soldiers in dingy, charming uniforms. He came presently to the Avenue de l'Observatoire, and he gave a sigh of pleasure at the magnificent, yet so graceful vista. He came to the gardens of the Luxembourg: children were playing, nurses with long ribbons walked slowly two by two, busy men passed through with satchels under their arms, youths strangely dressed. The scene was formal and dainty; nature was arranged and ordered, but so exquisitely, that nature unordered and unarranged seemed barbaric. Philip was enchanted. It excited him to stand on that spot of which he had read so much; it was classic ground to him; and he felt the awe and the delight which some old don might feel when for the first time he looked on the smiling plain of Sparta.

As he wandered he chanced to see Miss Price sitting by herself on a bench. He hesitated, for he did not at that moment want to see any one, and her uncouth way seemed out of place amid the happiness he felt around him; but he had divined her sensitiveness to affront, and since she had seen him thought it would be polite to speak to her.

"What are you doing here?" she said, as he came up.

"Enjoying myself. Aren't you?"

"Oh, I come here every day from four to five. I don't think one does any good if one works straight through."

"May I sit down for a minute?" he said.

"If you want to."

"That doesn't sound very cordial," he laughed.

"I'm not much of a one for saying pretty things."

Philip, a little disconcerted, was silent as he lit a cigarette.

"Did Clutton say anything about my work?" she asked suddenly.

"No, I don't think he did," said Philip.

"He's no good, you know. He thinks he's a genius, but he isn't. He's too lazy, for one thing. Genius is an infinite capacity for taking pains. The only thing is to peg away. If one only makes up one's mind badly enough to do a thing one can't help doing it."

She spoke with a passionate strenuousness which

was rather striking. She wore a sailor hat of black straw, a white blouse which was not quite clean, and a brown skirt. She had no gloves on, and her hands wanted washing. She was so unattractive that Philip wished he had not begun to talk to her. He could not make out whether she wanted him to stay or go.

"I'll do anything I can for you," she said all at once, without reference to anything that had gone before. "I know how hard it is."

"Thank you very much," said Philip; then in a moment: "Won't you come and have tea with me somewhere?"

She looked at him quickly and flushed. When she reddened her pasty skin acquired a curiously mottled look, like strawberries and cream that had gone bad.

"No, thanks. What d'you think I want tea for? I've only just had lunch."

"I thought it would pass the time," said Philip.

"If you find it long you needn't bother about me, you know. I don't mind being left alone."

At that moment two men passed, in brown velveteens, enormous trousers, and basque caps. They were young, but both wore beards.

"I say, are those art-students?" said Philip. "They might have stepped out of the *Vie de Bohème*."

"They're Americans," said Miss Price scornfully. "Frenchmen haven't worn things like that for thirty years, but the Americans from the Far West buy those clothes and have themselves photographed the day after they arrive in Paris. That's about as near to art as they ever get. But it doesn't matter to them, they've all got money."

Philip liked the daring picturesqueness of the

Americans' costume; he thought it showed the romantic spirit. Miss Price asked him the time.

"I must be getting along to the studio," she said. "Are you going to the sketch classes?"

Philip did not know anything about them, and she told him that from five to six every evening a model sat, from whom any one who liked could go and draw at the cost of fifty centimes. They had a different model every day, and it was very good practice.

"I don't suppose you're good enough for that. You'd better wait a bit."

"I don't see why I shouldn't try. I haven't anything else to do."

They got up and walked to the studio. Philip could not tell from her manner whether Miss Price wished him to walk with her or preferred to walk alone. He remained from sheer embarrassment, not knowing how to leave her; but she would not talk: she answered his questions in an ungracious manner.

A man was standing at the studio door with a large dish into which each person as he went in dropped his half franc. The studio was much fuller than it had been in the morning, and there was not the preponderance of English and Americans; nor were women there in so large a proportion. Philip felt the assemblage was more the sort of thing he had expected. It was very warm, and the air quickly grew fetid. It was an old man who sat this time, with a vast gray beard, and Philip tried to put into practice the little he had learned in the morning; but he made a poor job of it; he realized that he could not draw nearly as well as he thought. He glanced enviously at one or two sketches of men who sat near him, and wondered whether he would ever be able to use the charcoal with that mastery. The hour passed quickly. Not wishing to press himself upon Miss Price he sat down at some distance from her, and at the end, as he passed her on his way out, she asked him brusquely how he had got on.

"Not very well," he smiled.

"If you'd condescended to come and sit near me, I could have given you some hints. I suppose you thought yourself too grand."

"No, it wasn't that. I was afraid you'd think me a nuisance."

"When I do that I'll tell you sharp enough."

Philip saw that in her uncouth way she was offering him help.

"Well, to-morrow I'll just force myself upon you."

"I don't mind," she answered.

IV

On Tuesdays and Fridays masters spent the morning at Amitrano's, criticizing the work done. In France the painter earns little, unless he paints portraits and is patronized by rich Americans; and men of reputation are glad to increase their incomes by spending two or three hours once a week at one of the numerous studios where art is taught. Tuesday was the day upon which Michel Rollin came to Amitrano's. He was an elderly man, with a white beard and a florid complexion, who had painted a number of decorations for the State, but these were an object of derision to the students he instructed: he was a disciple of Ingres,[1] impervious to the progress of art and angrily impatient of that *tas de farceurs* whose names were Manet, Degas, Monet, and Sisley;[2] but he was an

s de farceurs, set of buffoons.
[1] Jean A. D. Ingres (1780–1867), French historical painter.
[2] Painters of the newer impressionistic or realistic schools.

excellent teacher, helpful, polite, and encouraging. Foinet, on the other hand, who visited the studio on Fridays, was a difficult man to get on with. He was a small, shriveled person, with bad teeth and a bilious air, an untidy gray beard, and savage eyes; his voice was high and his tone sarcastic. He had had pictures bought by the Luxembourg, and at twenty-five looked forward to a great career; but his talent was due to youth rather than to personality, and for twenty years he had done nothing but repeat his landscape which had brought him his early success. When he was reproached with monotony, he answered:

"Corot painted only one thing. Why shouldn't I?"

He was envious of every one else's success, and had a peculiar, personal loathing of the Impressionists; for he looked upon his own failure as due to the mad fashion which had attracted the public, *sale bête*, to their works. The genial disdain of Michel Rollin, who called them impostors, was answered by him with vituperation, of which *crapule* and *canaille* were the least violent items; he amused himself with abuse of their private lives, and with sardonic humor, with blasphemous and obscene detail, attacked the legitimacy of their births and the purity of their conjugal relations: he used an Oriental imagery and an Oriental emphasis to accentuate his ribald scorn. Nor did he conceal his contempt for the students whose work he examined. By them he was hated and feared; the women by his brutal sarcasm he reduced often to tears, which again aroused his ridicule and he remained at the studio, notwithstanding the protests of those who suffered too bitterly from hi attacks, because there could be no doubt that he wa

sale bête, dirty beast.
crapule, gluttony.
canaille, mob.

one of the best masters in Paris. Sometimes the old model who kept the school ventured to remonstrate with him, but his expostulations quickly gave way before the violent insolence of the painter to abject apologies.

It was Foinet with whom Philip first came in contact. He was already in the studio when Philip arrived. He went round from easel to easel, with Mrs. Otter, the *massière*, by his side to interpret his remarks for the benefit of those who could not understand French. Fanny Price, sitting next to Philip, was working feverishly. Her face was sallow with nervousness, and every now and then she stopped to wipe her hands on her blouse; for they were hot with anxiety. Suddenly she turned to Philip with an anxious look, which she tried to hide by a sullen frown.

"D'you think it's good?" she asked, nodding at her drawing.

Philip got up and looked at it. He was astounded; he felt she must have no eye at all; the thing was hopelessly out of drawing.

"I wish I could draw half as well myself," he answered.

"You can't expect to, you've only just come. It's a bit too much to expect that you should draw as well as I do. I've been here two years."

Fanny Price puzzled Philip. Her conceit was stupendous. Philip had already discovered that every one in the studio cordially disliked her; and it was no wonder, for she seemed to go out of her way to wound people.

"I complained to Mrs. Otter about Foinet," she said now. "The last two weeks he hasn't looked at

massière (lit., mace-bearer), manager.

my drawing. He spends about half an hour on Mrs. Otter because she's the *massière*. After all I pay as much as anybody else, and I suppose my money's as good as theirs. I don't see why I shouldn't get as much attention as anybody else."

She took up her charcoal again, but in a moment put it down with a groan.

"I can't do any more now. I'm so frightfully nervous."

She looked at Foinet, who was coming towards them with Mrs. Otter. Mrs. Otter, meek, mediocre, and self-satisfied, wore an air of importance. Foinet sat down at the easel of an untidy little Englishwoman called Ruth Chalice. She had the fine black eyes, languid but passionate, the thin face, ascetic but sensual, the skin like old ivory, which under the influence of Burne-Jones were cultivated at that time by the young ladies of Chelsea. Foinet seemed in a pleasant mood; he did not say much to her, but with quick determined strokes of her charcoal pointed out her errors. Miss Chalice beamed with pleasure when he rose. He came to Clutton, and by this time Philip was nervous too, but Mrs. Otter had promised to make things easy for him. Foinet stood for a moment in front of Clutton's work, biting his thumb silently, then absent-mindedly spat out upon the canvas the little piece of skin which he had bitten off.

"That's a fine line," he said at last, indicating with his thumb what pleased him. "You're beginning to learn to draw."

Clutton did not answer, but looked at the master with his usual air of sardonic indifference to the world's opinion.

"I'm beginning to think you have at least a trace of talent."

Mrs. Otter, who did not like Clutton, pursed her lips. She did not see anything out of the way in his work. Foinet sat down and went into technical details. Mrs. Otter grew rather tired of standing. Clutton did not say anything, but nodded now and then, and Foinet felt with satisfaction that he grasped what he said and the reasons of it; most of them listened to him, but it was clear they never understood. Then Foinet got up and came to Philip.

"He only arrived two days ago," Mrs. Otter hurried to explain. "He's a beginner. He's never studied before."

"*Ça se voit*," the master said. "One sees that."

He passed on, and Mrs. Otter murmured to him:

"This is the young lady I told you about."

He looked at her as though she were some repulsive animal, and his voice grew more rasping.

"It appears that you do not think I pay enough attention to you. You have been complaining to the *massière*. Well, show me this work to which you wish me to give attention."

Fanny Price colored. The blood under her unhealthy skin seemed to be of a strange purple. Without answering she pointed to the drawing on which she had been at work since the beginning of the week. Foinet sat down.

"Well, what do you wish me to say to you? Do you wish me to tell you it is good? It isn't. Do you wish me to tell you it is well drawn? It isn't. Do you wish me to say it has merit? It hasn't. Do you wish me to show you what is wrong with it? It is all wrong. Do you wish me to tell you what to do with it? Tear it up. Are you satisfied now?"

Miss Price became very white. She was furious because he had said all this before Mrs. Otter.

Though she had been in France so long and could understand French well enough, she could hardly speak two words.

"He's got no right to treat me like that. My money's as good as any one else's. I pay him to teach me. That's not teaching me."

"What does she say? What does she say?" asked Foinet.

Mrs. Otter hesitated to translate, and Miss Price repeated in execrable French.

"*Je vous paye pour m'apprendre.*"

His eyes flashed with rage, he raised his voice and shook his fist.

"*Mais, nom de Dieu*, I can't teach you. I could more easily teach a camel." He turned to Mrs. Otter. "Ask her, does she do this for amusement, or does she expect to earn money by it?"

"I'm going to earn my living as an artist," Miss Price answered.

"Then it is my duty to tell you that you are wasting your time. It would not matter that you have no talent, talent does not run about the streets in these days, but you have not the beginning of an aptitude. How long have you been here? A child of five after two lessons would draw better than you do. I only say one thing to you, give up this hopeless attempt. You're more likely to earn your living as a *bonne à tout faire* than as a painter. Look."

He seized a piece of charcoal, and it broke as he applied it to the paper. He cursed, and with the stump drew great firm lines. He drew rapidly and spoke at the same time, spitting out the words with venom.

Je vous paye, etc., I pay you to teach me.
bonne à tout faire, maid of all work.

"Look, those arms are not the same length. That knee, it's grotesque. I tell you a child of five. You see, she's not standing on her legs. That foot!"

With each word the angry pencil made a mark, and in a moment the drawing upon which Fanny Price had spent so much time and eager trouble was unrecognizable, a confusion of lines and smudges. At last he flung down the charcoal and stood up.

"Take my advice, Mademoiselle, try dressmaking." He looked at his watch. "It's twelve. *A la semaine prochaine, messieurs.*"

Miss Price gathered up her things slowly. Philip waited behind after the others to say to her something consolatory. He could think of nothing but:

"I say, I'm awfully sorry. What a beast that man is!"

She turned on him savagely.

"Is that what you're waiting about for? When I want your sympathy I'll ask for it. Please get out of my way."

She walked past him, out of the studio, and Philip, with a shrug of the shoulders, limped [1] along to Gravier's for luncheon.

"It served her right," said Lawson, when Philip told him what had happened. "Ill-tempered slut."

In the afternoon Philip thought he would go to the Luxembourg to see the pictures, and walking through the garden he saw Fanny Price sitting in her accustomed seat. He was sore at the rudeness with which she had met his well-meant attempt to say something pleasant, and passed as though he had not caught sight of her. But she got up at once, and came towards him.

A la semaine prochaine, until next week.

[1] Philip has a club foot, a deformity which has made him abnormally sensitive.

"Are you trying to cut me?" she said.

"No, of course not. I thought perhaps you didn't want to be spoken to."

"Where are you going?"

"I wanted to have a look at the Manet, I've heard so much about it."

"Would you like me to come with you? I know the Luxembourg rather well. I could show you one or two good things."

He understood that, unable to bring herself to apologize directly, she had made this offer as amends.

"It's awfully kind of you. I should like it very much."

"You needn't say yes if you'd rather go alone," she said suspiciously.

'I wouldn't."

They walked towards the gallery. Caillebotte's collection had lately been placed on view, and the student for the first time had the opportunity to examine at his ease the works of the impressionists. Till then it had been possible to see them only at Durand-Ruel's shop in the Rue Lafitte (and the dealer, unlike his fellows in England, who adopt towards the painter an attitude of superiority, was always pleased to show the shabbiest student whatever he wanted to see), or at his private house, to which it was not difficult to get a card of admission on Tuesdays, and where you might see pictures of world-wide reputation. Miss Price led Philip straight up to Manet's *Olympia*. He looked at it in astonished silence.

"Do you like it?" asked Miss Price.

"I don't know," he answered helplessly.

"You can take it from me that it's the best thing in the gallery except perhaps Whistler's portrait of hi mother."

She gave him a certain time to contemplate the masterpiece and then took him to a picture representing a railway-station.

"Look, here's a Monet," she said. "It's the Gare St. Lazare."

"But the railway lines aren't parallel," said Philip.

"What does that matter?" she asked, with a haughty air.

Philip felt ashamed of himself. Fanny Price had picked up the glib chatter of the studios and had no difficulty in impressing Philip with the extent of her knowledge. She proceeded to explain the pictures to him, superciliously but not without insight, and showed him what the painters had attempted and what he must look for. She talked with much gesticulation of the thumb, and Philip, to whom all she said was new, listened with profound but bewildered interest. Till now he had worshiped Watts and Burne-Jones. The pretty color of the first, the affected drawing of the second, had entirely satisfied his æsthetic sensibilities. Their vague idealism, the suspicion of a philosophical idea which underlay the titles they gave their pictures, accorded very well with the functions of art as from his diligent perusal of Ruskin he understood it; but here was something quite different: here was no moral appeal; and the contemplation of these works could help no one to lead a purer and a higher life. He was puzzled.

At last he said: "You know, I'm simply dead. I don't think I can absorb anything more profitably. Let's go and sit down on one of the benches."

"It's better not to take too much art at a time," Miss Price answered.

When they got outside he thanked her warmly for the trouble she had taken.

"Oh, that's all right," she said, a little ungraciously. "I do it because I enjoy it. We'll go to the Louvre to-morrow if you like, and then I'll take you to Durand-Ruel's."

"You're really awfully good to me."

"You don't think me such a beast as the most of them do."

"I don't," he smiled.

"They think they'll drive me away from the studio; but they won't; I shall stay there just exactly as long as it suits me. All that this morning, it was Lucy Otter's doing, I know it was. She always hated me. She thought after that I'd take myself off. I daresay she'd like me to go. She's afraid I know too much about her."

Miss Price told him a long, involved story, which made out that Mrs. Otter, a humdrum and respectable little person, had scabrous intrigues. Then she talked of Ruth Chalice, the girl whom Foinet had praised that morning.

"She's been with every one of the fellows at the studio. She's nothing better than a street-walker. And she's dirty. She hasn't had a bath for a month, I know it for a fact."

Philip listened uncomfortably. He had heard already that various rumours were in circulation about Miss Chalice; but it was ridiculous to suppose that Mrs. Otter, living with her mother, was anything but rigidly virtuous. The woman walking by his side with her malignant lying horrified him.

"I don't care what they say. I shall go on just the same. I know I've got it in me. I feel I'm an artist. I'd sooner kill myself than give it up. Oh, I shan't be the first they've all laughed at in the schools and then he's turned out the only genius of the lot. Art' the only thing I care for, I'm willing to give my whole life for it. It's only a question of sticking to it and pegging away."

She found discreditable motives for every one who would not take her at her own estimate of herself. She detested Clutton. She told Philip that his friend had no talent really; it was just flashy and superficial; he couldn't compose a figure to save his life. And Lawson:

"Little beast, with his red hair and his freckles. He's so afraid of Foinet that he won't let him see his work. After all, I don't funk it, do I? I don't care what Foinet says to me, I know I'm a real artist."

They reached the street in which she lived, and with a sigh of relief Philip left her.

V

But notwithstanding when Miss Price on the following Sunday offered to take him to the Louvre Philip accepted. She showed him *Mona Lisa*. He looked at it with a slight feeling of disappointment, but he had read till he knew by heart the jeweled words with which Walter Pater has added beauty to the most famous picture in the world; and these now he repeated to Miss Price.

"That's all literature," she said, a little contemptuously. "You must get away from that."

She showed him the Rembrandts, and she said many appropriate things about them. She stood in front of the *Disciples at Emmaus*.

"When you feel the beauty of that," she said, "you'll know something about painting."

She showed him the *Odalisque* and *La Source* of Ingres. Fanny Price was a peremptory guide, she would not let him look at the things he wished, and attempted to force his admiration for all she admired. She was desperately in earnest with her study of art, and when Philip, passing in the Long Gallery a window that looked out on the Tuileries, gay, sunny, and urbane, like a picture by Raffaelli,[1] exclaimed: "I say, how jolly! Do let's stop here a minute."

She said, indifferently: "Yes, it's all right. But we've come here to look at pictures."

The autumn air, blithe and vivacious, elated Philip; and when towards midday they stood in the great courtyard of the Louvre, he felt inclined to cry like Flanagan:[2] To Hell with art.

"I say, do let's go to one of the restaurants in the Boul' Mich' and have a snack together, shall we?" he suggested.

Miss Price gave him a suspicious look.

"I've got my lunch waiting for me at home," she answered.

"That doesn't matter. You can eat it to-morrow. Do let me stand you a lunch."

"I don't know why you want to."

"It would give me pleasure," he replied, smiling.

They crossed the river, and at the corner of the Boulevard St. Michel there was a restaurant.

"Let's go in here."

"No, I won't go in there; it looks too expensive."

She walked on firmly, and Philip was obliged to follow. A few steps brought them to a smaller restaurant, where a dozen people were already lunching on the pavement under an awning; on the window was announced in large white letters: *Déjeuner 1.25 vin compris.*

[1] Jean François Raffaelli, a French painter of the nineteenth century.
[2] One of the art-students.

"We couldn't find anything cheaper than this, and it looks quite all right."

They sat down at a vacant table and waited for the omelette which was the first article on the bill of fare. Philip gazed with delight upon the passers-by. His heart went out to them. He was tired but very happy.

"I say, look at that man in the blouse. Isn't he ripping!"

He glanced at Miss Price, and to his astonishment saw that she was looking down at her plate, regardless of the passing spectacle, and two heavy tears were rolling down her cheeks.

"What on earth's the matter?" he exclaimed.

"If you say anything to me, I shall get up and go at once," she answered.

He was entirely puzzled, but fortunately at that moment the omelette came. He divided it in two and they began to eat. Philip did his best to talk of indifferent things, and it seemed as though Miss Price were making an effort on her side to be agreeable; but the luncheon was not altogether a success. Philip was squeamish, and the way in which Miss Price ate took his appetite away. She ate noisily, greedily, a little like a wild beast in a menagerie, and after she had finished each course rubbed the plate with pieces of bread till it was white and shining, as if she did not wish to lose a single drop of gravy. They had Camembert cheese, and it disgusted Philip to see that she ate rind and all of the portion that was given her. She could not have eaten more ravenously if she were starving.

Miss Price was unaccountable, and having parted from her on one day with friendliness he could never tell whether on the next she would not be sulky and uncivil; but he learned a good deal from her: though she could not draw well herself, she knew all that could be taught, and her constant suggestions helped his progress. Mrs. Otter was useful to him, too, and sometimes Miss Chalice criticized his work; he learned from the glib loquacity of Lawson and from the example of Clutton. But Fanny Price hated him to take suggestions from any one but herself, and when he asked her to help after some one else had been talking to him, she would refuse with brutal rudeness. The other fellows, Lawson, Clutton, Flanagan, chaffed him about her.

"You be careful, my lad," they said, "she's in love with you."

"Oh, what nonsense," he laughed.

The thought that Miss Price could be in love with any one was preposterous. It made him shudder when he thought of her uncomeliness, the bedraggled hair and the dirty hands, the brown dress she always wore, stained and ragged at the hem: he supposed she was always hard up; they were all hard up, but she might at least be clean; and it was surely possible with a needle and thread to make her skirt tidy.

VI

Philip did not find living in Paris as cheap as he had been led to believe and by February had spent most of the money with which he started. He was too proud to appeal to his guardian, nor did he wish Aunt Louisa to know that his circumstances were straitened, since he was certain she would make an effort to send him something from her own pocket, and he knew how little she could afford to. In three months he would attain his majority and come into possession of his small fortune. He tided over the interval by selling the few trinkets which he had inherited from his father.

At about this time Lawson suggested that they should take a small studio which was vacant in one of the streets that led out of the Boulevard Raspail. It was very cheap. It had a room attached, which they could use as a bedroom; and since Philip was at the school every morning .Lawson could have the undisturbed use of the studio then; Lawson, after wandering from school to school, had come to the conclusion that he could work best alone, and proposed to get a model in three or four days a week. At first Philip hesitated on account of the expense, but they reckoned it out; and it seemed (they were so anxious to have a studio of their own that they calculated pragmatically) that the cost would not be much greater than that of living in a hotel. Though the rent and the cleaning by the *concierge* would come to a little more, they would save on the *petit déjeuner*, which they could make themselves. A year or two earlier Philip would have refused to share a room with any one, since he was so sensitive about his deformed foot, but his morbid way of looking at it was growing less marked: in Paris it did not seem to matter so much, and, though he never by any chance forgot it himself, he ceased to feel that other people were constantly looking at it.

They moved in, bought a couple of beds, a washing-stand, a few chairs, and felt for the first time the thrill of possession. They were so 'excited that the first night they went to bed in what they could call a home they lay awake talking till three in the morning; and next day found lighting the fire and making their own coffee, which they had in pyjamas, such a jolly business that Philip did not go to Amitrano's till nearly eleven. He was in excellent spirits. He nodded to Fanny Price.

"How are you getting on?" he asked cheerily.

"What does it matter to you?" she asked in reply.

Philip could not help laughing.

"Don't jump down my throat. I was only trying to make myself polite."

"I don't want your politeness."

"D'you think it's worth your while quarreling with me, too?" asked Philip mildly. "There are so few people you're on speaking terms with, as it is."

"That's my business, isn't it?"

"Quite."

He began to work, vaguely wondering why Fanny Price made herself so disagreeable. He had come to the conclusion that he thoroughly disliked her. Every one did. People were only civil to her at all for fear of the malice of her tongue; for to their faces and behind their backs she said abominable things. But Philip was feeling so happy that he did not want even Miss Price to bear ill-feeling towards him. He used the artifice which had often before succeeded in banishing her ill-humor.

"I say, I wish you'd come and look at my drawing. I've got in an awful mess."

"Thank you very much, but I've got something better to do with my time."

Philip stared at her in surprise, for the one thing she could be counted upon to do with alacrity was to give advice. She went on quickly in a low voice, savage with fury.

"Now that Lawson's gone you think you'll put up with me. Thank you very much. Go and find somebody else to help you. I don't want anybody else's leavings."

Lawson had the pedagogic instinct; whenever he found anything out he was eager to impart it; and because he taught with delight he taught with profit. Philip, without thinking anything about it, had got into the habit of sitting by his side; it never occurred to him that Fanny Price was consumed with jealousy, and watched his acceptance of some one else's tuition with ever-increasing anger.

"You were very glad to put up with me when you knew nobody here," she said bitterly, "and as soon as you made friends with other people you threw me aside, like an old glove" — she repeated the stale metaphor with satisfaction — "like an old glove. All right, I don't care, but I'm not going to be made a fool of another time."

There was a suspicion of truth in what she said, and it made Philip angry enough to answer what first came into his head.

"Hang it all, I only asked your advice because I saw it pleased you."

She gave a gasp and threw him a sudden look of anguish. Then two tears rolled down her cheeks. She looked frowsy and grotesque. Philip, not knowing what on earth this new attitude implied, went back to his work. He was uneasy and conscience-stricken; but he would not go to her and say he was sorry if he had caused her pain, because he was afraid she would take the opportunity to snub him. For two or three weeks she did not speak to him, and, after Philip had got over the discomfort of being cut by her, he was somewhat relieved to be free from so difficult a friendship. He had been a little disconcerted by the air of proprietorship she assumed over him. She was an extraordinary woman. She came every day to the studio at eight o'clock, and was ready to start working when the model was in position; she worked steadily, talking to no one, struggling hour after hour with difficulties she could not overcome, and remained till the clock struck twelve. Her work was hopeless. There was not in it the smallest approach even to the mediocre achievement at which most of the young people were able after some months to arrive. She wore every day the same ugly brown dress, with the mud of the last wet day still caked on the hem and with the raggedness, which Philip had noticed the first time he saw her, still unmended.

But one day she came up to him, and with a scarlet face asked whether she might speak to him afterwards.

"Of course, as much as you like," smiled Philip. "I'll wait behind at twelve."

He went to her when the day's work was over.

"Will you walk a little bit with me?" she said, looking away from him with embarrassment.

"Certainly."

They walked for two or three minutes in silence.

"D'you remember what you said to me the other day?" she asked then on a sudden.

"Oh, I say, don't let's quarrel," said Philip. "It really isn't worth while."

She gave a quick painful inspiration.

"I don't want to quarrel with you. You're the only friend I had in Paris. I thought you rather liked me. I felt there was something between us. I was drawn to you — you know what I mean, your club-foot."

Philip reddened and instinctively tried to walk without a limp. He did not like any one to mention the deformity. He knew what Fanny Price meant. She was ugly and uncouth, and because he was de-

formed there was between them a certain sympathy.
He was very angry with her, but he forced himself
not to speak.

"You said you only asked my advice to please me.
Don't you think my work's any good?"

"I've only seen your drawing at Amitrano's. It's
awfully hard to judge from that."

"I was wondering if you'd come and look at my
other work. I've never asked any one else to look at
it. I should like to show it to you."

"It's awfully kind of you. I'd like to see it very
much."

"I live quite near here," she said apologetically.
"It'll only take you ten minutes."

"Oh, that's all right," he said.

They were walking along the boulevard, and she
turned down a side street, then led him into another,
poorer still, with cheap shops on the ground floor,
and at last stopped. They climbed flight after flight
of stairs. She unlocked a door, and they went into
a tiny attic with a sloping roof and a small window.
This was closed and the room had a musty smell.
Though it was very cold there was no fire and no sign
that there had been one. The bed was unmade. A
chair, a chest of drawers which served also as a wash-
stand, and a cheap easel, were all the furniture. The
place would have been squalid enough in any case,
but the litter, the untidiness, made the impression revolting. On the chimney-piece, scattered over with
paints and brushes, were a cup, a dirty plate, and a
tea-pot.

"If you'll stand over there, I'll put them on the
chair so that you can see them better."

She showed him twenty small canvases, about
eighteen by twelve. She placed them on the chair,

one after the other, watching his face; he nodded as he looked at each one.

"You do like them, don't you?" she said anxiously, after a bit.

"I just want to look at them all first," he answered. "I'll talk afterwards."

He was collecting himself. He was panic-stricken. He did not know what to say. It was not only that they were ill-drawn, or that the color was put on amateurishly by some one who had no eye for it; but there was no attempt at getting the values, and the perspective was grotesque. It looked like the work of a child of five, but a child would have had some *naïveté* and might at least have made an attempt to put down what he saw; but here was the work of a vulgar mind chock full of recollections of vulgar pictures. Philip remembered that she had talked enthusiastically about Monet and the Impressionists, but here were only the worst traditions of the Royal Academy.

"There," she said at last, "that's the lot."

Philip was no more truthful than anybody else, but he had a great difficulty in telling a thundering, deliberate lie, and he blushed furiously when he answered:

"I think they're most awfully good."

A faint color came into her unhealthy cheeks, and she smiled a little.

"You needn't say so if you don't think so, you know. I want the truth."

"But I do think so."

"Haven't you got any criticism to offer? There must be some you don't like as well as others."

Philip looked round helplessly. He saw a landscape, the typical picturesque "bit" of the amateur.

an old bridge, a creeper-clad cottage, and a leafy bank.

"Of course I don't pretend to know anything about it," he said. "But I wasn't quite sure about the values of that."

She flushed darkly and, taking up the picture, quickly turned its back to him.

"I don't know why you should have chosen that one to sneer at. It's the best thing I've ever done. I'm sure my values are all right. That's a thing you can't teach any one, you either understand values or you don't."

"I think they're all most awfully good," repeated Philip. She looked at them with an air of self-satisfaction.

"I don't think they're anything to be ashamed of."

Philip looked at his watch.

"I say, it's getting late. Won't you let me give you a little lunch?"

"I've got my lunch waiting for me here."

Philip saw no sign of it, but supposed perhaps the *concierge* would bring it up when he was gone. He was in a hurry to get away. The mustiness of the room made his head ache.

VII

Then came the summer, and restlessness seized these young people. The blue skies lured them to the sea, and the pleasant breeze sighing through the leaves of the plane-trees on the boulevard drew them towards the country. Every one made plans for leaving Paris; they discussed what was the most suitable size for the canvases they meant to take; they laid in stores of panels for sketching; they argued about the merits of various places in Brittany. Flanagan and

Potter went to Concarneau; Mrs. Otter and her mother, with a natural instinct for the obvious, went to Pont-Aven; Philip and Lawson made up their minds to go to the forest of Fontainebleau, and Miss Chalice knew of a very good hotel at Moret, where there was lots of stuff to paint; it was near Paris, and neither Philip nor Lawson was indifferent to the railway fare. Ruth Chalice would be there, and Lawson had an idea for a portrait of her in the open air. Just then the Salon was full of portraits of people in gardens, in sunlight, with blinking eyes and green reflections of sunlit leaves on their faces. They asked Clutton to go with them, but he preferred spending the summer by himself. He had just discovered Cézanne,[1] and was eager to go to Provence; he wanted heavy skies from which the hot blue seemed to drip like beads of sweat, and broad white dusty roads, and pale roofs out of which the sun had burnt the color, and olive trees gray with heat.

The day before they were to start, after the morning class, Philip, putting his things together, spoke to Fanny Price.

"I'm off to-morrow," he said cheerfully.

"Off where?" she said quickly. "You're not going away?" Her face fell.

"I'm going away for the summer. Aren't you?"

"No, I'm staying in Paris. I thought you were going to stay too. I was looking forward . . . ."

She stopped and shrugged her shoulders.

"But won't it be frightfully hot here? It's awfully bad for you."

"Much you care if it's bad for me. Where are you going?"

[1] Paul Cézanne (1849–1906), leader of the Post-Impressionists in painting.

"Moret."

"Chalice is going there. You're not going with her?"

"Lawson and I are going. And she's going there, too. I don't know that we're actually going together."

She gave a low guttural sound, and her large face grew dark and red.

"How filthy! I thought you were a decent fellow. You were about the only one here. She's been with Clutton and Potter and Flanagan, even with old Foinet — that's why he takes so much trouble about her — and now two of you, you and Lawson. It makes me sick."

"Oh, what nonsense! She's a very decent sort. One treats her just as if she were a man."

"Oh, don't speak to me, don't speak to me."

"But what can it matter to you?" asked Philip. "It's really no business of yours where I spend my summer."

"I was looking forward to it so much," she gasped, speaking it seemed almost to herself. "I didn't think you had the money to go away, and there wouldn't have been any one else here, and we could have worked together, and we'd have gone to see things." Then her thoughts flung back to Ruth Chalice. "The filthy beast!" she cried. "She isn't fit to speak to."

Philip looked at her with a sinking heart. He was not a man to think girls were in love with him; he was too conscious of his deformity, and he felt awkward and clumsy with women; but he did not know what else this outburst could mean. Fanny Price, in the dirty brown dress, with her hair falling over her face, sloppy, untidy, stood before him; and tears of anger rolled down her cheeks. She was repellent. Philip glanced at the door, instinctively hoping that some one would come in and put an end to the scene.

"I'm awfully sorry," he said.

"You're just the same as all of them. You take all you can get, and you don't even say thank you. I've taught you everything you know. No one else would take any trouble with you. Has Foinet ever bothered about you? And I can tell you this — you can work here for a thousand years and you'll never do any good. You haven't got any talent. You haven't got any originality. And it's not only me — they all say it. You'll never be a painter as long as you live."

"That is no business of yours either, is it?" said Philip, flushing.

"Oh, you think it's only my temper. Ask Clutton, ask Lawson, ask Chalice. Never, never, never. You haven't got it in you."

Philip shrugged his shoulders and walked out. She shouted after him.

"Never, never, never."

VIII

Three months later

When Philip returned to Amitrano's, he found that Fanny Price was no longer working there. She had given up the key of her locker. He asked Mrs. Otter whether she knew what had become of her; and Mrs. Otter, with a shrug of the shoulders, answered that she had probably gone back to England. Philip was relieved. He was profoundly bored by her ill-temper. Moreover, she insisted on advising him about his work, looked upon it as a slight when he did not follow her precepts, and would not understand that he felt himself no longer the duffer he had been at first. Soon he forgot all about her. . . .

Then one morning when he was going out, the *concierge* called out to him that there was a letter. Nobody wrote to him but his Aunt Louisa and sometimes Hayward, and this was a handwriting he did not know. The letter was as follows:

Please come at once when you get this. I couldn't put up with it any more. Please come yourself. I can't bear the thought that any one else should touch me. I want you to have everything.

F. Price

I have not had anything to eat for three days.

Philip felt on a sudden sick with fear. He hurried to the house in which she lived. He was astounded that she was in Paris at all. He had not seen her for months and imagined she had long since returned to England. When he arrived, he asked the *concierge* whether she was in.

"Yes, I've not seen her go out for two days."

Philip ran upstairs and knocked at the door. There was no reply. He called her name. The door was locked, and on bending down he found the key was in the lock.

"Oh, my God, I hope she hasn't done something awful!" he cried aloud.

He ran down and told the porter that she was certainly in the room. He had had a letter from her and feared a terrible accident. He suggested breaking open the door. The porter, who had been sullen and disinclined to listen, became alarmed; he could not take the responsibility of breaking into the room; they must go for the *commissaire de police*. They walked together to the bureau, and then they fetched a locksmith. Philip found that Miss Price had not paid the last quarter's rent: on New Year's Day she had not given the *concierge* the present which old-established custom led him to regard as a right. The four of them went upstairs, and they knocked again at the door. There was no reply. The locksmith set to work, and at last they entered the room. Philip gave a cry and instinctively covered his eyes with his hands. The wretched woman was hanging with a rope round her neck, which she had tied to a hook in the ceiling fixed by some previous tenant to hold up the curtains of the bed. She had moved her own little bed out of the way and had stood on a chair, which had been kicked away. It was lying on its side on the floor. They cut her down. The body was quite cold.

IX

The story which Philip made out in one way and another was terrible. One of the grievances of the women-students was that Fanny Price would never share their gay meals in restaurants, and the reason was obvious: she had been oppressed by dire poverty. He remembered the luncheon they had eaten together when first he came to Paris and the ghoulish appetite which had disgusted him: he realized now that she ate in that manner because she was ravenous. The *concierge* told him what her food had consisted of. A bottle of milk was left for her every day and she brought her own loaf of bread; she ate half the loaf and drank half the milk at midday when she came back from the school, and Philip thought with anguish of what she must have endured. She had never given any one to understand that she was poorer than the rest, but it was clear that her money had been coming to an end, and at last she could not afford to come any more to the studio. The little room was almos bare of furniture, and there were no other clothes than the shabby brown dress she had always worn. Philip searched among her things for the address of some friend with whom he could communicate. He found a piece of paper on which his own name was written a score of times. It gave him a peculiar shock. He supposed it was true that she had loved him; he thought of the emaciated body, in the brown dress, hanging from the nail in the ceiling; and he shuddered. But if she had cared for him, why did she not let him help her? He would so gladly have done all he could. He felt remorseful because he had refused to see that she looked upon him with any particular feeling, and now these words in her letter were infinitely pathetic: *I can't bear the thought that any one else should touch me.* She had died of starvation.

ARABY

1916

North Richmond Street, being blind, was a quiet street except at the hour when the Christian Brothers' School set the boys free. An uninhabited house of two stories stood at the blind end, detached from its neighbours in a square ground. The other houses of the street, conscious of decent lives within them, gazed at one another with brown imperturbable faces.

The former tenant of our house, a priest, had died in the back drawing-room. Air, musty from having been long enclosed, hung in all the rooms, and the waste room behind the kitchen was littered with old useless papers. Among these I found a few paper-covered books, the pages of which were curled and damp: *The Abbot*, by Walter Scott, *The Devout Communicant*, and *The Memoirs of Vidocq*. I liked the last best because its leaves were yellow. The wild garden behind the house contained a central apple-tree and a few straggling bushes, under one of which I found the late tenant's rusty bicycle-pump. He had been a very charitable priest; in his will he had left all his money to institutions and the furniture of his house to his sister.

When the short days of winter came, dusk fell before we had well eaten our dinners. When we met in the street the houses had grown sombre. The space of sky above us was the colour of ever-changing violet and towards it the lamps of the street lifted their feeble lanterns. The cold air stung us and we played till our bodies glowed. Our shouts echoed in the silent street. The career of our play brought us through the dark muddy lanes behind the houses, where we ran the gauntlet of the rough tribes from the cottages, to the back doors of the dark dripping gardens where odours arose from the ashpits, to the dark odorous stables where a coachman smoothed and combed the horse or shook music from the buckled harness. When we returned to the street, light from the kitchen windows had filled the areas. If my uncle was seen turning the corner, we hid in the shadow until we had seen him safely housed. Or if Mangan's sister came out on the doorstep to call her brother in to his tea, we watched her from our shadow peer up and down the street. We waited to see whether she would remain or go in and, if she remained, we left our shadow and walked up Mangan's steps resignedly. She was waiting for us, her figure defined by the light from the half-opened door. Her brother always teased her before he obeyed, and I stood by the railings looking at her. Her dress swung as she moved her body, and the soft rope of her hair tossed from side to side.

Every morning I lay on the floor in the front parlour watching her door. The blind was pulled down to within an inch of the sash so that I could not be seen. When she came out on the doorstep my heart leaped. I ran to the hall, seized my books and followed her. I kept her brown figure always in my eye and, when we came near the point at which our ways diverged, I quickened my pace and passed her. This happened morning after morning. I had never spoken to her except for a few casual words, and yet her name was like a summons to all my foolish blood.

Her image accompanied me even in places the most hostile to romance. On Saturday evenings when my aunt went marketing I had to go to carry some of the parcels. We walked through the flaring streets, jostled by drunken men and bargaining women, amid the curses of labourers, the shrill litanies of shop-boys who stood guard by the barrels of pigs' cheeks, the nasal chanting of street-singers, who sang a *come-all-you* about O'Donovan Rossa, or a ballad about the troubles in our native land. These noises converged in a single sensation of life for me: I imagined that I bore my chalice safely through a throng of foes. Her name sprang to my lips at moments in strange prayers and praises which I myself did not understand. My eyes were often full of tears (I could not tell why) and at times a flood from my heart seemed to pour itself out into my bosom. I thought little of the future. I did not know whether I would ever speak to her or not or, if I spoke to her, how I could tell her of my confused adoration. But my body was like a harp and her words and gestures were like fingers running upon the wires.

One evening I went into the back drawing-room in which the priest had died. It was a dark rainy evening and there was no sound in the house. Through one of the broken panes I heard the rain impinge upon the earth, the fine incessant needles of water playing in the sodden beds. Some distant lamp or lighted window gleamed below me. I was thankful that I could see so little. All my senses seemed to desire to veil themselves and, feeling that I was about to slip from them, I pressed the palms of my hands together until they trembled, murmuring: "*O love! O love!*" many times.

At last she spoke to me. When she addressed the first words to me I was so confused that I did not know what to answer. She asked me was I going to *Araby*. I forget whether I answered yes or no. It would be a splendid bazaar; she said she would love to go.

"And why can't you?" I asked.

While she spoke she turned a silver bracelet round and round her wrist. She could not go, she said, because there would be a retreat that week in her convent. Her brother and two other boys were fighting for their caps, and I was alone at the railings. She held one of the spikes, bowing her head towards me. The light from the lamp opposite our door caught the white curve of her neck, lit up her hair that rested there and, falling, lit up the hand upon the railing. It fell over one side of her dress and caught the white border of a petticoat, just visible as she stood at ease.

"It's well for you," she said.

"If I go," I said, "I will bring you something."

What innumerable follies laid waste my waking and sleeping thoughts after that evening! I wished to annihilate the tedious intervening days. I chafed against the work of school. At night in my bedroom and by day in the classroom her image came between me and the page I strove to read. The syllables of the word *Araby* were called to me through the silence in which my soul luxuriated and cast an Eastern enchantment over me. I asked for leave to go to the bazaar on Saturday night. My aunt was surprised, and hoped it was not some Freemason affair. I answered few questions in class. I watched my master's face pass from amiability to sternness; he hoped I was not beginning to idle. I could not call my wandering thoughts together. I had hardly any patience with the serious work of life which, now that it stood between me and my desire, seemed to me child's play, ugly monotonous child's play.

On Saturday morning I reminded my uncle that I wished to go to the bazaar in the evening. He was fussing at the hall-stand, looking for the hat-brush, and answered me curtly:

"Yes, boy, I know."

As he was in the hall I could not go into the front parlour and lie at the window. I left the house in bad humour and walked slowly towards the school. The air was pitilessly raw and already my heart misgave me.

When I came home to dinner my uncle had not yet been home. Still it was early. I sat staring at the clock for some time and, when its ticking began to irritate me, I left the room. I mounted the staircase and gained the upper part of the house. The high, cold, gloomy rooms liberated me and I went from room to room singing. From the front window I saw my companions playing below in the street. Their cries reached me weakened and indistinct and, leaning my forehead against the cool glass, I looked over at the dark house where she lived. I may have stood there for an hour, seeing nothing but the brown-clad figure cast by my imagination, touched discreetly by the lamplight at the curved neck, at the hand upon the railings and at the border below the dress.

When I came downstairs again I found Mrs. Mercer sitting at the fire. She was an old, garrulous woman, a pawnbroker's widow, who collected used stamps for some pious purpose. I had to endure the gossip of the tea-table. The meal was prolonged beyond an hour and still my uncle did not come. Mrs. Mercer stood up to go: she was sorry she couldn't wait any longer, but it was after eight o'clock and she did not like to be out late, as the night air was bad for her. When she was gone I began to walk up and down the room, clenching my fists. My aunt said:

"I'm afraid you may put off your bazaar for this night of Our Lord."

At nine o'clock I heard my uncle's latchkey in the hall door. I heard him talking to himself and heard the hallstand rocking when it received the weight of his overcoat. I could interpret these signs. When he was midway through his dinner I asked him to give me the money to go to the bazaar. He had forgotten.

"The people are in bed and after their first sleep now," he said.

I did not smile. My aunt said to him energetically:

"Can't you give him the money and let him go? You've kept him late enough as it is."

My uncle said he was very sorry he had forgotten. He said he believed in the old saying: "All work and no play makes Jack a dull boy." He asked me where I was going and, when I had told him a second time, he asked me did I know *The Arab's Farewell to His Steed.* When I left the kitchen he was about to recite the opening lines of the piece to my aunt.

I held a florin tightly in my hand as I strode down Buckingham Street towards the station. The sight of the streets thronged with buyers and glaring with gas recalled to me the purpose of my journey. I took my seat in a third-class carriage of a deserted train. After an intolerable delay the train moved out of the station slowly. It crept onward among ruinous houses and over the twinkling river. At Westland Row Station a crowd of people pressed to the carriage doors; but the porters moved them back, saying it was a special train for the bazaar. I remained alone in the bare carriage. In a few minutes the train drew up beside an improvised wooden platform. I passed out onto the road and saw by the lighted dial of a clock that it was ten minutes to ten. In front of me was a large building which displayed the magical name.

I could not find any sixpenny entrance and, fearing that the bazaar would be closed, I passed in quickly through a turnstile, handing a shilling to a weary-looking man. I found myself in a big hall girded at half its height by a gallery. Nearly all of the stalls were closed and the greater part of the hall was in darkness. I recognized a silence like that which pervades a church after a service. I walked into the centre of the bazaar timidly. A few people were gathered about the stalls which were still open. Before a curtain, over which the words *Café Chantant* were written in coloured lamps, two men were counting money on a salver. I listened to the fall of the coins.

florin, two shillings.

Remembering with difficulty why I had come, I went over to one of the stalls and examined porcelain vases and flowered tea-sets. At the door of the stall a young lady was talking and laughing with two young gentlemen. I remarked their English accents and listened vaguely to their conversation.

"Oh, I never said such a thing!"

"Oh, but you did!"

"Oh, but I didn't!"

"Didn't she say that?"

"Yes. I heard her."

"Oh, there's a . . . fib!"

Observing me, the young lady came over and asked me did I wish to buy anything. The tone of her voice was not encouraging; she seemed to have spoken to me out of a sense of duty. I looked humbly at the great jars that stood like eastern guards at either side of the dark entrance to the stall and murmured:

"No, thank you."

The young lady changed the position of one of the vases and went back to the two young men. They began to talk of the same subject. Once or twice the young lady glanced at me over her shoulder.

I lingered before her stall, though I knew my stay was useless, to make my interest in her wares seem the more real. Then I turned away slowly and walked down the middle of the bazaar. I allowed the two pennies to fall against the sixpence in my pocket. I heard a voice call from one end of the gallery that the light was out. The upper part of the hall was now completely dark.

Gazing up into the darkness I saw myself as a creature driven and derided by vanity; and my eye burned with anguish and anger.

James Joyce, Dubliners

BOUND EAST FOR CARDIFF

1919

SCENE. *The seamen's forecastle of the British tramp steamer Glencairn on a foggy night midway on the voyage between New York and Cardiff. An irregular-shaped compartment, the sides of which almost meet at the far end to form a triangle. Sleeping bunks about six feet long, ranged three deep with a space of three feet separating the upper from the lower, are built against the sides. On the right above the bunks three or four portholes can be seen. In front of the bunks, rough wooden benches. Over the bunks on the left, a lamp on a bracket. In the left foreground, a doorway. On the floor near it, a pail with a tin dipper. Oilskins are hanging from a hook near the doorway.*

The far side of the forecastle is so narrow that it contains only one series of bunks.

In under the bunks a glimpse can be had of sea-chests, suit-cases, sea-boots, etc., jammed in indiscriminately.

At regular intervals of a minute or so the blast of the steamer's whistle can be heard above all the other sounds.

Five men are sitting on the benches talking. They are dressed in dirty patched suits of dungaree, flannel shirts, and all are in their stocking feet. Four of the men are pulling on pipes and the air is heavy with rancid tobacco smoke. Sitting on the top bunk in the left foreground, a Norwegian, Paul, is softly playing some folk-song on a battered accordion. He stops from time to time to listen to the conversation.

In the lower bunk in the rear a dark-haired, hard-featured man is lying apparently asleep. One of his arms is stretched limply over the side of the bunk. His face is very pale, and drops of clammy perspiration glisten on his forehead.

It is nearing the end of the dog-watch — about ten minutes to eight in the evening.

Cocky (a weazened runt of a man. He is telling a story. The others are listening with amused, incredulous faces, interrupting him at the end of each sentence with loud derisive guffaws). Makin' love to me, she was! It's Gawd's truth! A bloomin' nigger! Greased all over with cocoanut oil, she was. Gawd blimey, I couldn't stand 'er. Bloody old cow, I says; and with that I fetched 'er a biff on the ear wot knocked 'er silly, an' —— *(He is interrupted by a roar of laughter from the others.)*

Davis (a middle-aged man with black hair and mustache). You're a liar, Cocky.

Scotty (a dark young fellow). Ho-ho! Ye werr neverr in New Guinea in yourr life, I'm thinkin'.

Olsen (a Swede with a drooping blond mustache — with ponderous sarcasm). Yust tink of it! You say she wass a cannibal, Cocky?

Driscoll (a brawny Irishman with the battered features of a prize-fighter). How cud ye doubt it, Ollie? A quane av the naygars she musta been surely. Who else wud think herself aqual to fallin' in love wid a beauthiful, divil-may-care rake av a man the loike av Cocky? *(A burst of laughter from the crowd.)*

Cocky (indignantly). Gawd strike me dead if it ain't true, every bleedin' word of it. 'Appened ten year ago come Christmas.

Scotty. 'Twas a Christmas dinner she had her eyes on.

Davis. He'd a been a tough old bird.

Driscoll. 'Tis lucky for both av ye ye escaped; for the quane av the cannibal isles wad a died av the bellyache the day afther Christmas, divil a doubt av ut. *(The laughter at this is long and loud.)*

Cocky (sullenly). Blarsted fat-'eads! (*The sick man in the lower bunk in the rear groans and moves restlessly. There is a hushed silence. All the men turn and stare at him.*)

Driscoll. Ssshh! (*In a hushed whisper.*) We'd best not be talkin' so loud and him tryin' to have a bit av a sleep. (*He tiptoes softly to the side of the bunk.*) Yank! You'd be wantin' a drink av wather, maybe? (*Yank does not reply. Driscoll bends over and looks at him.*) It's asleep he is, sure enough. His breath is chokin' in his throat loike wather gurglin' in a poipe. (*He comes back quietly and sits down. All are silent, avoiding each other's eyes.*)

Cocky (after a pause). Pore devil! It's over the side for 'im, Gawd 'elp 'im.

Driscoll. Stop your croakin'! He's not dead yet and, praise God, he'll have many a long day yet before him.

Scotty (shaking his head doubtfully). He's bod, mon, he's verry bod.

David. Lucky he's alive. Many a man's light woulda gone out after a fall like that.

Olsen. You saw him fall?

David. Right next to him. He and me was goin' down in number two hold to do some chippin'. He puts his leg over careless-like and misses the ladder and plumps straight down to the bottom. I was scared to look over for a minute, and then I heard him groan and I scuttled down after him. He was hurt bad inside, for the blood was drippin' from the side of his mouth. He was groanin' hard, but he never let a word out of him.

Cocky. An' you blokes remember when we 'auled 'im in 'ere? Oh, 'ell, 'e says, oh, 'ell — like that, and nothink else.

Olsen. Did the captain know where he iss hurted?

Cocky. That silly ol' josser! Wot the 'ell would 'e know abaht anythink?

Scotty (scornfully). He fiddles in his mouth wi' a bit of glass.

Driscoll (angrily). The divil's own life ut is to be out on the lonely sea wid nothin' betune you and a grave in the ocean but a spindle-shanked, gray-whiskered auld fool the loike av him. 'Twas enough to make a saint shwear to see him wid his gold watch in his hand, tryin' to look as wise as an owl on a tree, and all the toime he not knowin' whether 'twas cholery or the barber's itch was the matther with Yank.

Scotty (sardonically). He gave him a dose of salts, na doot?

Driscoll. Divil a thing he gave him at all, but looked in the book he had wid him, and shook his head, and walked out widout sayin' a word, the second mate afther him no wiser than himself, God's curse on the two av thim!

Cocky (after a pause). Yank was a good shipmate, pore beggar. Lend me four bob in Noo York, 'e did.

Driscoll (warmly). A good shipmate he was and is, none bether. Ye said no more than the truth, Cocky. Five years and more ut is since first I shipped wid him, and we've stuck together iver since through good luck and bad. Fights we've had, God help us, but 'twas only when we'd a bit av drink taken, and we always shook hands the nixt mornin'. Whativer was his was mine, and many's the toime I'd a been on the beach or worse, but for him. And now —— (*His voice trembles as he fights to control his emotion.*) Divil take me if I'm not startin' to blubber loike an auld woman, and he not dead at all, but goin' to live many a long year yet, maybe.

Davis. The sleep'll do him good. He seems better now.

Olsen. If he wude eat something ——

Driscoll. Wud ye have him be eatin' in his condishun? Sure it's hard enough on the rest av us wid nothin' the matther wid our insides to be stomachin' the skoff on this rusty lime-juicer.

Scotty (*indignantly*). It's a starvation ship.

Davis. Plenty o' work and no food — and the owners ridin' around in carriages.

Olsen. Hash, hash! Marmalade, py damn! (*He spits disgustedly.*)

Cocky. Bloody swill! Fit only for swine is wot I say.

Driscoll. And the dish-wather they disguise wid the name av tea! And the putty they call bread! My belly feels loike I'd swalleyed a dozen rivets at the thought av ut. And sea-biscuit that'd break the teeth av a lion if he had the misfortune to take a bite av one! (*Unconsciously they have all raised their voices, forgetting the sick man in their sailor's delight at finding something to grumble about.*)

Paul (*swings his feet over the side of his bunk, stops playing his accordion, and says slowly*). And rot-ten po-tay-toes! (*He starts in playing again. The sick man gives a groan of pain.*)

Driscoll (*holding up his hand*). Shut your mouths, all av you. 'Tis a hell av a thing for us to be complainin' about our guts, and a sick man maybe dyin' listenin' to us. (*Gets up and shakes his fist at the Norwegian.*) God stiffen you, ye square-head scut! Put down that organ av yours or I'll break your ugly face for you. Is that banshee schreechin' fit music for a sick man? (*The Norwegian puts his accordion in the*

skoff, food.
lime-juicer, an English vessel (from lime-juice as preventing scurvy).

bunk and lies back and closes his eyes. Driscoll goes over and stands beside Yank. The steamer's whistle sounds particularly loud in the silence.)

Davis. Damn this fog! (*Reaches in under a bunk and yanks out a pair of sea-boots, which he puts on.*) My lookout next, too. Must be nearly eight bells, boys. (*With the exception of Olsen, all the men sitting up put on oilskins, sou'-westers, sea-boots, etc., in preparation for the watch on deck. Olsen crawls into a lower bunk on the right.*)

Scotty. My wheel.

Olsen (*disgustedly*). Nothin' but yust dirty weather all dis voyage. I yust can't sleep when weestle blow. (*He turns his back to the light and is soon fast asleep and snoring.*)

Scotty. If this fog keeps up, I'm tellin' ye, we'll no be in Cardiff for a week or more.

Driscoll. 'Twas just such a night as this the auld Dover wint down. Just about this toime ut was, too, and we all sittin' round in the fo'castle, Yank beside me, whin all av a suddint we heard a great slitherin' crash, and the ship heeled over till we was all in a heap on wan side. What came afther I disremember exactly, except 'twas a hard shift to get the boats over the side before the auld teakettle sank. Yank was in the same boat wid me, and sivin morthal days we drifted wid scarcely a drop of wather or a bite to chew on. 'Twas Yank here that held me down whin I wanted to jump into the ocean, roarin' mad wid the thirst. Picked up we were on the same day wid only Yank in his senses, and him steerin' the boat.

Cocky (*protestingly*). Blimey but you're a cheerful blighter, Driscoll! Talkin' abaht shipwrecks in this 'ere blushin' fog. (*Yank groans and stirs uneasily, opening his eyes. Driscoll hurries to his side.*)

Driscoll. Are ye feelin' any betther, Yank?

Yank (*in a weak voice*). No.

Driscoll. Sure, you must be. You look as sthrong as an ox. (*Appealing to the others.*) Am I tellin' him a lie?

Davis. The sleep's done you good.

Cocky. You'll be 'avin' your pint of beer in Cardiff this day week.

Scotty. And fish and chips, mon!

Yank (*peevishly*). What're yuh all lyin' fur? D'yuh think I'm scared to —— (*He hesitates as if frightened by the word he is about to say.*)

Driscoll. Don't be thinkin' such things! (*The ship's bell is heard heavily tolling eight times. From the forecastle head above the voice of the lookout rises in a long wail:* Aaall's welll. *The men look uncertainly at Yank as if undecided whether to say good-bye or not.*)

Yank (*in an agony of fear*). Don't leave me, Drisc! I'm dyin', I tell yuh. I won't stay here alone with everyone snorin'. I'll go out on deck. (*He makes a feeble attempt to rise, but sinks back with a sharp groan. His breath comes in wheezy gasps.*) Don't leave me, Drisc! (*His face grows white and his head falls back with a jerk.*)

Driscoll. Don't be worryin', Yank. I'll not move a step out av here — and let that divil av a bosun curse his black head off. You speak a word to the bosun, Cocky. Tell him that Yank is bad took and I'll be stayin' wid him a while yet.

Cocky. Right-o. (*Cocky, Davis, and Scotty go out quietly.*)

Cocky (*from the alleyway*). Gawd blimey, the fog's thick as soup.

Driscoll. Are ye satisfied now, Yank? (*Receiving no answer, he bends over the still form.*) He's fainted,

God help him! (*He gets a tin dipper from the bucket and bathes Yank's forehead with the water. Yank shudders and opens his eyes.*)

Yank (*slowly*). I thought I was goin' then. Wha' did yuh wanta wake me up fur?

Driscoll (*with a forced gayety*). Is it wishful for heaven ye are?

Yank (*gloomily*). Hell, I guess.

Driscoll (*crossing himself involuntarily*). For the love av the saints don't be talkin' loike that! You'd give a man the creeps. It's chippin' rust on deck you'll be in a day or two wid the best av us. (*Yank does not answer, but closes his eyes wearily. The seaman who has been on lookout, Smitty, a young Englishman, comes in and takes off his dripping oilskins. While he is doing this the man whose turn at the wheel has been relieved enters. He is a dark burly fellow with a rough stupid face. The Englishman steps softly over to Driscoll. The other crawls into a lower bunk.*)

Smitty (*whispering*). How's Yank?

Driscoll. Bether. Ask him yourself. He's awake.

Yank. I'm all right, Smitty.

Smitty. Glad to hear it, Yank. (*He crawls to an upper bunk and is soon asleep.*)

Ivan (*the stupid-faced seaman, who comes in after Smitty, twists his head in the direction of the sick man*) You feel gude, Jank?

Yank (*wearily*). Yes, Ivan.

Ivan. Dot's gude. (*He rolls over on his side an falls asleep immediately.*)

Yank (*after a pause broken only by snores — wit a bitter laugh*). Good-bye and good luck to the lot you!

Driscoll. Is ut painin' you again?

Yank. It hurts like hell — here. (*He points to t.*

lower part of his chest on the left side.) I guess my old pump's busted. Ooohh! (*A spasm of pain contracts his pale features. He presses his hand to his side and writhes on the thin mattress of his bunk. The perspiration stands out in beads on his forehead.*)

Driscoll (*terrified*). Yank! Yank! What is ut? (*Jumping to his feet.*) I'll run for the captain. (*He starts for the doorway.*)

Yank (*sitting up in his bunk, frantic with fear*). Don't leave me, Drisc! For God's sake, don't leave me alone! (*He leans over the side of his bunk and spits. Driscoll comes back to him.*) Blood! Ugh!

Driscoll. Blood again! I'd best be gettin' the captain.

Yank. No, no, don't leave me! If yuh do I'll git up and follow you. I ain't no coward, but I'm scared to stay here with all of them asleep and snorin'. (*Driscoll, not knowing what to do, sits down on the bench beside him. He grows calmer and sinks back on the mattress.*) The captain can't do me no good, yuh know it yourself. The pain ain't so bad now, but I thought it had me then. It was like a buzz-saw cuttin' into me.

Driscoll (*fiercely*). God blarst ut!

(*The Captain and the Second Mate of the steamer enter the forecastle. The Captain is an old man with gray mustache and whiskers. The Mate is clean-shaven and middle-aged. Both are dressed in simple blue uniforms.*)

The Captain (*taking out his watch and feeling Yank's pulse*). And how is the sick man?

Yank (*feebly*). All right, sir.

The Captain. And the pain in the chest?

Yank. It still hurts, sir, worse than ever.

The Captain (taking a thermometer from his pocket and putting it into Yank's mouth). Here. Be sure and keep this in under your tongue, not over it.

The Mate (after a pause). Isn't this your watch on deck, Driscoll?

Driscoll. Yes, sorr, but Yank was fearin' to be alone, and ——

The Captain. That's all right, Driscoll. (*Stares at his watch for a moment or so; then takes the thermometer from Yank's mouth and goes to the lamp to read it. His expression grows very grave. He beckons the Mate and Driscoll to the corner near the doorway. Yank watches them furtively. The Captain speaks in a low voice to the Mate.*) Way up, both of them. (*To Driscoll.*) He has been spitting blood again?

Driscoll. Not much for the hour just past, sorr, but before that ——

The Captain. A great deal?

Driscoll. Yes, sorr.

The Captain. He hasn't eaten anything?

Driscoll. No, sorr.

The Captain. Did he drink that medicine I sent him?

Driscoll. Yes, sorr, but it didn't stay down.

The Captain (shaking his head). I'm afraid — he's very weak. I can't do anything else for him. It's too serious for me. If this had only happened a week later we'd be in Cardiff in time to ——

Driscoll. Plaze help him some way, sorr!

The Captain (impatiently). But, my good man, I'm not a doctor. (*More kindly as he sees Driscoll's grief.*) You and he have been shipmates a long time?

Driscoll. Five years and more, sorr.

The Captain. I see. Well, don't let him move. Keep him quiet and we'll hope for the best. I'll read the matter up and send him some medicine, something

to ease the pain, anyway.   (*Goes over to Yank.*)
Keep up your courage!   You'll be better to-morrow.
(*He breaks down lamely before Yank's steady gaze.*)
We'll pull you through all right — and — hm — well
— coming, Robinson?   Dammit!   (*He goes out hurriedly, followed by the Mate.*)

Driscoll (*trying to conceal his anxiety*).   Didn't I tell
you you wasn't half as sick as you thought you was?
The Captain'll have you out on deck cursin' and
swearin' loike a trooper before the week is out.

Yank. Don't lie, Drisc.   I heard what he said, and
if I didn't I c'd tell by the way I feel.   I know what's
goin' to happen.   I'm goin' to —— (*He hesitates for
a second — then resolutely.*)   I'm goin' to die, that's
what, and the sooner the better!

Driscoll (*wildly*).   No, and be damned to you, you're
not.   I'll not let you.

Yank. It ain't no use, Drisc.   I ain't got a chance,
but I ain't scared.   Gimme a drink of water, will yuh,
Drisc?   My throat's burnin' up.   (*Driscoll brings the
dipper full of water and supports his head while he
drinks in great gulps.*)

Driscoll (*seeking vainly for some word of comfort*).
Are ye feelin' more aisy-loike now?

Yank. Yes — now — when I know it's all up.   (*A
pause.*)   You mustn't take it so hard, Drisc.   I was
just thinkin' it ain't as bad as people think — dyin'.   I
ain't never took much stock in the truck them sky-
pilots preach.   I ain't never had religion; but I know
whatever it is what comes after it can't be no worser'n
this.   I don't like to leave you, Drisc, but — that's
all.

Driscoll (*with a groan*).   Lad, lad, don't be talkin'.

Yank. This sailor life ain't much to cry about
leavin' — just one ship after another, hard work,

small pay, and bum grub; and when we git into port, just a drunk endin' up in a fight, and all your money gone, and then ship away again.   Never meetin' no nice people; never gittin' outa sailor-town, hardly, in any port; travelin' all over the world and never seein' none of it; without no one to care whether you're alive or dead.   (*With a bitter smile.*)   There ain't much in all that'd make yuh sorry to lose it, Drisc.

Driscoll (*gloomily*).   It's hell of a life, the sea.

Yank (*musingly*).   It must be great to stay on dry land all your life and have a farm with a house of your own with cows and pigs and chickens, 'way in the middle of the land where yuh'd never smell the sea or see a ship.   It must be great to have a wife, and kids to play with at night after supper when your work was done.   It must be great to have a home of your own, Drisc.

Driscoll (*with a great sigh*).   It must, surely; but what's the use av thinkin' av ut?   Such things are not for the loikes av us.

Yank.   Sea-farin' is all right when you're young and don't care, but we ain't chickens no more, and some-how, I dunno, this last year has seemed rotten, and I've had a hunch I'd quit — with you, of course — and we'd save our coin, and go to Canada or Argentine or some place and git a farm, just a small one, just enough to live on.   I never told yuh this, 'cause I thought you'd laugh at me.

Driscoll (*enthusiastically*). Laugh at you, is ut? When I'm havin' the same thoughts myself, toime afther toime.   It's a grand idea and we'll be doin' ut sure if you'll stop your crazy notions — about — about bein' so sick.

Yank (*sadly*).   Too late.   We shouldn'ta made this trip, and then —— How'd all the fog git in here?

Driscoll. Fog?

Yank. Everything looks misty. Must be my eyes gittin' weak, I guess. What was we talkin' of a minute ago? Oh, yes, a farm. It's too late. (*His mind wandering.*) Argentine, did I say? D'yuh remember the times we've had in Buenos Aires? The moving pictures in Barracas? Some class to them, d'yuh remember?

Driscoll (*with satisfaction*). I do that; and so does the piany player. He'll not be forgettin' the black eye I gave him in a hurry.

Yank. Remember the time we was there on the beach and had to go to Tommy Moore's boarding-house to git shipped? And he sold us rotten oilskins and sea-boots full of holes, and shipped us on a skysail-yarder round the Horn, and took two months' pay for it? And the days we used to sit on the park benches along the Paseo Colon with the vigilantes lookin' hard at us? And the songs at the Sailor's Opera where the guy played ragtime — d'yuh remember them?

Driscoll. I do, surely.

Yank. And La Plata — phew, the stink of the hides! I always liked Argentine — all except that booze, caña. How drunk we used to git on that, remember?

Driscoll. Cud I forget ut? My head pains me at the menshun av that divil's brew.

Yank. Remember the night I went crazy with the heat in Singapore? And the time you was pinched by the cops in Port Said? And the time we was both locked up in Sydney for fightin'?

Driscoll. I do so.

Yank. And that fight on the dock at Cape Town —— (*His voice betrays great inward perturbation.*)

---

kysail-yarder, a square-rigged vessel, distinguished by having a skysail, or sail above the usual equipment.

Driscoll (hastily). Don't be thinkin' av that now. 'Tis past and gone.

Yank. God. They say He sees everything. He must know it was done in fair fight, in self-defense, don't yuh think?

Driscoll. Av course. Ye stabbed him, and be damned to him, for the skulkin' swine he was, afther him tryin' to stick you in the back, and you not suspectin'. Let your conscience be aisy. I wisht I had nothin' blacker than that on my sowl. I'd not be afraid av the angel Gabriel himself.

Yank (with a shudder). I c'd see him a minute ago with the blood spurtin' out of his neck. Ugh!

Driscoll. The fever, ut is, that makes you see such things. Give no heed to ut.

Yank (uncertainly). You don't think He'll hold it up agin me — God, I mean.

Driscoll. If there's justice in hiven, no! *(Yank seems comforted by this assurance.)*

Yank (after a pause). We won't reach Cardiff for a week at least. I'll be buried at sea.

Driscoll (putting his hands over his ears). Ssshh! I won't listen to you.

Yank (as if he had not heard him). It's as good a place as any other, I s'pose — only I always wanted to be buried on dry land. But what the hell'll I care — then? *(Fretfully.)* Why should it be a rotten night like this with that damned whistle blowin' and people snorin' all round? I wish the stars was out, and the moon, too; I c'd lie out on deck and look at them, and it'd make it easier to go — somehow.

Driscoll. For the love av God don't be talkin' loike that!

Yank. Whatever pay's comin' to me yuh can divvy up with the rest of the boys; and you take my watch. It ain't worth much, but it's all I've got.

Driscoll. But have you no relations at all to call your own?

Yank. No, not as I know of. One thing I forgot: You know Fanny the barmaid at the Red Stork in Cardiff.

Driscoll. Sure, and who doesn't?

Yank. She's been good to me. She tried to lend me half a crown when I was broke there last trip. Buy her the biggest box of candy yuh c'n find in Cardiff. (*Breaking down — in a choking voice.*) It's hard to ship on this voyage I'm goin' on — alone! (*Driscoll reaches out and grasps his hand. There is a pause, during which both fight to control themselves.*) My throat's like a furnace. (*He gasps for air.*) Gimme a drink of water, will yuh, Drisc? (*Driscoll gets him a dipper of water.*) I wish this was a pint of beer. Oooohh! (*He chokes, he is convulsed with agony, his hands tearing at his shirt-front. The dipper falls from his nerveless fingers.*)

Driscoll. For the love av God, what is ut, Yank?

Yank (*speaking with tremendous difficulty*). S'long, Drisc! (*He stares straight in front of him with eyes starting from their sockets.*) Who's that?

Driscoll. Who? What?

Yank (*faintly*). A pretty lady dressed in black. (*His face twitches and his body writhes in a final spasm, then straightens out rigidly.*)

Driscoll (*pale with horror*). Yank! Yank! Say a vord to me for the love av hiven! (*He shrinks away from the bunk, making the sign of the cross. Then he comes back and puts a trembling hand on Yank's chest and bends closely over the body.*)

Cocky (*from the alleyway*). Oh, Driscoll! Can you ave Yank for arf a mo' and give me a 'and?

Driscoll (*with a great sob*). Yank! (*He sinks down

*on his knees beside the bunk, his head on his hands.
His lips move in some half-remembered prayer.*)

Cocky (*enters, his oilskins and sou'-wester glistening
with drops of water*). The fog's lifted. (*Cocky sees
Driscoll and stands staring at him with open mouth.
Driscoll makes the sign of the cross again.*)

Cocky (*mockingly*). Sayin' 'is prayers! (*He catches
sight of the still figure in the bunk and an expression of
awed understanding comes over his face. He takes off his
dripping sou'-wester and stands, scratching his head.*)

Cocky (*in a hushed whisper*). Gawd blimey!

THE CURTAIN FALLS

Eugene O'Neill, The Great God Brown, and Other Plays,
published by Horace Liveright. 1926.

PREFACE TO A BOOK OF FISHHOOKS

1919

This little book of flies and hooks and guts and
hackles, which was presented to us by a friend who
heard us say we liked to go fishing — we may as well
admit at once that it is full of riddles we cannot read.
We know nothing about trout and have no great ambition to learn. Fishing for trout has too much exertion
and bodily effort about it to be attractive. One
tramps about over rough country and gets one's self
wet in cold water, and tangles one's hook in one's hair
and ears, and all that sort of thing.

Our idea of fishing is to put all the exertion up to the
fish. If they are ambitious, we will catch them. If
they are not, let them go about their business. If a
fish expects to be caught by us, he has to look alive.
We give him his opportunity, and he must make the
most of it.

Most of our fishing, and the only fishing we ever really enjoyed, was done with a worm, a hook, a leaden sinker, a line, and a willow pole. We wouldn't know what to do with a reel. We expect a fish to eat the hook very thoroughly, to persist until he gets it well down, and then to signal us that all is well by pulling the float under water; a reel is superfluous; one flips the pole over one's head and the fish lands somewhere in the bushes behind.

A little quiet river or a creek, with low banks and plenty of big trees along the banks, is the only place to fish; and the fish should be mostly bullheads. Bullheads know their business; they hook themselves more completely and competently than any other fish. A bullhead will swallow the worm, the hook, and the lead sinker, a part of the line, and then grumble because he hasn't been able to eat the float and the pole. And you can leave it all up to him. You can sit in the shade and watch the float bobbing and jerking about in the serene consciousness that he will do a good job. When he pulls the pole itself out of the socket of earth into which you have jabbed the butt end of it, then is the time to interfere and bring him to land. Don't hold the pole yourself; it is too much trouble.

Being out of the water doesn't make much difference to the average bullhead. We don't suppose he could stand it more than two or three days, unless there was a damp wind blowing, but a few hours more or less are nothing to him. After having eaten as much of your fishing tackle as you will permit him to have before interfering, you might think that he would be a little dejected. But not so. You go to take the hook out of him, and he rushes at you and horns you, with a queer purring noise, and shows every disposition to fight it out on land.

And he seldom knows when he is dead. Often in the course of a day we have caught a bushel or so of bullheads and thrown them into the back of the buggy and driven home with them, five or six miles, maybe. Arrived at home, we would find them stiff and caked with dried mud and dust, and to all appearances dead, having been out of the water and jogging along in the hot afternoon sun for a couple of hours. But throw them into a barrel of water, and in a few minutes they were swimming around as if nothing had happened, grinning over the top of the barrel and begging for more worms and hooks and lead sinkers. Refreshed by his cool plunge, the beast was ready for another romp. The bullhead is not a beautiful fish, and has no claims to aristocracy, but he is enduring.

We never liked to fish from a boat. You have to row the thing about, and that is a lot of trouble. Select a big, shady tree that bends over a pool in some little inland stream, and lie down under the tree, and lie there all day, and fish and eat and smoke and chew tobacco and watch the dragon flies, and spit into the water. If you feel like swimming a little, all right — it doesn't particularly bother the bullheads. But it is a mistake to go to sleep.

If you go to sleep while you are loafing, how are you going to know you are loafing? And if you don't know it, what satisfaction is there in it? And it is also a mistake to think too deeply. If you do that, about the time you begin to get on the track of the secret of the universe some fool fish will hook himself, and you will have to attend to him.

Lie with your hat over your face, and watch

thoughts carefully from under the brim of it, as they come toward you out of the woods or up the creek. And if a thought that seems as if it were going to be too profound or troublesome tries to crawl up on you, shoo it away and wait for an easy thought. And when you get an easy thought, hold on to it, and think it for a long time, and enjoy it.

The best thoughts to have when you are fishing are the thoughts about what you would do if you had a million dollars. After a while you get sort of lenient toward the world, and unambitious, and think it's a little selfish of you to want a whole million, and say "Shucks! I'd be willing to take a hundred thousand!" And you think maybe if you roused up a little and looked over the edge of the bank you would see a streak of gold in the soil, and then you would go and buy that land of the farmer that owns it and get rich off of the gold. And then you remember that you don't know who owns the land and it would be considerable trouble to have to ask questions around and find out. So it doesn't seem worth while to look over the edge of the bank and see whether the gold is there, after all. And, anyhow, would it be fair to whatever farmer owns the land, to buy it knowing there was gold on it and never tell him? And what would you buy it with? If you borrowed money to buy it with, the fellow you borrowed the money from would likely get the biggest part of it, and you would have all your work and worry for nothing; and so you don't look to see if the gold is there. And then you get to thinking that probably there aren't many people honest enough to pass up a fortune like that just simply because somebody else owns it, and you admire yourself for being that honest.

You can find more things to admire yourself for, lying around fishing like that, if you pick your thoughts properly. Everybody ought to do it all the time and not work at anything else.

Don Marquis, in *Prefaces.* Reprinted by permission of the publishers, D. Appleton & Company, and of the author.

MONEY

1920

"As the world is, and will be, 'tis a sort of duty to be rich," wrote Lady Mary Wortley Montagu; and her words — which sound almost ascetic in our ears — were held to be of doubtful morality in the godless eighteenth century which she adorned and typified. Even Lady Mary endeavoured to qualify their greed by explaining that she valued money because it gave her the power to do good; but her hard-headed compatriots frankly doubted this excusatory clause. They knew perfectly well that a desire to do good is not, and never has been, a motive power in the acquisition of wealth.

Lady Mary did render her country one inestimable service; but her fortune (which, after all, was of no great magnitude) had nothing whatever to do with it. Intelligent observation, dauntless courage, and the supreme confidence which nerved her to experiment upon her own child — these qualities enabled her to force inoculation upon a reluctant and scandalized public. These qualities have lifted mankind out of many a rut, and are all we shall have to depend on while the world rolls on its way. When Aristotle said that money was barren, he did not mean that it was barren of delights; but that it had no power to get us to any place worth reaching, no power to

quicken the intellectual and spiritual potencies of the
soul.

The love of gold, the craving for wealth, has not
lain dormant for ages in the human heart, waiting for
the twentieth century to call it into being. It is no
keener now than it has always been, but it is ranker in
its growth and expression, being a trifle over-nourished
in our plethoric land, and not subjected to keen com-
peting emotions. Great waves of religious thought,
great struggles for principles and freedom, great births
of national life, great discoveries, great passions, and
great wrongs — these things have swayed the world,
wrecking and saving the souls of men without regard
for money. Great qualities, too, have left their impress upon the human race, and endowed it for all
the years to come.

The genius which in the thirteenth century found
expression in architecture and scholasticism, which in
the sixteenth and seventeenth centuries found expression in art and letters, finds expression to-day in
applied science and finance. Industrial capitalism,
as we know it now, is the latest development of man's
restless energy. It has coloured our times, given us
new values in education, and intruded itself grossly
into the quiet places of life. We should bear with it
patiently, we might even "admire it from afar," if
only we were sometimes suffered to forget. "Money
talks," and, by way of encouraging its garrulity, we
talk about money, and in terms of money, until it
would sometimes appear as if the currency of the
United States were the only thing in the country vital
enough to interpret every endeavour, and illustrate
every situation.

Here, for example, is an imposing picture in a Sunday paper, a picture full of dignified ecclesiastics and

decorous spectators. The text reads, "Breaking ground for a three-million-dollar nave." It is a comprehensive statement, and one that conveys to the public the only circumstance the public presumably cares to hear. But it brings a great cathedral down to the level of the million-dollar club-houses, or boat-houses, or fishing-camps which are described in unctuous and awe-stricken paragraphs. It is even dimly suggestive of the million-dollar babies whom reporters follow feverishly up and down Palm Beach, and who will soon have to be billion-dollar babies if they want to hold their own. We are now on terms of easy familiarity with figures which used to belong to the abstractions of arithmetic, and not to the world of life. We have become proudly aware of the infinite possibilities of accumulation and of waste.

For this is the ebb and flow of American wealth. It is heaped up with resistless energy and concentration; it is dissipated in broken and purposeless profusion. Every class resents the extravagance of every other class; but none will practise denial. The millionaire who plays with a yacht and decks his wife with pearls looks askance upon the motor and silk shirt of the artisan. The artisan, with impulses and ambitions as ignoble and as unintelligent as the millionaire's is sullenly aware that, waste as he may, the rich can waste more, and he is still dissatisfied. There is no especial appeal to manhood in a silk shirt, no approach to sweetness and light. It represents an ape-like imitation of something not worth imitating, a hopeless ignorance of the value and worth of money.

A universal reluctance to practise economy indicate a weakness in the moral fibre of a nation, a dangerou absence of pride. There is no power of the sou strong enough to induce thrift but pride. There is no quality stern enough to bar self-indulgence but the overmastering dictates of self-respect. There is no joy that life can yield comparable to the joy of independence. A nation is free when it submits to coercion from no other nation. A man is free when he is the arbiter of his own fate. National and individual freedom have never come cheap. The sacrifice which insures the one insures the other; the resolution which preserves the one preserves the other. When Andrew Marvell declined the bribe offered him "out of pure affection" by the Lord Treasurer, saying he had "a blade-bone of mutton" in his cupboard which would suffice for dinner, he not only held his own honour inviolate, but he vindicated the liberty of letters, the liberty of Parliament, and the liberty of England. No wonder an old chronicler says that his integrity and spirit were "dreadful" to the corrupt officials of his day.

There are Americans who appear to love their country for much the same reason that Stevenson's "child" loves the "friendly cow":

"She gives me cream with all her might
To eat with apple tart."

When the supply of cream runs short, the patriot's love runs shorter. He holds virulent mass-meetings to complain of the cow, of the quality of the cream, and of its distribution. If he be an immigrant, he probably riots in the streets, not clamouring for the flesh-pots of Egypt — that immemorial cry for ease and bondage — inasmuch as the years of his thraldom had been softened by no such indulgence; but simply because the image of the cow is never absent from his mind, or from the minds of those to whom he looks for guidance. The captain of industry and the agitator, the spendthrift and the spendthrift's wife who fling their money ostentatiously to the four winds of heaven, the working-man and the working-woman who exact the largest wage for the least labour, all are actuated by the same motive — to get as much and to give as little as they can. It is not a principle which makes for citizenship, and it will afford no great help in the hour of the nation's trial. Material progress and party politics are engrossing things; but perhaps Francis Parkman was right when he said that if our progress is to be at the mercy of our politics, and our politics at the mercy of our mobs, we shall have no lasting foundation for prosperity and well-being.

The tendency to gloat over the sight and sound of money may be less pervasive than it seems. It may be only a temporary predisposition, leaving us at heart clean, wise, and temperate. But there is a florid exuberance in the handling of this recurrent theme which nauseates us a little, like very rich food eaten in a close room. Why should we be told that "the world gapes in wonder" as it contemplates "an Aladdin romance of steel and gold"? The world has had other things to gape over in these sorrowful and glorious years. "Once a barefoot boy, now riding in a hundred-thousand-dollar private car." There is a headline to catch the public eye, and make the public tongue hang watering from its mouth. That car, "early Pullman and late German Lloyd," is to the American reader what the two thousand black slaves with jars of jewels upon their heads were to Dick Swiveller [1] — a vision of tasteful opulence. More intimate journalists tell us that a "Financial Potentate" eats baked potatoes for his luncheon, and gives

[1] Dick Swiveller, a poor clerk in Dickens's *The Old Curiosity Shop.*

his friends notebooks with a moral axiom on each page. We cannot really care what this unknown gentleman eats. We cannot, under any conceivable circumstance, covet a moral notebook. Yet such items of information would not be painstakingly acquired unless they afforded some mysterious gratification to their reader.

As for the "athletic millionaires," who sport in the open like — and often with — ordinary men, they keep their chroniclers nimble. Fashions in plutocracy change with the changing times. The reporter who used to be turned loose in a nabob's private office, and who rapturously described its "ebony centre-table on which is laid a costly cover of maroon-coloured silk plush," and its panelled walls, "the work of a lady amateur of great ability" (I quote from a newspaper of 1890), now has to scurry round golf-links, and shiver on the outskirts of a polo-field. From him we learn that young New Yorkers, the least and lowest of whom lives in a nine-hundred-thousand-dollar house, play tennis and golf like champions, or "cut a wide swathe in polo circles with their fearless riding." From him we learn that "automobile racing can show its number of millionaires," as if it were at all likely to show its number of clerks and ploughmen. Extravagance may be the arch-enemy of efficiency, but it is, and has always been, the friend of aimless excess.

When I was young, and millionaires were a rarity in my unassuming town, a local divine fluttered our habitual serenity by preaching an impassioned sermon upon a local Croesus. He was but a moderate sort of Croesus, a man of kindly nature and simple vanities, whom his townspeople had been in the habit of regarding with mirthful and tolerant eyes. Therefore it was a bit startling to hear — from the pulpit — that this amiable gentleman was "a crown of glory upon the city's brow," and that his name was honoured "from the Golden Gate to New Jersey's silver sands." It was more than startling to be called upon to admire the meekness with which he trod the common earth, and the unhesitating affability with which he bowed to all his acquaintances, "acknowledging every salute of civility or respect," because "like another Frederick II of Prussia" he felt his fellow-citizens to be human beings like himself. This admission into the ranks of humanity, however gratifying to our self-esteem, was tempered by so many exhortations to breathe our millionaire's name with becoming reverence, and was accompanied by such a curious medley of Bible texts, and lists of distinguished people whom the millionaire entertained, that we hardly knew where we stood in the order of creation.

Copies of this sermon, which was printed "in deference to many importunities," are now extremely rare. Reading its yellow pages, we become aware that the rites and ceremonies with which one generation worships its golden calf differ in detail from the rites and ceremonies with which another generation performs this pious duty. The calf itself has never changed since it was first erected in the wilderness — the original model hardly admitting of improvement. Ruskin used to point out gleefully a careless couple who, in Claude's picture of the adoration of the golden calf, are rowing in a pleasure boat on a stream which flows mysteriously through the desert. Indifferent to gold, uninterested in idolatry, this pair glide smoothly by; and perhaps the river of time bears them through centuries of greed and materialism to some hidden haven of repose.

Saint Thomas Aquinas defines the sin of avarice as "desire to acquire or retain in undue measure, beyond the order of reason." Possibly no one has ever believed that he committed this sin, that there was anything unreasonable in his desires, or undue in their measure of accomplishment. "Reason" is a word of infinite flexibility. The statisticians who revel in mathematical intricacies tell us that Mr. John D. Rockefeller's income is one hundred dollars a minute, and that his yearly income exceeds the lifetime earnings of two thousand average American citizens, and is equivalent to the income of fifty average American citizens sustained throughout the entire Christian era. It sounds more bewildering than seductive, and the breathless rush of a hundred dollars a minute is a little like the seven dinners a day which Alice in Wonderland stands ready to forego as a welcome punishment for misbehaviour. But who shall say that a hundred dollars a minute is beyond the "order of reason"? Certainly Saint Thomas did not refer to incomes of this range, inasmuch as his mind (though not without a quality of vastness) could never have embraced their possibility.

On the other hand, Mr. Rockefeller is responsible for the suggestion that Saint Paul, were he living to-day, would be a captain of industry. Here again a denial is as valueless as an assertion. It is much the habit of modern propagandists — no matter what their propaganda may be — to say that the gap between themselves and the Apostles is merely a gap of centuries, and that the unlikeness, which seems to us so vivid, is an unlikeness of time and circumstance, not of the inherent qualities of the soul. The multiplication of assets, the destruction of trade-rivalry, formed — apparently — no part of the original apostolic programme. If the tent-maker of Tarsus coveted wealth, he certainly went the wrong way about getting it. If there was that in his spirit which corresponded to the modern instinct for accumulation, he did great injustice to his talents, wasting his incomparable energy on labours which — from his own showing — left him too often homeless, and naked, and hungry. Even the tent-making, by which he earned his bread, appears to have been valuable to him for the same reason that the blade-bone of mutton was valuable to Andrew Marvell — not so much because it filled his stomach, as because it insured his independence.

"*L'amour d'argent a passé en dogme de morale publique*," wrote George Sand, whose words have now and then a strange prophetic ring. The "peril of Prosperity," to borrow President Hibben's alliterative phrase, was not in her day the menace it is in ours, nor has it ever been in her land the menace it has been in ours, because of the many other perils, not to speak of other interests and ideals, filling the Frenchman's mind. But if George Sand perceived a growing candour in the deference paid to wealth, to wealth as an abstraction rather than to its possessor, a dropping of the old hypocrisies which made a pretence of doubt and disapproval, a development of honoured and authorized avarice, she was a close observer as well as a caustic commentator.

The artlessness of the American attitude might disarm criticism were anything less than public sanity at stake. We appeal simply and robustly to the love of gain, and we seldom appeal in vain. It is not only that education has substituted the principle of getting on for less serviceable values; but we are bidden to

L'amour d'argent, etc., The love of money has become a dogma of popular morals.

purchase marketable knowledge, no less than marketable foodstuff, as an easy avenue to fortune. If we will eat and drink the health-giving comestibles urged upon us, our improved digestions will enable us to earn larger incomes. If we will take a highly commended course of horseshoeing or oratorio-writing, prosperity will be our immediate reward. If we will buy some excellent books of reference, they will teach us to grow rich.

"There are one thousand more millionaires in the United States than there were ten years ago," say the purveyors of these volumes. "At the present rate of increase, the new millionaires in the next few years will be at least twelve hundred. *Will you be one of them?*" There is a question to ask a young American at the outset of his career! There is an incentive to study! And by way of elucidating a somewhat doubtful situation, the advertisers go on to say: "Typical men of brains are those who have dug large commercial enterprises out of a copper mine, or transformed buying and selling into an art. You must take a leaf from the experience of such men if you would hold positions of responsibility and power."

Just how the reference books — chill avenues of universal erudition — are going to give us control of a copper mine or of a department store is not made clear; but their vendors know that there is no use in offering anything less than wealth, or, as it is sometimes spelled, "success," as a return for the price of the volumes. And if a tasteful border design of fat money-bags scattering a cascade of dollars fails to quicken the sales, there is no tempting the heart of man. Our covetousness is as simple and as easily played upon as was the covetousness of the adventurers who went digging for buried treasures on the unimpeachable authority of a soothsayer. The testimony offered in a New Jersey court that a man had bought some farmland because the spirit of a young negro girl had indicated that there was money hidden beneath the soil; the arraignment before a Brooklyn magistrate of two Gipsy women, charged with stealing the cash they had been commissioned to "bless," are proof, if proof were needed, that intelligence has not kept pace with cupidity.

The endless stories about messenger boys and elevator men who have been given a Wall Street "tip," and who have become capitalists in a day, are astonishingly like the stories which went their round when the South-Sea Bubble hung iridescent over London. Mankind has never wearied of such tales since Aladdin (one of Fortune's fools) won his easy way to wealth. Even the old dime novel with "Dare-Devil Dick," or "Jasper, the Boy Detective," for a hero, has been transmogrified into a "Fame and Fortune" series, with "Boys That Make Money" figuring vaingloriously on the title-page. Gone is the Indian brave, the dauntless young seaman who saved the American navy, the calm-eyed lad who held up a dozen masked ruffians with one small pistol. In their place we have the boy in the broker's office who finds out that "A. and C." stock will double its value within ten days; or the exploits of a group of juvenile speculators, who form a "secret syndicate," and outwit the wisest heads on Wall Street. The supremacy of youth — a vital feature of such fiction — is indicated when the inspired messenger boy gives a "pointer" to an old and influential firm of brokers, who receive it with glistening eyes and respectful gratitude. "I did not tip you in expectation of any compensation," observes the magnanimous and up-to-date young hero. "I simply felt it was my duty to prevent you from losing the profit that was bound to come your way if you held on a few days longer."

Our newspapers have told us (we should like to know who told the newspapers) that high prices are popular prices. It is fitting and proper that people who own the wealth of the world should pay a great deal for everything they buy. Shoppers with their purses full of money are affronted by any hint of cheapness or economy. This may be true, though it reminds me a little of a smiling Neapolitan who once assured me that his donkey liked to be beaten. One cannot, without entering into the mind of a donkey or of a rich American, deny the tastes imputed to them; but one may cherish doubts. It is true that "record prices" have been paid for every luxury, that the sales of furriers and jewellers have been unprecedented in the annals of our commerce, that the eager buying of rare books, pictures, and curios, flung on the markets by the destitution of Europe, has never been surpassed. One might wish that destitution anywhere (Vienna is not so far from New York, that no cry of pain can reach us) would dim our pleasure in such purchases. This does not seem to be the case. "'Tis man's perdition to be safe,"[1] and 'tis his deepest and deadliest perdition to profit by the misfortunes of others.

An American rhapsodist, singing the pæan of money in the pages of the *Bankers' Magazine*, says in its mighty name: "I am the minister of war and the messenger of peace. No army can march without my command. Until I speak, no ship of trade can sail from any port."

"Until I speak"! Always the emphasis upon that

[1] Emerson: 'Tis man's perdition to be safe, when for the truth he ought to die.

powerful voice which is so mute and inglorious without the compelling mind of man. When President Cleveland said that if it took every dollar in the Treasury, and every soldier in the United States Army, to deliver a postal card in Chicago, that postal card should be delivered, he was perhaps glad to think that the nation's wealth, like the nation's force, could be used to fulfil the nation's obligations. But back of wealth, and back of force, was purpose. When a man lays hand upon the "hilt of action," money stops talking and obeys.

Mr. Shane Leslie, shrinking sensitively from that oppressive word, "efficiency," and seeking what solace he can find in the survival of unpractical ideals, ventures to say that every university man "carries away among the husks of knowledge the certainty that there are less things saleable in heaven and earth than the advocates of sound commercial education would suppose." This truth, more simply phrased by the Breton peasant woman who said "*Le bon Dieu ne vend pas ses biens*," has other teachers besides religion and the classics. History, whether we read it or live in it, makes nothing clearer. Mr. Henry Ford is credited with saying that he would not give a nickel for all the history in the world; but though he can, and does, forbear to read it, he has to live in it with the rest of us, and learn its lessons firsthand. No one desired the welfare — or what he conceived to be the welfare — of mankind more sincerely than he did; and he was prepared to buy it at a handsome figure. Yet Heaven refused to sell, and earth, inasmuch as the souls of men are not *her* possessions, had nothing worth his purchase.

The price of war can be computed in figures; the

Le bon Dieu, etc., The good God does not sell his goods.

price of peace calls for another accountant. The
tanker, Gold Shell, which first crossed the "forbidden"
zone did more than a score of peace ships could have
done to secure the civilization of the world. Its plain
sailors who put something (I don't know what they
called it) above personal safety, and their plain captain who expressed in the regrettable language of the
sea his scorn of German pirates, were prepared to pay
a higher price than any millionaire could offer for
their own and their country's freedom. We know
what these men risked because we know what agoniz-
ing deaths the sailors on the tanker, Healdton, suffered
at Germany's hands. The Gold Shell seamen knew
it too, and met frightfulness with fearlessness. The
world is never so bad but that men's souls can rise
above its badness, and restore our fainting faith.

Mohammed prayed that he might be found among
the poor on the Judgment Day — a prayer echoed by
Saint Bernard, who took some pains to insure its being answered. Yet, as a mere abstraction, of what
worth is poverty? The jewel in the toad's head is as
glittering as adversity is sweet.[1] One has been well
likened to the other. Bishop Lawrence, undismayed
by the most humiliating page in our country's history,
seized a crucial moment in which to say very simply
and gallantly that Americans are not wedded to ease,
or enthralled by wealth. The time has come to prove
him in the right. God will not sell us safety. We
learned this much in the winter of 1917, when we dug
our mail out of an American steamer, and asked
Britain — Britain burdened with debt and bleeding
at every pore — to carry it over the sea. For our own
sake, no less than for the world's sake, we must show
that we coin money in no base spirit, that we cherish

[1] *As You Like It*, II, i, 12–14.

it with no base passion. The angel who looked too long at heaven's golden pavement was flung into hell.

Agnes Repplier, Points of Friction, first published in the Atlantic Monthly.

I WANT TO KNOW WHY

1921

We got up at four in the morning, that first day in the east. On the evening before we had climbed off a freight train at the edge of town, and with the true instinct of Kentucky boys had found our way across town and to the race-track and the stables at once. Then we knew we were all right. Hanley Turner right away found a nigger we knew. It was Bildad Johnson who in the winter works at Ed Becker's livery barn in our home town, Beckersville. Bildad is a good cook as almost all our niggers are and of course he, like everyone in our part of Kentucky who is anyone at all, likes the horses. In the spring Bildad begins to scratch around. A nigger from our country can flatter and wheedle anyone into letting him do most anything he wants. Bildad wheedles the stable men and the trainers from the horse farms in our country around Lexington. The trainers come into town in the evening to stand around and talk and maybe get into a poker game. Bildad gets in with them. He is always doing little favors and telling about things to eat, chicken browned in the pan, and how is the best way to cook sweet potatoes and corn bread. It makes your mouth water to hear him. When the racing season comes on and the horses go to the races and there is all the talk on the streets in the evenings about the new colts, and everyone says when they are going over to Lexington or to the spring meet ing at Churchill Downs or to Latonia, and the horse-men that have been down to New Orleans or maybe at the winter meeting at Havana in Cuba come home to spend a week before they start out again, at such a time when everything talked about in Beckersville is just horses and nothing else and the outfits start out and horse racing is in every breath of air you breathe, Bildad shows up with a job as cook for some outfit. Often when I think about it, his always going all season to the races and working in the livery barn in the winter where horses are and where men like to come and talk about horses, I wish I was a nig-ger. It's a foolish thing to say, but that's the way I am about being around horses, just crazy, I can't help it.

Well, I must tell you about what we did and let you in on what I'm thinking about. Four of us boys from Beckersville, all whites and sons of men who live in Beckersville regular, made up our minds we were going to the races, not just to Lexington or Louisville, I don't mean, but to the big eastern track we were always hearing our Beckersville men talk about, to Saratoga. We were all pretty young then. I was just turned fifteen and I was the oldest of the four. It was my scheme. I admit that and I talked the others into trying it. There was Hanley Turner and Henry Rieback and Tom Tumberton and myself. I had thirty-seven dollars I had earned during the win-ter working nights and Saturdays in Enoch Myer's grocery. Henry Rieback had eleven dollars and the others, Hanley and Tom, had only a dollar or two each. We fixed it all up and laid low until the Ken-tucky spring meetings were over and some of our men, the sportiest ones, the ones we envied the most, had cut out — then we cut out too.

I won't tell you the trouble we had beating our way on freights and all. We went through Cleveland and Buffalo and other cities and saw Niagara Falls. We bought things there, souvenirs and spoons and cards and shells with pictures of the falls on them for our sisters and mothers, but thought we had better not send any of the things home. We didn't want to put the folks on our trail and maybe be nabbed.

We got into Saratoga as I said at night and went to the track. Bildad fed us up. He showed us a place to sleep in hay over a shed and promised to keep still. Niggers are all right about things like that. They won't squeal on you. Often a white man you might meet, when you had run away from home like that, might appear to be all right and give you a quarter or a half dollar or something, and then go right and give you away. White men will do that, but not a nigger. You can trust them. They are squarer with kids. I don't know why.

At the Saratoga meeting that year there were a lot of men from home. Dave Williams and Arthur Mulford and Jerry Myers and others. Then there was a lot from Louisville and Lexington Henry Rieback knew but I didn't. They were professional gamblers and Henry's father is one too. He is what is called a sheet writer and goes away most of the year to tracks. In the winter when he is home in Beckersville he don't stay there much but goes away to cities and deals faro. He is a nice man and generous, is always sending Henry presents, a bicycle and a gold watch and a boy scout suit of clothes and things like that.

My own father is a lawyer. He's all right, but don't make much money and can't buy me things and anyway I'm getting so old now I don't expect it. He

sheet writer, a bookmaker's assistant who records the bets made.

never said nothing to me against Henry, but Hanley Turner and Tom Tumberton's fathers did. They said to their boys that money so come by is no good and they didn't want their boys brought up to hear gamblers' talk and be thinking such things and maybe embrace them.

That's all right and I guess the men know what they are talking about, but I don't see what it's got to do with Henry or with horses either. That's what I'm writing this story about. I'm puzzled. I'm getting to be a man and want to think straight and be O.K., and there's something I saw at the race meeting at the eastern track I can't figure out.

I can't help it, I'm crazy about thoroughbred horses. I've always been that way. When I was ten years old and saw I was going to be big and couldn't be a rider I was so sorry I nearly died. Henry Hellinfinger in Beckersville, whose father is Postmaster, is grown up and too lazy to work, but likes to stand around in the street and get up jokes on boys like sending them to a hardware store for a gimlet to bore square holes and other jokes like that. He played one on me. He told me that if I would eat half a cigar I would be stunted and not grow any more and maybe could be a rider. I did it. When father wasn't looking I took a cigar out of his pocket and gagged it down some way. It made me awful sick and the doctor had to be sent for, and then it did no good. I kept right on growing. It was a joke. When I told what I had done and why most fathers would have whipped me but mine didn't.

Well, I didn't get stunted and didn't die. It serves Harry Hellinfinger right. Then I made up my mind I would like to be a stable boy, but had to give that up too. Mostly niggers do that work and I knew father wouldn't let me go into it. No use to ask him.

If you've never been crazy about thoroughbreds it's because you've never been around where they are much and don't know any better. They're beautiful. There isn't anything so lovely and clean and full of spunk and honest and everything as some race horses. On the big horse farms that are all around our town Beckersville there are tracks and the horses run in the early morning. More than a thousand times I've got out of bed before daylight and walked two or three miles to the tracks. Mother wouldn't of let me go but father always says, "Let him alone." So I got some bread out of the bread box and some butter and jam, gobbled it and lit out.

At the tracks you sit on the fence with the men, whites and niggers, and they chew tobacco and talk, and then the colts are brought out. It's early and the grass is covered with shiny dew and in another field a man is plowing and they are frying things in a shed where the track niggers sleep, and you know how a nigger can giggle and laugh and say things that make you laugh. A white man can't do it and some niggers can't but a track nigger can every time.

And so the colts are brought out and some are just galloped by stable boys, but almost every morning on a big track owned by a rich man who lives maybe in New York, there are always, nearly every morning, a few colts and some of the old race horses and geldings and mares that are cut loose.

It brings a lump up into my throat when a horse runs. I don't mean all horses but some. I can pick them nearly every time. It's in my blood like in the blood of race-track niggers and trainers. Even when they just go slop-jogging along with a little nigger on their backs I can tell a winner. If my throat hurts and it's hard for me to swallow, that's him. He'll run like Sam Hill when you let him out. If he don't win every time it'll be a wonder and because they've got him in a pocket behind another or he was pulled or got off bad at the post or something. If I wanted to be a gambler like Henry Rieback's father I could get rich. I know I could and Henry says so too. All I would have to do is to wait 'til that hurt comes when I see a horse and then bet every cent. That's what I would do if I wanted to be a gambler, but I don't.

When you're at the tracks in the morning — not the race-tracks but the training tracks around Beckersville — you don't see a horse, the kind I've been talking about, very often, but it's nice anyway. Any thoroughbred, that is sired right and out of a good mare and trained by a man that knows how, can run. If he couldn't what would he be there for and not pulling a plow?

Well, out of the stables they come and the boys are on their backs and it's lovely to be there. You hunch down on top of the fence and itch inside you. Over in the sheds the niggers giggle and sing. Bacon is being fried and coffee made. Everything smells lovely. Nothing smells better than coffee and manure and horses and niggers and bacon frying and pipes being smoked out of doors on a morning like that. It just gets you, that's what it does.

But about Saratoga. We was there six days and not a soul from home seen us and everything came off just as we wanted it to, fine weather and horses and races and all. We beat our way home and Bildad gave us a basket with fried chicken and bread and other eatables in, and I had eighteen dollars when we got back to Beckersville. Mother jawed and cried but Pop didn't say much. I told everything we done except one thing. I did and saw that alone. That's what

I'm writing about. It got me upset. I think about it at night. Here it is.

At Saratoga we laid up nights in the hay in the shed Bildad showed us and ate with the niggers early and at night when the race people had all gone away. The men from home stayed mostly in the grandstand and betting field, and didn't come out around the places where the horses are kept except to the paddocks just before a race when the horses are saddled. At Saratoga they don't have paddocks under an open shed as at Lexington and Churchill Downs and other tracks down in our country, but saddle the horse right out in an open place under trees on a lawn as smooth and nice as Banker Bohon's front yard here in Beckersville. It's lovely. The horses are sweaty and nervous and shine and the men come out and smoke cigars and look at them and the trainers are there and the owners, and your heart thumps so you can hardly breathe.

Then the bugle blows for post and the boys that ride come running out with their silk clothes on and you run to get a place by the fence with the niggers.

I always am wanting to be a trainer or owner, and at the risk of being seen and caught and sent home I went to the paddocks before every race. The other boys didn't but I did.

We got to Saratoga on a Friday and on Wednesday the next week the big Mullford Handicap was to be run. Middlestride was in it and Sunstreak. The weather was fine and the track fast. I couldn't sleep the night before.

What had happened was that both those horses are the kind it makes my throat hurt to see. Middlestride is long and looks awkward and is a gelding. He belongs to Joe Thompson, a little owner from home who only has a half dozen horses. The Mullford Handicap is for a mile and Middlestride can't untrack fast. He goes away slow and is always way back at the half, then he begins to run and if the race is a mile and a quarter he'll just eat up everything and get there.

Sunstreak is different. He is a stallion and nervous and belongs on the biggest farm we've got in our country, the Van Riddle place that belongs to Mr. Van Riddle of New York. Sunstreak is like a girl you think about sometimes but never see. He is hard all over and lovely too. When you look at his head you want to kiss him. He is trained by Jerry Tillford who knows me and has been good to me lots of times, lets me walk into a horse's stall to look at him close and other things. There isn't anything as sweet as that horse. He stands at the post quiet and not letting on, but he is just burning up inside. Then when the barrier goes up he is off like his name, Sunstreak. It makes you ache to see him. It hurts you. He just lays down and runs like a bird dog. There can't anything I ever see run like him except Middlestride when he gets untracked and stretches himself.

Gee! I ached to see that race and those two horses run, ached and dreaded it too. I didn't want to see either of our horses beaten. We had never sent a pair like that to the races before. Old men in Beckersville said so and the niggers said so. It was a fact.

Before the race I went over to the paddocks to see. I looked a last look at Middlestride, who isn't such a much standing in a paddock that way, then I went to to see Sunstreak.

It was his day. I knew when I see him. I forgot all about being seen myself and walked right up. All the men from Beckersville were there and no one noticed me except Jerry Tillford. He saw me and something happened. I'll tell you about that.

I was standing looking at that horse and aching. In some way, I can't tell how, I knew just how Sunstreak felt inside. He was quiet and letting the nigbers rub his legs and Mr. Van Riddle himself put the saddle on, but he was just a raging torrent inside. He was like the water in the river at Niagara Falls just before it goes plunk down. That horse wasn't thinking about running. He don't have to think about that. He was just thinking about holding himself back 'til the time for the running came. I knew that. I could just in a way see right inside him. He was going to do some awful running and I knew it. He wasn't bragging or letting on much or prancing or making a fuss, but just waiting. I knew it and Jerry Tillford his trainer knew. I looked up and then that man and I looked into each other's eyes. Something happened to me. I guess I loved the man as much as I did the horse because he knew what I knew. Seemed to me there wasn't anything in the world but that man and the horse and me. I cried and Jerry Tillford had a shine in his eyes. Then I came away to the fence to wait for the race. The horse was better than me, more steadier, and now I know better than Jerry. He was the quietest and he had to do the running.

Sunstreak ran first of course and he busted the world's record for a mile. I've seen that if I never see anything more. Everything came out just as I expected. Middlestreak got left at the post and was way back and closed up to be second, just as I knew he would. He'll get a world's record too some day. They can't skin the Beckersville country on horses.

I watched the race calm because I knew what would

happen. I was sure. Hanley Turner and Henry Rieback and Tom Tumberton were all more excited than me.

A funny thing happened to me. I was thinking about Jerry Tillford the trainer and how happy he was all through the race. I liked him that afternoon even more than I ever liked my own father. I almost forgot the horses thinking that way about him. It was because of what I had seen in his eyes as he stood in the paddocks beside Sunstreak before the race started. I knew he had been watching and working with Sunstreak since the horse was a baby colt, had taught him to run and be patient and when to let himself out and not to quit, never. I knew that for him it was like a mother seeing her child do something brave or wonderful. It was the first time I ever felt for a man like that.

After the race that night I cut out from Tom and Hanley and Henry. I wanted to be by myself and I wanted to be near Jerry Tillford if I could work it. Here is what happened.

The track at Saratoga is near the edge of town. It is all polished up and trees around, the evergreen kind, and grass and everything painted and nice. If you go past the track you get to a hard road made of asphalt for automobiles, and if you go along this for a few miles there is a road turns off to a rummy looking farm house set in a yard.

That night after the race I went along that road because I had seen Jerry and some other men go that way in an automobile. I didn't expect to find them. I walked for a ways and then sat down by a fence to think. It was the direction they went in. I wanted to be as near Jerry as I could. I felt close to him. Pretty soon I went up the side road — I don't know why — and came to the rummy farm house. I was just lonesome to see Jerry, like wanting to see your father at night when you were a young kid. Just then an automobile came along and turned in. Jerry was in it and Henry Rieback's father, and Arthur Bedford from home, and Dave Williams and two other men I didn't know. They got out of the car and went into the house, all but Henry Rieback's father who quarreled with them and said he wouldn't go. It was only about nine o'clock, but they were all drunk and the rummy looking farm house was a place for bad women to stay in. That's what it was. I crept up along a fence and looked through a window and saw.

It's what gives me the fantods. I can't make it out. The women in the house were all ugly mean-looking women, not nice to look at or be near. They were homely too, except one who was tall and looked a little like the gelding Middlestride, but not clean like him, but with a hard ugly mouth. She had red hair. I saw everything plain. I got up by an old rose bush by an open window and looked. The women had on loose dresses and sat around in chairs. The men came in and sat on the women's laps. The place smelled rotten and there was rotten talk, the kind a kid hears around a livery stable in a town like Beckersville in the winter but don't ever expect to hear talked when there are women around. It was rotten. A nigger wouldn't go into such a place.

I looked at Jerry Tillford. I've told you how I had been feeling about him on account of his knowing what was going on inside of Sunstreak in the minute before he went to the post for the race in which he made a world's record.

Jerry bragged in that bad woman house as I know

Sunstreak wouldn't never have bragged. He said that he made that horse, that it was him that won the race and made the record. He lied and bragged like a fool. I never heard such silly talk.

And then, what do you suppose he did! He looked at the woman in there, the one that was lean and hard-mouthed and looked a little like the gelding Middlestride, but not clean like him, and his eyes began to shine just as they did when he looked at me and at Sunstreak in the paddocks at the track in the afternoon. I stood there by the window — gee! — but I wished I hadn't gone away from the tracks, but had stayed with the boys and the niggers and the horses. The tall rotten looking woman was between us just as Sunstreak was in the paddocks in the afternoon.

Then, all of a sudden, I began to hate that man. I wanted to scream and rush in the room and kill him. I never had such a feeling before, I was so mad clean through that I cried and my fists were doubled up so my finger nails cut my hands.

And Jerry's eyes kept shining and he waved back and forth, and then he went and kissed that woman and I crept away and went back to the tracks and to bed and didn't sleep hardly any, and then next day I got the other kids to start home with me and never told them anything I seen.

I been thinking about it ever since. I can't make it out. Spring has come again and I'm nearly sixteen and go to the tracks mornings same as always, and I see Sunstreak and Middlestride and a new colt named Strident I'll bet will lay them all out, but no one thinks so but me and two or three niggers.

But things are different. At the tracks the air don't taste as good or smell as good. It's because a man like Jerry Tillford, who knows what he does, could see a horse like Sunstreak run, and kiss a woman like that the same day. I can't make it out. Darn him, what did he want to do like that for? I keep thinking about it and it spoils looking at horses and smelling things and hearing niggers laugh and everything. Sometimes I'm so mad about it I want to fight someone. It gives me the fantods. What did he do it for? I want to know why.

Sherwood Anderson, The Triumph of an Egg

THE ART OF MORALS [1]

1923

That living is or may be an art, and the moralist the critic of that art, is a very ancient belief. It was especially widespread among the Greeks. To the Greeks, indeed, this belief was so ingrained and instinctive that it became an implicitly assumed attitude rather than a definitely expressed faith. It was natural to them to speak of a virtuous person as we should speak of a beautiful person. The "good" was the "beautiful"; the sphere of ethics for the Greeks was not distinguished from the sphere of æsthetics. In Sophocles, above all poets, we gather the idea of a natural agreement between duty and inclination which is at once both beauty and moral order. But it is the beautiful that seems to be most fundamental in τὸ καλόν, which was the noble, the honourable, but fundamentally the beautiful. "Beauty is the first of all things," said Isocrates, the famous orator; "nothing that is devoid of beauty is prized. . . . The admiration for virtue comes to this, that of all manifestation of life, virtue is the most beautiful." The supremely

[1] This essay is abridged. The omitted parts are mainly historical.

beautiful was, for the finer sort of Greeks, instinctively
if not always consciously, the supremely divine, and
the Argive Hera, it has been said, "has more divinity
in her countenance than any Madonna of them all."
That is how it came to pass that we have no word in
our speech to apply to the Greek conception; æsthetics for us is apart from all the serious business of life,
and the attempt to introduce it there seems merely
comic. But the Greeks spoke of life itself as a craft
or a fine art. Protagoras,[1] who appears to-day as a
pioneer of modern science, was yet mainly concerned
to regard living as an art, or as the sum of many crafts,
and the Platonic Socrates, his opponent, still always
assumed that the moralist's position is that of a critic
of a craft. So influential a moralist as Aristotle remarks in a matter-of-fact way, in his "Poetics," that if
we wish to ascertain whether an act is, or is not, morally right we must consider not merely the intrinsic
quality of the act, but the person who does it, the person to whom it is done, the time, the means, the motive. Such an attitude towards life puts out of court
any appeal to rigid moral laws; it meant that an act
must befit its particular relationships at a particular
moment, and that its moral value could, therefore,
only be judged by the standard of the spectator's
instinctive feeling for proportion and harmony. That
is the attitude we adopt towards a work of art. . . .[2]

As usually among the Greeks, it is only implicitly,
also, that we detect this attitude among the Romans,
the pupils of the Greeks. For the most part, the
Romans, whose impulses of art were very limited,
whose practical mind craved precision and definition,

---

[1] Protagoras (481–411 B.C.), a Greek Sophist philosopher.
[2] In the paragraphs omitted the author deals with Plotinus, an Alexandrian Greek mystic of the third century, A.D., who, he says, expressed the
Greek attitude in its loftiest aspect.

proved rebellious to the idea that living is an art; yet it may well be that they still retained that idea at the core of their morality. It is interesting to note that St. Augustine, who stood on the threshold between the old Roman and new Christian worlds was able to write: "The art of living well and rightly is the definition that the ancients give of 'virtue.'" For the Latins believed that *ars* was derived from the Greek word for virtue, ἀρετή.[1] Yet there really remained a difference between the Greek and the Roman views of morals. The Greek view, it is universally admitted, was æsthetic, in the most definite sense; the Roman was not, and when Cicero wishes to translate a Greek reference to a "beautiful" action it becomes an "honourable" action. The Greek was concerned with what he himself felt about his actions; the Roman was concerned with what they would look like to other people, and the credit, or discredit, that would be reflected back on himself.

The Hebrews never even dreamed of such an art. Their attitude is sufficiently embodied in the story of Moses and that visit to Sinai which resulted in the production of the table of the Ten Commandments which we may still see inscribed in old churches.[2] For even our modern feeling about morals is largely Jewish, in some measure Roman, and scarcely Greek at all. We still accept, in theory at all events, the Mosaic conception of morality as a code of rigid and inflexible rules, arbitrarily ordained, and to be blindly obeyed.

The conception of morality as an art, which Christendom once disdained, seems now again to be finding favour in men's eyes. The path has been made smooth for it by great thinkers of various complexion,

---

[1] Saint Augustine, *De Civitate Dei*, bk. IV, chap. XXI. — Author's note.
[2] Exodus, chaps. XXXI–XXXII.

who, differing in many fundamental points, all alike
assert the relativity of truth and the inaptitude of
rigid maxims to serve as guiding forces in life. They
also assert, for a large part, implicitly or explicitly,
the authority of art.

The nineteenth century was usually inspired by the
maxims of Kant, and lifted its hat reverently when it
heard Kant declaiming his famous sayings concerning
the supremacy of an inflexible moral law. Kant had,
indeed, felt the stream of influence which flowed from
Shaftesbury,[1] and he sought to mix up æsthetics with
his system. But he had nothing of the genuine artist's spirit. The art of morals was to him a set of
maxims, cold, rigid, precise. A sympathetic biogra-
pher has said of him that the maxims were the man.
They are sometimes fine maxims. But as guides, as
motives to practical action in the world? The maxims of the valetudinarian professor at Königsberg
scarcely seem that to us to-day. Still less can we
harmonise maxims with art. Nor do we any longer
suppose that we are impertinent in referring to the
philosopher's personality. In the investigation of
the solar spectrum personality may count for little;
in the investigation of moral laws it counts for much.
For personality is the very stuff of morals. The moral
maxims of an elderly professor in a provincial university town may have their interest. But so have
those of a Casanova.[2] And the moral maxims of a
Goethe may possibly have more interest than either.
There is the rigid categorical imperative of Kant; and
there is also that other dictum, less rigid but more

[1] Shaftesbury, Anthony Ashley Cooper, third Earl of (1671–1713). See
below in the text. (He is not to be confused with the first Earl or the
seventh, both of whom were also famous.)

[2] Casanova de Seingalt, Giovanni Jacopo (1725–98), an Italian adventurer
and complete cynic.

reminiscent of Greece, which some well-inspired person has put into the mouth of Walt Whitman: "Whatever tastes sweet to the most perfect person, that is finally right."

Fundamentally considered, there are two roads by which we may travel towards the moral ends of life: the road of Tradition, which is ultimately that of Instinct, pursued by the many, and the road of what seems to be Reason — sought out by the few. And in the end these two roads are but the same road, for reason is also an instinct. It is true that the ingenuity of analytic investigators like Henry Sidgwick [1] has succeeded in enumerating various "methods of ethics." But, roughly speaking, there can only be these two main roads of life, and only one has proved supremely important. It has been by following the path of tradition moulded by instinct that man has reached the threshold of civilisation: whatever may have been the benefits he derived from the guidance of reason he has never consciously allowed reason to control his moral life. Tables of commandments have ever been "given by God"; they represented, that is to say, obscure impulses of the organism striving to respond to practical needs. No one dreamed of commending them by declaring that they were reasonable.

It is clear how Instinct and Tradition, thus working together, act vitally and beneficently in moulding the moral life of primitive peoples. The "divine command" was always a command conditioned by the special circumstance under which the tribe lived. That is so even when the moral law is to our civilised eyes "unnatural." The infanticide of Polynesian islanders, where the means of subsistence and the

[1] Henry Sidgwick (1838–1900), English philosopher, author of *Outlines of the History of Ethics* (1886), etc.

possibilities of expansion were limited, was obviously a necessary measure, beneficent and humane in its effects. The killing of the aged among the Eskimos was equally a necessary and kindly measure, recognised as such by the victims themselves, when it was essential that every member of the community should be able to help himself. Primitive rules of moral action, greatly as they differ among themselves, are all more or less advantageous and helpful on the road of primitive life. It is true that they allow very little, if any, scope for divergent individual moral action, but that, too, was advantageous.

But that, also, is the rock on which an instinctive traditional morality must strike as civilisation is approached. The tribe has no longer the same unity. Social differentiation has tended to make the family a unit, and psychic differentiation to make even the separate individuals units. The community of interests of the whole tribe has been broken up, and therewith traditional morality has lost alike its value and its power.

The development of abstract intelligence, which coincides with civilisation, works in the same direction. Reason is, indeed, on one side an integrating force, for it shows that the assumption of traditional morality — the identity of the individual's interests with the interests of the community — is soundly based. But it is also a disintegrating force. For if it reveals a general unity in the ends of living, it devises infinitely various and perplexingly distracting excuses for living. Before the active invasion of reason living had been an art, or at all events a discipline, highly conven-

---

discipline. The author elsewhere suggests that an art (or science) that has ceased to grow is no longer an art (or science), but should be designated by another name, such as *discipline.* He gives as examples human anatomy and Hellenic sculpture.

tionalised and even ritualistic, but the motive forces of living lay in life itself and had all the binding sanction of instincts; the penalty of every failure in living, it was felt, would be swiftly and automatically experienced. To apply reason here was to introduce a powerful solvent into morals. Objectively it made morality clearer but subjectively it destroyed the existing motives for morality; it deprived man, to use the fashionable phraseology of the present day, of a vital illusion.

Thus we have morality in the fundamental sense, the actual practices of the main army of the population, while in front a variegated procession of prancing philosophers gaily flaunt their moral theories before the world. . . . Thus it comes about that abstract moral speculations, culminating in rigid maxims, are necessarily sterile and vain. They move in the sphere of reason, and that is the sphere of comprehension, but not of vital action. In this way there arises a moral dualism in civilised man. Objectively he has become like the gods and able to distinguish the ends of life; he has eaten of the fruit of the tree and has knowledge of good and evil. Subjectively he is still not far removed from the savage, oftenest stirred to action by a confused web of emotional motives, among which the interwoven strands of civilised reason are as likely to produce discord and paralysis as to furnish efficient guides, a state of mind first, and perhaps best, set forth in its extreme form by Shakespeare in Hamlet. On the one hand he cannot return to the primitive state in which all motives for living flowed harmoniously in the same channel; he cannot divest himself of his illuminating reason; he cannot recede from his hardly acquired personal individuality. On the other hand he can never expect, he can never even reasonably hope, that reason will ever hold in leash the emotions. It is clear that along neither path separately can the civilised man pursue his way in harmonious balance with himself. We begin to realise that what we need is not a code of beautifully cut-and-dried maxims — whether emanating from sacred mountains or from philosophers' studies — but a happy combination of two different ways of living. We need, that is, a traditional and instinctive way of living, based on real motor instincts, which will blend with reason and the manifold needs of personality, instead of being destroyed by their solvent actions, as rigid rules inevitably are. Our only valid rule is a creative impulse that is one with the illuminative power of intelligence.

At the beginning of the eighteenth century, the seed-time of our modern ideas, as it has so often seemed to be, the English people, having in art at length brought their language to a fine degree of clarity and precision, and having just passed through a highly stimulating period of dominant Puritanism in life, became much interested in philosophy, psychology, and ethics. Their interest was, indeed, often superficial and amateurish, though they were soon to produce some of the most notable figures in the whole history of thought. The third Earl of Shaftesbury, one of the earliest of the group, himself illustrated this unsystematic method of thinking. He was an amateur, an aristocratic amateur, careless of consistency, and not by any means concerned to erect a philosophic system. Not that he was a worse thinker on that account. The world's greatest thinkers have often been amateurs; for high thinking is the outcome of fine and independent living, and for that a professorial chair offers no special opportunities. Shaftesbury was, moreover, a man of fragile physical constitution, as Kant was; but, unlike Kant, he was not a childish hypochondriac in seclusion, but a man in the world, heroically seeking to live a complete and harmonious life. By temperament he was a Stoic, and he wrote a characteristic book of "Exercises," as he proposed to call what his modern editor calls the "Philosophical Regimen," in which he consciously seeks to discipline himself in fine thinking and right living, plainly acknowledging that he is the disciple of Epictetus and Marcus Aurelius. But Shaftesbury was also a man of genius, and as such it was his good fortune to throw afresh into the stream of thought a fruitful conception, in part absorbed, indeed, from Greece, and long implicit in men's minds, but never before made clearly recognisable as a moral theory and an ethical temper, susceptible of being labelled by the philosophic historian, as it since has been under the name, passable no doubt as any other, "Æsthetic Intuitionism."

Greek morality, it has been well said, is not a conflict of light and darkness, of good and evil, the clear choice between the broad road that leads to destruction and the narrow path of salvation: it is "an artistic balance of light and shade." Gizycki, remarking that Shaftesbury has more affinity to the Greeks than perhaps any other modern moralist, says that "the key lay not only in his head, but in his heart, for like can only be recognised by like."[1] We have to remember at the same time that Shaftesbury was really something of a classical scholar, even from childhood. . . .

"He seems," wrote of Shaftesbury his unfriendly contemporary Mandeville,[2] "to require and expect

[1] Georg von Gizycki, *Die Ethik David Hume's*, p. 11. — Author's Note.
[2] Bernard de Mandeville (1670–1733), a Hollander living in England,

goodness in his species as we do a sweet taste in grapes and China Oranges, of which, if any of them are sour, we boldly pronounce that they are not come to that perfection their nature is capable of." In a certain sense this was correct. Shaftesbury, it has been said, was the father of that new ethics which recognizes that Nature is not a mere impulse of self-preservation, as Hobbes [1] thought, but also a racial impulse, having regard to others; there are social inclinations in the individual, he realised, that go beyond individual ends. (Referring to the famous dictum of Hobbes, *Homo homini lupus*, he observes: "To say in disparagement of Man 'that he is to Man a wolf' appears somewhat absurd when one considers that wolves are to wolves very kind and loving creatures.") Therewith "goodness" was seen, virtually for the first time in the modern period, to be as "natural" as the sweetness of ripe fruit.

There was another reason, a fundamental physiological and psychological reason, why "goodness" of actions and the "sweetness" of fruits are equally natural, a reason that would, no doubt, have been found strange both by Mandeville and by Shaftesbury. Morality, Shaftesbury describes as "the taste of beauty and the relish of what is decent," and the "sense of beauty" is ultimately the same as the "moral sense." "My first endeavour," wrote Shaftesbury, "must be to distinguish the true taste of fruits, refine my palate, and establish a just relish in the kind." He thought, evidently, that he was merely using a metaphor. But he was speaking essentially in the direct, straightforward way of natural and primitive Man. At the foundation, "sweetness" and "good-

heretical writer, moralist, and satirist, author of the *Fable of the Bees*, probably directed against Shaftesbury's theories.

[1] Thomas Hobbes (1588–1680), philosopher and moralist.

ness" are the same thing. That can still be detected in the very structure of language, not only of primitive languages, but those of the most civilised peoples. That morality is, in the strict sense, a matter of taste, of æsthetics, of what the Greeks called αἴσθησις, is conclusively shown by the fact that in the most widely separated tongues — possibly wherever the matter has been carefully investigated — moral goodness is, at the outset, expressed in terms of *taste*. What is *good* is what is *sweet*, and sometimes, also, *salt*. Primitive peoples have highly developed the sensory side of their mental life, and their vocabularies bear witness to the intimate connection of sensations of taste and touch with emotional tone. There is, indeed, no occasion to go beyond our own European traditions to see that the expression of moral qualities is based on fundamental sensory qualities of taste. In Latin *suavis* is *sweet*, but even in Latin it became a moral quality, and its English derivatives have been entirely deflected from physical to moral qualities, while *bitter* is at once a physical quality and a poignantly moral quality. In Sanskrit and Persian and Arabic *salt* is not only a physical taste but the name for lustre and grace and beauty. It seems well in passing to point out that the deeper we penetrate the more fundamentally we find the æsthetic conception of morals grounded in Nature. But not every one cares to penetrate any deeper and there is no need to insist.

Shaftesbury held that human actions should have a beauty of symmetry and proportion and harmony, which appeal to us, not because they accord with any rule or maxim (although they may conceivably be susceptible of measurement), but because they satisfy our instinctive feelings, evoking an approval which is

aisthesis, perception by the senses.

strictly an æsthetic judgment of moral action. This instinctive judgment was not, as Shaftesbury understood it, a guide to action. He held, rightly enough, that the impulse to action is fundamental and primary, that fine action is the outcome of finely tempered natures. It is a feeling for the just time and measure of human passion, and maxims are useless to him whose nature is ill-balanced. "Virtue is no other than the love of order and beauty in society." Æsthetic appreciation of the act, and even ecstatic pleasure in it, are part of our æsthetic delight in Nature generally, which includes Man. Nature, it is clear, plays a large part in this conception of the moral life. To lack balance on any plane of moral conduct is to be unnatural; "Nature is not mocked," said Shaftesbury. She is a miracle, for miracles are not things that are performed, but things that are perceived, and to fail here is to fail in perception of the divinity of Nature, to do violence to her, and to court moral destruction. A return to Nature is not a return to ignorance or savagery, but to the first instinctive feeling for the beauty of well-proportioned affections. "The most natural beauty in the world is honesty and moral truth," he asserts, and he recurs again and again to the "beauty of honesty." "*Dulce et decorum est,* was his sole reason" he says of the classical pagan, adding: "And this is still a good reason." In learning how to act, he thought, we are "learning to become artists." It seems natural to him to refer to the magistrate as an artist; "the magistrate, if he be an artist," he incidentally says. We must not make morality depend on authority. The true artist, in any art, will never act below his character. "Let who will make it for you as you fancy," the artist declares; "I know it to be wrong. Whatever I have

Dulce et decorum est, sweet and seemly is it. — Horace, C. 3, 2, 13.

made hitherto has been true work. And neither for your sake or anybody's else shall I put my hand to any other." "This is virtue!" exclaims Shaftesbury. "This disposition transferred to the whole of life perfects a character. For there is a workmanship and a truth in actions."

Shaftesbury, it may be repeated, was an amateur, not only in philosophy, but even in the arts. . . . But if an amateur, he was an amateur of genius. He threw a vast and fruitful conception — caught from the "Poetics" of Aristotle, "the Great Master of Arts," and developed with fine insight — into our modern world. Most of the great European thinkers of the eighteenth and early nineteenth centuries were in some measure inspired, influenced, or anticipated by Shaftesbury. Even Kant, though he was unsympathetic and niggardly of appreciation, helped to develop the conception Shaftesbury first formulated. To-day we see it on every hand. It is slowly and subtly moulding the whole of our modern morality. . . .[1]

It has often been brought against the conception of morality as an art that it lacks seriousness. It seems to many people to involve an easy, self-indulgent, dilettante way of looking at life. Certainly it is not the way of the Old Testament. Except in imaginative literature — it was, indeed, an enormous and fateful exception — the Hebrews were no "aesthetic intuitionists." They hated art, for the rest, and in face of the problems of living they were not in the habit of considering the lilies how they grow. It was not the beauty of holiness, but the stern rod of a jealous Jehovah, which they craved for their encouragement

[1] The passage omitted traces Shaftesbury's influence upon subsequent philosophers (Leibnitz, Montesquieu, Diderot, Herder, Rousseau, Rodo, Croce), analyses the ideas of his disciples, Arbuckle and Hutcheson, and shows wherein they agree with the theories of Schiller, Goethe, and von Humboldt.

along the path of Duty. And it is the Hebrew mode of feeling which has been, more or less violently and imperfectly, grafted into our Christianity.[1]

It is a complete mistake, however, to suppose that those for whom life is an art have entered on an easy path, with nothing but enjoyment and self-indulgence before them. The reverse is nearer to the truth. It is probably the hedonist who had better choose rules if he only cares to make life pleasant. For the artist life is always a discipline,[2] and no discipline can be without pain. That is so even in dancing, which of all the arts is most associated in the popular mind with pleasure. To learn to dance is the most austere of disciplines, and even for those who have attained to the summit of its art often remains a discipline not to be exercised without heroism. The dancer seems a thing of joy, but we are told that this famous dancer's slippers are filled with blood when the dance is over, and that one falls down pulseless and deathlike on leaving the stage, and the other must spend the day in darkness and silence. "It is no small advantage," said Nietzsche, "to have a hundred Damoclean swords suspended above one's

hedonist, one who holds that pleasure is the chief good.

[1] It is noteworthy, however, that the æsthetic view of morals has had advocates, not only among the more latitudinarian Protestants, but in Catholicism. A few years ago the Reverend Dr. Kolbe published a book on _The Art of Life_, designed to show that just as the sculptor works with hammer and chisel to shape a block of marble into a form of beauty, so Man, by the power of grace, the illumination of faith, and the instrument of prayer, works to transform his soul. But this simile of the sculptor, which has appealed so strongly alike to Christian and anti-Christian moralists, proceeds, whether or not they knew it, from Plotinus, who, in his famous chapter on Beauty, bids us note the sculptor. "He cuts away here, he smooths there, he makes this line lighter, this other purer, until a living face has grown upon his work. So do you also cut away all that is excessive, straighten all that is crooked, bring light to all that is overcast, make all one glow of beauty, and never cease chiselling your statue until the godlike splendour shines on you from it, and the perfect goodness stands, surely, in the stainless shrine." — Author's note.

[2] "They who pitched the goal of their aspiration so high knew that the paths leading to it were rough and steep and long," remarks A. W. Benn (_The Greek Philosophers_, 1914, p. 57); "they said 'the beautiful is hard' — hard to judge, hard to win, hard to keep." — Author's note. The author is here using _discipline_ in the ordinary sense.

head; that is how one learns to dance, that is how one attains 'freedom of movement.'" [1]

For as pain is entwined as an essential element in the perfect achievement of that which seems naturally the most pleasurable of the arts, so it is with the whole art of living, of which dancing is the supreme symbol. There is no separating Pain and Pleasure without making the first meaningless for all vital ends and the second turn to ashes. To exalt pleasure is to exalt pain; and we cannot understand the meaning of pain unless we understand the place of pleasure in the art of life. In England, James Hinton [2] sought to make that clear, equally against those who failed to see that pain is as necessary morally as it undoubtedly is biologically and against those who would puritanically refuse to accept the morality of pleasure. It is no doubt important to resist pain, but it is also important that it should be there to resist. Even when we look at the matter no longer subjectively but objectively, we must accept pain in any sound æsthetic or metaphysical picture of the world.

We must not be surprised, therefore, that this way of looking at life as an art has spontaneously commended itself to men of the gravest and deepest character, in all other respects widely unlike. Shaftesbury was temperamentally a Stoic whose fragile constitution involved a perpetual endeavour to mould life to the form of his ideal. And if we go back to Marcus Aurelius we find an austere and heroic man whose whole life, as we trace it in his "Meditations," was a splendid struggle, a man who — even, it seems, unconsciously — had adopted the æsthetic criterion of moral goodness and the artistic conception of moral

[1] *Der Wille zur Macht*, p. 358. — Author's note.
[2] James Hinton (1822–1875), English surgeon and writer on moral and social questions.

action. Dancing and wrestling express to his eyes the activity of the man who is striving to live, and the goodness of moral actions instinctively appears to him as the beauty of natural objects; it is to Marcus Aurelius that we owe that immortal utterance of æsthetic intuitionism: "As though the emerald should say: 'Whatever happens I must be emerald.'" There could be no man more unlike the Roman Emperor, or in any more remote field of action than the French saint and philanthropist Vincent de Paul. At once a genuine Christian mystic and a very wise and marvellously effective man of action, Vincent de Paul adopts precisely the same simile of the moral attitude that had long before been put forth by Plotinus and in the next century was again to be taken up by Shaftesbury: "My daughters," he wrote to the Sisters of Charity, " we are each like a block of stone which is to be transferred into a statue. What must the sculptor do to carry out this design? First of all he must take the hammer and chip off all that he does not need. For this purpose he strikes the stone so violently that if you were watching him you would say he intended to break it into pieces. Then, when he has got rid of the rougher parts, he takes a smaller hammer, and afterwards a chisel, to begin the face with all the features. When that has taken form, he uses other and finer tools to bring it to that perfection he has intended for his statue." If we desire to find a spiritual artist as unlike as possible to Vincent de Paul we may take Nietzsche. Alien as any man could ever be to a cheap or superficial vision of the moral life, and far too intellectually keen to confuse moral problems with purely æsthetic problems, Nietzsche, when faced by the problem of living, sets himself — almost as instinctively as Marcus Aurelius or Vincent de Paul — at the standpoint of art. "Alles Leben ist Streit um Geschmack und Schmecken." It is a crucial passage in *Zarathustra*: "All life is a dispute about taste and tasting! Taste: that is weight and at the same time scales and weigher; and woe to all living things that would live without dispute about weight and scales and weigher!" For this gospel of taste is no easy gospel. A man must make himself a work of art, Nietzsche again and again declares, moulded into beauty by suffering, for such art is the highest morality, the morality of the Creator.

There is a certain indefiniteness about the conception of morality as an artistic impulse, to be judged by an æsthetic criterion, which is profoundly repugnant to at least two classes of minds fully entitled to make their antipathy felt. In the first place, it makes no appeal to the abstract reasoner, indifferent to the manifoldly concrete problems of living. For the man whose brain is hypertrophied and his practical life shrivelled to an insignificant routine — the man of whom Kant is the supreme type — it is always a temptation to rationalise morality. Such a pure intellectualist, overlooking the fact that human beings are not mathematical figures, may even desire to transform ethics into a species of geometry. That we may see in Spinoza, a nobler and more inspiring figure, no doubt, but of much the same temperament as Kant. The impulses and desires of ordinary men and women are manifold, inconstant, often conflicting, and sometimes overwhelming. "Morality is a fact of sensibility," remarks Jules de Gaultier; "it has no need to have recourse of reason for its affirmations." But to men of the intellectualist type this consideration is almost negligible; all the passions and affections of humanity

---

hypertrophied, enlarged, overgrown (by too much nutrition).

seem to them meek as sheep which they may shepherd, and pen within the flimsiest hurdles. William Blake, who could cut down to that central core of the world where all things are fused together, knew better when he said that the only golden rule of life is "the great and golden rule of art." James Hinton was for ever expatiating on the close resemblance between the methods of art, as shown especially in painting, and the methods of moral action. Thoreau, who also belonged to this tribe, declared, in the same spirit as Blake, that there is no golden rule in morals, for rules are only current silver; "it is golden not to have any rule at all."

There is another quite different type of person who shares this antipathy to the indefiniteness of æsthetic morality: the ambitious moral reformer. The man of this class is usually by no means devoid of strong passions; but for the most part he possesses no great intellectual calibre and so is unable to estimate the force and complexity of human impulses. The moral reformer, eager to introduce the millennium here and now by the aid of the newest mechanical devices, is righteously indignant with anything so vague as an æsthetic morality. He must have definite rules and regulations, clear-cut laws and by-laws, with an arbitrary list of penalties attached, to be duly inflicted in this world or the next. The popular conception of Moses, descending from the sacred mount with a brand-new table of commandments, which he declares have been delivered to him by God, though he is ready to smash them to pieces on the slightest provocation, furnishes a delightful image of the typical moral reformer of every age. It is, however, only in savage and barbarous stages of society, or among the uncultivated classes of civilisation, that the men of this type can find their faithful followers.

Yet there is more to be said. That very indefiniteness of the criterion of moral action, falsely supposed to be a disadvantage, is really the prime condition for effective moral action. The academic philosophers of ethics, had they possessed virility enough to enter the field of real life, would have realised — as we cannot expect the moral reformers blinded by the smoke of their own fanaticism to realise — that the slavery to rigid formulas which they preached was the death of all high moral responsibility. Life must always be a great adventure, with risks on every hand; a clear-sighted eye, a many-sided sympathy, a fine daring, an endless patience, are for ever necessary to all good living. With such qualities alone may the artist in life reach success; without them even the most devoted slave to formulas can only meet disaster. No reasonable being may draw breath in the world without an open-eyed freedom of choice, and if the moral world is to be governed by laws, better to people it with automatic machines than with living men and women.

In our human world the precision of mechanism is for ever impossible. The indefiniteness of morality is a part of its necessary imperfection. There is not only room in morality for the high aspiration, the courageous decision, the tonic thrill of the muscles of the soul, but we have to admit also sacrifice and pain. The lesser good, our own or that of others, is merged in a larger good, and that cannot be without some rending of the heart. So all moral action, however in the end it may be justified by its harmony and balance, is in the making cruel and in a sense even immoral. Therein lies the final justification of the æsthetic conception of morality. It opens a wider perspective and reveals loftier standpoints; it shows how the seeming loss is part of an ultimate gain, so restoring that harmony and beauty which the unintelligent partisans of a hard and barren duty so often destroy for ever. "Art," as Paulhan declares, "is often more moral than morality itself." Or, as Jules de Gaultier holds, "Art is in a certain sense the only morality which life admits." In so far as we can infuse it with the spirit and method of art, we have transformed morality into something beyond morality; it has become the complete embodiment of the Dance of Life.

Havelock Ellis, The Dance of Life, 1923, Chapter VI

NOTES

In these notes I have not as a rule given information which the reader can easily find for himself in such works as the *Dictionary of National Biography*, the Cambridge histories of literature, or an encyclopedia.

Section One — Middle Ages (1–61)

Pages 1–61. Few readers realize how much pleasure may be derived from such old books as are represented here. There is a provinciality of time as well as of place, and most people are provincial in being able to enjoy only what they look upon as up-to-date.

The best way to enjoy old literature is to try to put one's self into sympathy with it — with the times in which it was written, the person who wrote it, and the people for whom he wrote. This requires some effort of imagination and often some courage and industry, especially when the language and spelling are forbidding. But the rewards are great.

Page 1 (*Take Hede of Maydens*). De Glanville's little essay on girls is quite as interesting as when he wrote it, and it is even more amusing. I doubt whether his contemporaries saw anything to smile over in it. It was prepared originally as a page in an encyclopedia! But to-day the spelling, the diction, the turns of phrase, and the earnestness of the author all touch our sense of humor.

Page 2 (*A Prayer*). I have chosen this section of Chaucer's translation of Boethius's *Consolations of Philosophy* as an example of elevated prose of the Middle English period. Perhaps no other writer in English before 1550 could have written prose sentences of such varied structure and rhythm. The *Consolations* was an immensely influential book throughout the Middle Ages and on to the end of the sixteenth century. Both Alfred the Great and Queen Elizabeth translated it and it was well known to Shakespeare. It is written in the typical medieval form of the *vision*, an august woman (Philosophy) appearing to the author in a dream and expounding the old Greek maxim of "Know thyself."

PAGE 3 (*The Lady of the Land*). The problem of who really wrote *Mandeville's Travels* is very complex, and the reader should consult the *D.N.B.* about it. For centuries Mandeville was thought to have been an Englishman and the "Father of English Prose"; but we know now that the book is a French compilation of adventures, genuine and spurious. It abounds in tall stories, of which the *Lady of the Land* is fairly typical. Notwithstanding the crudity of the English, it has a certain pathos. The legend was used by William Morris in his fine narrative poem of the same title. The subject is very old, and is found in many ballads, such as "Kemp Owyne."

PAGE 5 (*The Book of Sir Balin le Savage*). Although the tale of Sir Balin is not so well known as some others in the *Morte Darthur*, it was used by both Tennyson and Swinburne. Swinburne follows Malory in outline, but Tennyson's idyll bears hardly any resemblance to the original except in the final incident.

Malory's tale is a characteristic prose romance of the late Middle English period, mysterious, rambling, somewhat incoherent, but adorned with passages of great beauty. Notice especially the opening of Chapter vi, and the incident, on page 27, in which Balin, hearing the blast of a horn, says, "That blast is blown for me; for I am the prize, and yet I am not dead." The conclusion of the tale is of course justly renowned.

The story is oddly uncertain in the handling, as if the author were not entirely sure just what story he had to tell. One is never quite aware what it is all about. It is clear, however, that Balin is a victim of fate. He is represented as a man of quick temper, who always does the wrong thing, though with good intentions. There is something admirable, nevertheless, about his quiet composure, his fortitude, his desire to help others, his loyalty to Arthur, and his clipped speech.

It has been maintained (see Professor Rhys's *The Arthurian Legend*) that Balin was originally a sun-hero and King Pellam king of the "other world," of darkness, enchantment, or faery. The dolorous stroke, then, represents the rays of the sun which penetrate the other world and destroy it. There is a similar incident — the destruction of Klingsor's castle — in Wagner's *Parsifal*. But the central idea of the story is very old and has a powerful human appeal. It is analogous to other situations in which dear friends kill each other: father and son (as Cuchulainn and Connla in ancient Irish, and Sohrab and Rustum in Persian); brothers-in-blood (in various Icelandic sagas and in such ballads as *Bewick and Graham*); and sworn friends (as in Chaucer's *Knight's Tale*, of Palamon and Arcite, modernized by Dryden). But the story of Balin and Balan is especially impressive because of the strain of fatality that runs through it.

It should be remembered that Balin's nickname, *le Savage*, means "wild" or "uncouth."

The great beauty of Malory's prose is the diction. It repays long study. His sentences are simply framed, and have an air of prattling that is deceptively childlike. He was a true artist, with considerable powers of narrative and characterization. His book was written a century before *Don Quixote* by one who, unlike Cervantes, loved and revered chivalry. He must, nevertheless, at times have felt the monotony of the adventures he was narrating for he often gives the impression of merely covering ground. But when his interest is really engaged he conceives so powerfully that some of his narratives have never been excelled by the innumerable poets who have used them.

PAGE 32 (*An Intimate Letter*). I owe this amusing letter to the *Oxford Book of English Prose*. It is hard to say just why Thomas Betson's desire that young Katherine should be a "good etter of her mete" in order that she may "waxe and grow fast to be a woman" tickles us, although I suspect that his spelling has a good deal to do with it. The entire letter gives the effect of having been rattled off and mailed without the slightest revision.

Such intimate glimpses of life five hundred years ago are not without their value, because they show that people were very like us. We have the same feeling of delighted surprise when we read the chatter of the Syracusan women (page 414), who lived in the third century B.C.

PAGE 35 (*Scenes from Reynard the Fox*). The main types of medieval literature have been aptly classified as *romance*, *vision*, and *satire*. The great romance of the period in England was the Arthurian cycle of chivalric legends; the great vision was the culminating poem of the Middle Ages, the *Divine Comedy* of Dante; and the great satire was the beast-epic, *Reynard the Fox*.

The last-named is a masterly satire, not only upon the feudal state and a corrupt church, but upon mankind in general. It represents an arch-rascal who, without a moral ideal or a trace of human compunction, is still fascinating; so fascinating, in fact, that James Anthony Froude wrote a very entertaining essay entitled, "Ethical Doubts concerning *Reineke Fuchs*." Another classical discussion of the book may be found in the Carlyle essay on "The German Literature of the Fourteenth and Fifteenth Centuries." But the literature concerning the Fox is immense and the reader should consult reference books about it.

The text which Caxton used is not the best version. Perhaps the finest is the German poetic text of 1544, which was admirably translated by Goethe and illustrated by the artist Kaulbach. Goethe called the poem a *Welt-Bibel* or Bible-of-this-World — that is to say, a universal handbook of the stupidity, weakness, cowardice, and sinfulness of mankind. Froude pronounces it "the most exquisite moral satire . . . which has ever been composed. It is not addressed," he says, "to a passing mode of folly or of profligacy, but it touches the perennial nature of mankind, laying bare our own sympathies, and tastes, and weaknesses, with as keen and true an edge as when the living world of the old Swabian poet winced under its earliest utterance." Of course both

Goethe and Froude were referring to the poetic version; but even in the "rude and symple englysshe" of Caxton some of its power can be felt.

The humor of the fable is persistent, though often very bitter. Notice the description, on page 37, of the funeral cortège of the good hen Coppen and of her burial, on page 39; Bellyn's diffidence about shriving the Fox, on page 53, and Nobel's tendency to blame his own credulity upon his queen, on page 58.

I am sorry that in condensing the story I have not been able to illustrate fully the admirable spirit with which some incidents are narrated. I hope that what I have given will prompt the student to read the whole. The account of the visits of Bruin and Tybert to Malperduis and the story of Reynard's mortal combat with Isegrim are superb, but they do not illustrate Reynard's astonishing dialectic and sophistry as well as the chapters I have given.

Chaucer's *Nonne's Priest's Tale* is a genuine Reynard episode, although he chose to call the Fox Rossel. Many of the episodes were afloat in European literature as early as the time of Æsop and some of them can be traced back to the Sanskrit. A modern version of Caxton's translation was published by Joseph Jacobs in 1895 with an excellent introduction.

SECTION TWO — RENAISSANCE (62–131)

PAGES 62–131. "The history of the earlier Elizabethan prose," says Professor Saintsbury, "if we except the name of Hooker, in which it culminates, is to a great extent the history of curiosities of literature — of tentative and imperfect efforts, scarcely resulting in any real vernacular style at all. It is, however, emphatically the Period of Origins of modern English prose, and as such cannot but be interesting." And in somewhat the same vein Henry Craik writes: "The achievements of the Elizabethans did not belong, in any large part, to the domain of prose. What they did in that domain was, at the best, to show what were the possibilities of English prose. . . . All that was hardest of attainment it would seem that the Elizabethans had attained. What they wanted we might judge was but a trick of art. . . . The poets and the dramatists of the age completed their work quickly, and attained, by leaps and bounds, to the consummate perfection of their diction. But prose style grows more slowly; and its growth is hindered rather than quickened by the very variety of its subject.

In the selections in this section I have tried to illustrate the main styles cultivated in the sixteenth century, from the "hifalutin" rhetoric of the title-pages to the simple realism of Deloney. In perhaps no other century can we find so great a variety, though every tendency then shown can be traced quite down to our own time. It might almost be said, for example, that Carlyle's style sometimes shows what euphuism might have been in the hands of a writer of genius (see the passage beginning at page 345). But although euphuism was the most spectacular mode, it was too affected to endure. It is in writers like Ascham, Foxe, Raleigh (in his narratives), and above all Hooker that we see the beginnings of what is usually called standard prose.

PAGE 62 (*The Burghers of Calais*). John Bourchier, Lord Berners, was Chancellor of the Exchequer under Henry VIII and it was at the king's command that he executed his noble translation of the *Chronicles* of Froissart. The passage in the text is a good example of early Tudor prose, honest, straightforward, and manly, though it is not entirely representative of Berners's manner, because he was inclined to be flowery. Some doubts have been cast upon the accuracy of Froissart in narrating the incident of Calais, and historians have said that the burghers were not so heroic as they appear here. But the story is a good one, and it seems rather too bad to spoil it.

PAGE 66 (*What They Laughed at*). These three little jokes are in the vein of medieval *fabliaux*, though these latter were written in verse. No jests were quite so good as those concerning priests and women, and such folk-tales contrast oddly with the religious and chivalric literature of the upper classes.

Page 69 (*A Very Godly Letter*). A boy of ten in the sixteenth century was about as mature as one of twenty to-day, and Sir Henry's letter to little Philip is in no way different from many other letters to children. His excellent advice, which reminds one of Polonius's to Laertes, followed a prevalent literary mode. A more elaborate example is Lord Burleigh's letter to his son, Robert, written about 1598, often named as the earliest independent essay in English. Such epistolary essays on the ordering of life were suggested by the "books of conduct" which were fashionable during the Renaissance, and they point the way to Lord Chesterfield's letters to his son and his stepson, in the eighteenth century. Lady Mary's postscript is a pleasant human touch. It was the custom for wives even then to add postscripts to their husbands' letters. Sir Thomas Browne's wife, Dame Dorothy, almost always added one when he wrote to a member of the family.

Pages 72–76 (*Lady Jane Grey*). Ascham's style is noteworthy for its plainness. His *Scholemaster* is a little landmark in English education, for his ideas on the teaching of Latin were enlightened and he advocated humane methods in the classroom. His other book, *Toxophilus* (Lover of the Bow) is still curious as a treatise on archery. He seems to have been a lovable man.

Foxe's *Book of Martyrs* used to be in every devout Protestant household. It is, as Professor Manly calls it, "an unrelieved orgy of blood and bitterness," and the pictures which adorned it in many editions must have frightened whole generations of children from their sleep. It is also one of the most prejudiced and unjust books ever written. It was primarily directed against Queen Mary and the Catholics of the sixteenth century.

Pages 76–81 (*Flowers of Rhetorick*). These three examples should make quite clear what is meant by *Euphuism*. Euphuism, which takes its name from Lyly's novel, *Euphues*, was an affected and highflown kind of writing, characterized by the continual use of figures of speech, especially similes,

and allusions to mythology and medieval science and superstition; and by an equally continual use of balance, antithesis,
and climax.   It is easy to make fun of such writing, and yet
there is no doubt that in its care for sentence-structure and
particularly in its observance of the balanced and periodic
constructions it rendered a valuable service to English prose.

The style of Gosson and Lyly and Greene is so different
from any written to-day that it offers an interesting and useful study.   It is the most artificial style in English and makes
that of modern rhetorical writers, like Macaulay and Meredith seem easy and natural; and yet the young student of
writing, although he will never seek to imitate anything so
false, may obtain hints concerning effective expression from
it.

PAGE 77.   It is interesting to compare Gosson's anecdotes
of animals here with Darwin's on pages 454–59.   At first
glance the connection may seem fanciful; and yet it should
not be forgotten that Gosson's statements about bees,
cranes, geese, and woodcocks, although used by him merely
as literary ornaments, passed for science in the Middle Ages,
and for a long while afterwards.   Darwin is quite as much
concerned with making a point as Gosson, but it is a scientific
point, while Gosson's point is a moral lesson.   The difference
between modern rationalism and medieval allegory is really
a measure of the difference between the two ages.

PAGE 78.   Professor Saintsbury says of this letter: "No
better specimen of him can be given than from the letter
commendatory to the *Hecatompathia*."   It is certainly
euphuism of the purest.

PAGE 80.   I have given these title-pages only because they
are amusing.   They show with what a fine fury our Elizabethan ancestors could write when they abandoned themselves.

PAGE 81 (*Menaphon*).   Greene in *Menaphon* is an avowed
disciple of Lyly (as was Lodge, in *Rosalynde*, upon which
Shakespeare based *As You Like It*).   There is something very

charming about the pastoral airs and graces of this romance, in which shepherds talk like philosophers and princesses impersonate shepherdesses. To enjoy it one must forget all our modern notions about realism and naturalness. It should be remembered, however, that the artificial pastoral has always flourished among sophisticated people and that such writing as this appealed most strongly to the court-circle. I have given so much of *Menaphon* because it furnishes an excellent example for comparison and contrast with the pastoral comedies of Shakespeare. The dialogue on pages 95–97 is especially characteristic of what Professor Arber (see page 98) calls "the fine-filed talk of the English court." Greene, by the way, was a very interesting person, a playwright of some genius, a writer of excellent lyrics, and an authority on rogues and vagabonds.

PAGE 99 (*The Last Fight of the Revenge*). This narrative is popularly remembered because Tennyson used it in his poem, *The Revenge: A Ballad of the Fleet.* It is customary to praise Raleigh's prose, and that he could write superbly is proved by the famous paragraph on death (page 196); and yet, as the present narrative shows, he was not always coherent. Perhaps the best-known eulogy of his prose is that of Thoreau: "Sir Walter Raleigh might well be studied, if only for the excellence of his style, for he is remarkable in the midst of so many masters. There is a natural emphasis in his style, like a man's tread, and a breathing space between the sentences, which the best of modern writing does not furnish. . . . You have constantly the warrant of life and experience in what you read." In one sense that is quite true. Samuel Daniel, a contemporary of Raleigh, wrote in his *Musophilus*:

> What good is like to this:
> To do worthy the writing, and to write
> Worthy the reading, and the world's delight?

and such writing as Raleigh's has the quality found in Hakluyt's *Voyages* everywhere, of doing first and writing afterwards. And yet to say that such writing is better in general than the best of our day is extravagant. Thoreau was riding a hobby.

PAGES 107–08 (*Laws of Nature* and *The Search*). Hooker's style is sometimes heavy, bare, and labored: and yet it is perhaps true that nobody before Dryden (except Shakespeare) wrote prose so modern. Notice his handling of the long sentence.

PAGE 109 (*An Elizabethan Wife*). Deloney's novel in praise of shoemakers deserves to be better known. It is an entirely unassuming narrative, but is full of a sunny gentle temper. It should be compared with Dekker's pleasant comedy, *The Shoemaker's Holiday*. The character of the officious but loving wife is admirably drawn.

PAGE 115 (*The Watch*). I have included this Dogberry scene as an example of excellent burlesque. Shakespeare, like most dramatic geniuses, loved nonsense, and when he could find people who were naturally nonsensical, he wrote with a delighted chuckle. I wished to include the still finer scenes between Falstaff and Justice Shallow, in *Henry IV*, Part 2, but they were too long.

PAGE 118 (*The Art of Acting*). This speech of Hamlet is really an essay. Many years ago William Archer sent out a questionnaire to prominent actors in England, France, and America, asking them for opinions on the art of acting, and published the results in a book, *Masks or Faces*. The upshot of all his labor was that Hamlet had said everything essential. The sentence which he commends above all is that on page 118: "In the very . . . whirlwind of your passion, you must acquire and beget a temperance," etc.

PAGE 119 (*On the Art of Conferring*). From the time of Berners's translation of Froissart early in the sixteenth century to Urquhart's translation of Rabelais and Motteux's of *Don Quixote*, near the end of the seventeenth, English literature was enriched by a great series of foreign works. Many of these have been English classics ever since. Among them are Chapman's Homer, Fairfax's Tasso, and Florio'

Montaigne. The main reason for the esteem in which they are held is their nervous, racy diction; for they are seldom accurate and sometimes take great liberties with their originals. Florio's Montaigne, particularly, in spite of the publication of more careful translations (like the recent one of George B. Ives), is still the most read.

I am afraid that the selection I have given will prove hard reading, for Florio is seldom more incoherent, but I chose it as very characteristic of Montaigne. Indeed, it gives the keynote of his entire books of *Essais* and therefore of his character. It deserves thoughtful reading, because it abounds in wise and curious reflections and perhaps shows why the kind of talk he loved has become so rare in our time.

PAGE 125 (*The Sleep-Walker*). This scene, which Lamb thought the greatest of its length ever written, is particularly interesting because it is written in prose. It is usually said that Shakespeare wrote his less inspired and less passionate scenes in prose; and it is a curious question why he chose to use it here, changing to verse in the prosy reflections of the Doctor at the end. The manner in which he uses retrospect in Lady Macbeth's speeches has always been admired, for through the queen's disordered mind are floating recollections of the murders of Duncan, Banquo, and Lady MacDuff. Read with the requisite imagination, the scene is tremendous in its suggestions.

PAGE 128 (*Of Painting the Face*). This homily on the use of cosmetics is very amusing, in spite (perhaps because) of the solemnity of the author. He was apparently a Puritan totally devoid of a sense of humor, and his use of argument is more industrious than convincing. It should be remembered that in Elizabethan times men painted as well as women. Perhaps that custom suggests the next step in modern progress.

SECTION THREE — SEVENTEENTH CENTURY
(1600–1700)

In the seventeenth century, the artificial rhetoric of the Elizabethan period was not only further cultivated, but in some authors reached a pitch of extravagance scarcely excelled before. But more characteristic of the century were two streams of tendency, represented by Milton and Browne on the one hand and Walton and Bunyan on the other, to write learnedly or popularly, the results being known as the simple and the ornate styles.

The contribution of the century to the development of prose has not been recognized of late as it should be. Our present-day admiration of plain realism has made us praise the masculine style of Dryden and the clarity and directness of the eighteenth-century prose which he anticipated; and the same admiration has made us slow to admire the gorgeous Latinity of Browne and Milton and the tremendous periods of Jeremy Taylor. And yet these men were great artists, who treated prose in much the same spirit as poets, weaving intricate fabrics of style in which they chose words as a painter lays on colors and framed their sentences and paragraphs with something of an architectural grandeur. In so doing they at least exhibited the emotional powers of prose, practicing subtle rhythms, ransacking the vocabulary for expressive words, and experimenting in tone and in total effect.

It has been customary to say that the style of such men is often greater than their matter. One might maintain, for example, that Browne's great periods are poorly expended upon such a subject as mummies; but his subject is only ostensibly mummies: it is really mutability and the vicissitudes of things. That is a great subject, and his later paragraphs in the fragment given below (page 181) are a sublime prose-poem on the decay of a nation.

Of course, at the beginning of the century two great monuments of prose defy classification — the King James *Bible* and the works of Bacon. Bacon is little read, except in the *Essays* and these are written in a compressed style of his own invention; but the *Bible*, which contains prose as gorgeous as Browne's and as simple as Bunyan's, has been the greatest single force in shaping the minds and the styles of subsequent writers. A careful reading of the selections of the seventeenth century may easily be a revelation to the student of the varieties and potencies of English style.

PAGE 132 (*The Story of Joseph*). Tolstoy, in his *What Is Art?* argues that this narrative is the greatest story in the world, because it has appealed to all sorts and conditions of men and is equally appealing to high and low, learned and ignorant, young and old, wise and simple. It furnishes a perfect example of the kind of sincerity for which he pleaded. There is no slightest attempt to work up the incidents or to arouse a specious emotional effect. The events are told as simply, even baldly, as possible, as if the unknown author had a definite artistic theory that such a story would carry its own effect without any help from description, characterization, or comment, such as one finds in a modern novel. It is interesting to ask one's self what a modern novelist would do with such a story.

PAGE 154 (*The Prodigal Son*). Without doubt this is the most famous story ever written. It is, in fact, the germ of an entire European literature of tales, novels, poems, and plays, and it is quite as likely as ever to inspire new literature today. A parable is a generalized story, in which typical characters do certain things which suggest a moral or religious generalization. It is, moreover, an inherently probable story, as a rule, although, as in *Dives and Lazarus*, it occasionally becomes imaginative. It has always been the favorite device used by great moral teachers, like Plato and Christ, for the inculcation of their principles in simple and interesting form. Disguised by realistic detail it has also been used by certain literary artists, like Hawthorne and Poe (see page 356), to convey a philosophic or moral idea in attractive guise.

PAGE 157 (*Charity*). This famous essay illustrates a more consciously eloquent style than those Biblical passages that precede. Nothing could be finer than the combination of powerful simple words and an intricate rhetoric; for, like the *Gettysburg Address*, this great passage is not so simple as it looks. One feels in it the consuming earnestness and fervor of Paul, but also his oratorical skill. — I have given it in the old spelling, because most students have never realized what the original Bible pages looked like.

PAGE 158 (Bacon's *Essays*). After Bacon had published the little volume of ten essays in 1598, he continued for nearly thirty years to revise, add, and subtract, and to write new essays; and I thought it would be interesting to give the famous *Of Studies* in its earliest and latest forms for comparison. For the modern reader the earlier form contained everything essential and the additions contain little new wisdom. This, however, was not always so by any means. For a more extended study the student should consult Professor Arber's *A Harmony of the Essays*, in which not only all of the English editions are given in parallel but the variations in the Latin text are put down in footnotes.

PAGE 161 (*Of Discourse*). Compare with Montaigne's *On the Art of Conferring* (page 119) and *The Burden of Much Talking* (page 239). For a more complete picture of the "wisest, brightest, meanest of mankind" one should read such essays as *Of Cunning*, *Of Friendship*, and *Of Gardens*, in which he gives himself more scope. In *Of Truth*, as in parts of *The Advancement of Learning*, he expresses a noble enthusiasm for the right and good, however he may have failed always to practice it.

PAGES 170–77 (*A Child*, *A Young Gentleman*, and *The Good Schoolmaster*). The first two of these are examples of the character-writing which amounted to a fad at the time; the third is a transitional form, the character-essay, between the character proper and the later essay. It will be seen that Fuller, in the italicized sentences, has written a character which he develops sentence by sentence. The classic original of the type was the *Characters* of Theophrastus. In *On a Child* Earle has written not only with wit but with delicate feeling and has anticipated something of the sentiment of Vaughan's *The Retreat* and Wordsworth's *Intimations* ode (both given in the *College Book of Verse*).

PAGE 177 (*Life, Sleep, and Dreams*). I have said something of Browne above. The present selection illustrates not so much of his eloquence as his ingenuity. He had a questing mind to which literally nothing was without interest, and he was an amusing mixture of shrewdness and credulity. He is a representative man of the period when medieval pseudoscience was dying and modern science was being born; and he was never able fully to perceive the difference. His *Religio Medici* is so skeptical that it is hard to see how he escaped persecution — the characteristic work of a doctor — and yet it is also full of a simple faith. The two tendencies toward doubt and belief run through all his writings. He was a lovable soul and was one of the greatest writers of English prose.

PAGE 181 (*On Mummies*). In the earlier paragraphs one almost suspects that one is reading a parody of Browne's style, but on page 183 begins a passage that has always seemed to me one of the greatest in English prose. It should be read aloud, with due attention to the rhythm and to the atmospheric effect of the great words. Milton, in his nativity hymn, and Shelley, in *Ozymandias*, have produced a comparable effect, but their verse is no better than this prose, which is indeed written in the spirit of poetry. Young readers are often intolerant of the use of long words, such as are a special feature of Browne's style, because they consider such use pedantic; and no doubt pedantry was a fault of many of the writers of the age, including Browne himself. And yet, when he is inspired, Sir Thomas, like Milton, uses a Latinized diction mingled with simple Saxon words with truly tremendous effect. To dismiss all such passages as pedantic is to miss a great æsthetic pleasure.

PAGE 185 (*Of Myself*). Cowley enjoyed a great reputation as a poet in his lifetime, but is to-day remembered only for three or four lyrics and the book of essays from which the present one is taken. His prose is not only historically significant as inaugurating the familiar style, but is very pleasing on its own account. *Of Myself* is really an *apologia* or explanation of why he is as he is — a man who in the midst of wars and exile and busy with state affairs always longed for the solitude he sings about so sweetly in his verse.

PAGES 191–95 (*Table-Talk, etc.*). John Seldon was one of the most erudite men of his age and a character of impressive independence and wisdom. He also, as these passages prove, had a keen wit and abundant humor. It would be hard to find more common sense clothed in a more amusing phrasing. He is especially notable for his use of homely comparison, which because of its aptness becomes a form of wit. It is this which makes his observations read like folk wisdom, such as one finds in the best popular proverbs.

PAGES 199–200 (*Sentences and Paragraphs*). I have included these excerpts in order to round out the reader's impression of the richness of seventeenth-century prose. The famous paragraph on the death of Raleigh and the less well-known but quite as impressive one of Donne will bear much study, as will the sentence of Taylor, in which the rhythm and even the syntax can be not too fancifully compared with the flight of the lark described. The other examples, from Walton and Bunyan, illustrate the less intellectual and gentler prose of the period.

SECTION FOUR — EIGHTEENTH CENTURY
(1700–1800)

The eighteenth century is usually called the great prose century. In it the realistic novel, the prose satire, the essay, and the prose comedy all reached a quality hardly excelled since, and prose in general attained some of the clarity, ease, and order usually ascribed to the French. As a change from the pedantry, incoherence, and wildness of much that had gone before, this was an advantage, and yet, with the attainment of qualities that are usually praised as the best prose qualities, it lost the poetic fervor and imaginative color of the better earlier writing. It remained for the nineteenth century to combine these two tendencies — towards reason and imagination — into a prose that was at once correct and powerful, rational and moving.

PAGE 201 (*Ned Softly*). This essay and *The Fine Lady's Journal* (page 218) are examples of the quiet and good-natured satire in which Addison was a very skillful practitioner. They are written with such simple ease that one might suppose them easy to write; and yet in their perfect tact and balance of qualities they belong to a type of composition very rarely successful. Addison hardly ever achieves much power but he also hardly ever is merely tame, except to an immature or jaded taste. His rule in writing was to be "simple, but not obvious," and, within the range he set himself, it is a good rule. Austin Dobson suggests that this pleasing bagatelle may have been suggested by a scene in Molière's *Les Précieuses Ridicules*.

PAGE 206 (*The Vision of Mirza*). An example of the eighteenth-century "moral tale" and rather a trite example, I admit. And yet it is so characteristic of the thinking of the time — which though not very religious was *very* moral, at least on paper — that I could not omit it. Many good critics have admired it, and yet it seems to me to contain little true imagination, but rather a kind of mathematical ingenuity that is commonly found in a person of low imaginative power. The allegory is too neat, too hard in outline and detail. One would suppose that those who admire it are prosy persons. And yet it is, as I have said, entirely characteristic of the age of Queen Anne.

PAGE 211 (*A Day's Ramble*). Austin Dobson, in a note on this naïve essay, wonders what Steele's wife, Prue, thought of her husband's philanderings. The narrative has more detail than do most similar essays of the time, and yet very little compared with those of Leigh Hunt, who wrote much in the style of Steele. The reader who wishes to obtain a vivid picture of London street-life should read Swift's *A Summer Shower* and Gay's *Trivia: or, The Art of Walking the Streets of London*, and should study carefully such plates of Hogarth as "The Distressed Poet" and "The Distressed Musician."

PAGE 218 (*The Fine Lady's Journal*). See above, note on page 201.

PAGE 223 (*Pope Rides with His Bookseller*).   Perhaps the most attractive writing of the eighteenth century is found in familiar letters, journals, and diaries.   The letters of Horace Walpole (see page 258), Lady Mary Wortley Montagu, Gray, and Cowper (see page 306); the journals or diaries of Evelyn and Pepys (though these two were Restoration writers) and Fanny Burney are only the best-known; for great numbers of other persons have left intimate records less complete but equally readable.   This amusing letter of Pope proves that his humor could be devoid of malice.   He enjoys Lintot as a curious human specimen and writes what is really a little essay upon him.   The letter has less self-conscious polishing than most of his.   It also opens a window into a past age.   The account of the devices of the publishers in 1716 may be compared with those of the same fraternity in 1779 by turning to Sheridan's *Mr. Puff* (page 296).

PAGE 228 (*The European Yahoos*).   Christopher Morley says of this passage: "Have you read, since the war, Gulliver's 'Voyage to the Houyhnhnms'? . . . Swift's satire, which the textbook writers all tell you is so gross and savage as to suggest the author's approaching madness, seems tender and suave by comparison with that we know to-day."

PAGE 240 (*Of Avarice*).   An example of the moral essay, so much written at the time.   It is instructive to compare Hume's handling of a general topic with Bacon's.   Hume is suave, temperate, and genial and his essay is carefully outlined.   It is a gentlemanly kind of writing, in which the author aims quite as much at the avoidance of any cheap appeal, on the one hand, as at the avoidance of dullness, on the other.   His use of the fable (pages 243–44) is very characteristic of the age.

PAGE 245 (*The Making of a Merchant*).   These passages, which are quite devoid of any literary ambition on the part of the author, nevertheless reveal an upright and likable character and give interesting glimpses of a period.   Concerning the diary Leigh Hunt says: "Hutton of Birmingham (as he is familiarly called) combined, in a remarkable manner, prudence with enterprise, industry with amusement, and the love of books with devotion to business, and all because he was a thorough human being of his class, probably from causes anterior to his birth. Not that his father was a person of any very edifying description. His son gives the following amusing account of him: 'Though my father was neither young, being forty-two, nor handsome, having lost an eye, nor sober, for he spent all he could get in liquor, nor clean, for his trade was oily, nor without shackles, for he had five children, yet women of various descriptions courted his smiles, and were much inclined to pull caps for him.' But this squalid Lothario probably supplied him with wit and address, and his mother with thought and a good constitution.

"William Hutton was the son of a poor wool-worker. He was brought up as a poor weaver, had not a penny in the world, became a bookbinder under the poorest auspices, and ended with being a rich man, and living in wealth and honour to the age of ninety-two. The passages selected are from a life of him written by himself, and in the original are accompanied with a great deal of additional matter, all worth reading, and in the course of which he gives an account of the rise and progress of his courtship of Mrs. Hutton, here only intimated. He was one of the sufferers from the Riots of Birmingham (which he has recorded), and author of amusing Histories of that town and of Derby . . . ." (*A Book for a Corner.*)

PAGE 258 (*A King's Levee*). Another example of the admirable letters of the time. Walpole was an amusing mixture of dandy, wit, dilettante, writer, printer, shrewd man of the world, and cynic. No more entertaining letters exist than his or any that give so varied and accurate a picture of a time. His description of the funeral has a certain rugged power, and few masters of the novel could better convey the mixture of sublimity and ridiculousness than he does here.

PAGE 262 (*The Story of Le Fever*). Imbedded in the chaotic mass of *Tristram Shandy* is a little group of immortal characters — Mr. and Mrs. Shandy, Dr. Slop, My Uncle

Toby, Corporal Trim, the Widow Wadman — whose humors have delighted the world. The story of Le Fever lacks the humor and nonsense of other parts of the novel, but I chose it because it is complete in itself. It also exemplifies very well the delicacy of Sterne's style and its inimitable ease and naturalness. Sterne was an avowed sentimentalist, but the pathos of this story of a dying soldier is not sentimental.

PAGE 274 (*The Tortoise*). White's *Selborne* is like Walton's *Compleat Angler*, an honest unpretentious work that has become a classic simply because it has the indefinable quality called charm. White was a country rector who made a hobby of nature-study in a time when professional writers, if they wrote of nature at all, wrote of it romantically or sentimentally. He merely put down the facts as he saw them, but with a quiet enthusiasm that warms them. His book has gone through countless editions and has been in its turn the hobby of many loving students who have annotated and illustrated it with tireless care. He might be taken as a parable of the truth that anything truly seen and perfectly recorded has value. If, moreover, the writer has, as he had, a lovable personality, serene, finely simple, and honest, such a record is lasting.

PAGE 278 (*Boswell as Bear-Leader*). This passage is especially rich as comedy because of the revelation of Boswell's character and technique, as well as of Johnson's temperament. Note how vividly the scenes are seen and described: Boswell handling Johnson with gloves (page 279); Johnson in his library (page 280); Johnson in the window-seat (page 282); Wilkes ingratiating himself with Johnson (page 283); Wilkes with the candle before the print (page 290). It is all admirable comedy, as good as a scene in a play of the time.

PAGE 291 (*Johnson against Garrick*). This little-known skit is really only slightly burlesqued. Reynolds has merely developed the hint of Boswell (page 285): "Johnson would let nobody attack Garrick but himself, as Garrick said to me." Davy had been a pupil of Johnson at Lichfield and had accompanied him on his journey to London. One rose to be the greatest actor, the other the autocrat of letters. Reynolds, who possessed a fine vein of humor, knew them both intimately and, although he honored and loved them both, he was quite aware of their foibles. The imitation of Johnson's dogmatism and his intimidating manner is perfect, being merely heightened enough to make it amusing.

PAGE 293 (*The Ephemera*). An example of the fable or parable so much cultivated. Franklin was a typical eighteenth-century man of genius, learned, skeptical, suspicious of enthusiasm, common-sense; and yet a cultivator of the amenities of life and of a polished style.

PAGE 296 (*Mr. Puff*). This scene is really complete, for it introduces Mr. Puff's tragedy, which is a wild parody of the heroic plays and romantic tragedies. It serves well enough as an example of the easy, natural dialogue of the classic comedy, though its purpose is essentially satiric. One of the greatest features of Sheridan's plays is the purity of the language. Here in ten pages is hardly a word that is not in good use to-day. And the manner of speech, though it is that of men of the world, is perfect in rhythm, ease, and naturalness. Such manner and diction are a great preservative of drama. It is amusing to reflect that the art of puffing, though its technique may have changed, is by no means lost to the present age, and that some of Mr. Puff's devices are quite as effective to-day as then.

PAGE 306 (*A Poet Receives a Commission*). A fair example of Cowper's admirable letters — admirable for their simple naturalness and intimacy. Some one has said that he introduced whimsicality into English literature. His letters certainly have some of the qualities of the personal essay of the next century.

SECTION FIVE — NINETEENTH CENTURY (1800–1900)

Literary historians divide the nineteenth century into two (or, occasionally, three) periods: the Romantic Period (to

about 1830) and the Victorian Era (to 1880). Whether the
last two decades of the century constitute a separate period
is as yet uncertain, though there is a tendency to consider
them as really belonging to the modern period or the twentieth century.

The prose of the Romantic Period is perhaps best represented by the novels of Scott and the essays of Lamb, Hazlitt,
and De Quincey. But during the same years works were produced, such as the novels of Jane Austen and Thomas Love
Peacock and the *Imaginary Conversations* of Landor, which
were classic rather than romantic in inspiration. I regret that
I was unable to include examples of the prose of the three
writers just mentioned, but considerations of interest or of
space prevented my doing so. The selections I have given,
however, do, I hope, represent the main current of prose.
The revolutionary spirit of the era reached its greatest expression in the poets, Shelley and Byron; the æsthetic and
philosophic appreciation of nature, in Wordsworth.

During the Victorian Era every possible type and form of
prose was written; but, if one seeks the main quality or mood
of that time, one finds it perhaps to have been *moral earnestness*. It is the moving force of the so-called Victorian
Prophets, Carlyle, Ruskin, and Arnold, and of the major
poets and novelists. Humanitarian sympathy and æsthetic
appreciation of nature, both great thought-movements of the
age, met, at the mid-century, the new biological science and
both were enriched by it, even though the doctrine of evolution precipitated a new stage in the "conflict of science and
religion," which still disturbs many minds. It has been
maintained that the only new art-form in literature produced
during the century was the short story. The familiar essay
was less successfully cultivated than during the Romantic
Period, but the more formal essay, discussional, critical,
opinionative, argumentative, became one of the chief vehi-
cles for the expression of the moral earnestness of which I
have spoken. I found it impracticable to include passages
from the Victorian novel, but all readers of this book have
read novels by Dickens, Thackeray, and George Eliot. I

have included some examples of short narrative, however, for reasons indicated below. In prose drama the entire century was wofully deficient until the translation of Ibsen and the success of the Irish Movement in the eighties and nineties set the dramatist free from the imitation of classical and Elizabethan models.

By 1880 the Victorian earnestness seemed to have spent itself and reactionary movements, such as the "æsthetic" and "decadent" appeared to mark its death. But at the same time new vitalizing influences made themselves felt, and some of these have affected the literature of the present century profoundly. Chief among these was a new realism, remotely no doubt the child of science but immediately of Continental influences, Scandinavian, French, and Russian. The eighties and nineties were years of groping and experiment; as we see now, a seed-time for the growths of the present era. As such they have attracted much attention of late and have come to appear much more important than they were formerly thought to be.

PAGE 309 (*Proverbs*). These proverbs have been seldom reprinted, but they represent quite well the philosophy of their author. Blake was remarkable as artist, poet, and mystic; his influence has been widespread; and he is one of the strangest and most fascinating figures in English literature. The reader should not fail to acquaint himself with Blake's pictures.

PAGE 310 (*Poetry*). I have gathered here a few of the classic pronouncements concerning poetry in a period when poetry roused to a new life. Certain of these sentences, particularly of Wordsworth, Coleridge, and Shelley, have influenced æsthetics ever since. Of course they express a romantic view of poetry which has constantly been challenged, sometimes as mystical, sometimes as extravagant, sometimes as incomprehensible. It has been maintained that they allow insufficient place to the intellectual and formal elements in poetry, that they describe the spirit of poetry rather than the art. And yet a careful reading even of these meager excerpts will show that the romantic critics (especially Coleridge) held no limited or merely visionary opinions of the art they practiced. There is probably no single critical work in the language so profound or so generally sound as the *Biographia Literaria*.

PAGE 317 (*My First Play*). An example of the reminiscent essay — perhaps the easiest sort to write. It is not one of Lamb's greatest, but is perhaps one most full of suggestions for the young writer.

PAGE 323 (*Poor Relations*). Certainly one of Lamb's finest essays, especially notable for the variety and nicety of its diction. It is also interesting as showing how skillfully Lamb used materials from his own life for illustration.

PAGE 332 (*On Going a Journey*). Compare with Thoreau's *Walking, and the Wild* (page 395). This is one of the greatest of essays, interesting, vivid, provocative, and full of the quality which Hazlitt valued most, *gusto*. Hazlitt is as full of ideas as a nut of meat. He has not the charm which has made Lamb the most popular of essayists, and he lacks Lamb's odd humor; but he has an astonishingly fertile mind and a vigorous personality that appeal more powerfully to some readers. He is the most quotational of modern authors — an inveterate reader of old books and passionately fond of great poetry. But he also loved the active life, wrote superbly of games, prize-fights, walking-tours — was in short a vagabond at heart. He also wrote with fire and insight of painting. A remarkable man who deserves to be better known than he is.

PAGE 345 (*Natural Supernaturalism*). After much searching and hesitation, I decided to include this chapter from *Sartor Resartus*, because it is good reading for youth. It raises and discusses many topics which thoughtful young people struggle with and, while it may not answer many questions, at least presents with tremendous vigor a view of life and of the world which does not receive the attention it should to-day. This view is essentially poetic, inspired by awe and wonder; and yet there is more than a little of canny

Scotch shrewdness in it too. Carlyle's astounding style is well represented. It is not to be imitated, but it is certainly to be enjoyed. He is one of the writers who, like Browning and Hugo and Richter, of the three qualities of style, clearness, force, and beauty, strove constantly for the second. But he did not always do so. When he chose he could write as calmly and clearly as any one else. In *Sartor* and the *French Revolution* he is really writing poetry.

PAGE 356 (*Shadow — A Parable*). Probably the finest piece of prose Poe ever wrote. His purpose is to achieve atmosphere and he succeeds better than in some of his more elaborate tales. It is curious to reflect that there is some reason to believe that Poe wrote *Shadow* as parody or burlesque.

PAGE 360 (*Gifts*). This little essay is very characteristic of Emerson in its idealism, its ingenuity, and its lofty contempt of ordinary human motives. It has a little of what Barrett Wendell called his "serene insolence." And yet he is not be to taken too solemnly. I suspect that he sometimes had his tongue in his cheek. But the essay has a kind of translucency and a noble sweetness.

PAGE 364 (*Literature of Knowledge and Power*). The famous distinction made here has real value and the essay is a good example of De Quincey's analytical power. Like Emerson and Ruskin, he had a very ingenious mind, full of theories and original distinctions. The present selection, however, is not at all representative of his work as a conscious stylist. For that one should read *The English Mail-Coach* or the *Suspiria de Profundus*. A third style or manner is that of the *Confessions of an English Opium-Eater* — his greatest and most famous book.

PAGE 370 (*The Seeing Eye*). These passages from *Modern Painters* are no more notable as examples of eloquent prose than as examples of close observation. Ruskin was once pronounced "the most analytical mind in Europe"; and his analytical powers can be discerned here. But he was also one of the most observing men in Europe, uniting the sense of fact of a scientist with the sense of values of a poet. The passage on *Leaves, Lichens, and Mosses* is very beautiful, and yet it is a fine example of that "pathetic fallacy" which Ruskin named and analyzed. Ruskin is one of the greatest masters of the sentence. Notice the structure and rhythm of the sentences in the last paragraph on page 378.

PAGE 379 (*The Wind on the Heath*). The passage is taken from one of the most enjoyable of picaresque novels, all about gipsies, horses, boxing, taverns, and the open road.

PAGE 380 (*Oliver Goldsmith*). An example of the short biography, written by a man who loved his subject. Some may think Thackeray a trifle sentimental. Such readers will prefer Macaulay's essay on the same subject. Still, Thackeray's is a good model, because he is concerned not merely with facts but with making us see Oliver as the lovable, erring, ridiculous, pathetic genius he was.

PAGE 395 (*Walking, and the Wild*). The original essay is perhaps three times as long as the part I have given, but it is so desultory and disjointed that it has hardly any unity at all. Thoreau was original enough by nature, and yet he sometimes gives the effect of trying to be still more so. He is the type of intellectual nonconformist. At his best he writes with a raciness that seems like the smell of ploughed land or wood-smoke. The passage about the cockerel on page 403 is very characteristic, both in its poetic appreciation of natural sights and sounds and in its touch of extravagance. And the opening sentences of the same paragraph express his doctrine (which he shared with Emerson) of the vital importance of the present moment. Experience is entirely here and now, and the richest life is that which extracts from every passing day the richest experience. (Compare Emerson's *Days*, in the *College Book of Verse*.)

PAGE 405 (*In the Mediterranean*). This little-known essay of Lowell is an excellent example of the lighter kind of writing which at the same time is not really trivial. Mr. X. is a character of the simplest and yet one cannot help sharing

Lowell's zest in making his acquaintance. And the portrait is very skillfully painted, without a trace of condescension or arrogance.

PAGE 412 (*Pagan and Medieval Religious Sentiment*). Primarily an argument, the discussion is conducted with such richness of illustration that the reader almost forgets that the author is making a point. The essay represents Arnold at his best. He is serious without being solemn and entertaining without ever losing sight of his main purpose. The contentions are important and the criticism of religious sentiment is very instructive. And I was glad to include the essay because of the two excellent translations from Theocritus and Saint Francis. The version of the *Syracusan Gossips* seems to me the finest in English.

PAGE 433 (*A Cynic's Apology*). It is interesting to compare the tone of this essay with that of Arnold's. Of course, Stephen was not a cynic: he merely adopts the name applied to him by his critics and then humorously defends it: he is really thinking of what he would have called "high thinking and plain speaking." Bernard Shaw somewhere suggests that "cynic" is a word that we apply to any one whose opinions we do not approve of; and Benjamin Jowett, in one of his letters, maintains that cynicism is always bad, because it is necessarily a negative attitude. Stephen is really defending social criticism, and his manner of doing so is a model of wit, urbanity, and good humor. Notice too how well-stored his mind is, with quotation, illustration, example, and analogy.

PAGE 449 (*The Death of Socrates*). This famous account of an incident has touched the hearts of men more than any other except that of the passion of Jesus.

PAGE 454 (*The Ascent of Man*). A fine specimen of scientific writing, in which the facts and conclusions from them are almost the sole concern of the writer. Darwin is really engaged in establishing a theory, and his purpose is essentially argumentative; but he knew that his conclusions were unwelcome to many readers and he carefully avoided giving unnecessary offense. The passage is an admirable model of persuasion, in which the qualities are not showy and yet are impressive because of the modesty, honesty, and thoroughness of the author. Particularly interesting is the analysis of the growth of a moral sense in animals and man (pages 460–64). It is closely reasoned and, whether or not it contains the whole truth, is perfectly clear and comprehensible. It is remarkable how a piece of prose so quiet and impersonal is still so revealing of the temperament of the writer that one might from it alone construct a fairly complete portrait of a naturalist. The concluding sentence (page 465) should be pondered. It is important because in it Darwin states this theory of evolution. Many criticize him without having ever taken the trouble to read what he himself said.

PAGE 465 (*A Crisis in My Mental History*). An example of autobiography. As the confession of a young man of twenty, even though Mill was an astoundingly precocious young man, it is noteworthy, because of the nobility of his character and the depth of his feelings. The earlier chapters of the *Autobiography*, which recount the course of his strange education, are more curious and exciting than the present one, but less valuable to a young reader. They should be read, however; and might be compared with profit with Ruskin's account of his strange childhood, given in *Præterita*. Mill's father, James Mill, was a man of great ability and learning but deficient in imagination. He no doubt loved his son, but he suffered from the delusion of Richard Feverel's father (in Meredith's *The Ordeal of Richard Feverel*), who believed that a father might take the place of Providence or of Nature in the training of a child. He therefore reared John by a system, in which, as the present passage explains, the intellect was developed at the expense of the emotions and affections. The consequence was that John, at the age of twenty, suffered the kind of disillusionment that is usually reserved for middle age. How he found himself through the reading of poetry helps one to understand the value of poetry and poets to mankind.

PAGE 479 (*Classic and Romantic*). I have followed, with some changes, the abridgement of Professor Raymond Alden. All of Pater's main contentions are given, and the omitted portions are mostly illustrative. The contentions are not difficult for the young reader to comprehend, although he may be bewildered by the array of references to books which he has not read. The distinction which forms the drift of the essay is of the utmost importance to students of literature and, while some of Pater's views may have been controverted or emended, the discussion still remains one of the classics of criticism.

PAGE 491 (*El Dorado*). The theme of the essay is found in the sentence: "To be truly happy is a question of how we begin and not of how we end, of what we want and not of what we have." Christian moralists would no doubt condemn this as a pagan doctrine, and there was certainly a good deal of the pagan in Stevenson. But, as his friend Henley said, there was also a good deal of Scotch Calvinism. Here, although the little essay has a philosophic basis, he is not concerned with being complete or exhaustive, but with being provocative. He is singing the praises of aspiration, and perhaps his eulogy of spiritual pioneering needs the correction of Thoreau's doctrine of the importance of the present moment of experience. (See page 403.) The great fault of Stevenson's essay style is preciosity and self-consciousness, a fastidious or finicking search for the effective word. This essay shows the fault a little.

PAGE 494 (*Fame's Little Day*). Miss Jewett is now admired more highly that at any time since her first vogue. Her stories reflect the art of perfect naturalness. Her style never gets in the way of her story, and at first both style and story may impress the reader as commonplace. Her full quality cannot be conveyed by a single story; but *Fame's Little Day* will serve as a model of quiet realism, in which the characters are permitted to express their unconscious humor and their solid, homely character with very little comment by the author. In spite of its low tone, also, the story has excellent structure. It is divided into three episodes and the part of the young reporter as *deus ex machina* binds all together. It also has a theme of deep significance: the influence of a trifling incident upon two lives; for the reporter's little joke really affected the lives of Mr. and Mrs. Pinkham, not only for a week, but in all probability for the rest of their years.

PAGE 505 (*On the Stairs*). I included this gruesome little story as an example of the modern technique, in which such principles as immediacy, economy, and the single point-of-view are used with skill to produce an effect of impressive irony. It might be maintained that the portrayal of a woman like Mrs. Curtis is hardly worth the effort and that a study of such degraded ideals as hers is a waste of time. On such a question there is likely to be no agreement. But all readers must admit that the technique of the story is admirable. It offers an interesting comparison in this respect with *Fame's Little Day*. The latter is told in episodes, moves from place to place, and covers several days in its action; the former is built like a Greek play, with strict observance of the unities of time, place, and action.

PAGE 510 (*The Song of the Minster*). I selected this beautifully written parable as representing a third kind of story, in which fantasy and a poetic treatment are used to clothe a moral meaning. It has the quality of a legend, but is more skillfully told than most primitive legends. The author, after a brief explanatory introduction, is able to confine his story to one time and one place and attain a powerful emotional climax by simply following the course of the supernatural music until it reaches a grand crescendo. He deserves praise, too, for avoiding the use of archaic or Biblical English and for relying upon good modern words for his effect.

The three short stories just discussed, with the examples in the following section of the book, offer sufficient material for a fairly complete study of short-story technique.

SECTION SIX — TWENTIETH CENTURY (1900–1923)

During the quarter-century just passed, the main movement in literature has been a development of the realism which came into vogue during the eighteen-nineties. Its purpose may be described as the attempt in art to give an illusion of actual life and, in the hands of most writers who were not great masters, it has been little more than a style, even a trick, which consisted in selecting words and sentence-forms that are used by people in real life. For the masters it was a deeper thing than style, because it reflected a philosophy of life which refused to recognize as truth anything that could not be scientifically proved. This aspect of realism is usually called *Rationalism*. In literature in its extreme form it has been called *Naturalism*.

The realistic tendency in writing is easily recognized in the novel, short story, and drama, and even in poetry; and in the selections that follow it is well represented. But, like all other literary theories pushed too far, strict realism has proved hampering to creation. In the drama, for example, it was found that the restriction of the play to the speech and action and themes of real life prevented the dramatist from expressing much of that in which the old poetic drama was most powerful and significant. Attempts to revive the poetic drama were persistent all through the 19th century, but were never successful. The dramatists of the present have kept to prose, but have tried to regain some of the elevation and richness of the Elizabethan drama by means of fantasy (Dunsany), or a rhythmical stylistic prose (Synge), or the use of symbolism, masks, soliloquy, or some other non-realistic convention (O'Neill). In the novel and short story, too, there has been a growing use of fantasy. Such works are as a rule realistic in thought or spirit (indeed, all great literature must be) though not in form or style.

If we seek to name the peculiar character of the best contemporary literature, we shall probably not be far wrong if we name it as courageous and honest. The 20th century has been determined to know and to tell the truth about life. If the 19th century was remarkable for moral earnestness, the 20th is quite as remarkable for intellectual earnestness — which is possibly the same thing, with a shift from conduct to ideas. Its mood is that of science, which pursues the truth, or at least the facts, at any price, "no matter whom it hurts." Artistically this mood has led to a hatred of all forms of artificial plotting in fiction, "licenses" and conventions in poetry; and to a freedom of discussion hardly known before in the history of English literature.

Novels like Maugham's *Of Human Bondage* (see p. 575), stories like Anderson's "I Want to Know Why" (p. 654), are characteristic of the age in their simple unpretentious style, their absence of any apparent manipulation of incidents, and their frank statement of facts, whether these are beautiful or are not. Such discussional essays as Babbitt's "On Being Original" (p. 516), Russell's "The Place of Science" (p. 563), and Ellis's "The Art of Morals" (p. 666), are essentially modern in their defense of humanism, scientific rationalism and a new-old ethics, respectively. The light essays of Chesterton and Marquis (p. 536 and p. 636) and the more serious essay of Agnes Repplier (p. 640), are examples of a form in which the present century has been particularly rich, and the passages from Beerbohm and Stephens (p. 540 and p. 548) represent what stage-people call "stylized" art, in which, by departing from the customary speech of ordinary life, the author produces a fresh effect. Beerbohm does it directly, by the use of a fastidious, somewhat affected style, which is nevertheless very witty and beautiful; Stephens, indirectly, by recording what the old woman says in her own words and rhythms, but without any realistic dialectic spelling.

Probably the only new art-form invented and developed in the present century is the one-act play. It is true that Molière used it three centuries ago and that it has not been unknown in the period since; but in our era it has been immensely cultivated and at times with power and beauty. In *The Lost Silk Hat* (p. 553) and *Bound East for Cardiff* (p. 621), examples of realistic fantasy and humor, on the one hand, and of hard realism, on the other, exhibit the extremes of the type. Such a play as Synge's *The Riders to the Sea*, which I could not include, would illustrate the use of a poetic prose in an artfully developed style and rhythm, as Dunsany's *The*

Queen's Enemies or *King Argimenes* would illustrate romantic fantasy.

PAGE 516 (*On Being Original*). I felt that nothing could be more appropriate to introduce the last section of the book than this criticism of the period. Professor Babbitt is one of the most learned and philosophical upholders of the attitude of life called *humanism*, and "On Being Original" is a remarkably intelligible statement of what that attitude is. Read with the essays of Bertrand Russell and Havelock Ellis, it will give the young reader a valuable insight into some of the most discussed questions and problems of the present. No one of these is "easy reading." The best way to read them is not to be frightened by their learning, as shown in the illustrations and allusions, but to look for the main drift throughout. This is never in doubt, though the array of names may be disconcerting. Such reading is valuable, too, as giving the reader a measure of his own ignorance. For such authors as these, the entire world of books and men lies open as if it were one book. They seem to have read everything, and yet to have assimilated it all. The reason is that they are thinking men, for whom reading and experience are merely an arena for the activities of their minds. They never succumb to their learning. It has been said that "knowledge is power"; and that is true. But for many men it is merely weight and the more they have of it the less intelligence they show. There is a fine exhilaration, then, in reading the works of men who have amassed vast hoards of knowledge and yet carry it easily and use it as a means and not an end. In order to do this nothing is more useful than to have a theory of life in which one believes, because then every new fact or opinion becomes a ratification or a challenge. Each of the three writers has a theory which he has spent his life in presenting and enforcing, and it gives to his work coherence and interest and power.

In the present essay nothing is more valuable than the discussion of originality itself, because it wholesomely analyses current misconceptions and champions older and probably sounder conceptions. For many readers Professor Babbitt's contention will seem quite novel, though it is really as old as human culture. It is, in fact, the very heart of humanism as this appears in art.

PAGE 536 (*On Lying in Bed*). A humorous essay with a sub-current of seriousness. For over thirty years Chesterton has been a champion of conservatism or, as he calls it, orthodoxy; and in whatever form he may write — essay, biography, criticism, fantastic romance, detective story, or poetry — a philosophic basis is perceptible. His favorite device in the essay is to assume a paradoxical attitude, turning some popular belief or assumption inside out or upside down, and then arguing from this new point of view. He loves nonsense, deals brilliantly in half-truths — in short argues for the conventional in an unconventional way. In the preface to *Tremendous Trifles*, from which book the present essay is taken, he discusses essay-writing.

PAGE 540 (*Zuleika Dobson*). A brilliant pen-portrait of a coquette. Zuleika is a music-hall actress who visits Oxford, where all of the students fall in love with her and all commit suicide at the same moment by drowning. At the end Zuleika is preparing to move to Cambridge. The novel is an elaborate *jeu-d'esprit*, of a kind very little cultivated in English. Beerbohm is master of a delicately ironic prose of classical purity, lightness, and polish. He is best known as a writer of the light essay and as a caricaturist of great humor and originality.

PAGE 548 (*An Old Woman of the Roads*). A character-sketch of mingled humor, pathos, and poetry. *The Crock of Gold*, from which the passage is taken, is one of the most original books of the present century, clearly a work of genius. It is a fantasy of artfully mingled modes, nonsense, poetry, realism, romance, legend, and wisdom, all fused by a beautiful style.

PAGE 553 (*The Lost Silk Hat*). A little drama of what may be called realistic fantasy, in which a somewhat preposterous situation is presented in everyday speech. Notice how the entrances of the three pedestrians lead up to three climaxes. The episodes of the Laborer and the Clerk are disposed of quickly; that of the poet is developed at length. Lord Dunsany is best known as a writer of romantic melodramas written in poetic prose and of short stories dealing with a mythology which he invented himself.

PAGE 563 (*The Place of Science in a Liberal Education*). Interesting as a contemporary discussion of a subject first argued by Huxley a half-century ago. Huxley's ablest opponent was Matthew Arnold, who upheld the classical or humanist view, in its essentials that of Irving Babbitt (see pp. 516 ff.). With the present essay it would be interesting to compare Mr. Russell's other essay, *Science*, recently published in *Whither Mankind?* Bertrand Russell is a noted mathematician whose researches long ago led him into philosophy, and as a philosopher he has been one of the most influential speculators of the period.

PAGE 575 (*The Story of Fanny Price*). A story in novelette length, written in the modern realistic manner. The novel, *Of Human Bondage*, from which I have extracted Fanny's pathetic history, is generally considered one of the finest of the past quarter-century. It is the biography of Philip Carey, who, suffering from the deformity of a clubfoot, has become somewhat morbidly diffident, and its theme is mainly his search for some consistent meaning in life. To read it after reading *Tom Jones* and *Pendennis* is a valuable intellectual experience for a young man or woman, as well as an illuminating study of three conceptions of realism in three centuries. *The Story of Fanny Price* is a fine example of pathos without sentimentality. The author makes his heroine about as unattractive as a girl could well be, and yet she never forfeits the reader's sympathy.

PAGE 613 (*Araby*). A narrative sketch that is still much more than a sketch. Such writing has sometimes been called "story without plot," but the phrase is not very apt, because, although the narrative is almost devoid of the elements of suspense and surprise, it holds the reader's interest by its perfect naturalness, the accurately observed detail, and, especially, the unstressed pathos of the boy's deferred hope. Such stories were seldom written in English before the present century. The greatest master of the type is Anton Chekov.

PAGE 621 (*Bound East for Cardiff*). One of a group of one-act plays of the sea, all taking place on the Glencairn and involving the same group of characters. Others are *The Moon of the Caribbees* and *The Long Voyage Home*. Since writing them Mr. O'Neill has experimented in many techniques and manners, but has probably not excelled the simple strength and verity of these transcripts from his life as a sailor. The present little drama is perhaps not as successful as a stage-play as one or two others, because such a prolonged death-scene puts too severe a strain upon both the actor who impersonates Yank and upon the audience; but it holds interest strongly in the reading. Questions that occur are: Are the characters really individualized or are they only types? Does the realism of the language prevent any suggestion of sentimentality in the incidents? Is the use of dialect necessary? Has the play any underlying theme?

PAGE 636 (*A Preface to a Book of Fishhooks*). A light essay, built up almost entirely of whim. The success of such writing consists partly in complete naturalness of style and partly in the selection of such whims as the reader will view good-naturedly, even though he may not share them. The theme is in the sentence, "Our idea of fishing is to put all the exertion up to the fish," which suggests the lazy man's philosophy that follows. This is not an easy type of essay for most people to write, even though it reads like mere prattle, because it expresses, without affectation or shame, the essence of a personality. Most young writers attempting the type unconsciously suggest a feeling of superiority to other people, or an affectation of oddity that is not real, or a smart manner, or a literary, precious flavor. Whether Mr. Marquis avoids all of these dangers will be a matter of opinion. But whatever we may think of this essay, any one who is familiar with his work in general recognizes in it very rare traits of originality, humor, and wisdom. He is also an excellent poet.

PAGE 640 (*Money*). A third type of essay, lying somewhere between "On Lying in Bed" and "A Preface to a Book of Fishhooks," on the one hand, and "On Being Original" and "The Place of Science," on the other. Miss Repplier's purpose is not mainly to be amusing, but to be instructive, and yet she aims at a more popular treatment than either Mr. Babbitt or Mr. Russell. She is one of the leading writers of what may be called the discussional or provocative essay. Her method gives the impression of being a kind of mosaic-work, in which she first collects data, apt quotations, anecdotes, reminiscence, and allusions, all of which illustrate or further her thesis. The success of such writing must depend largely upon the common-sense truth of what is said and upon the interest which strong opinions honestly held must always have. She does not hesitate to be ironical or sarcastic, because to irritate a reader is one of the best ways to break through his indifference and to arouse him to thought.

PAGE 654 (*I Want to Know Why*). An impressive example of the short story in the modern style. There is no obvious manipulation of incidents to make an effect. The author considers his theme important and interesting enough to carry without literary tricks or devices. And yet, the more the story is studied, the more artistic, even artful, the technique appears. The boy who narrates it has never taken a course in short-story writing, and has never heard anything about immediacy, economy, single effect, unity of plot or tone; and yet he tells his story remarkably well, one might say by just naturally floundering through it. His artlessness (which is not the author's) gives the final touch of realism to what he tells; and the author skillfully uses the boy's ignorance of technique to give to the story the only suspense it has. This suspense all lies in the question, "Just what did happen to the boy at Saratoga?" a question the answer to which he constantly defers and yet constantly refers to vaguely. But of course it is the *meaning* of the story that makes it impressive.

PAGE 666 (*The Art of Morals*). There is no subject that young readers love to discuss more than morals, and that is why I have included this discussion of a new-old ethical philosophy. Mr. Ellis's views are noble, but probably too indefinite (see p. 682) for popular adoption, even for popular comprehension. But they afford a ground for discussion. Merely to ponder upon such sentences as those quoted on page 685 — "Art is often more moral than morality itself," and "Art is in a certain sense the only morality which life admits" — is highly valuable and educative; and the central thesis, that life may be and should be lived as an art, is a new idea to many persons who have always thought of morals as a collection of Thou shalts and Thou shalt nots.

INDEX

OF SUBJECTS, TYPES, FORMS, AND TECHNIQUE

Subjects are printed in SMALL CAPITAL letters. The index is not exhaustive, and many of the entries are merely suggestive.

The purpose of this index is to provide teachers and students with examples, *in their context*, of methods and devices and of sentences, paragraphs, and literary forms. In general only those subjects have been listed which are treated at some length in the text.

INDEX

OF AUTHORS AND TITLES